# SPLINTERED VISIONS

## Lucio Fulci and His Films

# SPLINTERED VISIONS

## Lucio Fulci and His Films

**by Troy Howarth**

**With Special Collaboration**
**by Mike Baronas**

**Midnight Marquee Press, Inc.**
**Baltimore, Maryland, USA, London, U.K.**

Interior layout by Susan Svehla
Cover Design by Tim Paxton
Cover Art is from the Italian poster for *Zombie* (1979), produced and distributed by Variety Film Distribuzione; artwork is unsigned but is possibly the work of "Symeoni" / Sandro Simeoni.



ISBN 978-1-936168-53-8 (Color Edition)
ISBN 978-1-936168-61-3 (Black and White Edition)
Library of Congress Catalog Card Number 2015909290
Manufactured in the United States of America
First Printing September, 2015

For Lucio
and Richard Johnson

**German poster for *Zombie*, which utilizes the same artwork as the Scandinavian; artist unknown.**

# Table of Contents

# Acknowledgements

I am indebted to the assistance, feedback, support and all-around collaboration of many people in the writing of this book. First and foremost, I would like to extend a hearty thank you to Mike Baronas. When it comes to all things-Fulci, there simply isn't anybody out there with more passion or greater knowledge than Mike. Not only did he contribute an excellent appreciation of Fulci and his work, he also proved to be a treasure trove of information. Mike's research encompassed interviews with just about every person imaginable who had some connection with Fulci and I am grateful to him for allowing me access to these marvelous quotes and insights. In addition to providing transcripts of some interviews, which are being published for the first time in this book, Mike also put me in contact with a number of Fulci's colleagues, thus enabling me to interview them first hand. Mike also provided a plethora of rare images, many of which are included in this book. Mike's tireless dedication to this project has earned him a well-deserved "collaboration" credit on this book; it simply would not have turned out nearly so well without him.

Mike's "partner-in-crime," Kit Gavin, also deserves a special note of thanks for his dedication to keeping the Fulci legacy alive. Kit was instrumental in tracking down many of the people associated with Fulci's work in the first place and I (and the world of fandom at large!) am therefore very much in his debt. Kit also took some of the candid photographs that are used in this book, for which he also has my thanks.

My good friend in Italy, Roberto Curti, again proved to be invaluable with fact-checking and providing information on lesser-known titles. Roberto provided a review of Fulci's comedy mini-series *Un uomo da ridere*, which is more than a mere review—it helps to contextualize Fulci's place in Italian cinema at that time and serves as something of an overview of the director's place in the realm of Italian film comedy, a part of Fulci's career which has been overlooked by fans for far too long. Roberto also was of tremendous assistance in providing translations for the Fulci films that are unavailable in English to date.

The actor Brett Halsey agreed to provide a foreword for this volume, for which he has my gratitude. In addition to being an accomplished actor, Mr. Halsey is also a fine writer, as anybody who has ever read his novels—including *Magnificent Strangers* and *A Grave Misunderstanding*—will readily attest. He is also a genuinely friendly and down-to-earth human being and I thank him for taking the time to share some of his memories of working with Fulci.

The impeccable soundtracks composed by Fabio Frizzi distinguish many of Fulci's best films. I am therefore delighted to have secured the services of *Maestro* Frizzi, who provided an afterword for this text. He has been extremely busy of late with various concert appearances, but has readily given his time to provide a tribute to his late friend and collaborator.

Steve Fenton again lent his considerable talents to helping to proofread and edit the manuscript and also gave freely of his time when it came to contributing images and helping to clean up images provided by other sources. Steve's patience and generosity is much appreciated.

The Maltese Twins, Mario and Roderick Gauci, were of great help in editing and proofing the manuscript, as they have done on my previous endeavors. Mario and Roderick's exacting eye (for they seem to function as one!) caught many potentially embarrassing errors and they have my gratitude for their hard work and dedication.

Actor and filmmaker Scooter McCrae (*Shatter Dead*, 1994) was fortunate enough to spend the weekend attending to Fulci's needs when the ailing director was in New York for his first—and as fate would have it, final—American festival appearance. I am deeply grateful to him for taking the time to recount some of his memories of this experience in this book.

The idea of incorporating some newly commissioned artwork seemed a good way of varying the "look" of the layout somewhat; finding an artist who was willing to come through and deliver the goods, however, proved more difficult. I enlisted the services of Scott Hoffman when I happened to see a sample of his artwork online. Scott was commissioned to do several pieces for the book, but his enthusiasm for the project and for Fulci's body of work prompted him to volunteer to go above and beyond—he has provided a piece of artwork for each and every film Fulci directed. Scott has my sincere gratitude for his hard work and positive energy.

Michal Poplawski and Peter Jilmstad were both of great help with regards to finding images. I am deeply grateful to them for their kindness and generosity.

Jon Kitley provided some great shots of Fulci at his only American convention appearance in New York in 1996. I am very grateful for these valuable additions to the book.

Jason Slater provided me with some rare behind-the-scenes stills, which were provided to him by Lucio Fulci and the late David Warbeck. Jason also provided a copy of the English-language screenplay translation for *Zombie*, which was given to him by the film's English dubbing director, the late Nick Alexander. He has my gratitude for donating these rare items for the benefit of this book.

Michele de Angelis, who served as Fulci's assistant director on such films as *Touch of Death*, *The Ghosts of Sodom*, *The House of Clocks* and *The Sweet House of Horrors*, provided me with some continuity snapshots from the set of *Touch of Death*.

I am also grateful to Lucas Balbo, whose extensive image archive yielded some great stills from some of the more obscure Fulci titles. Also, thanks to Joshua Randell, who donated a couple of images, as well as to Andrea Rossi, who provided some shots of Fulci's gravesite in the *Prima Porta* cemetery in Rome.

Fulci super-fan Mark Jason Murray provided some images from the cast reunion of *The House by the Cemetery* from 2011 and the *City of the Living Dead* cast reunion from 2010; in addition to being a huge fan of Fulci's work, he has also helped to promote and preserve his legacy. Mark's line of "bobble head" figures includes a couple pertaining to Fulci's works (including one of the *Maestro* himself, which continues to look balefully down on me as I write these words!) and can be purchased from this website: www.cultcollectibles.com. Mark also runs a website devoted to the actress Catriona MacColl, who featured so prominently in three of Fulci's most beloved horror films; it can be located at: www.catrionamaccoll.com.

The images contained in this book are the property of their respective authors, production companies and/or copyright owners; they are reproduced here solely in the interest of publicity and educative purposes.

Tim Paxton worked overtime to provide the beautiful cover for this book. Tim's work already graced my two-part study of the *giallo* film—*So Deadly, So Perverse*—and I look forward to working with him on future projects, as well. The iconic Italian poster artwork for *Zombie* provided the focal point of the cover design for this book, but despite our best efforts, we have not been able to determine the identity of the artist responsible; it has been suggested that it may have been the work of the late "Symeoni"/Sandro Simeoni, but that is mere speculation. We doff our caps in respect to whomever it was who devised this stark but beautiful artwork and it, too, is reproduced here in the spirit of publicity and educative purposes.

A good book needs a good title and I struggled on this front for a long time. Fulci's work is so diverse and encompasses so many genres and I didn't want to go down the route of predictability by simply paying lip service to his better-known horror movies. I finally reached out for suggestions among my friends on Facebook and was gratified when author Wayne Maginn made the suggestion of *Splintered Visions*. It just fits—and I am grateful to Wayne for coming up with the idea.

The following people were interviewed by me for this book, and they all have our thanks for cooperating and sharing their thoughts: Al Cliver, Silvia Collatina, Carlo De Mejo, Giannetto De Rossi, Geretta Geretta, Antonella Interlenghi, the late and much-missed Richard Johnson, Zora Kerova, Marina Loi, Giovanni Lombardo Radice, Ray Lovelock, Catriona MacColl, Paolo Malco, Jared Martin, Cinzia Monreale, Franco Nero, Beatrice Ring and Venantino Venantini. The following interviews were conducted by Mike Baronas (sometimes in collaboration with Kit Gavin) and are being published here for the first time: Florinda Bolkan, Barbara Cupisti, the late Frances Nacman, Andrea Occhipinti, the late Carlo Rambaldi and Jean Sorel. Adrienne Larussa did not have time to do a new interview, but graciously provided me with a copy of her career-length interview with Tim Ferrante from the magazine *The Phantom of the Movies' Videoscope*; relevant quotes as provided with proper accreditation. Steve Fenton and Dennis Capicik kindly donated their out-of-print interview with Brett Halsey, which touches upon so many facets of his career in addition to his work with Lucio. Fulci fanatic Lionel Grenier runs a marvelous French website devoted to the *maestro*, titled luciofulci.fr, and he graciously allowed me to print his interviews with Michele de Angelis, Lara Naszinski and Roberto Sbarigia, in addition to providing some information on Fulci's lesser-known career as a writer of short stories and magazine articles. Any comments from Fulci's friends and collaborators that are not credited to a specific source in the footnotes were culled from the DVD *Paura: Lucio Fulci Remembered Vol. 1*, which was created and compiled by Mike Baronas; these comments are utilized here with Mike's blessing.

In addition to these many fine and invaluable collaborators, I would also like to extend special thanks to the following people: Rita and Marisa Agostini, Mark Thompson Ashworth, Jenn, Jessica and Jacob Baronas, Douglas Bowers, Jared and Jacquie Burnworth, Tony M. Clarke, Horace Cordier, Pierpaolo De Mejo, Franco Di Girolamo, Gav Ellinger, Camilla Fulci, Eric McNaughton, Mark and Miranda Murray, Matt Gemmell Robertson, Tim Wickens and Chris Workman. Each and every one of them were of help to this project—some of them simply by being there to act as sounding boards when needed and they have my undying gratitude for this.

I would also like to extend a special thank you to my ever-supportive parents, Gary and Diane Howarth, and to my wonderful publisher Midnight Marquee Press, Inc. (Gary Svehla and A. Susan Svehla, whose design work is again much in evidence). It is the support and enthusiasm of the Svehlas and the many people thanked in this section that make writing these books a special treat. I would also be remiss if I neglected to thank Stephanie Kazamek, who not only puts up with my passion for genre movies—but actively takes an interest in them, as well. I am very grateful to have you in my life.

Ordinarily, this would be where I would move on to the next section, but I need to take a moment for an extra word of special thanks. As many of you holding this volume are aware, we attempted to bring you a special limited edition hardcover printing of this book; it was an uphill battle and we ultimately were defeated, but a number of devoted Fulci fans put their money where their mouths were and paid up front to try and make this dream become a reality. I would like to take a moment to thank all of you who have not already been thanked earlier on in this section: Archer Avenue Productions, Denis Beresford, Elmar Berger, John Cooper, Bruce Crelin, Richard Doyle, Michael Duffield, David Dunn, Brian Frederick, Keith Gamble, Paul Grove, Andrew Hale, Michael and Victoria Hall, David Hallmark, Donald Isom, Lee Karr, James Killough, Marco Lanzagorta, Brandon McQuatters, John Melligh, David Munoz, Celeste Padilla, David Parker, Gary Patry, Lawrence Raffel, Douglas G. Rednour, Merlyn Roberts, James Rodriguez, Matthew Saunders, Mark Savage, Matthew Shimkus, Daniel Snoke, Greg Sonier, John Stell, Damin Toell, Yamagata Tsuruoka, Jamie Tutino, Thomas Ullrich, Carlos Villar, Robert Weiner and Russ Weissenburger.

# Author's Preface

To the public at large, the name Lucio Fulci is at best obscure. Among horror fans and cult film enthusiasts, his reputation looms large, albeit with tremendous controversy attached. For some, he is the supreme "Godfather of Gore." For others, he is a low-talent hack who made his name following templates established by such filmmakers as Dario Argento and George A. Romero. Sadly, few seem to fully appreciate the entire length and breadth of his filmography, the diversity of which is frequently amazing.

My own introduction to Fulci came at an early age, though it would take many more years for his name and legacy to become known to me. *The Black Cat* (1981), one of his less visceral late period horror movies, was something of a staple on the USA Network in the 1980s and it certainly made an impression, though not necessarily for the best of reasons: these were the days of panning and scanning (or outright cropping) of widescreen movies on TV and Fulci's widescreen vistas and fetishistic close-ups suffered accordingly. I didn't really realize what I was seeing at the time, but all those squashed close-ups of people's eyes lingered in the mind as an oddity, to say the least. A little later, some of the image-heavy books on horror movies I was devouring as a child featured some memorably nasty stills from *Zombie* (1979) and *The House by the Cemetery* (1981). These images carried much more impact than the usual picture from the more genteel Hammer and Universal horrors, which dominated my attention, and they couldn't help but make an impression for that reason. As time went by and I became more invested in studying the horror film, I began to realize that Fulci was a name of some weight—but at this stage in the game, the general critical consensus was far from favorable. I couldn't help but form the admittedly unfair impression that he was a no-talent hack who relied on generous helpings of gore and sadism as a means of compensating for a general lack of ability in other areas. Certainly, nothing I read in the studious likes of Phil Hardy's *The Encyclopedia of Horror Films* did anything to correct that impression; for Hardy and his stable of august writers (including Kim Newman and Tom Milne), Fulci represented the sad decline of the Italian horror film from the glory days of Riccardo Freda and Mario Bava. Yet, it was my interest in Bava that would

**Lucio Fulci (center) jokes around with (from left to right) unknown, David Warbeck and producer Fabrizio De Angelis; photo courtesy of Jason Slater.**

encourage me to give Fulci (and others of his ilk) a proper chance. I acquired copies of some of his best-known films—in state-of-the-art widescreen, no less—and began to familiarize myself with his work. The rest, as they say, is history.

Fulci's place in the canon of great horror filmmakers is nowhere near so assured as that of Bava or Argento, but there is every reason to argue that he is among the least properly appreciated directors of his era. His range is truly astonishing: He directed comedies, musicals, sword and sorcery fantasies, *poliziotteschi*, horror, *gialli*, sci-fi, Westerns, erotica ... and what's more: he did them all *well*. Fulci never set out to become enshrined as a director of horror films, but he took to the genre like a duck to water and never bemoaned his lot. After struggling for so many years, seeing so many films of which he was proud dwindle and die at the box-office, the surprise success of *Zombie* came as a much-needed relief. The film was a smash hit across the globe, even if critics savaged it, and it pointed to a new direction for his then-fledgling career. More trials and tribulations would await, but the floodgates of gore and carnage had opened; there was no going back, even if Fulci had a mind to do so. From the point of view of the mainstream press, being associated with horror films was bad enough—but add in the constant allegations of unoriginality and out-and-out plagiarism that greeted his work and it's easy to see that Fulci's battle was destined to be an uphill one. It didn't matter that Fulci's so called "living dead" films owed precious little to those of Romero; the point was, Romero's films (principally *Dawn of the Dead*, 1978, which had been co-financed by Argento) led the way and as such, Fulci was destined to exist in his shadow. A similar problem plagued the director earlier in his career when his stylish and mature *gialli* (baroque Italian thrillers with a predisposition to the lurid and the irrational) were compared unfavorably to those of Argento.

Fulci's renaissance as a purveyor of potent screen violence earned him a place in cinema infamy, especially in the U.K., where no less than three of his films ended up on the notorious "video nasties" list. More will be discussed with regards to this lamentable episode in the history of censorship in the chapter devoted to Fulci's splattery watershed movie *Zombie*, but in essence the list arose out of public furor over the ease with which minors could conceivably get hold of violent and/or salacious materials due to the emergence of the home video revolution. Many of Fulci's films had already been censored for theatrical release, but it proved harder to keep tabs on what the various video labels were providing as the home video boom took off with full force. Lead by moral crusader Mary Whitehouse—who would later admit that she had never even *seen* any of these films—a group of irate citizens hounded parliament until some career-minded politicians saw the potential to grab headlines. Thus, the Obscene Publications Act was instituted and Fulci's *Zombie* (known in the U.K. as *Zombie Flesh Eaters*), *The Beyond* and *The House by the Cemetery* found themselves labeled as well and truly obscene. By contrast, *City of the Living Dead* somehow managed to escape classification as a true "video nasty," but local members of the police force looking to enforce the strict guidelines of the Obscene Publications Act pulled it often from the shelves. Fulci's nihilistic *giallo The New York Ripper* would fare even worse, being denied both a theatrical and home video release in any form for many years. No doubt Fulci relished the controversy in the spirit of "there's no such thing as bad publicity," but in the eyes of some of the more pious and genteel members of the press, this merely served to cement the director's reputation as a purveyor of filth—a pornographer of violence, in fact.

Filmmakers are often judged—at least in the short run—by their more recent works, and sadly it is here that Fulci is at his most vulnerable. He spent roughly the last decade of his career battling various physical ailments that drained his cash supply and made it necessary for him to work when he would have been better off recuperating and regaining his strength. Never one to shrink away from a challenge, he threw himself into various projects, but they were invariably cash-strapped and time simply was not on his side; as such, many of these later films don't only feel impoverished, they feel half-finished. Less sympathetic viewers have interpreted this as carelessness on Fulci's part, but the reality is that he simply didn't have the energy, the stamina or the support of his most talented and valuable collaborators to make the very best out of these projects. When confronted with works like *The Ghosts of Sodom* (1988) or *Demonia* (1990), even the most sympathetic of Fulci's fans tend to groan and retreat to discussing their favorites among his earlier works; there's good reason for this, as it is indeed difficult to make a particularly compelling case for these films. That being said, Fulci's flair for the absurd and the audacious is still evident sporadically in these films and it is not difficult to believe that if they had come at a better time in his life, he may well have given them the kind of treatment which distinguished his best work. Unfortunately, this is all merely theorizing and at the end of the day, his final works served to put a final nail in his coffin (metaphorically speaking) where the critics were concerned.

When Fulci passed away in 1996, he was on the cusp of a potential comeback thanks to the intervention of former rival Dario Argento. *The Wax Mask*, based on a story by Gaston Leroux, promised to offer a major shot-in-the-arm to the fledgling Italian horror industry, with its dream teaming of Argento as producer and Fulci as writer-director. Sadly, it was not meant to be and Fulci would die of complications related to diabetes before production commenced; the film that emerged in 1997 was radically overhauled by Sergio Stivaletti, Fulci's replacement in the director's chair, and the best bits in it appear to have originated from Fulci's original screenplay. Obituaries were typically condescending, dismissing much of his output as gory and nonsensical, and very few saw fit to acknowledge his long and varied career in the film business. From his origins as a production assistant and screenwriter, Fulci dabbled in many genres and crossed the paths of some of the most interesting and eclectic talents in the Italian film scene.

Of course, it would be unfair to suggest that I am the first writer to delve into the muddy waters of Fulci's legacy. The first in-depth appreciation of Fulci that I ever read came courtesy of a booklet *Beyond the Gates*, written by the late, lamented Chas. Balun, published at the time of Fulci's death. It was a slim book, but it was the first to give some sense of Fulci's full background as a filmmaker. A few years later, Stephen Thrower delivered *Beyond Terror: The Films of Lucio Fulci*. Published by FAB Press in the U.K., this handsomely illustrated tome took a more scholarly approach and provided a truly well rounded approach to its subject. To date, it remains the most impressive volume on Fulci and his work written in the English language. In Italy, at least two significant volumes have been published: *Il terrorista dei generi: Tutto il cinema di Lucio Fulci* by Paolo Albiero and Giacamo Cacciatore and *Lucio Fulci: Il poeta della crudeltà* by Antonio Bruschini and Antonio Tentori. Fulci's gory horror films have, of course, been the subject of much appreciation and study in genre-oriented magazines such as *Fangoria*. Suffice it to say, I doff my proverbial cap at all the writers who have come before me in this field and I can only hope to have brought something a little different to the table that will prove interesting and illuminating on the topic.

It is my hope that this book will shed some light on some of the less familiar facets of Fulci's career, while paying proper tribute to his best-known genre work, as well. There's no getting around the fact that Fulci's popularity among fans with a taste for the extreme and the confrontational is as strong as ever, but along with the nasty, gleefully sadistic streak which runs through so much of his work, there is also a distinctive voice tempered with ironic humor and a flair for creating a richly atmospheric and tactile environment. It goes without saying that this is a study of Fulci's films, but it is also very much an *auteur* study at heart. Yes, the *auteur* approach has its problems and limitations, but it also has merit where applicable. In addition to directing, Fulci also had a very heavy hand in the writing of many of his films. He is not always credited in this capacity, but he wrote screenplays (invariably in collaboration, as is the norm in the Italian film industry) long before he was directing narrative features and his sense of story and structure would invariably serve him well as a director. It is not my contention that Fulci was a tortured genius slaving away in solitude: film is a collaborative medium, after all, and it is for this reason that many critics have turned their backs on the *auteur* theory. At its worst, the *auteur* theory is narrow-minded and overly simplistic, attaching great importance to the director at the expense of other key collaborative figures. I hope to steer clear of this pitfall by acknowledging—indeed, playing up—the presence of the key creative talents who worked closely with Fulci throughout his career, but inevitably it does boil down to the basic hypothesis that Fulci's films were uniquely his own.

This book does not seek to offer the final word on Fulci and his work. It's my sincere hope that no such book ever surfaces, thus necessitating more and more critical works to emerge that are dedicated to his uneven but impressive filmography. As this text will hopefully make clear, Fulci was a well-read, cultured and sophisticated artist; he was also notoriously volatile and eccentric, making him a man who inspired as much controversy among those who knew him as he did among the critics who generally trashed his work. The odds of Fulci ever being recognized as a great director among the critical intelligentsia is unlikely, to say the least; however, if this book helps to further a serious consideration of his talents among the more sympathetic numbers of genre-oriented critics and scholars, then so much the better. Ultimately, there is much more to his work than may initially be apparent and it's my aim to draw some attention to some of these facets, without, hopefully, being too solemn or pedantic about it. What Fulci would have made of such an exercise is open to speculation. Given his penchant for the blunt and the fiery, however, I think it is safe to assume that his overall take on critics in general can be summed up in three choice words: Fuck them all.

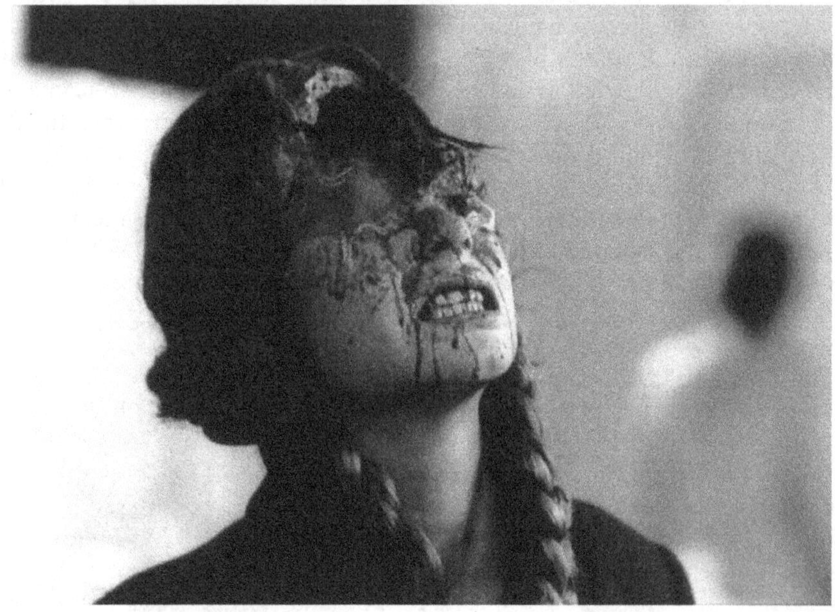

**Extreme imagery such as this—from *The Beyond*—became Fulci's trademark.**

# Introduction
## by Brett Halsey

I am very happy that Troy Howarth has written this book. I have been waiting for a book that offers an honest, candid look at a talented, friendly and very complicated man. I starred in four films with Lucio Fulci, and treasure the memory of each one of them. I came to truly like and admire Lucio as a director, an actor and as a friend.

I first met the "Godfather of Gore" in Spain on the morning of our first day of shooting *The Devil's Honey*. He was very frail from a series of debilitating illnesses, but his eyes and voice were as bright and strong as a healthy young bull. I soon learned that his gruff exterior was a façade. He had a great sense of humor and an infectious smile that he was quick to share with those he liked.

I have been fortunate enough to work with the directors most associated with Fulci—Riccardo Freda, Mario Bava, Dario Argento and Luigi Cozzi. Maybe I liked working best with Fulci because with his love for acting, we shared a similar point of view. *Touch of Death* is one of my favorite films, because we took a script that was almost a straight thriller (*giallo*) and turned it into a sort of black comedy.

Lucio Fulci has his critics, but as we all know, it is far easier to criticize than to create. He was an artist who loved his work and has earned his honored place in movie history.

Brett Halsey
Laguna Woods, Calif.

**Brett Halsey and Lucio Fulci (right) in between takes on the set of *The Devil's Honey*.**

# My Maestro & His Galloping Cadavers
## by Mike Baronas

Enigmatic visions created by European horror artisans made up the American VHS boom of the mid-1980s and such searches struck an everlasting chord with a niche demographic who retain these films in their blood. Directors with household names today—Argento, Bava, Naschy, Lenzi, Franco, et al.—once had sought after, and often elusive, treasures at the neighborhood mom-and-pop video store. Discovery became an almost taboo activity, as the content of these films was always unsavory. Obsession followed soon thereafter and hunting for such films became a Saturday morning ritual. Never one to pass on an in-stock copy of new stateside arrivals such as *Day of the Dead* or *The Re-Animator*, I always tried to include an *Invasion of the Flesh Hunters/Cannibal Apocalypse*-esque rental for good measure in hopes of finding a movie that made me as uneasy as the first dance with my *Maestro*.

It was *The Gates of Hell/City of the Living Dead* that captured my 15-year-old imagination and has only tightened its grip since, dragging me down a lifelong path of Lucio Fulci worship (or what I deem as being a "Fulcifarian") that continues to this day. Since you are holding this book in your hands, you certainly don't need me to explain the film's disconcerting attributes.

Awkward high school years soon gave way to a larger community of like-minded college friends that I was able to pummel with just the right film to tap into their fears while preaching the good word of Lucio. While multiple viewings of the same gorefests—namely *Zombie*, *The House by the Cemetery*, *The Seven Doors of Death* and the aforementioned *Gates*—were always a blast with the uninitiated, I yearned to see more of Fulci's atmospheric offerings.

It was the early '90s when I began my half-horror, half-metal magazine *G.A.S.P. etc.* and, again, I found folks out there with similar interests, namely Mark Jason Murray, who was doing his own fanzine at the time called *Shocking Images*. A kindred Fulcifarian, Mark was instrumental in providing me with the fix I so desired. Through tape trading, he accumulated titles that spanned the director's entire career and proceeded to dub and send me copies of everything in his collection. Many difficult hours were spent enduring static-riddled Franco and Ciccio slapstick taped from RAI television to attempting to decipher politically charged sex comedies from a time and country (not to mention language) that escaped me. A fan of the Sergio Leone "Man With No Name" staples, I found much more enjoyment in Fulci's Spaghetti Westerns—*Massacre Time*, *Four of the Apocalypse*, *Silver Saddle*, and, in many respects, his *White Fang* films—which allowed the director to finally uncork his more brutal and sadistic visions. Fulci carried these sentiments over to one of his personal favorite works, the torture-laden period piece *Beatrice Cenci*. He pushed the envelope even further with his now classic *gialli*—*A Lizard in a Woman's Skin*, *Don't Torture a Duckling* and *The Psychic*—and allowed his internal pot to boil over onto the screen from that point forward.

**Mike Baronas with Catriona MacColl, one of Fulci's favorite actresses.**

While I gravitated to Fulci's darker offerings, I finally began to piece together the breadth of what the man was capable. He was a true chameleon in his ability to ride the ever-changing cinematic trends in such a grueling industry for over 40 years. My appreciation and respect for his body of work prompted me to want to find out more about the man himself. Back in 1996 I had that chance, even when Mother Nature decided to bury New York City under 20 inches of snow on January 7 where the *Fangoria* "Weekend of Horrors" was taking place. Lucio was the guest of honor in his first ever U.S. convention appearance at the Hotel Pennsylvania (I remember this only because it was the first and last time I stayed anywhere that stacked telephone books to hold up one corner of my bed) and he was mobbed by fans after his panel on Saturday. I stood in line for what seemed an eternity to finally have an obviously agitated Lucio sign my *Gates of Hell* one-sheet and move on to the next item passed in front of him. He never looked up. He never acknowledged my existence. Shaking it off quickly, I chalked it up to a probable language barrier and/or jet lag issue. I approached his wrangler about possibly doing an interview with Lucio for *Alternative Cinema Magazine* and was told to speak with someone on *Fangoria*'s staff. No go there. I decided to try and confront him *mano a mano* and waited until the now exhausted director finished his signing and made his way to the elevator. As we ascended in silence, I was overcome with the inability to say anything. There were so many questions that the man admiring my *Zombie* t-shirt at arm's length could answer. But the words never came out and an important life lesson about hesitation would soon be learned as the elevator doors closed behind him. Later that evening I had a drink with a staff member from Creation Entertainment (the convention's financial backer) and told her my tale of woe. She assured me that she could arrange a chat after Lucio's panel the following afternoon. My excitement upon waking the next morning was short-lived as the local New York television stations were tweaking over the amount of expected snow that had just begun to coat the pavement outside. I quickly had to weigh my options and the responsible side of me won out by determining that chances were quite good that *Fangoria* would have Fulci back again in short order given his appearance's popularity. With that, I escaped from New York and beat the bulk of the blizzard back to Massachusetts.

**Mike Baronas camps it up with Dakar, who appeared in *Zombie*.**

Lucio Fulci passed away two months later on March 13, 1996, from diabetic shock.

Needless to say, the death of my *Maestro* had haunted me for years thereafter with an overwhelming need to keep his name and body of work alive and in the public eye. But how? What could a mere fanboy who couldn't speak a lick of Italian do?

I credit my next steps to Stephen Thrower's gorgeous 1999 tome *Beyond Terror: The Films of Lucio Fulci* for what it *didn't* include, specifically who the late director was and what made him tick. Thus began my quest to locate and interview as many folks who worked with and knew Fulci over the years and pull together my own book to serve as a companion of sorts. I made some initial inroads via phone and fax and connected with English-speaking cast members such as Jared Martin, Brett Halsey, Giovanni Lombardo Radice and Florinda Bolkan, but I soon hit a wall with that dreaded language barrier. It was around this time that I became acquainted with a knowledgeable newsgroup poster named Kit Gavin and over the course of several chats I saw my dream begin to take shape. Kit spoke 3 or 4 languages, including Italian, and had the same level of enthusiasm for European cinema. We could seriously give Fulci's legacy an informed shot now I thought to myself.

It was also around this time that I met Lucio's daughter Antonella online and we emailed each other at length. She informed me that she was going to be a guest at the horror convention 'Cult-Con 2000' in Tarrytown, New York with genre greats such as Ruggero Deodato and Claudio Simonetti. It turned out to be a small yet very meaningful event to me in the years to come, as it was the birthplace of some lifelong friendships and, sadly, betrayals.

While Kit and I continued to amass contact details for the ultimate Fulci collaborator list, I received an email out of the blue from Mark Jason Murray about a New York company who was going to begin licensing Eurocult classics we grew up with on DVD. They were looking for paraphernalia for their debut title that happened to be Lucio's 1990 nunsploitation offering *Demonia*. As luck would have it, I had star Brett Halsey's recollections that I was willing to share. This was the beginning of my three-year partnership with Media Blasters' "Shriek Show" line of releases as a Supplement Producer. Together with Kit and his invaluable resources in tow, we were able to convince the powers that be to send us off on my first of eight trips to Bella Roma, in September 2001.

I met Kit at Heathrow where he appropriately held a picture of Lucio to greet me. After a few days in London where we secured interview times for our debut DVD project together—Deodato's *Last Cannibal World* or, as Shriek Show released it, *Jungle Holocaust*—I landed in Europe for the first time. I was filled with nervous energy for this newfound job opportunity and the prospect of meeting many of those I grew up with on VHS who worked alongside my *Maestro* during down time for our tribute book.

We stayed with a friend of Kit's during that extended two-week period, who happened to be a voice-over actor named Ian Danby who also appeared in Joe D'Amato's *Absurd* and as the announcer in Fulci's *Rome, 2072 A.D.: The New Gladiators*. A man who enjoyed enormous jugs of wine, Danby was very kind to allow us to come and go as we pleased and thankfully offered us a meal now and again. We budgeted poorly this first trip and ended up dining primarily from the jar of peanut butter I brought from home. We also walked endlessly to appointments in the Roman heat as we only had enough to get around via public transportation, which was often and literally miles away from our destinations. Despite these inconveniences, I felt an immediate connection with Rome. Not a drop of Roman blood in me, but I felt instantly at ease upon our arrival.

I can never forget the very first on-camera interview we conducted. It was with the late, great Ivan Rassimov at his home, just outside of Rome. We cordially sat and listened to him relay memories of an often-difficult shoot, while 4,300 miles away two planes smashed into New York City's World Trade Center, sending both skyscrapers crumbling to the ground.

Needless to say, everyone we met from that point forward was even more "molto simpatico" and equally concerned about what lay ahead for the world. We were less than one week into our almost three week adventure and thankfully we had the good fortune to meet face-to-face with some of my cinematic Fulci-related heroes—namely Paolo Malco, Giovanni Lombardo Radice, Carlo De Mejo, Venantino Venantini, Andrea Occhipinti, Fabrizio Jovine, Dagmar Lassander—for both the book project and to keep my mind occupied on things other than the tragedy back home. I would be remiss not to bestow eternal thanks to the incredibly kind and generous Sacha Maria Darwin for a lifesaving dinner and that magic elixir known as grappa that cured Kit of a nasty bout of food poisoning.

All things considered, I was enthralled with what Kit and I accomplished on that first trek. Not only did we record an audio commentary with Ruggero Deodato and shot interviews with leading men Rassimov and Massimo Foschi of *Jungle Holocaust*, we left with a fistful of audiocassettes filled with historic memories of those we had met for our book. The plan was to cull them down into individual Q&As as well as show the public what these stars looked like today by including an ancillary DVD compilation with each answering one question that I shot on camera: "What is your fondest memory of Lucio?"

**Lucio Fulci signs a poster for *City of the Living Dead* (aka *The Gates of Hell*) for Mike Baronas.**

Highlights during that time in my life were many. Some that instantly come to mind include presenting Florinda Bolkan with a bouquet of flowers and receiving a big kiss square on the lips, enjoying the most elegant meal of my life (with gold flatware no less) on Dagmar Lassander's veranda, awkwardly smoking hash with Frances Nacman in her bathroom, meeting AL FUCKING CLIVER (!!!), drinking what Kit recalls as being "Peruvian firewater" before noon with Dakar, giggling as the little white dog an egotistical Fabio Testi carried around with him pissed all over his shirt, slurping down a homemade strawberry smoothy made by Catriona MacColl at the café she and her husband owned at the time in one of the most picturesque places I'd ever visited—and many more tales that could fill a book all on its own.

Subsequent trips also saw us digging deeper and locating those that worked behind the scenes alongside my *Maestro,* all of whom praised Fulci's on-set craftsmanship; everything from his technical knowledge of a camera's intricacies to his extraordinary (and usually bombastic) ability to run the whole show when necessary. It was during these later visits when multiple interviewees informed us that they were instructed *not* to speak to us. It seems I had made an error in judgment describing my concept much too freely, and a curiously similar book to our own was already in the works by an Italian author busy spreading misinformation. Thankfully, many celebrities we met felt everyone should have access to their memories of Lucio. Pensive speculation surrounding this situation remains, as an olive branch can only be extended so many times.

**Mike Baronas with Sacha Maria Darwin, who appeared in Fulci's *Touch of Death* and *Voices from Beyond*.**

It took over a decade, but shortly before *Splintered Visions* began taking shape, one of the most elusive and important people in Lucio's life entered mine. I had always hoped to have some level of family input, so connecting with the daughter who worked side-by-side on the majority of her father's later projects put the wind back into my sails. Camilla Fulci, the victim of a horse riding accident in her youth, rose above her challenges and was being groomed to take over the family business. While she served in multiple capacities on Lucio's films until his perplexing and untimely death, it is still nearly impossible for Fulci's youngest to speak freely about any of that.

It has been many moons since I was last in Rome. The decline in Shriek Show titles and my growing family trumped any further international trips starting about 10 years ago. Work on the book also came to an abrupt halt around then as well. It wasn't until years later when I began watching some of the video tributes by those I had met when the heart of my entire project revealed itself. The collective responses to "What is your fondest memory of Lucio?" proved to be a worthwhile standalone memorial and I ended up releasing the 4-hour *Paura: Lucio Fulci Remembered* on DVD in 2008. I optimistically titled this as "Volume 1" as there were obviously many more folks to speak with about my *Maestro,* and decided to put my efforts into bringing Italy to America for a change.

I saw my first worthwhile foray into the world of conventions by utilizing the frequent flier miles I accumulated going back and forth to Europe and bringing Giovanni Lombardo Radice to assist in the promotion of my DVD. We did a marathon of four shows in five weekends around the U.S., peppering a couple with Ruggero Deodato and Catriona MacColl appearing alongside us. This new venture met with enough success that I continue to import a wide variety of Eurohorror icons to the convention circuit. As it seems to have always been, money is secondary to what's really important here. Not only does it help to keep this beloved genre alive, but has proven to many of my actor friends—many of whom wanted to escape the memories of these low-budget video nasties—how worthwhile their contributions were from the love and admiration they receive from their fans. It has also proven to be a great avenue to reunite those who haven't worked or seen each other in decades as I've done with cast reunions for *Zombie, City of the Living Dead* and *The House by the Cemetery,* to name a few. The perks for a geek like me continue as well by being able to do things like bring Catriona back to visit said *House* at the conclusion of a convention appearance in Massachusetts, for example. I like to think that I'll always enjoy dipping my toe into this amazing world that my *Maestro* opened the doors to.

I'm most thankful to my friend Troy Howarth for embracing my years of work and utilizing much of it within these pages. Yet another Fulcifarian dream comes to fruition.

Mike Baronas
December 2014

# Beginnings

It all began with a woman. As Fulci would later explain:

> I used to work as an art critic while studying medicine, though I was interested in films. Then, one day, I fell in love with a woman who, after a while, dropped me because I wasn't well enough off. She came from an impoverished family, which had been wealthy and for those times—in the aftermath of the war—still were comfortably off. I remember I was going home in the train, there was a gentleman sitting opposite me reading a paper and an advertisement on the back said that the Centro Sperimentale [Note: Rome's film school] were going to be reopened. So, I decided to apply and Luchino Visconti examined me and admitted me to the school, where I managed to win his lasting esteem and that of his assistants, Antonioni, Pietrangeli and others.[1]

**Lucio Fulci, aged 9, in his school uniform; photo courtesy of Joshua Randell.**

In another interview, he would adjust the story ever so slightly. When asked where his passion for the cinema originated from, he replied:

> A woman, of course. You know, I used to be a doctor once, and I had a great passion for films. My favorite hobby, it was. One day, I had this huge argument with my head physician, so I left the hospital in a very bad mood and went home. My woman abandoned me on that very day, so I got on the bus, read about courses at the Centro Sperimentale and decided I was going to change my life. And I sure did.[2]

Fulci would learn the ins and outs of filmmaking at the Centro Sperimentale program and his determination to succeed would soon lead him to breaking into the film industry.

Lucio Fulci was born in Rome, in the Trastevere neighborhood, on June 17, 1927. His mother Lucia came from a reputable family from the city of Messina, in Sicily. Her family had a quarter of German blood in it, as Lucia's mother was related to the family of Professor Robert Koch, recipient of the 1905 Nobel Prize for Medicine.[3]

She had fallen for a man but her relatives opposed the relationship, so she left her family and joined him in Rome. However, Lucia and her lover separated before Lucio's birth. Lucio grew up with his mother and the housekeeper, and started his studies at the Convitto Nazionale, and then, at the start of the WWII, his mother had him move to Venice, at the local Naval College, where he had some success as a soccer player. Lucio returned to Rome before the end of the war, and enrolled at the Liceo Classico Giulio Cesare. Fulci was a politically committed adolescent, close to the Communist Party. One of his classmates was another future film director, Pasquale Festa Campanile. According to his peers, Fulci was a very intelligent student—but as a person, he presented as shy and rather shabby, with a blatant disregard for his personal appearance.[4]

After finishing high school, Lucio was already an ardent cinephile and was well versed in art and music, as well. However, his mother did not approve of his interests and tried to persuade him to continue his studies and become a lawyer. Eventually he ended up studying medicine as a compromise of sorts, while in the meantime cultivating his passion for the arts. He collaborated on several prestigious publications, besides earning his living with more trivial employments—one of the more colorful being when he acted as an assistant to a French fakir named Burma, who used to lock himself into a glass shrine and fast for days, amidst snakes (which Lucio bought at a local market). Dressed in a badly assembled suit which only vaguely resembled a tail-coat and armed with a microphone, Lucio addressed the passers-by and praised Burma's extraordinary self-control and resistance.[5] It was all a puff, of course, but it appealed to Fulci's love of the dramatic. Fulci would never pursue acting as a serious, primary profession, but he loved performing. This manifested itself on set, where he would frequently indulge in dramatic explosions of temperament, as well as in the occasional cameo roles he would perform for other directors, before ultimately playing a number of roles (normally uptight authority figures) in his own films; this would climax when he played himself, or more accurately a variation on himself, in the self-reflexive *Nightmare Concert (A Cat in the Brain)*.

He started off, like so many, working his way up the ladder. Soon after finishing his apprenticeship with Centro Sperimentale, he made the acquaintance of Demofilo Fidani. Fidani would go on to become a not-so-well-regarded director of Italian genre fare, notably Spaghetti Westerns that he would direct under the name of Miles Deen, but at this stage in the game he was starting off in the art department. He also netted a prestigious, albeit uncredited, job assisting Visconti on *La Terra Trema* (1948), one of the great Italian Neorealist pictures. In addition to working as a production designer and art director, Fidani was also responsible for putting together documentaries on various topics. Fulci's ambitious, outgoing character apparently impressed him and Fidani made him an offer. "He called me to make three [documentaries], with my friend Carletto Romano.[6] The titles were: *Una lezione al sistema*, featuring Fulvio Bernardini[7], about soccer; *Il sogno di Icaro*, about flight, and another, which I produced, about my painter friends, and with the participation of Massimo Girotti, *Pittura italiana del dopoguerra*. Carletto Romano directed and I took care of the sound."[8] Very little information survives about these early documentaries, but it would seem that they followed this order: *Una lezione al Sistema* (1948), *Il sogno di Icaro* (1948), *Pittori italiana del dopoguerra* (1948, which, as Fulci notes, was directed by Romano), *Pittori in provincia* (1949) and two back-to-back assignments devoted to one of Fulci's passions—sailing: *100,000 metri cubi* (1949) and *Zona di porta fluviale* (1949), but the latter two were never completed. Fulci would revisit the format years later with *I giovani e il lavoro* (1958), *Non sono d'accordo: Intervista a Ciccio Ingrassia e Franco Franchi* (1964) and *Tecnica della regatta* (1971). The first of these later credits would come just before he made the transition to directing his own feature films, while the second saw him highlighting the career of the comic duo who would become so inextricably linked to his early days as a director; they were both part of a newsreel series titled *Settimana Incom*, which were put on as an appetizer before the main course at the cinema. The latter would again allow him to explore his fascination with all things maritime. It should be noted that these documentaries did not necessarily arise out of a passionate desire to draw attention to special interests or hobbies. As Gino Moliterno explains in his epic *Historical Dictionary of Italian Cinema*, there were economic perks involved:

**Lucio Fulci at the Centro Sperimentale, where he studied films and filmmaking.**

> Full-length documentary filmmaking was provided by the Italian government itself, which in 1947 passed a law that introduced both a significant financial subsidy and a legal obligation on exhibitors to screen nationally produced documentaries together with feature films on at least 80 days each year. The immediate result was a massive increase in the annual number of documentaries, rising approximately from 250 in 1948 to 1,150 in 1955, the year in which the law was due to expire (it was, in fact, extended to 1962).[9]

In a sense, it would seem that Fulci was progressing with rapid speed; after all, he was only 21 years old and was already directing. These early works enabled Fulci to hone his craft and learn more of the practical side of making films, but they hardly did much to further his career and didn't earn him much in the way of money. Given that he wasn't going to get rich making specialized documentaries for regional audiences, he needed to find a way to further his experience while earning enough to keep body and soul together. To that end, he started working as an assistant director.

**Italian poster for *The Sins of Pompeii* (1950), on which Fulci served as an uncredited assistant director. Artwork by Martinati.**

He and Fidani would be united on the French-Italian co-production *Sins of Pompeii* (1950), a variation on the eruption of Mount Vesuvius. Fulci would go uncredited on the release prints, but he acted as an assistant to the second unit director, Aldo Vergano.[10] The film provided Fulci with his first intimate glimpse of the problems of mounting and executing an ambitious production filled with extras and special effects. However, he would not earn his first official feature film screen credit until 1952, when he made his first of many films with a man whose role in Fulci's career cannot possibly be over-estimated. Indeed, the gentleman in question would provide a dual role for the young aspiring filmmaker: not only would he help him to establish himself as an artist, he would also become the father figure young Lucio never had.

Stefano Vanzina, also known as Steno, was born in Rome in 1915. He became a popular satirist and cartoonist before breaking into films in 1939. He initially worked as a screenwriter and assistant director, collaborating frequently with the writer-director Mario Mattoli on a string of popular comedies and melodramas. As a screenwriter, he displayed a sharp sense of humor but was also at ease with such populist genres as swashbucklers; among his many credits was Riccardo Freda's popular hit *Return of the Black Eagle* (1946), which marked the screen debut of Gina Lollobrigida, in an uncredited bit part.[11] In 1949, he made the transition to directing with a series of films co-signed by the equally formidable Mario Monicelli (1915-2010), who would go on to direct the Oscar-winning *Big Deal on Madonna Street* (1958) and *Casanova 70* (1965), among others. The Steno/Monicelli films would include *Al diavolo la celebrità* (1949), *Totò cerca casa* (1950) and *Vita da cani* (1950), the latter of which contains some interesting credits of its own. The cinematographer on the film was future "King of Italian Horror" Mario Bava, with whom Fulci

**DVD sleeve for *Totò e i re di Roma*, Fulci's first collaboration with the director Steno.**

would later become good friends, and the cast includes early appearances by Lollobrigida (billed this time!) and Marcello Mastroianni. These early works proved to be successful and Steno would eventually split from Monicelli and direct features on his own, continuing to work steadily as a director until his death in 1988.

**Logo for *Settimana Incom*, a popular newsreel series for which Fulci did some of his first directing work.**

Fulci first collaborated with Steno on *Totò e i re di Roma* (1951). However, the film encountered problems with the censors and would not be released until later; Fulci was not credited on the final prints. He came to be involved in the project in an unusual way, as he would later explain in an interview: The original assistant director, Mario Marinari, was fired for becoming sexually involved with a female extra that Steno was hoping to seduce, so the director needed another assistant in a hurry and Fulci simply happened to be at the right place at the right time.[12] Other films starring Totò followed, including *Totò in Color* (1952). As the title indicates, it was sold on the gimmick that it was the first to feature the legendary comic (born Antonio Griffo Focas Flavio Angelo Ducas Comneno de Curtis di Bisanzio Gagliardi [!] in 1898) in color. Indeed, the film is of even greater historical significance as being the first major commercial Italian film to be filmed entirely in color.[13] In addition to assisting Steno, for which he finally received an onscreen credit as "Assistant Director," Fulci can also be seen playing a young man on a train who is desperately trying to get some sleep; it was the first of several unbilled cameo appearances Fulci would make for Steno, with later appearances including *Cinema d'altri tempi* (1953), *Un Americano a Roma* (1954) and *Piccola posta* (1955). Fulci was also rumored to have contributed some ideas to the script for *Totò in Color*, but he received no official credit in this capacity. Steno was taken with the ambitious Roman and took him under his wing. He would continue to work as an assistant director for the better part of the decade, often contributing to the screenplays of the films he was working on; he would develop a solid reputation as a screenwriter and this would indeed become the focal point of his career as the decade unfolded. As an assistant, he found one of his more prestigious assignments when he was hired to be Roberto Rossellini's assistant on the comedy-drama *Dov'è la libertà...?* (1954), again starring Totò.[14] This grim but amusing picture featured Totò as a barber with a jealous streak who commits a murder; he is released back to society after being imprisoned for 22 years and ultimately finds that he prefers life behind bars. The morbid dark humor of the film surely appealed to Fulci, whose own darker sensibilities would go untapped for many years. Even so, he was working steadily as a screenwriter and assistant director and things were definitely looking up.

But what of the woman whose rejection started it all? With typically wry humor, Fulci would say:

> Anyway, I bumped into that lady again 10 years later, by which time I was working as Steno's assistant and had written several scripts; I was sitting on the pavement with [cinematographer] Tonino Delli Colli in the Spanish Square waiting for the crew to arrive so we could shoot a particular scene and she happened to pass by. When she saw me, she came over looking as elegant as ever and, with an air of compassion asked me, "What are you doing these days?" Some poor folks just don't get to the cinema very often![15]

**Italian *locandina* for *Totò a colori*, Italy's first major production to be photographed entirely in color; artwork by Bob DeSeta.**

Notes:

1. Albiero, Paolo and Giacomo Cacciatore, *Il terrorista dei generi. Tutto il cinema di Lucio Fulci* (Rome: Un Mondo a Parte, 2004) pp. 19-20.
2. *Ibid.*
3. *Ibid.*
4. Palmerini, Luca M. and Gaetano Mistretta, *Spaghetti Nightmares*, (Key West: Fantasma Books, 1996), p. 58.
5. Curci, Loris, *Shock Masters of the Cinema*, (Key West: Fantasma Books, 1996), p. 68.
6. Carlo Romano (1908-1975) was a prolific Italian character actor (he played the role of Michele Curti in Federico Fellini's *I Vitelloni*, 1953) and vocal artist. He also dabbled in screenwriting and worked as an assistant to Alessandro Blasetti on the ambitious *peplum*, *Fabiola* (1949). However, he is arguably best remembered as the Italian voice of Jerry Lewis; he also dubbed Eli Wallach, Jason Robards and Rod Steiger into Italian in Sergio Leone's *The Good, The Bad and The Ugly* (1966), *Once Upon a Time in the West* (1968) and *Duck, You Sucker* (1971), respectively.
7. Fulvio Bernardini (1905-1984) was a famous ex soccer player and coach. As a player, he was part of the Italian team that won a bronze medal at the 1928 Summer Olympics; he also coached the Italian national team from 1974 to 1975.
8. Fulci interviewed in the documentary *La notte americana del dott. Lucio Fulci*, directed by Antonietta De Lillo.
9. Moliterno, Gino, *Historical Dictionary of Italian Cinema* (Metuchen: The Scarecrow Press, Inc., 2008), p. 118.
10. Aldo Vergano (1897-1957) was a prolific screenwriter whose filmography extends back to the 1920s. He also worked sporadically as a director. He directed the important Neorealist drama *Il sole sorge ancora* (1946), but his career went downhill after *I fuorilegge* (1949), based on the exploits of Sicilian outlaw Salvatore Giuliano (whose story would be immortalized in the Francesco Rosi masterpiece *Salvatore Giuliano*, 1962), was compromised by squeamish censors.
11. Federico Fellini is rumored to have collaborated on the script without credit, as well.
12. Fulci interviewed in the documentary *La notte americana del dott. Lucio Fulci*, directed by Antonietta De Lillo.
13. That said, the first Italian film shot in color was the religious drama *Mater dei* (1950), directed by Emilio Cordero and about the life of the Virgin Mary.
14. The film had a very troubled production: Rossellini abandoned the project before it was completed. Rumors flew fast that Mario Monicelli stepped in to finish it, but he denied this. There was also a rumor that Federico Fellini directed some scenes, and Fulci was also reported in several sources to have directed part of the picture in Rossellini's absence. Interestingly, for a man who was not shy about speaking about his involvement in films, Fulci never made any such claims about doing this himself.
15. Palmerini, Luca M. and Gaetano Mistretta, *Spaghetti Nightmares*, (Key West: Fantasma Books, 1996), p. 58.

# Fulci the Screenwriter

Note: Since this is an English-language publication, I have endeavored to refer to the films under review by their best-known English-language titles. In some cases, this is simply not possible: many of Fulci's early movies were never officially released in English-speaking provinces. In those instances, the titles are listed in Italian. Some of Fulci's films are known under different English-language titles—for example, *City of the Living Dead* and *The Gates of Hell* are one-and-the-same—and in those cases I have settled on the more popular variant. Other titles are often abbreviated for home video, but I have elected to go with the actual onscreen titles: thus, it is *Rome, 2072 A.D.: The New Gladiators*, not *The New Gladiators*, and *Nightmare Concert (A Cat in the Brain)*, not *A Cat in the Brain*. I have also decided not to get bogged down in attaching dates to the films under review every time one of them is referenced; however, films not under review will have the date of release mentioned in brackets—for example, *Deep Red* (1975) or *Dawn of the Dead* (1978), etc.

## L'uomo, la bestia e la virtù (1953)

Directed by Stefano Vanzina (as Steno); Produced by Antonio Altaviti and Luigi De Laurentiis; Screenplay by Vitaliano Brancati, Lucio Fulci, Jean Josipovici and Stefano Vanzina (as Steno), based on the novel by Luigi Pirandello; Director of Photography: Mario Damicelli; Editor: Gisa Radicchi Levi; Music by Angelo Francesco Lavagnino and P.G. Redi; Assistant Directors: Lucio Fulci and Sergio Leone

Main Players: Totò (Professor Paolino); Orson Welles (Captain Perella, The Beast); Viviane Romance (Assunta Perella); Mario Castellani (The Doctor); Franca Faldini (Mariannina)

*Professor Paolino is engaged in an affair with Assunta, the wife of the rough and ill-tempered Captain Perella. When their relationship results in an unwanted pregnancy, Paolino must think of a way to make it look as though the Captain is the father. The Captain, meanwhile, has been exerting himself with mistresses on his trip—but unless Paolino is able to arrange an amorous rendezvous between the surly sea dog and his neglected wife, the affair will be exposed …*

Luigi Pirandello (1867-1936) was the son of well-to-do parents. He was especially close to his beloved mother, and when he discovered that his father was being unfaithful to her, it caused a deep rift between father and son. His own love life was complicated, as well: he fell in love with his cousin and the ensuing relationship was the root of more familial conflict before the romance was ultimately accepted. Pirandello would not follow through with the plan to marry his cousin, but he would eventually marry a shy, retiring woman who nevertheless possessed a bitter streak of jealousy. It is perhaps not surprising that the specter of family dysfunction and infidelity should loom over a number of his most famous works, including *Liolà* (1916), *Il gioco delle parti/The Rules of the Game* (1918) and *L'uomo, la bestia e la virtù/The Man, The Beast and The Virtue* (1919); the latter was reportedly written during a period of great personal grief for the writer, as his wife succumbed to mental illness and was eventually institutionalized. That is not to suggest that his main interest was in matters of sex and fidelity, however, whereas in reality his characters were often driven by a crisis of identity. In this regard, one may point to a play like *Sei personaggi in cerca d'autore/Six Characters in Search of an Author* (1921) as being a better representation of his complex, often challenging approach to character and structure compared to his more lighthearted sketches alluded to above. Pirandello's flair for the comic and the absurd was surely influenced by his chaotic, often stressful life, which included such noteworthy honors as being awarded the Nobel Prize for Literature in 1934.

**Orson Welles digs into the pasta ... and the scenery ... in *L'uomo, la bestia e la virtù.***

Lucio Fulci had almost certainly contributed to screenplays prior to this film. He began his association with his mentor and *maestro*, Steno, in 1951 with the comedy *Totò e i re di Roma*. Fulci's quick wit and eagerness to advance in his chosen profession made a good impression on Steno, who recognized his talent and was happy to capitalize on any good ideas the young man brought to the table. *Totò in Color* and *Totò and the Women* (both 1952) continued their collaboration, which reached another plateau with the release of *L'uomo, la bestia e la virtù*. Steno took credit as primary screenwriter, but Fulci's contributions were formally recognized in his credit for collaborating on the script. The precise nature of Fulci's contributions to these early works can only be guessed at, but the somewhat cynical, at times grotesque, nature of the material surely appealed to his dark sense of humor.

Another significant name in the screenwriting credits is that of Vitaliano Brancati (1907-1954), an acclaimed novelist who also dabbled in screenwriting. He rose to prominence with the success of the book *Don Giovanni in Sicily* (1941) and risked the displeasure of *Il Duce* with his satire *Gli anni perduti/The Lost Years* (written in 1936, published in 1941), which presented a sharply comedic and less-than-flattering portrait of Italy's reigning dictator, Benito Mussolini. As a screenwriter, his credits included Riccardo Freda's *Don Cesare di Bazan* (1942), Alessandro Blasetti's *Fabiola* (1949), William Dieterle's *Volcano* (1950) and Roberto Rossellini's *Voyage to Italy* (1954). His writings have also been adapted into several successful films, including Mauro Bolognini's *Il bell' Antonio* (1960) and Marco Vicario's *The Sensuous Sicilian* (1973).

The film makes great use of Totò's screen image as the dignified fool. Totò's screen presence is predicated on the notion of self-mockery. He conveys tremendous gravity and dignity on the exterior, but internally his characters—almost always a variation on the same basic theme—are at war. Often times, the characters he played were amoral or at the very least morally ambiguous. Their ambitions override their good judgment and this could sometimes yield comic results, which were very bitter indeed. In this film, his character—Professor Paolino—is essentially a well-meaning sort. Emphasis must be placed on the "essentially," however, as he is also governed by cowardly self-interest. He's been carrying on with the lonely and emotionally fragile Assunta, even if he is now doing everything in his power to ensure the stability of her marriage. His desire to help Assunta is by no means selfless, however: He has inadvertently made the poor girl pregnant, and if he doesn't succeed in tricking her hulk of a husband into making love to her while he's back in town, the awful truth will be revealed. Totò's facility for making his often-despicable characters endearing cannot be praised too highly. In the hands of a lesser performer, characters like Professor Paolino can become oily and unctuous to an off-putting degree. Totò's mannerisms border on caricature but never descend into over-the-top extremes. His carefully calculated performance, guided by Steno's sure and steady hand, helps to anchor the film while also providing some well-timed laughs.

The great Orson Welles played the boorish Captain Perella with relish. Welles enters the film at the midpoint—he literally makes his first appearance at the start of the "secondo tempo"[1]—and his broad interpretation threatens to lunge the film into a more obvious form of farce. He plays very well off Totò, however, and the two actors do a splendid job of milking their interactions for all the laughs they are worth while still keeping the potential for violence in the foreground. Welles was reportedly not impressed with the film or its director, but this does not manifest itself in a disinterested performance. As reported by Christopher Frayling in his book *Sergio Leone: Something to Do With Death*, Welles would later grumble, "None of the dialogue made any sense at all. Complete *non sequiters*."[2] The mercurial writer-director-actor was in Italy around this time because of his production of *Othello*, which was finally completed and released in 1952. When the production was shut down for a few days due to problems with the Agfacolor process, Welles snatched up second assistant Sergio Leone (1929-1989)—later to become one of the leading lights of Italian popular cinema—and put him to work as his assistant on an unidentified project which is now lost to the mists of time.[3] Fulci apparently did not make so much of an impression on the grumpy star, but the young cineaste nevertheless relished being in the great man's presence and the film would provide him with his first screen credit as a writer; the film may not have been a rip-roaring success, but things were looking up.

The distinguished French actress Vivian Romance (1912-1991) was cast in the role of Assunta, but she lacks the earthy qualities one would ideally like to see in the role. She tends to disappear into the scenery somewhat and cannot hope to compete with the antics of Totò or Welles. Her presence in the film was regarded as a major coup, however, though she makes virtually no impression except when Steno and company go out of their way to make her character look ridiculous during the seduction scenes.

For Steno, dealing with the various egos on set was a less-than-thrilling experience:

> It was Ponti who pegged away with the idea of *L'uomo, la bestia e la virtù*, perhaps because Pirandello allowed him to have such renowned actors as Welles and Romance. It was an attempt at an international cast that actually didn't work. The result was a hybrid. However, I wrote the script with Brancati: I did not allow myself to put things at random, but called the greatest Sicilian novelist and scriptwriter, who certainly knew a lot about Pirandello. [...] During shooting, one day Welles asked me, "What am I doing between a Neapolitan and a French woman?" Then I asked him why he signed the contract, and he replied, "Because I'm hungry, that's why!" However, he never caused any trouble, never tried to interfere. Actually, it was I who sometimes asked him his advice. One day, finally he gave me advice on something and then immediately added, "Remember, you should never listen to what actors suggest." After finishing a scene, he always went back to his dressing room. I think he was writing something about *Moby Dick*.[4] When we were ready to shoot and we had to call him over, everyone tried to avoid disturbing him, as they had a sacred respect for him. He always behaved like a great gentleman. He is one of those directors who, when working as actors for another director, behave like guests and not hosts.[5]

Fulci, on his part, was not filled with optimism, either, as he would later reveal:

**Italian *fotobusta* detail: Orson Welles as Captain Perella in *L'uomo, la bestia e la virtù*.**

> I said it from the very beginning that it was a bad move. Brancati and I wrote the script. Totò did not want to do it, but had signed a contract with Ponti and De Laurentiis, and could not refuse. The play never really worked on stage, why should it have to work on film? It cost a lot of money and did not make a cent. And all the trouble and pains in the ass we had during shooting, mostly because of Romance's husband (whom the crew used to call "Pallesecche" [Dried Balls]). And she wasn't easy, either. I once asked Welles "Why did you do this film?" "Because I'm desperate!" He had to run away from Hollywood after *The Lady from Shanghai* (1947). Since the film went way beyond schedule, Ponti did not pay him anything extra, and he snuck away from the set a few days before shooting ended. He just couldn't stand it anymore; he kept running away. In that period he started his affair with Mori [Paola Mori] after the disasters with Padovani [Lea Padovani, another of Welles' love affairs] in *Othello* (1952). Welles and Totò got along well together. At first Ponti used to say, "What will happen with Totò?" and I told him: "Well, Totò is going to eat him alive in two minutes!" and that's what happened in the film, since Welles ended up being Totò's sidekick, and gave him the pretexts for his jokes. Welles wanted to act in Italian. Totò would say: "Better to do it in English. I understand it better!" Poor Totò. I remember we were driving in Trastevere and our car was stopped by a crowd. People kept telling him: "Totò, make us laugh!" and he replied, "I am exhausted, you can't imagine how exhausted I am." He was a sad character.[6]

Even so, the young cineaste was understandably in awe working with Welles and was often amused by his antics:

> Welles used to take me with him during his trips. At night, he could eat about 40 oranges. He had a flat in Naples, Mori stayed in one room while he stayed in the other, writing and working on the films he wanted to make. He even shot a brief scene for *Mr. Arkadin* (1955), in Naples, right in the middle of all of us. One night, at one o'clock, he took command of a boat and drove it personally, and Steno was seasick! He lived on oranges. One night I counted him eating 47 of them—he scared me! And he was full of debts! When he left Naples, his suitcases were put on auction. Back to the film, Welles said that having such a comedian as Totò play that character which he described as—I remember it quite well since he even wrote a report for Steno about that—"sinister and despicable," was a tremendous mistake. He had written a 60-page report, in English, about the film. It was translated by a secretary, and who knows if Steno kept a copy of it. And the report ended with these words, "Why are we doing this film?"[7]

*L'uomo, la bestia e la virtù* may not have been the happiest of experiences for anybody involved, but it is a diverting and frequently amusing film. Steno's flair for comedic situations is particularly evident in the more grotesque set pieces—Paolino making Assunta up to look like a parody of a common hussy in the hopes of piquing the Captain's amorous interest; the protracted attempts to get the Captain to eat the cake which is laced with a stimulant—and he paces the film very well.

For all that, Pirandello's heirs were less-than-pleased with the film. They rightly regarded it as a simplistic distillation of the play's themes (which it is, admittedly) and objected to the way in which it frequently ignored Pirandello's original conception: For example, the animal theme implicit in the title is only partly hinted at in the film, whereas it was Pirandello's idea that the actors in the stage production should be made up to resemble animals which were symbolic of the characters' inner nature. Censorship woes also took the edge off of the more bawdy humor and what was left on screen seemed to Pirandello's heirs as very poor indeed, if not downright criminal. The film was a failure critically and commercially and was eventually withdrawn from circulation and became impossible to see for many years. A print was eventually unearthed and aired on the RAI network in the early 1990s; sadly, the only currently available print is in black-and-white, thus making it impossible to accurately assess the quality of Mario Damicelli's cinematography.

Notes:
1. Italian films are invariably broken into two halves—*primo tempo* and *secondo tempo*—with an intermission in the middle.
2. Frayling, Christopher, *Sergio Leone: Something to Do With Death*, (London: Faber and Faber, Inc., 2000), p. 60.
3. *Ibid*, p. 61.
4. In 1955, Welles started work on a highly experimental film titled *Moby Dick Rehearsed*. The concept was that a group of actors gather together to rehearse a production of Herman Melville's classic story; the actors would mime actions without the benefit of any props. Welles headed the assembled cast (starring as an actor who was playing Captain Ahab), which included future stars such as Patrick McGoohan, Christopher Lee and Joan Plowright appeared. Like so many of Welles' films, it was never completed.
5. Faldini, Franca and Goffredo Fofi, *L'avventurosa storia del cinema italiano raccontata dai suoi protagonisti*, 1935-1959, (Milan: Feltrinelli 1979), p. 292.
6. *Ibid*, p. 293.
7. *Ibid*.

## *Ci troviamo in galleria (1953)*

Directed by Mauro Bolognini; Produced by Luigi Carpentieri and Ermanno Donati; Screenplay by Mauro Bolognini (as Bolognini), Sandro Continenza (as Continenza), Lucio Fulci (as Fulci), Stefano Vanzina (as Steno) and Luigi Viganotti (as Viganotti), from a story by Fede Arnaud (as F. Arnaud) and Alberto Liberati (as A. Liberati); Director of Photography: Mario Scarpelli; Editor: Mario Serandrei; Music by Carlo Rustichelli; Songs: *Quanno staje cu mme'; Ho gli occhi tuoi; Duska; 'O ciucciariello; Gigolette; Grazie dei fior; Cherie; Quizas quizas quizas; Nannì (Una gita a li castelli)*—All performed by Nilla Pizzi.

Main Players: Nilla Pizzi (Caterina Lari); Carlo Dapporto (Ignazio Panizza detto Gardenio); Sophia Loren (Marisa); Mario Carotenuto (Il commendator Tittoni); Gianni Cavalieri (Sep); Alberto Sordi (Mario Pio del telefono)

*Gardenio is an old-time entertainer who has been reduced to putting on third-rate variety shows in provincial towns. He is pressured into allowing the youthful and vivacious Caterina to perform and her singing voice turns her into an overnight sensation. The two fall in love and are married, but ultimately they go in different directions …*

*Ci troviamo in galleria* is a good old-fashioned Italian melodrama with comic and musical elements. It is perhaps most successful in its evocation of a provincial atmosphere, loaded with eccentric types including wannabe artists and breathless hangers-on. The story focuses on a small-time theatrical troupe that travels from one small town to the next, just barely making enough to get by but finding satisfaction in the reactions of the crowd. They are the ultimate examples of "big fish in a small pond," even if it sometimes just means that they are first in line to receive rotten tomatoes thrown at them when an act doesn't go over very well. The film pays attention to character and detail and allows the various caricature types—the prima donna, the hack comedian, etc.—to register as realistic human beings. This aspect helps to distract one from the fact that the story—devised by Fede Arnaud and Alberto Liberati—borrows more than a little from the superior *Variety Lights* (1950), a film best-known today as the directing debut (albeit in collaboration with Alberto Lattuada) of Federico Fellini. The film follows a similar trajectory: The manager of a small theatrical troupe falls in love with a talented amateur who rises to stardom.

In a sense, the film can also be seen as a good-natured variation on the popular Hollywood standby *A Star is Born*. First filmed in 1937 by director William A. Wellman and starring Janet Gaynor and Fredric March, it told of an ill-fated romance between a matinee idol (March) who falls in love with and marries a young ingénue (Gaynor). The matinee idol's popularity wanes due to his alcoholism, while the ingénue becomes a much bigger star. However, just to prove that original ideas are few and far between, *A Star is Born* bears more than a passing resemblance to an earlier drama by director George Cukor titled *What Price Hollywood?* (1932). In any event, *A Star is Born* was a big hit in 1937 and netted an Oscar for its original story (which must have irked Cukor and company!) and nominations for director Wellman and actors Gaynor and March. Two remakes followed, the first and best of which (directed by George Cukor, appropriately enough!) emerged in 1954, with Judy Garland and James Mason scarfing up well-deserved Oscar nominations. The less said about the ill-fated 1976 update, directed by Frank Pierson and starring Barbra Streisand and Kris Kristofferson, the better. In any event, the basic theme of romance upset by professional success definitely links to this film, though the overall treatment is far more downbeat and cynical in these American productions compared to the generally sweet-natured disposition of *Ci troviamo in galleria*.

**Italian poster for *Ci troviamo in galleria*; artwork by Averardo Ciriello.**

Leading lady Nilla Pizzi (1919-2011) was hired more for her singing abilities than anything else. She belts out quite a few tunes and definitely has a lovely voice, but as an actress she is not the most compelling screen presence. She enjoyed some popularity on screen in the 1950s, but her film career was never so prolific—or successful—as her singing and recording career. Her biggest hit was undoubtedly *Grazie dei fiori*, for which she won the San Remo Festival; inevitably, she performs the song in this film, as well. Director Mauro Bolognini had some uncertainties about her suitability for the role, as he later revealed:

I just finished *Processo alla città* where I was the assistant director. Donati and Carpentieri called me and offered me to direct a film with a very popular singer, Nilla Pizzi. The story they had was basically centered on this female singer: little by little, though, we managed to change it quite a bit, and focused on the vaudeville setting, and it became *Ci troviamo in galleria*. I didn't know Nilla Pizzi; I had never seen her even though I often heard her songs on the radio. Donati and Carpentieri were enthusiastic about her, and showed me a beautiful pic of her, where she had a wonderful face and a gorgeous slim body. I said, "Well, if she just can act a little bit, we're good!" It was only when I went to pick her up at the station that I realized it was a photomontage: From the train came down this lady who had the same beautiful face as the picture, but a

**Italian *fotobusta* for *Ci troviamo in galleria,* with a young—and gorgeous—Sophia Loren on the left.**

> thick neck and a corpulent figure. I have to say that in that moment I felt lost. But then Nilla smiled at me, and it was such a sweet and warm sympathetic smile that I immediately decided that I didn't care if the body was not up to my expectations, it was her facial expressions that counted, and it was so much better that way. It took me some time to understand how I could release her from her many complexes: for instance, when she sang she would not move her arms because she felt it was not appropriate for the "lady of Italian music." Therefore she looked wooden in front of the microphone.[1]

Carlo Dapporto (1911-1989) is more successful as the hack comedian who falls in love with Pizzi's character. He brings an oily, unctuous charm to the role and is very convincing as the type of small-time entertainer he is supposed to be embodying on screen.

However, it is luscious sex siren Sophia Loren who ends up stealing every scene she is in. Loren's distinctive brunette hair was dyed red for the role of the bitchy and vindictive Marisa, but the various neck-plunging outfits she wears ensure that she is the center of attention whenever she is on screen. Born in Rome in 1934, she came to the attention of producer Carlo Ponti when he spotted her in a beauty contest when she was only 14 years old; despite an age gap of 22 years, they would become an item and the two would marry in 1966. Loren broke into films making small but eye-catching appearances in a variety of now-obscure Italian films. She ascended to lead actress status around 1953, though she is decidedly in "second banana" capacity in this film. Loren's stunning looks and genuine acting talent would eventually make her one of the major stars of Italian cinema; this, in turn, would lead to international stardom in major productions such as Anthony Mann's *El Cid* (1961) and *The Fall of the Roman Empire* (1964). She won an Oscar—the first ever awarded to a non-English-speaking role—for her sensitive performance in Vittorio De Sica's harrowing *Two Women* (1960) and was nominated again in De Sica's *Marriage, Italian Style* (1964). She also won an honorary Oscar for her significant body of work in 1991. Loren made a powerful impression on Fulci, who would also contribute to the screenplay for another early role for her in *Un giorno in pretura* (1954). He once reflected on working with the soon-to-be-legendary actress:

> Loren was in *Ci troviamo in galleria,* Bolognini's first film, which I had written. The part had been offered to Marisa Merlini, who thought it was unsuitable for her, and refused it. Then we took Loren, who was making one B-flick after another, and threw her into the film. Bolognini said, "Well, yes, she's not bad!" I came on the set to watch them shoot a scene with her doing a dance routine, and you could really feel she had everything it took to be a star; boy, she definitely did![2]

In addition to Loren, the other major name in the cast is undoubtedly Alberto Sordi. Born in Rome in 1920, Sordi entered films while still in his teens and became a major star of Italian cinema. He specialized in playing comic layabout types, notably in Federico Fellini's *The White Sheik* (1952) and *I Vitelloni* (1953). His path first crossed with that of Fulci on the set of the ill-fated *Totò e i re di Roma* (1951). He later became a successful director before passing away in 2003. His role in this film is a minor cameo, but it allows him to offer yet another variation on his slimy would-be gigolo routine.

Director Mauro Bolognini made his debut with this film. Bolognini was born in Tuscany in 1922. He started off in films as the assistant director to the Neorealist filmmaker Luigi Zampa, assisting the latter on such films as *Anni difficili* (1948) and *The White Line* (1950). After *Ci troviamo in galleria,* he gradually developed an excellent reputation for his sumptuous period films. His first major success was *Wild Love* (1955), but the likes of *Il bell' Antonio* (1960), *That Splendid November* (1969), *The Murri Affair* (1974) and *The Venetian Woman* (1986) were more indicative of his output. He remained active until the mid-1990s and died in 2001.

The crew includes a couple of familiar names working in relatively minor capacities. Assistant director Antonio De Teffé was born in Rome in 1929; he appears to have made his debut working on this picture, but within the next couple of years he would change careers and go in front of the camera as an actor. In the 1960s he would adopt the *nom de plume* of Anthony Steffen and appear in a number of popular Spaghetti Westerns (*Django the Bastard,* 1969), horror films (*An Angel for Satan,* 1966) and *gialli* (*The Night Evelyn Came Out of the Grave,* 1971). He died in 2004. The assistant editor was Ornella Micheli, who would go on to become one of the best editors in popular Italian cinema. She would later work with Fulci on a number of projects that he directed, beginning with *Le massaggiatrici* (1962) and culminating with *The Psychic* (1977).

Notes:
1. Faldini, Franca and Goffredo Fofi, *L'avventurosa storia del cinema italiano raccontata dai suoi protagonisti*, 1935-1959, (Milan: Feltrinelli, 1979), p.270.
2. *Ibid*, p. 275.

## *Un giorno in pretura* (1954)

Aka *A Day in Court*

Directed by Stefano Vanzina (as Steno); Produced by Gianni Hecht Lucari, Dino De Laurentiis (uncredited) and Carlo Ponti (uncredited); Screenplay by Sandro Continenza, Lucio Fulci, Alberto Sordi, Stefano Vanzina (as Steno) and Giancarlo Viganotti, from an idea by Lucio Fulci; Director of Photography Marco Scarpelli; Editor: Giuliana Attenni; Music by Armando Trovajoli; Assistant Directors: Lucio Fulci and Paolo Heusch

Main Players: Peppino De Filippo (Magistrate Salomone Lorusso); Silvana Pampanini (Luisa); Alberto Sordi (Nando Moriconi); Sophia Loren (Anna); Tania Weber (Elena); Leopoldo Trieste (Leopoldo); Walter Chiari (Don Michele)

*Magistrate Lorusso presides over four different cases:* "Adultery in 16mm" *deals with Elena, who brings charges against her husband but is hiding a secret of her own;* "The Priest and the Prostitute" *deals with Don Michele, a priest who claims that he was taken advantage of and beaten up by a prostitute and her pimp;* "Indecent Exposure" *focuses on a man brought up on charges of public nudity; and* "Lustful Lieutenant" *deals with a middle-aged prostitute who is revealed to have something of a history with the Magistrate …*

Lucio Fulci had a larger than usual presence in the making of *Un giorno in pretura*. In addition to collaborating on the script and serving as the assistant to Steno, he is also credited with devising the idea for the scenario. Such a credit is definitely a feather in his cap, for the film is one of the more imaginative comedies he worked on at this stage in his career.

The film utilizes the anthology format to good effect. This concept extended back in Italian cinema well beyond this film, with Roberto Rossellini directing *L'amore* (1948) and contributing to such pictures as *We, The Women* (1953) and *Mid-Century Loves* (1954). However, the format would become particularly popular in the 1960s. Producers saw it as a good way of cramming as much headline-grabbing talent as possible into one long, rambling show—thus, films like *Boccaccio '70* (1962, directed by Vittorio De Sica, Federico Fellini, Mario Monicelli and Luchino Visconti), *The Witches* (1967, directed by Mauro Bolognini, De Sica, Pier Paolo Pasolini, Franco Rossi and Visconti) and *Spirits of the Dead* (1968, directed by Fellini, Louis Malle and Roger Vadim) could be sold not only on the basis of their starry casts, but by virtue of their lionized filmmakers, as well. Coming as it does relatively early in the cycle, *Un giorno in pretura* isn't quite as flashy and extravagant, but that is not entirely a bad thing in itself.

As usual with anthologies, the segments vary in effectiveness. The opening segment, "Adultery in 16mm," tackles the theme of voyeurism. There are some chuckles to be had as the courtroom proceedings degenerate into a veritable circus as the sexy Elena (Tania Weber) is humiliated by the projection of some "home movies" taken by her peeping Tom of a husband. The sequence is relatively brief and doesn't make a tremendous impression, but as opening acts go it's diverting enough. Next is the suggestively titled "The Priest and the Prostitute," which can be seen as an early draft of Fulci's decidedly ambivalent attitude towards the Catholic Church and its representatives. The humor is not nearly so stinging as it would be in later variations on the theme in his own films, however, and ultimately the priest, Don Michele (Walter Chiari), does

**Italian poster for *Un giorno in pretura*; artwork by Averardo Ciriello.**

**Italian *fotobusta* for *Un giorno in pretura*; artist unknown.**

not emerge as completely villainous—even if his sanctimonious exterior is somewhat punctured by the end of his testimony. "Indecent Exposure" focuses on Nando Moriconi (Alberto Sordi), a somewhat dim but well meaning Roman who is obsessed with everything American. The character proved popular with audiences and would become something of a signature role for the great Alberto Sordi; he, Steno and Fulci would continue to develop the character in their next collaboration, the hugely successful *Un Americano a Roma*. In this admittedly slight but amusing segment, Moriconi is showing off for some local kids. They encourage him to take a swim in a local river and do his Tarzan impression. Stripping down to his birthday suit, he dives in and makes such a commotion that it attracts the attention of the police. He manages to escape but ends up gate crashing a party, where his nudity causes him no small measure of embarrassment. Sordi's expert comedic timing is put to excellent use, and Steno and cinematographer Marco Scarpelli get around censorship difficulties by implying nudity through suggestive camera placements and artful use of shadowy lighting. The final segment, "Lustful Lieutenant," explodes the sanctity of the court system by revealing that the seemingly upstanding Magistrate (Peppino De Filippo) passing moral (and legal) judgment over the cases has had a past association with the prostitute placed on trial in his courtroom.

The cast includes memorable appearances by Alberto Sordi and Sophia Loren, who were then recurring players in Fulci's early credits, but the gifted Neapolitan comedian Peppino De Filippo carries the picture. De Filippo is very effective showing the different sides of the Magistrate—pompous, fussy, self-righteous one moment, salacious and leering the next—and provides the film with its center. The two-faced hypocrisy of the character is central to the film's gently sardonic anti-authoritarian theme but De Filippo is careful to ensure that the character does not become completely off-putting. Born in 1903, he originally studied to be a musician but a chance encounter with Totò coincided with his decision to go into acting. He initially performed in vaudeville settings, having formed a theatrical troupe with his brother Eduardo and his sister Titina, both of whom would go on to film careers of their own. He began appearing in films in the 1930s and gradually became a popular presence in Italian comedies and melodramas. He top-lined Fellini's directing debut, *Variety Lights* (1950), and later reteamed with the *Maestro* on what is arguably his best-known film role, as the sexually frustrated and prudish protagonist of his segment "The Temptation of Dr. Antonio" in *Boccaccio '70*. De Filippo also appeared in a number of comedies with Totò, establishing an onscreen partnership that would result in his name being used in such titles as *Totò, Peppino e la... malafemmina* (1956), *Totò, Peppino e le fanatiche* (1960) and *Totò, Peppino e... la dolce vita* (1962), the latter of which was also co-written by Fulci. He made his last film appearance in Sergio Corbucci's *giallo* parody *Atrocious Tales of Love and Death* (1979) and passed away in 1980.

As for the character of Nando Moriconi, played so memorably by Sordi, he would prove sufficiently popular to generate further screen adventures, including the aforementioned *Un Americano a Roma* (1954). Inevitably, when a character becomes popular with the public, a general rush surges among different participants in the film production to claim paternity. Steno later explained:

> The whole sketch had been conceived by Sordi. However, it was Lucio Fulci, as far as I recall, that introduced the idea of this guy from Rome who speaks in a sort of funny Americanized slang—he took inspiration from a guy [...] who called himself Blacky Nothon, who talked that way and had everybody rolling on the floor laughing. That's my recollection, despite Sordi denying it.[1]

Fulci was quite rightly proud of his accomplishment and was increasingly annoyed at Sordi's tendency to claim it as his own creation:

> I must say that Sordi, who rarely interfered with the script, used to "color" the character a bit, but he certainly did not ad-lib. On the other hand, he was not a pain in the ass. And I'm speaking of early Sordi: in those days he would thank the Lord when they cast him for a film. He was not famous yet. He took a million *lira* for *Un giorno in pretura*, six or seven for *Un Americano a Roma*. [...] Sordi was not a guy who ad-libbed on set. Totò did—he was a genius of invention. All he needed was a bare-bone scenario. Sordi, Tognazzi, Manfredi, are "comédiens," but not old-style comedians. [...]
>
> I invented the character of Nando Moriconi, the American in Rome, for Sordi. Steno is my witness on that [...]. I took inspiration from Mimmo Rotella, who today is a rather famous painter, who had been to Kansas City, and used to say, "How do you say that in Italian?" Come on, you were born in Bari! Talk like you eat ...
>
> So, I invented the character and me and Continenza wrote the sketch. Sordi was paid one million, since nobody wanted him back then. He had done *Mamma mia, che impressione* and was shooting *I vitelloni*. [...] First day on set: the Marana sketch [Note: the Marana is the spot of the river Tiber where Sordi goes skinny-dipping]. I remember that I shot a little bit of that as well, since Steno had other things to do, and Steno and me were like father and son. When the film was finished and edited, we screened it to Ponti and De Laurentiis. The film was too long, and we had to cut out a sketch. Ponti and De Laurentiis, at the same time: "Cut Sordi's bit!" [...] Whereas Silvana Mangano, who was sitting behind her husband [De Laurentiis], told him: "Come on, don't you see this part is the only good one in the film?" Ponti and De Laurentiis sold the film to Mosco, thinking they would rip him off, whereas the movie grossed millions, much to their regret. Then Sordi reprised the character in another film, and recently in *Di che segno sei?* (1975), without giving us a cent. To Sordi, we had nothing to do with it, the character was the actor's invention, and Continenza and I were "two guys who used to hang around Steno."[2]

Notes:

1. Faldini, Franca and Goffredo Fofi, *L'avventurosa storia del cinema italiano raccontata dai suoi protagonisti*, 1935-1959, (Milan: Feltrinelli, 1979), p. 286.
2. *Ibid*, p. 287.

## *Un Americano a Roma* (1954)

Aka *An American in Rome* (unofficial English-language translation)

Directed by Stefano Vanzina (as Steno); Produced by Dino De Laurentiis and Carlo Ponti; Story and Screenplay by Sandro Continenza, Lucio Fulci, Ettore Scola, Alberto Sordi and Stefano Vanzina (as Steno); Director of Photography: Carlo Montuori; Editor: Giuliana Attenni; Music by Mario Abbado and Angelo Francesco Lavagnino (as A.F. Lavagnino); Assistant Director: Lucio Fulci

Main Players: Alberto Sordi (Nando Moriconi); Maria Pia Casilio (Elvira); Giulio Calì (Nando's Father); Ilse Petersen (Molly); Rocco D'Assunta (Commissario)

Cameo appearance: Lucio Fulci (Boy listening to music on record player)[1]

*Nando is a layabout who is obsessed with all things American. He does his best to mimic what he believes is typical of "the American way" and concocts an elaborate plan to realize his dream of visiting the United States: He will go to the Coliseum and threaten to commit suicide if the American Embassy does not intercede and send him to America ...*

Lucio Fulci, Steno and Alberto Sordi were left with no doubt that they were on to a good thing when the "Indecent Exposure" episode of *Un giorno in pretura* proved popular with audiences. Fulci had based the character of the America-obsessed Nando Moriconi on a real-life acquaintance, and he and his collaborators were quick to realize that there was more mileage to be had out of the character. The resulting film, appropriately titled *Un Americano a Roma*, would prove to be a major hit, helping to solidify Steno as one of Italy's premier comedy directors and Sordi as one of the country's top box-office draws. If anybody was "left behind" in the ensuing success, sadly, it was Lucio Fulci. He would continue to work steadily as a screenwriter and assistant director, but felt that he was not properly recognized or appreciated for his contribution; as would so often be the case during so much of his career, he would exist in the shadow of a larger, more popular figure—in this case, he was seen as subservient to Steno and later on when he started making thrillers and horror films, he would often be referred to as a poor man's imitation of Dario Argento or George A. Romero. Such trivialization of his gifts would come to embitter Fulci in later years, though he continued to soldier on and add creative ideas to films even when he was not properly recognized for doing so.

**Italian poster art for *Un Americano a Roma*; artist unknown.**

The film expands on the character of Moriconi, but is careful to repeat elements that had proved popular in the earlier film. Thus at one point, the hapless Moriconi finds himself hired as a nude model for an English artist; not realizing what is being asked of him, he rebels when an interpreter explains that he is expected to remove his clothes. Inevitably, things do not go as planned and Moriconi finds himself "streaking" his way through the city and crashing the filming of a live broadcast about Italian art. It may not be humor of the most highbrow variety, but it works and Sordi and company certainly milk the situation for everything it is worth.

In a sense, Moriconi is emblematic of the European idealization of America, which was particularly prevalent among the Allies following the devastation of World War II. The Marshall Plan (or The European Recovery Plan) had been implemented by the United States as a means of helping to rebuild Europe, and as part of this initiative, there was also a major influx of American films being distributed; in Italy, for example, American films had been suppressed under the Fascist regime, but now all bets were off and audiences thrilled to seeing the glitz and glamour of Hollywood product. To the war-ravaged Europeans, America looked to be a symbol of hope and prosperity. Many believed that the average American owned fancy sports cars, smoked expensive cigars and lived in rambling mansions on streets paved with gold. The importing of American films, with their iconic movie stars exuding cool and confidence, also played into this notion. No matter that poverty and an inability to get ahead in life was also rampant in the United States—it was the fantasy ideal that mattered, and many Europeans latched onto this idea as a means of dealing with their own feelings of hopelessness and despair. Moriconi is, by the admission of his frustrated parents, a complete and total failure. He is a wastrel with delusions of grandeur. Sooner than soil his hands with manual labor, he plays at being an artist. Unfortunately, he lacks in artistic inspiration and talent. He is convinced that he has soaked up American culture by watching American movies—even if they have been dubbed into Italian. Moriconi brags to his friends that he is fluent in American English, but his sense of the language can best be summed up as rambling incoherently in a nasally drawl. Sordi is particularly amusing when he bursts into "American" singing mode, offering up inept (and completely unintelligible) imitations of American singers, or when he struts about in full-blown John Wayne mode, acting like he is impervious to harm. He also does his damndest to reject his Italian heritage by mocking local cuisine and playing at being an expert in "authentic" American food; at one point he slathers a piece of bread with marmalade, mustard and yogurt, saying that this is how a typical American would do it, but the results are inedible and he reluctantly dives into a plate of pasta instead. The character could easily become tiresome at any point, but he retains a sharp comic edge throughout. His pathetic dreams of earning a free ticket to Hollywood compels him to pull a ridiculous public stunt which causes his family no small measure of embarrassment; tellingly, sooner than work towards this goal, his aim is to get there for free—as always, it is his belief that the wealth and prosperity of the American people will compel them to intervene on his behalf, thus playing into an entitlement mentality which speaks of his own over-inflated ego. Ultimately, it is Moriconi's inability to accept reality that makes him a strangely endearing, even pitiable, figure. The climax sees him sustaining a head wound which the doctors believe will "cure" him of his mania for all things American; a final voice-over reveals that his obsessions are still in place, however, and Steno indulges in a clever sight gag which allows Sordi to wipe the "*Fine*" credit from the screen in favor of spelling out a good, old-fashioned "The End" credit—just like in Hollywood movies.

A number of the same crew reunited from *Un giorno in pretura* to make this film. Fulci again collaborated on the script with Steno, Sordi and his friend and colleague Sandro Continenza. Born in Rome in 1920, Continenza broke into films as a screenwriter in the late 1940s. He worked on the scripts of a number of films starring Totò throughout the 1950s and first collaborated with Fulci on the screenplay for *Ci troviamo in galleria*. Fulci and Continenza would continue to collaborate on such scripts as *Sins of Casanova* and *Piccola posta* (both 1955) and Continenza would later return to collaborate on the script for Fulci's acerbic political satire, *The Eroticist* (1972). His other credits include such standout genre fare as Mario Bava's *Hercules in the Haunted World* (1961), Franco Giraldi's *Sugar Colt* (1967), Romolo Guerrieri's *The Double* (1971), Jorge Grau's *The Legend of Blood Castle* (1973) and *Let Sleeping Corpses Lie* (1974) and Enzo G. Castellari's *The Inglorious Bastards* (1978). He died in 1996.

Another distinguished name found among the screenwriters is that of Ettore Scola. Born in Trevico in 1931, he started off as a screenwriter in the 1950s. He would cross paths with Fulci again on *Totò nella luna* (1958) and would go on to collaborate on the scripts for such distinguished titles as Antonio Pietrangeli's *Hungry for Love* (1960) and Dino Risi's *Il sorpasso* (1962). He started directing films in 1964 and would go on to win much acclaim for the likes of *We All Loved Each Other So Much* (1974), *Down and Dirty* (1976; for which he won the Best Director award at Cannes), *A Special Day* (1977), *Macaroni* (1985) and *The Dinner* (1998).

With the success of *Un Americano a Roma*, Sordi became one of Italy's most popular—and highly paid—film stars. He would go on to distinguish himself in a number of critically-acclaimed films, including several for director Mario Monicelli, including *The Great War* (1959, which was nominated for an Academy Award as Best Foreign Film), *An Average Little Man* (1977) and *Il marchese del Grillo* (1981). He also began directing films, with some measure of success, including *Incontri proibiti* (1998), which would prove to be his last picture. He reprised the role of Nando Moriconi one last time in Sergio Corbucci's comedy anthology film *Di che segno sei?* (1975), but inevitably Fulci didn't receive any special credit or recognition for having devised the character in the first place. As Steno would later recount, this resulted in a lawsuit: "Then Sordi reprised the character recently in *Di che segno sei?*, making him the gorilla of a Milanese entrepreneur, but without asking anyone the authorization. So Fulci and Continenza sued him. However, I remember that when I suggested Sordi to be cast as this character who in *Un giorno in pretura* had to remain naked, Ponti and Gianni Hecht replied 'Are you crazy? Let's cast Walter Chiari, who at least is good-looking!'"[2]

**Italian *locandina* for *Un Americano a Roma*; artwork by Piovano / Studio Paradiso.**

Speaking of good-looking, it should be noted that *Un Americano a Roma* marked the screen debut of Swiss-born sexpot Ursula Andress, who would go on to attain screen immortality as the first big-screen "Bond girl" in Terence Young's epochal *Dr. No* (1962). In an audio interview included among the supplements on the Shriek Show DVD release of Fulci's later film *Touch of Death*, Fulci claims to have been involved in a sexual relationship with Andress at this time; whether it was really true or just wishful thinking is unknown, however!

Notes:
1. A round-faced, bespectacled Fulci, with a full head of hair, is seen during a party scene. When Moriconi bumps into him, he asks of Fulci, "Damn, what are you? A porcupine?"
2. In this sense, one can't help but be reminded of the story of how Sergio Leone came up with the title *Duck, You Sucker* for his 1971 film. At one stage, Leone had intended to produce the film, with Peter Bogdanovich directing. Bogdanovich quizzed Leone on the use of this rather bizarre expression in the script and Leone reportedly was insistent that this was a typical American expression—no matter that Bogdanovich, being an American, was completely unfamiliar with it.
3. Faldini, Franca and Goffredo Fofi, *L'avventurosa storia del cinema italiano raccontata dai suoi protagonisti*, 1935-1959, (Milan: Feltrinelli, 1979), p. 286.

## *Totò all'inferno (1955)*

Aka *Totò in Hell*

Directed by Camillo Mastrocinque (as Mastrocinque); Produced by Alfredo De Laurentiis and Carlo Ponti; Screenplay by Antonio De Curtis (as Totò), Italo De Tuddo, Lucio Fulci, Luigi Mangini, Camillo Mastrocinque, Vittorio Metz and Francesco Nelli, from a story by Antonio de Curtis (as Totò); Director of Photography: Aldo Tonti; Editor: Gisa Radicchi Levi; Music by Pippo Barizza

Main Players: Antonio de Curtis [as Totò] (Antonio Marchi / Marc' Antonio); Maria Frau (Cleopatra); Fulvia Franco (Wife); Dante Maggio (Pacifico); Franca Faldini (Maria)

*Antonio is fed up with his life of crime and attempts suicide on several occasions. Finally he is successful and finds himself in Hell, where he is revealed to be the reincarnation of Marc Antony. Satan, jealous of his lusty relationship with Cleopatra, plots revenge. In order to escape his wrath, Antonio flees back to Earth, where things take an even more surreal turn ...*

Fulci continued his association with Totò, but this time Steno was not to be found in the director's chair. Indeed, Fulci was very nearly in charge this time around, but things did not pan out that way. According to the book *Il terrorista dei generi: Tutto il cinema di Lucio Fulci*, Fulci stepped in to take over directing the ending of *Totò a colori* (1952) and producer Carlo Ponti was so impressed with his efficiency that he earmarked him as a talent worth watching. When *Totò all'inferno* was in its early stages of pre-production therefore, Ponti offered Fulci the chance to direct his first feature. Surprisingly, Fulci elected not to take him up on his offer as he had hoped to make his debut with a picture which would not be so bound up in the identity of its star performer[1]; amusingly, Fulci would later make his directing debut with *I ladri* (1959) ... starring Totò. The resulting film is more of a collection of sketches than a coherent narrative, but it offers up some memorable set pieces and gave its star ample rein to display his comic timing.

Totò's versatility on screen allowed him to embody different comic attributes, ranging from the stereotypical simpleton in over his head to the scheming scoundrel with a Machiavellian streak. No matter what his character name, he generally was playing some variation on this basic template—and as far as the public was concerned, the character was very much "Totò." The actor's willingness to make himself look ridiculous, often while adopting a posture of extreme self-importance, made him something of a combination of the fool and the straight man. Comic teams such as Laurel and Hardy and Abbott and Costello—or, perhaps more appropriately in this context, Franco and Ciccio—drew a lot of mileage out of this concept, with the marginally more intelligent member of the team reacting with exasperation as the clown continued to display a bottomless capacity for stupidity. In the case of Totò, he essentially performs the two functions simultaneously; his droll reactions and line readings can be remarkably subtle one moment, while his bug-eyed expressions and hysterical attempts at self-preservation take him to the brink of pantomime. This is certainly evident throughout *Totò all'inferno*, as his willingness to embrace the more unsavory aspects of his character. His portrayal of Antonio Marchi,

**Italian *fotobusta* for *Totò all'inferno*, with the star's hair(piece) literally standing on end.**

whose failure in life extends even to bungling his attempts at suicide, is wonderfully amoral and wickedly funny.

The screenplay is a loosely structured series of sketches and anecdotes. Totò's attempts at committing suicide in the early scenes point to the willingness of the filmmakers to make light of a particularly heavy concept in Catholic cultures. He tries gassing himself, but the gas has been shut off. He throws himself from his apartment window, but a passing group of furniture movers inadvertently break his fall. He then decides to drown himself, but a firm warning is posted in his chosen spot that forbids people from drowning themselves in the area, so he decides to hatch another scheme. At that point, he appears to inadvertently succeed when the bridge he is walking on collapses beneath him. From there, the film moves to its scenes in Hell, where Totò is eventually put on trial for his immortal soul. This makes for some further comic sketches as his shady past is revealed; there's a hysterical scene in which the comic abuses a bully in a bar by finding every excuse to "accidentally" slap the man, as well as a great sequence detailing his bungled attempts at being a stick-up artist, which results in him losing the few items he manages to steal and most of his own personal possessions as well. The echoes of *The Devil and Daniel Webster* in the trial scenes are unmistakable. Written by Stephen Vincent Benet and first published in 1937, that story dealt with a Faustian bargain between a poor farmer and one Mr. Scratch who, of course, is revealed to be The Devil incarnate. The story was first filmed in 1941 by William Dieterle and is revered for is magnificent portrayal of the devil by the great Walter Huston. However, it is not only *The Devil and Daniel Webster* which is evoked in this scenario; one cannot also help but be reminded of Dante's *Inferno*, which comprises the opening act of Dante Alighieri's epic poem *The Divine Comedy*, which dates from the 14th century. In the hands of Fulci and his co-writers, however, these lofty literary antecedents merely serve as a springboard for broad comedy.

**Detail from an Italian *fotobusta* for *Totò all'inferno*; the Devil made Totò do it.**

The film's visualization of Hell is somewhat disappointing. It's clear that the art department had a field day, but the sets look like one-dimensional backdrops and the extras are encouraged to prance about as if in a Halloween pantomime act. Director Camillo Mastrocinque and cinematographer Aldo Tonti seem unable to breathe much life into these set pieces and they come off as rather stilted as a result. Arguably a stronger director-cinematographer team—ideally, Steno (or, yes, Fulci) and Mario Bava, for example—would have been able to turn the scenes in Hell into a visual *tour-de-force*, but apart from the novelty of garish color (the scenes on Earth are tinted blue), they never attain an inner reality or any sense of genuine atmosphere.

Director Camillo Mastrocinque was born in Rome in 1901. He wore a number of different hats during his lengthy cinematic career. He did some work as an art director (some sources credit him with contributing to the silent epic *Ben-Hur: A Tale of the Christ*, 1925, but this seems a fanciful claim at best) but worked chiefly as a screenwriter and director beginning in the 1930s. He also worked very sporadically as a character actor, making a later appearance in one of Fulci's earlier directing gigs, *Gli imbroglioni* (1963). As a director, his work tended towards the solid rather than the inspired. He put Totò through his paces in 11 films in total, in addition to garnering some critical acclaim for the likes of *Le vie del cuore* (1942) and *Lost in the Dark* (1949), the latter starring the great Neorealist filmmaker Vittorio De Sica. He would go on to direct two very different Italian Gothics: *Terror in the Crypt* (1964) was a stiff and stodgy retelling of Sheridan LeFanu's *Carmilla* featuring Christopher Lee in red herring mode, while *An Angel for Satan* (1966) is an underrated gem with one of Barbara Steele's most striking performances. He remained active until his death in 1969.

Notes:

1. Albiero, Paolo and Giacomo Cacciatore, *Il terrorista dei generi: Tutto il cinema di Lucio Fulci* (Rome: Un mondo a parte, 2004), p. 26.

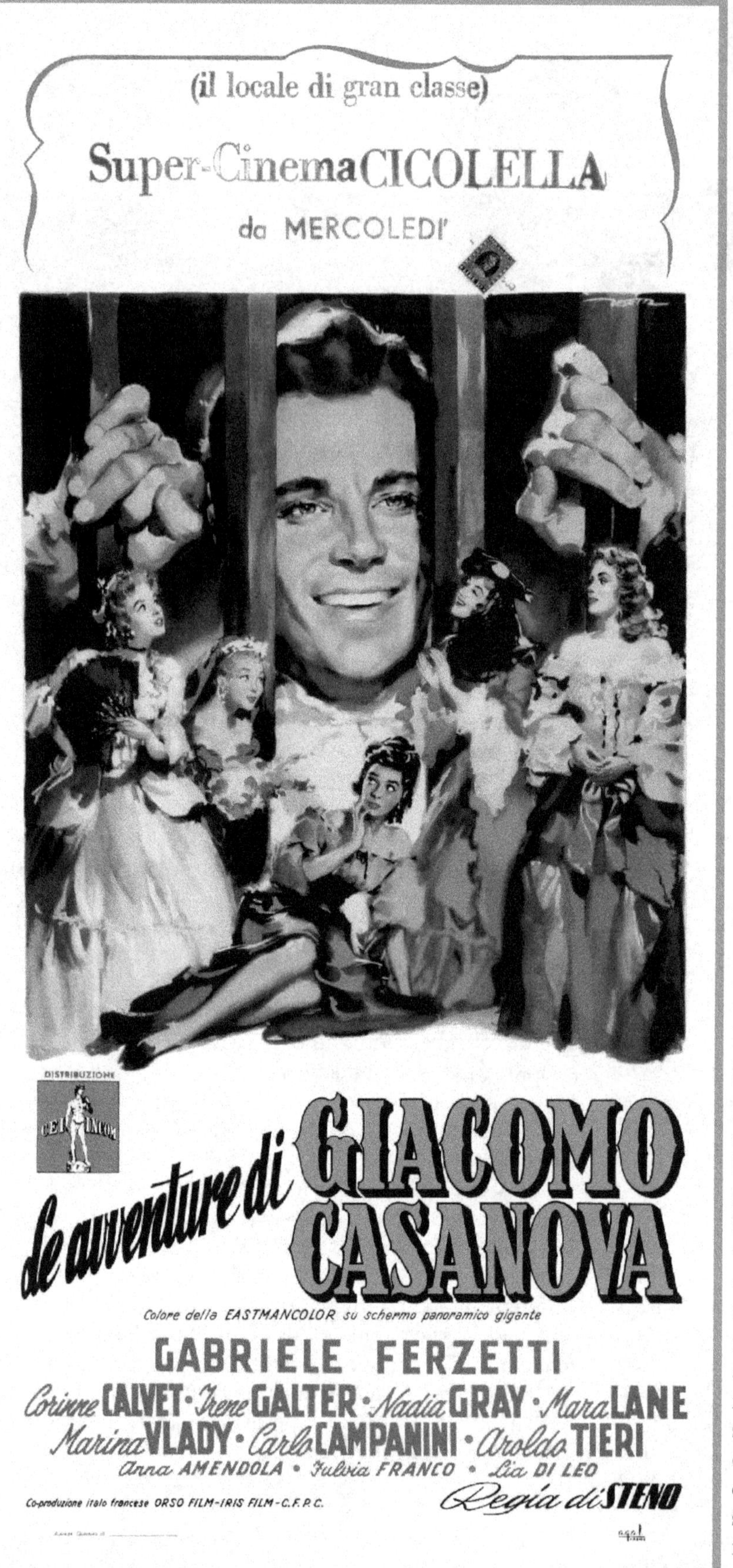


**Italian *locandina* for *Sins of Casanova*; artwork by Bob DeSeta.**

## *Sins of Casanova (1955)*

Aka *Le avventure di Giacomo Casanova*

Directed by Stefano Vanzina (as Steno); Produced by Emo Bistolfi, Elio Gagliardo and Dario Sabatello; Screenplay by Emo Bistolfi, Gian Bistolfi, Sandro Continenza, Lucio Fulci, Mario Guerra, Carlo Romano and Stefano Vanzina (as Steno); Director of Photography: Mario Bava; Editor: Giuliana Attenni; Music by Angelo Francesco Lavagnino (as Francesco Lavagnino); Assistant Director: Lucio Fulci

Main Players: Gabriele Ferzetti (Giacomo Casanova); Corinne Calvet (Louse de Châtillon); Irene Galter (Dolores); Nadia Gray (Teresa); Mara Lane (Barbara)

*Dashing playboy Giacomo Casanova woos various young women and runs afoul of their spouses, families and suitors. He is eventually arrested and thrown in prison, where he reminisces about his life and loves …*

Long before his name came to be associated with amorous adventures, Giacomo Casanova lived a rather placid and unremarkable existence. He was born in Venice in 1725 to parents who thrived in the world of the theater; his father died when he was only eight years old and his mother was too busy touring with theatrical troupes to care for him, so he was raised by a caring grandmother. He began to explore his sexual urges as a teenager and put his quick wit and intellect to work by attending university to become a lawyer. He eventually abandoned his legal pursuits and made a brief attempt at living a humble existence in a seminary. This, too, fell by the wayside and the young man decided to switch gears altogether and try his hand at everything from being a professional gambler to pursuing a career in music. He soon won the support of a wealthy patron when Casanova saved the older man's life. It was during this period of wealth and leisure that Casanova truly blossomed into the lady's man of lore, and he began seducing women of all social stations with enviable success. Unfortunately, he also attracted the attention of some powerful enemies and was imprisoned on charges of blasphemy. He managed to escape from prison and fled to France, where he set out to find another patron to support him in the manner to which he had become accustomed. Casanova's knowledge of alchemy and the occult had already landed him in hot water, but he saw it as a good tool to persuade the gullible of his "power" and indeed it proved very successful at doing just that. Casanova was also utilized as a spy, earning large sums of money in the process that allowed him to finance his lavish lifestyle. He finished his years acting as a librarian to a wealthy Count in Bohemia; during this time, he wrote his memoirs, which were published posthumously for the first time in the 1800s; Casanova died in 1798.

It's easy to see why Casanova's story continues to inspire such fascination. His life was anything but ordinary and his exploits brought him into contact with many distinguished artists and statesmen. To reduce his accomplishments to a series of bedroom encounters is to tell only part of the tale, but let's face it, it was his spectacular success in the *boudoir* that attracts the most attention. The name Casanova is synonymous with the art of seduction and many are the aspiring lothario who have looked to him for inspiration. To date, there have been approximately 100 appearances of the character of Casanova on film; these range from semi-faithful adaptations of his memoirs to fanciful variations that utilize the name and very little else. The earliest known "proper" version of his life story emerged in Hungary in 1918 and featured a young actor known as Arisztid Olt in the supporting cast; a few years later, Olt would move to Hollywood and change his name to Bela Lugosi. In the 1950s, another soon-to-be horror icon would add the character to his list of credits when Vincent Price made a cameo as debt-ridden Casanova in *Casanova's Big Night* (1954). The following year, Lucio Fulci would find himself contributing to a colorful and imaginative version of the story, as well.

**Casanova (Gabriele Ferzetti) works his magic.**

*Sins of Casanova* was an ambitious undertaking for director Steno. The film called for the best craftsmanship that money could buy and, while it was by no means a lavish spectacle in terms of available financing, it benefitted from a top-notch team of technical artisans. Chief among these is the great cinematographer Mario Bava. Born in San Remo in 1914, Bava was the son of silent film cinematographer and special effects artist Eugenio Bava. Mario determined to break into the business despite the protestations of his father and made his debut as a cinematographer with Roberto Rossellini's short subject *Il tacchino prepotente* (1939). Bava's stock rose throughout the 1940s as he demonstrated a singular gift not only for providing lush imagery on a shoestring, but also for his tremendous flair for creating cheap but convincing visual effects. By the time he photographed *Sins of Casanova*, he was already one of the country's foremost cinema technicians. He and Fulci struck up a fast friendship—they were both rather shy and ironic in nature, but whereas Bava was known for being soft-spoken and gentlemanly on the set, Fulci would develop a reputation for being anything but gentlemanly. As fate would have it, their names would become inextricably linked as they both developed into film directors with a flair for horror and the macabre. The notoriously acerbic Fulci was sufficiently impressed by Bava that he always referred to him as "the great Mario Bava" and the influence the self-effacing cinematographer-turned-director would have on Fulci would prove tremendous. Bava's legacy as a film director is finally being properly recognized and includes such gems as *Black Sunday* (1960), *The Three Faces of Fear* (1963, heavily re-cut and re-edited for English-language consumption as *Black Sabbath*), *Blood and Black Lace* (1964) and *Kill, Baby ... Kill!* (1966). He died in 1980, a few months shy of his 66th birthday.

Bava's lush imagery gives the film a tremendous boost. He and Steno make great use of the frame, with individual shots evoking the great art works of the period, while also utilizing a mobile camera to judicious effect. However, it's in the dazzling use of color that Bava really exceeds himself. One need look no further than the bedroom seduction of one character by Casanova, illuminated by the multi-colored lighting emanating from fireworks playing off of the colored glass windows; the effect is eye-catching and flashy in the best sense of the term and helps give the scene an appropriate sparkle. There are also some

**A rare image of *Sins of Casanova* cinematographer Mario Bava dining with his wife Iole and children Lamberto and Elena in the 1950s; courtesy of Mike Baronas.**

marvelously rendered close-ups and tracking shots which anticipate the more deliriously romantic moments in Bava's later psychological horror film as a director, *The Whip and the Body* (1963). As Fulci later recalled, Bava's artistry took a little time, much to the irritation of the producer, which nearly led to a catastrophe on set:

> Once, while we were shooting *Casanova*, we were in a huge room, and Bava had to light it for a party scene. And it took a lot of time … you know, at that time they had those "brutes" (Note: This was the nickname for the very powerful and hot arc lights) … meanwhile, the producer, Sabatello—a very nice man but definitely not intelligent, perhaps the only dumb Jew on Earth—kept asking: "What time is it? Where are we?" Then Bava replied: "It's time that I leave!" Steno and I were frightened! I told Sabatello: "Come on, get out of here for a minute!" And we went to calm Bava down, because if he'd have left the set we'd be in big trouble.[1]

In addition to Bava's cinematography, the film is graced with excellent sets and costumes. Steno, usually more comfortable in contemporary comedic fare, proves to be quite at home in this kind of stylized *milieu*. He paces the action very well and gets fine performances from his actors. He is also able to skirt around the more overtly crude elements of the scenario through the use of witty transitions, such as an emphasis on statues in amorous poses or the use of clocks to signify that Casanova's latest sexual encounter is lasting well into the wee hours of the morning.

The screenplay does not pay much lip service to the more colorful aspects of Casanova's story, being instead a lively and ribald exploration of his amorous activities. The occult angle is completely missing and the court intrigue angle is also tossed by the wayside, but within the parameters of what it sets out to achieve, the writers (including Fulci) did their job admirably. Compared to some of the other versions of the story—including a recent adaptation from 2005 starring the late Heath Ledger—it is admirable in its focus and efficiency. Steno and company do not waste any time and the economy of filmmaking and storytelling ensures that the movie never outstays its welcome.

Gabriele Ferzetti gives an excellent performance as Casanova. The script shies away from the more colorful aspects of the character, preferring instead to emphasize his sexual prowess and keen sense of wit and intellect. In the film's landscape, he is representative of youth and virility; the women he seduces are invariably attached to older, far duller men. The implication is that they are not satisfied in their relationships, thus allowing Casanova a foothold to come in and provide them with a bit of excitement. One amusing scene sees the local men of the village crossing themselves when they hear his name; as such, he can almost be read as a sexual vampire of sorts, preying upon not-so-innocent females and leaving them hungry and looking for more. Ferzetti's handsome looks and obvious charm are ideally suited to the role and he does not let the film down. Born in Rome in 1925 as Pasquale Ferzetti, he began appearing in films in the early 1940s. He made an uncredited appearance in Riccardo Freda's version of *Les Misérables* (1948) and appeared in Alessandro Blasetti's epic *Fabiola* (1949) before rising to greater prominence (and popularity) in the early 1950s. He scored a major international success with his lead role in Michelangelo Antonioni's enigmatic *L'Avventura* (1960) and went on to appear in such international co-productions as John Huston's *The Bible: In the Beginning ...* (1966) and the James Bond adventure *On Her Majesty's Secret Service* (1969). He also gave a terrific performance as the crippled and embittered railroad tycoon in Sergio Leone's masterpiece *Once Upon a Time in the West* (1968). Ferzetti later appeared in Fulci's *giallo The Psychic* (1977) and has more recently been seen in Edoardo Leo's critically acclaimed *18 Years Later* (2010).

Sadly, for all its merits, *Sins of Casnova* became an instant whipping boy for the Italian censors. As recounted in the book *Visioni proibite: I film vietati della censura italiana (1947-1968)*, the problems the film encountered with the censors made it an obvious target of ridicule; a joke of the period has a couple stopping to see what times the picture is playing—upon noting that the movie is running every 15 minutes, the intrigued spectators remark upon how it has been subjected to "a few cuts" and is therefore suitable for the public again.[2] The film was originally passed by the censors and released in December of 1954, but Secretary of State Oscar Luigi Scalfaro (who would go on to become the ninth President of the Italian Republic from 1992 to 1999) decided that the film was "insulting to the modesty, morality and decency" of the public and had it withdrawn.[3] At that point, it was subjected to heavy cutting. Some new scenes were hastily filmed to help patch up the damage, but the controversy over the suppression of the original edit was already beginning to wage. Scalfaro found support among conservatives and staunch supporters of the Catholic Church, but he was still moved to defend his position in a radio statement issued on March 11, 1955. As recounted in *Visioni proibite*, his speech went thus:

> I understand how people who are concerned that their interests are affected, have to complain. Because of this I tried personally to see if it was possible to somehow mitigate the damage itself, but each person sensitive to the moral laws that are the basis of every healthy human society will have to agree that I would gravely fail towards my duty if, in my position, I had neglected such an impressive and vast array of citizens who believe in the necessity and urgency to protect society from every kind of moral and civic disintegration.[4]

After much negotiating and back-and-forth between the opposing factions, *Sins of Casanova* went into general release in 1955. It was reportedly released in America in 1957, but if an English dub was ever prepared, it has since disappeared into obscurity. Seen today, the film appears mild and good-natured, though the French print includes some more salacious material (including some female nudity) that surely would have caused Scalfaro to suffer an apoplectic fit had he seen it.

Notes:
1. Romagnoli, Michele, *L'occhio del testimone*, (Bologna: Granata Press, 1992), p. 47.
2. Curti, Roberto and Alessio Di Rocco, *Visioni proibite: I film vietati della censura italiana (1947-1968)*, (Turin: Lindau, 2014), p. 281.
3. *Ibid*, p. 282.
4. *Ibid*, p. 284.

## *Piccola posta (1955)*

**A detail enlargement from an Italian *fotobusta* for *Piccola posta*: Rodolfo (Alberto Sordi) preys upon one of the residents of his crooked nursing home.**

Aka *Piccola posta, ovvero: Cercasi vecchia con dote*

Directed by Stefano Vanzina (as Steno); Screenplay by Sandro Continenza, Lucio Fulci and Stefano Vanzina (as Steno); Director of Photography: Tonino Delli Colli; Editor: Giuliana Attenni; Music by Raffaele Gervasio

Main Players: Alberto Sordi (Rodolfo Vanzino); Franca Valeri (Lady Eva); Sergio Raimondi (Giorgio Cappelli); Anna Maria Pancani (Franchina); Peppino De Filippo (Gigliotti); Nanda Primavera (Lady Eva's Mother)

Cameo appearance: Lucio Fulci (Young man with glasses)

*Lady Eva is a Polish noblewoman who dispenses romantic advice in a popular newspaper column. At least, that is what she wants the public to believe. And believe it, they do; the public laps up her column, with some people being particularly devoted to it. However, her own love life is unfulfilling, as the veterinarian she is smitten with does not even realize she exists ...*

*Piccola posta* continues the anthology structure of *Un giorno in pretura*. The narrative is tied together by the figure of Lady Eva, a sort of European version of a "Dear Abby" style newspaper columnist. She doesn't deal exclusively in matters of the heart, but by and large her specialty is romantic advice, generally of the tritest variety. Though superficially light and fluffy, the film is distinguished by

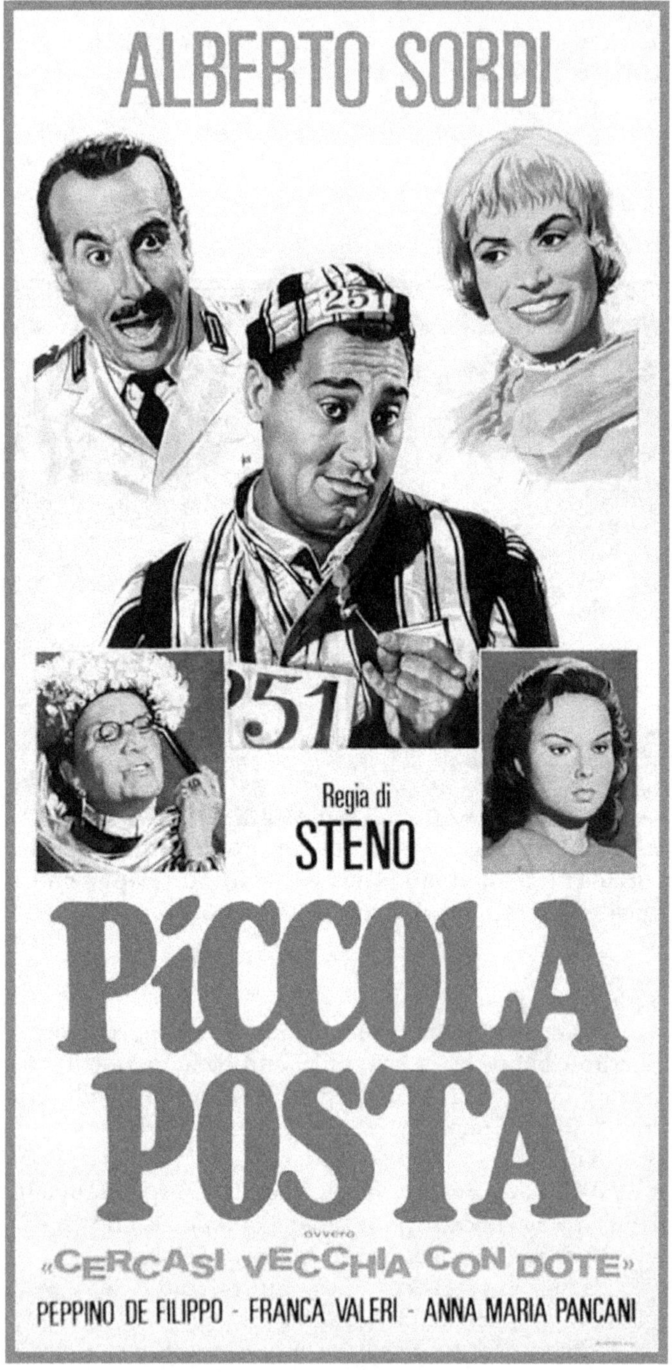


**Italian *locandina* for *Piccola posta*; artist unknown.**

an underlining sense of misanthropy that rejects romantic conventions.

The most interesting—and darkly amusing—segment focuses on the character of Rodolfo Vanzino, played by Alberto Sordi. Rodolfo is a completely irredeemable lout, a (so-called) nobleman fallen on hard times who runs a nursing home for the aged and infirm. Sordi's portrayal of the opportunistic character is a minor masterpiece in its own right, equaling his memorable interpretation of Nando Moriconi in his earlier collaborations with Steno and Fulci. Yet, whereas Moriconi was rather likable in his naïveté, Rodolfo is not the least bit sympathetic. He is not above mistreating his clientele so as to speed them off to the great beyond in the hopes of collecting their insurance monies, and the way in which he interacts with them, barking orders and condescending to them as if they were children, is as amusing as it is horrific. Rodolfo is also in the habit of extorting money from his elderly charges. Sordi's expert comic timing combined with his willingness to embrace the unsavory aspects of the character makes his scenes stand out in relief compared to the rest of the picture.

Deceptive appearances run rampant throughout the film. Rodolfo is no more a Baron than Lady Eva is a Polish noblewoman. Eva adopts this disguise to help give an air of worldly authority, but her readers are not aware of the fact that she is every bit as mixed-up as they are. She approaches her column with the best of intentions, but her advice lands a number of people in hot water—for example, she advises an elderly millionaire to go into Rodolfo's crooked nursing home—and her own love life is something of a joke, as well. In order to attract the attention of the veterinarian with whom she is in love, she decides to open a *salon* for dogs ... but this inevitably does not pan out well and some of the dogs escape and cause a ruckus. The plot strands come together at the end as the various characters are assembled at the police station.

Steno had nothing but praise for Alberto Sordi at this stage in the game:

> At the time when we worked together, Sordi was very nice, very helpful and absolutely not a pain in the ass. He became such (and I'm saying it in a positive way) later on, when he came up with his own ideas and showed that he was right [...]. However, I didn't sense his invasiveness, maybe because I liked him so much that I allowed him to impose his ideas without minimally opposing. Well, sometimes I left him too much room, as in *Piccola posta*, since he was lots of fun with his stories about and with old women, to the point that I completely forgot what the audience might or might not like.[1]

Franca Valeri gives a charming performance as Lady Eva. Valeri makes the character human and endearing, even as her words of "wisdom" land more and more people into trouble. She is therefore emblematic of the better aspects of human nature, especially when compared to the vile Rodolfo. The fact that her good intentions tend to produce bad results is key to the film's darker undercurrent, suggesting that Steno and his collaborators do not have much faith in Good Samaritan types, especially when they are put up against ruthless and cunning characters like Rodolfo. Valeri was born in Milan in 1920. She made her film debut with a small role in *Variety Lights* (1950), before becoming a more prominent presence on screen toward the end of the decade. She first worked with Fulci on *Totò a colori* (1952), on which he served as assistant director. Valeri won critical acclaim for her role in Mauro Bolognini's *Arrangiatevi* (1959), starring Peppino De Filippo (who also appears in this film) and Totò, for which she was nominated for her first of three Silver Ribbon awards from the Italian National Syndicate of Film Journalists. She was also memorable for Dino Risi in *Il segno di Venere* (1955), which also featured Alberto Sordi. Valeri has also worked extensively on stage and remains active in both films and the theater to this day, despite advancing age and suffering from Parkinson's disease.

The film also benefits from some good black-and-white cinematography courtesy of Tonino Delli Colli. Delli Colli was born in Rome in 1922. He entered films as a camera operator in the early 1940s and graduated to director of photography status in 1944. His early credits run the gamut from operettas and melodramas to broad comedies. He earned the distinction of photographing the first major Italian production to be filmed entirely in color, the aforementioned *Totò a colori* (1952). Delli Colli photographed several of Pier Paolo Pasolini's most significant films, including *Accattone* (1961) and *The Gospel According to St. Matthew* (1964), but found his biggest international success when he began collaborating with Sergio Leone. He took over from Massimo Dallamano as Leone's cinematographer of choice on such films as *The Good, The Bad and the Ugly* (1966), *Once Upon a Time in the West* (1968) and *Once Upon a Time in America* (1984). He also worked with such major *auteurs* as Lina Wertmüller (*Seven Beauties*, 1975), Roman Polanski (*Bitter Moon*, 1992), Marco Ferreri (*Tales of Ordinary Madness*, 1981) and Federico Fellini (*Ginger and Fred*, 1986). His last credit was Roberto Benigni's critically-acclaimed *Life is Beautiful* (1997), for which he won a David as Best Cinematographer at the David di Donatello Awards. Delli Colli died in 2005. As a final piece of trivia, he was married to the statuesque actress Alexandra Delli Colli, who would appear so memorably as the ill-fated nymphomaniac who encounters the crazed killer in Fulci's notorious *The New York Ripper* (1982).

Notes:
1. Faldini, Franca and Goffredo Fofi, *L'avventurosa storia del cinema italiano raccontata dai suoi protagonisti*, 1935-1959, (Milan: Feltrinelli, 1979), p. 286.

## *La ragazza di via Veneto* (1955)

Directed by Marino Girolami; Produced by Bruno Bolognesi; Screenplay by Lucio Fulci, Roberto Gianviti, Marino Girolami and Bruno Valeri, from a story by Bruno Valeri; Director of Photography: Carlo Montuori; Music by Carlo Innocenzi

Main Players: Anna Maria Moneta Caglio (Anita); Carlo Giustini (Spartaco); Giulio Calì (Anita's Father)

*Anita and Spartaco are deeply in love, but they are too poor to do anything about it. Anita works as a laundress, while dreaming of becoming a model; Spartaco is a small-time amateur boxer who dreams of going professional. As Anita reaches out to achieve her dream, the jealous Spartaco, fearful that this kind of success will cause her to lose interest in him, sets out to sabotage her every move. Will their love be able to survive these conflicts?*

*La ragazza di via Veneto* is a relatively minor entry in Fulci's early screenwriting filmography. It's basically a melodrama with a few comic elements and it lacks the acerbic edge and sense of wit that distinguishes the films he was collaborating on with Steno around this same time.

The scenario offers up the usual star-crossed lovers. Both Anita and Spartaco come from humble surroundings, and in their own way, they each aspire to better themselves. However, Spartaco, perhaps being emblematic of the more parochial and closed-minded side of Italian males, is a born chauvinist who wishes to get the girl—and be the proverbial breadwinner as well. It's not enough for him to love Anita and to try and make her happy—he has to accomplish this on his own terms and this extends to trampling on her own dreams. Anita's dream of making a name as a model is a threat to his macho image and the only way he can handle being with her is to therefore block her attempts at success at every turn. Anita is no wilting wallflower, however, and it does not take her long to realize that her love for Spartaco should not come equipped with a desire to please his every whim. She possesses a strong independent streak, thus providing the film with its dramatic core as she fights to assert herself.

**Anna Maria Moneta Caglio as Anita; *La ragazza di via Veneto* was her shot at film stardom.**

Amid all this lofty-sounding "battle of the sexes" action, there's also time for a little lowbrow humor courtesy of Spartaco's emotionally arrested friends. Spartaco and his cronies are juveniles at heart, even if the former plays at being very tough and in control of his own actions. As he and his aimless friends drift through the city and poke fun at everything they do not comprehend, they remind one of the so-called "*Vitelloni*" of Federico Fellini's 1953 film of the same name; in common with that group of delinquents, they have reached a point in their lives where drifting from day to day is no longer acceptable and they must learn to cope with the idea of embracing adulthood and pursuing their own destiny.

A key scene in this respect occurs when Spartaco and his friends crash Anita's first fashion show. They sit in the audience and mutter wisecracks about the fashions and the decidedly effeminate designer and M.C., and then when it is Anita's chance to shine, they pipe up and show "support" by essentially trying to turn the entire affair into a big joke. Spartaco and his friends may see it as Anita playing "grown up," but she is not laughing—this is what she wants out of her future, whether her boyfriend and his companions approve of it or not, and she is not likely to forget the humiliation in a hurry. Spartaco, for his part, is hopeful that he can win her back by falling back on juvenile tactics like trying to make her jealous, but it is apparent that they are headed in very different directions. This being a fairly conventional romance, however, there's little doubt that they will ultimately patch up their differences and find true love.

Director Marino Girolami handles the film with efficiency but little in the way of style or originality. There are good ideas to be found in the screenplay and its characterizations, but Girolami's conventional, somewhat humdrum approach prevents it from ever rising above the ordinary. Girolami does a nice job of showcasing a refreshingly "normal" view of Rome, as opposed to over-indulging in the usual travelogue images, and the film certainly does not overstay its welcome.

Girolami was born in Rome in 1914. He started off as an actor, screenwriter and assistant director, then began directing his own films in the early 1950s. Girolami was something of a jack of all genres, dabbling in many different forms without ever really distinguishing himself in any of them; he did competent work, but seldom was it anything more than that. He would follow in Fulci's footsteps, first by putting the comics Franco and Ciccio through their paces in several films (including *Due rrringos nel Texas*, 1967), then by helming an early cash-in on the success of Fulci's *Zombie* (1979), titled *Zombie Holocaust* (1980). He died in 1994. Girolami's family also achieved some distinction in the film industry: his brother Romolo changed his surname to Guerrieri and went on to direct such genre fare as *The Sweet Body of Deborah* (1968) and *The Double* (1971). Romolo served as his brother's assistant on this film, along with another future genre filmmaker, Emilio Miraglia, who is best known for directing the thrillers *The Night Evelyn Came Out of the Grave* (1971) and *The Red Queen Kills Seven Times* (1972). Girolami's two sons also went into the business: the eldest, Ennio, would work as an assistant director and actor (he can be seen as the store detective who accosts shoplifter Ania Pieroni in Dario Argento's *Tenebrae*, 1982), while the younger, Enzo, would change his name to Enzo G. Castellari and become one of the most prominent action filmmakers in Italian cinema; among his credits are such gems as *Street Law* (1973) and *The Big Racket* (1976).

The film is also notable as the first collaboration between Fulci and fellow screenwriter Roberto Gianviti. Gianviti's date of birth is not known, but he broke into films around 1953 and would work within many of the popular genres: comedies like *Totò a Parigi* (1958), adventures like *Terror of the Red Mask* (1960), *pepla* like *The Vengeance of Ursus* (1961), Westerns like *Have a Good Funeral, My Friend ... Sartana Will Pay* (1970), *gialli* like *Seven Blood-Stained Orchids* (1972) and so on. He and Fulci would go on to work on a number of different screenplays, including *The Two Crusaders* (1968) and some of Fulci's most notable works as a director, including *Beatrice Cenci* (1969), *A Lizard in a Woman's Skin* (1971) and *Don't Torture a Duckling* (1972). He remained active until the late 1990s and died in 2001.

Leading lady Anna Maria Moneta Caglio gives a rather flat and listless performance as Anita, thus hurting the film's dramatic impact. Caglio's movie career began and ended with this effort, but her biography is by no means run-of-the-mill. She attained instant celebrity (and infamy) as the sole witness in the high profile Montesi Scandal. Twenty-year-old Wilma Montesi was found dead on the Torvajanica beach, located in Rome, on April 11, 1953. Caglio testified that Piero Piccioni dragged the girl to the shore. He was a composer and musician who was the son of the Ministry of Foreign Affairs, Attilio Piccioni, the candidate who was set to succeed Alcide De Gasperi as Prime Minister. Piero Piccioni was acquitted four years later, but his father's career was ruined by the trial. Moneta Caglio, thanks to the notoriety the newspapers had given her (they dubbed her "The Black Swan," owing to her long neck and the black dress she wore to the trial), became a sort of public figure for a period of time. She was the lover of Marquis Montagna (who had organized the wild party which led to Wilma Montesi's death) and used her newfound fame to land the leading role in *La ragazza di via Veneto*. After that, she disappeared from view.[1] Accused and acquitted Piero Piccioni, on the other hand, would go on to a long and successful career as a film composer; among his many credits were Elio Petri's *The 10th Victim* (1965), Luchino Visconti's *The Stranger* (1967), Radley Metzger's *Camille 2000* (1969) and Francesco Rosi's *Christ Stopped at Eboli* (1979); he died in 2004 at the age of 82. The murder of Wilma Montesi remains unsolved.

Fulci rightly regarded the film as a slight diversion, but the film's notorious leading lady certainly made an impression:

> I was called by a producer called Bolognese to revise the script of *La ragazza di via Veneto*, written by minor, terrible scriptwriters, one of whom was to literally die of hunger, the poor man [Note: Fulci is possibly referring to Bruno Valeri]. There was this woman, Caglio, who looked rather modest; she was the opposite of the *femme fatale* that the newspaper had described her as being. The producer thought he would make money out of using her in the film, whereas it flopped. Caglio was a rather squalid character, anyway. Once, when somebody addressed her in a rather insulting way, she burst out laughing and said, "Beware, I'm gonna tell that to the police!" Apart from this, she never mentioned the story that made her famous. As an actress, she just could not play the lead; she simply did not exist. The movie didn't have any trouble, since it was a nondescript story, about the girl who moves to Rome to make money, but the producer possibly had given his word (or was forced) not to mention the Montesi murder at all.[2]

Actress-singer Nilla Pizzi performs the title song, and she also appears briefly in the film; she had formerly toplined *Ci troviamo in galleria* (1953).

Notes:
1.http://press.uchicago.edu/Misc/Chicago/668487.html
2. Faldini, Franca and Goffredo Fofi, *L'avventurosa storia del cinema italiano raccontata dai suoi protagonisti*, 1935-1959, (Milan: Feltrinelli, 1979), p. 278.

## *Io sono la Primula Rossa (1955)*

Directed by Giorgio Simonelli; Produced by Giovanni Amati; Screenplay by Lucio Fulci, Gastone Ramazzotti, Giorgio Simonelli, Raffaele Sposito and Stefano Vanzina (as Steno), based on "The Scarlet Pimpernel" by Baroness Emma Orczy; Director of Photography: Carlo Bellero; Editor: Nino Baragli; Music by Mario Nascimbene

Main Players: Renato Rascel (Sir Archibald); Kerima (Lola); Luigi Pavese (James); Flora Medini (Lady Elisabeth); Lauro Gazzolo (Chiffon)

*France, 1793: As the revolution reaches its bloody peak, an English nobleman who conceals his identity behind the guise of The Scarlet Pimpernel, fighting back against violence and tyranny. Meanwhile, another English nobleman, Sir Archibald, travels to France in the hopes of escaping the interference of his wife and mother-in-law, while finding a new bevy of mistresses. Sir Archibald is mistaken for the elusive Pimpernel and is summarily arrested and put on trial; only the real Pimpernel can save him …*

*The Scarlet Pimpernel* originated on stage in London in 1903. Written by Emma Orczy, it initially did not find much favor with audiences—but Orczy would tinker with the material and find another backer, who produced the show in 1905. At this point, it became a huge hit and went on to be performed over one hundred times in its original run. Inspired by the success of the play, Orczy decided to put the story out in novel form; it was originally published not long after the play's success, in 1905. Orczy, born in Hungary in 1865, immigrated to England with her parents when she was only 15 years old. She took up writing after the birth of her first child, hoping to supplement her husband's modest income, but she only had minor success prior to *The Scarlet Pimpernel*; after its commercial (if not critical) success, she and her family were able to live out their days in luxury. She would go on to write about a dozen sequels focusing on the character of Sir Percy Blakeney (or members of his family), a foppish English aristocrat who helps rescue French nobility from the guillotine during the French Revolution. She died in 1947. Her most popular creation was brought to the cinema no less than 15 times, beginning as early as 1917. The best-known adaptation emerged from England in 1934 and featured Leslie Howard as Sir Percy and Raymond Massey as his nemesis Chauvelin. The most significant of the later versions was titled *The Elusive Pimpernel* (1950) and featured David Niven in the title role, with the beloved team of "The Archers" (Michael Powell and Emeric Pressburger)

**Italian *fotobusta* for the very obscure *Io sonno la Primula Rossa*, highlighting star Renato Rascel; artist unknown.**

assuming the writing, producing and directing honors. A popular Broadway musical made its debut in 1997 and parodies have been seen everywhere from *Daffy Duck* cartoons and British *Carry On* comedies to a recent episode of the popular children's animated series *Phineas and Ferb*.

Lucio Fulci and his mentor Stefano Vanzina (Steno) had a hand in adapting this parody, but the film has become virtually impossible to screen in recent years. It does not appear to have been a popular success commercially and neither Fulci nor Steno appears to have been moved to discuss it in interviews. At the time of this writing, it is one of only two films written or directed by Fulci which is unavailable to view in any form—the other being *Sanremo – La grande sfida* from 1960.

The film was a vehicle for comic actor Renato Rascel. Born in Turin in 1912, Rascel was the son of accomplished opera singers and indeed his early years saw him poised to follow in their footsteps. The lure of performing was too strong, however, and he began appearing in films in 1942. He achieved favor with audiences early on and went on to win acclaim for his performances in such films as Alberto Lattuada's *The Overcoat* (1952, for which he won a Silver Ribbon from the Italian National Syndicate of Film Journalists) and Mario Soldati's *Policarpo* (1959, for which he won Best Actor at the David di Donatello Awards). He appeared opposite Christopher Lee in Steno's horror spoof *Uncle Was a Vampire* (1959) and appeared in Vittorio De Sica's *The Last Judgement* (1961). He made his final appearance in Franco Zeffirelli's star-studded mini-series *Jesus of Nazareth* (1977) and died in 1991.

Director Giorgio Simonelli was born in Rome in 1901. His credits stretch all the way back to the end of the 1920s and he initially worked primarily as an editor and screenwriter. He began directing in 1934, establishing himself as a competent journeyman who was at home in various genres. He directed quite a few films featuring the comedy team of Franco and Ciccio, who would dominate the early part of Fulci's directorial career, as well; among his many vehicles with them were *The Amazing Doctor G* (1965), *I due sanculott* and *I due figli di Ringo* (both 1966). He died in 1966.

## *Totò nella luna (1958)*

Aka *Totò in the Moon*

Directed by Stefano Vanzina (as Steno); Produced by Mario Cecchi Gori; Screenplay by Sandro Continenza, Ettore Scola and Stefano Vanzina, from an original story by Lucio Fulci and Stefano Vanzina; Director of Photography: Mario Scarpelli; Editor: Giuliana Attenni; Music by Alexander Derevitsky (as Alessandro Derevitsky)

Main Players: Antonio de Curtis [as Totò] (Pasquale Belafronte); Sylva Koscina (Lidia); Ugo Tognazzi (Achille Paoloni); Sandra Milo (Tatiana); Luciano Salce (Von Braun); Richard McNamara (Campbell); Jim Dolen (O'Connor)

*American scientists are determined to put a man on the Moon despite the interference of extra-terrestrial intelligence. It is believed that only primates are capable of surviving on the moon, however, due to a substance secreted in their blood known as glumonium. When it is discovered that the dim-witted Achille has glumonium in his blood, a plan is hatched to convince him to go into space. The devious Pasquale becomes aware of the plan, however, and is determined to capitalize on it …*

During the height of the Cold War, America and the former Soviet Union engaged in a so-called "space race," the two super powers vying for supremacy in the uncharted terrains of outer space. As scientists and engineers sweated around the clock trying to build rockets which could take people into space, the public's imagination was thoroughly captivated: Who would be the first to succeed in attaining this goal, and would it be possible to inhabit other planets? In 1955, both countries announced plans to launch satellites within the next two to three years. In 1957, the Soviets achieved their dream: Sputnik 1 was successfully put into orbit. Smarting from this public humiliation, the U.S. then set out to become the first country to launch a human being into space. In 1961, the Soviets again emerged victorious when they sent Yuri Gagarin into orbit in the Vostok 1, which made a successful orbit around the Earth; he became the first person to go into space. Not to be outdone in such a fashion, the Americans launched a spaceship, the Freedom 7, into space a mere three weeks later; Alan Shepherd therefore became the first American to go into outer space. After that, then-President of the U.S., John F. Kennedy, launched an initiative to send an American to the moon. This would finally reach fruition in 1969, when the Apollo 11 made a successful landing; the crew was comprised of Neil Armstrong, Michael Collins and Edwin "Buzz" Aldrin. Armstrong would take the famous first step, which was broadcast to record-capacity audiences the world over. To this day, the public fascination with the mysteries of outer space remains undimmed

**Italian *fotobusta* for *Totò nella luna*; the sexy, half-naked women do not figure in the actual film.**

and, as science and technology continue to develop, the potential of more and more unexplored terrain and universes remains a tantalizing challenge in the offing.

Films about the mysteries of space can be traced back to the early days of cinema, with Georges Méliès' *A Trip to the Moon* (1902) offering an imaginative and witty vision of the first rocket being fired at the moon's surface. Fritz Lang's ambitious *Woman in the Moon* (1929) provided a more serious and speculative account of the first mission into outer space, but it was something of an expensive failure in its day. In the 1950s, science fiction became the rage due to fears over the hydrogen bomb. As school kids in the United States were put through "duck-and-cover" drills to prepare them for the eventuality of a nuclear attack, people across the world were growing more and more fearful of the terrifying outcome of such a catastrophe. This fear manifested itself in a series of films focusing on animals and insects mutated by atomic power (*Them!*, 1954; *Tarantula*, 1955, etc.), as well as heavily codified thrillers which addressed the loss of identity and the pressure to conform wrought by the Cold War (*Invasion of the Body Snatchers*, 1956, being the classic example). As the decade wore on, filmmakers began to explore the more humorous potential of such scenarios and soon various comic actors found themselves being launched into space, as it were. *Abbott and Costello Go to Mars* (1953) supplied a rather cheap and cheerful variation on this formula and the Italians soon got in on the act when Totò literally beat the Americans to the moon by more than a decade.

The story was devised by Steno and Fulci, but the latter did not participate in the creation of the finished script. Instead, a different group of writers—including the talented Ettore Scola and Sandro Continenza, who had already collaborated with Fulci and Steno on other scenarios—were entrusted with the task of helping Steno to bring Italy's number one comic into the space age. Totò would take co-writing credit on a number of his vehicles, but his name does not appear in the writing credits this time. Indeed, his presence in the film is somewhat minimized in favor of the character of Achille, a space-obsessed would-be science fiction author played by Ugo Tognazzi. The title is by no means misleading, but compared to some of his other vehicles for Steno, Totò seems somewhat ill-used in this film.

The plot relies a great deal on miscommunication and language barriers. The American agents looking to utilize Achille as the first man on the moon, due to his having a rare substance peculiar to chimpanzees in his blood stream (don't ask), are at a loss when faced with the wheeling-and-dealing Pasquale (played by Totò). Neither side really understands the other and poor Achille is trapped in the middle, desperately hoping to find success with his schlocky sci-fi stories while also winning the esteem of Pasquale, who is about to become his father-in-law. Totò plays up the language aspect beautifully, notably during the scene in which he negotiates with the American agents for a percentage of the money Achille is to be paid if he agrees to go into space. He believes that they are offering to pay for the American rights to Achilles' books, whereas they believe that he is playing hardball with them to guarantee Achilles' willingness to become the first man to go to the moon. The crossed wires of communication yield some very funny exchanges and inevitably have dire consequences for Pasquale and the hapless Achille.

When the film finally reaches its destination, as it were, it offers up an imaginative and charmingly naïve portrait of the moon. Art director Giorgio Giovannini (who would go on to work on such Mario Bava films as *Black Sunday*, 1960, and *Black Sabbath*, 1963) and cinematographer Marco Scarpelli (who also photographed *Un giorna in pretura* and *Ci troviamo in galleria*) work wonders with minimal resources and present an impressively stylized landscape. Steno's flair for visual humor manifests itself throughout and if the visualization of the aliens as animated, floating eyes, invisible to the human characters and communicating telepathically, is a little disappointing, they are sensibly played for goofiness and therefore come off better than their counterparts in many serious sci-fi films of the period.

For once, Totò is overshadowed by one of his co-stars, in this instance the gifted Ugo Tognazzi. Tognazzi's charming performance as Achille provides the film with its heart and soul. Totò's Pasquale is pure greed and cunning, whereas Achille represents the dreamer. He is very funny in the film and also proves to be an endearing protagonist. Tognazzi was born in 1922 and began his career on the stage. He made his film debut in 1950 and became a major star as the decade unfolded. He won much acclaim for his work in such films as Dino Risi's *I mostri* (1963) and Pietro Germi's *The Climax* (1967), as well as several films for Marco Ferreri, including *The Conjugal Bed* (1963), *The Wedding March* (1965) and, most famously, *La Grande Bouffe* (1973). Well-known for playing macho types, he went against type when he played Michel Serrault's lover in the hit comedy *La Cage aux Folles* (1978); the film's success led to two sequels, in which he also appeared. He won Best Actor in Cannes for his lead role in Bernardo Bertolucci's *Tragedy of a Ridiculous Man* (1981) and directed several films throughout the 1960s and 1970s; he died in 1990.

Fulci may not have been as deeply involved in the writing of this project, but he was far from idle during this period. 1958 saw him embarking on an important chapter of his personal life. He married his wife Marina that year; the couple would remain together for 11 years. Their union would result in the birth of two daughters: Antonella would be born in August 1960 and Camilla would follow in July 1963.[1] Their union would end tragically, but for the time being things were looking very bright indeed for Fulci.

Notes:
1. Some sources allude to a third daughter, who reportedly died in a car crash, but this has not been confirmed.

## *Guardia, ladro e cameriera (1958)*

Aka *Maid, Thief and Guard*

Directed by Stefano Vanzina (as Steno); Produced by Dino De Laurentiis; Story and Screenplay by Sandro Continenza (as Continenza), Lucio Fulci (as Fulci) and Stefano Vanzina (as Steno); Director of Photography: Riccardo Pallottini; Editor: Gisa Radicchi Levi; Music by Lelio Luttazzi

Main Players: Gabriella Pallotta (Adalgisa Pellicciotti); Nino Manfredi (Otello Cucchiaroni); Fausto Cigliano (Amerigo Zappitelli); Bice Valori (Countess); Mario Carotenuto (Professor)

*Otello attempts a robbery on New Year's Eve, but does not reckon on the presence of the maid, Adalgisa. The two fall for each other, but the nosy night watchman, Amerigo, is not about to let the romance blossom ...*

Fulci continued his association with his mentor Steno with this slight but amusing comedy. The set-up is contrived, to say the least, but the film nevertheless benefits from Steno's energetic direction and some excellent comic set pieces.

Beneath the surface of lightness and frivolity, there is a darker undercurrent. The film continues the exploration of the conflict between the older generation and their younger counterparts. In this film's *milieu*, the older generation has fallen into stagnation: They are driven by an obsession with surface gloss and the appearance of success. The young, on the other hand, are aimless and indolent, thus making them easy prey for their more cynical and amoral elders. Otello is a typical drifter in this setting; he is not a bad person, *per se*, but he has no clue what he will be doing with his life and allows himself to be pulled into a scheme by a shifty underworld figure known as The Professor. The latter rallies these young people to carry out his robberies, thus saving some potential embarrassment by using them to ensure that the coast is clear before he ever enters the scene. One doesn't want to make too much out of this set-up, as it really isn't a particularly serious or deep exploration of this theme, but these elements do

**Title card frame grab from *Guardia, ladro e cameriera***

bubble beneath the surface, thus giving the film a slightly jaundiced quality to accompany its lighter, more frivolous elements.

Steno handles the material with tremendous aplomb. There are some superb sequences highlighting his unobtrusive but effective directorial style. In particular, the sequence wherein Otello is forced to scale a high wall in order to gain access to the apartment earmarked for the robbery is simultaneously suspenseful and amusing—and even a little bit scary, if one suffers at all from acrophobia. The depiction of the New Year's Eve festivities is lively throughout, providing an ideal backdrop for the story of mistaken identity and bungled criminal endeavors.

Cinematographer Riccardo Pallottini, who would later photograph *Massacre Time* (1966) for Fulci, works well with the widescreen, black-and-white format. One cannot help but be reminded of a later mixture of drama and acerbic comedy also photographed in this format, namely Billy Wilder's *The Apartment* (1960). The connection is purely coincidental, of course, but it does point to the effectiveness of playing potentially intense sequences against a setting that is rife with joy and laughter. Steno's firm control of pacing also ensures that the film moves at a very good rhythm and seldom puts a foot wrong; only a couple of overly padded sequences designed to allow Fausto Cigliano (as the night watchman, Amerigo) to show off his singing talents threaten to slow things down.

The actors are all very well cast and effective in their roles. Nino Manfredi is superb as the hapless Otello. It would have been easy to make the character into a total fool, but Manfredi and Steno see to it that he retains his humanity, even if it is sometimes at the expense of his dignity. His attempts at deceiving the maid, Adalgisa, are charmingly inept and the way he gradually succumbs to his feelings for her never comes off as forced or insincere. Manfredi was born in Castro dei Volsci in 1921. He made his film debut in 1949 and soon proved himself adept in comedy as well as heavy drama. Manfredi was also much in demand as a dubbing performer; for example, he dubbed Marcello Mastroianni in some of his early roles, including *Paris is Always Paris* (1951), in addition to dubbing Sergio Raimondi in *Piccola posta*. Manfredi won acclaim for his performances in such films as Dino Risi's *Il gaucho* (1965), Franco Brusati's *Bread and Chocolate* (1974), Alberto Bevilacqua's *Eye of the Cat* (1975) and Ettora Scola's *Ugly, Dirty and Bad* (1976). He also directed a handful of films, including the critically-acclaimed *Between Miracles* (1971), which was nominated for the Palme D'Or at the Cannes Film Festival and netted prizes as Best First Time Director at Cannes and at the Italian Golden Globes. He died in 2004.

Gabriella Pallotta brings great charm to her role as Adalgisa. Pallotta's appealing screen presence makes the love story believable, and she also displays a nice, light comedic touch where appropriate. Pallotta was born in Rome in 1938 and originally trained to be a concert pianist before making an auspicious debut in Vittorio De Sica's *The Roof* (1956). The Italian National Syndicate of Film Journalists nominated her as Best Actress for that film. She followed that with an appearance in Michelangelo Antonioni's *Il grido* (1957) and went on to earn a Golden Globe nomination for her role in *The Pigeon That Took Rome* (1962), starring Charlton Heston. She made her last film appearance in 1977, after which she retired from the business.

*Guardia, ladro e cameriera* would mark an important moment of transition for Lucio Fulci. After years of working in Steno's shadow, Fulci decided the time had come to make the transition to directing. As he would later explain, his main motivator was money: "[…]I began to direct films […] for the simple reason that I'd got married and had no money to live on […]."[1] Fulci would continue to write screenplays for other filmmakers as time wore on, helping to supplement his income and allowing himself to continue to dabble in subjects he might not be deemed suitable to direct himself. But by the time he collaborated on his next project for another director, he was already well on his way to establishing himself as a promising young talent among Italian commercial filmmakers.

Notes:
1. Palmerini, Luca M. and Gaetano Mistretta, *Spaghetti Nightmares* (Florida: Fantasma Books, 1996), p. 58.

## *Sanremo—La grande sfida* (1960)

**Italian poster for *Sanremo—La grande sfida*, notable for being the only instance of Fulci (bottom right) getting his face on the advertising for a movie until he took the lead role in his own film, *Nightmare Concert* (*A Cat in the Brain*).**

Directed by Piero Vivarelli; Produced by Giovanni Addessi, for ERA Cinematografica and Aronfilm; Story and Screenplay by Giovanni Addessi, Piero Accolti, Lucio Fulci, Francesco Thellung and Piero Vivarelli; Director of Photography: Giuseppe La Torre; Editor: Gabriele Varriale; Music by Piero Umiliani

Main Players: Mario Carotenuto; Adriana Celentano; Sergio Bruni; Fausto Cigliano; Tony Dallara; Jula De Palma; Mina; Domenico Modugno; Joe Sentieri; Teddy Reno; Vania Protti; Odorado Spadaro

Cameo appearance: Lucio Fulci

*Two record labels try to out-do each other in an effort to win the coveted prize at the annual San Remo music festival …*

*Sanremo – La grande sfida* is a mixture of documentary and genteel comedy, built around the 10th San Remo music festival. The festival originated in 1951 and was designed to give musicians an opportunity to unveil and perform never-before-heard songs; at the end of the festival, a winner would be selected. The goal of the festival was to try and help rebuild San Remo's economy in the lean postwar years and it proved to be a resounding success. The festival continues to be held to this day. For this film, director Piero Vivarelli took a film crew to the festival and recorded some of the highlights; Fulci participated in this work and was rewarded with a special credit as "technical supervisor." Fulci also plays a small role in the film and is credited with co-writing the screenplay.

As a director, Fulci began dabbling in the musical genre around this same time, often in collaboration with Piero Vivarelli. Their collaboration would yield such films as *I ragazzi del juke-box* and *Urlatori alla sbarra*, both of which also feature the comic actor Mario Carotenuto, who is featured in this film playing one of the greedy record executives. Vivarelli had a significant hand in the writing of those films and also served as Fulci's assistant on the latter. More on Fulci's relationship with Vivarelli and the musical genre can be found in the reviews for those titles alluded to above. In any event, *Sanremo – La grande sfida* marked Vivarelli's debut as a director. Sooner than risk over-stretching, he put much of his emphasis on the content of the picture and in dealing with the actors, while Fulci leant his technical expertise to the production. As Vivarelli would later recall, while reflecting on working with Fulci:

> [He was] a bit mad, but he had technical skills like no one else […]. Lucio used to shoot with an eye on what the editing would be like. And it was an absolutely modern editing, especially on the songs, like a video clip. Only, he did it 30 years before the video clip. So he was an absolute precursor. […] The funny thing is that Lucio never had the success he deserved – even when he made horror films, which were no lesser than those by Argento. I don't know why … perhaps he was too good … I mean, he always solved all the technical problems in a snap, and

there are many of them while shooting a film. If you look again at certain shots, they are quite difficult. Whereas someone else would take six, seven weeks, he did it in four. On one hand, this allowed him to work more. On the other, it depreciated him. Otherwise, there's no explanation...[1]

The film has never been released on video and has only surfaced on Italian television in recent years, but it would appear that Fulci's technical input was confined to helping to co-ordinate the filming of the various performance pieces. As a piece of trivia, one of the songs that Fulci co-wrote with Vivarelli for Adriano Celentano was entered into the competition: *Blue jeans Rock*. The big winner at the festival that year, however, was *Romantica*, written by Renato Rascel—the star of Fulci's other "lost" project, *Io sono la Primula Rossa*—and Dino Verde. This was the second consecutive year that a song co-authored by Verde won the festival; incidentally, he also had a hand in *Piove (Ciao, ciao bambina)*, which claimed the prize in 1959.

Another piece of trivia worth noting: The continuity person was Umberto Lenzi, who would later become another popular and prolific director in the Italian genre community. Born in Tuscany in 1931, Lenzi broke into films in the late 1950s; he made his directing debut with the seldom-seen *Mia Italida stin Ellada* (1958), then worked his way through many of the popular genres in later years. He dabbled in *pepla* (*Samson and the Slave Queen*, 1963), spy yarns (*008: Operation Exterminate*, 1965), *fumetti* (*Kriminal*, 1966), war movies (*Desert Commandos*, 1967), *gialli* (*Orgasmo*, 1968), *polizziotteschi* (*Almost Human*, 1974), horror movies (*Nightmare City*, 1980) and so on. He and Fulci became friendly during the making of this film and they would remain so for the remainder of the latter's life.

Notes:
1. Albiero, Paolo and Giacomo Cacciatore, *Il terrorista dei generi: Tutto il cinema di Lucio Fulci* (Rome: Un mondo a parte, 2004), p. 41.

## *Totò, Peppino e... la dolce vita* (1961)

Directed by Sergio Corbucci; Produced by Gianni Buffardi and Mario Mariani; Screenplay by Bruno Corbucci (as B. Corbucci), Giovanni Grimaldi (as G. Grimaldi) and Mario Guerra (as M. Guerra), from a story by Lucio Fulci (as L. Fulci) and Stefano Vanzina (as Steno); Director of Photography: Alvaro Mancori; Editor: Renato Cinquini

Main Players: Antonio de Curtis [as Totò] (Antonio Barbacane); Peppino De Filippo (Peppino); Mara Berni (Elena); Francesco Mulé (Guglielmo); Rosalba Neri (Magda); Jacqueline Pierreux (Jacqueline); Antonio Pierfederici (Oscar)

**Italian *locandina* for *Totò, Peppino e ... la dolce vita*; artwork by R. Olivetti.**

*Antonio is sent to Rome by his grandfather with a simple goal: He must bribe local politicians to divert the building of a new highway so that it cuts through their little village, thus increasing real estate value. However, Antonio is soon seduced by the sweet life in the big city and loses sight of his goal. His cousin Peppino is then sent to get things under control, but it does not go as planned ...*

***Totò, Peppino e ... la dolce vita*: Antonio (Totò) hawks his wares on the streets of Rome.**

Federico Fellini's *La dolce vita* (1960) was no ordinary movie; it captured something on celluloid that other films had never managed to capture. It provided a snapshot of a particular time of happiness and prosperity in Rome, while also allowing viewers a glimpse of the seedier aspects of the so-called "sweet life." The story focused on a scandal journalist, played by Marcello Mastroianni, whose life is turned upside down in the course of a week; he encounters love, loss and the promise of sex with a blonde goddess (Anita Ekberg) and a spiritual awakening, which may or may not make him a better person by the end of the picture. The film's frank sexuality and unsparing portrayal of the problems lurking beneath the glittering surface of the rebuilt ruins of the Eternal City created a sensation. It landed in serious trouble with censors in many countries and would be banned in Spain until after the death of Dictator Generalissimo Francisco Franco. The film would go on to win a number of prestigious awards (including Palme D'Or at the Cannes Film Festival) and its popularity would introduce certain terms into the popular vernacular; chief among these is *paparazzi*, a name specific to scandal-hungry news photographers, deriving their name from the character called Paparazzo, played in the film by actor Walter Santesso.

Inevitably, the film's popularity resulted in numerous homages and parodies, some more overt than others. The film's imagery can be seen being quoted in such pictures as Giuseppe Tornatore's *Cinema Paradiso* (1988), Woody Allen's *Celebrity* (1998) and Sofia Coppola's *Lost in Translation* (2003), while Spanish filmmaker Jess Franco would pay tribute to its infamous orgy scene in his masterpiece *Venus in Furs* (1969). Given that so many of Totò's movies were built upon the success of other films, it is hardly surprising that he should have done a film specifically indebted to Fellini's model. Steno and Fulci devised the story, perhaps with the idea that the former should direct, but by the time the film went into production, it was future Spaghetti Western specialist Sergio Corbucci who was sitting in the director's chair. The end result is a little over-eager, perhaps, but is still loaded with genuine laughs.

Totò and Peppino De Filippo first crossed paths while working in the theater and their obvious chemistry resulted in their being paired for a number of pictures. They weren't exactly a comedy act à *la* Abbott and Costello, for example, but the two men possessed extraordinary comic timing and played off each other beautifully. Titles such as *Totò, Peppino e la ... malafemmina* (1956), *Totò, Peppino e i fuorilegge* (1956) and *Totò, Peppino e le fanatiche* (1960) played up their partnership to good box-office, and this film followed in that tradition. Using Fellini's satire as a starting point, the story crams in references to "hot button" topics like prostitution and narcotics but uses them as a counterpoint to the charmingly naïve antics of the two middle-aged country bumpkin figures who are clearly out of their depth in the excesses of contemporary Rome.

The film includes some absolutely brilliant comic set pieces. The best involves Totò and Peppino doing their best to impress a couple of American women who are trying to make their husbands jealous. The two men put on all the courtly airs in an attempt to seduce the much younger women, but they only succeed in making themselves look foolish. They wreck the nightclub furniture, get into fights with the clientele and, best of all, Totò reacts hysterically when he sees a flambé being prepared at one of the adjoining tables—thinking the table to be on fire, he uses a bottle of seltzer to attack the blaze, creating chaos in the process. The two comedians are clearly in their element improvising their way through such sequences and the film definitely benefits as a result.

The supporting cast includes an early appearance by the sultry and beautiful Rosalba Neri. She plays a character clearly coded to be a prostitute and even at this early stage in the game she brings a tremendous, smoldering sensuality to the part. Born in Forlì in 1939, Neri came to public attention when she won a beauty pageant. She decided to give acting a try and made her debut in 1956. As a graduate of the Centro Sperimentale di Cinematografica, she sometimes found herself being credited on films for quota reasons—there were incentives given to films to utilize school talent and many times the actors and actresses credited were only present in name only. Many of her early roles were minor walk-on or bit parts, but gradually she began to score juicier roles by the early 1960s. She impressed in Raoul Walsh's *Esther and the King* (1960), co-directed and photographed by Fulci's friend and colleague Mario Bava, and is rumored to have appeared in Bava's *Hercules in the Haunted World* (1961), though if she does actually appear in the finished film it is not clear in which role. She appeared in a number of Spaghetti Westerns like *Johnny Yuma* (1966) and *Days of Violence* (1967), but she really began to rise to prominence in more exploitation-minded fare at the end of the decade. Jess Franco featured her most memorably in his woman-in-prison epic *99 Women* (1969) and the De Sade adaptation *Justine* (1968), and she also appeared in such sleazy *gialli* as *Top Sensation* (1969) and *Amuck* (1972), in which she shared a memorably steamy love scene with Barbara Bouchet. Neri also top-lined such sex-infused Gothic horrors as *Lady Frankenstein* (1971) and

*The Devil's Wedding Night* (1973). Producers were eager to capitalize on her nubile figure and she was only too willing to oblige, but Neri also displayed genuine acting ability and elevated many films with her presence. She retired from films in the mid-1980s and the Italian exploitation scene, because of her absence, was all the poorer.

Director Sergio Corbucci was born in Rome in 1926. He broke into films as a screenwriter and director in the early 1950s. Corbucci dabbled in many genres before achieving his breakout success with the violent Spaghetti Western, *Django* (1966). The film introduced a theme typical of his work: A flawed protagonist who endures much torture and torment during the course of the narrative. He would continue to deliver outstanding Westerns throughout the 1960s and 1970s, including *The Great Silence* (1968), *The Mercenary* (1968), *The Specialists* (1969) and *Compañeros* (1970). He also did good work in other genres, including *The Beast* (1974) and *Atrocious Tales of Love and Death* (1979). His last theatrical feature would be co-written by Fulci, *Night Club* (1989), and Corbucci suffered a fatal heart attack in 1990, just five days shy of his 64th birthday.

Corbucci would later recall:

> In the scriptwriting phase, Totò gave almost no contribution at all. But as soon as he showed up on the set, he came up with one idea after another, invented jokes and sight gags, and could radically change for the best even the most banal scene. *Totò, Peppino e la dolce vita* was a very messed-up film, produced by Totò's relatives, his daughter and her husband, and I was hired to replace Camillo Mastrocinque, who had had an argument with them and left the film. I didn't know anything, hadn't even read the script; there was a scene in a bar, and on a piece of paper I read that Totò and Peppino would sit at a table and talk. But it did not specify about what. I told him: "I just came over and this is all I have, but I'm groping in the dark! What are we going to do with this scene?" Totò, calmly, told me to leave it to him. So, ad-libbing from scratch, while I followed them with the camera, Peppino ordered champagne from a waiter, who suggested to him Moët & Chandon, and Totò invented an extraordinary sketch by turning "Moët & Chandon" into "Mo' esce Anto" [Note: in Neapolitan dialect: "Antonio's coming"] and going on with the verbal wordplay for several minutes. Everyone in the crew was rolling on the floor laughing, and on occasions like that all the electricians and grips ended up applauding him because they had such a great time.[1]

Notes:

1. Faldini, Franca and Goffredo Fofi, *L'avventurosa storia del cinema italiano raccontata dai suoi protagonisti*, 1935-1959, (Milan: Feltrinelli, 1979), p. 290.

## *Letto a tre piazze (1961)*

Directed by Stefano Vanzina (as Steno); Screenplay by Bruno Baratti, Sandro Continenza, Lucio Fulci, Stefano Vanzina (as Steno) and Vittorio Vighi, from a story by Bruno Baratti, Lucio Fulci and Vittorio Vighi; Director of Photography: Alvaro Mancori; Editor: Giuliana Attenni; Music by Carlo Rustichelli

Main Players: Antonio de Curtis [as Totò] (Antonio Di Cosimo); Peppino De Filippo (Professor Peppino Castagnano); Nadia Gray (Amalia); Cristina Gaioni (Prassede); Gabriele Tinti (Nino)

*Antonio and Amalia are separated when the former goes to fight for his country. When he does not return from the war, he is believed to have died. Amalia marries again, but Antonio is not dead. When he returns, Amalia's life is thrown into chaos …*

The romantic literary cliché of the husband lost in the war who returns to upset his wife's new life gets the comic treatment in this vehicle for Toto and Peppino De Filippo. The set-up is exploited to its full comic potential, happily, and allows the two comics to have a field day.

Totò was nearing the end of his life by the time he toplined *Letto a tre piazze* (which translates roughly as *Triple-Sized Bed*). In 1956, he was afflicted with an eye infection. Sooner than cancel his tour dates or back out of any film contracts, he allowed the condition to deteriorate; he went almost completely blind as a result. Though he was undergoing a number of personal problems—including coping with the death of his son, who was born prematurely in 1954—he continued to soldier on and do what he did best; make people laugh. Totò's popularity remained undimmed throughout the 1960s and he began to appear in more adventurous fare for "intellectual" filmmakers like Pasolini; *Hawks and Sparrows* (1966) was a particularly memorable title in this category, one which proved beyond the shadow of a doubt that Totò's gifts were not restricted to more "populist" comedic fare. Even if he had not begun doing such ambitious projects, however, he would still remain firmly entrenched in the annals of Italian cinema as one of the most gifted and memorable of their many screen comics.

The role of Antonio Di Cosimo is, naturally, tailor-made for the actor. He has spent many years in captivity in Russia and has become so accustomed to praying to a portrait of Joseph Stalin that he has brought it home with him, like a lucky charm, and continues the ritual nightly. Like so many of Totò's other characters, Di Cosimo is emblematic of the common man. He has good intentions and the ambition to carry his plans through, but the deck is stacked so high against him that he can barely keep his head above water. Di Cosimo is a much more sympathetic character than some of the other roles he played in films co-written by Fulci, though he is by no means presented in an idealized manner. Like so many Totò figures, he is comical in his pomposity and there are times when his

**Italian poster for *Letto a tre piazza*; artwork by R. Olivetti.**

common sense deserts him and he is reduced to acting like a total buffoon.

As usual, he had tremendous chemistry with his longtime sparring partner, Peppino De Filippo. De Filippo's Professor Castagno is all bluff and bluster. He displays an obvious jealous streak with regards to his wife—though in fairness, he has good reason: His shady attorney really does have his eye on her—and is definitely accustomed to ruling the roost in his classroom, but he is not presented in an unsympathetic manner, either. Catagnano is no match for the wily Di Cosimo, but he is not about to give up his "marital rights," either.

The key set piece involves Di Cosimo's first night home. He is obliged to share a bed with the Professor while the wife keeps to herself on the couch. As the two men attempt to adjust to the awkwardness of the situation, Totò and De Filippo pour every ounce of their experience performing on stage into the scene. The end result is a comic *tour-de-force* which climaxes with a wonderfully outré nightmare sequence in which Di Cosimo envisions a Biblical scenario: Castagnano and Di Cosimo in full Egyptian dress, appearing before King Solomon, pleading their case of "ownership" of their mutual wife, Amalia. Solomon's decision is to split the poor woman in two, leading the men to bicker over who will get which half. The notion of reducing the wife to a possession that can be split into desirable sections speaks volumes about the way in which the two men view their "beloved" and could well be indicative of a general commentary on Italian chauvinism in general.

Steno rightly selected that scene for special praise when he was asked of his memories of making the movie:

> In *Letto a tre piazze* there's a scene where Totò and Peppino sleep in the same bed so as no one sleeps with their mutual wife. We shot with live sound, with film cans of 300 meters each [Note: approximately 10 or 11 minutes in length], and we had the feeling that Totò would ad-lib something. Peppino just had to pretend he had fallen asleep, Totò would watch him, and that was that, we'd cut. But Totò kept looking at Peppino, and since he didn't hear "cut" Peppino opened his eyes again, and Totò started adlibbing: "You know, the more I look at you, the more I like you?" and from then on a whole scene was born. Totò did some terrific and incredibly funny things, admirably assisted by Peppino. Totò and Peppino had a feeling that came from their times in the Neapolitan stage comedies. Today no one would be able to do such things. Those takes went on for minutes, without any single cut, and were all improvised, without ever failing a comic timing.[1]

Totò and De Filippo inevitably dominate the proceedings, but there are a couple of interesting faces in the supporting cast, as well. Nadia Gray gives a good performance as Amalia. The character isn't as well developed as all that—perhaps appropriate given the way she is basically objectified by the protagonists—but Gray gives her dignity and intelligence. Gray was born in Hungary in 1923 as Nadia Kujnir-Herescu. She left her homeland in the late 1940s during the period in which Communism swept the country, and then she made her way to Paris, where she began to hone her craft as an actress. She made her film debut in 1949 and enjoyed an eclectic run of films, including Federico Fellini's *La dolce vita* (1960), Peter Sellers' *I Like Money* (1961) and Michael Carreras' *The Maniac* (1963). She made her last appearance in an episode of the cult British TV series *The Prisoner* in 1967 and died in 1994.

A very young Gabriele Tinti plays the minor role of the family chauffeur. The role doesn't give him much to do, but Tinti's charisma and charm is evident even at this early stage of his career. He was born in Molinella in 1932 and began appearing in films in the early 1950s. Tinti appeared in a number of *pepla* (Carlo Campogalliani's *Goliath and the Barbarians*, 1959) and historical epics (*Esther and the King*, 1960, directed by Raoul Walsh and Mario Bava), in addition to appearing in such scattershot international fare as Robert Aldrich's *The Flight of the Phoenix* (1965) and René Clément's *Rider on the Rain* (1970). One of his oddest assignments came when he was cast as an Italian immigrant in the American sitcom *Mayberry R.F.D.*, a spin-off of the hugely popular *The Andy Griffith Show*. Tinti would later marry the beautiful Laura Gemser, whose "exotic" looks were properly exploited in the *Black Emanuelle* series, in which he was a frequent co-star. Tinti's other appearances included everything from Paolo Cavara's *The Wild Eye* (1967) to Mario Bava's *Lisa and the Devil* (1973); he also appeared in one of the films "presented" by Fulci, *The Murder Secret* (1988). He died in 1991.

According to an interview with Fulci included on the Shriek Show DVD release of *Touch of Death*:

> I was supposed to direct [*Letto a tre piazza*]. In fact, [Angelo] Rizzoli called me to do this movie and the producer [Franco] Magli told me: "Fulci, if you do this movie, I will pay your four million *lire*." I'd never seen such money! Then he said, "Now you write the screenplay and we'll pay you another three million, then you come sign the director's contract." I went over, feeling fine, and I found Magli crying because he couldn't steal any more and he said, "He doesn't want you!" I asked whom he was talking about and he says, "Totò! I can't tell you why, but he doesn't want you!" I was very surprised because Totò was like a father to me. Anyway, it was all over.

After this, Steno and Fulci would go their separate ways. Fulci would always acknowledge his debt to his mentor but felt—rightly or wrongly—that he had spent too many years laboring in his shadow. Steno would often acknowledge Fulci's contributions in print, but Fulci rightly recognized that being seen as an assistant to a renowned filmmaker was not the same thing as being properly appreciated as an artist. He would continue to do sporadic screenwriting work on projects he did not direct, of course, but even by this stage he already considered himself a director, first and foremost.

Notes:
1. Faldini, Franca and Goffredo Fofi, *L'avventurosa storia del cinema italiano raccontata dai suoi protagonisti (1960-1969)*, (Milan: Feltrinelli, 1981), p. 184.

## I'll Kill Him and Return Alone (1967)

Aka *El hombre que mató a Billy el Niño; ...E divenne il più spietato bandito del sud; A Few Bullets More; The Man Who Killed Billy the Kid*

Directed by Julio Buchs; Produced by Silvio Battistini and Ricardo Sanz; Screenplay by Julio Buchs, Federico De Urrutia, Lucio Fulci and José Mallorquí, from a story by Julio Buchs and Federico De Urrutia; Director of Photography: Miguel Fernández Mila; Editor: Cecilia Gómez and Magdalena Pulido; Music by Gianni Ferrio

**Spanish handbill for *I'll Kill Him and Return Alone*; artwork by "Jano"/ Francisco Fernández Zarza..**

Main Players: Karl Hirenbach [as Peter Lee Lawrence] (Billy the Kid); Fausto Tozzi (Pat Garrett); Dyanik Zurakowska (Helen); Gloria Milland (Billy's mother); Carlos Casaravilla (Murphy)

*Billy the Kid is living a peaceful life with his mother. When Tom McGregor rapes the mother, Billy retaliates by killing him. Billy is eventually caught and put on trial for murder, but he escapes. Pat Garrett is elected to capture him again and it is apparent that one of them will not survive the eventual showdown ...*

The man who was eventually known as Billy the Kid was born in New York City under the name of William Henry McCarty, Jr; his date of birth has been given as anywhere from 1859 to 1861. He would later change his name to William H. Bonney and killed for the first time when he was in his late teens. Plenty of legends have attached themselves to him and his exploits—some sources indicate that he killed nearly two dozen men, whereas more recent evidence points to a far more "modest" sum of about eight people. Similarly, it has often been reported that the man who is reputed to have brought about the end of his life, Sheriff Pat Garrett, was a good friend of the outlaw; in fact, it would seem that they were not friends at all. Old legends die hard, however, and the more popular fabrications and exaggerations have inspired any number of different stories and cinematic adventures. What is for certain is that Billy the Kid died of a gunshot wound on July 14, 1881; depending on the true date of his birth, he was anywhere from his late teens to his early 20s at the time. Garrett's role in the death of Billy the Kid is more or less certain, but the precise nature of their final showdown has been the source of much speculation: In some versions, he and his men ambushed the outlaw, while in others Garrett brought Billy to justice in a more fair-handed *mano-a-mano* scenario.

Given that he remains one of the most popular, indeed mythic, figures of the Old West, it's hardly surprising that Billy the Kid's exploits have been dramatized many times over on the screen. The earliest known version, simply titled *Billy the Kid*, was made in America in 1911; this version is now believed to be lost. King Vidor staged an ambitious version under the same title in 1930, with Johnny Mack Brown as the outlaw and Wallace Beery as Pat Garrett; the film was photographed in an early widescreen process, though it only survives in a standard aspect ratio edition. Western superstar Roy Rogers got his crack at playing the character in *Billy the Kid Returns* (1938), while Robert Taylor and Brian Donlevy essayed the roles of Billy and Garrett in a 1941 Technicolor remake of *Billy the Kid*, directed by David Miller. The low-budget Producers Releasing Corporation backed a series of serializations of Billy the Kid adventures throughout the 1940s, initially starring Bob Steele in the title role; former *Flash Gordon* Buster Crabbe would later take over the holster. Perhaps the most infamous version came from Howard Hughes (with help from an uncredited Howard Hawks), who channeled his obsession with giant breasts into the bosom heaving "sexy Western" *The Outlaw*, produced in 1941. Censorship problems over Jane Russell's gravity-defying bosoms would keep the film out of circulation until 1943, by which time some of the more salacious material had been cut. The film was not widely released until 1946, when it had almost attained legendary status. Jack Beutel played Billy the Kid in the film, but the statuesque Russell inevitably overshadowed him; Thomas Mitchell played Garrett, while Walter Huston co-starred as Doc Holliday. *The Left Handed Gun* (1958), directed by Arthur Penn from a screenplay by Gore Vidal, offered a more sober take on the story and featured Paul Newman in one of his best early performances. The notoriously troubled *One-Eyed Jacks* (1961), started by Stanley Kubrick and ultimately taken over by star Marlon Brando, was a version in everything but name; the film was derived from a screenplay by Rod Serling, though it was ultimately heavily re-written by others, including Sam Peckinpah. The latter, of course, would go on to direct the

***I'll Kill Him and Return Alone*: Billy the Kid (Karl Hirenbach, aka Peter Lee Lawrence) draws on an opponent as Helen (Dyanik Zurakowska) clutches his arm.**

elegiac *Pat Garrett and Billy the Kid* (1973), which is generally accepted as the best (if not always the most strictly true-to-reality) screen version; Kris Kristofferson and James Coburn played Billy and Garrett in this gem, which was unfortunately butchered for its original theatrical release, though it has since been more-or-less restored according to Peckinpah's intentions. Lost amid these better-known versions is the Spaghetti Western *I'll Kill Him and Return Alone*.

English-language prints do not credit him, but apparently Lucio Fulci did have a hand in writing the screenplay for the film. The story plays fast and loose with the facts, but is notable for offering a more ambiguous portrait of the final showdown between Billy and Garrett. In this version, Billy is prepared to give up the outlaw life in favor of eloping with the girl he loves. Garrett reluctantly agrees to let him go, but only if he removes his guns. Billy trusts Garrett, so he agrees to the terms, rendering himself vulnerable; as his guns hit the ground, one of his enemies, laying in wait, seizes the opportunity to gun him down. Garrett is therefore left to live with the knowledge that he inadvertently killed his good friend; his faith in the law is destroyed and he wanders from town to town, desperately trying to escape his past.

As Spaghetti Westerns go, this one is neither among the best nor the worst. Director Julio Buchs handles the material with efficiency but he never instills the sense of poetry that is evident in the best films of the subgenre. The settings and costumes are credible enough, but somehow the movie never creates a powerful sense of atmosphere. It really only comes to life during its action sequences; Buchs and his technical team do a terrific job during the various gunfights, so the picture at least delivers the goods where it counts the most.

The somewhat bland central performance by Peter Lee Lawrence as Billy the Kid creates the film's major deficiencies. Lawrence has the right naïve, open-faced look for the part, but his transition from good-natured farmhand to cold-blooded avenging angel lacks conviction. There is also a frankly gratuitous love story grafted on involving Billy's relationship with his boss' daughter, played by the lovely Dyanik Zurakowska. If the two actors had demonstrated genuine chemistry, then perhaps this subplot would have yielded better results; as it stands, however, one gets the feeling of marking time, waiting for the next gunfight.

Lawrence was born in Bavaria in 1944, as Karl Hirenbach—though note, some sources give the spelling of the surname as Hyrenback or Hyrenbach. He made his way to Italy in the 1960s, where he made his film debut with a small, unbilled appearance as Colonel Mortimer (Lee Van Cleef)'s ill-fated brother-in-law in Sergio Leone's *For a Few Dollars More* (1965). He became something of a staple figure in Spaghetti Westerns, appearing in such titles as Alfonso Brescia's *Day of Violence* (1967) and Tulio Demicheli's *Sabata the Killer* (1970). In 1969, he married the actress Cristina Galbó (*Let Sleeping Corpses Lie*, 1974) and then in 1972 he began suffering from severe headaches; specialists found that he had a brain tumor and attempted to cure the malady via surgery, but the cancer spread and he died in 1974.

Pat Garrett is well played by veteran character actor Fausto Tozzi. He latches on to the character's moral ambiguity and plays this aspect up for all it is worth. He was born in Rome in 1921 and began appearing in films in the early 1950s. He portrayed more than a few villains in his time and appeared in everything from Henry Levin's *The Wonders of Aladdin* (1961) and Mario Bava's *Knives of the Avenger* (1966) to Anthony Mann's *El Cid* (1961) and Carroll Ballard's *The Black Stallion* (1979); the latter was Tozzi's final film. He died in 1978.

Director Julio Buchs was a solid, all-purpose journeyman. His work seldom rose above the solidly average, but within that level he managed to create some entertaining work. Buchs was born in Madrid in 1926. As the son of silent movie director José Buchs, he grew up in the midst of film production; it did not take him long to follow in his father's footsteps. He entered the Spanish film industry in the early 1940s, working as a production assistant and assistant director, then made his directing debut in 1962. He started turning his attention to Spaghetti Westerns in the mid-'60s, helming such titles as *Django Does Not Forgive* (1966) and *A Bullet for Sandoval* (1969). Interestingly, Fulci is often credited with co-directing the latter, but star George Hilton has denied this in interviews. Buchs also directed the unusual psychedelic thriller *Perversion Story* (1969, not to be confused with Fulci's film of the same title!), starring Brett Halsey and Romina Power, and co-wrote such borderline "Spanish *gialli*" as *Alta tensión* (1972) and *Evil Eye* (1975). He died in 1973.

## *I due crociati (1968)*

Aka *The Two Crusaders*

Directed by Giuseppe Orlandini; Produced by Fulvio Lucisano; Screenplay by Lucio Fulci, Roberto Gianviti and Dino Verde, from a story by Roberto Gianviti; Director of Photography: Franco Delli Colli; Editor: Enzo Micarelli; Music by Coriolano Gori (as Lallo Gori)

Main Players: Franco Franchi (Franco di Carrapipi); Ciccio Ingrassia (Ciccio Visconte di Braghelunge); Janet Agren [as Janet Ahgren] (Clorinda); Fiorenzo Fiorentini (Ciccio's counselor); Umberto D'Orsi (Goffredo di Buglione)

*Viscount Ciccio is furious when the people on his land refuse to pay any more taxes. He enlists the aid of Franco to act as an enforcer, but he proves to be completely useless. Meanwhile, the Crusades continue to wage but their combined ineptitude sets the cause back a little …*

Having spent the better part of his early directorial career putting the comedy team of Franco Franchi and Ciccio Ingrassia through their paces, Lucio Fulci eventually

**DVD sleeve for the IIF Home Video release of *I due crociati*; artwork by by Renato Casaro.**

decided to part ways with them and explore fresh terrain. His decision was a brave one. After all, their films were ridiculously popular and they provided Fulci with a steady cash flow. However, if he ever wished to be taken seriously as a writer-director, he knew changes were necessary and so he decided to risk the potential fall out. *I due crociati* would be the last of his scripts for the duo to go before the cameras and by this stage in the game he was content to pass directing duties on to another.[1]

The film utilizes the Crusades as a backdrop, with Ciccio cast as the inept son of a once-proud ruler (also played by Ingrassia) who attempts to rule with an iron fist but is unable to gain any respect. He seeks the services of Franco to act as his "muscle," but predictably he proves ill equipped to the task and the two men are eventually imprisoned and pressed into service on behalf of the Roman Catholic Church. In the film's chaotic and comedic *milieu*, the Christian warriors are not presented in an entirely favorable light. The emissaries of the Church, including Franco and Ciccio, are arrogant and inept as they go about the task of trying to enforce their religion on others. Indeed, with the "assistance" of Franco and Ciccio, the plan to conquer Jerusalem is almost spoiled altogether. The Muslim characters aren't depicted with any particular depth, but they at least appear to be competent with regards to the task at hand.

Like so many Franco and Ciccio films, the script is constructed to allow for a variety of comedic episodes, some of which are more successful than others. One amusing sequence involves the ill-fated application of some early submarines, but the various battle scenes are never really convincing. It would be expecting too much, perhaps, to derive any real suspense or excitement out of the spectacle of the two buffoons waging battle in chain mail, but a little more flair in the staging of these sequences would have gone a long way towards redeeming the picture.

Compared to the pictorial flair and sense of comic timing that Fulci brought to his own Franco and Ciccio comedies, this one suffers due to the slack and rather indifferent staging of director Giuseppe Orlandini. His approach is generally flat and functional, with little care put into the *mise-en-scene*. He briefly seemed poised to become a successor of Fulci's with the comedy team, as he also helmed *I due vigili* (1967), *I due maggiolini più matti del mondo* (1970), *Il clan dei due Borsalini* (1971) and *Continuavano a chiamarli... er più e er meno* (1972), but he retired from directing after the latter title. The absence of a strong, distinctive director would inevitably hurt Franco and Ciccio's later works, but it did not impact their standing at the box-office; for all intents and purposes, their long and fruitful screen association ended with *Farfallon* (1974), a parody of Franklin J. Schaffner's *Papillon* (1973).

The supporting cast includes a couple of faces familiar from Fulci's later works. The beautiful, Swedish-born Janet Agren is somewhat uncomfortably cast as a female Crusader; she looks great in the costume but seems ill at ease during her swordfights. This was only her second screen appearance and she would return for the far more interesting role of Sandra in *City of the Living Dead*. Fabio Testi plays the role of the warrior who enlists (i.e., bullies) Franco and Ciccio into serving in the Crusades; he doesn't have much to do, truth be told, but his career would later take off in a big way and he would top-line *Four of the Apocalypse* and *Contraband* for Fulci.

Notes:

1.Of course, Fulci would reteam with Ciccio Ingrassia on *Young Dracula* (1975) and with Franco Franchi on the TV show *Buonasera con* (1978) and the mini-series *Un uomo da ridere* (1980), but by that point, the two comics had parted ways.

## *Double Face (1969)*

Aka *A doppia faccia; Liz & Helen; Das Gesicht im Dunkeln*

Directed by Riccardo Freda (as Robert Hampton); Produced by Oreste Coltellacci; Screenplay by Riccardo Freda (as Robert Hampton) and Paul Hengge, from a story by Lucio Fulci, Romano Migliorini and Gianbattista Musset-

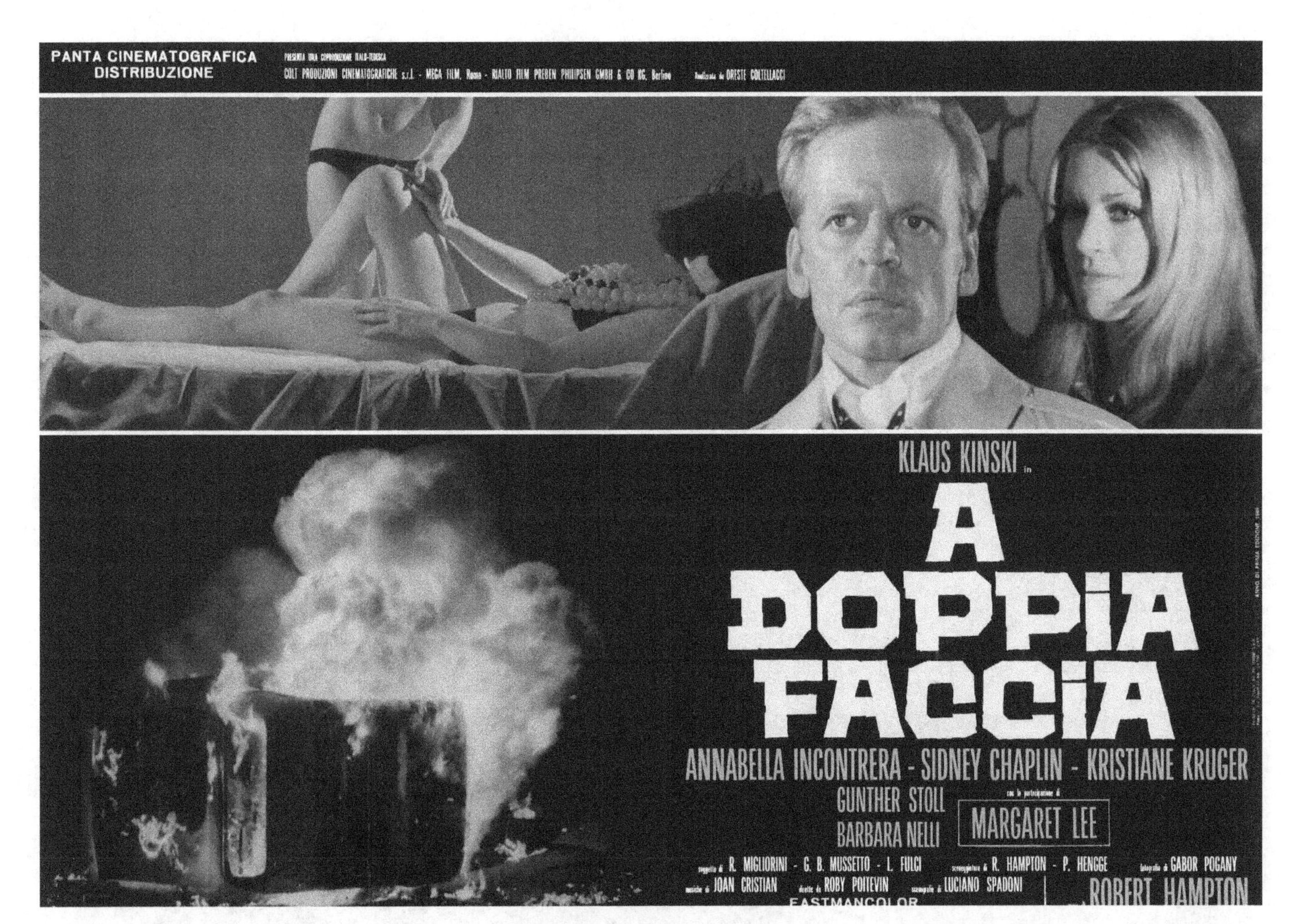


**Italian *fotobusta* for *Double Face.***

to; Director of Photography: Gábor Pogány; Editor: Anna Amedei and Jutta Hering; Music by Nora Orlandi (as Joan Christian)

Main Players: Klaus Kinski (John Alexander); Christiane Krüger (Christine); Margaret Lee (Helen Alexander); Günther Stoll (Inspector Stevens); Sydney Chaplin (Mr. Brown); Luciano Spadoni (Inspector Gordon); Annabella Incontrera (Liz)

*Industrialist John Alexander falls in love with Helen and they are married. After two happy years, the couple has grown apart and both are involved in affairs: John with his secretary Alice and Helen with her friend Liz. When Helen dies in an explosion, John falls under suspicion, so he must do everything he can to clear his name and find the murderer. His quest leads him to a dark underground of drugs and pornography ...*

This Italian/West German production was one of several *gialli* that were marketed in Germany as Edgar Wallace *krimi*. Considering the flagging quality of Rialto's own product (as evidenced by *The Man With the Glass Eye*, 1969, or *The Dead Woman from the Thames*, 1971), no doubt a truly superior offering such as this would have come as a welcome relief. However, as with other "*faux krimi*" like *The Bird With the Crystal Plumage* (1970) or *What Have You Done to Solange?* (1972), *Double Face* is a *krimi* in name only—but it is most definitely a fine example of a *giallo*.

The film takes its cue from the success of Michelangelo Antonioni's *Blow Up* (1966) and Umberto Lenzi's *Orgasmo* (1968) in its tale of sex, drugs and duplicity in Swinging London. The melancholy tone and refusal to glamorize the "free-spirited" lifestyle of the period, however, point to an altogether different approach on the part of Riccardo Freda. For him, the film is a dark drama with elements of the Gothic lurking at the edge of the frame; John Alexander's obsession for his dead wife cannot help but remind one of Freda's earlier anti-hero, the perverted Dr. Bernard Hichcock, the necrophiliac protagonist of *The Terror of Dr. Hichcock* (1962). Despite the modern setting, the film has a stately, old-fashioned air. Clearly, unlike some of his contemporaries, Freda regarded himself as a fish out of water in this very contemporary setting; to his credit, sooner than blindly embrace it and steep the film in "far-out" clichés, he steps back and observes it quizzically, as if to suggest that the surface allure of this new-found freedom comes at the expense of something deeper and more noble.

Freda wrote the screenplay in collaboration with Paul Hengge, from a story by Fulci, Romano Migliorini and Gianbattista Mussetto. The plot hangs together very well

**German lobby card for Double Face: Liz (Antonella Interlenghi) and Helen (Margaret Lee) are more than just friends.**

and the emphasis on the underground porno loop circuit was a novel touch for its time. The meta-cinematic connotations of this are addressed slyly and without hypocrisy; like the stag films that John finds himself confronted with, commercial flicks like the *giallo* trade on images of sensationalized sex and nudity. *Double Face* is no different in this regard, and it is to Freda's credit that he resists sermonizing against the "evils" of pornography, preferring instead to address any criticism towards the seedy individuals who conspire to make John's life a living hell. The film is ultimately a rare *giallo* that is both surprising and genuinely affecting on a human level. It is easy to care about John and his plight, even if he is a deeply flawed "hero" at best.

The film is graced with some gorgeous cinematography courtesy of Freda's regular collaborator Gábor Pogány, while the soundtrack by Nora Orlandi is one of the finest ever to grace a *giallo*. Production values are very good on the whole, but the film admittedly gets off to a rocky start with some less-than-convincing special effects work, notably the toy car used to fake the car accident, some very dodgy rear-screen projection to simulate John and Helen's honeymoon and a patently phony race-track sequence with plenty of stock footage. Once the film settles into the narrative proper, however, there are no such distractions. A pretty neat matte shot towards the end of the film creates the illusion of St. John's Cathedral, and one cannot help but wonder if Freda's friend and collaborator Mario Bava dropped by to contribute that particular shot.

Director Riccardo Freda was born in Alexandria, Egypt, in 1909. A student of art history, he was lured to filmmaking in the 1930s, first as a writer and assistant director. He made the transition to directing with *Don Cesare di Bazan* (1942) and scored a major success with the massively popular *Return of the Black Eagle* (1946). Freda favored historical movies and sword-and-sandal adventures, but together with Mario Bava, he conceived Italy's first horror film of the sound era, *I vampiri* (1957), a picture with distinct *giallo* overtones. Freda made it on a bet, hardly an uncommon occurrence in his career, and guaranteed to have the film completed in 12 days. Ten days in, it was apparent that he was not going to be able to complete work to his satisfaction and, after quarreling with the producers, left the production in Bava's hands; the cinematographer and special effects artist cut corners, sought out stock footage and managed to complete the movie on time. The film's box-office failure convinced Freda that Italian audiences could not accept the idea of an Italian horror film, so he would start signing his subsequent genre credits with the pseudonym, Robert Hampton. Freda would undertake *Caltiki the Immortal Monster* (1959) with an eye towards compelling the unambitious Bava to make a final move to the director's chair; abandoning the film once more, this time after only a few days of shooting, it was again taken over by an uncredited Bava. Throughout the 1960s, Freda would dabble in films as something of a pastime. He was independently wealthy and had a good track record (literally) betting on horses, which he also bred, so he was in the position of being able to walk whenever productions became too much of a headache. He saw his most noteworthy films of the period, including *The Terror of Dr. Hichcock, The Ghost* (1963) and *Double Face*, through to completion but his output would slow down in the 1970s. He directed the *giallo The Iguana With the Tongue of Fire* (1971) but hid behind an obscure pseudonym (Willy Pareto), reportedly because he had not finished the picture himself and would deny having much to do with the bizarre ghost story *Tragic Ceremony* (1972), though his name was listed in the credits.[1] He completed his last effort, *Murder Obsession* (1980), and would sit out the rest of the decade, save for offering advice to disciples like director Bertrand Tavernier. He made a surprise return to the director's chair with *Revenge of the Musketeers* (1994), but quarreled with the producers early on and Tavernier was brought in to take over the film. Freda died in 1999, at the age of 90.

Klaus Kinski, the infamous *enfant terrible* of European cult cinema, carries *Double Face*. Born in Poland in 1926, Kinski started off acting on stage and made his film debut in the late 1940s. His peculiar looks and fiery intensity made him a natural for villains, and the actor was notorious for squabbling with directors and co-stars alike. Even so, his obvious talent and box-office appeal kept him in movie roles for decades. He would appear in important films for the likes of David Lean (*Dr. Zhivago*, 1965) and Billy Wilder (*Buddy Buddy*, 1981), but found his biggest success, artistically, collaborating with maverick German filmmaker Werner Herzog on a series of intense movies, including *Aguirre, the Wrath of God* (1972) and *Nosferatu the Vampyre* (1979). Theirs was a love/hate relationship and it has been rumored that Herzog and Kinski both secretly plotted to kill each other at different points. Herzog even made a documentary about their relationship, titled *My Best Fiend* (1999). Kinski enjoyed a more harmonious relationship with genre filmmakers like Jess Franco and Antonio Margheriti, both of whom used him on several occasions without encountering any untold drama when dealing with him. It is hard to imagine that the actor, with his hair-trigger disposition and fondness for temper tantrums struck up much of a friendly relationship with the notoriously despotic Freda, but nothing has ever been reported of their collaboration, be it good, bad or indifferent. The results on screen are quite good, however, with Kinski giving a relaxed, unaffected performance as a man clinging to the last shred of his sanity. It is a sympathetic performance from an actor who was often called upon to foam at the mouth playing stock villains. Kinski's unpredictable antics continued throughout the 1980s and rumors abound of his being clinically insane and of possibly even having sunk so low as to have molested his own daughters, Paola and Nastassja; the latter, of course, would become an actress in her own right. Kinski died of a heart attack in 1991 at the age of 65. The supporting cast includes Sydney Chaplin, the son of the legendary Charlie Chaplin, and the gorgeous Margaret Lee, who gives a strong performance as the mysterious Helen. Lee, born in England in 1943, immigrated to Italy in the 1960s and got her start playing mostly decorative roles in *pepla* and spy thrillers. She would go on to appear in the sleazy *giallo Slaughter Hotel* (1971, also starring Klaus Kinski) and appeared in Jess Franco's *The Bloody Judge* (1969) and *Venus in Furs* (1969, again with Kinski). Lee also appeared in Fulci's *Gli imbroglioni, The Maniacs* and *I due pericoli pubblici.* She retired from acting in the mid-'80s.

Notes:

1. Newman, Kim, ed. *The BFI Companion to Horror* (London: British Film Institute, 1996), p. 128.

## Hector the Mighty (1972)

Aka *Ettore lo fusto*

Directed by Enzo G. Castellari; Produced by Edmondo Amati and Raoul Katz; Screenplay by Enzo G. Castellari, Sandro Continenza, Lucio Fulci and Leonardo Martin, from the book *Il re dei mimiduti* by Henri Viard and Bernard Zacharias; Director of Photography: Guglielmo Mancori; Editor: Vincenzo Tomassi; Music by Francesco De Masi

Main Players: Philippe Leroy (Hector); Giancarlo Giannini (Ulysses); Rosanna Schiaffino (Helen); Vittorio De Sica (Cardinal Giove); Michael Forest (Achilles); Haydée Politoff (Criseide); Aldo Giuffre (Agamemnon); Vittorio Caprioli (Menelaus); Giancarlo Prete (Patroclo 'Clo-Clo')

*Hector resists selling his land to the Cardinal because he has opened a successful and highly profitable brothel on it. This lands him in hot water with Agamemnon and Menelaus, who send their enforcers Ulysses and Achilles to do battle with him…*

The Helen of Troy story gets a modern face-lift in this over-the-top comedy, which is loosely based upon the book *Il re dei mimiduti*, published in 1966. The film contains ample irreverent humor and an anti-clerical theme that is typical of Fulci's work, but some of the more interesting elements are underplayed in favor of broad slapstick.

In this updated interpretation of the story, "Horny" Hector operates a thriving brothel on a piece of land coveted by Cardinal Giove. The Cardinal collaborates with his minions to come up with a plan to get the land away from Hector and eventually the plot to kidnap Helen in order to trigger a small gang war comes into play. The political dimensions of the scenario are explicit early on, but this aspect becomes more muted as the story unfolds; it's almost as if Fulci and his co-writers lost faith in their vision and decided to fall back on action scenes and over-the-top comedy instead.

Indeed, according to Fulci, he was originally in line to direct the picture himself but he was not convinced by the subject matter. In an interview included on the Shriek Show DVD release of *Touch of Death*, Fulci says:

> [Edmondo] Amati loved the novel and asked me to do a movie version. At the time I had a contract with Amati. When I realized the story was bullshit—the Trojan War set on the Côte d'Azur—I thought of everything I could do not to do it, telling Amati that I didn't know how to shoot it. So he said, "We'll give it to Castellari!" Castellari was loved by vulgar people […] Vulgarity doesn't mix with culture.

In the hands of director Enzo G. Castellari, the film's tone vacillates wildly. Castellari packs in a number of weird, outré camera angles to play up the artificiality of the whole concept, but he tends to be a little slack with the pacing. At nearly two hours, the film is simply much too long. The action scenes—notably a protracted fight on motorcycles between Hector and Clo-Clo—are very well staged and demonstrate Castellari's flair in that area. Unfortunately, much of the comedy is broadly overplayed and tends to grate after a while.

**Detail enlargement from the Italian *fotobusta* for *Hector the Mighty*: Giancarlo Giannini as Ulysses (at left), with Haydée Politoff and Orchidea de Santis providing "eye candy" on the right.**

On the upside, the starry cast invests the film with considerable interest. Some of the actors succumb to the temptation to mug and leer their way through the proceedings, but the more low-key performances by Philippe Leroy and Giancarlo Giannini are a joy. Leroy is excellent as the oily Hector. He portrays him as a low-life pimp, but also manages to make him oddly endearing. Given the nature of the people he is up against, he can hardly be seen as the film's villain; indeed, there really are no heroes or villains in this irreverent variation on the story. Similarly, Giannini is wonderfully deadpan as the unctuous and deceptive Ulysses. Far from reminding one of the noble warrior of Homer's epic poem *The Odyssey*, he is a shifty opportunist who plays the two warring factions against each other in search of a little wealth and security. Among the rest of the cast, Rosanna Schiaffino comes off reasonably well as a sexually promiscuous Helen, while the great Vittorio De Sica steals his too-few scenes as the hypocritical Cardinal. One of the film's best jokes occurs when the Cardinal's minion informs him that a writer named Homer wishes to write a story about him and wishes to call it *The Iliad*; the Cardinal takes offense, however, thinking the proposed title is "The Idiot."

Unfortunately, for every laugh earned, there are more that fail to come off. A more restrained approach may have yielded better satire, but the desire to play things big and go for slapstick tends to stop the material dead in its tracks. Fulci, for his part, would delve more successfully into the realm of political satire the same year with the much superior *The Eroticist*.

Philippe Leroy was born in Paris in 1930. He made an auspicious debut as one of the inmates in Jacques Becker's powerful prison drama *Le Trou* (1960), and then he started showing up in Italian films like Riccardo Freda's *Caccia all'uomo* (1961) and Warren Kiefer's *Castle of the Living Dead* (1964). He would top-line Tinto Brass' unusual Spaghetti Western *Yankee* (1966) and played one of his most interesting characters in Piero Schivazappa's arty *Femina ridens* (1969). Leroy would appear in a number of *poliziotteschi*, as well, including Fernando Di Leo's *Caliber 9* (1972) and Umberto Lenzi's *Gang War in Milan* (1973). More recently he appeared as the alchemist who assists Asia Argento in Dario Argento's controversial *Mother of Tears* (2007). He remains an active presence in the European film scene.

Giancarlo Giannini was born in La Spezia in 1942. After making his debut in Ernesto Gastaldi's claustrophobic *giallo Libido* (1965), he went on to appear in such diverse fare as Alberto Lattuada's *Fraulein Doktor* (1969), Paolo Cavara's *Black Belly of the Tarantula* (1971) and Sergio Corbucci's *The Beast* (1974). However, it was his association with art house *auteurs* like Luchino Visconti (*The Innocent*, 1976) and Lina Wertmüller (*Seven Beauties*, 1977, for which he was nominated for an Oscar as Best Actor) which catapaulted him to the forefront of Italian screen actors. Giannini would go on to appear in a number of major productions, including Ridley Scott's *Hannibal* (2001) and the James Bond adventures *Casino Royale* (2006) and *Quantum of Solace* (2008), in which he had a scene-stealing role as double agent Rene Mathis. He has been feted many times during his long and varied career and remains much in demand to this day. One of his more unusual credits, incidentally, came when he dubbed Jack Nicholson for the Italian release of *The Shining* (1980), a task for which he was handpicked by writer/producer/director Stanley Kubrick.

Director Enzo G. Castellari was born in Rome in 1938. The son of director Marino Girolami, he was born as Enzo Girolami but changed his surname to avoid comparisons with his father. Castellari displayed a verve for action early on and would go from directing Spaghetti Westerns (*Johnny Hamlet*, 1968) to *poliziotteschi* (*Street Law*, 1974) to dystopian sci-fi (*1990: Bronx Warriors*, 1982) with equal flair. His prolific output has earned him a loyal following among genre cineastes and the heavy promotion of his name by superstar fan Quentin Tarantino has helped to keep his name alive in recent years. He remains active, though his output has slowed due to the general decline of film production in Italy.

*Hector the Mighty* is by no means a bad film, but it falls short of its potential; the presence of so many interesting names in the credits seems to promise so much more, but taken as a lighthearted diversion it certainly has its moments.

## The Trap (1985)

Aka *La gabbia*

Directed by Giuseppe Patroni Griffi; Produced by Juan L. Isasi and Ettore Spagnuolo; Screenplay by Lucio Fulci, Concha Hombria, Roberto Leoni and Alberto Silvestri, based on a story by Francesco Barilli; Director of Photography: Juan Amaros and Hans Burmann; Editor: Sergio Montanari; Music by Ennio Morricone

Main Players: Laura Antonelli (Marie Colbert); Tony Musante (Michael); Florinda Bolkan (Helene); Blanca Marsillach (Jacqueline); Cristina Marsillach (Young Marie)

*Marie has a torrid, S/M-tinged relationship with the sadistic Michael. When he abandons her, Marie is driven by a lust for revenge. Fifteen years later, their paths cross again and Marie is not about to miss out on an opportunity to get back at him. However, her daughter/conspirator, Jacqueline, is attracted to him and proceeds to complicate matters ...*

*The Trap* is something of a companion piece to Fulci's own S/W melodrama, *The Devil's Honey* (1986). However, while the latter film goes much further into the themes of depravity and potential redemption, *The Trap* is an altogether more introspective and elliptical work.

**Image insert from the Italian DVD release of *The Trap*: Michael (Tony Musante) and Marie (Laura Antonelli) reacquaint themselves.**

Based on a story by the gifted filmmaker Francesco Barilli (whose psychological horror movie *The Perfume of the Lady in Black*, 1974, is often mislabeled as a *giallo*), the story deals with selfishness and its consequences. Michael engages in a fling with the younger Marie, but he has no interest in her beyond seeing her as a sexual plaything. Once that aspect of the relationship grows tiresome, he moves on and she is left to lick her wounds. The perpetually immature Michael goes through a couple of marriages and continues to keep his eye open for easy sexual conquests; for Marie, however, life is not so simple—she, too, marries but her husband passes away and the memories of how Michael abandoned her are not quickly forgotten. When she sees the opportunity to finally get back at him, she cannot resist—but her fatal mistake lies in involving her young, sexually frustrated daughter, Jacqueline. The latter is won over by Michael's easy charm and the ensuing complications are not destined to end well for anybody concerned.

While Fulci's subsequent foray into erotica was saddled with a very low budget and often-inadequate production resources, it would seem that no such problems presented themselves on this film. Director Giuseppe Patroni Griffi was an old hand at dealing with scenarios involving complex sexual and emotional relationships and he was able to assemble an interesting and eclectic cast for the picture. In 1969, Patroni Griffi directed a similarly erotic film titled *The Love Circle*, which featured Tony Musante, Florinda Bolkan and a haunting music score by Ennio Morricone; for *The Trap*, he saw fit to invite Musante, Bolkan and Morricone back into the fold and the results are almost as effective. Interestingly, that earlier film had been co-written by Fulci's long-time "rival" in the field of Italian horror, Dario Argento.

*The Trap* is not nearly as sexually explicit as the salacious advertising seemed to promise, but it is a sensual and lively piece of filmmaking. The characters are well drawn and expertly realized by an enthusiastic cast. Patroni Griffi paces the film in a leisurely manner, but the end result is never dull. The use of elliptical editing scenes, with various flashbacks shown as tantalizing, ambiguous glimpses, helps to keep the suspense piqued throughout. The various sexual encounters are appropriately kinky, including sequences of the mother and daughter exposing themselves to the bound Michael, driving him to the point of insanity as he desires nothing more than to have his way (as usual) and touch them.

Tony Musante gives an excellent performance as Michael. The character is not particularly sympathetic and Musante does not go out of his way to make apologies for him. Michael is a spoiled, self-centered egomaniac. He can be very charming when he wants to be, but he has very little empathy and compassion. He views women as sexual objects and it is this objectification that leads to his downfall. Musante, born in Connecticut in 1936, started off as a teacher before catching the acting bug. He got his start doing theater work, and then began appearing on TV in the early 1960s. He gained attention for his back-to-back appearances in Larry Peerce's *The Incident* (1967), playing one of the young thugs terrorizing passengers on a New York subway, and Gordon Douglas' *The Detective* (1968). From there, he made a transition to Italy, appearing alongside Franco Nero in Sergio Corbucci's *The Mercenary* (1968) and Patroni Griffi's *The Love Circle*. Argento was impressed with his work in the latter and hired him to play the lead in his debut as a director, *The Bird with the Crystal Plumage* (1970). Back in America, Musante blew his chance at the big time when he clashed with the producers of a new show called *Toma* (1973-1974); he was removed from the show and replaced with Robert Blake, who achieved much success on the newly rechristened *Baretta*, which ran from 1975 to 1978. Even so, Musante continued to appear in many films and TV shows, remaining active until his death in 2013.

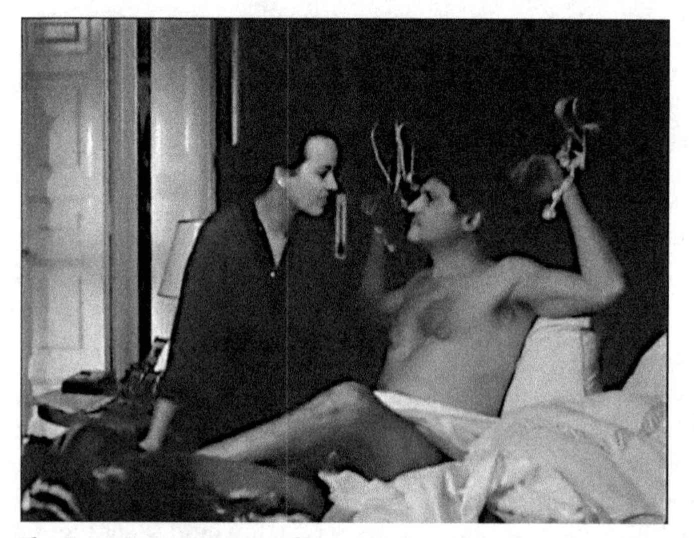

***The Trap* is not as sexually explicit as this scene implies.**

Laura Antonelli is also very good as the avenging angel, Marie. One's sympathy is firmly on her side, even considering the extremes she goes to in order to teach Michael a lesson. Antonelli is able to clue the viewer into her emotional turmoil without becoming unduly melodramatic, and the film is all the more effective due to her poise and restraint. Antonelli was born in Istria, then part of Italy but now recognized as part of Croatia, in 1941. Like Musante, she got her start as a teacher, but then moved into acting. She made her cinema debut with a role in Mario Bava's unfortunate *Le spie vengono dal semi-freddo* (1966), but would go on to become a major star thanks to such salacious fare as Massimo Dallamano's *Venus in Furs* (1969) and Pasquale Festa Campanile's *Secret Fantasy* (1971); films such as this traded on her beauty and her willingness to disrobe for the camera, but it was evident that she also possessed genuine acting ability. Luchino Visconti cast her in a pivotal role in his final film, *The Innocent* (1976), and she also received much critical acclaim for her role in Salvatore Samperi's *Malicious* (1973). Antonelli also appeared in Fulci's blend of sexy comedy and political satire, *The Eroticist* (1972). She reprised her role from *Malicious* in *Malice 2000* (1991), after which she disappeared from the screen. That same year, she endured a personal catastrophe when the police raided her home and reportedly found cocaine in her possession. She was charged with intent to deliver and was sentenced to house arrest. She maintained her innocence and eventually had the verdict overturned in 2006, at which point all charges were dropped and she was financially compensated for her troubles.

The beautiful Blanca Marsillach played Jacqueline, who also starred in *The Devil's Honey*, while the young Marie is played in flashbacks by her sister, Cristina Marsillach. Cristina was born in Madrid in 1963. She made her film debut in 1983 and went on to star opposite Tom Hanks in the tearjerker *Every Time We Say Goodbye* (1986) before playing her best-known role, as the sexually frustrated soprano Betty in Dario Argento's superior *giallo Opera* (1987). She and Argento clashed during the filming and she developed a reputation for being a bit of a diva. Cristina remained active in films until the 1990s, at which point she retired from the screen to focus on running a school for actors in Madrid.

Director Giuseppe Patroni Griffi was born in Naples in 1921. The son of a well-to-do, upper-crust family, he would go on to much acclaim for his work in the world of theater and the opera. His film career was comparatively sporadic, but he started off as a screenwriter in the 1950s before turning to directing in 1963. He would only direct a handful of movies, but they revealed him to be a filmmaker of style and distinction. *The Trap* was his last theatrical feature; he would follow it up with the mini-series *La romana* (1988), adapted from the book by Alberto Moravia. He died in 2005.

Unfortunately, the man who originally conceived the project viewed the resulting movie as a total failure. In an interview, Francesco Barilli recalled how his original concept, titled *L'Occhio*, got away from him:

> *L'Occhio* was another project I really cared about. I wrote it to show people that you can do a movie on a shoestring budget, and make good money out of it. The idea came to me because of a guy I knew, who lived in a house in Rome that no art director in the world could ever dream of. It was a huge abandoned villa that this hippie had transformed into a beautiful nightmare. It was haunting, stunning and gloomy at the same time. All the windows were sealed with tape and so on. By the way, I had used that house on *Perfume* [*of the Lady in Black*]: It's Mario Scaccia's apartment. I wrote *L'Occhio* thinking of that particular house. It was the story of a horrible old hag—I wanted the renowned painter Novella Parigini for the role—who lives secluded in this incredible place. One day, looking out the window, she sees a beautiful young man passing by. She lures him into the house and never lets him go. It was not a completely original story, as William Wyler had done something similar with *The Collector* [1965], but Stephen King hadn't written *Misery* yet. I showed the script to a producer and he told me: "Hey, this is going to be expensive, we need U.S. coproduction!" I said, "Look, it's a very low-budget thing, I'm even going to shoot it with a hand-held camera! It'll make lots of money ... " I had planned to make it a low-budget, minimalistic horror movie—*L'Occhio* would cost 240 million *liras*, which was a ridiculous sum—but they wanted Shelley Winters in the lead ... I couldn't believe my ears. So I eventually dropped the project, then one day Patroni Griffi phoned me and said: "Well, I read your script and really loved it. I'd like to make a movie out of it." He offered me lots of money, and made *La gabbia*, which is a totally different film from the one I had in mind. Let's talk frankly here, that movie sucks. Instead of a macabre story it looks like a third-rate, soft-porn version of *Death in Venice* [1971, directed by Luchino Visconti]. It was squalid. And it flopped.[1]

Fulci shared Barilli's sentiments, noting that he lost out on directing the film at the last second because of scheduling conflicts with his *giallo*, *Murder-Rock: Dancing Death*. In an interview included on the Shriek Show DVD release of *Touch of Death* (1988), he was characteristically blunt:

> I was supposed to direct it [...] It was a movie that they turned into bullshit! Griffi was crooked, he didn't even call when I left the project—a director inheriting a movie should at least call the previous director asking for explanations, but he didn't. Neapolitan asshole!

Notes:
1. Curti, Roberto, *Interview with Francesco Barilli*, "Offscreen," (Volume 15, Issue 12, December, 2011), retrieved from http://offscreen.com/view/francesco_barilli_interview

## *Night Club (1989)*

Directed by Sergio Corbucci; Produced by Claudio Bonivento; Screenplay by Sergio Corbucci and Massimo Franciosa, from a story by Giovanni Fago, Lucio Fulci and Luciano Martino; Director of Photography: Sergio D'Offizi; Music by Giorgio Chierchiè and Guido Pistocchi

Main Players: Christian De Sica (Walter Danesi); Mara Venier (Luciana); Massimo Wertmuller (Ragionier Piero Grassi); Sergio Vastano (Commendator Consalvo Balestretti); Roberto Ciufoli (Ragionier Ottavio Grassi)

*Rome, 1960: Piero and Ottavio dream of opening a swanky nightclub but are not able to raise sufficient capital. None too*

*wisely, they turn to the dishonest Walter Danesi, who agrees to give them the necessary funding. Walter proceeds to use the club as a cover for his call-girl service …*

Beginning with its opening credits sequence illustrated with images of the "Hollywood on the Tiber," *Night Club* establishes itself as a bittersweet slice of nostalgia. The story by Giovanni Fago, Luciano Martino (brother of director Sergio Martino, one of Fulci's chief "rivals" in the *giallo* genre of the 1970s) and Fulci uses a factual backdrop for its tale of failed dreams in Italy's movie capital.

The film uses the release of Federico Fellini's *La dolce vita* (1960) as its starting point. It's difficult to fully appreciate it today, but Fellini's film was the cinematic event of the day. Its scandalous depiction of sex, drugs and psychological and emotional unrest coupled with a magical sense of glamour made it a controversial film, especially where the censors were concerned, but audiences couldn't get enough of it. Viewers around the globe thrilled to the spectacle of gorgeous Anita Ekberg doffing her high heels for a walk through the Trevi Fountain and its frank depiction of sexual and narcotic indulgences made many anxious to get a piece of "the sweet life" for themselves. Of course, many viewers failed to realize that Fellini's film was a cautionary tale at heart; they preferred to focus, instead, on the glitz and the glamour, unaware that the film was not wholeheartedly endorsing the behavior it was dramatizing. The characters in *Night Club* are typical of this mentality. They see the film as a sort of documentary and they are determined to cash in on it while also sampling some of the things it dramatized so effectively.

**Italian entertainer Fred Buscaglione modeled himself after gangsters seen in American films; his death in a car crash is recreated for the climax of *Night Club*.**

At the heart of the tale are two rather naïve brothers, Piero and Ottavio, who hit upon the idea of opening a night club which would cater to the kind of lavish indulgences seen in Fellini's film. They lack much experience in business, however, so they turn to the shady Walter (played by Christian De Sica, the son of the great actor/director Vittorio De Sica) for added financing. Always the opportunist, Walter sees the nightclub as a perfect venue for his prostitution ring. Inevitably, things do not pan out as well as Piero and Ottavio had envisioned—but for a brief period of time, they do manage to live a bit of the lifestyle they so enjoyed seeing in the film; appropriately enough, this turns into a case of "be careful what you wish for," as they realize that these kinds of excesses are not all they are cracked up to be.

The film concludes with a recreation of a tragic event which sums up the film's theme; on February 3, 1960, singer and actor Ferdinando "Fred" Buscaglione (played in the film by Michele Seccia) was killed in an automobile accident near the U.S. Embassy in Rome. Buscaglione—who had appeared in Fulci's first films as a director, *I ladri* and *I ragazzi del juke-box* (both 1959)—was one of the most popular entertainers in the Italian music scene at that time. He took inspiration from the "tough guy" antics of mobsters seen in American films and literature (he was a particular devotee of Mickey Spillane, in fact), so the fact that he died so close to "American soil" was a fitting irony. In the context of the film, his death serves as a sober reminder that the good times were bound to come to an end sooner or later. Whether the characters really learn anything from their brief but flashy sojourn into the world of nightclubs and glamour is open to speculation, but the bittersweet tone of the final scenes ends the film on a comparatively somber note.

*Night Club* would end up being the last feature film directed by the gifted Sergio Corbucci. He would make one more effort for television, and then die the following year. Appropriately enough, he and Fulci had first collaborated on another title indebted to *La dolce vita*; the Fulci-scripted, Corbucci-directed *Totò, Peppino e… la dolce vita*. Corbucci displays a good feel for period detail, but the film is somewhat spoiled by bland TV movie-like cinematography from the normally reliable Sergio D'Offizi. A few indifferently staged nightclub musical numbers serve to slow the pace, but for much of the running time the film is humorous and engaging. The extended party sequence which degenerates into a drunken orgy is, of course, indebted to Fellini's model and the vacillating tone between comedy and drama is also very much in line with its model. The end result may not be as vividly cinematic as Corbucci's best movies, but it is still of interest for its evocation of a very particular period in Italian filmmaking.

## *The Wax Mask* (1997)

Aka *M.D.C. – Maschera di cera*

Directed by Sergio Stivaletti; Produced by Dario Argento, Giuseppe Colombo and Fulvio Lucisano; Screenplay by Lucio Fulci and Daniele Stroppa, from a screen story by Dario Argento, Lucio Fulci and Daniele Stroppa, based on the story "Waxwork Museum" by Gaston Leroux; Director of Photography: Sergio Salvati; Editor: Paolo Benassi; Music by Maurizio Abeni

Dedicated to the memory of Lucio Fulci

Main Players: Robert Hossein (Boris Volkoff); Romina Mondello (Sonia Lafont); Riccardo Serventi Longhi (Andrea Conversi); Aldo Massasso (Inspector Lanvin); Gabriella Giorgelli (Aunt Francesca)

*Sonia witnesses the brutal murder of her parents by a killer wearing a mask and with a claw for a hand. As an adult, Sonia becomes convinced that there is a connection between the killing of her parents and the lifelike exhibits in a new wax museum run by the mysterious but brilliant Boris Volkoff. As people begin to disappear and the police prove inefficient, Sonia launches her own investigation …*

Lucio Fulci's later years were full of professional disappointments and personal hardships. Diabetes ravaged his body and a bout of hepatitis came very close to killing him. The financial and physical toll this took on him cannot be overestimated. Fulci went from being a larger-than-life figure to being reduced to a shadow of his former self. His sharp tongue and biting wit remained intact, but he was frail and looked older than his years. Fulci's long-standing professional rivalry with Dario Argento, then recognized as Italy's premiere specialist in the field of horror and suspense, extended all the way back to the 1970s, when films like *A Lizard in a Woman's Skin* (1971) were seen as "rip-offs" of Argento's innovative *gialli*, like *The Bird with the Crystal Plumage* (1970). Argento's biographer Alan Jones recalls on the commentary track for the Blue Underground edition of *Bird* that there was a period when mentioning Fulci's name was *verboten* in Argento's presence.

UM FILME DE DARIO ARGENTO
GABRIELLA GIORGELLI
ROBERT HOSSEIN
SONIA TOPAZIO
MASSIMO VANNI
MUSEU DE HORRORES
WAX MASK
MORTOS E VIVOS... COMO NÃO CONFUNDI-LOS NESTE LUGAR

**VHS sleeve for the Brazilian DVD release of *The Wax Mask*, from Alpha Filmes; artist unknown.**

Fulci, never shy to speak his mind, was the more vocal of the two. "I think Dario is a great artisan who considers himself an artist," he opined, "as opposed to Hitchcock who was a an artist who considered himself an artisan. This is the flaw that will make Argento go on repeating the same things. He's very good on the public relations side […] Every one thinks he's a very good writer and a very bad director, whereas, in fact, it's the other way around!"[1] Fulci's potshots almost certainly got back to Argento on a regular basis, but the latter tended to avoid discussing the older filmmaker in interviews. However, the two men had encountered each other in different venues in happier days, so when Argento saw Fulci when the latter was at his lowest ebb, his heart went out to him. "I was one of the guests of honor at the Rome Fanta Festival in 1994, and I was shocked to see Fulci turn up in a wheelchair looking so ill, tired and in a bad state generally. I will be perfectly honest, up until this time there was no love lost between Fulci and myself. I always felt he had copied my signature style in his *giallo* pictures […] and our paths never crossed socially or business wise. But my heart went out to him when I saw him in such a dreadful physical condition. […] His agent told me he was about to have a serious hospital operation—which the agent paid for because Fulci couldn't afford to—and I knew the best recovery therapy would be to get him working again."[2] Leaving aside the obvious fallacy of Fulci having "copied" Argento's style in his own *gialli*—Argento's approach was cool and detached, compared to Fulci's fire and brimstone—Argento is nevertheless to be commended for letting bygones be bygones. He decided to back Fulci in a project of his choice designed to serve as a "comeback" for the "Godfather of Gore." Sadly, the best of intentions did not pay off as planned.

Initially there was talk of doing an updated version of *The Mummy*, with Fulci working with Argento and his long-time collaborator Dardano Sacchetti on the screenplay.[3] This eventually fell by the wayside, at which point Fulci had an inspiration to remake the André de Toth classic *House of Wax* (1953) starring Vincent Price. The film had been a huge hit internationally back in the day and it has long been rumored that it was the film's success in Italy which inspired Riccardo Freda and Mario Bava to make *I vampiri* (1957), which would become the first Italian horror film of the sound era. Argento liked the idea and arranged for them to screen copies of the de Toth film, as well as the original 1933 *Mystery of the Wax*

**The mysterious killer strikes in *The Wax Mask.***

or should he make the film and dedicate it to his memory? The latter path was chosen, but it seems that Argento himself was never seriously interested in taking over directing duties himself. Instead, he turned to 40-year-old special effects artist Sergio Stivaletti. Stivaletti joined the Argento camp when he created make-up effects for *Phenomena* (1985), which in turn earned him the difficult task of creating the multitude of make-up effects for the Argento-produced, Lamberto Bava-directed *Demons* (1985) and its hastily produced sequel *Demons 2* (1986). Stivaletti's work on these films established him as a veritable *maestro* in the field, and he soon developed an

*Museum*, which was the film that got the whole ball of wax rolling in the first place. Fulci and his collaborator Daniele Stroppa also hit upon the idea of using Gaston Leroux's short story "The Waxwork Museum" as their official source of inspiration, lest they run into any problems with Warner Bros. with regards to copyright infringement.[4] According to Alan Jones, the collaboration between Argento and Fulci proved to be heated, with one aspect being a particularly touchy topic, specifically onscreen violence. Surprisingly, Fulci was not particularly interested in playing up his reputation as "The Godfather of Gore" and was more intrigued by the possibilities of making an old-fashioned, atmosphere-driven horror movie. Argento was not convinced and kept trying to increase the gore quota; the two men fought like hell over it, but Fulci was eventually left with no choice but to acquiesce.[5] Argento controlled the purse strings and was in a position to cripple the project, after all, so Fulci was not about to jeopardize his best chance of getting back into the game.

Unfortunately, the pre-production phase dragged on interminably while Argento tinkered over post-production and promotional duties on his own "Italian comeback" *giallo*, *The Stendhal Syndrome* (1996).[6] Fulci became more and more desperate as the clock ticked; he was in bad shape financially and the prospect of his comeback film possibly slipping away from him was too much to bear. Argento continued to assure Fulci that they were on track and that he needed to be patient, but nobody could have foreseen what would happen next: Fulci died on March 13, 1997 as a result of complications from his diabetes. Argento was then faced with the inevitable quandary: Should he continue with the project without Fulci,

urge to begin directing films. Argento felt he would be a logical choice to take over the film and wasted little time in making him the proverbial offer he couldn't refuse. As Stivaletti recalled, "I was shocked when Dario called [...] I had been looking for a chance to direct and thought it would be with my own film and script. [...] I was in the right place at the right time; I accepted the offer."[7] The rest, as they say, was history. Stivaletti made some significant changes to Fulci's original script and did his best to make the film a homage, while still being in his own style. He and Argento even hired Fulci's eldest daughter, Antonella, to serve as an assistant art director.

*The Wax Mask* opens with a bit of childhood trauma, as a little girl witnesses the brutal murder of her father; a kindly police inspector arrives later and promises to find the culprit. Fans of Argento will recognize this as the setup for his own later *giallo*, *Sleepless* (2001). The film then moves full force into the era of the Belle Époque in Paris, as Stivaletti and his collaborators emphasize the beauty and excess of the era to counterpoint the grisly goings-on in the story. Once again, Argento fans will recognize a similarity to one of his other films, in this instance his reviled take on *The Phantom of the Opera* (1998). Argento may have felt that Fulci was copying him in his *gialli*, but clearly he was not above borrowing from others, as well.

The story hews fairly closely to de Toth's model: a demented genius kidnaps various members of polite society so that he can use their bodies in his waxworks museum. The public is fascinated by how lifelike the figures are, and for good reason: They are actually human beings coated in wax. A sick twist to the story reveals that the mad Boris Volkoff (Robert Hossein[8]) uses a special chemical compound to keep the unwilling models in a state of suspended animation while they are put on display; as such, they are aware of everything that is going on around them, but they are unable to react. One of the film's most effective sequences sees the ineffectual heroine (Romina Mondello) accidentally knocking out the hidden "feeding tube" from one of the figures, thus allowing it to regain some perfunctory body movement; it's a moment of "body horror" which wouldn't be out of place in a David Cronenberg movie.

**Boris Volkoff (Robert Hossein) is taken with Sonia (Romina Mondello) in *The Wax Mask.***

It is well known that Stivaletti made some significant changes to the script: Fulci was interested in mood and atmosphere, whereas Stivaletti (who makes a cameo appearance as a satisfied customer at a brothel) naturally tailored the material to suit his interest in special effects. This manifests itself in the slightly silly finale, which contains more than a whiff of James Cameron's *The Terminator* (1984) as the exposed (literally!) Volkoff is reduced to a bloodthirsty automaton. Up until that point, however, the film is sober and well made. One sequence shot apparently as Fulci intended involves a character being faced with a *doppelgänger* of sorts and climaxes with a spurt of blood spraying onto a gramophone record, which causes the needle to come to a screeching halt. It's a magnificent sequence, no matter who devised it. The film benefits from superior production design by Massimo Antonello Geleng and first-rate cinematography by Fulci's long-time collaborator Sergio Salvati. Salvati's use of shadow and vivid primary colors makes it one of the last truly rich-looking Italian horror films to date; Argento would have been wise to have employed him on his lavish remake of *The Phantom of the Opera*, truth be told.

If the film falls apart during its final scenes and suffers from some less-than-convincing computer-generated effects, it still offers up ample mood and some rich imagery. One can only guess at what Fulci might have done with the film, or what it could have done to bolster his flagging career, but the film still provided him with an opportunity to attach his name to one last worthy example of a genre with which his name had become synonymous.

Notes:
1. Palmerini, Luca M. and Gaetano Mistretta, *Spaghetti Nightmares* (Florida: Fantasma Books, 1996), p. 61.
2. Jones, Alan, *Dario Argento: The Man, The Myths & The Magic* (Godalming: FAB Press, 2012), p. 237.
3. In fact, according to the website luciofulci.fr, Fulci had planned to do a new version of the 1932 horror film directed by Karl Freund and starring Boris Karloff as far back as 1980, following the production of *Contraband*; that project also fell by the wayside.
4. Jones, Alan, *Dario Argento: The Man, The Myths & The Magic* (Godalming: FAB Press, 2012), p. 237.
5. *Ibid.*
6. Argento's desire to expand his business empire to America prompted him to relocate to Pittsburgh to make his segment of *Two Evil Eyes* (1990) and then to Minneapolis to make *Trauma* (1993). Since neither film was well received, his return to Italy was greeted with a veritable blitz of excited publicity; the resulting film was not entirely well received, but there were darker days to come in light of the failure of *The Phantom of the Opera*.
7. Jones, Alan, *Dario Argento: The Man, The Myths & The Magic* (Godalming: FAB Press, 2012), p. 238.
8. Veteran voice actor Robert Rietty, director of the English track, dubbed Hossein in the English version. Incidentally, Hossein also starred in and directed the Dario Argento-scripted Spaghetti Western *Cemetery Without Crosses* (1969).

# Films Directed by Fulci

## 1959

### *I ladri (Italy/Spain)*

Aka *Contrabando en Nápoles; The Thieves* (unofficial English-language translation)

Directed by Lucio Fulci; Produced by Roberto Capitani and Luigi Mondello, for Fénix Cooperativa Cinematográfica and ICM; Story and Screenplay by Marcello Coscia, Lucio Fulci, José Gallardo, Ottavio Jemma, Nanni Loy, Marino Onorati and Vittorio Vighi; Director of Photography: Manuel Berenguer and Carlo Fiore; Editor: Juan Pisón and Gino Talamo; Music by Carlo Innocenzi; Song: *Che notte,* performed by Fred Buscaglione

Main Players: Antonio de Curtis [as Totò] (Commissario Di Sapio); Giovanna Ralli (Maddalena); Armando Calvo (Joe Castagnato); Giacomo Furia (Vincenzo Scognamiglio); Enzo Turco (Brigadiere Nocella); Roberto De Simone [as Renato De Simone] (American Agent); Fred Buscaglione (Himself)

*Petty thief Vincenzo steals a case of jam from the harbor in Naples, not realizing that it contains gold coins from an ambitious heist. Vincenzo's wife, Maddelana, realizes that the coins are connected to a mobster, Joe Catagnato, who is under suspicion for the theft. Hoping to get in on the action, Vincenzo and Maddalena contact Catagnato and set out to help him regain his stolen property. They do not count on the intervention of the dogged Commissario Di Sapio, however …*

***I ladri*; original artwork by Scott Hoffman.**

Producer Carlo Ponti had offered Lucio Fulci the opportunity to direct *Totò all'inferno* (1955), but Fulci was reluctant to make his debut directing a vehicle for a popular comedian. His concern was that doing something like that would be counter-productive to his desire to be taken seriously as an *auteur* filmmaker. Fulci had already spent the early part of his career in the shadow of his mentor, Steno, and was not about to become equally anonymous as a director, as well. However, by 1959, Fulci was married; he and his wife had plans to start a family of their own—his first daughter would be born in August of 1960—and money became more of a pressing concern. He finally decided that the time was right to make the transition to directing; he was already a well-regarded assistant and screenwriter, after all, so if the resulting film did not go over well, he at least had options on which to fall back. *I ladri* would not be a vehicle for any one comic performer, thus allowing Fulci to put himself forward as the film's true author, but he would hedge his bets, just the same: The cast would still include Totò in a character role, even if the narrative was carried by other characters.

A Spanish/Italian co-production with a predominantly Spanish crew, *I ladri* was filmed over a period of approximately five weeks in Spain in order to satisfy the Spanish co-producers. Fulci was happy to make the trip in the interests of getting his directing career off the ground and approached the project with enthusiasm. However, things were not entirely smooth behind the scenes, as he later explained:

> In Spain, for my first film with Totò, I realized that the local producer, Marcos, was a thief and a crook. One day I was shooting a panning shot, and, while I was moving from left to right, they were taking away the furniture. "What's happening?" Then the producer, [Luigi] Mondello, told me: "They're taking away the furniture because Marcos did not pay the rent." […] I made that film under terrible conditions […] However, before shooting started and blissfully unaware of what would happen to me, I went to Mondello's office […] after I sat down, Mondello addressed the secretary: "Aha, Fulci's

here. Go get a few IOUs ready, so we can give him an advance!" The next day I was on the set.[1]

In essence, *I ladri* is a comic variation on the sort of witty caper films popularized by Jules Dassin's *Rififi* (1955). The notion of seeing a group of characters coming together to plot and execute the perfect crime has all the ingredients of great entertainment. Inevitably, tensions within the group lead to a falling out, causing the entire project to crumble to pieces. In Fulci's take, there is little doubt that he is on the side of the thieves; they are a rather pathetic bunch and are essentially looking to finally get a leg up in life, sooner than continue to scrape by with the bare minimum. By contrast, the police are presented as weak and ineffectual. Indeed, they are presented as fools. In one scene, Catagnato pretends to be drunk in order to get himself arrested, thus providing himself with a fool-proof alibi, but his attempts at getting the police to act are unsuccessful—he hurls insults and staggers, but they only take exception when he decides to insult Naples' football team.

The thieves are presented as a literal family unit: Maddalena, Vincenzo and their relatives are all "in the business," as it were, and like so many families, they spend much of their time bickering and getting on each other's nerves, though their familial bond is ultimately very strong. There is genuine warmth and affection in the way these characters are presented. They may be thieves, but their transgressions are on a very petty level; they do not have much beyond each other's company and it is entirely understandable that they should jump on the possibility of coming into a major cash flow, even if they aren't going to go about it in the most honorable of ways. It is the intrusion of the American gangster, Castagnato, which throws things off and brings about their downfall. The family may argue and bicker with one another, but there is genuine affection and loyalty between them; Castagnato feels no such loyalty and as a result has no problem in screwing them over in an attempt to save his own skin.

The scenes with the police have a very different feel and tempo and seem to have been included to give Totò something to do. That is not to say that these sequences do not work—Totò's natural charisma and comic timing ensures that these diversions are not a waste—but they do not feel entirely unified with the material that surrounds them. As portrayed by Totò, Commissario Di Sapio is an arrogant buffoon. He mispronounces the name of his long-suffering subordinate and he arrogantly asserts that he has "an ace up my sleeve" even as he seems to be bumbling in the dark. Ultimately, he does prove to have some insight and resourcefulness, but this could simply be a matter of dogged determination ultimately paying off with a bit of luck. One of his first scenes sees him dressing down (so to speak) an exotic dancer whose routine has resulted in an elderly patron having a heart attack. Di Sapio puffs his chest and acts indignant, but his leering expression and tendency to address the woman while staring at her breasts reveals that he is a hypocrite. Di Sapio blusters his way through the narrative, ignorant of much of what is going on around him, and cannot be seen as a "hero" in any sense of the term. In a move typical of Fulci's anarchic streak, the conventional heroic figures (i.e., the police) are marginalized and made to look ridiculous, while the conventional villains (i.e., the thieves) are rendered in a more positive light.

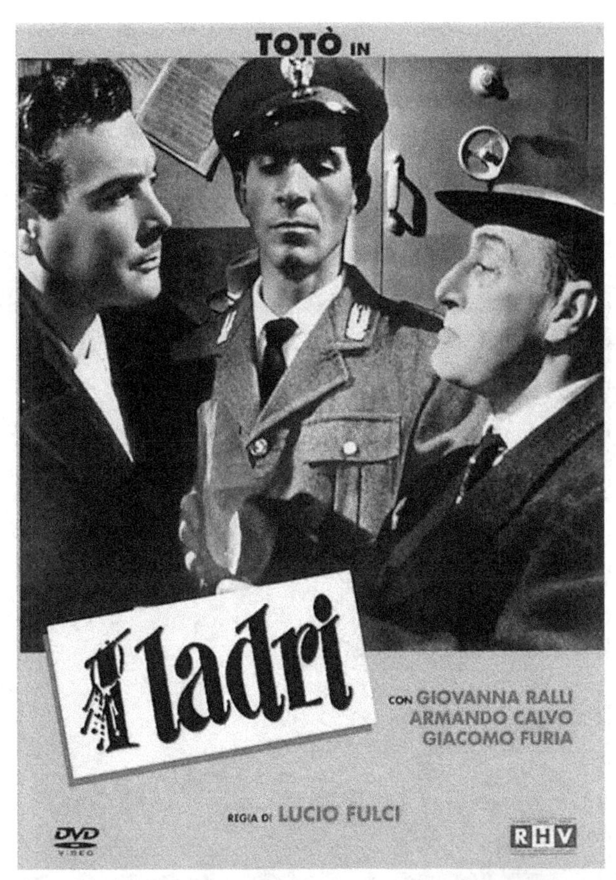


**DVD sleeve for the Italian release of *I ladri*, through RHV.**

Fulci handles the material with confidence and aplomb. He and cinematographer Manuel Berenguer[2] make good use of mobile camera work and precise but unfussy compositions throughout. Fulci does not announce himself as a major stylist his first time out of the gate, but he displays a solid understanding of pace, tempo and comic timing, which was surely informed by his years of working with Steno. As time wore on and he became more adventurous, he would begin to experiment more with flashy visual devices—split-screen, deep focus, etc.—but in *I ladri*, he keeps things simple and to the point. This works very well for the story, which is fairly unassuming and straightforward. Fulci would later describe the film as "a big flop,"[3] but its commercial failure did not prevent him from forging forward in his new career path. Deep down he may have desired to make personal "artistic" films, but in the interests of keeping body and soul together he decided to continue making commercial movies; he would still be able to put his personality into these projects, of course, but it would establish a precedent for critics who would continue to treat him with a lack of respect.

Notes:
1. Romagnoli, Michele, *L'occhio del testimone*, (Bologna: Granata Press 1992), p. 48.
2. Some sources indicate that Carlo Fiore assisted Berenguer (whose credits include everything from Nicholas Ray's biblical epic *King of Kings*, 1961, to Gordon Hessler's *Murders in the Rue Morgue*, 1971), but Berenguer is credited as chief camera operator on Italian prints. Another camera assistant is Angelo Lotti, who would go on to become a cinematographer in his own right; his credits include Jess Franco's *Venus in Furs* (1969).
3.http://www.shockingimages.com/fulci/interview2.html

## *I ragazzi del juke-box* (Italy)

Aka *The Juke-Box Kids* (unofficial English-language translation)

Directed by Lucio Fulci; Produced by Giovanni Addessi and Elios Vercelloni, for Era Cinématografica; Screenplay by Lucio Fulci, Vittorio Vighi and Piero Vivarelli; Director of Photography: Carlo Montuori; Editor: Gabriele Varriale; Music Credits: *A squarciagola* sung by Tony Dallara; *Sono pazzo di te* sung by Tony Dallara; *Ti dirò* sung by Tony Dallara; *Brivido blu* sung by Tony Dallara; *Per un bacio d'amor* sung by Tony Dallara; *Condannami* sung by Tony Dallara; *Dimmelo con un disco* sung by Betty Curtis; *With all my heart* sung by Betty Curtis; *Lontano da te* sung by Betty Curtis; *Buondì* sung by Betty Curtis; *Sofisticata* sung by Fred Buscaglione; *Il dritto di Chicago* sung by Fred Buscaglione; *Bambole d'Italia* sung by Fred Buscaglione; *I ragazzi del juke-box* sung by Adriano Celentano; *Il ribelle* sung by Adriano Celentano; *Il tuo bacio è come un rock* sung by Adriano Celentano; *Vorrei saper perchè* sung by Adriano Celentano; *Odio tutte le vecchie signore* sung by Gianni Meccia; *Ciao ti dirò* sung by I Campioni.

Main Players: Mario Carotenuto (Commendatore Cesari); Elke Sommer (Giulia Cesari); Antonio De Teffè (Paolo Macelloni); Betty Curtis (Betty); Giacomo Furia (Gennario); Yvette Masson (Maria Davanzale); Adriano Celentano (Adriano); Fred Buscaglione (Fred); Gianni Meccia (Jimmy); Tony Dallara (Tony)

Cameo appearance: Lucio Fulci (Festival organizer)

*Commendatore Cesari runs a music publishing company, but his tastes are a little too old-fashioned to suit his daughter Giulia. She suggests bringing on some more modern rock 'n' roll acts to the label, but Cesari will not hear of it. The conflict reaches a peak when Giulia arranges a festival of rock music, which causes such a scandal that Cesari is arrested. With her father out of the picture, Giulia takes over the family business and begins promoting the rock 'n' roll singers to great success …*

It may seem an oversimplification, but the musical genre can be divided into two basic camps: the "performance musical" and the "fantasy musical." In the former, the narrative is structured around musical acts as part of nightclub routines and the like; in the latter, characters express their inner thoughts through song. *I ragazzi del juke-box* – filmed under the title *Ti dirò… che mi piaci* (*I'll Tell You … That I Like You*) – belongs to the former camp. In many respects, it's similar to the *rock 'n' roll* musicals which were being made in England and America around the same time, including Roy Lockwood's *Jamboree!* (1957) and Richard Lester's *It's Trad, Dad!* (1962). In a way, these films are hopelessly dated when viewed through a contemporary lens, but they are important in understanding the social upheaval caused by the emergence of rock music.

Elements of rock music can be traced as far back as the 1930s. It is generally accepted that it grew out of Southern Jazz music, which became more and more popular throughout the 1940s. No art form is born in a vacuum, of course, and different music historians have different theories on the precise chronology of rock's birth into popular culture. Most will agree, however, that changes in technology—in terms of both the instruments used and in the emergence of independent record labels, which came to challenge the safely established majors—facilitated the rise of this new and aggressive style of music. By the early 1950s, the term "rock and roll" entered into the popular lexicon thanks in large part to the popular radio disc jockey Alan Freed, who used the term in his broadcasts; he did not originate the term, of course, but his use of it to describe the music on his broadcasts made an impression on his youthful listeners, and it stuck.

**Italian *locandina* for *I ragazzi del juke-box.***

*I ragazzi del juke-box* is more specifically linked to the genre known as *musicarello*; indeed, it has been described as the starting point of the form, which would continue to grow and then die off in the 1960s. Unlike American musicals, which were often carried by older actors and were designed to rope in a substantial audience, these films were explicitly made by and for the young. Fulci was only 32 at the time of production, which probably made him seem relatively "mature" compared to the target audience, but never mind: He was still a youthful filmmaker and the film would focus on younger characters, often with an aim towards making the older generation look stuffy and downright foolish by comparison. These films also differed in terms of their inspiration; many of the big American musical films of the 1950s and '60s were based on established Broadway shows, while the *musicarelli* were based on currently popular songs—they wouldn't use these songs to inspire the plot, *per se*, but if, say, Adriano Celentano had a hit tune out like *Il tuo bacio è come un rock*, to pick but one example, then the film would be most likely to incorporate said tune, front and center. In essence, these *musicarelli* did things the opposite way compared to their Hollywood counterparts. American musical films would hope to create toe-tapping hits with their musical numbers, whereas the Italian films were expected to appeal to public sentiment by utilizing already-established popular numbers. Thus, while the likes of *The King and I* (1956) or *Oklahoma!* (1955) came with the seal of approval of Broadway success and could be counted upon to appeal to audiences of all age brackets, *musicarelli* like *I ragazzi del juke-box* would sink or swim based on their ability to draw in the youth market.

*I ragazzi del juke-box* is an innocuous enough film, but it has a serious theme at its core. Specifically, it addresses the generation gap and the manner in which rock music helped to give a voice to the younger generation, thus allowing them to get out from under their oppressive elders. This idea is dealt with in a sprightly fashion in the film, so it doesn't do to treat it too gravely. The conflict between the stuffy Commendatore Cesari, whose respectable label caters to more traditional tastes, and his rebellious young daughter Giulia is neatly established early on. Giulia is introduced cutting loose in a youth club, taking in the rock music so deplored by her father, while the elder Cesari is depicted as something of a hapless despot in the confines of his company. Giulia is shown as a sympathetic character from the beginning—she may be rebelling against her father's staid, old-fashioned sensibilities, but she is hardly out of control in doing so. She is not the usual "juvenile delinquent" type presented in more conservative "teen" fare of the period—she is simply a normal young girl looking to make her own way in the world. The film makes it clear on which side of the equation Fulci's sympathies lie: Giulia is spunky, intelligent and resourceful, while her father is something of a middle-aged buffoon. Viewers accustomed to the accusations of misogyny, which would be so routinely leveled against Fulci's later horror films, will be surprised by the positive and respectful manner in which Giulia is represented here. She, not her out-of-touch fuddy-duddy of a father, is the wave of the future; and in addition to having her wits about her in terms of what she wants to do with her life, she also proves to be a canny and resourceful businesswoman, which inevitably surprises her father, while still making him proud.

***I ragazzi del juke-box*; original artwork by Scott Hoffman.**

Fulci was certainly the main authorial "voice" in the film, but one must not underestimate the presence of screenwriter Piero Vivarelli, either. Vivarelli was born in Tuscany in 1927 and went on to have a successful career as a songwriter, in addition to struggling to preserve his artistic integrity in the film business. In this capacity, he wrote a couple of hit numbers for Adriano Celenatano, including *24,000 baci* and *Il tuo bacio è come un rock*, the latter of which is featured in this film. In 1960, he created a popular Italian radio show titled *La coppa del jazz*, which highlighted his love of jazz music. A committed Communist, he was reportedly the only member of the Italian chapter of the party to receive official recognition by Castro himself. In films, he contributed to everything from Sergio Corbucci's *Django* (1966) and Aristide Massaccesi's *Emanuelle in America* (1977) in a screenwriting role. His work as a director includes the popular *fumetti Mister X* (1967) and *Satanik* (1968), as well as the weird sex-horror-art film hybrid *The Snake God* (1970). He died in Rome in 2010. Given his background in the music scene, it is not unreasonable to suggest that his voice was as strong as that of Fulci's in developing the scenario and the overall attitude towards the characters. Fulci collaborated with Vivarelli in writing the lyrics for the afore-mentioned *Il tuo bacio è come un rock* and he also wrote lyrics for the afore-mentioned song *24,000 baci*, which was featured in Vivarelli's *musicarello Io bacio… tu baci* (1961), but it would seem that Fulci's own musical tastes were more geared towards jazz. In any event, when Fulci returned to the genre the next year with *Urlatori alla sbarra*, he would again have Vivarelli on board as screenwriter. That same year would also see them collaborating on *Sanremo – La grande sfida*, which has already been covered in an earlier section of this book.

Much of the running time is devoted to the musical acts themselves. Various popular entertainers of the period are given ample exposure, notably Fred Buscaglione and Adriano Celentano. Buscaglione had already featured in Fulci's debut, *I ladri*, and would go on to lose his life at the too-young age of 38 when he was involved in a fatal car crash in February of 1960, an event later explicitly alluded to in Sergio Corbucci's *Night Club* (1989; co-scripted by Fulci); Buscaglione's persona of an "American-style" gangster with a fondness for women and whiskey is prominently on display as he swaggers his way through several musical numbers. Buscaglione proves to be an engaging and likable actor, making his sudden death all the more regrettable. Adriano Celentano (born 1938) modeled himself after Elvis Presley and became a major sensation in the process; he would also become a popular and prolific presence on screen, top-lining successful films like Pietro Germi's *Serafino* (1968) as well as Dario Argento's atypical period comedy adventure *Le cinque giornate* (1973), which would prove to be a rare box-office flop for both men. Celentano also tried his hand at directing, notably with the unusual musical film *Yuppi du* (1975), which was entered into competition at Cannes and has become a cult item. Celentano doesn't have as much screen time beyond performing his numbers, but his charisma during those scenes make it obvious why he became such a popular presence in the Italian music scene and remains so to this day.

Fulci would later recall casting Celentano and the impact it would have on the singer's career:

> Immediately after *I ladri*, which was a big flop, I didn't have any work offer until one day Ugo Pirro came over and asked me to make *I ragazzi del juke-box*. Pirro was a very serious and distinguished gentleman […] and so I accepted. *I ragazzi del juke-box* was a low-budget film and the so-called stars were Tony Dallara and Betty Curtis. One day, Vighi, Vivarelli (who was the musical expert and my assistant) and I were discussing about the casting and Vivarelli said, "You know, there is a watchmaker in Milan who's quite good. His name is Adriano Celentano and he sings *Io sono ribelle*." Then Pirro replied, "Call him over, we'll make a screen test." A few days later he showed up and was very shy and awkward, and kept saying, "Good morning *dottore*, good day *dottore*" [Note: Although *dottore* is Italian for doctor, it is used in this context as a sign of respect by lower-class individuals towards upper-crust types with presumably superior education.] and shook everybody's hands. Since Vighi played the ukulele and always had it with him, he handed it to the guy and asked him to show us what he could do. Celentano started: "*Sono un ribelle … sono un ribelle …*" (I am a rebel… I am a rebel) and I whispered, "Let's cast this one." A few days later Vivarelli, Celentano and I met for the rehearsals and he said, "Let's write a song together, eh?" and started whistling a melody. Vivarelli and I wrote the words of what became *Il tuo bacio è come un rock*. We filmed the song and Celentano sang live (whereas the others used playback) and then overdubbed it.

> Some time later, during the preparation of a scene with Buscaglione [...] I heard someone in the studio whistling that song. So I thought that maybe we did it right this time ...[1]

An interesting cast filled the dramatic roles capably, with Elke Sommer handily stealing the show as the spunky Giulia. Born in Berlin in 1940 as Elke Schletz, she was discovered by director Vittorio De Sica while she was on holiday with her family in Italy. Changing her surname to Sommer, she made her film debut in Giorgio Bianchi's *Men and Noblemen* (1959), which also starred De Sica; *I ragazzi del juke-box* was her second picture. She would go on to appear in Fulci's next film, *Urlatori alla sbarra* (1960) and began appearing in more international fare in the 1960s, including Mark Robson's Hitchcock *pastiche The Prize* (1963, for which she was nominated for a Golden Globe as the "Most Promising Newcomer") and Blake Edwards' *A Shot in the Dark* (1964), starring Peter Sellers as Inspector Clouseau. She would go on to star in two films for Mario Bava: *Baron Blood* (1972) and *Lisa and the Devil* (1973). She would also film some additional scenes for the latter, when it was overhauled and re-edited by producer Alfredo Leone (with a reluctant Bava co-operating only up to a point) as *The House of Exorcism* (1975). Sommer is a radiant and charming presence in this film and she has great chemistry with her onscreen love interest, played by future Spaghetti Western stalwart Antonio De Teffè; he would later change his name to Anthony Steffen and top-line such movies as Sergio Garrone's *Django the Bastard* (1969) and Emilio Miraglia's *The Night Evelyn Came Out of the Grave* (1971). De Teffè/Steffen was a rather wooden presence in his later films, but he is surprisingly relaxed here, even managing to convey some genuine charm; how much of this was due to Fulci's direction is open to speculation, but he certainly makes a better impression than usual. Fulci makes an appearance as a music promoter and even manages to give himself a few lines; he would go on to play more substantial roles in his own films over time.

*I ragazzi del juke-box* is by no means "essential Fulci," but it shows a light-hearted, amiable side to the director that is rather endearing. As a time capsule of the social changes afoot in the late 1950s, it is not without interest. Within its own admittedly unambitious parameters, it accomplishes its goals with style and a sense of fun.

**Urlatori alla sbarra*; original artwork by Scott Hoffman.**

Notes:

1. Romagnoli, Michele, *L'occhio del testimone*, (Bologna: Granata Press 1992), pp. 59-60.

# 1960

## *Urlatori alla sbarra (Italy)*

Aka *Howlers of the Dock* (unofficial English-language translation)

Directed by Lucio Fulci; Produced by Giovanni Addessi, for Era Cinématografica; Story and Screenplay by Giovanni Addessi, Lucio Fulci, Vittorio Vighi and Piero Vivarelli; Director of Photography: Gianni Di Venanzo; Editor: Gabriele Varriale; Music by Piero Umiliani; Songs: *Nessuno*, performed by Mina; *Blue Jeans Rock*, performed by Adriano Celentano; *Ruskaja*, performed by Adriano Celentano; *Ritroviamoci*, performed by Joe Sentieri; *Vorrei sapere perchè*, performed by Mina; *Precipito*, performed by Brunetta; *Arrivederci*, performed by Chet Baker; *Un brivido blu*, performed by I Brutos; *Dopo l'amore l'odio*, performed by Umberto Bindi; *I soldati delicati*, performed by Gianni Meccia; *Mai più*, performed by Adriano Celentano; *Non so parlare*, performed by Joe Sentieri; *Tintarella di luna*, performed by Mina; *Whisky*, performed by Mina; *Milioni di scintille*, performed by Joe Sentieri

Main Players: Adriano Celentano (Adriano); Mina Anna Mazzina [as Mina] (Mina); Joe Sentieri (Joe the Red); Elke Sommer (Giulia Giommarelli); Chet Baker (Chet, the American); Giacomo Furia (Gubellini)

*A group of friends hang out and indulge in their love of rock music and dancing. Their antics prove annoying to the older people in the neighborhood, some of whom band together and try to put a stop to such frivolity ...*

Fulci's second *musicarello* is considerably lighter on plot than the first. Much of the running time is devoted to the various singers—the so-called *urlatori*, or howlers, as the older generation was prone to dismissing them—as they perform their songs and the scenario (again with the input of Piero Vivarelli) doesn't allow for much in the way of character development. Once again a young daughter and her stuffy father are at odds—Elke Sommer and Mario Carotenuto play the roles establishing a further continuity with the earlier film, even if they are not playing the same characters—and, here too, all will be resolved happily by the final fade-out.

Even so, there is a touch of the anarchic in Fulci's approach that lends credence to his oft-expressed desire to work within genres and explode them from within. The film opens with a charmingly naïve montage depicting various forms of "shouting" from the times of the cavemen to the spectacle of long-winded politicians holding

**Italian *locandina* for *Urlatori alla sbarra*; artwork by Serafini.**

forth from their soap-boxes in Parliament. The purpose is to illustrate the connection between this mode of expression and the so-called howling of the rock singers, which stands in contrast to the "proper" singing lionized in more classical venues. Fulci depicts the "howlers" as a sort of family unit; they virtually live together and never seem to interact with anybody outside of their circle. Their attitude towards rock and jazz is almost religious, an attitude summed up neatly (and humorously) by the sight of a young girl lighting a candle beneath the portrait of Louis Armstrong in one scene.

Fulci brings considerable style and energy to the various musical set pieces. Some of the cutting seems to anticipate the later trend in music videos, with cuts occurring in synch with the beats of the music in some scenes. Fulci rightly recognizes that the main draw is the performers, so he wastes no time putting them front and center. Adriano Celentano has a considerably more prominent presence this time, singing such hit tunes as *BlueJeans Rock* and *Ruskaja*. His Elvis-inspired routine is definitely engaging: he swaggers with authority and his energetic style is in perfect harmony with Fulci's camerawork and staging. Superstar Mina (born 1940; full name: Mina Anna Mazzini) is also prominently on display, performing a number of tunes, including *Whisky* and *Tintarella di luna*. Mina's pretty looks and expressive voice made her a sensation during this time frame and Fulci was surely fortunate to have her so prominently featured in the film; he definitely makes good use of her presence and her songs are among the more melodic and affecting heard in the picture. Mina's personal life would unfortunately overshadow her popularity, however, when an affair with married actor Corrado Pani led to an unexpected pregnancy; she was attacked in the press for the indiscretion and retired from public view under ignominious circumstances. She continues to perform on various recordings, but no longer makes any public appearances or appears in any live venues.

The film also features the legendary jazz musician Chet Baker (1929-1988). Baker was a brilliant trumpet player, but he also possessed an expressive voice, which is put to good use in the film. A life-long fan of jazz music, Fulci was only too happy to have Baker along for the film. Fulci recounted his memories of how he came to be involved in the project in an audio interview included on the DVD release of *Touch of Death* (1988):

> Here's the story of Chet Baker: he was in terrible shape, so Vivarelli and I helped him and he told us that he needed money. We asked him, "Would you like to do a movie with us?" So we told him to sing *Arrividerci* and then go to sleep. He was always sleeping! He was a junkie living in fleabag hotels. So he did this movie with us and then we found him a job at the Rupe Tarpea, which was a club full of whores, but he didn't understand shit. He worked in this club with an Italian band who loved him. After a week, he took the money and left.

True to Fulci's description, Baker looks very sleepy and out of it in the film, and the many shots of him yawning or taking a nap were surely sarcastic on the director's part. Baker would die under mysterious circumstances when he fell out of a window while visiting the Netherlands; ample quantities of narcotics were found in his system, but it has never been definitively established if it was an accident,

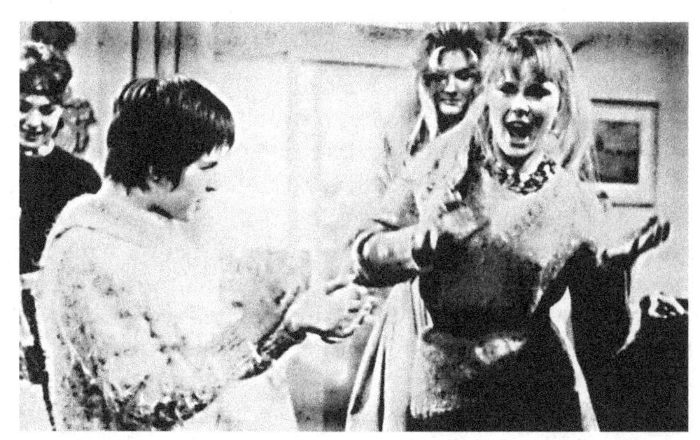

**Mina and Elke Sommer cut a rug in *Urlatori alla sbarra.***

suicide or something more sinister. Clips of Baker in the film would later be used in the critically acclaimed documentary about his life, titled *Let's Get Lost* (1988).

Piero Vivarelli recalled how his shared love of music with Fulci made their collaboration a happy one:

> Both Lucio and I loved jazz. From jazz to blues, from blues to rhythm-and-blues and rock, it's not a huge step. In a sense, theoretically we were already rockers! [...] In both *I ragazzi del juke-box* and *Urlatori*, if you pay attention to it, there is a common element—that is the small house surrounded by huge tower blocks, because the building speculators were invading Rome. In that small house there are these youths making their music, and thanks to their success they manage to keep the house ... in hindsight, it's like Frank Capra's *You Can't Take It with You*. We remade *You Can't Take It with You*, even though changing it in various ways, in both *I ragazzi del juke-box* and *Urlatori*, and then with my own film *Io bacio ... tu baci*. So we created this new genre. Those who paid the ticket to see the film did not just like one record or one singer, but a whole range of singers. Because we had all of them in the film: Dallara, Celentano, Betty Curtis, Mina [...][1]

Fulci would later speak of his experience dealing with the recording side of the industry:

> In that film, Celentano sang another tune which we labeled *Flamenco rock* since we had to write the lyrics yet. Eventually, Vivarelli and I came up with that line, which went like "*10,000 baci*" (10,000 kisses). When we arrived in Milan to shoot [...], we met Rapetti [Note: Giulio Rapetti, a renowned Italian lyricist who used the pen-name Mogol], who listened to the melody and said, "Why 10,000 kisses? Make it 24,000, it sounds better." That year, with that song we came second at the San Remo Festival and Mogol showed up demanding the author's rights [....]. All occasions are good to ask for money ...[2]

Cinematographer Gianni Di Venanzo gives the film an appropriately slick and stylish look, which is hardly surprising when considering his pedigree as one of Italy's foremost lighting cameramen. He would go on to photograph some of the most significant Italian films of the 1960s, including Michelangelo Antonioni's *La notte* (1961) and *L'eclisse* (1962), Francesco Rosi's *Salvatore Giuliano* (1962) and *Hands Over the City* (1963) and Federico Fellini's *8 ½* (1963) and *Juliet of the Spirits* (1965). Tragically, he died very young, from hepatitis, in 1966; he was only 45 years old. His assistant on the film was the young Erico Menczer, who would go on to photograph such Fulci films as *Operation St. Peter's* (1967) and *Beatrice Cenci* (1969). Menczer would later recall that Fulci's tempestuous presence on set was already in place on this film:

> I met Fulci on the set of *Urlatori alla sbarra*; I was Di Venanzo's camera operator. It was the first of the four films I did with him, three as director of photography. He was already the "usual" Fulci [...], he had a hell of a time with those young actors. He was frightful, made them toe the line, yelled four-letter words ... he was angry with everyone ... when Mina, who was an 18-year-old girl, or Barilli were not around, he used to badmouth them in their absence. [...] There was also Carotenuto, who wouldn't allow you to say anything to him. He was a great actor, huge and with personality, you could not dispute him. He was quite a character. And Fulci had a lot of respect for true actors.[3]

Unfortunately for Fulci, the film encountered some unexpected problems with the censors. Some of the more sexually suggestive bits of innuendo were toned down, some overt political references were removed and perceived "blasphemy" was avoided through the removal of the line, "Jesus, Mary and Joseph!" and ultimately the film was given a restricted rating, meaning that nobody under the age of 16 was permitted to see the film. Given that this effectively barred a large portion of the intended audience, this cut down on the film's box-office returns; it also pointed to the kinds of woes Fulci would begin to encounter in his later works, when his darker impulses began to take hold.

Fulci would spend the following year working on other people's projects and it would take until 1962 for him to sign his name to another film of his own.

Notes:

1. Albiero, Paolo and Giacomo Cacciatore, *Il terrorista dei generi. Tutto il cinema di Lucio Fulci* (Rome: Un Mondo a Parte, 2004) pp. 35-36.
2. *Ibid*, p. 38.
3. Romagnoli, Michele, *L'occhio del testimone*, (Bologna: Granata Press 1992), p. 60.

## 1962

### *Colpo gobbo all'Italiana (Italy)*

Aka *Getting Away With It The Italian Way* (informal English title); *Hunchback Italian Style* (unofficial English-language translation); *La rubia tuvo la culpa*

Directed by Lucio Fulci; Produced by Mario Carotenuto for Era Cinématografica; Story by Mario Carotenuto; Screenplay by Bruno Corbucci, Beppo Costa and Giovanni Grimaldi; Director of Photography: Alfio Contini; Editor: Mariella Ercoli and Franco Fraticelli; Music by Piero Umiliani; Songs: *La nottola di notte* and *Quello che bolle in pentola*, performed by Gianni Meccia.

Main Players: Mario Carotenuto (Nando Paciocchi); Andrea Checchi (Orazio Menicotti); Hélène Chanel (Blonde); Gina Rovere (Gina); Gabriele Antonini (Ennio)

*Orazio is a night watchman whose impeccable record is spoiled one night when a pretty blonde distracts him from his duty; a bank is robbed, but he has time enough to try and find the culprit and cover up the crime in order to save his reputation. He turns to Nando, a reformed criminal who now runs a thriving business. In order to keep his past buried and to retrieve his own money, which was stolen in the robbery, Nando agrees to form a group of former colleagues to help Orazio. The thieves locate the stolen money and then must break into the safe in order to replace it before the bank opens again on Monday morning …*

**Colpo gobbo all'Italiana; original artwork by Scott Hoffman.**

Following a brief period away from directing, Fulci found himself in the position of becoming a gun for hire. The true *auteur* of *Colpo gobbo all'Italiana* is not Fulci, but rather popular writer/actor Mario Carotenuto (1916-1995), who concocted the story in addition to producing and playing one of the lead roles.[1] No doubt Carotenuto was moved to select Fulci based on his experiences working with the director on *I ragazzi del juke-box* and *Urlatori alla sbarra*, but he may well have had opportunity to regret his decision: Fulci would later recall that they did not see eye-to-eye, resulting in a strained experience.[2]

In many respects, the film is closer in spirit and tone to *I ladri* than to Fulci's more recent directing work. The film finds him returning to the colorful caper genre, with the spectacle of kids indulging in their passion for rock 'n' roll nowhere to be seen. The film unfolds in a seedier version of Rome teeming with petty thieves and prostitutes. For all that, it is oddly antiseptic, almost naïve in its approach. None of the criminal class on display represent any kind of a threat: They are the nicest, most kind-hearted group of thieves you could ever hope to meet.

In the film's idealized universe, the night watchman character is on friendly terms with the criminals. More than that, they are actively in cahoots with each other. Given that the thieves never stoop to anything too awful, they will inevitably be useful to Orazio as he attempts to salvage his honor. If the film has a major failing, it rests in its inability to give any edginess to the characters. Orazio, Nando and the rest are basically a group of well-intentioned schmucks; one is never in doubt of their basic decency and there's therefore little suspense generated, simply because we know that they will band together and see to it that everything will be all right in the end.

That said, one doesn't wish to be too hard on the movie. Despite its lack of suspense, it works quite effectively as a well-paced caper comedy. The final safe-cracking sequence doesn't have the requisite spark, arguably, but it is still very well-staged by Fulci, who utilizes appropriately dramatic camera angles, while cinematographer Alfio Contini—in his first assignment for Fulci—plays up the atmospherics via some excellent lighting effects. The character vignettes are frequently charming and the film benefits enormously from the charismatic performance of Andrea Checchi as the luckless Orazio. Checchi's mix of world-weary despair and deadpan comedy helps to give a bit of depth to the character. As for Carotenuto, he makes for an appropriately ambiguous presence: Nando has built his business on his ill-gotten gains and relishes the status symbols he has acquired, notably a curvaceous wife of whom he is insanely jealous. Nando may condescend to the other thieves, but of course he is ultimately no better than they are.

Fulci's background in rock music manifests itself with some songs performed by Gianni Meccia, but they are strictly background fare; the film does not stop in its tracks for any performance numbers. One can see Fulci growing and becoming more and more confident as a stylist; while his approach in *I ladri* was fairly staid and conventional, this film shows him utilizing more mobile camera work and striking compositions. There's a marvelous scene in which some of the thieves are playing cards, for example, with Fulci and Contini covering the scene via a continuous dolly shot that encircles the men as they try to outsmart each other. The use of low-key lighting gives the film the appropriate *noir* ambience. Indeed, one can't help but be reminded of some of the classic *noir* caper films of the era, notably John Huston's *The Asphalt Jungle* (1950) and Stanley Kubrick's *The Killing* (1956), both of which starred rugged Sterling Hayden as an ex-con looking to make one final score. The material doesn't allow for the kind of world-weary cynicism that infected those American efforts, but there are traces of their stylistic influence in the way Fulci envisions the gang and their *milieu*. The occasional touch of gritty realism stands in stark contrast to the happy-go-lucky nature of the material, but the clash never becomes too jarring.

**Cover for the soundtrack album for *Colpo gobbo all'Italiana*, through RCA Victor.**

The film also benefits from a very good music score by Piero Umiliani. Umiliani was born in Florence in 1926. He graduated from the conservatory in Florence and went on to make a name for himself in the burgeoning jazz scene of the 1950s. He made an auspicious film debut with his score for Mario Monicelli's acclaimed *Big Deal on Madonna Street* (1958)—certainly the best of the many Italian caper spoofs—and first worked with Fulci on *Urlatori alla sbarra*. His hit tune *Mah nà mah nà*, written for the film *Sweden: Heaven and Hell* (1968), summed up his approach: Light and insanely catchy, with nonsensical lyrics, it is the type of song that refuses to budge from the subconscious once it has been heard. It would prove to be a very popular song indeed and would be used in various contexts, most famously as a recurring piece on *The Benny Hill Show*. Speaking of catchy tunes, they don't come much catchier than *Quello che bolle in pentola*, which is memorably featured as background accompaniment to a couple of scenes in this film. Umiliani would go on to score several more comedies for Fulci, including *Oh! Those Most Secret Agents* (1964) and *I due pericoli pubblici* (1965). He would also score several films for Fulci's friend, Mario Bava: *The Road to Fort Alamo* (1964), *Roy Colt & Winchester Jack* and *Five Dolls for an August Moon* (both 1970). He remained active until the early 1980s and died in 2001.

Amid the supporting cast, there is a performer who was linked to a project Fulci is reported to have been tied to during this timeframe. Milanese comic actor—and later director—Gino Bramieri appears in a small role in this film and would go on to play the title role in *Nerone '71* (1962). Lucio Fulci apparently was attached to the film early on but was ultimately replaced by journeyman Filippo Walter Ratti. Ratti, whose career finished with the tacky *giallo Crazy Desires of a Murderer* (1977), never made much of a name for himself and *Nerone '71*, like the rest of his filmography, has disappeared into the murky waters of obscurity.[3]

*Colpo gobbo all'Italiana* lacks the bite one associates with Fulci's best work, but it is an enjoyable diversion, just the same. Viewers looking to chart his growing assuredness as a filmmaker will find much to enjoy in his staging and pacing of the action. As a comedy, it also offers some genteel laughs along the way. Fulci's next comedy, however, could never be described as genteel. Indeed, it would mark an important step in his career and would begin an association with a comedy team who would top-line more of his films than any other actor.

Notes:

1. That said, in *Il terrorista dei generi. Tutto il cinema di Lucio Fulci* (Paolo Albiero and Giacomo Cacciatore, Rome: Un Mondo a Parte, 2004, p. 46), Carotenuto's daughter insists that her father worked on the script with Fulci and that the other names credited had nothing do to with it.
2. In the audio interview included on the Shriek Show DVD of *Touch of Death*, Fulci brushed the film aside fairly quickly, noting: "I quarreled with Carotenuto… It's an OK movie, but nothing special."
3. Thanks to Jason Slater for revealing this information about *Nerone '71* via email.

## *I due della legione (Italy)*

Aka *Those Two in the Legion* (unofficial English-language translation)

Directed by Lucio Fulci; Produced by Danilo Marciani, for Sicilia Cinematografica, Titanus and Ultra Film; Screenplay by Roberto Bianchi Montero, Bruno Corbucci, Dino De Palma, Giancarlo Del Re, Lucio Fulci, Giovanni Grimaldi, Antonio Leonviola and Arnaldo Marrosu, from a story by Roberto Bianchi Montero and Antonio Leonviola; Director of Photography: Alfio Contini; Editor: Mario Serandrei; Music by Luis Bacalov (as Luis Enriquez); Songs: *Saïda* composed by Ennio Morricone and performed by Rosario Borelli

Main Players: Franco Franchi (Franco Cocuzza); Ciccio Ingrassia (Ciccio Fisichella); Alighiero Noschese (Mustafa Abdul Bey); Rosalba Neri (Lina); Aldo Giuffrè; Maria Teresa Vianello

Cameo appearance: Lucio Fulci (German on train)

*Two idiotic con men become mixed up in a murder when a local mob boss with whom they had fallen out turns up dead. Looking to escape imprisonment, they attempt to flee the country. They follow the advice of an eccentric German, who assures them that a wonderful life awaits them in the Foreign Legion. They sign up and find it's not what it's cracked up to be, but their commanding officer, hearing of their troubles with the law, mistakes them for brave men of adventure and sends them in to thwart a weapons smuggling ring…*

***I due della legione*; original artwork by Scott Hoffman.**

*I due della legione* is something of a game change for Fulci. He had resisted the idea of making films built around the presence of popular comics when he first set out to direct, but some box-office disappointments and professional setbacks, combined with the need to provide for his family, made him change his tune. As Fulci later explained in an interview included on the Shriek Show DVD release of *Touch of Death,*

> I invented Franchi's and Ingrassia's characters […] because they did *L'onorata società* (1961) first, which was their first movie. *I due della legione* was my screenplay and it had made the rounds. So I wanted to offer the two guys a contract, but Modugno came and said, "I'm making a film with them!" So they signed a contract to do *L'onorata società*, a total flop. Then [Bruno] Corbucci adapted my screenplay for Franco and Ciccio, but he screwed up by making Franchi the smart one and Ingrassia the dumb one. After the first day of shooting, I told Ingrassia, "What are you doing? Franco's the dumb one!" Ingrassia always says that the duo was invented that night. Once the movie was finished, at a cost of 62 million *lire*, Titanus distributed it. Lombardo saw it and said, "It's crap. Chuck it." The film hit theaters in the middle of August. […] [*I due della legione*] earned four billion *lire*.

Fulci is hardly exaggerating: Franco and Ciccio would become a force to be reckoned with thanks to the success of this film. For better or for worse, Fulci would find himself joined at the hip of the comedy duo and for the next several years, the majority of his films would make ample use of their presence. It would seem that the union was a happy one at the time, but in later years the caustic filmmaker would be far more critical. In what is reported to be his last published interview, for example, Fulci described them as "horrible rip-offs of Laurel and Hardy."[1] That may seem fair enough as far as descriptions go, but there is something a little disingenuous about Fulci's late-period desire to distance himself from the pair of Sicilian clowns. More than likely it was the latter-day cult adulation he received in a very different genre which prompted him to adopt this attitude, but there is no getting around the facts: without Franco and Ciccio, Lucio Fulci's career would have evolved very differently. Next to Steno, they were arguably the most significant "happening" in his early career and his sure and steady hand behind the camera would also result in their best films. Other filmmakers would try their hand with the duo, with mixed results, but Fulci's films have a sense of pace and energy that is frequently lacking in their other efforts. Whether he would have been loathe to admit it or not, the team's gimmick of parodying popular genres and trends had its similarities to Fulci's own desire to "explode" genres from within; the three of them together would therefore produce some surprisingly inspired comedy.

Franco Franchi (born in 1928) and Ciccio Ingrassia (born in 1922) both emanated from Palermo. They first crossed paths in the early 1950s, when they were both struggling to earn a living in the Sicilian theatrical circuit. Audiences warmed to their routines and they then made the inevitable transition to movies. Truth be told, Franchi

**Italian *fotobusta* for *I due della legione*: Franco and Ciccio pose as sheiks.**

had already played some small roles in minor Italian films of the 1950s, but they were first paired together in Mario Mattoli's *Appointment in Ischia* (1960), which was written by Fulci's old friends and colleagues Roberto Gianviti and Vittorio Metz; indeed, this was probably where they first came to his attention. They showed up late in the story as comical smugglers, but they would not be stuck playing second (or indeed third-and-fourth) fiddle for long. Riccardo Pazzaglia cast them in the mob comedy *L'onorata società*, but as Fulci notes above, the results were not entirely successful. *I due della legione* set their routine in stone, with Ciccio as the marginally more intelligent and dignified of the two, and Franchi working his rubbery face mercilessly as the clown. Audiences lapped up their vehicles: For Fulci, they would appear in no less than a dozen pictures, many of which would remain among the most popular of the director's career in Italy. It is difficult for American audiences to appreciate them for the simple fact that so much of their comedy was rooted in social commentary, albeit in a very broad key. If Totò was able to do a similar thing with an air of dignity, Franco and Ciccio were strictly for the masses. This is evident in their filmographies: While the duo would be paired with Totò in Pier Paolo Pasolini's segment ("Che cosa sono le nuovole?") of the anthology film *Capriccio all'Italiana* (1968), they would get far fewer opportunities to work with "serious" filmmakers, whereas Totò's comic genius was never really in doubt. They would go on to appear together in approximately 130 films (!) released between 1964 and 1974, after which they went their separate ways. Fulci would reteam with Franchi on the mini-series *Un uomo da ridere* (reviewed later in this book by Roberto Curti), while Ingrassia would find much critical acclaim playing the love-lorn uncle who cries so memorably, "I want a woman!" from atop a tree in Federico Fellini's *Amarcord* (1973); he was also used to excellent effect in Elio Petri's brilliant *Todo Modo* (1976).[2] The two would reteam in Michele Massimo Tarantini's *Crema cioccolato e pa ... prika* (1981) and the Taviani Brothers' *Kaos* (1984). Franchi died in 1992; Ingrassia followed in 2003.

The film also features an early role for the beautiful Rosalba Neri. Neri had already crossed paths with Fulci on *Totò, Peppino e... la dolce vita* (1961), but *I due della legione* marked the first time she was witness to his gruff manners while directing. As she later recalled in an interview:

**The near-sighted sultan (Alighiero Noschese) woos Franco and Ciccio in one of their less likely disguises.**

> [H]e wasn't kind, but saying that he treated us badly would be too much. He had unfriendly manners, that's all [...] I think that Fulci behaved that way to make a strong impression on other people ... he also had this threatening look.[3]

Like so many of the comic duo's films, *I due della legione* is of marginal interest to non-Italian viewers. The movie is built upon their routines and it really boils down to a matter of personal taste as to whether they are very funny or not. Some of the jokes fall flat, which is hardly surprising when one considers how chaotically and aggressively the material is presented, but there are some legitimately funny moments as well. One such sequence sees Franco hurriedly packing his bag in order to leave town while Ciccio ponders whether it is wise to do so; every time Ciccio says it is best to leave, Franco begins stuffing things into the case, but whenever Ciccio changes his mind, Franco dutifully returns the items to the dresser ... this continues for a good while and becomes more and more amusing as the scene unfolds. Fulci sensibly adopts a low-key style during these routines, lest any fancy camera work get in the way of their timing and rhythm. Another highlight occurs when the duo is quizzed by the frazzled Legion commander; it doesn't take the latter long to realize that neither man is exactly cut out for officer duty, but the way in which they play off of each other and drive the poor man around the bend is quite funny. Fulci is sometimes as guilty as the duo of trying too hard for belly laughs, falling back on the use of fast-motion for comedic effect—this technique was dated even at the time and it certainly hasn't aged very well. On the whole, however, Fulci works capably in tandem with the duo to get the best out of the material. Indeed, the director even casts himself in a small but crucial role and manages to hold his own against them; he plays the German farmer who advises the boys to join the Foreign Legion. Fulci is appropriately eccentric in the role, but he doesn't go in for the kind of rubber-faced antics typical of his stars. The end result is well crafted and doesn't overstay its welcome.

Notes:

1. Berger, Howard, "The Prince of Italian Terror," *Fangoria*, July 1997, p.63
2. Ingrassia would also reteam once more with Fulci, playing a wizard in *Young Dracula*.
3. Gomarasca, Manlio and Davide Pulici, *99 donne: Stelle e stelline del cinema italiano*, (Milan: Media World, 1999), p. 268.

## *Le massaggiatrici (Italy/France)*

Aka *The Masseuses* (unofficial English-language translation); *Les Faux Jetons; Mit Damenbedienung*

Directed by Lucio Fulci; Produced by Luigi Carpentieri and Ermanno Donati, for Gallus Films and Panda Films; Story and Screenplay by Oreste Biancoli, Italo De Tudo, Vittorio De Tudo and Antoinette Pellevant; Director of Photography: Guglielmo Mancori; Editor: Ornella Micheli; Music by Coriolano Gori (as Lallo Gori)

Main Players: Sylva Koscina (Marisa); Cristina Gaioni [as Cristina Gajoni] (Iris); Valeria Fabrizi (Milena); Philippe Noiret (Bellini); Ernesto Calindri (Ing. Parodi); Franco Franchi (Franco the Usher); Ciccio Ingrassia (Ciccio the Usher); Louis Seigner (Cipriano Paolini)

*Two businessmen attempt to win the contract to build a new YMCA in Rome. To that end, they enlist the services of a beautiful masseuse, Marisa, to seduce the head of the Catholic organization in charge of the project. The ploy proves to be successful, but everybody ends up with more than they bargained for when the vice squad is called in to investigate the masseusse's business…*

*Le massaggiatrici* is Fulci's first overtly political film. The director, who identified himself as a diehard Marxist, especially in his younger years, thoroughly enjoyed lambasting the Italian political scene and he would often return to the themes of hypocrisy and corruption in his later work.

Fulci embarked on the film right after completing *I due della legione;* he had no way of knowing just how successful the earlier effort would be, but he rightly recognized that Franco and Ciccio were to become lucky charms in his career. Thus, he brought them in to carry the film through its last act. Its eventual failure at the box-office seemed to confirm that he was better off casting them in lead roles, but Fulci remained fond of some of the film's more morbid humor. In particular, he once alluded to the plot device of the characters being forced to fool the public into thinking that a dead man is still alive as one that he was especially pleased with; indeed, he would argue that this pre-dated the surprise American box-office hit *Weekend at Bernie's* (1989).[1] The parallel is not entirely without merit, but while the later film used this one joke as a pretext for 90 minutes of strained comedy—to say nothing of the inevitable 1993 sequel—here it is used only in the last act; not surprisingly, the gag works better in this context and helps to end the film on a pleasingly morbid and cynical note.

Compared to the Franco and Ciccio comedies he would spend much of the remainder of the decade directing, *Le massaggiatrici* is positively understated. That's not to say that there isn't plenty of mugging for the camera—don't forget, Franco and Ciccio show up late in the day—but much of the humor is considerably more biting. The characters of Paolini and his right-hand man, Bellini, are made the butt of the bulk of the film's political jokes. Paolini is introduced recording a speech in which he pontificates about morality and the need for reform in what has become a corrupt society. He is pompous and condescending. He is also a raging hypocrite who changes his tune very quickly when Marisa shows off her shapely legs. Similarly, Bellini is a preening buffoon who waits on Paolini hand and foot; he seems to share his boss' priggish mentality, but this is also a façade. He, too, will crumble when the possibility of some easy sex is waved in front of him. Fulci and his writers (including the gifted Oreste Biancoli [1897-1971], whose credits include everything from Vittorio De Sica's Neorealist masterpiece *Bicycle Thieves*, 1948, to Riccardo Freda's misanthropic Gothic *The Ghost*, 1963) make it very plain that the men in power, who hide behind an illusion of piety, are little more than money-grubbing bastards. They are also depicted as being emblematic of the Christian Democratic party, which was wielding power in Italy at that time and would continue to maintain a stronghold until the mid-1990s. By extension, the womanizing nature of the male characters can be seen as a swipe at Italian machismo, that frequently manifests itself in the cliché of men treating their wives like Madonnas while seeking out whores to satisfy their "baser" instincts.

The film definitely kicks into high gear in the last act: Paolino suffers a fatal stroke while visiting Marisa and her co-workers; between the excitement over being around such beautiful women and the sudden arrival of the vice squad to raid the premises, it is only a matter of time before he goes into sensory overload, anyway. Bellini discovers the death and he also comes to make use of the masseusses' services. Always the politician, Bellini realizes that the death of his mentor in such a "squalid" *milieu* could be disastrous. Thinking quickly, he enlists the girls to help him in staging a more politically convenient demise. The

***Le massaggiatrici;* original artwork by Scott Hoffman.**

scenes of Bellini and his associates scrambling through the *noir*-ish landscape with the dead body of Poalino stuffed in the trunk have real style and energy. Fulci and cinematographer Gugliemo Mancori (who would also photograph Fulci's next film, *Uno strano tipo*) make the best of the moody nighttime ambience to play up the more macabre aspects of the sequence. It is not all shadows and political jabs for long, however; soon enough Franco and Ciccio are in the mix, playing hapless night watchmen who inadvertently become mixed up in the plot. A little Franco and Ciccio can typically go a long way, but their scenes are very amusing without feeling like a pointless digression.

**Behind the scenes of *Le massaggiatrici*.**

Sylva Koscina, Cristina Gaioni and Valeria Fabrizi play the title characters. They are emblematic of the fantasy-level "working girls" so frequently depicted on screen, whereas the hard-bitten call girls seen walking the streets in the opening scenes are closer to reality. The three actresses display good comic timing in addition to being stunning to look at. The distinguished French actor Philippe Noiret played Bellini. Fulci would later insist that this was Noiret's first film, but in reality he had been appearing in bit roles since the late 1940s. Born in 1930, he established himself as a reliable character actor before attaining stardom in Yves Robert's *Very Happy Alexander* (1968). His later career highlights would include Marco Ferreri's controversial *La Grande Bouffe* (1973) and Giuseppe Tornatore's Oscar-winning *Cinema Paradiso* (1988); ironically, the actor Tornatore originally had in mind for the part played by Noiret in the latter was ... Ciccio Ingrassia. Noiret is rumored to have regarded *Le massaggiatrici* as his worst-ever film; a harsh critique, if true, but given Fulci's reputation for clashing with his actors, anything is possible. Noiret died in 2006.

The crew includes the first appearance of a man who would become a key part of Fulci's team for the next several years. Giovanni Fago (born in Rome in 1933) took on the role of Fulci's first assistant director on this film and he would continue to act in that capacity for the next several years, assisting Fulci on *Gli imbroglioni, The Maniacs, I due evasi di Sing Sing, 002 operazione luna, Come inguaiammo l'esercito, I due parà, Come svaligiammo la banca d'Italia, Massacre Time, Come rubammo la bomba atomica* and *Il lungo, il corto, il gatto*. Soon after parting ways with Fulci, he would transition to directing films on his own, including the *poliziottesco Kidnap* (1974) starring Henry Silva and Gabriele Ferzetti.

*Le massaggiatrici* also marked the first time one of Fulci's films was edited by Ornella Micheli. She and Fulci hit it off—amazing, considering the reputation he had for terrorizing females, in particular—and she would go on to edit a whopping 18 features for the director. They would part ways after *Silver Saddle* in 1978, at which point Fulci's preferred editor of choice became the equally gifted Vincenzo Tomassi.

The hectic workload Fulci was adopting at this time ensured that he would have a taste of success and defeat almost simultaneously: *I due della legione* would open to tremendous box-office success in August of 1962, while *Le massaggiatrici* was released a mere month later and was, in his own words, "a complete flop."[2] None of this affected the director's forward momentum, however.

Notes:

1. Audio interview with Lucio Fulci, conducted by Pier Maria Bocchi and Andrea Bruni, included on the Shriek Show DVD release of *Touch of Death*.
2. *Ibid.*

# 1963

## *Uno strano tipo (Italy)*

Aka *The Strange Type* (unofficial English-language translation); *Un tipo extraño; Ein seltsamer Typ*

Directed by Lucio Fulci; Produced by Giovanni Addessi, for Giovanni Addessi Cinematografica; Story and Screenplay by Lucio Fulci and Vittorio Metz; Director of Photography: Guglielmo Mancori; Editor: Ornella Micheli; Music by Detto Mariano; Songs: *Stai lontana da me; Pregherò; Amami e baciami; Il tangaccio; Grazie prego scusi; L'ombra nel sole*, all performed by Adriano Celentano

Main Players: Adriano Celentano (Peppino/Himself); Claudia Mori (Carmelina); Donatella Turi (Emanuela Mazzolani); Luigi Pavese (M. Mazzolani); Rosalba Neri (Marina); Aldo Caponi [as Don Backi] (Himself); Mario Brega (Gas Station Attendant)

*Adriano goes to the resort town of Amalfi to perform a few concerts. Despite never having been there before, he receives a hostile welcome from the locals, many of whom act like he has taken advantage of them. Carmelina accuses him of impregnating her and refusing to accept his responsibilities. Adriano tries to leave, but his fiancée, Emanuela, and her business tycoon father come to join him and he feels he must go on with the show. Unbeknown to him, the dimwitted Peppino has actually been impersonating him and will continue to make complications for him during his stay in Amalfi…*

Fulci's final brush with the *musicarello* is a much more plot-driven film than its predecessors. It's also far more farcical in tone, making it something of a hybrid of the *musicarello* with the broad slapstick antics evident in his comedies of the period.

The film is carried by Adriano Celentano, who is called upon to stretch his acting muscles far more extensively than he had in Fulci's first two *musicarelli*. Instead of just relying on his natural screen presence, he is faced with the task of creating two clearly defined characters. He portrays himself as an easy-going, decent sort who is ill equipped to deal with the unusual situation he finds himself in. He is devoted to his girlfriend and does his best to fulfill the desires of his long-suffering manager; he also treats his band members as equals and does not condescend to them. Whether this was true to Celentano as he was in real life is open to debate, but within the context of the film it establishes him as a likable and endearing protagonist. By contrast, his portrayal of Peppino is straight out of the Franco and Ciccio school of mugging for the camera. Whether this was Celentano's concept or was imposed by Fulci is not known, but if the viewer can get past the pantomime aspect of the performance, he is to be congratulated for making the character so completely distinct from his regular persona. Peppino is a nitwit and

**Italian *locandina* for *Uno strano tipo*; the artist's name is illegible.**

a sex maniac who is manipulated into deceiving the public by a shady con man; as such, he is not the villain of the piece, *per se*. When the charade is ultimately exposed, one can't help but feel a little sorry for Peppino who, after all, is a mere pawn. Fulci and cinematographer Guglielmo Mancori utilize some effective split-screen effects to sell the illusion of the two Celentanos appearing on screen together, but the real pressure to deliver was on the actor—and while his portrayal of Peppino may seem a bit strained and hammy, it indicates a willingness to immerse himself in a character role which would allow him to become a popular screen performer in addition to trading on his reputation as a recording artist.

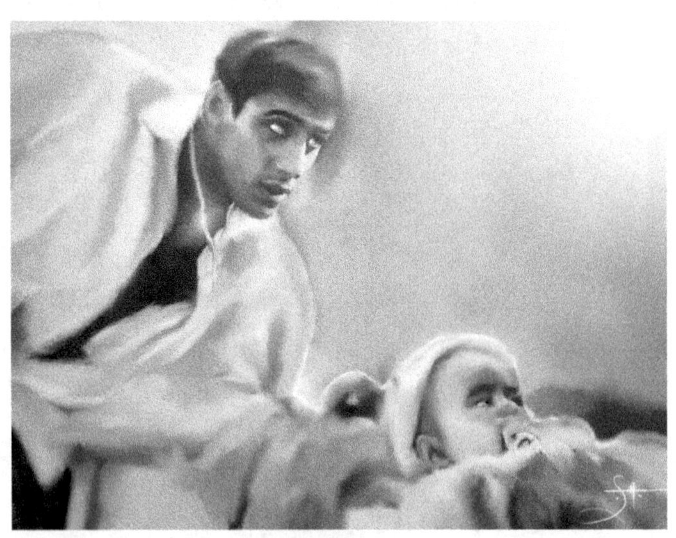
**_Uno strano tipo_; original artwork by Scott Hoffman.**

In addition to offering Celentano a more substantial acting challenge, *Uno strano tipo* was also important for him on a more personal level. As Fulci later recalled,

> This was where Celentano and Claudia Mori met. One day Celentano asked my wife, who was pregnant with my daughter Camilla, "Do you think I can fuck her?" My wife answered, "Try it, Celentano!" So they fell in love.[1]

Celentano and Mori would be married the following year and they remain together to this day.

Fulci handles the material with energy and style. His use of composition is skillful throughout: He does not waste a frame in advancing the narrative. The musical interludes are well staged and, while gags are on the slim side for the first hour or so, there are some genuine belly laughs in the last third. Things really take off in this last section of the film, with the frenetic pacing working in perfect harmony with the various plot developments. The most amusing sequence, undoubtedly, shows Peppino being forced into performing on stage, even though he can't sing; his con man partner tries to get around this by having him lip-synch to a recording, with predictably disastrous results. It may not be revolutionary in its concept, but in execution these farcical set pieces cannot be faulted.

*Uno strano tipo* is not a typical *musicarello*, but it has elements in common with that genre. The presence of Celentano and the use of popular songs is certainly indicative of the trend, but the music is never prioritized as much in this context as it had been in *I ragazzi del jukebox* or *Urlatori all sbarra*. The film also steers clear of the generational conflict subtext that had been so important in those earlier films. It's conceivable that the absence of Piero Vivarelli in the screenwriting department may have influenced the different tone and style this particular picture took. Vivarelli, after all, had a more significant background in the music industry than Fulci ever did. Even so, Fulci and his co-writer Vittorio Metz manage to come up with something a little different, thus ensuring that *Uno strano tipo* stands out from the rest of the pack. The subgenre would continue to proliferate throughout the '60s, but the upheaval of social unrest signaled by the student riots of 1968 would more or less kill off the genre; suddenly, fluffy, superficial films such as this were no longer appealing to their target audience and tougher, more politically committed pictures would take their place. This would be Fulci's last brush with this sort of material. He would spend the bulk of the decade putting Franco and Ciccio through their paces, while gradually working his way towards fresh pastures which would open his work up to a broader, more international audience.

Notes:
1. Audio interview with Lucio Fulci, conducted by Pier Maria Bocchi and Andrea Bruni, included on the Shriek Show DVD release of *Touch of Death*.

**Italian poster for _Uno strano tipo_; artist unknown.**

## *Gli imbroglioni (Italy/Spain)*

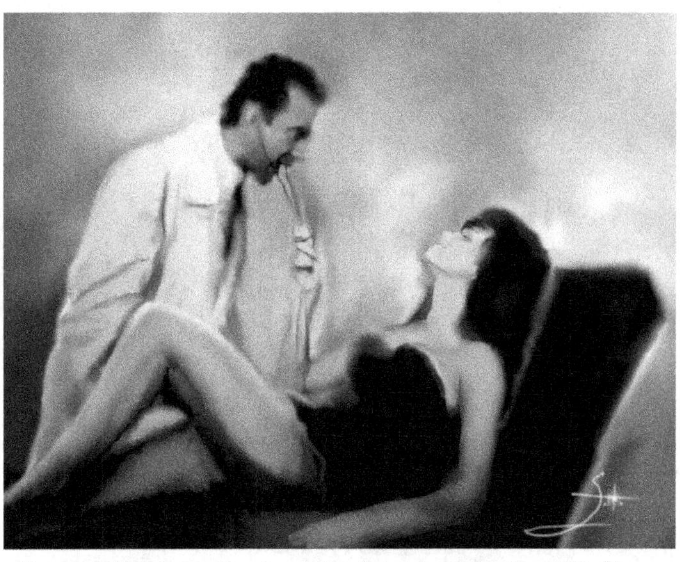

**Above: *Gli imbroglioni*; original artwork by Scott Hoffman. Below: Italian poster for *Gli imbroglioni.***

Aka *The Swindlers* (unofficial English-language translation); *Los Mangantes*

Directed by Lucio Fulci; Produced by Sergio Iacobis and Dario Sabatello, for Produzioni D.S., Tecisa and Titanus; Screenplay by Franco Castellano [as Castellano] (segment: Medico e fidanzata), Lucio Fulci, Mario Guerra, Giuseppe Moccia [as Pipolo] (segment: Medico e fidanzata) and Vittorio Vighi, from an idea by Franco Castellano [as Castellano] and Giuseppe Moccia [as Pipolo]; Director of Photography: Alfio Contini and Tino Santoni; Editor: Gisa Radicchi Levi; Music by Carlo Rustichelli; Songs: *La ballata degli imbroglioni*, composed by Giorgio Gaber and Umberto Simonetta; *Roma nun fa' la stupida stasera* and *Ciumachella de Transtevere*, composed by Pietro Garinei (as Garinei), Armando Trovajoli and Riccardo Giovannini (as Giovannini); *Gokart twist*, composed by Ennio Morricone and Pilantra

Main Players: Franco Franchi (Salvatore Di Carmine/Rizzo/Sposito); Ciccio Ingrassia (Napoleone Palumbo/Nostradomine/Roccanera); Walter Chiari (Doctor Corti); Antonella Lualdi (Sister Celestina); José Luiz López Vázquez (Judge); Raimondo Vianello (Tabanelli); Dominique Boschero (Mrs. Taverna); Aroldo Tieri (Taverna); Luciana Gilli (Liliana Ferri); Elio Crovetto (Gustav Schultz); Claudio Gora (Spianelli); Camillo Mastrocinque (Spianelli's Lawyer); Umberto D'Orsi (Lucarini); Margaret Lee (Adelina)

*A judge presides over six cases. In the first, a pair of Sicilians are brought up on charges of swindling an antiquarian; in the second, Taverna, the chairman of a football club, attempts to bribe Tabanelli; in the third, Sister Celestine is brought up on charges of indecency for embroidering ladies underwear for a local shop; in the fourth, Lucarini brings charges against the two Sicilians for disrupting a rally; in the fifth, Doctor Corti is accused of improper behavior by his estranged girlfriend, Liliana and in the sixth, the two Sicilians are accused of trying to fraud a German tourist and his daughter by staging a fake archeological dig…*

If the set-up for *Gli imbroglioni* sounds familiar, it should: It is basically a retread of Steno's *Un giorno in pretura*, right down to the presence of Walter Chiari in the cast. The earlier film had been very successful and Fulci was surely looking to replicate that success when he helped to devise the scenario for this film. It isn't quite on the same tier, but it is very amusing in its own right.

Like so many anthologies, this one is hindered by the uneven quality of the stories. One can't help but feel that Fulci and company would have done better cutting the stories down to only three, instead of indulging in several rather minor and forgettable skits, with the really "meaty" stories strewn throughout. The segments involving the underwear-embroidering nun and the shifty football club captain are more or less disposable. They aren't particularly funny and they aren't given enough screen-time to develop into anything more than frivolous bits of trimming. Fortunately, the other segments are much more successful in both concept and execution.

Franco and Ciccio become the *de facto* leads by virtue of their presence in three out of the six segments. The joke is that they have several different names owing to the fact that their grandfather was a bigamist. In their first segment, they attempt to outwit an antique dealer: Ciccio pretends to be an eccentric Count looking for a particular piece of antique furniture, while Franco pretends to be a vagabond who just happens to have said piece of furniture for sale. It's a slight segment—more of a sketch, really—but it allows the boys to expand on their con man routine from *I due della legione* and offers up a few chuckles. Their second segment, in which they disrupt a rally, is far and away their most trivial contribution to the film but it, too, has its share of lowbrow laughs. The most successful of their segments involves their plan to rip off a German tourist by staging a fake Etruscan tomb, complete with a mummy—and since nobody else is in a hurry to volunteer for the gig, it's Franco who gets covered in the bandages. All hell breaks loose when Franco pretends to return to life. It's a genuinely of Franco and Ciccio. The two men also tried their hand at directing, racking up about two-dozen credits between 1964 and 1993. Their contribution to *Gli imbroglioni* results in the film's most substantial and thought provoking segment. Chiari is in excellent form as the doctor who may or may not be chronically unfaithful to his adoring fiancée. Fulci directs the segment with quiet authority, milking laughs from the material without going too far over-the-top. Chiari's subtle performance stands in contrast to the antics of Franco and Ciccio, and the segment is all the more effective because of it. As the two sides go back and forth telling their own version of the truth, it becomes clear that both sides are doing everything they can in order to make the other look as bad as possible. As usual in these matters, the truth lies somewhere in the middle. Fulci's cynical outlook is in perfect harmony with this rather bitter portrait of Italian machismo gone awry and the segment provides the film with some real substance to go along with the jokes. In terms of laughs, the sequence of Chiari attending the funeral of his girlfriend's favorite aunt is hard to beat: The football-obsessed doctor smuggles a transistor and listens to the game via headphones; he becomes so worked up over the game that he begins shouting out.

**Enlarged detail from the *fotobusta* for *Gli imbroglioni*: Ciccio tries to swindle some tourists while Franco pretends to be a reanimated mummy.**

funny segment, visually sure-footed and featuring Franco and Ciccio at their most inspired. Perhaps distilling their routine to smaller doses was the key to bringing out their best qualities, but in any event their contributions to the film become perhaps the most genuinely amusing of their screen career. For Fulci, the bit with the fake mummy proved prophetic: He would later attain notoriety with his depictions of the living dead on screen, albeit in a much more serious key.

However, Fulci did not write the cleverest segment. "Medico e fidanzata" is a *Rashomon*-style examination of the truth, featuring Chiari as a doctor who may or may not be a pillar of society. The segment was devised and written by the acclaimed screenwriting team of Franco Castellano and Giuseppe Moccia, known best simply as Castellano and Pipolo. Castellano (1925-1999) and Moccia (1933-2006) met when they were employed on the satirical newspaper *Marc'Aurelio*, which was also famous for launching such talents as Federico Fellini. The two men hit it off and began collaborating on screenplays in 1958; among their many credits were two further collaborations with Fulci: *The Maniacs* and *I due pericoli pubblici*. They also had a hand in writing Luciano Salce's *The Fascist* (1961), Dino Risi's *Thursday* (1964) and the all-star anthology *Viva Italia!* (1977), directed by Mario Monicelli, Dino Risi and Ettore Scola; they also contributed to Mario Bava's unfortunate misfire *Le spie vengono dal semi-freddo* (1966), which saw the great filmmaker floundering amid the slapstick

**The beautiful Dominique Boschero models some outlandish fashions in *Gli imbroglioni*.**

*Gli imbroglioni* is also notable as the film debut of the distinguished production designer Dante Feretti. Feretti (born in Rome in 1943) worked as a set decorator on this film, but within the next few years he would climb the ranks to art director and production designer. His impeccable eye would enrich such films as Pier Paolo Pasolini's *The Canterbury Tales* (1972) and *Salò, or the 120 Days of Sodom* (1975), Elio Petri's *Todo Modo* (1975), Federico Fellini's *Orchestra Rehearsal* (1978) and *City of Women* (1980) and Terry Gilliam's *The Adventures of Baron Munchausen* (1988). In recent years he has become the production designer of choice for director Martin Scorsese, for whom he designed *The Age of Innocence* (1993), *Casino* (1995), *Gangs of New York* (2002) and *Hugo* (2011), among others; he won his third Oscar for *Hugo*, having already taken home statuettes for his work on Scorsese's *The Aviator* (2004) and Tim Burton's *Sweeney Todd: The Demon Barber of Fleet Street* (2007).

*Gli imbroglioni* underwent some difficulties with the Italian censors, as recounted in the book *Visioni proibite: I film vietati della censura italiana (1947-1968)*:

Submitted to the censors on August 7, 1963, Fulci's film is reviewed and rejected the next day: For the Commission "it contains numerous scenes contrary to morality [..] especially in the episode containing the unseemly parody of the funerary religious ceremony and the litany of the dead, by deformation of the words that compose it, replaced by others of a different kind." [...] In addition, in the same episode, the Commission noted, "other sequences are clearly indecent, such as the highlighting of the effect of admiration expressed by Walter Chiari to the passage of provocative female beauties with the dizzying elevation of his portable radio as well as the actor's obscene gesture during that funeral."[1]

Fulci decided to revisit the anthology format with his next picture and of course, Franco and Ciccio were destined to get back in on the act, as well.

Notes:
1. Curti, Roberto and Alessio Di Rocco, *Visioni proibite: I film vietati della censura italiana (1947-1968)*, (Turin: Lindau, 2014), p. 441.

# 1964

## *The Maniacs* (Italy/Spain)

Aka *I maniaci*

Directed by Lucio Fulci; Produced by Ferruccio Brusarosco, for Hesperia Films S.A., Tecisa and Produzioni Associate; Screenplay by Franco Castellano (as Castellano), Giuseppe Moccia, Lucio Fulci and José Gutiérrez Maesso, from a story by Franco Castellano (as Castellano), Giuseppe Moccia, Vittorio Viechi and Tonino Guerra; Director of Photography: Alfio Contini and Riccardo Pallottini; Editor: Ornella Micheli (as Ornella Micheli Donati); Music by Ennio Morricone and Carlo Rustichelli; Songs: *La mia mania*, performed by Gianni Morandi; *Ma neanche per idea*, performed by Michele; *Sono un ragazzo*, performed by Roby Ferrante; *Stelle e sogni*, performed by Barbara Baldassare; *Eravamo amici*, performed by Dino; *Cosa rimane alla fine di un amore*, performed by Nico Fidenco; *Pel di carota*, performed by Rita Pavone; *Mezzanotte*, performed by Mario Rigual and Pedro Rigual; *Ogni volta*, performed by Paul Anka

Main Players: Walter Chiari (Sicilian Hitchhiker/Driver/Pasquale Taddei/Nightclub client); Enrico Maria Salerno (Castelli); Barbara Steele (Barbara/Brugnoli's Wife); Franco Franchi (Thief #1); Ciccio Ingrassia (Thief #2); Raimondo Vianello (Mr. Brugoli/Giulio Errani/Paolo/Milcozzi); Franco Fabrizi (Stipa); Umberto D'Orsi (Ilario Baietti/Friar Egisto/Milanese Businessman); Gaia Germani (Carla); Franca Valeri (The Wife); Vittorio Caprioli (The Husband); Corrado Olmi (The Husband); Aroldo Tieri (Bonfanti); Margaret Lee (Rosalie); Alicia Brandet (The Maid)

*The film features a series of comedic sketches highlighting the absurdity of Italian life, ranging from a devout football fan who puts his wife's honor on the line for the sake of a bet, a writer looking to find a wider audience who decides to embrace lewd subject matter and a couple of thieves who find themselves stuck in the middle of an elaborate game of bed-hopping when the house they break into turns out to be busier than they had anticipated...*

*The Maniacs* continues the anthology structure of *Gli imbroglioni*. Unlike that film, however, this one does not attempt to aim for any kind of a linking device. It is a series of sketches, many of them of the madcap variety. Happily, many of the segments are legitimately amusing.

In essence the film goes from one brief skit to a lengthier, more substantial segment. The general aim is to highlight the absurdities of Italian life, as evidenced in the machismo of the culture in particular. Fulci and his co-writers do not pull any punches and their targets include everything from the obsession with sports to the so-called highbrow pillars of Italian culture. The end result does not aim for any kind of narrative cohesion; indeed, it can be seen as sort of a cinematic forerunner to popular American sketch comedy shows as *Rowan & Martin's Laugh-In* (1967-1973), which adopted a similarly irreverent attitude in a sketch comedy format. In this respect, however, the film's most likely influence was Dino Risi's popular anthology *I mostri* (1963), which was similarly madcap in its approach.

**Barbara Steele, the so-called Queen of Italian Horror, makes an appearance in *The Maniacs*; original artwork by Scott Hoffman.**

The opening segment, "L'elaborazione," is a cute diversion which shows a driver getting his car fitted out with all the fancy trimmings and being rigged for top speed at a garage; as he pulls away, it is revealed that the

**Italian *locandina* for *The Maniacs*; artist unknown.**

car in question is a hearse. There isn't much meat to this segment—but as an appetizer it's amusing, albeit predictable.

Up next is "Lo sport," which features Raimondo Vianello in a marvelous comedic performance as Giulio Errani, a petty despot in his work environment who abuses his underlings daily. Errani claims to have no interest in anything other than his work, but in truth he is a rabid fan of Italian football. While arguing with a fellow fan at a game, he promises to "pimp out" his wife if his favorite player does not make a goal. The player fails to come through and he decides to go through with the bet to save his honor; unfortunately for him, one of his underlings, Stipa, is out cruising for action at this same time. The segment highlights Errani's hypocrisy, showing him to be a tyrant and a sexist who would sooner put his wife in danger than sacrifice face when it comes to his number one passion, football. Vianello's expert performance helps to make this one of the film's most genuinely amusing segments; perhaps unsurprisingly, he was also a fan of the game in real life and even conducted the football-related TV talk-show *Pressing* between 1991 and 1999.

"Il sorpasso" casts Walter Chiari as a hothead who takes offense when another vehicle attempts to surpass him on the highway. Chiari successfully conveys the man's fragile ego as he goes from pretending to not care if he is overtaken to succumbing to blind fury as the other vehicle speeds by; the punch line is that Chiari failed to realize that the lights creeping up behind him were from a plane taking off from a local airport.

"L'hobby" deals with an "open marriage" scenario. Barbara is accustomed to sharing her husband with Carla, but when it looks like the husband is two-timing them both, all bets are off. They follow the man to one of his assignations and are surprised by their discovery: The husband, tired of dealing with the drama of trying to please two women, has joined an amateur football team. The segment is slight and not terribly funny, but it does provide a rare opportunity to see horror icon Barbara Steele trying her hand at light comedy. Steele acquits herself reasonably well, but Fulci was not impressed; when asked about working with the actress, he bellowed, "A terrible actress! *Mamma mia*! An incredibly bad actress!"[1] Steele, for her part, reportedly has no memory of working with Fulci.

"I consigli" continues the theme of fractured marriages, with a bickering couple out for a drive. The wife needles the husband incessantly, leading to a car crash, which claims their lives. Not exactly the cheeriest set-up for a comedy sketch, perhaps, but there is humor to be found in the interplay between real-life husband-and-wife team Raimondo Vianello and Sandra Mondaini.

"La protesta" casts Chiari and Aroldo Tieri as friends who spend their time bemoaning the state of Italian politics, be it in wartime, under the reign of Mussolini or as they age into old men. No matter how much they complain, however, they always end up toeing the party line. The two actors do a splendid job of bringing these two professional crepehangers to life and the bit with them being summoned to appear before *Il Duce* is memorably irreverent.

"Il pezzo antico" is a slight and more or less disposable segment, in which Franca Valeri and Vittorio Caprioli play a married couple who go around looking to rip off unsuspecting people who own priceless antiques. Their hobby knows no bounds, so when a kindly Friar takes them in, they even set out to take advantage of him. The Friar will inevitably have the last laugh. Umberto D'Orsi, looking remarkably like Victor Buono (*What Ever Happened to Baby Jane?*, 1962), is wryly amusing as the Friar; he had already appeared in *Gli imbroglioni* and would go on to work with Fulci again, notably on *Beatrice Cenci* (1969).

Fulci was proud of the next segment, "La parolaccia," and it is easy to see why. The segment allows Fulci to poke fun at the hypocrisy of the intelligentsia, which looks down on so-called "popular" culture while venerating works that are frequently more sensationalistic in nature, even if they hide behind a veneer of respectability. The character of the successful writer, Castelli, is particularly interesting. He is arrogant, conceited and completely lost in his own world. When the naive but well-meaning Baietti comes to seek his advice on his latest manuscript, he is ill-prepared for his colleague's response; Baietti is attempting to write a heart-felt story with depth and feeling, but Castelli advises him to throw out the good intentions and play down to the public's love for sex. Only by doing this, he says, will artists be able to change society for the better. Baietti takes him at his word and is shocked when Castelli subsequently attacks his work as "pornography" in public. From the gag of Castelli's dog being named Pier Paolo to the notion of the "artistic" author trading on sensationalism for its own sake, it is clear that Fulci is looking to point out the hypocrisy that exists in criticism and the arts. The director would later recall:

> There was a wonderful sketch with Enrico Maria Salerno and Umberto D'Orsi about swear words. The movie wasn't bad, but it was badly distributed. There were a series of sketches, but the most important was "La parolaccia," in which D'Orsi played a failed novelist who visits his friend, who is successful, like Pasolini, thanks to the bad language. The novelist explains that he is writing a story about partisans and the friend says, "What partisans! You must write about ass, pussy, etc." So he puts these bad words in the story but the censors tear the book apart. The title of his book was *The Mountain Said No*, a very Victorian title, but for the money he changes it to *The Mountains Said Screw You*.[2]

The segment also benefits from the expert performances by Salerno and D'Orsi: The former verges on caricature but makes Castelli into a properly despicable presence, while the latter lends sincerity to his portrayal of an idealistic author who decides to sell out and loses his self-respect in the process.

"Lo strip" is another one-joke concept, in which Chiari plays a twitchy pervert who goes from one strip club to another before returning home and applying what he has learned by putting on a striptease himself. Fulci pushes things as far as bare skin is concerned; there's no actual nudity, but the various erotic routines go about as far as the censorship would allow. The problem with the segment is, it's just not very funny.

"Le interviste" plays on the pat terminology of politicians, as a political spokesman gives the same canned response over and over again as one scandal after another breaks out. As political humor goes, this is pretty facile stuff; Fulci would address the hypocrisy of the system far more successfully in his later film, *The Eroticist*.

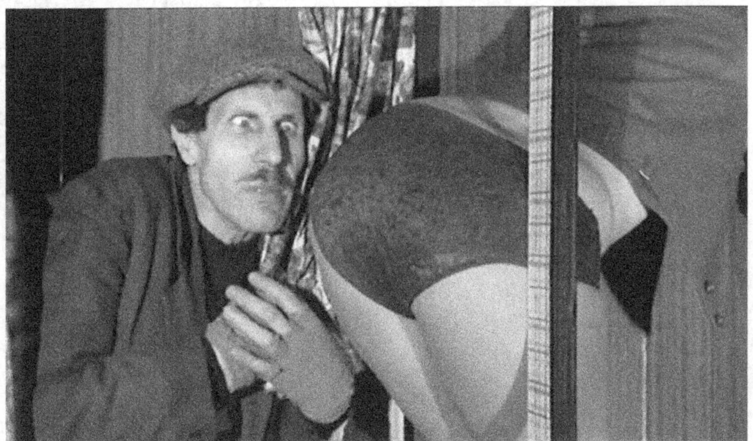

**Ciccio gets an eyeful in *The Maniacs*.**

"L'autostop" is much better. In it, D'Orsi plays a driver who picks up a vagrant played by Chiari. The two men exchange only a few words openly, with much of the segment's dialogue conveyed through voice-overs. D'Orsi seems well intended in his desire to help a less fortunate man, but he ultimately reveals himself to be superficial and condescending. The vagrant, on the other hand, is unable to get past his own ignorant stereotypical thinking and begins to panic that the other man is a homosexual looking to take advantage of him. The segment concludes when both men panic and run from the car, which continues on its journey unattended.

"La cambiale" presents two socially conscious couples who are looking to out-do each other at every turn. Fulci and his writers side with the henpecked husbands, who are compelled to start filling out IOUs in order to satisfy their wives' extravagant whims. Apart from addressing the social reality of people getting in way over their heads

in debt in order to attain a more desirable lifestyle, the segment doesn't contribute much to the overall picture and the jokes are weak.

Lastly, "Il week-end" presents Franco and Ciccio as bungling—what else—burglars who get more than they bargained for when they break into a house they believed was going to be empty. The maid is having a romantic tryst with a soldier and the husband returns early with his mistress, hoping for a little extra-marital fun. Ciccio is wryly amusing as he tries to maintain his dignity, but Franco mugs like usual; Margaret Lee and Alicia Brandet help to amp up the erotic angle, both actresses coming as close to actual nudity as possible, but the game of revolving bedroom doors is a bit tired, causing the film to limp to a rather tired close.

If only all the segments had been on the same tier as "Lo sport," "La parolaccia" and "L'autostop," *The Maniacs* would emerge as a classic of its kind. As it stands, it's an uneven but charming exercise. Fulci's flair for bringing manic energy to comic scenarios is evident throughout and the excellent cast helps to give the film some real credibility.

Once again, Fulci found himself in conflict with the censors due to some of the more suggestive material, but only one cut was finally insisted upon before the film was given a restricted rating for Italian audiences: A shot of the book cover featuring the obscene title alluded to by Fulci in the interview quoted above was censored, having been deemed inappropriate for viewers.[3]

Notes:

1. Audio interview with Lucio Fulci, conducted by Pier Maria Bocchi and Andrea Bruni, included on the Shriek Show DVD release of *Touch of Death.*
2. *Ibid.*
3. http://www.italiataglia.it/home

# Giannetto De Rossi Interview by Troy Howarth

The following interview with make-up effects artist Giannetto De Rossi was conducted by email from December 4, 2014 to December 9, 2014. *Maestro* De Rossi is best known among horror afficianados for his gore effects in later Fulci fare like *Zombie* and *The Beyond*, but they first worked together on *The Maniacs*. He has my thanks for taking the time to discuss his remarkable film career with us.

**Troy Howarth**: Where did your interest in make-up and special effects start?

**Giannetto De Rossi**: My interest in make-up started with my birth. Both my father Alberto and grandfather Camillo were make-up artists. My family has been in show business for over a 100 years. We're probably the oldest family in world cinema. My interest in trick effects started during the shooting of *Doctor Faustus*, a film with Elizabeth Taylor and Richard Burton. I had to render the characterizations of the Hellish figures. I took inspiration from the painter Bosch and it was exhilarating. Since then I pursue work that stimulates me to improve my capabilities!

**TH:** You first worked with Lucio Fulci very early on in your career in the comedy *The Maniacs* ... what do you recall of working on that film? What was your first impression of Lucio as a director and as a person?

**GD**: Yes, my first time working with Fulci was on *The Maniacs*. It was a comic anthology with various popular actors of the period. At that time, Fulci was already an excellent director and scriptwriter (as a writer he also penned *Un Americano a Roma* with Alberto Sordi, a great Italian actor). Lucio was well prepared as a director and a very cultured man, sensitive and with a great sense of humor. He didn't bother with "life's frivolities" and, in fact, he was not very mindful of fashion or his own image. After that film we lost sight of one another, but I believe that we both had mutual respect.

**TH:** Not long after that you worked on *Once Upon a Time in the West* for Sergio Leone ... what was Leone like to work with? Charles Bronson was in that film and also in *The Valachi Papers*, which you also worked on ... do you have any memories of him?

**GD**: Leone was a very great director with the fantasy and purity of a child. This can be seen from observing the way he "dresses" and "presents" his characters. One only needs to recall Charles Bronson's appearance in the film. He is sitting on a bench in the saloon playing the harmonica and, when the light of an oil lamp illuminates him, he appears to us as if in a dream. I worked with Bronson three times, but he was a man of few words, grumpy, introverted but actually very shy. I only spoke to him a couple of times but I believe we liked each other a lot.

**TH**: Your next film with Fulci was another comedy, *The Eroticist*. You had to work extensively with Lando Buzzanca on that film to make him look like the politician Colombo ... was this Fulci's direction to you? *The Eroticist* got into some trouble with the Italian censors, also due to its political content; did you have a feeling it would be a controversial movie?

**GD**: On that film, Fulci asked me to make up Buzzanca to resemble [Italian] minister Colombo. I must say the make-up worked very well and, yes, there were minor censorship problems and a political uproar. The budget was adequate and the faith Lucio had in my regard was so great that he allowed me to visualize and render the art direction of the dream sequence. Just think that I created the sculpture of a tree trunk made from naked women embracing. I had a lot of fun.

**TH**: You worked with Jorge Grau on the zombie movie *Let Sleeping Corpses Lie* ... do you have any memories of working with Grau? Did Grau have a specific idea of what he wanted the zombies to look like, or were they designed on your own?

**American lobby card for Sergio Leone's *Once Upon a Time in the West* (1968).**

**Candid shot of Giannetto De Rossi and his wife Marina; courtesy of Mike Baronas.**

GD: I remember Grau as a very sweet man with a grand personality. The look of the zombies was my idea, likewise with the make-up effects. Usually the directors, bless them, had faith in my capabilities.

TH: You next did an epic film for Bernardo Bertolucci, *1900*. What are some of the challenges of doing a big film like that compared to working on small films? What is Bertolucci like to work with? Donald Sutherland was in *1900* and you would work with him again on Fellini's *Casanova* ... do you have any memories of working with him?

GD: *1900* is one of the films I recall with the greatest fondness. For me big and low-budgeted films were the same because I've worked often on major and small films. The most important thing for me was that my brain would be stimulated. Bertolucci is, for me, one of Italy's greatest-ever directors. I've never worked with anyone who "moved" the camera the way he did. In *1900* I created an infinity of diverse make-ups, aging, characterizations and some very difficult make-up effects, which thanks to the extraordinary lighting of my friend Vittorio Storaro, have made "history." At first my relationship with Donald Sutherland was tense because he wanted to have his bald cap and wig made in the U.S. I proposed to him that he sit for two make-up tests, one with the American stuff and another with the things I had prepared. I did the first test using the latter and in the end Donald apologized for having doubted me, and we put aside the American stuff and became friends.

TH: Tell us a bit about working with Fellini ... how hands-on was he with regards to the "look" of Casanova?

GD: For Donald's look in *Casanova*, Fellini made me a sketch. One of the prerogatives Fellini had was that of exasperating the aesthetic "defects" of the actors. Being aware of this, I interpreted his design and, after a false nose and chin, a bald cap and a pair of eyebrows attached to the middle of his forehead, I devised Casanova's make-up. Let me tell you an amusing anecdote. I love coming to work an hour prior to the start of applying make-up because I need time to "prepare" myself. The trouble was that Donald did the same thing. So I began to anticipate my arrival by half-an-hour, then an hour, but so did Donald so we decided to come to Cinecittà—and play chess for two hours before turning to make-up. The sad thing was that Donald almost always won.

TH: Next came your most iconic collaboration with Lucio Fulci, *Zombie*. Do you recall how you came to be involved with the film? This in turn led to your collaborating on *The Beyond* and *The House by the Cemetery* ... Did you and Fulci become closer during this time?

GD: I think that on *Zombie* I was called up by the producers but, obviously, following Fulci's approval. The most important thing in the film was finding the look of the zombies. The producers wanted to recycle the make-up of the Romero film that had come out in theaters the previous year. Lucio, who was going through a lean period in his professional career, had agreed ... but I did not. I thought that for our film it was vital to have shocking make-up effects and some terrifying zombies. I did a make-up test of a zombie and the producers weren't all that convinced, but Lucio was ... and the film was a success, thanks also to my zombies. The most gratifying make-up effect for me was undoubtedly the Karlatos eye perforation. Rather than friendship, great affection and respect existed between Lucio and me. Working in the cinema makes it very hard to nurture friendships because it entails absurd working hours and often takes you abroad (at least that was what happened to me). Lucio had a great sense of humor and we always had a lot of laughs. Of course, I was also witness to his "outbursts" which were never deliberate. In truth Lucio loathed superficiality and laziness.

**TH**: I love the make-up design for Dr. Freudstein in *The House by the Cemetery* ... was that a mask or was it done with appliances? Do you have any favorite memories of working on *The Beyond* or *The House by the Cemetery*? Did you design the contact lenses worn by David Warbeck, Catriona MacColl and Cinzia Monreale in *The Beyond* or was that done by one of your associates? If so, do you remember who designed them?

**GD**: I honestly don't recall the make-up for Dr. Freudstein because I didn't do it. Maybe I gave a few suggestions but nothing more. Of *The Beyond* I remember very well the scene with the "nail" also because I was the one holding the fake head. The funniest episode was when the nail came out of the head dragging the eye, blood and various liquids with it, the joints of the blood containers gave out and I, who was sitting underneath the head, got splashed all over with an outburst of blood. The design of the lenses was mine. Even the choice of colors and the painting I did myself by hand.

**Donald Sutherland, made up to by Giannetto De Rossi to look properly grotesque, in Fellini's *Casanova*.**

**TH**: Speaking of trusted associates, you have often worked with your wife Mirella ... was she present on the set of many of your films with Fulci?

**GD**: My wife and inspirational muse, Mirella, has worked with me on virtually all the films I made with Fulci. Mirella had a lovely rapport with Lucio. Both having a strong sense of humor (I'm more "boorish"), Lucio, when he had something funny to say, went directly to my wife ... and they had a lot of laughs.

**TH**: You stopped working with Fulci after *The House by the Cemetery*; why was that? Did you keep in touch with Fulci in his later years? Did he ever confide in you about his many illnesses and problems that he had in his final years?

**GD**: Why didn't I work with Fulci anymore? Well, there's no reason. Unfortunately, when he offered me a film I had already signed up for some other project. I have to confess, however, that every time I had to turn him down I was truly sorry. As I've already told you, the cinema is a stupendous job that gives you a lot, but it does take away some things. In fact I had no more contact with Lucio even though I was aware of his troubles and illnesses.

**TH**: You worked on *The Man in the Iron Mask* with Leonardo Di Caprio, Jeremy Irons and John Malkovich ... did you enjoy working on that film and do you have any memories of the cast?

**GD**: Recollections of the cast of *The Man in the Iron Mask*? Well, that's easy. Leonardo, a youngster with a great talent, Jeremy, an impeccable professional, John, very reserved, Gerard, a crazy ham but with a great instinctive talent, Gabriel, a great actor and an exceptional human being. And on top of everything ... my Iron Mask. It was really beautiful.

**TH**: How about working with Alexandre Aja on *Haute Tension*, for which you provided some memorable splatter effects?

**GD**: I'm very happy to have worked with Alexandre Aja. I love working with enthusiastic and passionate youngsters. In *Haute Tension* I believe I contributed considerably to the film's success. Alexandre was happy and I was even more so, because working with young people keeps me young, as well.

**TH:** *Maestro* De Rossi—thank you for your time!

**GD**: I'd like to end this interview by telling you that for me it was an honor working with Lucio and I'm very happy he has never been forgotten—he deserves this tribute. Hugs. *Ciao.*

***I due evasi di Sing Sing*; original artwork by Scott Hoffman.**

## *I due evasi di Sing Sing (Italy)*

Aka *Two Escape from Sing-Sing* (unofficial English-language translation); *Das Großmaul*

Directed by Lucio Fulci; Produced by Mega Film and Turris Film; Screenplay by Mario Ciorciolini and Lucio Fulci, from a story by Mario Ciorciolini; Director of Photography: Bitto Albertini (as Adalberto Albertini); Editor: Ornella Micheli; Music by Ennio Morricone (as Ennio Moriconi)

Main Players: Franco Franchi (Franco); Ciccio Ingrassia (Ciccio); Arturo Dominici (Attanasia); Gloria Paul (Molly); Livio Lorenzon (Tristan)

*Franco and Ciccio inadvertently prevent a hit on mob boss Attanasia. The violent Attanasia rewards the duo by welcoming them into his circle. He promotes Franco as a boxer, putting him into rigged matches to protect him; when Franco's ineptitude becomes too much to bear, Attanasia sees to it that Franco will not survive his next match. The plan backfires and Attanasia finds himself in the middle of a gang war, for which Franco and Ciccio will take the blame; they are then imprisoned in Sing Sing and sentenced to death in the gas chamber …*

Fulci's next film with the Sicilian comedy team would prove to be one of his most popular films among Italian viewers; he would later refer to it as "Ciccio and Franco's greatest success"[1] in an interview. It's difficult to figure out what made certain Franco and Ciccio films more popular than others, but it is possible that the film's light-hearted approach to poking fun at the Mafia may have endeared it to local audiences. In any event, it does not seem to be one of Fulci's more effective comedies, even if it packed in audiences at the time of its release.

Franco and Ciccio are cast in their usual hapless idiot roles. They aren't really con men this time, thus inviting more overt audience sympathy, but they never really stray far from their usual screen persona. Ciccio is the brains of the team—if such a term can be applied in this context—whereas Franco sputters and mugs while playing the fool. This time the action is set in America, with the two comedians cast as immigrants looking for their piece of the American dream. Like so many immigrants, they do not find things to be as easy or welcoming as they had imagined. There is the kernel of a serious theme in this idea, but Fulci and his collaborators do not make much out of it. The goal is principally to allow Franco and Ciccio to cut loose and do their usual shtick, so anything of more weight or substance is bound to get the short shrift by comparison. Even so, without wanting to read too much into what is ultimately a bit of baggy pants farce, the theme of wide-eyed immigrants being disappointed by the harsh realities of American life gives the film an added subtext that is interesting.

Fulci and co-writer Mario Ciorciolini (the man who devised the story in the first place) depict America as a place of violence, turmoil and corruption. Attanasia has built an empire on the ruins of slaughtered opponents and he ensures his own safety by bribery and murder. One amusing sequence has him watching television: Upon seeing a politician claiming that he is going to crack down on organized crime, he makes a phone call and the man is summarily shot to death on the air; this gag is all the more daring given the fact that President John F. Kennedy had been assassinated a year before, and his death was also broadcast on live television. Whether Fulci and Ciorciolini were looking to reference that tragic event or not is open to speculation, but they were certainly aware of what had happened and were at the very least unconcerned with upsetting viewers by alluding to it in such a fashion. Of course, truth be told, they were also well aware that the film's chances of securing a release in English-speaking territories was slim to nil, anyway; Franco and Ciccio were very much an Italian phenomenon and it would be a while before Fulci would make a film which would secure that kind of distribution.

One would assume from the title that much of the action was set in the prison, but in fact only the opening and end sequences are set in Sing Sing. Located on the east bank of the Hudson River in New York, Sing Sing Correctional Facility opened in 1826 and would become one of the more notorious prisons in the United States. Julius and Ethel Rosenberg, accused of selling sensitive information to the Soviets, were executed in the electric chair at Sing Sing in 1953, though their method of execution was ultimately discontinued on the grounds of being inhumane. Indeed, Franco and Ciccio believe that they will be electrocuted and try to save themselves by causing a short circuit, not realizing that the gas chamber was, by then, the preferred method of capital punishment. The would-be execution scene is actually one of the few genuinely amusing scenes in the picture: The two men cling to their cells

**Italian *locandina* for *I due evasi di Sing Sing*; artist unknown.**

and refuse to come out, then they feign bravery when they believe that they have outwitted the warden and his staff. This kind of morbid comedy is definitely up Fulci's alley, so it's hardly surprising that sequences such as this work especially well in context.

The film also benefits from the presence of the reliable character actor Arturo Dominici. Dominici is properly intimidating as the short-tempered Attanasia. While there is never any doubt that Franco and Ciccio will ultimately best him, he makes for a fierce antagonist and plays the role deadly seriously. Dominici (1918-1992) enjoyed an eclectic career on screen, working for such directors as Antonio Margheriti (*Castle of Blood*, 1964), Damiano Damiani (*Confessions of a Police Captain*, 1971) and Elio Petri (*Investigation of a Citizen Above Suspicion*, 1970). He is best remembered, however, for his iconic appearance as the vampire Javutich in Mario Bava's *Black Sunday* (1960).

*I due evasi di Sing Sing* is enjoyable enough for what it is, but it lacks the bite and edge of Fulci's best comedies. It is not even the most memorable of his vehicles for Franco and Ciccio, though it definitely has some amusing sequences and moves at an energetic pace.

Notes:
1. Audio interview with Lucio Fulci, conducted by Pier Maria Bocchi and Andrea Bruni, included on the Shriek Show DVD release of *Touch of Death*.

## *Oh! Those Most Secret Agents (Italy)*

Aka *002 agenti segretissimi*; *Wir, die Trottel vom Geheimdienst*; *Worst Secret Agents*

Directed by Lucio Fulci; Produced by Antonio Colantuoni, for Mega Film; Screenplay by Lucio Fulci (as L. Fulci), Vittorio Metz (as V. Metz) and Amedeo Sollazzo (uncredited), from a story by Vittorio Metz; Director of Photography: Bitto Albertini (as Adalberto Albertini); Editor: Ornella Micheli; Music by Piero Umiliani; Song: *Cerco un ragazzo per un giorno d'estate*, written by Lucio Fulci (as Fulci) and Piero Umiliani (as Umiliani) and performed by Gisella Ferrini

Main Players: Franco Franchi (Franco); Ciccio Ingrassia (Ciccio); Ingrid Schoeller (Wife); Carla Calò (Russian

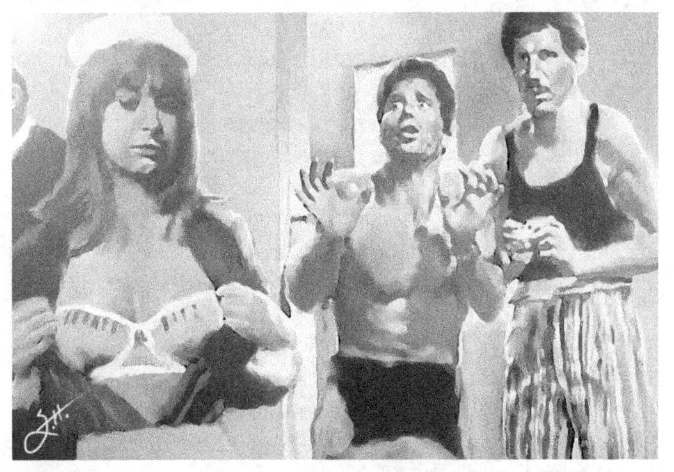

**_Oh! Those Most Secret Agents_; original artwork by Scott Hoffman.**

**American poster for *Oh! Those Most Secret Agents!*; artist unknown.**

Agent); Aroldo Tieri (Husband); Annie Gorassini (Maid); Mary Arden (Russian Spy)

*Franco and Ciccio are petty thieves who get lured into serving as spies. Unbeknown to them, while drugged, a microfilm containing sensitive information has been hidden in one of Franco's many cavities. The two hapless would-be spies are then sent off, ignorant to what has happened to them, as dueling world powers target them and attempt to retrieve the microfilm…*

The international success of Terence Young's *Dr. No* (1962) unleashed a craze for spy thrillers. The James Bond films started on a serious note, but as the decade wore on they would become more and more gimmicky; audiences really responded to this, making films like *Goldfinger* (1964) and *Thunderball* (1965) box-office smashes. Producers the world over responded with other spy franchises of their own: Dean Martin suited up as Matt Helm, Richard Johnson put a two-fisted spin on Bulldog Drummond, Michael Caine found stardom as Harry Palmer and James Coburn played up the camp angle in the Derek Flint series. More "artistic" minded filmmakers would attempt to take the genre in more serious directions, resulting in such grim and realistic pictures as Martin Ritt's *The Spy Who Came in from the Cold* (1965) and Sidney Lumet's *The Deadly Affair* (1966). No matter what the tone or approach, there's no denying that spying was good for business in the 1960s and it's no small wonder: The growing paranoia over the nuclear capabilities of the Soviet Union had already lead to a major showdown with the United States in 1962; the Cuban Missile Crisis nearly ended in devastation but fortunately cooler heads ultimately prevailed. The fear over a possible nuclear Armageddon gave rise to literature and films which would approach the topic seriously—*Fail-Safe*, written by Eugene Burdick and Harvey Wheeler, published in 1962 and adapted into a film of the same name in 1964, directed by Lumet—and ones which would highlight man's basic absurdity by playing up the grotesque humor of it all—most famously, Stanley Kubrick's *Dr. Strangelove, or: How I Learned to Stop Worrying and Love the Bomb*, 1964, which was very loosely based on Peter George's straightforward Cold War thriller *Red Alert*, published in 1958. As these spy films and nuclear war scenarios proliferated at the box-office, it was only a matter of time before the Italians got in on the act as well. Given that Franco and Ciccio were already a steady box-office draw, it is hardly surprising that they were among the first to dabble in the genre. *Oh! Those Most Secret Agents* would be the first of several Cold War-themed spy comedies starring the Sicilian duo, two of which would be directed by Fulci. The later entries were Giorgio Simonelli's *The Amazing Doctor G* (1965) and Mario Bava's *Le spie vengono dal semi-freddo* (1966), which American International Pictures would mercilessly re-edit and release in the U.S. as *Dr. Goldfoot and the Girl Bombs*. Fulci would then return with *Come rubammo la bomba atomica* (1967), by which point the formula had run its course. To say that Fulci's first contribution to the cycle was the best of the lot is damning it with faint praise, but truth be told, it emerges as one of the team's more endearing movies.

For Fulci, the film marks a few significant firsts. For one thing, it is his first effort to be photographed in color. While he had worked on Italy's first widely released color film *Totò in Color* (1952), it took him a while to finally direct one of his own in color. For another, it appears that *Oh! Those Most Secret Agents* was his first to secure any kind of a release in the United States. No doubt its then-timely satire of the spy genre made it an easier sell to American distributors, none of whom could have cared less about the antics of a couple of Sicilian con men. In this context, the theme is the thing—and it helped to give the movie a wider commercial exposure than the team's earlier vehicles. Allied Artists released the film in the United States in 1965 and, while it didn't exactly set the box-office on fire, it nevertheless set a brief trend of seeing the comedy duo's movies released in America. And lastly, it represents the first time Fulci was granted a special "A Film by Lucio Fulci" credit, which appears before the title; the success of his pictures was making it clear that he was a director with a good sense of what the public wanted and, as such, he certainly earned this sign of authorship and respect.

As usual, Franco and Ciccio are cast as inept con men. They struggle and barely scrape by and there's no indication that they would ever knowingly hurt anybody; they are simply looking to survive in an unforgiving society that has no place for them. As such, the deck is stacked against them and the audience is encouraged to take pity on them as they are put upon, time and time again. They are drafted into acting as spies and they really don't comprehend the danger that this entails. All they can see is the potential to earn some money and perhaps use their position to impress the ladies. When they are sent to a ritzy hotel, for example, they have no clue how to behave or how to fit in. Ciccio does his best to encourage Franco to watch and observe the classy ladies and gentlemen, but it is all for naught. They mistake the hotel porter for an admiral, the staff holding out their hand as a friendly desire to shake hands, and even use the hotel room's bidet for a fish tank. To say they are out of their element is most definitely an understatement!

The humor is of the usual lowbrow variety, but much of it is actually successful. There is an amusing sequence in which the KGB sends in a couple of shapely female agents to seduce them, but they are still stinging from a nasty sunburn suffered on the beach, so they reject their advances. As the two men apply ointment to each other and try to cool their blistering skin, the KGB officers listen in via concealed microphones in the bathroom. The conversation and accompanying moans of pain and pleasure that accompanies as they rub the lotion on one another causes the ladies to mistake the pair for a couple of homosexuals, so they send in a couple of body builders right out of an Italian *pepla* to do the job the two female agents failed to complete. It's not exactly sophisticated humor, but it hits all the right notes and is genuinely funny. Even Franco's customary mugging seems a little more restrained than usual, much to the film's benefit.

There is also use made of a super computer that reflects the growing unease with science and technology at the time. The notion of computers with the ability to think independently was certainly not a novel concept in 1964 and it would soon reach its apotheosis in Stanley Kubrick's *2001: A Space Odyssey* (1968). In this film, the main innovation was to give the computer a libido, thus causing it to overheat every time a well-rounded bottom is waved in front of its face.

Fulci and cinematographer Bitto Albertino give the film a slick, stylish veneer. The color photography is attractive to look at throughout. The use of vivid primary colors is pleasing to the eye and Fulci's usual sense of dynamic frame composition is very much in evidence. The film moves at a good pace and never succumbs to any needless *longeurs*. Ultimately, the real fun lies in seeing Fulci poking fun at spy thriller conventions, again demonstrating his irreverent attitude and his desire to knock the competition down a peg by showing up the inherent absurdity in such scenarios. This would later climax in his exaggerated approach to violence and viscera in his gory horror films, but for now he was still biding his time until he could break free of Franco and Ciccio—in essence, the "monster" he had helped create—and establish himself as a thoughtful director of other genre fare. In the meantime, however, *Oh! Those Most Secret Agents* would go on to gross over a billion *lire* at the box-office, putting it in the same blockbuster category as *I due evasi di Sing Sing*, so further reunions with Franco and Ciccio were definitely in the cards.

## *I due pericoli pubblici (Italy)*

Aka *Two Public Enemies* (unofficial English-language translation)

Directed by Lucio Fulci; Produced by Aster Film; Story and Screenplay by Franco Castellano (as Castellano), Lucio Fulci and Giuseppe Moccia (as Pipolo); Director of Photography: Alfio Contini; Editor: Ornella Micheli; Music by Piero Umiliani

Main Players: Franco Franchi (Franco Introlia); Ciccio Ingrassia (Ciccio Introlia); Margaret Lee (Floriana); Linda Sini (Dora); Riccardo Garrone (The Baron)

Cameo appearance: Lucio Fulci (Sailor who shouts at Franco and Ciccio)

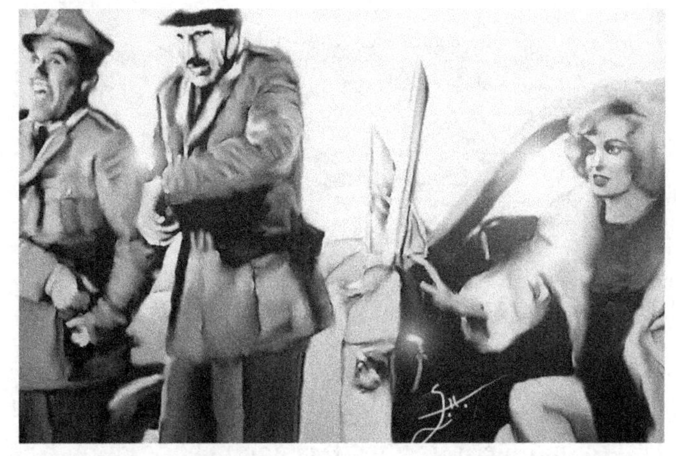

***I due pericoli pubblici*; original artwork by Scott Hoffman.**

*Brothers Franco and Ciccio are hired by a phony Baron to act as servants at a gala he is hosting. It turns out the party is a ruse designed to allow the Baron to rob from his unsuspecting guests. When Franco and Ciccio inadvertently spoil his plans, they are pressured by his mob buddies into coming up with a way to repay their debt. Their attempts at earning some quick cash are doomed to fail, however …*

Fulci's next film starring Franco and Ciccio is a worthy follow up to *Oh! Those Most Secret Agents.* Indeed, it is one of the better films they made together. This is all the more impressive when one considers Fulci's claim that the production was rushed and he was obliged to finish filming in a scant 15 days.[1] Happily, the haste with which it was assembled does not manifest itself on screen, apart from the decision to revert to black-and-white photography, which seems an odd regression after the colorful look of their previous outing with Fulci. It feels like a polished and quietly accomplished little movie.

For a director known for being aggressive and downright rude to his actors at times, Fulci apparently had a more "simpatico" relationship with Franco and Ciccio. Art director Umberto Turco once commented:

> Fulci had a subordinate relationship with the two comedians, since they were the bosses … […] the films he did with Franco and Ciccio were shot in four weeks, three with the two stars and one without them. The comic couple wanted to get rid of each film in three weeks because they had to immediately start another one afterwards, and Fulci was conditioned by that. The progress of the shoot depended not as much on Ciccio […] but mainly on Franco, who tended to be prevaricating, as all the great comedians are. The script was not regarded as Gospel and was changed according to the jokes and gags they came up with. Sometimes there were hassles, and Fulci had to find a compromise, because Franco's personality was very strong, and since the film would be made only if the two comedians were happy, it was inevitable that the director ended up a bit conditioned by that. They respected him very much and he respected them and found the right key to approach them. Whereas with the other directors, Franco and Ciccio often had arguments and discussions. With Fulci, they were more satisfied.[2]

**Franco and Ciccio try to fleece the public, with mixed results.**

The screenplay by Castellano, Pipolo and Fulci again serves as a pretext for allowing the Sicilian duo to do their time-honored routines. There is nothing very new or fresh on display on that level, but the routines are lively and many of the jokes are genuinely funny. The pace is occasionally allowed to go slack when Fulci pays lip service to the admittedly thin and unbelievable story, but when focusing on the comedy routines it often hits the right notes.

The first really standout comic set piece involves Franco walking into traffic in order to fake getting hit by a car; it's Ciccio's job to play a concerned onlooker who just happens to be an attorney. As Franco attempts to overcome his fear of physical harm and makes his way sheepishly into the traffic, it's evident that the plan is not going to come off very successfully. He eventually manages to fake an accident by throwing himself in front of a car, which has already braked to a standstill, and Ciccio then intervenes with the appropriate air of self-importance. The two actors play off of each other beautifully here, each of them playing to their particular strengths as comedians: Franco as the hapless coward and Ciccio as the pompous ass.

Later on, in a moment of respite, they enjoy a nerve-calming cigarette together, not realizing that the cigarette has been laced with marijuana. The two men encounter the kind of hallucinatory experiences that only occur in movies made by people with no first-hand knowledge of what it is really like to get stoned—Fulci, it should be noted, was notoriously intolerant of drug use and would lash out at actors on his sets if he got it into his head that they were smoking pot between takes. The charming naïveté of the set-up gives way to some broad humor, as the two men imagine the other as a desirable woman and take each other into their arms—at which point, an irate sailor played by Fulci himself shouts abuse at them. This kind of lowbrow, vaguely homophobic humor is not uncommon in this style of comedy, but it never comes off as unduly parochial or mean-spirited in its intent.

Another memorable sequence occurs towards the end, when the two dimwits disguise themselves as military types—with Franco as a German officer who comes off as a cross between Lionel Atwill's Inspector Krogh in *Son of Frankenstein* (1939, memorably spoofed by Kenneth Mars in Mel Brooks' *Young Frankenstein*, 1974), and Peter Sellers' portrayal of Dr. Strangelove in the Stanley Kubrick film of 1964. The latter was likely the chief inspiration, as the film was more of a current reference point, but the disguise allows Franco to do some of his funniest work. He spouts out gibberish in a bad German accent, uses his "mechanical" arm to slap an underling repeatedly and struts about trying to look intimidating; the addition of a Hitler mustache only adds to the general air of absurdity. Given that the Franco and Ciccio films often suffer from Franco's tendency towards vigorous overacting, it is a pleasant surprise finding him in such good form throughout much of the picture.

**Franco and Ciccio impersonate a pair of Friars and offer spiritual advice to some women in distress.**

The finale is properly ironic: The two brothers are killed in an explosion and make their way to the pearly gates. They are about to be admitted when the halo over the archangel's head catches Franco's eye and he reaches out to steal it; old habits die hard, after all. Fulci and his collaborators were never unduly concerned with maintaining continuity from one Franco and Ciccio film to the next, so it wasn't exactly a big deal to kill them off for once, even in a jokey fashion such as this. Much like Abbott and Costello (the team they most closely resemble, even if Fulci compared them to Laurel and Hardy), they were always playing variations on themselves—and yet, they were never really *quite* the same characters from film to film.

Fulci's flair for the absurd serves the movie well. The film is never remotely credible, nor is it really intended to be. It's a manic cartoon brought to life and this suits the comedy team very well. As noted, there's a little more expository dialogue than one would have wished, but once that is dispensed with the film settles into a nice madcap rhythm. Not all of the vehicles Franco and Ciccio made as a team were created equal, of course, and not even all of Fulci's films with them were of a particularly high caliber, but the ones that do work—such as this—can provide some insight into their extreme popularity with Italian audiences. This popularity extended to a documentary on the duo which Fulci directed around this time: titled *Non sono d'accordo. Intervista a Ciccio Ingrassia e Franco Franchi*, it was released to theaters through the *Settimana Incom* newsreel series in December of 1964; the most interesting sight Fulci's cameras were able to capture for the piece was a visit to Cinecittà by the great writer-director Billy Wilder, whom Fulci held in great esteem. The spectacle of seeing Fulci film the renowned Hollywood filmmaker as he chatted to Franco and Ciccio about the finer points of comedy surely bordered on the surreal. Around this same period, Fulci is also reported to have started work on *Il gaucho* (1964), starring Vittorio Gassman and Nino Manfredi. For reasons unknown, however, he was ultimately replaced by Dino Risi; the resulting film proved to be a bigger critical hit than most of Fulci's films and would net Manfredi a Golden Goblet as Best Actor.[3]

Notes:
1. Audio interview with Lucio Fulci, conducted by Pier Maria Bocchi and Andrea Bruni, included on the Shriek Show DVD of *Touch of Death*.
2. Albiero, Paolo and Giacomo Cacciatore, *Il terrorista dei generi: Tutto il cinema di Lucio Fulci* (Rome: Un mondo a parte, 2004), p. 64.
3. Thanks to Jason Slater for revealing this information about *Il gaucho* via email.

# 1965

## *Come inguaiammo l'esercito (Italy)*

Aka *How We Got into Trouble with the Army* (unofficial English-language translation)

Directed by Lucio Fulci; Produced by Five Film; Screenplay by Roberto Gianviti and Amedeo Sollazzo, from a story by Alfonso Brescia and Franco D'Este; Editor: Ornella Micheli

Main Players: Franco Franchi (Franco Piscitello); Ciccio Ingrassia (Sergeant Camilloni); Remo Germani (Nick Moroni); Alicia Brandet (Catherine); Gina Rovere (Mariuccia); Umberto D'Orsi (Hamlet); Andrea Scotti (Captain)

*Nick Moroni, a popular singer, is called upon to do his duty in the Army. While there, he learns that his wife, up-and-coming actress Catherine, is planning to pursue her dream of success in America—and that she intends taking their infant son with her. Moroni retaliates by kidnapping the child and bribing his friend Franco to hide it in the barracks. Things become complicated when Sergant Camilloni, who has it in for Franco, starts sticking his nose in ...*

They are given special guest star billing, but don't let that fool you: *Come inguaiammo l'esercito* is every inch a vehicle for Franco and Ciccio; incidentally, a feature-length documentary tribute to the duo which debuted at the 2004

***Come inguaiammo l'esercito*; original artwork by Scott Hoffman.**

Venice Film Festival was entitled *Come inguaiammo il Cinema Italiano: La vera storia di Franco e Ciccio*. The comedy is a little more genteel, even family-oriented, this time around as the boys become mixed up in a plot involving a baby. As usual, one's tolerance for broad slapstick and obvious jokes will determine whether or not it is very funny, but the film definitely contains some nice touches and is amusing enough on its own terms.

The film represented something of a reunion between Fulci and the comedy duo, following a few vehicles that had been entrusted instead to Giorgio Simonelli. These films—including *Due mafiosi nel Far West* (1964)—had proved to be less successful at the box-office. Worried that they might be losing some of their favor with the public, the team thought long and hard about how to proceed and it was reportedly Ingrassia who came to the realization that Fulci had been responsible for their biggest box-office triumphs, so they reached out to him to continue their collaboration.[1] Fulci had had nothing to do with the development of the story and screenplay, but the film did allow him to reconnect with his old friend and collaborator Roberto Gianviti, who would go on to become a more prominent part of Fulci's career later on. Ingrassia's suspicions would be verified when the film was released in 1965 and pulled in a substantial sum at the Italian box-office.

The narrative is split between Franco and Ciccio and the young couple played by Remo Germani and Alicia Brandet. Germani was a popular singer in Italy at the time and he made his film debut playing the role of Nick Moroni in this film. He is not the most interesting screen presence and the film definitely suffers from his rather bland, wooden performance, but Brandet (who had already appeared in *Gli imbroglioni* and *The Maniacs*) helps to pick up the slack. It's Moroni's job to belt out a number of tunes, while it's up to Franco and Ciccio to provide the laughs. Ciccio is wonderfully condescending and snide as the short-tempered Sergeant who has his eye on becoming a General. He abuses Franco verbally at every turn and is also given a rare chance to play a would-be ladies' man as he tries to wine and dine a former flame. Unfortunately for him, he places his confidence in Franco and enlists him to pose as his servant with disastrous results. The intended seduction ends with the woman leaving in tears, indicating that she left behind a memento of their previous tryst. Franco, who has brought the baby along to keep it safe while he participates in the charade, has no choice but to go along when Ciccio finds the baby and assumes that this is the memento and that he is indeed the father. The plot pretty much revolves around a game of revolving babies from this point on as Franco tries to save his own skin while trying to satisfy both Moroni and the Sergeant.

The strong suit of the Franco and Ciccio comedies was never really in the clever wordplay. They were a more visually oriented team and it's for this reason that Fulci proved to be their ideal director: Fulci understood the need to keep things simple and direct in this context. Sooner than intrude upon their routines by trying to impose flashy camerawork, he allows the spectator to sit back and observe as they go through their well-rehearsed paces. This time, however, there are some clever verbal gags to go along with the slapstick. Late in the film, the duo are involved in some military maneuvers overseen by a General from NATO by the name of MacKee. In Italian, however, the name MacKee sounds very much like "Ma chi," which translated into English as "But who?" This inevitably leads to some breakdowns in communication as the General tries to communicate with them during the course of the maneuvers. Not surprisingly, perhaps, Fulci regarded the final scenes involving the maneuvers to be the funniest set piece he ever directed.[2]

Fulci's flair for the exaggerated and the ridiculous is much in evidence. The film plays out in a wonderfully over-the-top fashion, with no real attempt towards verisimilitude. The director recognizes the need for this type of material to be handled with the right combination of visual simplicity and energetic pacing and he never lets the material down. It takes a little while for the story to get on course, but once it does the film never really lets up and it builds to an appropriately goofy finale which perfectly sums up the chaotic, even anarchic spirit of this type of broad comedy.

The use of music is also rather interesting. Composer Ezio Leoni (working for the first and last time for Fulci) provides a number of songs implemented into the general score of the picture. The songs serve to comment on the action as it unfolds. It's not a unique device to use music in this fashion, but it was a first in the context of Fulci's cinema and, as such, it points towards the later use of the ballads in the score for his Western *Four of the Apocalypse*.

Fulci did not take a screenwriting credit this time, but the story was co-authored by future director Alfonso Brescia. Brescia was born in Rome in 1930 and started working in films in the late 1950s as an assistant director. He began contributing to screenplays in the early 1960s and this was one of his earliest credits in that capacity; he would also

**Italian poster for *Come inguaiammo l'esercito*; artwork by Bob DeSeta.**

contribute to the story for Fulci's *Come svaligiammo la banca d'Italia*. Brescia turned to directing around this time, as well, specializing in *pepla* (*The Magnificent Gladiator*, 1964) and Spaghetti Westerns (*The Colt is My Law*, 1966) before establishing himself as a purveyor of sleaze in the 1970s. He would direct two of the sequels to Fulci's hugely successful *White Fang* (1973): *Zanna Bianca e il cacciatore solitario* and *White Fang and the Gold Diggers*, both from 1975. From there, he would find lasting cinematic infamy with his series of *Star Wars* (1977) rip-offs, including *Star Odyssey* (1979) and the porno hybrid *Beast in Space* (1980). Brescia died in 2001.

Fulci would spend the remainder of the year putting Franco and Ciccio through their paces, but a change was in the air and an opportunity to attain greater recognition from a wider audience (if not necessarily from the critics) suddenly seemed within reach.

Notes:
1. Albiero, Paolo and Giacomo Cacciatore, *Il terrorista dei generi: Tutto il cinema di Lucio Fulci* (Rome: Un mondo a parte, 2004), p. 64.
2. Fulci interviewed in the documentary *La notte americana del dott. Lucio Fulci*, directed by Antonietta De Lillo.

## *002 operazione luna* (Italy/Spain)

Aka *002 Operation Moon* (unofficial English-language translation); *Dos cosmonautas a la fuerza*

Directed by Lucio Fulci; Produced by IMA Productions and Ágata Films S.A.; Story and Screenplay by Vittorio Metz and Amedeo Sollazzo; Director of Photography: Tino Santoni; Editor: Pedro del Rey; Music by Coriolano Gori (as Lallo Gori); Song: *A Schiffo Finisce*, written by Lucio Fulci and Amadeo Sollazzo

Main Players: Franco Franchi (Franco/Colonel Paradowsky); Ciccio Ingrassia (Ciccio/Major Borovin); Mónica Randall (Mischa Paradowsky); Linda Sini (Leonidova); Ignazio Leone (Sergio)

*Russian astronauts Colonel Paradowsky and Major Borovin are sent into space, but when it appears that their spacecraft has disintegrated, the head of the Russian space program determines to save face by finding look-alike replacements and firing them into space without attracting attention. The plot goes more or less as planned, thanks in no small measure to finding the astronauts' identical (albeit inept) twins named Franco and Ciccio. The two idiots are successfully sent into space and come back safely; the only problem is, their Russian "comrades" also return safe and sound …*

Fulci would later recall that his next two films with Franco and Ciccio—*002 operazione luna* and *I due parà*—were made under tighter restrictions than usual. "I shot it together with *I due parà*, both movies in seven weeks," he later claimed.[1] The tight schedule apparently also extended to impoverished budgets, which is doubly unfortunate in this context since, on the face of it, *002 operazione luna* is one of the more ambitious films to star the comic duo. Fulci would fall back on his ingenuity and that of his technical crew and they were able to create some memorable images in the process. As he later recalled:

> I shot the spaceship's take-off with four lights. Everybody asked me, "How the fuck did you do it?"

***002 operazione luna*; original artwork by Scott Hoffman.**

**Italian *locandina* for *002 operazione luna*; artwork by Averardo Ciriello.**

> That scene is a source of pride for me! Because we were out of money, when they were in the cosmos, the cosmos was made with a black cloth all over the stage, with a lot of little bulks on the floor for stars. We shot it in slow-motion.[2]

Fulci's memory is actually a little fuzzy here: the take-off is accomplished via stock footage, but the images of Franco and Ciccio floating around in space are effectively rendered, especially considering the meager means at the director's disposal.

Truth be told, the title is more than a little misleading. Viewers expecting a spy spoof or a space opera are bound to be very disappointed. It takes forever for the boys to finally be launched into space and much of their journey is conveyed in a frankly uninteresting visual manner, lending credence to Fulci's claims that there simply wasn't enough money in the budget; most of the outer space footage is set inside a space capsule without windows, so the audience is expected to just accept the notion that they are in outer space on faith. When the duo finally decides to leave the capsule, they float around free-form in a way that anticipates some imagery in Stanley Kubrick's *2001: A Space Odyssey* (1968), but within a few minutes they are back in the capsule and headed back to Earth.

On the plus side, there are some memorable sequences worth savoring. The opening is a minor *tour-de-force* of directing and mime acting as Franco and Ciccio break into a villa and attempt a robbery. The extended sequence is performed entirely without dialogue. The timing and comic skill the two actors display in this sequence lends credence to their popularity among Italian audiences; for once they aren't relying on shouting and manic gestures trying to be funny. Fulci seems to be completely in his element in this sequence, finding interesting ways to frame the action without going overboard to draw attention to his own cleverness.

Once the film gets back to Earth, as it were, it focuses on a *doppelganger* theme as the two nitwits are sent home to the wives of the real astronauts. Much confusion erupts, inevitably, and in time the two Russian look-alikes get added into the mix as well. The most interesting thing about this section of the film is seeing Franco stretch himself by playing two separate and distinct characters. Unlike Ciccio, who could be relied upon to aim for a more low-key and subtle performance, Franco is typically firing on all cylinders. For the fans who really love this kind of thing, this is key to the appeal; for those who aren't so sold on it, his incessant mugging can be the breaking point. He doesn't exactly veer far from his usual persona overall, but when playing the straight-laced Colonel Paradowsky, he is far more restrained than usual. It's something of a relief seeing him in such a low-key light, quite frankly, but inevitably this side of his performance is short-lived; by the end of the film, he will be back to his usual routine of pulling faces and shouting his lines in "comic" desperation.

*002 operazione luna* is one of only two forays that Fulci would make into the realm of science fiction. Other directors like Antonio Margheriti would dabble extensively in the genre, making fantastic visions of outer space with very little resources, but it does not seem to have been a type of storytelling that really appealed to Fulci. He would return to the genre later with *Rome, 2072 A.D.: The New Gladiators*, but the results were indifferent. *002 operazione luna* is therefore, by default, his most successful contribution to science fiction, even if its actual fantasy elements are rather muted by comparison. With a bigger budget and a little more time, perhaps Fulci and his crew could have made more of these elements, but within the parameters of what is there on screen, it is a respectable and sporadically amusing picture in its own right.

Notes:
1. Audio interview with Lucio Fulci, conducted by Pier Maria Bocchi and Andrea Bruni, included on the Shriek Show DVD release of *Touch of Death*.
2. *Ibid*.

## *I due parà* (Italy/Spain)

Aka *The Two Parachutists* (unofficial English-language translation)

Directed by Lucio Fulci; Produced by IMA Productions and Ágata Films S.A.; Story and Screenplay by Vittorio Metz and Amedeo Sollazzo; Director of Photography: Tino Santoni (as Clemente Santoni); Editor: Pedro del Rey; Music by Piero Umiliani

Main Players: Franco Franchi (Franco Impallomeni); Ciccio Ingrassia (Ciccio Impallomeni); Umberto D'Orsi (American Ambassador); Roberto Camardiel (General Jose Limar); Mónica Randall (Rosita); Luis Peña (Alvardo Garcia)

*Franco and Ciccio are small-time performers who decide they have had enough of scraping to get by in their small village. They turn their eyes toward conquering America, where they hope to finally find their fame and fortune. Unfortunately for them, they book a flight on the wrong plane and find themselves in South America, where they run afoul of a dictator and his military goons …*

Lucio Fulci was surely beginning to feel as if he was the ringmaster of the Franco and Ciccio circus by this stage in his career. Beginning with *I due della legione*, he helped to shape their onscreen persona and guided them through many of their best and most profitable comedies. Like so many marriages, it went through its good and bad periods, but 1965 saw them spending more time together than usual: Fulci directed no less than three films for them in rapid succession, with the latter two being made at breakneck speed back-to-back, with much the same supporting cast and crew. As such, it's not entirely surprising that some signs of fatigue were starting to become evident by the time of *I due parà*.

The scenario by Vittorio Metz and Amedeo Sollazzo feels a trifle warmed-over, with bits and pieces of earlier Franco and Ciccio films thrown into the pot and reheated for good measure. There is even a touch of the autobiographical for the team, as the opening scenes depicting their attempts at entertaining the public on the street refers back to their origins in show business. Some of the gags are funny, but many of them fail to elicit the desired response. Worse still, the story—such as it is—seems to amble and ramble with little purpose other than killing time until the next comic set piece. Even Fulci's direction feels somewhat perfunctory, if not completely uninspired. The bits of manic inspiration evident in the last few Franco and Ciccio films are not as prevalent this time and the tight pacing is also allowed to go slack.

One of the few really inspired visual moments occurs when the camera pulls back from the oversized portrait of the South American dictator, General Limar, and reveals Limar sitting at his desk, striking the exact same pose. Fulci clearly knew it was a funny touch, as he repeats it later, this time with Franco sitting in front of a much smaller portrait and making the exact same expression. Jim Abrahams, David Zucker and Jerry Zucker, in their phenomenally successful disaster film send-up *Airplane!* (1980), restaged this inspired sight gag to tremendous effect. Fulci's penchant for sight gags such as this confirm his talent and flair for the comedy genre, even if the film as a whole finds him coasting through the assignment on auto pilot. In fairness, however, the stress and strain of making two films back to back under such difficult circumstances was bound to take its toll—and if *I due parà* seems listless and half-hearted, then at least its companion feature, *002 operazione luna*, gave a better indicator of the director's strengths in this area.

Fulci would later play up the film's low budget in interviews, causing him to make a highly fanciful claim: "The producers were out of money, so for one scene poor Franchi had to eat a real light bulb; there was no money in the budget to make one out of sugar glass."[1] It's a colorful anecdote, but the film does not support it.. There is indeed a scene where Franco eats glass—albeit a bottle of wine,

**_I due parà_; original artwork by Scott Hoffman.**

**Italian poster for *I due parà*.**

not a light bulb—but it's quite obvious that the bottle is not made of real glass. As was so often the case with Fulci, he knew the value of playing things up in interviews; the truth was all well and good, but a really colorful lie could be that much more interesting and he was only too willing to comply. Even so, there's little doubt that his basic point was correct: Money was tight and, as such, things sometimes had to be done in a half-assed manner. This is especially evident in the scene demonstrating the "bulletproof glass," which the General uses to protect himself in bed. In order to convey the illusion of the glass being hit by bullets, paint pellets were used. Tighter editing and more careful lighting might have made the visual come off more convincingly, but as it stands the effect is none-too-convincing.

Fulci's morbid, absurdist sense of humor is really only evident in the final scene: Franco and Ciccio finally escape from South America and believe that they are being sent to their desired destination, only to discover that they have been drafted into the U.S. army and are on their way to Vietnam. It's just as well, however, that the seemingly inevitable *How We Fooled The Viet Cong* never materialized. Even so, the anti-American streak that runs throughout the film is particularly interesting on a subtextual level; far from being granted access to the American dream, the boys are ruthlessly manipulated by a corrupt American politician (played by Umberto D'Orsi, one of the director's favorite character actors) who will stop at nothing to ensure that he continues to get as much graft money as possible. The character is emblematic of a bigger problem in American society, which Fulci would continue to explore in later films like *The New York Ripper*; the notion of the cut-throat society in which people sacrifice empathy for their own selfish interests. This element helps to bring an overtly political dimension to the film, which was unique in Franco and Ciccio's comedies up until that time. Beyond that, much of the film is comprised of scenes of characters screaming at each other for the sake of comedy, and Fulci only seems to take much of an interest when he's finally given an opportunity to stage something exciting like a skirmish. The action scenes, quite unlike anything he had staged till then, reveal him to be confident and capable in that area and would finally bear fruit the following year, with *Massacre Time*.

*I due parà* would remain Fulci's final film to be photographed in black-and-white.

Notes:
1. Audio interview with Lucio Fulci, conducted by Pier Maria Bocchi and Andrea Bruni, included on the Shriek Show DVD of *Touch of Death*.

# 1966

## *Come svaligiammo la banca d'Italia (Italy)*

Aka *How We Robbed the Bank of Italy*

Directed by Lucio Fulci; Produced by Anteos and Fono Roma; Screenplay by Lucio Fulci, Roberto Gianviti and Amedeo Sollazzo, from a story by Alfonso Brescia; Director of Photography: Fausto Rossi; Editor: Nella Nannuzzi; Music by Coriolano Gori (as Lallo Gori)

Main Players: Franco Franchi (Franco); Ciccio Ingrassia (Ciccio); Lena von Martens (Marilina); Mirella Maravidi (Rosalina); Mario Pisu (Paolo); Umberto D'Orsi (Commissioner); Fiorenzo Fiorentini (Romoletto, also known as "Evil Genius")

*Paolo is a criminal mastermind known to the authorities as "Maestro." Part of his skill lies in never getting caught. Unfortunately for him, his brothers Franco and Ciccio have not inherited his abilities. While Paolo is away putting the finishing touches on an ambitious robbery, Franco and Ciccio uncover his plans and decide to beat him at his own game. They decide to rob the Bank of Italy on their own in order to prove their own cunning and ability; things inevitably do not go according to plan…*

Fulci's next vehicle for Franco and Ciccio is one of his most unusual. The duo is again cast as inept brothers, but the supporting cast does much of the heavy lifting. For

***Come svaligiammo la banca d'Italia*; original artwork by Scott Hoffman.**

once, Franco and Ciccio sit out long stretches of action while their equally inept underlings go about trying to commit the ambitious robbery.

Fortunately, the supporting players are up to the challenge and bring something oddly endearing to their characters. For example, Fiorenzo Fiorentini is in marvelous form as the so-called "Evil Genius" who helps to put the plot into motion. Fiorentini's portrayal of the stammering, football-obsessed petty crook is marvelously detailed and adds some color to the proceedings. Franco and Ciccio, for their part, are in good form. They don't stray far from their established routines, but that is not necessarily a bad thing. By this stage in the game, there is something almost oddly comforting in seeing the two play off each other: They may be grating at times, but on those occasions where they are truly effective, the results are amusing. There is a nice bit, for example, when they are in a rush to let their respective spouses into their apartment, but they get so caught up in the action that Ciccio gets locked outside; he knocks on the door and Franco lets him back in, causing the latter to get locked out; and so forth.

Fulci works in some acerbic jabs at the Church, as well. Paolo keeps his blueprint for his perfect crime in a hollowed-out copy of the Bible, for example. Later, Franco and Ciccio take a tour of the portraits of their ancestors, most of whom are notorious thieves; the black sheep, however, is hidden behind a curtain and it is revealed to be a priest. Fulci's distrust of organized religion and its relationship to Italy's corrupt political scene would inform a number of his later films, most notably *Beatrice Cenci* and *Don't Torture a Duckling*.

The caper format works very well. The plot is actually solidly constructed and the manner in which the robbery is carried out is properly ingenious. Franco and Ciccio would never have been able to construct such a plan on their own, of course, but in stealing the idea from their far cleverer (and more dangerous) older sibling, they remain true to their screen image as con men and tricksters. The delicious final irony is that—for once—they actually succeed in their goal. Most Franco and Ciccio films end with a bitter twist in which they are put upon one last time (or even killed!) before the fade-out, but Fulci and his collaborators veer from that formula this time. It may be a matter of pure dumb luck, but Franco and Ciccio really do succeed in robbing the Bank of Italy and they are able to enjoy the comfort of their loot and the company of their spouses without any hint of a final comeuppance. It could be that Fulci and company simply decided that the time was right for the boys to get a little peace and quiet for once, but whatever the motivation, it proves to be an oddly satisfying finale.

As usual for the comic duo, the film's plot was inspired by the success of another film: Marco Vicario's *Seven Golden Men* (1966), which also spawned a sequel by the same director titled *Seven Golden Men Strike Again* (1966). The success of Vicario's films resulted in a brief spate of heist thrillers in Italy, though the success was not exactly felt the world over. According to Fulci's assistant, Giovanni Fago, "*Seven Golden Men* had just come out and we wanted to make a spoof of it. We shot it entirely in the studio, even the tunnels."[1]

If the production values are any indicator, *Come svaligiammo la banca d'Italia* was clearly shot on a higher budget than the preceding Franco and Ciccio comedies directed by Fulci. The production looks slick and well mounted throughout. This is Fulci's first film in the widescreen Techniscope process and he took to the format like a duck to water. The wider-than-usual frame allows for many extra details, and Fulci and his cinematographer, Fausto Rossi, do not miss any opportunities to exploit this. The "portrait shots" beloved by so many fans in Fulci's later films—tight close-ups on an actor or actress in the foreground with the extra space carefully filled in the background—are already in evidence. The director also gets to cut loose visually during the fireworks sequence, wherein the robbery starts to go wrong and an order is misunderstood, causing some fireworks to be set off underneath the bank. As the fireworks explode in all directions, the image over-flows with imaginative color and use of light and shadow. It's a visually arresting set piece that shows Fulci's willingness to experiment with the Baroque when the opportunity presents itself. Lallo Gori's cool, jazzy score anticipates Riz Ortolani's truly exceptional work on the director's later *giallo Perversion Story*, and the combination of suspense and comedy is skillfully achieved from beginning to end. The film is definitely one of Fulci's best with Franco and Ciccio, and he would move from it to what was arguably his first truly mature major work, in a very different genre.

Notes:

1. Albiero, Paolo and Giacomo Cacciatore, *Il terrorista dei generi. Tutto il cinema di Lucio Fulci* (Rome: Un Mondo a Parte, 2004), p. 70.

## *Massacre Time (Italy)*

Aka *The Brute and the Beast; Colt Concert; Le colt cantarono la morte e fu... tempo di massacro; Las pistolas cantaron la muerte; Django – Sein Gesangbuch war der Colt*

Directed by Lucio Fulci; Produced by I.F. Produzioni Cinematografiche and Mega Film; Story and Screenplay by Fernando Di Leo; Director of Photography: Riccardo Pallottini; Editor: Ornella Micheli; Music by Coriolano Gori (as Lallo Gori); Song: *A Man Alone (Come Back Some Day)*, performed by Sergio Endrigo

Main Players: Franco Nero (Tom Corbett); George Hilton (Jeffrey Corbett); Nino Castelnuovo (Jason "Junior" Scott); Linda Sini [as Lynn Shane] (Brady); Giuseppe Addobbati [as John M. Douglas] (Mr. Scott); Tom Felleghy (Murray); Rina Franchetti (Mercedes)

*Tom Corbett is called home after having been away for many years. There he is reunited with his estranged brother, Jeffrey, who is now an alcoholic. Tom discovers that a tycoon named Mr. Scott has taken over much of the town, including Jeffrey's ranch. Worse, his son Jason is a sadist who instills fear into the people. There are more surprises in store for Tom, however, including a revelation about his relationship with the Scott clan ...*

It is a common misconception that the so-called Spaghetti Western (i.e., Italian Westerns) sprung up out of nowhere with the arrival of Sergio Leone's *A Fistful of Dollars* (1964). Truth be told, the Italians had been dabbling in the genre since the silent days. Giacomo Puccini may well be the one to claim paternity to the very first Italian Western, with his 1910 opera *La fanciulla del West* and the first known Italian Western film emerged three years later: *La Vampira Indiana.* The director of that film was one Vincenzo Leone, the father of future genre superstar Sergio Leone. In the late 1950s, some comedy vehicles for Walter Chiari and Ugo Tognazzi utilized Western themes; among these were *La sceriffa* (1959), directed by Roberto Bianchi Montero and *Un dollaro di fifa* (1960). Other, more straight-faced examples of the genre included *Gunfight at Red Sands* (1963), directed by Ricardo Blasco and *The Road to Fort Alamo* (1964), directed by Mario Bava, but it was undoubtedly the success of *A Fistful of Dollars* that triggered the flood of Westerns that followed. The film made a superstar out of a minor American television actor named Clint Eastwood and producers wasted no time in finding other actors to follow in his footsteps. Americans like Mark Damon, Cameron Mitchell and Lee Van Cleef would find success top-lining these films, while Italian actors like Giuliano Gemma and Gianni Garko would attain popularity in the genre as well. Of all the "homegrown" Italian Western stars, however, the most popular was undoubtedly Franco Nero. He rose to prominence playing the lead in Sergio Corbucci's *Django* (1966) and it was this role which prompted Lucio Fulci to cast him in his first Spaghetti Western: *Massacre Time.* The film displayed a capacity for violence only hinted at in Fulci's earlier work and it would prove to be prophetic on that level. At the time, it was seen as just another Spaghetti Western, but it now stands out as one of the best of the period; Fulci would revisit the genre sporadically but with impressive results, making *Four of the Apocalypse* in 1975 and *Silver Saddle* in 1978. The latter marked the death knell of the Spaghetti Western; very few would emerge from that point on, but there is no shortage of titles for fans to sift through if they are so inclined: literally hundreds, ranging from the sublime to the ridiculous, would be made during that relatively brief window of time.

***Massacre Time*; original artwork by Scott Hoffman.**

The gifted Fernando Di Leo wrote the screenplay for *Massacre Time.* Di Leo was born in San Ferdinando di Puglia in 1932 and entered films in the early 1960s, as a screenwriter and assistant director. His contribution to the evolution of the Spaghetti Western is significant: he had a hand (albeit uncredited) in writing *A Fistful of Dollars* and *For a Few Dollars More* (1965) for Leone and also was involved in the writing of Duccio Tessari's *The Return of Ringo* (1965), Franco Giraldi's *Seven Guns for the MacGregors* (1966) and Sergio Corbucci's *Navajo Joe* (1966), among others. Di Leo would go on to become a director, specializing in hard-bitten *poliziotteschi* like *The Italian Connection* and *Caliber 9* (both 1972); he died in 2003. His expertly written and constructed screenplay gave Fulci a strong foundation to work from and the director was clearly excited by the material, rising to the occasion with energy and stylistic aplomb. Fulci would later claim that he pushed Di Leo to make things as violent as possible, but the writer refuted this:

> I don't know anything about Fulci's claims that he insisted that I write a very violent movie: All that's in the film, including Junior dressed in white, was already in the script. Fulci only directed well what was already on the page. [...] The script was good and ready and he liked it the way it was, otherwise I'd complied to his demands if there had been any.[1]

The film opens with a lush panning shot that accentuates the beauty of the landscape; in the background the viewer can hear the sound of barking dogs. Fulci cuts jarringly from this idyll to a closer view of a group of hunters. The scene takes a darker, more disturbing turn when it becomes evident that the creature being hunted is not an animal but a frightened man pleading for his life. The character of Jason presides over the action—Fulci and Di Leo establish him immediately as a sadist who completely lacks empathy. Jason's preferred weapon is not the revolver, but a whip—a kinky touch that underlines the savage thrill he gets out of being cruel. Jason whips the poor man, drawing blood from his face; the latter runs for his life, but is caught by Jason's vicious dogs, who proceed to tear him to pieces. Fulci doesn't pull any punches in this scene; his pragmatic streak would eventually make him one of Italian cinema's most notorious purveyors of graphic screen violence. The sequence concludes with the man's blood dirtying the mountain stream.

From here, the script goes about setting up the basic conflict: Tom Corbett, a decent man looking to make his own way in life, is called back to his familial home because his family is in danger. He dutifully responds to the message and finds that his hometown is in the grip of fear: Mr. Scott has taken control of the area and his brand is on virtually every building and establishment. Tom's relationship with his brother Jeffrey is strained: The latter has succumbed to self-pity and alcoholism and does not wish to continue any kind of a relationship with his sibling. The two men work through their differences and ultimately work together for the greater good. Tom is the typically stoic and upright Western hero, but he is not depicted in glittering and heroic terms; he is just an ordinary man fighting for what is right. Jeffrey is considerably more complex, but his less admirable qualities are counterbalanced by the charm and wit that George Hilton brings to his performance. For once, Franco Nero (as Tom) finds himself being outshone on screen; this had not been an issue in *Django*, nor would it be in his subsequent Westerns, but here he has the less interesting role and Hilton does not miss any opportunities to outclass him on screen.

**Italian *locandina* for *Massacre Time*; artwork by "Symeoni"/Sandro Simeoni.**

The Scott clan is particularly interesting. The patriarch (played by character actor Giuseppe Addobbati, known to genre fans as the frightened innkeeper in Mario Bava's *Kill, Baby ... Kill!*, 1966) is stern but reasonable. He has taken over the town, but he does not bully or terrorize its inhabitants; he simply uses his position and his access to money to buy what he wants, with no questions asked. By contrast, his son Jason is an unrepentant psychopath. The two men are basically flipsides of the same coin, an idea visualized by Fulci when he has the two men play a duet together on the piano. Jason is cruel and sadistic, but he loves his father and wants the same kind of love in return. The son's excesses, however, repulse the father. The would-be "daddy's boy" eventually rebels by taking his father's life, an act of patricide which is timed to coincide with the revelation that the older man is also the real father of Tom. In a sense, Jason's kinky psychosexual characterization is something of an echo of Indio (Gian Maria Volontè) in the Di Leo-scripted *For a Few Dollars More*. Indio's vice was marijuana (which somewhat naively causes him to suffer from hallucinations), but Jason's is pure unbridled sadism. Both characters are denoted by their twitchy mannerisms and both seem to derive genuine pleasure from hurting others.

Tom and Jason are given two major showdowns. The first is a truly nasty set piece in which the former underestimates the latter and just barely lives to suffer the consequences. Tom sees the immaculately dressed, vaguely

**Italian *locandina* for the 1977 rerelease of *Massacre Time*; artwork by Renato Casaro.**

effeminate Jason as being an easy target and provokes him into a fight. Jason responds by utilizing his favored weapon, the whip. Here again, as had been the case in *Django* (1966) and would continue to be the case in later Westerns, Nero's screen image embraces the masochistic: He is whipped and bloodied and beaten to a pulp. Tom is defeated, but only momentarily; he is still able to walk away, promising to return another day. This he does at the end, as he and Jeffrey unite to take on Jason and his minions. As the two (half) brothers proceed to decimate the gang, Jason's inherent cowardice begins to take hold. The two men—already revealed to be brothers—are then left to duke it out, with Jason using unfair tactics to try and defeat Tom, but it is all for naught: He is finally killed, leaving Tom to continue working towards building a better relationship with his other half-brother, Jeffrey.

Fulci expertly contrasts the beauty of the settings with the violence inherent in the material. This is evident right from the beginning, with its pastoral imagery giving way to bloodshed. In this respect, it reminds one of the opening of Michael Reeves' powerful historical horror film *Witchfinder General* (1968), which opens on a similar setting. The first violent showdown between Tom and Jason is similarly structured: Tom crashes a polite society gathering, with men and women dressed in their finest clothes, where he finally runs afoul of Jason. When Tom retires from the beating, bruised and bloodied, he bumps into a young man in a clean white suit, staining the jacket with his blood.

The film is beautifully realized from start to finish: Riccardo Pallottini's expert color cinematography helps to belie the film's low budget and Fulci shows tremendous assuredness in staging the action scenes. The characters are well drawn and engaging and the actors do a splendid job. Nero is ideal as the world-weary but compassionate hero. Born in San Prospero Parmense in 1941, he made his way to Rome and got his big break in films courtesy of legendary filmmaker John Huston, who cast him as Abel in his epic *The Bible: In the Beginning …* (1966). Nero would become one of Italy's biggest movie stars and his facility in speaking English also allowed him to appear in such American fare as Joshua Logan's *Camelot* (1967), where he met his long-time companion, actress Vanessa Redgrave. Nero remains an active presence in films and was recently featured in a cameo role in Quentin Tarantino's Spaghetti Western homage *Django Unchained* (2012). Nero would go on to appear in two more films for Fulci—*White Fang* and *Challenge to White Fang*—but he was not the original choice to play the role here. According to Fulci:

> George Martin was supposed to play the lead, but fate, as Buñuel has said, rules life. The Spanish co-production pulled out because they said the movie was too violent. […] One day as I was looking through stills, I found a very good-looking boy […] He was acting in a Western called *Django*.[2]

Despite working with Nero again, Fulci remained singularly bitter and acerbic with regards to the star, though Nero himself has nothing but good things to say about the director (see interview). Fulci continued:

> So I called this fucking bastard—a lot of people think he's an asshole—yeah, I could go through life insulting Mr. Nero because he swindled me badly on at least four occasions … Anyway, I called

him and he asked for four million *lire*, which was nothing at all.[3]

Perhaps the "baggage" Nero brought with him as an up-and-coming star angered Fulci, but his tone on the subject would never vary in interviews; Nero may have helped to bring Fulci's films a little more international commercial viability, but the director did not have to be happy about it.

For the role of the hard-drinking Jeffrey, Fulci took a chance on a newcomer:

> Then I found a Uruguyan from commercials called George Hilton, a real gentleman. His important career began then and he's very grateful to me because he knows where to give due.[4]

**German lobby card for *Massacre Time*: George Hilton as Jeffrey Corbett prepares to do battle.**

George Hilton was born in Montevideo in 1934. He started off acting on stage and in films and TV in South America before making his way to Italy in the early 1960s. He would later refer to *Massacre Time* as his first film in Italy, but in fact he had already top-lined the swashbuckler *The Masked Man Against the Pirates* (1964) and appeared in a small role in *The Amazing Doctor G* (1966), starring Fulci's old comrades, Franco and Ciccio. Nevertheless, *Massacre Time* is the first film to really test his acting abilities and he rises to the occasion beautifully. Jeffrey could easily have been reduced to the usual colorful alcoholic rogue, but Hilton keeps the character's inner suffering visible and makes him an endearing presence. He would later recall Fulci in an interview,

> He was a difficult man to work with. [...] He was a great director and I owe a lot to him. But he had an overbearing personality and that could be difficult. From one point of view, that was the best film I made.[5]

Despite their mutual respect for one another, Hilton never worked with Fulci again. Hilton would later provide a clue for this when he explained that, while he respected Fulci as a filmmaker, he was not as keen on him as a person:

> Artistically he was, I have to say, very talented, very demanding. On a human level, less brilliant. On a human level, he was an odd man with a strange personality. To be honest, we could never develop a friendship because he was quite unstable. I liked him less. As an artist, my hat goes off to him, but as a man, I have to say there was a lot less admiration.

Nino Castelnuovo, who was born in Lecco, Lombardy in 1936, played the flamboyant villain. He was quite popular for a time, in demand for both arthouse – Luchino Visconti's *Rocco and his Brothers* (1960) and Jacques Demy's *The Umbrellas of Cherbourg* (1964) – and commercial fare – the Dario Argento-scripted Spaghetti Western *The Five-Man Army* (1969) and the sleazy *giallo Strip Nude for Your Killer* (1975). He proves to be a worthy foil for Nero and Hilton and easily steals many of their scenes.

American International eventually released *Massacre Time* in the United States, but they changed the title to *The Brute and The Beast* and gave it a release in 1968. Producers Samuel Z. Arkoff and James H. Nicholson were dissatisfied with the English soundtrack prepared by the dubbers in Rome, however, so they had the film completely revoiced. Beyond that, however, the film was presented uncut. This was only Fulci's second picture to cross the Atlantic, but more would eventually follow. The title of *Massacre Time*, incidentally, derived from a book by Franco Enna. The book was a thriller rather than a Western, but Di Leo knew a good thing when he saw it and utilized it—before going on to adapt the story itself for the Mino Guerrini *giallo Date for a Murder* (1967).

Notes:
1. Albiero, Paolo and Giacomo Cacciatore, *Il terrorista dei generi. Tutto il cinema di Lucio Fulci* (Rome: Un Mondo a Parte, 2004), p. 72.
2. Audio interview with Lucio Fulci, conducted by Pier Maria Bocchi and Andrea Bruni, included on the Shriek Show DVD release of *Touch of Death*.
3. *Ibid.*
4. *Ibid.*
5. "From *Massacre Time* to *A Bullet for Sandoval*: The George Hilton Interview," included on the Wild East DVD release of *Massacre Time/ The Brute and The Beast*.

# Franco Nero Interview by Troy Howarth

The following interview with Franco Nero was conducted by phone on September 23, 2014. *Signor* Nero has my sincere thanks for taking the time to discuss his lengthy career and his thoughts about working with Lucio Fulci.

**Troy Howarth**: What made you want to become an actor?
**Franco Nero**: When I was a boy, when I was about five, six, seven years old, I was reading always of horsemen on a white horse ... and that image was always in my mind when I was a boy. And I said to myself, one day I want to be an actor, so I can be on the horse, the white horse. (*laughs*)
**TH**: Were there any actors in particular you admired at that time?
**FN**: No, because I was a boy at the time. And then, when I was seven, I accepted to do a play at school. And that was my first experience.

Then when I was about 13, 14 or 15, that was when I started to go see movies for the first time. And of course, you know, I liked many American actors at that time. I remember my favorite was Spencer Tracy, when I saw *The Old Man and the Sea* (1958) by Hemingway.

And then I saw the musical *West Side Story* (1961). I must have seen that about 50 times! (*laughs*) There were two musicals; one was *West Side Story*, and the other was *Seven Brides for Seven Brothers* (1954). I must have been about 16, 17—I was crazy about them.

And so then I said, I want to be an actor. So I started to organize plays for students at school. My hometown was Parma. And of course, the students there were saying, "You wanna be an actor? You will stay here all your life!" I said, "No, you will see one day!" (*laughs*)
**TH**: And they certainly did! (*laughter*)
**FN**: So then I went to Milan, I went to University ... I worked ... But in the meantime, I went to an acting school: Piccolo Teatro di Milano. That was the best acting school in Italy, directed by Giorgio Strehler. And that's it. On weekends, I went back to Parma and I formed a little music group. And I used to sing in small provinces for nothing ... I don't know (*laughs*) ... $5, $10, but it was a lot of fun and I used to imitate all the American singers like Sinatra, Perry Como, Dean Martin. And I was singing in English while inventing the words. The people said, "He seems English!" but, you know, I would sing the first line correctly, then the rest was all invented. (*laughs*)
**TH**: And nobody knew...
**FN**: No, they didn't know. Only once, there was an American couple and they said, "What the hell are you saying?!" and I said, "Shut up! You are ruining my show!" (*laughs*) That was very funny, but anyway ...

I went into the army. In the army I organized plays for the soldiers. Then I came to Rome and it all started there.
**TH**: Your film career really began to take off in the mid-1960s ...
**FN**: I started much earlier. At the end of the '50s, in Milan they said, "They are making a movie and the producer is looking for young boys," and I said I want to go! So I went there and the director looked at me and said "Now, can you say a few lines?" I said yes, and I said a few lines for him; I must have been 18.

Then I came to Rome when I was about 21 or 22. To get some money to survive on, I used to help a photographer. He used to photograph paintings. One day there was an assistant director for John Huston working at DeLaurentiis Studios and he came to see .... No, no, it was a photographer friend of the guy I was working with and he looked at me and said, "Can I take some photos of you? Some close-ups?" And I said, okay, why not? Well, these photos ended up on the desk of John Huston. Then John Huston wanted to meet me. So, they asked if I could go to the hotel where he was staying and I went there. I knocked at the door and the door opened: It was a big room with many people, many women, and John Huston looked at me and said, "Oh good boy, now undress!" I said, what do you mean, undress? He said, "*Undress*!" (*laughs*) So I started to undress little by little ... I was down to my underwear and he said, "Turn, turn ... okay, good!" And the next day they called me and said, "John Huston wants you to play Abel in *The Bible* (1966)." (*laughs*)
**TH**: Quite a start! Well, what was John Huston like?
**FN**: He was great. I owe him everything, because he is the man who taught me English. I would go to see him every day and he was my teacher in a way. He said, (*imitating Huston's deep voice*) "You have to learn English because you have a great physique; for playing not only Italians, but you can play anything!" And he gave me recordings of Shakespeare, spoken by John Gielgud, Laurence Olivier, Michael Redgrave and Ralph Richardson ... you know, the typical great English actors. And I learned Shakespeare phonetically, without knowing what I was saying.

So one day, a little later, John Huston was in London. John Huston met Joshua Logan and had dinner and Logan said, "You know, I am doing this big musical, *Camelot*, and I don't want Richard Burton and Julie Andrews, I want somebody new." So John Huston said, "I have the right actors for you: Richard Harris, who played Cain in *The Bible*, and Franco Nero, who played Abel in *The Bible*." And Logan said, "Well, I don't know them." And Huston said, "You should meet them." And of course, Richard Harris was in London and it was easy. But I was doing a Western

**Franco Nero as Django, one of the great antiheroes of the Spaghetti Western.**

at that time and they called me and said, "You have to go to London to meet this director." So I went there and I met him and he started to talk a lot and he made me talk a lot in English, and he said, "You know, John is right. Physically you are perfect to play Lancelot. But you know, this is a big movie, very expensive, and I cannot risk taking you, to hire you, because your English is not very good. I'm sorry." So I started to walk towards the door. When I reached the door, I turned and I said, "But Mr. Logan, I know Shakespeare in English!" He said, "What do you mean, you know Shakespeare? You don't know how to speak proper English! Okay, let's hear it!" So I started and for a half-hour I recited Shakespeare in English: "All the world's a stage and all the men and women merely players …" I went on and on and he went crazy! He said, "If you know how to speak Shakespeare, you know how to say a few bloody lines in the movie! Okay!" (*laughs*) So John Huston, I owe him everything, in a way.

**TH**: What do you remember of your co-stars in *Camelot* (1967), Richard Harris and David Hemmings?

**FN**: Well, Richard Harris, as you know, we worked together in *The Bible*. I knew him already, and he was so happy when they chose me to play Sir Lancelot. He was very happy. I had a lovely time with both of them.

David was always on the phone. He was always trying to do other things, like production … (*laughs*) He was a very busy, busy actor.

**TH**: Prior to that you had done a bunch of Spaghetti Westerns, including one you made with Lucio Fulci …

**FN**: Wait, wait! I forgot, let me tell you, when they called me to meet Joshua Logan in London, I was shooting a Western with Lucio Fulci in Abruzzo, in the center of Italy.

**TH**: So you were making *Massacre Time*?

**FN**: Right, it was called *Massacre Time*.

**TH**: Now, *Django* (1966) came prior to *Massacre Time*?

**FN**: Yes. *Django* was just before. And before that there was also *Texas, Adios* (1966).

**TH**: And you did one with Joseph Cotten, called *The Tramplers* (1965).

**FN**: Yes, I did that with Albert Band. Albert Band was the assistant to John Huston on *The Bible*. And he wanted me in that movie.

**TH**: Do you remember how *Django* came about?

**FN**: Well, *Django* came about in a very easy way. I was in the car with Elio Petri because his wife was my agent and somebody was talking about hiring me to play the lead in *Django*. And I said, "Oh, Elio, me in a Western? I am an actor from the Piccolo Teatro … I want to do serious movies!" He said to me, "Do people know you?" I said, no. He said, "So you have nothing to lose. Just do it!" (*laughs*) So I accepted his advice. I know that [Sergio] Corbucci saw me in a movie; I think it was called *Hired Killer* (1966).

**TH**: *Hired Killer*, yes.

**FN**: Yes, with Robert Webber, a movie that was shot in New York and France. Corbucci saw it and said, "I would love

**American lobby card for *Massacre Time* with Franco Nero ready for action.**

to have this actor. He has the right face to play Django." But the other producers said, "No, no!" The one wanted Mark Damon. The other wanted a Spanish actor … I think his name was Peter Martell, or something like that.

**TH**: Peter Martell, yes.

**FN**: Yeah, so they were fighting—the two producers and the director, Corbucci, were fighting. And one of the producers, Manolo Bolognini, said, "Listen. These three actors are all unknown. So, we will go to the distributor with a photo, a close-up of each of them, and we go to Fulvio Frizzi, the guy who was in charge of the distributor, Euro International Film." So they went there and said, "You pick the face you like for Django." And (*laughs*) he put his finger on my photo. That's it.

**TH**: Was this the first time you met Sergio Corbucci?

**FN**: Yeah, yeah.

**TH**: And you went on to make more films with him, obviously … Do you have any particular memories of him?

**FN**: Well, I have so many great memories. Corbucci was a very funny man, very ironic. He had great humor. In the morning he would say, "Okay, how many people are we going to kill today?" One guy would say 10, another would say, no, 15. Cobucci would say, no, 25! (*laughs*)

Corbucci was like a boy. He was joking and he never liked to shoot early in the morning, because he used to go to bed late in the evening. He used to go out. (*laughs*) So he was always coming late to the set. So we used to wait on the set for him. And he was always late, so one day he arrived and he said, "I know, I know! There was a problem this morning, my tire went flat and I had an important phone call!" Every day he had an excuse. So, he said to me, "You know Franco, all these people are here waiting for me." I said, yes, they are waiting for you to shoot! And he said, "Well, they are waiting to shoot, but let me tell you something: You need an idea before you can shoot. And I don't have an idea yet. So let's go to the bar and get something to drink." (*laughs*) But at the end of the day, he always finished with no problem. Always.

**TH**: Did you have a particular favorite of all the movies you made with him?

**FN**: No, not particularly, because I always had a lot of fun with him … you know, *Django*, *The Mercenary*, *Compañeros* … you know, they were all wonderful and I always loved to work with him.

**TH**: After that came *Massacre Time* for Lucio Fulci. Do you remember how you came to be cast in that film?

**FN**: Well, I got cast because *Django* had been filmed and *Texas, Adios* had come out, so my name was all over, so they hired me for Lucio Fulci. And I said I would do it, and you know why? Because Elio Petri told me that when they were very young, already young directors, he said, "The most talented of all of us was Lucio Fulci."

**TH**: Really?

**FN**: Yeah. Elio said, "But you know, we wanted to suffer and make *auteur* movies." You know, Elio Petri won the Oscar for *Investigation of a Citizen Above Suspicion* (1970).

**German lobby card for *Massacre Time;* Tom (Franco Nero) and Jeffrey take a stand.**

I did a movie with Elio called *A Quiet Place in the Country* (1968), with Vanessa Redgrave. Elio Petri was one of the top Italian directors.
**TH**: Very much so, yes.
**FN**: But he said to me, "You know, Franco, when we were like 23, 24, Lucio was the most intelligent of us. But he didn't want to suffer. So he accepted to do commercial movies." (*laughs*) So that's it.
**TH**: Right. Before this, he had pretty much only made musicals and comedies.
**FN**: Yeah, he did comedies; he wanted to do commercial movies instead of *auteur* movies.
**TH**: Fulci had a reputation for being really tough on his actors, for being very temperamental. Did you find him to be that way?
**FN**: No, no. Lucio Fulci was a big liar. Like Fellini, you know? They liked to lie. Every day when we had dinner, Lucio loved to talk a lot and he always had a cigarette in his mouth and the ashes would go all over his pull-over … all over, the place was full of ashes and we had to clean him. (*laughs*) And he was saying a lot of bullshit, but we all believed it! You know, "I had dinner with John Fitzgerald Kennedy!" He was a bullshitter, but he was good.

He loved teasing the actors. He was kidding an actor that was not very special; he was stiff. He said, "You know that actor is like a block of wood. He's like a *Carabiniere*!" (*laughs*) I'm not going to tell you the names, but he was very funny. Lucio was like Corbucci: full of humor. He was very funny, very, very funny.
**TH**: Was *Massacre Time* a low-budget movie?
**FN**: Oh yeah, the movie was low budget. Yes.
**TH**: What do you remember about your co-star, George Hilton?
**FN**: Well, George Hilton was a very nice man. He came from South America. I think he was doing *fotoromanzi* … you know?
**TH**: Yes.
**FN**: He was hired because he was very inexpensive. (*laughs*) They were always trying to pay actors very little. But he had a good face, so he was very good for the movie. And he was very, very nice, a nice man.
**TH**: Do you have any memories of the cinematographer, Riccardo Pallottini?
**FN**: Oh yeah, yeah. He was very good. Pallottini was a great cinematographer.
**TH**: Was it a difficult film to shoot?
**FN**: Well, you know, when you do action scenes, it's tough, but I enjoyed it very much.
**TH**: You didn't get to do your own English dubbing on early films like *Django* and *Massacre Time*; at what point did you start doing your own dubbing?
**FN**: I started to do the English dubbing right after. I did my own dubbing in Corbucci's movies like *The Mercenary* and *Compañeros*. But earlier, we were not shooting in English. We shot in Italian, so they had to find specialized dubbers for the English.
**TH**: So *Massacre Time* was not filmed in English?
**FN**: No, it was in Italian. *Django* was in Italian, too.
**TH**: That's interesting. I always understood that these films were primarily filmed in English …
**FN**: Right, but earlier on, the first three Westerns were in Italian … no actually, *The Tramplers* was filmed in English.
**TH**: Was that to accommodate the English-speaking actors like Joseph Cotten?
**FN**: Well, you know there was Joseph Cotten, there was the son of Robert Mitchum, Jim Mitchum … so they decided to do it in English.
**TH**: Do you remember if *Massacre Time* was popular at the box-office when it came out?
**FN**: Yes, it was very successful.
**TH**: Did you know that it was sold in Germany as a *Django* film?
**FN**: Yes, in Germany they used to call all of my films *Django* … I did a movie like *Day of the Owl* (1968), about the Mafia, and they called it *Django with the Mafia* … When I did *The Shark Hunter* (1979)—*Django The Shark Hunter* … (*laughs*) They used to call all my movies *Django*, yes.
**TH**: But you only did one real sequel to *Django*, about 20 years after the first one?
**FN**: Yeah, I did *The Return of Django* or *Django Strikes Back* (1987) or something like that.
**TH**: What did you think of that one?
**FN**: Ah, it was so-so. It was all right, but it was not a great movie. We shot the movie in Colombia. I mean the idea was good. The bad guy was on a boat on the river. (*laughs*) It was all right.
**TH**: You worked with Donald Pleasence on that film … do you remember much about him?
**FN**: Yes, he was a wonderful actor. We had a good time together.
**TH**: Around the same time you made *Django* and *Massacre Time* you made a horror film with Mino Guerrini called *The Third Eye* (1965) …
**FN**: That was a little before *Django*, yes.
**TH**: Do you remember much of that film? It hasn't received a lot of exposure in the U.S.
**FN**: Well (*laughs*) I remember the producer got some money from a girl in the movie, Gioia Pascal; her father gave them some money and they made the movie in just a few days. Mino Guerrini was great. He was a journalist. He changed his name to … I don't remember…
**TH**: James Warren.
**FN**: Ah, James Warren, yes! And he was good. Mino Guerrini was a good director and he knew what he was doing. He shot it very well.
**TH**: Another great director you worked with, who sadly passed away recently, was Damiano Damiani. Do you have any special memories of him?
**FN**: Damiani was a big man. He used to be a boxer. (*laughs*) He used to hire people from the streets. He used to combine professional actors and people from the streets. So he used to act out scenes for everybody. At that time, there

was no direct sound, so he was yelling behind the camera all the time.

Damiani and I did some great movies, then I turned down a TV movie he did called *The Octopus* (1984). It was a big TV series but I didn't want to do it, so that was the end of our collaboration. And then a few years ago, before he died, he wanted to do a movie in America with me ... and I would have done it for him, but he couldn't get the money to do it. It was to be called *Eyes*. It was set in the world of prostitution in New York.

**TH**: You next worked with Fulci almost a decade later on the two *White Fang* films. Did he specifically ask for you for these movies?

**FN**: Yes, yes. He wanted to work with me and the producers liked the idea. Both of those films were so successful. This is why we did a second one. The first one was so successful all over the world, so they decided to do a second one. Fulci said, "You know, Franco, years ago I wanted to be an *auteur* and write my own films, but now when they give me a script that I like, I sometimes shoot it better that way. Because I feel I try to be very professional and technical and sometimes they come out pretty well." (*laughs*)

**TH**: The two *White Fang* films were shot in Austria, is that right?

**FN**: Yes.

**TH**: Was it difficult shooting on location?

**FN**: No. I mean, it was cold, very cold, but we enjoyed it. I remember I used to have my son, who was little then, and my two daughters Natasha and Joely [Richardson] were also there and they stayed with me. It was a great atmosphere on those movies, a wonderful atmosphere.

And then of course, they wanted me to repeat that atmosphere with the dog! (*laughs*) And you know, I stayed with the dog and worked to create a special bond with the dog. And of course, sometimes I would be asleep in bed and the dog would hear something and would come over and start licking my face. *Ahhhhh*! (*laughter*) But it was wonderful, wonderful.

**TH**: Did you or Fulci have any problems working with the animals on those films?

**FN**: No. Well ... there was a problem, I think, when it came to shoot the scene with the bear and the dog; that was not an easy scene.

**TH**: What do you remember of some of your co-stars, like Virna Lisi, Fernando Rey and John Steiner?

**FN**: John Steiner was fantastic. That is the reason why we worked together again on these films; we had worked together with Damiani [Note: the film was *The Case is Closed, Forget It*, 1971] and he was fantastic. And then later on he decided he didn't want to be an actor any more. He went to Los Angeles to be a real estate agent. Actually I saw him in Los Angeles. He said he is very happy.

Virna was a beautiful lady, a lovely woman, and she had her son there, and I had my children, so we were like a big family.

Fernando Rey was unique. I think we did like 10 movies together. And so I used to say to Fernando Rey, "Fernando Rey plus Franco Nero equals success!" (*laughs*) And he laughed at that. I met Fernando on [Luis] Buñuel's movie, *Tristana* (1970). But Fernando was fantastic. I remember when we were in Spain, he used to take care of my son. We would go out, Vanessa, my wife, and his wife—and we left our son at his house with Fernando. He was always very, very kind. I remember I used to say, Fernando, why do you always have that beard? It was not a full beard, what do you call it?

**TH**: A goatee.

**FN**: Goatee, yes. He said, "Because if I cut it off, my face looks like shit." (*laughs*)

**TH**: You mentioned *Tristana*... what was Buñuel like to work with?

**FN**: Oh Buñuel was the best. Fantastic. When I did *Tristana*, he never called me Franco. He was against the dictator in Spain, [Generalissimo Francisco] Franco. He did not like that name, so he used to call me Nero. He was fantastic. He told me many stories of how he tried to kill Franco and how he did not succeed. He was always asking me to bring in a bottle of Fernet Branca from Italy.

I have many, many stories, but I will tell you a very funny story. He was a genius. He was the only director in the world who could cut a movie in three days. And he never used music in movies. The music was the barking of dogs, bells ringing ... He was a genius. But like all geniuses, he was childish. One day we were filming in the square in Toledo and everybody was preparing to shoot and he was very nervous. I said, what's happening, Luis? He said, "Somebody took my bag!" And we were worried because we thought maybe it had the script or his notes. So we looked around and finally we found the bag. So, like a boy, he picked up the bag and clutched it to his chest. (*laughs*) So everybody went back to work and he looked around to make sure nobody was looking at him, and he walked to the side of the square, where he thought nobody could see him, and he sat on the bench and finally opened the bag. I followed him and saw finally when he opened it, it contained a ham sandwich and he started to eat it. (*mimics eating furiously*) He pulled out a bottle of Coca-Cola, with a cork in it. In the bottle was red wine and he started drinking. And I said, Luis, what are you doing?! And he started to yell, "Oh Nero, *please*! Don't tell anybody I am hungry!" (*laughs*) He was like a child.

And then, I remember, he was going to do a movie in Spain called *The Monk* but he couldn't make it. He sold the script to the French producers and they said they wanted Peter O'Toole for the lead. And Buñuel said, "No! I give you the script on one condition: Nero *must* play the lead!" So they cast me.

**TH**: Were you happy making *The Monk* (1972)?

**FN**: Yes, yes! It was mostly filmed in Paris, in a studio.

**TH**: After *Challenge to White Fang*, you did not make any more movies with Fulci ... did you keep in touch with him?

**FN**: Well, I kept in touch a little, but then he died. All these directors, like Corbucci and Fulci, they all died on me. It's been a long time since he died. Actually, Fulci called me because he wanted me for a thriller, but I couldn't do it.
**TH**: Do you remember which film?
**FN**: I don't remember which one. I don't know, maybe the one with Jean Sorel but I am not sure.[1]
**TH**: Do you remember hearing about when he died?
**FN**: You know, I think I was away when he died. I heard about his death. I'm sorry I couldn't go to his funeral. But it's always so sad when somebody you know very well dies, especially since I don't think … how old was he when he died? I don't remember?
**TH**: He was 68 when he died.
**FN**: Yeah, so it's a great pity.
**TH**: He had diabetes.
**FN**: Yeah, he was sick for a while.
**TH**: Are his films still popular in Italy?
**FN**: Now? No, no, nobody remembers them. Unfortunately.
**TH**: Around that time, you started working a lot with Enzo Castellari…
**FN**: Yeah, yeah. We did more than 10 movies together, yes.
**TH**: My favorite was *Street Law* (1974) … do you have any particular memories of working with him?
**FN**: Well, we are still working together. We are planning to do two movies together.
**TH**: Oh really?
**FN**: Yeah. One is a Western, and we are preparing to do a movie about boxing—child boxing. So we hope to do these two movies. But Enzo and I are like brothers after more than 40 years of great collaborations.

By the way, let me tell you a funny line that Corbucci used to say to the lighting cinematographer. He used to say, "You better light those two blue lakes"—those lakes would be my eyes—"because if you light them well, they will make me a lot of money!" (*laughs*)
**TH**: You worked on so many different films, it would take forever to go through all your credits …
**FN**: I have made about 200 movies! (*laughs*)
**TH**: I was going to ask about a few actors I particularly like that you have worked with … one of them was William Holden on *21 Hours at Munich* (1976)?
**FN**: Fantastic. Fantastic. I worked with many, many American actors. Many American stars. William Holden, when I was a boy, when I started seeing movies, my favorite actor was William Holden. I must have seen *Picnic* (1955) 20 times. He was beautiful. When we worked together, I used to kiss him on the mouth. (*laughs*) I said, "Billy, you don't know how much I love you, you are my *hero*!" He was so happy. We had an incredible relationship. We used to go out every night together for dinner. We used to eat at the place where we were staying. I remember I used to give some suggestions to the director and Bill would say, "Now,

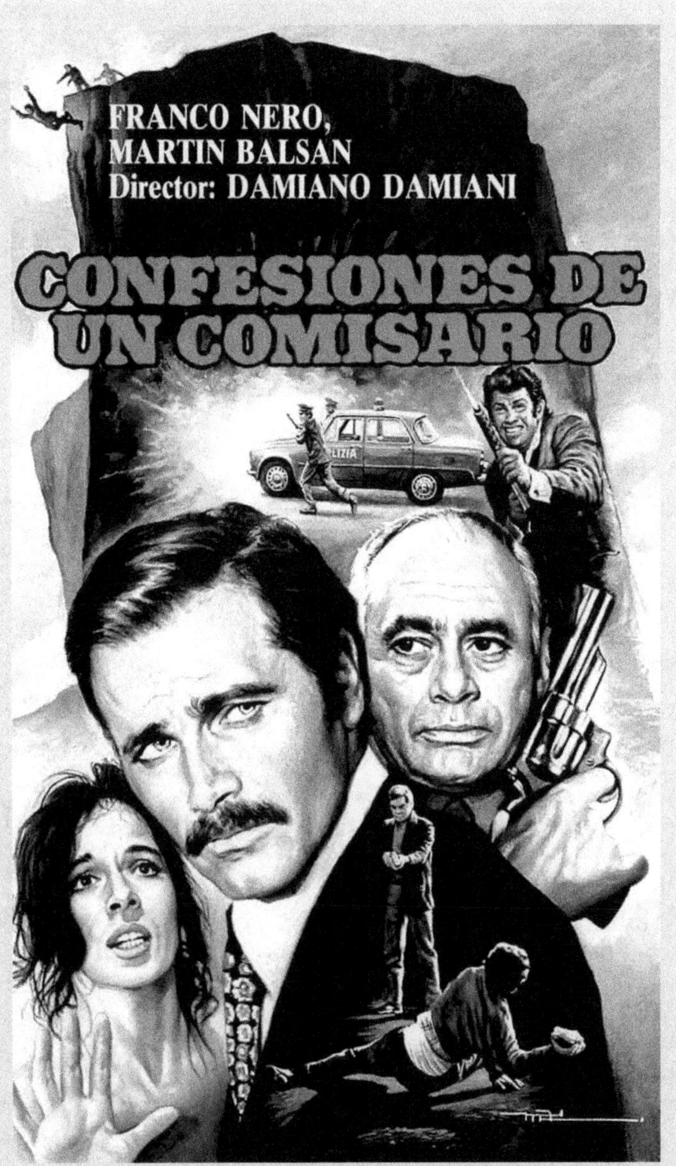


**Spanish poster for Damiano Damiani's *Confessions of a Police Captain* (1971); artwork by Mac.**

you better listen to Franco! He says the right things!" (*laughs*)

But apart from that, one day Castellari came to the set to visit because we were planning to do *Keoma* (1976). And Enzo said, "Oh Franco, can you manage to get Billy to play your dad in *Keoma*?" So I said, "Billy! What do you think about doing a Western?" "Oh that would be great! I can get into shape again!" (*laughs*) But then he had to go back to America and it was not possible.

And actually, in America, I went to see him in Palm Springs. He was crazy about me. He invited me to Kenya. He had a place there. And when I heard about his death, I really cried. You know how he died? I will tell you. He started to have a great relationship with Stefanie Powers. She was on the set with us. And he stopped drinking because of her; it was wonderful. He had a house in Malibu and, from what I hear, he had a fight with her. He was in Malibu all by himself and he got drunk. He was coming down the stairs and he slipped and hit his head on the edge of a table. He cut himself on the temple and he bled to death. I went to his funeral.

**TH**: That's so tragic. He wasn't very old, either.

**FN**: He wasn't old. He was maybe in his 60s. Tragic.

**TH**: On *The Salamander* (1981), you worked with Christopher Lee.

**FN**: Oh yes. Christopher is Italian. He used to say, (*mimicking Christopher Lee's deep voice*) "Franco, I am *Italiano*. I am a Count!" (*laughs*) He spoke Italian *perfectly*. *Perfetto*! And he was talking all the time; he loved to talk *all the time*. I loved it when he was talking. He said his best friend in America was Muhammad Ali. Muhammad Ali would call him just to talk on the phone many times.

Anyway, I loved him. And he played my father in *The Pirate* (1978). I chose him for that part and I suggested him for the part in *The Salamander*. I suggested him and Tony Quinn in *The Salamander*. Then when I did a movie in Sweden a few years later called *The Girl* (1987), I wanted him in the movie, so he came to Stockholm and did three days with me.

**TH**: How about Telly Savalas … you did a film with him called *Redneck* (1973).

**FN**: (*laughs*) Telly Savalas was fantastic. He never liked to go to sleep. I would say, "Telly! You better learn your lines! Your acting in this movie can get you an Oscar, if you give a great performance." "Yeah, yeah, Franco, okay!" (*laughs*)

He loved to play cards. When he was in Rome, I used to take him to see boxing matches. He loved to go see boxing matches. So Telly was another great man, a great man.

**TH**: Did you enjoy making *Die Hard 2* (1990)?

**FN**: You know, it was all right … Nothing special. It was just a movie. (*laughs*) I remember that the director, Renny Harlin, was from Finland and he said I was his idol as a kid.

**Italian *locandina* for Silvio Narizzano's *Redneck* (1973); artwork by Ermanno Iaia.**

The producer, Joel Silver, used to go to a studio in Los Angeles and his accountant was also my accountant. And my accountant used to say, "Franco, I would like posters from your movies—but from the Eastern countries, like Romania, Czech Republic, Russia." So I used to send him posters from my movies, with my name really huge. (*laughs*) And he used to hang these posters in the corridor of his office. One day Joel Silver was there and he said, "Fred, do you know this guy?" "Of course, he is my client," he said. And Silver said, "I want him!" You know, how Americans say, (*mimics American accent*) "I want him!" And that was *Die Hard*. They approached me and I said, "No, I cannot do this movie." Joel Silver says, "What do you mean?! I am the biggest fucking producer in the world!" I said, "I'm sorry, but I'm about to do a movie in Sicily with Vanessa and Fernando Rey." In English it was called *A Breath of Life* (1990). And he said, "Tell me when you have to shoot it." And I said it was, I don't remember now, four or five weeks. So he said, "Okay, I'll tell you what I am going to do. I will fly you to Los Angeles. You work three days with me. Then you go back and do your fucking movie, and then you come back in six weeks and finish my movie." And so we did it. (*laughs*)

**TH**: You also worked with Lamberto Bava on a movie called *The Dragon Ring* (1994) … what was he like to work with?

**FN**: Yeah. Lamberto was a wonderful man, very sweet, professional. We decided to make my character have the long hair and beard … I remember, I played the King. It was nice. We shot a bit in Morocco and then in the Czech Republic. We used to go to work every morning in the Czech Republic and there was a park with all the best animals … a zoo. Fantastic.

**TH**: You also tried your hand at directing with a picture called *Forever Blues* (2005) … did you enjoy directing?

**FN**: It was tough, because I was the producer, I was the director, I was the actor and I was the writer. So it was very tough, but I think I did a good job and I got many prizes for the movie.

**TH**: Are you planning on directing anything else?

**FN**: Oh yeah, yeah. Well, I directed two or three other movies but I didn't put my name on them. I'm not going to name them, but I plan to direct two movies. One is about a blind man … I don't want to say too much about the story. The other is a movie that Elio Petri wrote for me when I was younger, called *The Hostage*. And I am planning to do that as a director, but the other one about the blind man, I will act and direct, both.

**TH**: What was your experience like working with Quentin Tarantino on *Django Unchained* (2012)?

**FN**: Well, it was a lot of fun working with Quentin. He loved me. I first met him when I was doing a movie with Penelope Cruz in which she played my daughter. It was called *Talk of Angels* (1998). And Penelope said to me, "Tomorrow I am going to the festival at San Sebastian." The next day when she came back she said, "You know Franco, I met a young director named Quentin Tarantino. When I told him I was working with you, he said, 'You have to bring him here! He is my idol!'" (*laughs*) So I knew that he was a fan of mine, in a way. And then we met finally one day in Rome and had lunch. He told me that when he was 14, he started to work in a video shop and he studied my movies and he knew *alllllll* my movies: unbelievable! (*laughs*) And he started to say lines from my movies and he quoted music from my movies. Unbelievable! So at the time Enzo Castellari and I were planning to do a Western and I said, "You have to do a cameo." He said, "Okay, I will do it!" But that didn't happen.

**Nero makes a memorable cameo appearance in Quentin Tarantino's Oscar-nominated Spaghetti Western homage *Django Unchained* (2012).**

And then, he called me and said, "I am doing this movie as a tribute to Sergio and to you, so you have to be in the movie!" I said, "Well I don't know, I haven't read the script." (*laughs*) And he sent me the script and I couldn't see any parts, apart from the German that Christoph Waltz did fantastically; he was great in it. So I said, "I don't know. Maybe we can do something else." My idea for a cameo was for Django to occasionally have a flashback in which you see a horseman with the black cape and hat coming slowly towards the camera. And this would be seen throughout the movie, then at the end the horseman stops in front of the camera and the black boy's mother says, "That is your dad." (*laughs*) Tarantino said, "Let me think." But after a while he called back and said "That doesn't work. In real life he could be the father of a black boy, but not in the film!" (*laughs*) Then finally we met in Los Angeles and I decided to do it. I must say, even if he cut a lot—I did a cameo but the movie was very long—during the shooting he would say to the other actors, "You know, Franco Nero was the biggest star in the world together with Charlie Bronson and Clint Eastwood! He's amazing!" (*laughs*) And he used to put the music from the original *Django* on the set and he also showed the original *Django* to the crew. He used to hire a cinema in New Orleans. He was great.

One day, since he said he knew all of my movies, I said, now I am going to see if he knows this movie! So I said, "Listen Quentin, do you know about a movie called *I diafanoidi vengono da Marte* (1966; English title: *War of the Planets*)?" He said, "Yes! Anthony Dawson! Antonio Margheriti!" Unbelievable! So, he knew even that movie! (*laughs*)

**TH**: The rumor is you're about to make another *Django*.

**FN**: Well, they are planning to do a movie in America and I said that if they can get the money, I would do it. I told them, don't wait too many years, because I will be too old! (*laughs*)

**TH**: That covers everything I wanted to ask. I want to thank you very much for talking to me; I've been a very big fan of yours for some time.

**FN**: You're welcome! *Ciao.*

Notes:

1. As per http://www.luciofulci.fr/en/filmographie/trance, the film in question was to have been titled *Trance* and was scheduled to be filmed in June 1983 for producer Piermaria Romano. That Nero was unable to accept the offer during a time when Fulci's career was starting to hit a bad patch may well explain some of the negative feelings the director felt towards his star. Did the project fall apart in light of Nero's rejection of the offer? One can only make guesses. In any event, the film was not made.

# 1967

## *Come rubammo la bomba atomica (Italy/Egypt)*

Aka *How We Stole the Atomic Bomb* (unofficial English-language translation)

Directed by Lucio Fulci; Produced by Copro Film, Five Film and Fono Roma; Story and Screenplay by Gian Paolo Callegari, Alessandro Continenza (as Sandro Continenza), Roberto Gianviti and Amedeo Sollazzo; Director of Photography: Fausto Rossi; Editor: Nella Nannuzzi; Music by Coriolano Gori (as Lallo Gori)

Main Players: Franco Franchi (Franco); Ciccio Ingrassia (Ciccio, also known as No. 87); Julie Menard (Cinzia); Eugenia Litrel (Modesty Bluff); Youssef Wahbi (Doctor Yes); Franco Bonvicini (Derek Flit); Adel Adham (James Bomb)

*Italian fisherman Franco is working off the coast of Egypt when he witnesses an American plane crashing into the ocean. Unbeknown to Franco, the plane is carrying an atom bomb. The incident attracts the attention of the secret service as well as that of SPECTRALIS, a shady organization devoted to evil on a global scale. Franco is abandoned by his crew and washes ashore, where a SPECTRALIS agent named Ciccio abducts him. The agent tries to compel Franco to reveal everything he knows, but it does not go as planned, and ultimately Franco must answer to the mysterious and all-powerful Dr. Yes ...*

Following the high of *Massacre Time*, Fulci went back to work with Franco and Ciccio. He would later claim that he stepped in as a sort of traffic cop on the set of *I due figli di Ringo* (1966), a rather limp Spaghetti Western parody signed by Giorgio Simonelli. As Fulci later explained,

> I shot *I due figli di Ringo* without signing it because Simonelli got sick. The producer said, "Why don't you sign it?" I said because the movie belongs to the director who prepares it, what the fuck do I know about it? [...] I didn't care about finishing it. Every week they said, "Don't worry, Simonelli is coming back." A month later they told me that Simonelli was dead.[1]

**Come rubammo la bomba atomica; original artwork by Scott Hoffman.**

A viewing of the film is enough to justify Fulci's reluctance to sign the film, which is a tired retread of the usual Franco and Ciccio routines in an Old West setting. (Note: The film is not reviewed in depth here because it is not accepted as part of Fulci's "official" canon of credits and even he downplayed his involvement in the picture as insignificant.) The credits give co-director status to Giuliano Carnimeo, who was Simonelli's assistant on the picture. More than likely Franco and Ciccio insisted upon having a more seasoned hand guiding the ship and thus reached out to Fulci to do the job, but Carnimeo would go on to become a not-uninteresting director in his own right; among his credits is the stylish *giallo The Case of the Bloody Iris* (1972).

Fulci followed this favor up with another "official" Franco and Ciccio vehicle. This time, the film was a co-production with Egypt, which at least allows for some colorful travelogue views of an "exotic" landscape. Indeed, the landscape was a little too colorful for the two stars. According to Fulci's assistant, Giovanni Fago, the duo was terrified of flying and insisted upon importing their own food and water for fear that the local cuisine was infected with some terrible malady![2] Beyond that it is pretty much just another spy spoof, though this time the debt to the James Bond canon is even more obvious than usual.

Franco plays a dual role this time, as he also makes an appearance playing his own (elderly) father. Not a lot of difference is to be found between the two performances, however, and by this stage in the game, his propensity for frantic mugging is more than a little tiresome. As usual, Ciccio comes off much better, playing yet another variation on his pompous cretin routine.

The best set piece involves Ciccio's attempt to extract information from Franco. Ciccio does his best to be properly threatening and frightening, but it is all in vain: Not only is Franco a complete idiot, he truly doesn't know anything of value, anyway. In order to raise the stakes, Ciccio decides to break out a newly devised instrument of torture: a sort of makeshift ass-kicking machine. Franco is intrigued and asks for a demonstration; Ciccio, always polite, decides to oblige and ends up getting his own butt kicked in the process.

Later in the film, barely disguised variations on popular fixtures of the spy/*fumetto* genre are introduced. These include a trio of secret agents known as James Bomb, Derek Flit and Modesty Bluff. The obvious reference points are Bond, Flint and Modesty Blaise, the latter of whom was brought to the screen with uneven results by director Joseph Losey in a film of the same name in 1966. The joke

**Italian *locandina* for *Come rubammo la bomba atomica*; artwork by Bob DeSeta.**

in this context is that the three spies are even more inept than Ciccio, which is admittedly no small feat!

Another key set piece involves their meeting with Dr. Yes, an obvious allusion to Ian Fleming's super villain Dr. No (played by Joseph Wiseman in the seminal 1962 film of the same name). Dr. Yes is convinced that Franco and Ciccio are now in cahoots and decides to play a trick on them in the hope of scaring them into revealing the whereabouts of the atom bomb. Dr. Yes insists that the bomb is needed to complete his revivification of The Queen of the Dead. The two dimwits manage to outwit the evil genius by giving him a phony bomb, but their celebration is short-lived: The mummified remains of the Queen spring back to life. However, this turns out to be a deception; the mummy is actually Flit in disguise and, together with his comrades Bomb and Bluff, he helps the boys to escape from the evil madman. The revived body may be a joke, but it is yet another precursor of the zombie imagery which would become so prominent in Fulci's later horror films.

The finale is memorably ironic: The American government, embarrassed by the loss of the bomb, issues a statement saying that there were no nuclear warheads aboard the plane. Franco and Ciccio, however, discover the bomb in the former's fishing nets and take it as a play for power. They are then able to use this discovery to become very wealthy, living out their days on a private island, with the bomb aimed towards civilization should anybody decide to cramp their style. Here again, the duo have managed to attain an unusual degree of success in their scheming; while most Franco and Ciccio films end with their plans going up in smoke, here they have achieved their goal and are in a position of power.

Fulci stages the action with some manic energy, but the tired jokes and unduly complicated plot get in the way of things. *Come rubammo la bomba atomica* has a few amusing scenes and ideas scattered about, but for the most part it is definitely on the lower rung of Fulci's comedies. The director would gamely go forward for one more collaboration with the Sicilian duo, but by this point the bloom was off the rose; it could be that the experience of making something like *Massacre Time* had him itching to move on to fresh pastures, but no matter what the reason, a significant change was about to occur in Fulci's career as a filmmaker.

Notes:

1. Audio interview with Lucio Fulci, conducted by Pier Maria Bocchi and Andrea Bruni, included on the Shriek Show DVD release of *Touch of Death*.
2. Albiero, Paolo and Giacomo Cacciatore, *Il terrorista dei generi: Tutto il cinema di Lucio Fulci* (Rome: Un mondo a parte, 2004), p. 80.

## *Il lungo, il corto, il gatto (Italy)*

Aka *The Tall, The Short, The Cat* (unofficial English-language translation)

Directed by Lucio Fulci; Produced by Five Film and Fono Roma; Screenplay by Gian Paolo Callegari, Roberto Gianviti, Marino Girolami and Amedeo Sollazzo; Director of Photography: Guglielmo Mancori; Editor: Nella Nannuzzi; Music by Coriolano Gori (as Lallo Gori)

**Italian *locandina* for *Il lungo, il corto, il gatto*; artwork by Aller.**

Main Players: Franco Franchi (Franco); Ciccio Ingrassia (Ciccio); Ivy Holzer (Gina); Giusi Raspani Dandolo (Contessa); Ivano Staccioli (Il Gatto); Daniele Vargas (American Inspector)

*Franco and Ciccio work as servants for an eccentric Countess who believes that her late husband has been reincarnated as her pet cat. They are expected to wait on the animal hand and foot and its tendency to escape and cause mischief presents locals with an opportunity to cash in by claiming that the cat has caused damages and they deserve to be paid out of the Countess' deep pockets. When it transpires that the cat had impregnated another kitten, the Countess dies of grief. Franco and Ciccio celebrate by kicking the despised animal out of the house, but upon the reading of the will they have a terrible shock; the Countess has provided for them only on condition that they continue to care for the cat, whose exact measurements and specifications have been recorded and are in possession of her attorney, who plans to enforce the rules of the will. Franco and Ciccio must then move heaven and earth to retrieve the cat …*

*Il lungo, il corto, il gatto* is a significant film in Fulci's filmography, but not for any reasons pertaining to its quality. It marked the end of the road for Fulci and the comedy team of Franco Franchi and Ciccio Ingrassia. The two comedians were still a big box-office draw—though their biggest successes, invariably directed by Fulci, were already behind them. Fulci had grown tired of being known as "Franchi and Ingrassia's director" for a number of reasons. He had already put them through variations on the same basic jokes and routines more times than he would care to count. The material was getting thinner and thinner. And worst of all, they insisted upon maintaining a degree of control over their films that prevented Fulci from really developing as an artist. *Massacre Time* had offered a welcome respite and demonstrated that he was a talent deserving of far more than labored slapstick and the director was determined to forge ahead on his own. He would contribute to the screenplay for *I due crociati*, released the following year, but *Il lungo, il corto, il gatto* marked his final time directing the duo on screen. That said, he would reunite with the two actors on a couple of different occasions: Ingrassia would appear in a supporting role in his horror comedy *Young Dracula*, while Franchi would be at the center of the mini-series *Un uomo da ridere*, which Fulci directed just prior to his career re-energizing thanks to the world-wide box-office success of *Zombie*.

Based on the title, one would assume that the film is a spoof of Sergio Leone's epic *The Good, The Bad and The Ugly*, which was a major box-office smash in 1966. Franco and Ciccio made a career out of parodying pop culture phenomena, but in fact the title is virtually the only link to Leone's classic (and in any case, the duo would spoof the Leone film outright in their very next outing—*The Handsome, the Ugly and the Stupid* [1967]—directed by Giovanni Grimaldi). The theme of characters grasping for wealth is another common plot point, and there is also an amusing spoof of the showdown sequence in Leone's film, with Franco squaring off against the cat, but beyond that the two storylines are completely different.

On the face of it, the pleasingly quirky set-up should yield some real laughs. The characters vary from the greedy—Franco and Ciccio—to the downright pathetic—the Countess. However, none of them manage to generate any genuine audience empathy. The Countess is so ridicu-

***Il lungo, il corto, il gatto;* original artwork by Scott Hoffman.**

lous in her beliefs that one can never take her seriously; even when she dies, it is played for laughs. The chilly tone aptly reflects the lack of humanity in the characters, but this is not particularly interesting in and of itself. If anything, it just makes it difficult to care what happens to whom or why.

Fulci's direction is blandly efficient but never reaches the levels of inspiration evident in his better films with the duo. One can sense that he is growing bored with these assignments at this stage and certainly it is hard to blame him for this. Franco and Ciccio may have brought him a level of commercial stability and a steady income, but they also stifled him creatively. The two actors were now in the habit of bringing along a writer by the name of Amedeo Sollazzo, whom Fulci recalled as their preferred gag writer.[1] Sollazzo (1931-1971) began working on the team's films with *Oh! Those Most Secret Agents*, but it seems that his role in the screenplays became more prominent as he gained the trust of Franco and Ciccio. In time, Fulci's contributions would therefore become less and less valuable to the team. Fulci would work in bits of craziness where he could, but the duo had final approval on what was included in their films and it's not likely that this degree of creative control sat well with the director. Fulci therefore approaches this film with an air of weary resignation: He makes a professional job of it, working in the occasional stylistic flourish where he can, but for the most part it lacks the sheer, frenetic energy of his best comedy work.

Ultimately, *Il lungo, il corto, il gatto* is neither fish nor fowl. It's not among the worst films Franco and Ciccio made, nor is it among their best. For Fulci, it represents another paycheck gig; it doesn't give him the chance to really shine, but he does the best he can under the circumstances. As such, he is able to finally divorce himself from Franco and Ciccio with his dignity intact. And most assuredly, better things lay ahead. Within the context of his filmography, it can however be seen as a precursor to his later—and much superior—Edgar Allan Poe homage, *The Black Cat* (1981).

Notes:
1. Audio interview with Lucio Fulci, conducted by Pier Maria Bocchi and Andrea Bruni, included on the Shriek Show DVD release of *Touch of Death*.

## *Operation Saint Peter's (Italy/France/West Germany)*

Aka *Operazione San Pietro; Au diable les anges; Die Abenteuer des Kardinal Braun*

Directed by Lucio Fulci; Produced by Turi Vasile, for Ultra Film, Marianne Productions and Roxy Film; Story and Screenplay by Adriano Bolzoni, Ennio De Concini, Lucio Fulci, Roberto Gianviti and Paul Hengge; Director of Photography: Erico Menczer; Editor: Elisabeth Kleinert-Neumann, Ornella Micheli and Gabrielle Reinecke; Music by Ward Swingle and The Swingle Singers

Main Players: Lando Buzzanca (Napoleone); Jean-Claude Brialy (Cajella); Edward G. Robinson (Joe Ventura); Heinz Rühmann (Cardinal Erik Braun); Uta Levka (Samantha); Christine Barclay (Marisa); Pinuccio Ardia (The Baron); Ugo Fangareggi (Agonia); Dante Maggio (The Captain); Wolfgang Kieling (Poulain); Herbert Fux (Targout); Virgilio Gazzolo (Schultz, the Cardinal's secretary)

*The Baron, Agonia and The Captain are three small-time crooks looking to make it big. While pulling off a bank heist, they inadvertently penetrate a prison cell and release Napoleone, who presents himself as a master criminal. The four men band together and hatch a scheme to steal Michelangelo's Pietà, which is on display at Saint Peter's Cathedral. Stealing the statue is no problem, but trying to sell it proves to be more difficult. Their troubles become compounded when American gangster Joe Ventura gets wise to what they are trying to do. Ventura and his femme fatale Samantha steal the Pietà and try to cash in on it themselves, but the Vatican is not about to be outfoxed so easily ...*

Fulci's first film, post-Franco and Ciccio, is an elaborate heist comedy. As the director was quick to admit, it was a cash-in on a popular box-office hit: Dino Risi's *The Treasure of San Gennaro* (1966) was a light-hearted caper comedy about a pair of American thieves (played by Harry Guardino and Senta Berger) who talk a group of Italians (including Totò and nominal star Nino Manfredi) into helping to steal the treasure of San Gennaro. Risi's film offered the right mixture of comedy, romance and suspense, making it a hit with audiences and critics alike. Nothing spells success like imitations and, not for the last time, Fulci found himself riding on the success of another filmmaker. This aspect of Fulci's career has often resulted in him being unfairly maligned as a copycat, but in truth there is no shame in using a popular success to inspire your own work; the only shame is in being slavishly imitative, which is not something Fulci can truly be accused of.

**Italian *locandina* for *Operation Saint Peter's*; artwork by Giuliano Nistri.**

*The Treasure of San Gennaro* was likewise co-written by screenwriter Ennio De Concini (1923-2008), who earned an Oscar for his work on Pietro Germi's *Divorce—Italian Style* (1961). De Concini also leant his talents to everything from Mario Bava's *Black Sunday* (1960) to Tinto Brass' *Salon Kitty* (1976), but there was at least one filmmaker who was resolutely unimpressed by his talents: Lucio Fulci. As the director would later recall:

> The producer's pet was De Concini, who ruined two of my movies.[1] That's what I think of De Concini, who is considered a genius. Gianviti and I wrote the last scenes, which are the funniest part of the movie; De Concini wrote the rest. I did it because they finally paid me a lot of money.[2]

Regardless of Fulci's take on De Concini, *Operation Saint Peter's* benefits from a clear, concise and coherent narrative. The story is engaging and the characters are a colorful lot.

The material is rife for the kind of anti-clerical sentiment that is evident in so many of Fulci's other movies, but it does not go far in this direction. If anything, the film is one of the sweetest-natured that Fulci ever directed. Whether this was down to De Concini or Fulci is open to speculation, of course, but the Church does not escape entirely unscathed. The film touches on the way in which great works of art have been commercialized and prostituted by the Vatican. The Pietà is on display at Saint Peter's Cathedral, but when the viewer is first introduced to this locale, it is covered up because it is a day of worship. That does not stop the guide from reminding people that there are nice picture postcards available in the gift shop—at a reasonable price, of course. Inevitably, Fulci shows a brash American bribing his way to seeing the statue up close. The beauty of the artwork itself is secondary to the price it can fetch and this is certainly crucial to the plot, as well. The Pietà is therefore reduced to being just another piece of desirable merchandise; its value rests not in whatever spiritual comfort it may possess, but in the inflated price tag it will surely fetch.

The clergy is also shown to be hypocritical, if not entirely corrupt. In one scene, Napoleone is forced into going to confession by his girlfriend, Marisa. He tells the priest that he has sinned, to which the priest said that everybody sins these days. He clarifies further by saying that he has stolen, to which the priest replies that stealing is the way of the world and not to worry about it. However, when he reveals that he has stolen from the church, the priest becomes stern: "That's more serious." Napoleone then reveals that he has stolen from the Vatican: "That's much more serious." The implication is clear; the church cannot concern itself with petty theft committed in the moral cesspool of regular society, but when it encroaches on their "turf," this needs to be addressed much more severely.

Beyond these touches, however, Fulci and company are surprisingly gentle with the church. That is not to say that they are not made to look a bit ridiculous. From the special phone linked in with the Pope—complete with celestial muzak playing as the Pope prepares to address the Cardinal—to the final scenes showing the different congregations trying to outdo each other as they do battle with Ventura and attempt to retrieve the precious statue, Fulci doesn't miss an opportunity to play up the absurdity of the church and its representatives. This, however, does not come at the expense of making them look completely debased or corrupt. True, there are strong implications of greed and moral hypocrisy (notably in the scenes depicting the various "holy men" and their feigned reactions of moral outrage when presented with the female body) but ultimately they are depicted as a force for good in an otherwise corrupt society. Fulci's own distrust of the church had not fully developed at this time and would likely be influenced by the tragedies which would befall him in his personal life just a couple of years after this film, so if the satire seems a bit muted or even safe, it pays to remember that the man who made this film was in a happier place compared to the man who made, say, *Don't Torture a Duckling*.

The film builds to a truly crazed finale that benefits enormously from the input of the distinguished stunt coordinator Rèmy Julienne. Born in France in 1930, Julienne entered movies in the mid-1960s as a stunt performer and co-coordinator. He became renowned for his flair for staging and executing high-speed chase sequences, a function he performed in such films as Peter Collinson's *The Italian Job* (1969), Henri Verneuil's *The Burglars* (1971), Stuart Rosenberg's *Love and Bullets* (1979), John Glen's *For Your Eyes Only* (1981) and many others. He last worked on Ron Howard's *The Da Vinci Code* (2006). Julienne's flair for bringing off seemingly impossible stunts is much in evidence as the various interested parties attempt to reach the Pietà before Ventura carts it off for good. Using motorcycles and cars, the various priests, monks and thieves take to the streets and nearly do each other in—all in the name of the Lord, of course. This kind of elaborate stunt work was relatively new in Fulci's films, but he integrates it well into the action and does not allow logic to get in the way of a good sight gag. This freewheeling, anarchic approach recalls the stronger elements of his Franco and Ciccio comedies, notably the not-entirely-dissimilar *Come svaligiammo la banca d'Italia*.

The film marks the first of three collaborations between Fulci and lead actor Lando Buzzanca. Born in Palermo in 1935, Buzzanca dropped out of school in order to pursue his dream of becoming an actor. He made his debut with an uncredited bit in William Wyler's *Ben-Hur* (1959) before perfecting the routine of the lower-class Italian immigrant struggling to make ends meet in a world he does not entirely comprehend. He appeared in Pietro Germi's *Divorce—Italian Style* and *Seduced and Abandoned* (1964), then rose to more prominent parts in such films as Antonio Pietrangeli's *The Magnificent Cuckold* (1964) and Alberto Lattuada's *Don Juan in Sicily* (1967). He also worked with Fulci's mentor, Steno, on the comedy *Letti sbagliati* (1966) and was of the opinion that Fulci out-classed his role model:

> Fulci used to speak wonders about Steno, but I did not agree with his assessment, even though I recognized that his comedies had great value. That was because I saw Steno's limits. Fulci had a great quality as a director: he filmed like a God. He had a sense of framing and camera movement that I've never seen in anyone else. Perhaps I found this quality only in Marco Vicario, another one who did not repeat the same shot twice. Fulci was extraordinary, he always challenged himself, even though it meant risking that he would fall down flat. That's because he was a very, very cultured man, but when making movies the sense of criticism prevailed over culture.[3]

Buzzanca gives an excellent performance as the outwardly cool but inwardly spineless Napoleone in this film. His understated approach to comedy stands in stark contrast to the baggy pants excesses of Franco and Ciccio and works to the film's advantage. He would go on to top-line two of Fulci's final comedies for the big screen, *The Eroticist* and *Young Dracula*.

The legendary Edward G. Robinson played Joe Ventura. Robinson's screen legacy almost doesn't require an introduction, so to keep it brief; he was born as Emanuel Goldenberg in Romania in 1893, then immigrated with his family to the United States in the early 1900s. He worked sporadically in silent films before establishing himself as a tough talking, swaggering mobster in such early gangster classics as *Little Caesar* (1931) and *The Last Gangster* (1937). A committed leftist, he grew to be uncomfortable with essaying such roles and made a concerted effort to change his screen image by tackling more benign characters in the likes of *The Amazing Dr. Clitterhouse* (1938) and *Dr. Ehrlich's Magic Bullet* (1940). John Huston's classic *Key Largo* (1948) provided him with another memorable gangster characterization and Robinson also excelled in a number of hard-boiled *noir* thrillers, including Billy Wilder's *Double Indemnity* (1944), and Fritz Lang's *The Woman in the Window* (1944) and *Scarlet Street* (1945). Robinson remained active until his death in 1973, making a memorable, scene-stealing appearance in the cult sci-fi flick *Soylent Green* (1973) with Charlton Heston; he died a matter of weeks after wrapping his scenes in that picture and was awarded a posthumous honorary Oscar for his imposing body of work. Robinson's screen image is lampooned in this film, and not always in a particularly kind way. Joe Ventura is emblematic of another era—a time in which "gentlemen" gangsters wore natty suits and commanded respect from *maître d*'s as well as from their underlings—and in a sense, time has passed him by. Ventura is, in short, a dinosaur. The formerly intimidating mob boss is now bordering on senility and is so badly affected by post-traumatic stress disorder that he slips into a child-like state every time he hears three knocks—the knocks sending him into flashback mode to a particularly nasty gangland beating he suffered at the hands of his so-called friends. Ventura rallies late in the action and regains some of his former dignity, but by the end of the picture he is back to his usual impotent self once more. One would imagine that working with a legend like Robinson was intimidating for Fulci, but in fact he did not even want Robinson in the picture: when producer Turi Vasile sprung the news on the director that Robinson had been cast in the part, Fulci was incredulous: "But he's pushing 80!" Fulci was obviously concerned that the actor would be ill equipped to handle the demanding role, but Robinson rose to the challenge like a perfect professional. Even so, Fulci was characteristically terse and demanding. In one scene, Robinson improvised a bit of business by removing his coat, prompting Fulci to stop the take and yell at the veteran actor to knock it off. Robinson replied by saying he had done something similar in a John Ford movie. Fulci's reply? "What the fuck do I care?!"[4] Buzzanca would later recall that some of Fulci's frustrations boiled down to a language barrier: "[Fulci] did not know a word of English! We were all acting in English and he didn't understand it!"[5] Fulci's script supervisor, Rita Agostini[6], would later provide another possible reason for Fulci's difficulties with Robinson: "Lucio did not love actors that much, and also had difficulties with foreign languages, so he had to discuss with people whom he did not understand directly. For someone like him it was a huge nuisance. On the set, he used to call them with unthinkable ... and unrepeatable names!"[7]

The bewitching Uta Levka played Ventura's *femme fatale*. She is effective in the role, conveying an air of slinky eroticism as well as a sly sense of humor; she also provides the first (albeit brief) flash of nudity in a Fulci film. Born in Germany in 1942, Levka appeared in several of the popular German-made Edgar Wallace *krimis*, including *The Sinister Monk* (1965) and *The Hunchback of Soho* (1966), before claiming the lead role in Radley Metzger's sexed-up take on the Prosper Mérimée opera *Carmen*, titled *Carmen, Baby* (1967). Following her turn for Fulci, she would relocate to England and appear in a few films for American International Pictures, including two for director Gordon Hessler: *The Oblong Box* (1969) and *Scream and Scream Again* (1970), both top-lining genre superstars Vincent Price and Christopher Lee. Levka walked away from films in the early 1970s and evidently her experience working with Fulci is not high on her list of favorite memories. Levka would later claim in an interview that during the filming, she retired to bed for a night of much-needed rest; much to her surprise, another person entered the bed and sidled up beside her—panic-stricken, she turned on the light and found that it was Lucio Fulci, who was clearly smitten by her and had more on his mind than running lines for the next day's filming. She threw him out of the room and the following day, she found herself being treated differently by the director, who would often stop perfectly good takes to dress her down in front of the crew. She finally had enough and snapped back that he was being unpleasant "just because I wouldn't let you stay with me in bed last night." Fulci had not anticipated this reaction and gave her a dirty look, but from that moment on he left the actress in peace.[8] Rita Agostini had a very different recollection of Fulci's relationship with Levka, however, which could lend some credence to the idea of the actress having a personal grudge which compelled her to invent the incident:

> There was a German actress in the film, a bit cross-eyed, who had been imposed [by the producer]. And he despised the people that were imposed on him. What's more, he hated her because she always spent too much time in make-up [...] Lucio called her "*la cessa*" [Note: *cesso* means "toilet," *cessa* is the female declination, meaning a person who is as ugly as a toilet], and he did it explicitly. He yelled: "Send me *la cessa*!"[9]

Whether one chooses to believe Agostini or Levka, there's no doubting that the relationship between Fulci and the actress was strained, adding yet another complication to an already difficult production.

In spite of the problems he encountered in filming for the first time in English, Fulci would later point to *Operation Saint Peter's* as the film which caught the eye of producer Edmondo Amati, who would bankroll some of Fulci's most significant films of the late '60s and early '70s.

Notes:

1. De Concini also wrote *Four of the Apocalypse*.
2. Audio interview with Lucio Fulci, conducted by Pier Maria Bocchi and Andrea Bruni, included on the Shriek Show DVD release of *Touch of Death*.
3. Albiero, Paolo and Giacomo Cacciatore, *Il terrorista dei generi. Tutto il cinema di Lucio Fulci* (Rome: *Un Mondo a Parte*, 2004), p. 87.
4. Giusti, Marco, *Stracult*: *Dizionario dei film Italiani* (Milano: Frassinelli, 2004), p. 586.
5. Albiero, Paolo and Giacomo Cacciatore, *Il terrorista dei generi. Tutto il cinema di Lucio Fulci* (Rome: Un Mondo a Parte, 2004), p. 87.
6. This was Agostini's first collaboration with Fulci; she would go on to serve in the same capacity on such films as *The Eroticist*, *The Psychic*, *City of the Living Dead*, *The Beyond*, *The New York Ripper* and *Manhattan Baby*.
7. Albiero, Paolo and Giacomo Cacciatore, *Il terrorista dei generi. Tutto il cinema di Lucio Fulci* (Rome: Un Mondo a Parte, 2004), p. 87.
8. Huber, Uwe, "Die braven Rollen interessierten mich nie," *Splatting Image*, March 2001, #45, p.19-25.
9. Albiero, Paolo and Giacomo Cacciatore, *Il terrorista dei generi. Tutto il cinema di Lucio Fulci* (Rome: Un Mondo a Parte, 2004), p. 87.

# 1969

## *Perversion Story (Italy/France/Spain)*

Aka *Una sull'altra; One On Top of the Other; Nackt über Leichen*

Directed by Lucio Fulci; Produced by Edmondo Amati, for Empire Films, Les Productions Jacques Roitfeld and Trébol Films C.C.; Screenplay by Lucio Fulci, Roberto Gianviti and José Luiz Martínez Mollá; Director of Photography: Alejandro Ulloa; Editor: Ornella Micheli; Music by Riz Ortolani

Main Players: Jean Sorel (Dr. George Dumurrier); Marisa Mell (Susan Dumurrier/Monica Weston); Elsa Martinelli (Jane); Alberto De Mendoza (Henry Dumurrier); John Ireland (Inspector Wald); Faith Domergue (Martha); Riccardo Cucciolla (Benjamin Wormser); Jean Sobieski (Larry)

Cameo Appearance: Lucio Fulci (Handwriting Expert)

*George Dumurrier runs a successful clinic in San Francisco, but his reputation is tarnished by his desire to grab headlines at all costs by making fantastic claims. His marriage to Susan is strained and the woman's health is precarious at best. George carries on an affair with Jane, but she is anxious that he leaves Susan and devotes himself to her. When Susan dies unexpectedly, George finds himself on the shortlist of suspects. Things take an unusual turn when he discovers that a stripper by the name of Monica Weston bears an uncanny resemblance to his "late" wife. Might she actually be Susan in disguise and could it be that George is being set up for an appointment in the gas chamber? ...*

*Operation Saint Peter's* went into release at the end of December 1967. It proved to be a success but Fulci did not find himself on the receiving end of a barrage of offers for work. He contributed to the screenplays for the Franco and Ciccio comedy *I due crociati* and the Riccardo Freda *giallo Double Face;* the latter proved to be particularly significant, as it offered his first direct association with the Italian thriller. Around the same time, producer Edmondo Amati, who had been impressed by *Operation Saint Peter's*, approached him. As Fulci explained:

> I'm an honest man so I must say that Romolo Guerrieri did a movie called *The Sweet Body of Deborah* (1968), a *giallo* invented and produced by Luciano Martino. Anyway, one day the lawyer, Pietravalle, was talking with Amati in his office. I thought they had finished when I heard Amati say, "Fulci is intelligent, he's smart, a good director." And Pietravalle said, "He's a good goalie." [...] When Piatravalle came out of the office, I didn't speak to him, I was ready to cry. I never met him again. [...] Amati looked at me and said, "We have a contract; what do you want to do?" So I went to Gianviti on my knees and told him we had to invent something. He said, "We like thrillers, let's write one!" So we wrote *Perversion Story.*[1]

Fulci's anecdote is significant: He had been directing films for 10 years, but to many people he was seen as a hack who guided comedians like Franco and Ciccio through their paces. *Massacre Time* had demonstrated a flair for the cruel and the poetic only hinted at in his comedy work, but it was a one-off. He had not been given an opportunity to follow through on its promise, having retreated to the safety of Franco and Ciccio before breaking free to make another light-hearted caper comedy. Fulci was already in his 40s and had yet to really prove himself as a serious artist; the time had come to get serious and do something different. And so, taking a cue from the success of Guerrieri's *giallo* (which was met with far more audience acceptance than Mario Bava's seminal work in the genre, *The Girl Who Knew Too Much,* 1963, and *Blood and Black Lace*, 1964), Fulci and Gianviti concocted a scenario with ample doses of sex and duplicity; the humor would be of the pitch black variety and effectively the "old Lucio Fulci" of comedies would pass into oblivion.

**Italian poster for *Perversion Story*; artwork by Renato Casaro.**

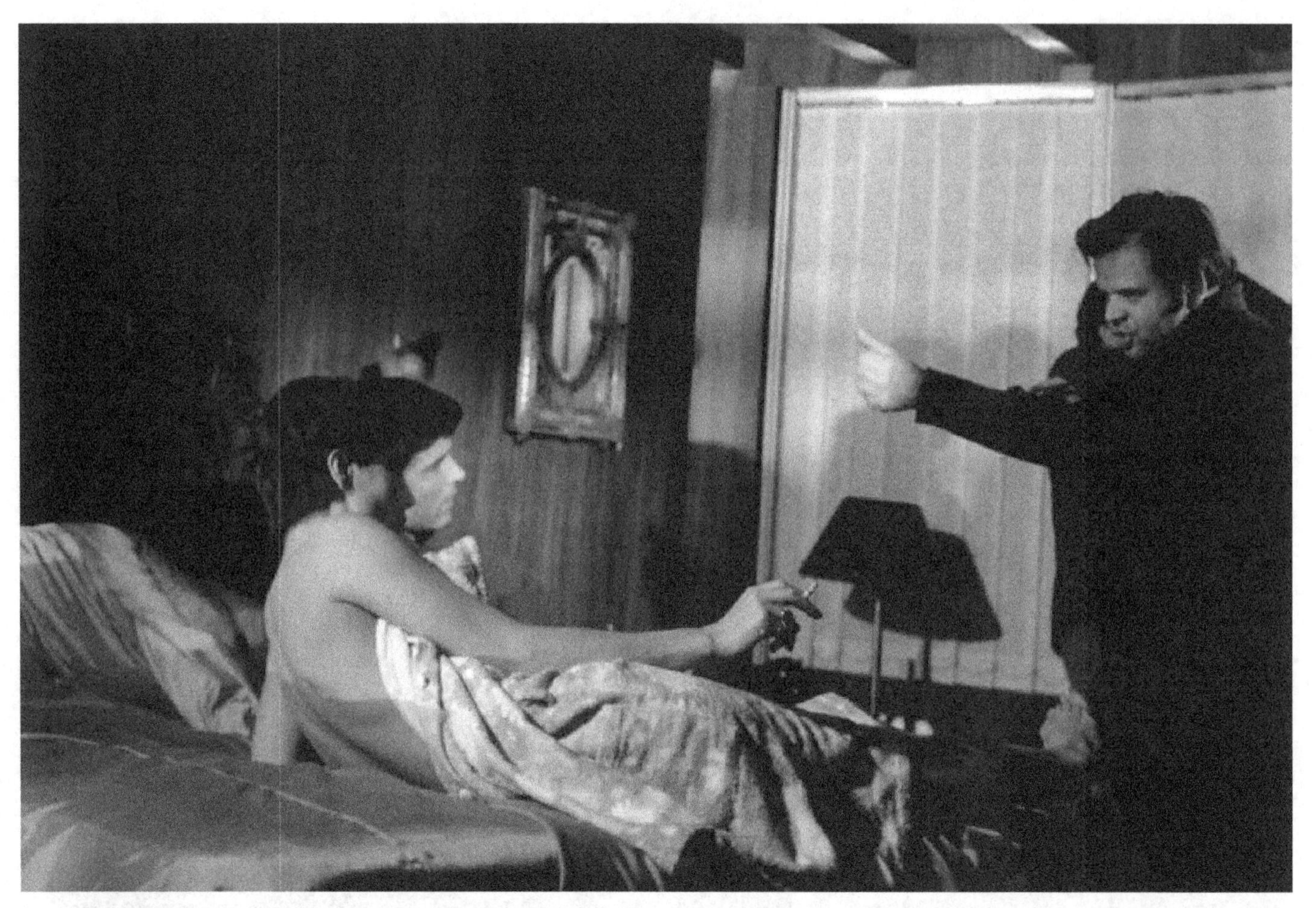

**Rare behind-the-scene glimpse of Lucio Fulci (right) directing Elsa Martinelli and Jean Sorel in their lovemaking scene.**

For the benefit of the uninitiated, the *giallo* is a very particularly Italian brand of murder mystery. The genre got its official start in the cinema with the release of Mario Bava's *The Girl Who Knew Too Much* in 1963, but it is important to note that the film did not spring out of nowhere: Italian thrillers had been around since the silent era, truth be told, but Bava was the first filmmaker to really define what would come to be known as the *giallo*. The genre's moniker derives from the series of lurid paperback thrillers published by Mondadori, which were distinguished by their yellow (*giallo*) covers, invariably illustrated with an image of a woman (often clad in a sexy negligee) being menaced by a knife or gun-wielding assailant. These books included Italian translations of works by Agatha Christie as well as hard-boiled detective novelists like Raymond Chandler. Italian novelists got in on the act, too, and copies of the books would fly off the shelves with regularity. In cinematic terms, antecedents to Bava's first attempt can be traced to such *auteurs* as Alfred Hitchcock and Fritz Lang, as well as to the lovably lurid *krimi* films produced in Germany, based on the stories of British author Edgar Wallace. In purely generic terms—for what exactly does or does not constitute a proper *giallo* film is often the topic of spirited debate—*gialli* are Italian thrillers with an emphasis on the lurid or the violent. Putting it even more simply, there are two basic "types" of gialli: the "bad people trying to drive a virtuous person insane" and the "killer in black slashing up young women" strains. Fulci would dabble in both, but his first efforts—the aforementioned *Double Face* and *Perversion Story*—are readily identifiable as belonging to the former variety. These films owe a tremendous debt to Henri-Georges Clouzot's *Les Diaboliques* (1955), a twist-laden thriller that knocked audiences for a loop and retains much of its terrifying impact to this day. Bava helped to define the *giallo* in cinematic terms, but his films did not attract much attention when they were originally released. The genre would really capture the imagination of viewers with the release of Dario Argento's debut *The Bird with the Crystal Plumage* (1970); the film cleaned up at the box-office and led to a series of *gialli* with imitative titles, including Fulci's own *A Lizard in a Woman's Skin* and *Don't Torture a Duckling*. Fulci would buck at the implication that he was borrowing anything explicitly from Argento and indeed many critics would do well to remember that Fulci beat the younger director to the punch, unleashing his first *giallo* a year before Argento burst onto the scene with his own first effort. In any event, the genre would peak in the 1970s, but *gialli* continue to be made to this day.

*Perversion Story* takes its cue from the novel *D'entre les morts*, written by the renowned crime fiction duo of Pierre Boileau and Thomas Narcejac. The story had been famously adapted for Alfred Hitchcock's masterpiece *Vertigo* (1958). Sensibly, Fulci and Gianviti saw fit to not hew close to Hitchcock's model, and the similarities between the two films are more subtle than heavy-handed.

The story hinges on the concept of the deceptive nature of appearances. The film's superficial, self-centered protagonist is a faithless husband whose life is turned upside-down by the sudden passing of his wife. His grief is not motivated by a sense of remorse, however. He is simply concerned (and rightly so) that he will somehow be implicated in the death and that this will upset his plans of starting a new life with his lover, Jane. When he encounters the sultry Monica, he is unable to tell for sure whether or not it is really his wife for one simple reason: He is so self-centered and egotistical that he never really got to know the woman in the first place. The ensuing games of sexual manipulation owe a stronger debt to the likes of *The Sweet Body of Deborah* than to the Hitchcock film, though the two pictures share a similarly melancholy disposition.

The plotting is exceedingly clever and logical, lending credence to Fulci's later assertion that his *gialli* were more coherent than those of many of his contemporaries. The character of George is initially smug and unlikable, but as the story unfolds and his world starts to crumble around him, it is hard not to feel for him. Similarly, Monica is an exceedingly fascinating figure, one that the audience can never be certain whether she is a legitimate *femme fatale* or simply a pawn in a very cruel game. The finale works remarkably well on several levels. For one, the drama is sufficiently strong that one becomes legitimately engrossed in it on an emotional level. For another, Fulci and Gianviti (as Fulci would later explain, José Luiz Martínez Mollá was credited solely to appease the Spanish co-producers and had no input into the script[2]) work in a series of very clever twists and turns that not only surprise but also make perfect sense in context. The revelation that Susan and Monica are one and the same could easily have come off as hackneyed, but it works thematically, as well. George would never catch on to the scheme for the simple reason that he is too arrogant and superficial to really pay much attention to the woman (or women) with whom he is having sex. He is therefore the ideal patsy in a scheme orchestrated by his jilted wife and his long-suffering older brother, Henry. In a way, one can't help but admire Henry and Susan for their ingenuity, but they failed to take the presence of another jilted individual into the equation: The lonely and pathetic Benjamin has become so obsessed with Susan in the form of Monica that he would sooner kill her and her lover than lose her for good. The end result is very satisfying indeed.

Fulci's direction is flashy in the best sense of the term. He utilizes every stylistic device at his disposal as if to emphasize the superficial and glitzy lifestyle of his flawed protagonists. His use of visual tricks like split-screen and split diopter shots anticipates the later work of Brian De Palma, who would be equally praised and damned for his use of such stylistic flourishes. Fulci keeps the action moving at a steady pace and also ensures that the film works on a dramatic level, thus preventing it from becoming a mere exercise in style. Production values are consistently excellent and Fulci and cinematographer Alejandro Ulloa makes fine use of the San Francisco locales, including the gas chamber at San Quentin. The overall impact is greatly enhanced by an outstanding, dynamic score by Riz Ortolani.

The film is also well served by a fine cast. Leading man Jean Sorel had already established himself as the *giallo*'s premiere superficial cad in *The Sweet Body of Deborah* and he would continue to play such roles, in both an unsympathetic and sympathetically put-upon key, in later *gialli* like Fulci's own *A Lizard in a Woman's Skin* and Romolo Guerrieri's *The Double* (both 1971). He is very effective as the smug George, seamlessly moving from untrustworthy playboy to hero-in-distress. Marisa Mell played the dual roles of Monica Weston and Susan Dummurier. She offers ample evidence of her acting ability while also being given plenty of opportunities to show off her tremendous looks and physique, notably during the stunning striptease sequence set to Ortolani's blaring music. Mell was born in Austria in 1939 and made her first (uncredited) film appearance in 1954. She would appear in the *krimi Puzzle of the Red Orchid* (1962), with Christopher Lee, Ken Russell's feature film debut *French Dressing* (1964) and as one of the many women in Marcello Mastroianni's life in Mario Monicelli's *Casanova 70* (1965). Mell's extraordinary looks caught the attention of casting directors in Hollywood, but she turned down an offer to relocate to America, fearing she would lose control of her career. Her most iconic role came when Mario Bava cast her as Eva Kant in his pop-art classic, *Danger: Diabolik* (1968); interestingly, the leading roles for the latter film had originally been earmarked for both her *Perversion Story* co-stars, Sorel and Elsa Martinelli, when the film was first set to be made by British director Seth Holt in 1964. Mell's later career would be dominated by far too many films which sought to exploit her body rather than her acting ability, and the actress grew rather embittered as a result. She would appear in the *gialli Devil's Ransom* (1970) and *Seven Blood-Stained Orchids* (1972), but much of her later output was geared towards the sexploitation market. She died in 1992 at the age of 53. Elsa Martinelli is also in very good form as George's lover, Jane. Martinelli was born in 1935 and got her start in films in the early 1950s. Her combination of good looks and genuine acting ability netted her leading roles in such films as Roger Vadim's *Blood and Roses* (1960) and Howard Hawks' *Hatari!* (1962), as well as all-star "international" productions like Orson Welles' *The Trial* (1962) and *The V.I.P.s* (1963), opposite Richard Burton, Elizabeth Taylor and Welles. Her career slowed down in the 1970s and she

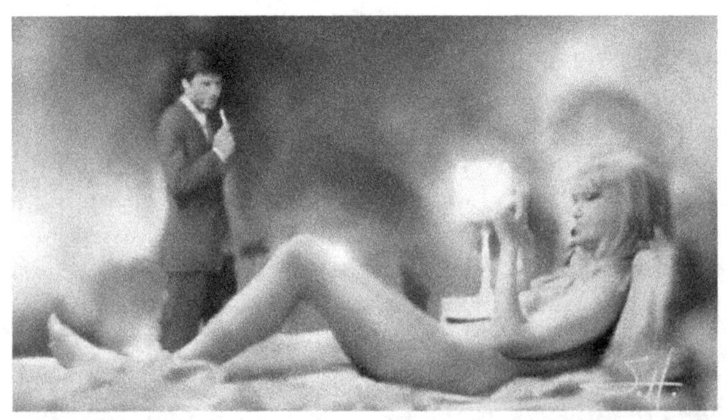

**Above: *Perversion Story*; original artwork by Scott Hoffman.**
**Below: Fulci directs Elsa Martinelli and Marisa Mell.**

would only appear sporadically in films during the '80s and '90s; her last credited appearance was in an Italian TV series from 2005, *Orgoglio*. Alberto De Mendoza makes his first of many *giallo* appearances in the role of George's more serious brother, Henry. De Mendoza is very effective and his role grows in stature and interest as the film unfolds. He was born in Argentina in 1923 and made his earliest screen appearances as a child actor in the 1930s. He became a familiar face in genre fare of the 1970s, including a scene-stealing turn as a demented monk in the Christopher Lee/Peter Cushing film *Horror Express* (1972) and a rare leading role in the striking post-apocalyptic thriller *The People Who Own the Dark* (1976), with Paul Naschy. He would later re-unite with Fulci on *A Lizard in a Woman's Skin*, playing the sardonic sidekick of inspector Stanley Baker. He remained active in films until his death in 2011. The supporting cast includes such fine character actors as John Ireland and Riccardo Cucciolla. Ireland fares better here than he had in Alberto De Martino's *The Insatiables* (1969) and plays his role as the tough but fair detective investigating George with conviction. Cucciolla is outstanding as the lovelorn Benjamin Wormser, whose obsession with Monica is bound to turn out badly. Cucciolla's film career would encompass winning the best actor prize at Cannes for his turn as Nicola Sacco in Giuliano Montaldo's *Sacco and Vanzetti* (1971) and starring as the harassed kidnap victim in Mario Bava's troubled *Rabid Dogs* (1974). He died in 1996. Cameo spotters will be pleased to note the first onscreen appearance of Fulci in several years, playing the handwriting expert who provides testimony in one scene.

The outstanding jazzy music score by Riz Ortolani must be noted. Ortolani would go on to score *Don't Torture a Duckling* and *Rome, 2072 A.D.: The New Gladiators* for Fulci, and the two men enjoyed a harmonious collaboration. As the composer later explained,

> Lucio Fulci was a dear man, a very talented and fine director. We first met because he was a music lover. [...] As a musician, I was musically free [working with Fulci] because, as a director, he appreciated and understood and loved music.

Born Riziero Ortolani in 1926, he got his start as a conductor for RAI radio and then scored his first film in 1954. Ortolani hit pay dirt with the acclaimed score for *Mondo Cane* (1962), earning him his first of two Oscar nominations for the song "More." He would contribute the soundtracks to Antonio Margheriti's early horror films *The Virgin of Nuremberg* (1963) and *Castle of Blood* (1964), in addition to such Euro Westerns as *Old Shatterhand* (1964), *Day of Anger* (1967) and *The Hunting Party* (1971). Ortolani would compose memorable scores in other genres, as well, including Damiano Damiani's splendid *poliziottesco Confessions of a Police Captain* (1971) and Ruggero Deodato's infamous *Cannibal Holocaust* (1980). His other *giallo* credits include Umberto Lenzi's *So Sweet ... So Perverse* (1969) and Armando Crispino's *The Dead Are Alive* (1972). Ortolani's music would be re-used by lifelong fan Quentin Tarantino on the soundtracks for his films *Kill Bill Vol. 2* (2004), *Inglourious Basterds* (2009) and *Django Unchained* (2012). He remained active until his death in January 2014.

As a final note of trivia, the film exists in at least two different edits. The most commonly available English-language print is titled *Perversion Story* and clocks in at an abbreviated 97 minutes; the fully uncut version, titled *One On Top of the Other*, runs 10 minutes longer. The differences between the two edits are basically down to dialogue scenes; the longer cut does not include any more violent or salacious material.

*Perversion Story*'s success helped to establish that Fulci's talents could extend well beyond slapstick fare and it would allow him to move into an even more ambitious project. As is so often the case in his career, however, things have a way of souring quickly ...

Notes:
1. Audio interview with Lucio Fulci, conducted by Pier Maria Bocchi and Andrea Bruni, included on the Shriek Show DVD release of *Touch of Death*.
2. *Ibid.*

## Beatrice Cenci (Italy)

Aka *The Conspiracy of Torture; Liens d'amour et de sang; Die Nackte und der Kardinal*

Directed by Lucio Fulci; Produced by Giorgio Agliani, for Filmena; Screenplay by Lucio Fulci and Roberto Gianviti; Director of Photography: Erico Menczer; Editor: Antonietta Zita; Music by Angelo Lavagnino and Silvano Spadaccino

Main Players: Adrienne Larussa (Beatrice Cenci); Tomas Milian (Olimpio Calvetti); Georges Wilson [as George Wilson] (Francesco Cenci); Mavie (Lucrezia); Antonio Casagrande (Don Giacomo Cenci); Ignazio Spalla [as Pedro Sanchez] (Catalano); Raymond Pellegrin (Cardinal Lanciani); Umberto D'Orsi (Inspector); Massimo Sarchielli (Gasparro)

*Italy, 1559: Brutal nobleman Francesco Cenci rules over his serfs and his family with an iron fist. He is well known for his savage temper and his fondness for dispensing harsh punishments on people who cross him. One night, while drunk, he rapes his daughter Beatrice. She then conspires with her lover, the servant Olimpio, to avenge her honor. Olimpio hires a thug known as Catalano to kill the patriarch. The plan is carried off, but suspicions are soon raised and Olimpio, Beatrice and the rest of the family find themselves being tortured by the Cardinal's minions ...*

After having taken some genteel potshots at the Catholic Church in *Operation Saint Peter's*, Fulci was given the freedom to make his most personal and savage film to date. *Beatrice Cenci* is based on a historical incident, involving the trial and execution of a young woman who murdered her abusive, oppressive father. With its mixture of tragedy and court intrigue, it was a story cut out for motion pictures and it was first adapted in 1909 by director Mario Caserini, who cast his wife Maria Caserini in the title role. Guido Brignone directed another version in 1941, with German actress Carola Höhn taking on the title role. Prior to the Fulci version, however, Riccardo Freda directed the well-known adaptation in 1956, with Micheline Presle as Beatrice. As one might expect from Freda, his version was pictorially splendid and dramatically distant. The story held great interest for Fulci and he jumped at the chance of bringing the story to the screen. As he later explained, "When they asked us to do this movie, we studied a lot."[1] Fulci's devotion to the project is evident on screen; the attention to detail is meticulous, the period is beautifully evoked and the film is executed with a sweep of style and romanticism that is simultaneously epic and intimate. Fulci would often refer to it as one of the films he was proudest of and it is easy to see why; it is definitely one of his finest achievements.

The film opens with a bit of sadism, which evokes the opening scenes of *Massacre Time*. Francesco Cenci and his right-hand man, Gasparro, have apprehended a man accused of stealing from the estate. Francesco unleashes his vicious dog on the man and sits back and watches in amusement as the man scurries for his life; he is trapped in an enclosure, however, so it is only a matter of time until

**Italian *locandina* for *Beatrice Cenci*; artist unknown.**

the animal catches him. Fulci hones in on the spectacle of brutality, showing close-ups of the dog tearing at the man's throat; images such as this would later recur in *The Beyond*. The director's flair for detail is evident in the scene, as he cuts from the gruesome image of the man's savaged throat to a close-up of Gasparro biting his lip in shock. Francesco ultimately shows "mercy" by having Gasparro put the man out of his misery with a dagger; Fulci shows Francesco walking away from the execution from a high angle, which then booms down as he is startled by the sound of the man's dying scream.

Fulci and co-writer Roberto Gianviti give the film an intricate structure, with flashbacks within flashbacks. It is a testimony to their skill and clarity as screenwriters that this never comes across as arbitrary or confusing. Indeed, the structure helps to preserve elements of suspense and surprise even as it sets up the tragic inevitability of the finale: One does not hold out hope that there will be a last minute intercession which will spare Beatrice and her family. However, the full violence of Francesco's beastly nature is not shown all at once. His cruelty towards the thief establishes him as a bastard of the highest order, but worse is still to be revealed.

**German lobby card: Olimpio (Tomas Milian) and his beloved Beatrice (Adrienne Larussa).**

Like so many noblemen, especially of the period, Francesco is in league with the Church. Truth be told, Francesco has no use for the Church beyond the protection it can afford. He is not a spiritual man and is not above indulging in a little casual blasphemy when it suits him. When he is visited by one of the Cardinal's emissaries, he makes it clear that his relationship with the Church is purely financial. At one point it is suggested that Francesco's comments may be offensive to the Almighty, prompting him to quip, "Let Him plug his ears!" The relationship between Francesco and the Church is nevertheless mutually beneficial. Presented with the option of going to jail for some of his offenses, Francesco is able to buy his way out of it by agreeing to give up some of his money and property. The Church's representatives are satisfied with this arrangement and even acknowledge the moral hypocrisy in private; in public, however, they are sure to play up the notion that Francesco has been properly humbled and is truly sorry for having strayed from the path of righteousness.

However, it is the rape of Beatrice that really pushes Francesco into the realm of the monstrous. He attempts to break her strong will by bullying her, but she refuses to bend. One night, fuelled by drinking, he decides to take things to the next level and attacks her. The scene is appropriately horrific and disturbing. Fulci does not sexualize or trivialize Beatrice's feelings in this scene. She fights back and does what she can to defend herself, but Francesco is simply too big and strong for her to overcome. Here again, Fulci focuses on disturbing details as a means of conveying the true horror of the situation. As Francesco looms over Beatrice, his eyes glazed over with alcohol, he drips with perspiration over her exposed flesh. Sensual touches such as this give the scene a dramatic potency but never reduce the set piece to the sort of sexualized rape fantasy that would become such a key motif in later Italian exploitation fare.

When Beatrice enlists the help of Olimpio to kill her father, the viewer cannot help but be on her side. Fulci emphasizes his stoic qualities to an extent that some critics have accused him of presenting her in a callous and unsympathetic fashion. This seems a gross misreading of his intentions. If anything, the film adopts something of a feminist approach, with Beatrice ultimately being far stronger than her male counterparts. Brutalized by her father, but he never succeeds in breaking her spirit. Olimpio and Catalano cower at the idea of killing the man in his sleep, but she pushes and drives them on, offering to do it if they are too scared to complete the task. Fulci leaves us in no doubt that she is fully capable of it—and certainly, she has more than ample justification for doing so. Beatrice is not an unsympathetic figure, but her tendency to keep her feelings bottled-up—a typical trait in people who have survived traumatic events such as rape—expresses an inner strength and resolve which makes her truly heroic.

The murder of Cenci is built up with great suspense. The old man sleeps, having been drugged, and Olimpio and Catalano bicker back and forth on how they are going to proceed. Fulci does not play this for comedy, however, this is a grim and serious business. They finally steel themselves and get to work, Olimpio covering Francesco's mouth with his hand and Catalano delivering two knife thrusts, the first being to the eye, the second to the throat. The use of eye violence is particularly interesting in this context, as it is an element that would recur many times over in Fulci's later work, most notably *Zombie*. Fulci would often comment on this, stating that the eyes had to go first because they have seen too much. In a sense, Fulci was also evoking the great surrealist filmmaker Luis Buñuel, whose experimental film (co-directed with Salvador Dalí) *Un Chien Andalou* (1929) included a sequence of an eyeball being bisected by a razor blade. In the context of a film such as *Beatrice Cenci*, the image has been sometimes criticized as being a piece of overdone sensationalism, a misstep in an otherwise strong film, but psychologically it makes perfect sense. In order to punish Francesco for seeing his daughter as a sexual object, his sight has been taken away from him. In any event, it's a tough and brutal set piece that serves as a primer of sorts for the bloodshed to come in later Fulci films.

The sequences of Olimpio and Beatrice being tortured by the emissaries of the Church are also very potent. Olimpio suffers the brunt of the treatment. He refuses to betray his beloved and suffers mightily for it. He is stretched on the rack, branded with an iron and has his limbs twisted and broken. He is reduced to a quivering, paralyzed mess. The pains of the torture eventually have the desired effect, however, and he tells the tribunal what they want to know. He eventually recants, but the damage has been done. He dies knowing that he has failed the woman he loved. Beatrice is then subjected to similar tortures. She holds up better under duress and is not prepared to incriminate herself or her family for their role in the murder, but once again she is let down by the weakness of others: Her brother Giacomo and her stepmother Lucrezia crack under pressure and she finally gives in to the demands for answers. The brutality of the tortures underlines the hypocrisy of the Church, which seeks to make an example of the Cenci clan while ultimately condemning their souls to hell. Beatrice is beheaded, but this final indignity is kept off-camera; the truly horrific final act is the hypocritical decision of the Pope to "absolve" Beatrice of her sins, and to release the youngest sibling, Bernardino, from his life sentence—after the Church has been paid off from the remainder of the estate, of course.

Fulci often referred to the French playwright Antonin Artaud as a major inspiration and this is particularly evident in this film. Artaud, born in Marseille in 1896, came to prominence for creating the so-called "Theatre of Cruelty." He suffered from major bouts of depression and mania for much of his life and channeled his psychological demons into his plays, which would often depict protracted sequences of pain, torture and suffering. As he once explained,

> The Theatre of Cruelty has been created in order to restore to the theater a passionate and convulsive conception of life, and it is in this sense of violent rigor and extreme condensation of scenic elements that the cruelty on which it is based must be understood. This cruelty, which will be bloody when necessary but not systematically so, can thus be identified with a kind of severe moral purity which is not afraid to pay life the price it must be paid.[2]

Artaud also believed firmly in the concrete reality of dreams and fantasies, putting as much stock in them as in the so-called "real world." Peter Brook would adapt Artaud's concepts into his scandalous production *Marat/Sade* (1964), which would later be made into a film of the same name in 1966—starring two actors who would later work with Fulci, no less: Patrick Magee and John Steiner. Artaud's collection of essays, *The Theatre and Its Double*, remains in print to this day; he died in Paris in 1948. Fulci's repeated allusions to Artaud could conceivably be an attempt to intellectualize his fondness for strong sequences of violence, but this is arguably unfair to him and his methodology. Fulci's approach to screen violence is remarkably consistent; he shows it as rough, brutal and, above all, sudden and unexpected. The narrative does not call for these sequences to be depicted in such a long and drawn-out manner, but for Fulci they represent an attempt to confront the horrors of everyday reality. Sooner than trivialize these actions and present them in a more sanitary fashion, he shows them for what they are. Man, ultimately, is a collection of veins, nerves and organs—and the final destruction of this collection is as savage as it is inevitable.

And what of Fulci's own spirituality and beliefs? He was certainly raised as a member of the Catholic Church, but he would later tell interviewers that, "I'm a man who searches for God and who has doubts."[3] As such, this sounds closer to agnosticism than out-and-out atheism. Fulci's issues with the Church are therefore more rooted in political corruption than they are in spiritual contempt. Faith, for Fulci, is not necessarily a bad thing in itself, but the way in which the Church positions itself in the community, draining unsuspecting, trusting people dry of their hard-earned money and resources, is the greatest sin of all. It is also possible that his problems with the Church were deepened during the making of this film. As he later explained, "The movie's cursed because my wife died tragically as I was editing."[4] Allegations of impropriety by Uta Levka during the making of *Operation Saint Peter's* to one side, it seems that Fulci enjoyed a happy marriage with his wife Marina. Out of the blue, during this period, things took a tragic turn:

> We were engaged for a long time [...] We were happy with our lives. My wife underwent some tests and, unexpectedly, cancerous polyps were found. I didn't understand. After a more thorough examination, it was determined that nothing could be done. One day I went out. When I returned, my mother met me at the door. She said, "Marina is dead. She killed herself with gas."[5]

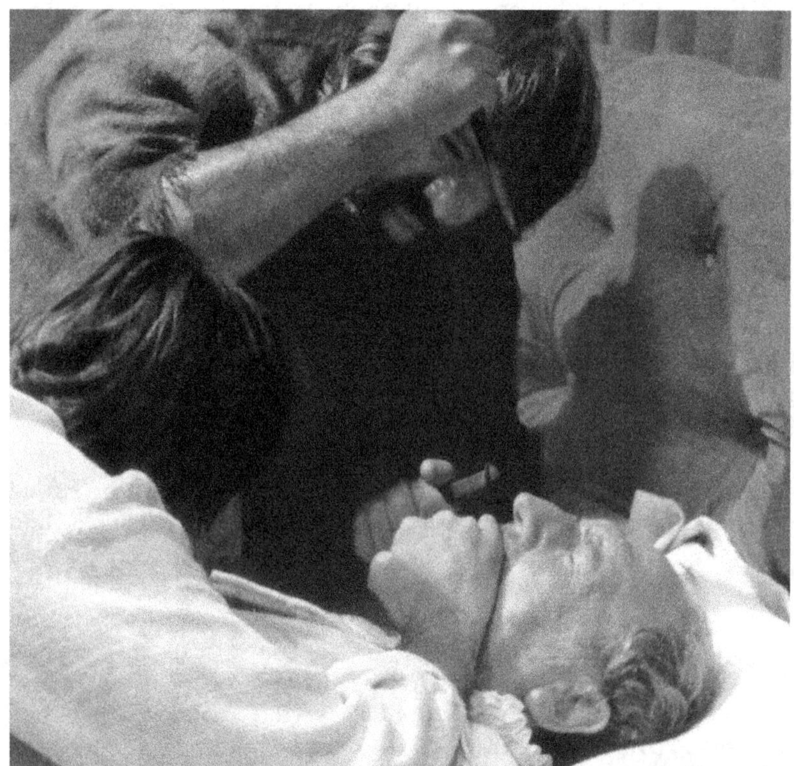
**Fulci's first instance of eye violence, as Catalano (Ignazio Spalla) and Olimpio murder Francesco (Georges Wilson).**

Suicide is, of course, a cardinal sin according to the Catholic faith and it is unlikely that Fulci was able to cope with this loss with much support from the Church. He suddenly found himself widowed and responsible for the care of his two young daughters. If this ended up darkening his disposition, this can hardly be surprising. [6]

Even so, for Fulci, the film represented a pinnacle in his career. He was justifiably proud of the finished product. The film is loaded with interesting imagery, striking cinematography courtesy of Erico Menczer (in his penultimate collaboration with Fulci) and exacting costume design and art direction. Unlike many of his contemporaries, who used period pieces as an opportunity to celebrate the pretty and the poised, Fulci presents a more realistic portrait of the period. Part of the action is set during the depths of the summer: The characters are clearly uncomfortable in their heavy period costuming, pulling at their collars, fanning themselves and literally dripping with perspiration. As the weather turns cold, the stone walls and floors of the castle become frigid. Far from coming off as an idealized never-never land, this period of history is presented as harsh and unforgiving, which is all the more appropriate given the nature of the subject matter. Fulci paces the film beautifully and jumps backwards and forwards in chronology without ever losing the narrative thread. In short, the film demonstrates him to be a filmmaker of great power and authority.

The film is well served by its excellent cast. Adrienne Larussa is absolutely perfect as the proud and beautiful Beatrice. She was born in New York City in 1948 and made her way to Italy in the late 1960s, hoping to start an acting career. She made a couple of minor films prior to landing this plum role. Unfortunately, the film did not prove to be a pleasant experience for the young actress:

> My agent told me I was going to Rome to make the movie! It was summertime and he warned me not to have a tan because Beatrice had to have fair skin. Tomas Milian [...] I was told he was a very big star at the time, but it meant nothing to me. [...] We never had a warm and fuzzy relationship. [...] [Fulci] was gruff, but very focused. He wasn't fond of my tactics or me. I'd walk off the set because I had a contract stating my workday was 12 hours. And when the 11-and-a-half hour arrived, I told someone to tell Fulci that he had 30 minutes more time with me and then I was out of there. The only interaction I would have with him was while being directed.[7]

Larussa later recalled the filming of the rape scene:

> The nude scene in *Beatrice Cenci*—it was in my contract that I didn't do nudity ... Lucio and I didn't get along that well. We did not scream and yell at each other. We sort of had a quiet dislike for each other. So the day they were filming the nude scene, I show up on set to see what my stand-in is going to look like, and it is this very, very fuzzy pudgy ... and I'm there like (mimics shock) and I take a look at him and he just ... grinned and walked away.

Fulci was typically outspoken and abrasive in his comments about the actress and would confirm that the rape scene was something of a sticking point with them:

> Adrienne Larussa was an incredible slut! She gave me a lot of trouble on the rape scene, then she goes and fucks De Paolis in the garden![8]

Fulci may have had personal reasons to dislike Larussa, but he could hardly have complained about her performance: She rises to the occasion and carries the film with poise and dignity. None of her subsequent acting roles—including a small part in Nicolas Roeg's *The Man Who Fell to Earth* (1976)—would provide her with such a challenge and she ultimately retired from the profession and went into real estate.

The male leads are played by two of Fulci's favorite actors: Tomas Milian and Georges Wilson. Milian gives a moving performance as the simple and devoted Olimpio. He was born in Cuba in 1932. He emigrated to the U.S. in the 1950s and, inspired by James Dean's performance in *East of Eden* (1955), joined up with the Actors' Studio, where he learned his craft. Milian would find success in the theater but decided to pursue movie work, initially appearing in "intellectual" films in Italy like Mauro Bolognini's *The Big Night* (1959), Luchino Visconti's segment of the anthology *Boccaccio '70* (1962) and Francesco Maselli's *Time of Indifference* (1964). Looking to diversify, Milian accepted a plum role in Sergio Sollima's splendid Spaghetti Western *The Big Gundown* (1966), opposite Lee Van Cleef; the film was a huge hit and made Milian into a major star in Italian popular cinema. He would go on to appear in such Spaghetti Westerns as Sollima's *Face To Face* (1967) and Giulio Questi's *Django Kill!* (1967), as well as maximizing his popularity with Italian audiences with his appearances in such *poliziotteschi* as *Bandits in Milan* (1968), *Almost Human* (1974), *Silent Action* (1975) and *The Cop in Blue Jeans* (1976). He would re-unite with Fulci on *Don't Torture a Duckling* and *Four of the Apocalypse*, thus allowing him to play major roles in three of Fulci's personal favorite films. Milian began appearing in more American films and TV shows in the 1980s and scored a major late-career triumph with his role as drug kingpin General Salazar in Steven Soderbergh's Oscar-winning *Traffic* (2000). The quirky and outspoken Milian got along uncommonly well with Fulci. In an interview included on the Anchor Bay DVD release of *Four of the Apocalypse*, he said:

> Poor Lucio. I liked Lucio very much. [...] He suffered. And I always feel for people that suffer. [...] The problem is that his persona—the problems that he had with actors and the movies that he selected to do—his sadism. When a person truly tries to destroy himself, you know? [...] But talent, he did have. My God, if you gave Lucio a very, very well written script, you would have had a beautiful movie. He was a fantastic technician.[9]

Fulci, never one to dispense praise easily, was equally impressed with Milian, calling him "a wonderful actor and a great friend."[10] Fulci was similarly effusive over Georges Wilson, who gives a stellar performance as the depraved Francesco Cenci. Born in France in 1921, he began appearing in films in the late 1940s. He also had a distinguished reputation as a theater actor and served as the director of France's Théâtre national de Chaillot from 1963 to 1972. He was nominated for a BAFTA for his work in Henri Colpi's *The Long Absence* (1961) and also appeared in such notable international productions as Walerian Borowczyk's *Blanche* (1971), Richard Lester's *The Three Musketeers* (1973) and Jacques Demy's *Lady Oscar* (1979), which starred one of Fulci's most beloved actresses, Catriona MacColl. He died in 2010. Fulci later described Wilson as "an amazing actor and he was great as old Cenci."[11] They would reunite for *Don't Torture a Duckling*.

Unfortunately for Fulci, *Beatrice Cenci* did not make any kind of an impact at the box-office. The film received poor distribution and did not garner a U.S. release until 1976, at which point it was retitled *A Conspiracy of Torture*; the English dub was the work of veteran dubber Nick Alexander[12], who would become a common presence on the English tracks of many of Fulci's later horror films. The combination of the film's box-office failure with the loss of his wife proved to be a terrible setback for Fulci; he would not be given another chance to direct a feature for nearly two years, at which time producer Edmondo Amati decided to take another chance on him and give him another *giallo* to direct.

Notes:

1. Audio interview with Lucio Fulci, conducted by Pier Maria Bocchi and Andrea Bruni, included on the Shriek Show DVD release of *Touch of Death*.
2. Bentley, Eric, ed., *The Theory of the Modern Stage*, (Penguin, 1968), p.66.
3. Palmerini, Luca M. and Gaetano Mistretta, *Spaghetti Nightmares* (Florida: Fantasma Books, 1996), p. 58.4. Audio interview with Lucio Fulci, conducted by Pier Maria Bocchi and Andrea Bruni, included on the Shriek Show DVD release of *Touch of Death*.
5. Balun, Chas., *Beyond the Gates: A Tribute to The Maestro*, (San Leandro: Blackest Heart Books, 1996), p. 25.
6. Fulci would remarry twice: he married German bit part actress Ursel Erbez in 1971; she can be seen as the red-headed police woman in *A Lizard in a Woman's Skin*. They divorced some time later. And circa 1981, he married African-American actress Violet Jean, who can be seen as the nurse in *The New York Ripper*. That marriage also ended in divorce. Thanks to Kit Gavin for this information.
7. Ferrante, Tim, "*Giallo* Gal Adrienne Larussa," *The Phantom of the Movies' Videoscope*, #88, p. 27
8. Audio interview with Lucio Fulci, conducted by Pier Maria Bocchi and Andrea Bruni, included on the Shriek Show DVD release of *Touch of Death*.
9. Quoted from "Fulci of the Apocalypse" (2001) featurette included on the Anchor Bay DVD release of *Four of the Apocalypse*, directed by Gary Hertz.
10. Audio interview with Lucio Fulci, conducted by Pier Maria Bocchi and Andrea Bruni, included on the Shriek Show DVD release of *Touch of Death*.
11. *Ibid.*
12. Alexander provided the English voice for Al Cliver in such Fulci films as *Zombie*, *The Black Cat* and *Rome, 2072 A.D.: The New Gladiators*, among many other credits. He can be heard voicing several background characters in *Beatrice Cenci*. He died in 2004.

# 1971

## *A Lizard in a Woman's Skin (Italy/Spain/France)*

Aka *Una lucertola con la pelle di donna; Una lagartija con piel de mujer; Le venin de la peur; Schizoid*

Directed by Lucio Fulci; Produced by Edmondo Amati, for Apollo Films, Atlándia Films and Les Films Corona; Screenplay by Lucio Fulci, Roberto Gianviti, José Luis Martínez Mollá and André Tranché, from a story by Lucio Fulci and Roberto Gianviti; Director of Photography: Luigi Kuveiller; Editor: Vincenzo Tomassi and Giorgio Serrallonga; Music by Ennio Morricone

Main Players: Florinda Bolkan (Carol Hammond); Stanley Baker (Inspector Corvin); Jean Sorel (Frank Hammond); Leo Genn (Edmond Brighton); Alberto De Mendoza (Sergeant Brandon); Edy Galleani [as Edy Gall] (Joan Hammond); Silvia Monti (Deborah); Anita Strindberg (Julia Durer); Jorge Rigaud (Dr. Kerr)

*Carol Hammond is plagued by recurring dreams involving her hedonistic neighbor, Julia Durer. She turns to her therapist, Dr. Kerr, for guidance but he does not see any cause for concern. When Julia turns up dead, in a scenario eerily like one of her dreams, Carol becomes a likely suspect for Inspector Corvin. Carol's barrister father, Edmund Brighton, does everything in his power to clear her name and Inspector Corvin is forced to release her when another person is killed ...*

Following the suicide of his wife and the commercial failure of *Beatrice Cenci*, Lucio Fulci hit a low spot. Offers were not flying at him and money was tight.

> When my wife died, I couldn't touch the money because everything was registered in her name; I couldn't even pay for the funeral. Amati called and said, "Do three movies with me and I'll pay you 20 million *lire* each." It wasn't a great offer, but I had to accept.[1]

The first of the proposed trilogy—which would ultimately encompass *Don't Torture a Duckling* and *The Eroticist*, as well—was Fulci's second *giallo*, *A Lizard in a Woman's Skin*. The film allowed him to utilize every trick at his disposal and helped to get his career back on solid ground.

According to those who knew him, Lucio Fulci had a deep distrust of psychoanalysis. In her introduction to Chas. Balun's *Beyond the Gates*, Fulci's daughter Antonella writes:

> He hated whoever tried to put some order in his life. This was the reason why he almost drove crazy one of his fiancées. She was a very rational, well-known psychiatrist who believed in her job. Dad kept telling her psychiatrists are just a bunch of suckers. Nevertheless, she talked to him for hours explaining to him that he was the victim of unresolved conflicts with his mother. According to her, he hated women because of these conflicts. Dad let her speak, nodding and pretending he was very interested in her opinion. Then, he told her to *fuck off*! [...] That's how he was. If he thought you were trying to take control of his life, he rebelled against you and treated you as badly as he could.[2]

As such, it should come as no surprise that *A Lizard in a Woman's Skin* is one of several films in his *oeuvre* that basically makes nonsense of the psychiatric profession as a whole. Whether one agrees with his take on the field is a subjective call, but the film finds him working at the peak of his powers. If only his subsequent career would have allowed him to work on a similar scale, with access to as many gifted collaborators as he had at his disposal here, it is likely he would be remembered more fondly by *cinéastes* outside of the gore-hound circle.

In many respects, the film is a classical mystery, Agatha Christie-style. Fulci would later quip that he found Dario Argento's thrillers to be sloppy in their construction but brilliant in their execution, whereas he found his own *gialli* to be too "mechanical" in their structure.[3] Fulci's assessment of his own work only becomes a problem, however, if we subscribe to the notion that a good thriller need not be beholden to logic and an inevitable outcome. Fulci's approach may not be quite as fanciful as that of Argento's, but he is by no means reticent when it comes to indulging in cinematic flights of fancy. His handling of the material is consistently stylish and inventive, employing fluid camerawork, dynamic editing and a keen eye for composition and detail. The film is also graced with plenty of dream sequences, which truly allow the director's vivid imagination full reign. The end result is one of the most stylish *gialli* of its period and one of the director's finest films.

The story plays on the contrast between the real and the imagined as well as the repressed versus the uninhibited. Carol is a rigid, proper, high society English woman. She observes convention and seems to have an idyllic life, with a handsome and successful husband, a tastefully decorated and well-appointed home and a father who is about to transition from a distinguished career as a barrister to a more high profile position in the world of politics. Her dreams, however, reveal a wealth of repressed desires and fantasies, and she imagines a Sapphic relationship with her "loose" upstairs neighbor, the stunning Julia Durer (in this context, it is interesting to note that leading man Jean Sorel is best-remembered for playing the husband of Catherine Deneuve, the frigid protagonist with a similarly sexually active imagination in Luis Bunuel's *Belle de Jour*, 1967). The complications inherent in such a schism cause her to seek psychiatric help, but the question that lingers for much of the film is whether she secretly desired a relationship with Julia or if her dreams really do speak of a subconscious battle between convention and desire, with convention triumphing when Julia is killed off in one of her dreams. Of course, this being a *giallo*, the murder is not confined to the dream world; it happens for real, too. Fulci leads the viewer on a labyrinthine journey in which one can never be sure if Julia was responsible for the murder or if she is being set up by an unscrupulous outside agent.

The title makes it quite clear that the producers were hopping on the Dario Argento bandwagon, but it makes sense in context—to reveal its meaning would give the game away, however, for those who have not had the chance to see the film for themselves. Fulci's approach to the material is at once bracingly garish and experimental, yet beholden to the principles of logic and coherence. Whereas Argento might have been willing to throw caution to the wind and work in more unrealistic elements, Fulci refuses to allow anything to get in the way of developing the story to its natural conclusion. The dream sequences allow for plenty of trippy imagery, but that is fair enough: They are dream sequences, after all. The director's flair for the grotesque emerges in shocking images of eviscerated dogs in a laboratory setting, while his propensity for tactile effects adds to the growing tension, as in the moment when a panic-stricken Carol clenches her fist so tight that her long nails draw blood from the palm of her hand. All told, the film points to the direction his career would later take, with a series of visceral horror films, while also establishing beyond a shadow of a doubt that his talents extended well beyond staging splashy gore sequences.

**Italian poster for *A Lizard in a Woman's Skin*; artist unknown.**

One of the common criticisms leveled against Fulci by his detractors, many of whom are only familiar with one phase of his long and varied career, is that his films make no sense. A viewing of this one should be enough to dispute such nonsense. Fulci artfully treads the line between the realistic and the surreal, contrasting the real and the imagined in a way that is clear and coherent, while still introducing elements of doubt in the viewer. The film progresses to a finale that has been criticized for its lack of spectacle, but truly it is the ending the film needs. The last piece of the jigsaw fits into place and the impression is akin to the kind of classical detective stories that interested Fulci the most, where the "wow factor" comes from an unexpected revelation rather than from an over-the-top bit of action or mayhem.

*A Lizard in a Woman's Skin* is graced with lush production values. The sets and art direction are of a high standard, while Luigi Kuveiller's lighting creates ample atmosphere. Kuveiller (1927-2013) served as a camera operator on everything from Michelangelo Antonioni's *L'Avventura* (1960) to Warren Keifer's *Castle of the Living Dead* (1964) before becoming one of Italy's top cinematographers. He shot many of Elio Petri's most significant films—including *We Still Kill the Old Way* (1967) and *Investigation of a Citizen Above Suspicion* (1970)—and also worked with such diverse filmmakers as Paul Morrissey (*Flesh for Frankenstein*, 1973; *Blood for Dracula*, 1974), Billy Wilder (*Avanti!*, 1972) and Dario Argento (*Le cinque giornate*, 1973; *Deep Red*, 1975). He returned to the Fulci fold later with *The New York Ripper*. The camerawork by Ubaldo Terzano, Mario Bava's long-time camera operator, is elegant where needed and appropriately jarring when trying to convey Carol's frazzled mental state. Fulci had begun exploring the

**Photo montage from the Italian pressbook for *A Lizard in a Woman's Skin* which plays up the film's erotic content.**

possibilities of handheld camerawork on *Operation Saint Peter's* and it is used here, as elsewhere, to convey a sense of dramatic urgency. The technique jars with the otherwise elegant camerawork utilized in other scenes, but this is precisely the point; similarly, the use of split diopter effects to create a sense of deep focus allows one to appreciate the importance of different pieces of visual information within the same frame. Fulci also implements more split-screen effects, something which American filmmaker Brian De Palma would also utilize in his own *giallo*-esque thrillers and horror films, including *Sisters* (1973) and *Carrie* (1976). The special effects by Carlo Rambaldi are consistently convincing, as well; indeed, the effects involving the disemboweled dogs proved so realistic that Fulci was reportedly brought up on charges of animal cruelty and was only released when Rambaldi was able to produce the prop dogs as evidence! Ennio Morricone's score is another gem from a composer whose prolific output in this period did nothing to sap his creativity.

The film is also blessed with expert editing by the gifted Vincenzo Tomassi. Born in Lazio in 1937, Tomassi began working in films in the late 1960s; one of his first assignments was editing the Eurospy adventure *Mexican Slayride* (1967) for Riccardo Freda. Tomassi would go on to edit no less than 17 films for Fulci between 1971 and his death in 1993; indeed, Fulci's *Voices from Beyond* would be the last film he ever worked on. The relationship between directors and their editor is frequently undervalued in film studies: In many respects, films are made in the editing room. A good editor can take mediocre footage and inject it with energy, just as an inept editor can be handed the most beautiful footage imaginable and make a mess out of it. Next to the similarly long-running and prolific relationship between Fulci and Tomassi's predecessor, Ornella Micheli, Tomassi would have a more significant role in helping to shape and define the director's style and rhythm on screen than any other collaborator.

Florinda Bolkan is excellent in the central role. She conveys the character's frail emotional and mental state very well but is never reduced to the level of a one-dimensional victim. She was born in Brazil in 1941 and made her film debut with a small role in the star-studded comedy *Candy* (1968) starring Ewa Aulin. She rose to prominence thanks to Luchino Visconti, who cast her in his controversial exploration of Nazism, *The Damned* (1969). From there, she landed a key role as the murder victim in Elio Petri's Oscar-winning *Investigation of a Citizen Above Suspicion* (1970). She won three David di Donatello awards in rapid succession for her work in Giuseppe Patroni Griffi's *The Love Circle* (1969) and Enrico Maria Salerno's *The Anonymous Venetian* (1970) and *Cari genitori* (1973). Bolkan would reteam with Fulci on his next *giallo, Don't Torture a Duckling* (1972). According to Fulci, she was not the first actress lined up for the part, but he couldn't have been happier with the way things panned out.

> Florinda Bolkan wasn't slotted for the movie, but then [Giuseppe] Patroni Griffi's movie was canceled. [...] We sent her the script. Then Pasquale Festa Campanile, my ex-schoolmate, said to her, "You're not going to work with Fulci, are you? The guy who does Franchi and Ingrassia?!" She told me this story on the third day of shooting. [...] We became good pals. [...] She is an amazing actress, very focused.[4]

The distinguished Welsh actor Stanley Baker is also in great form as the sardonic but sympathetic Inspector Corvin. Baker manages to make the character into a credible human being while also conveying great efficiency and competence in his job as an investigator. Baker (1928-1976) entered films in the 1940s and established himself as a tough, two-fisted, blue-collar type in such films as

*The Cruel Sea* (1953), *Hell Drivers* (1957) and *Violent Playground* (1958). Baker would also collaborate with expatriate American director Joseph Losey on a series of fascinating films, including *The Criminal* (1960), *Eva* (1962) and *Accident* (1967). He appeared in a number of major films throughout the 1960s and moved into production with the acclaimed historical epic *Zulu* (1964). *A Lizard in a Woman's Skin* was a relatively rare foray for him into Italian genre cinema; he was knighted in 1976, shortly before succumbing to lung cancer at the too-young age of 48. Leo Genn, a distinguished veteran of British films dating from the 1930s onwards, played Carol's father quite beautifully. Genn (1905-1978) was a familiar presence from such classic films as Laurence Olivier's *Henry V* (1944), Sidney Gilliat's *Green for Danger* (1946) and Anatole Litvak's *The Snake Pit* (1948), which is generally regarded as the first truly sympathetic portrayal of mental illness and psychiatry in a Hollywood film. He was nominated for an Oscar for *Quo Vadis?* (1951) and began drifting into genre films in the 1960s, thanks to appearances in such Harry Alan Towers productions as *Ten Little Indians* (1965), *Circus of Fear* (1966) and Jess Franco's *The Bloody Judge* (1969). Genn does a splendid job of playing the very stiff-upper-lip Edmond Brighton, conveying an undercurrent of sly humor while showing genuine concern for his daughter. Jean Sorel, Alberto De Mendoza and Jorge Rigaud had already worked with Fulci on *Perversion Story* and they lend great support here, with De Mendoza proving particularly impressive as Baker's sidekick, who is always ready with a quip. The stunningly beautiful Anita Strindberg makes quite an impression as the mysterious Julia Durer. Strindberg does not have the benefit of any dialogue, but her presence is deeply felt. She is dressed memorably in fetish boots and very little else, and performs her various scenes with wild abandon. Strindberg would go on to play a small role in Fulci's next film, *The Eroticist*. Penny Brown and Mike Kennedy play the two hippies who dog Carol's dreams. Brown, born in Texas in 1941, gravitated to the Italian film scene in the mid-1960s. She played a number of minor roles prior to landing the flashy role of Jenny in *Lizard*. Brown would go on to make an uncredited appearance in Federico Fellini's delirious *City of Women* (1980) before re-uniting with Fulci on *Rome, 2072 A.D.: The New Gladiators* in 1984. Kennedy (whose real name is Michael Volker Kögel) was born in Germany in 1944. He moved to Spain in the mid-1960s, where he found popularity as the lead singer of the rock group *Los Bravos*. As an actor, he made only a handful of film appearances, of which this one is probably the best known.

***A Lizard in a Woman's Skin*; original artwork by Scott Hoffman.**

Both Brown and Kennedy had positive experiences working with Fulci. Kennedy recalled him as "a very hard worker. He couldn't really show his tenderness—or maybe when he showed it too deeply, maybe it was something he liked to hide." Brown would get to know the director a little better, having worked with him on two occasions, and she summed him up thus:

> All the memories I have of Lucio are extremely fond. He was very intense and a very interesting person. He liked me and I liked him and we worked very well together. I always felt very good with him. He always made me feel special.

*A Lizard in a Woman's Skin* became the second of Fulci's films to be picked up for release in the United States by American International Pictures (AIP). AIP changed the title to the more generic-sounding *Schizoid* and removed some of the gorier and more sexually provocative material; all in all, about eight minutes of material was trimmed. To this day, various home video editions represent different edits of the film, with the U.K. DVD release from Optimum presenting the most complete version to date.

For Fulci, *A Lizard in a Woman's Skin* proved to be a success, thus making up for the commercial failure of *Beatrice Cenci*. As he would later recall, the film:

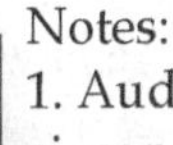

> … came out at the same time as *The Cat O'Nine Tails*, which was perhaps one of the best films of Argento's "thriller" period. Films about animals were the only ones at that time to have any success. [*Lizard*] made eight million *lire* at Rome's *Rouge et Noir* cinema, which was a real triumph for those days [...].[5]

Notes:

1. Audio interview with Lucio Fulci, conducted by Pier Maria Bocchi and Andrea Bruni, included on the Shriek Show DVD release of *Touch of Death*.
2. Balun, Chas., *Beyond the Gates: A Tribute to The Maestro*, (San Leandro: Blackest Heart Books, 1996), p. 7.
3. Thrower, Stephen, *Beyond Terror: The Films of Lucio Fulci* (Guildford: FAB Press, 1999), p. 70.
4. Audio interview with Lucio Fulci, conducted by Pier Maria Bocchi and Andrea Bruni, included on the Shriek Show DVD release of *Touch of Death*.
5. Palmerini, Luca M. and Gaetano Mistretta, *Spaghetti Nightmares* (Florida: Fantasma Books, 1996), p. 59.

# Jean Sorel Interview by Mike Baronas and Kit Gavin

Mike Baronas and Kit Gavin conducted the following interview with actor Jean Sorel on February 4, 2003. The topic of the discussion was focused on *A Lizard in a Woman's Skin*, as Sorel does not have as many memories with regards to his first film with Fulci, *Perversion Story*. We thank him for taking the time to answer these questions.

**Mike Baronas and Kit Gavin**: So what attracted you to a movie with such a colorful title?

**Jean Sorel**: I did not choose the title, of course. At that time, in Italy, they chose movie titles that were very, very long; and the longer the title, the better it was. And this is a ridiculous thing that lasted for several years. I did another movie in Italy with a very long title. It was called *Kill Me Quick, I'm Cold!* (1967). It starred Monica Vitti. And the title was very long. (Note: the original title was *Fai in fretta ad uccidermi... ho freddo!*) We never understood why Italian producers or distributors wanted to have titles that long, because the longer it is, the less you remember. Short titles … you remember them quite well. That's the explanation; that's it.

**MB/KG**: Was it a big taboo because there are scenes with Bolkan with a lesbian theme … ?

**JS**: Yes. Now this is perfectly normal, but back then these were the first movies that were sexually explicit, where you could see love scenes and homosexuality being addressed. Italian films started to get a bit daring. We were starting then, so there were a lot of them. You could often see them in mystery movies, which were somewhat erotic. All this is completely related to a period of Italian moviemaking.

**MB/KG**: Do you remember much of how the film came together?

**JS**: No, but as I told you previously, they were professionally made movies, with professional actors. Everybody you see in the cast was experienced. These were very professional movies, with a professional director and professional producers.

**MB/KG**: And the locations of that film around London and so forth?

**JS**: Yes, this was a sort of fashion, so to speak. We did not shoot much in the studio at the time, except for a scene or two, which we did in the studio with Leo Genn. Otherwise, all the rest was in natural environments. If you needed sets, the production could rent them at a very low price; for example, the gas chamber (Note: in *Perversion Story*). You could rent anything you wanted. It was then much more interesting for the producer, the director and even the actors to play in taboo places. Shooting in a gas chamber, playing scenes in the gas chamber, nobody can imagine that. All that filmmaking was done that way.

**MB/KG**: Tell us about your leading ladies.

**JS**: I met Florinda during the filming of the movie I did with Visconti (Note: *Sandra* aka *Of a Thousand Delights*, 1965), because she was then starting her career. And Florinda made a movie later on with Helmut Berger, the boy who was living with Visconti at the time (Note: *The Damned*, 1969). She was a well-known actress and everybody expected a lot from her. She was talented and people thought that she had done a lot. And for her, it was important to play in commercial movies. Because the film worked well, it was a great success commercially; it is good for actors to appear in successful movies. [Elsa] Martinelli was already better known; she had made lots of movies and was a model and had starred in American movies. So, as an actress, she was well known. (Note: Martinelli co-starred with Sorel in *Perversion Story*.)

**MB/KG**: And Stanley Baker?

**JS**: I think that Stanley was involved as part of the English co-production. Because in these movies, there were a few French people, a few Italian people, a few English people, a few Spaniards … It was like in Godard's movies. There was a Godard movie where he placed four actors of different nationalities, side by side, and he said it is an Italian co-production; this is all they did in the movie, nothing more. Stanley Baker did magnificent movies. He had starred in films for [Joseph] Losey, he had worked with very important people. He was a stupendous actor who had a great reputation. I think that the producers picked well-known people in the hopes of securing worldwide distribution. They were sold all over because of the actors, because of the subject matter. They traveled all over.

**MB/KG**: And Alberto De Mendoza?

**JS**: Mendoza was a very nice fellow and he was very well known in Spain. He was also well known in Argentina. Italian movies had a huge following in Argentina, in South America and Brazil, so they needed actors who were well known down there.

**MB/KG**: And Silvia Monti?

**JS**: Monti was a wonderful girl—Italian and a superb woman. She is now married to an Italian who is immensely rich and powerful… I forget his name… De Benedetti! She had a significant career, then enjoyed a significant life as well.

**MB/KG**: Ely Galleani?

**JS**: I do not recall her.

**MB/KG**: The petite blonde.
**JS**: Ah yes, the petite blonde. She was Italian. It must have been one of her first movies because I do not remember her very well.
**MB/KG**: What do you remember of Lucio Fulci?
**JS**: Fulci was a great professional. He was a very intelligent and cultivated man, who had a perfect knowledge of the trade. He wrote numerous scripts, which he sold to other people. He wrote many treatments that were made into movies by other directors. Lucio was perfect for this sort of film, because he knew exactly what he wanted from the actors, locations, even from the co-production people. He chose everything. He was a pro, a great professional. He was not seen as a serious artist who did personal movies, but he was a professional with great talent.
**MB/KG**: Do you remember anything in particular about the filming of *Lizard in a Woman's Skin*?
**JS**: I remember Leo Genn. Genn was a marvelous fellow. In movies, you remember the people you work with. Genn was fantastic. Galleani, we talked about her previously. I remember an extraordinary castle, a very beautiful English castle, where we were shooting the movie; it belonged to an old English family. And it was an absolutely magnificent place. There is something magical about moviemaking: As soon as you see a camera in the streets, as soon as you see a projector, you can go everywhere, you enter where you want. People are still fascinated by the process of making movies. If you have a camera, people are fascinated by it.

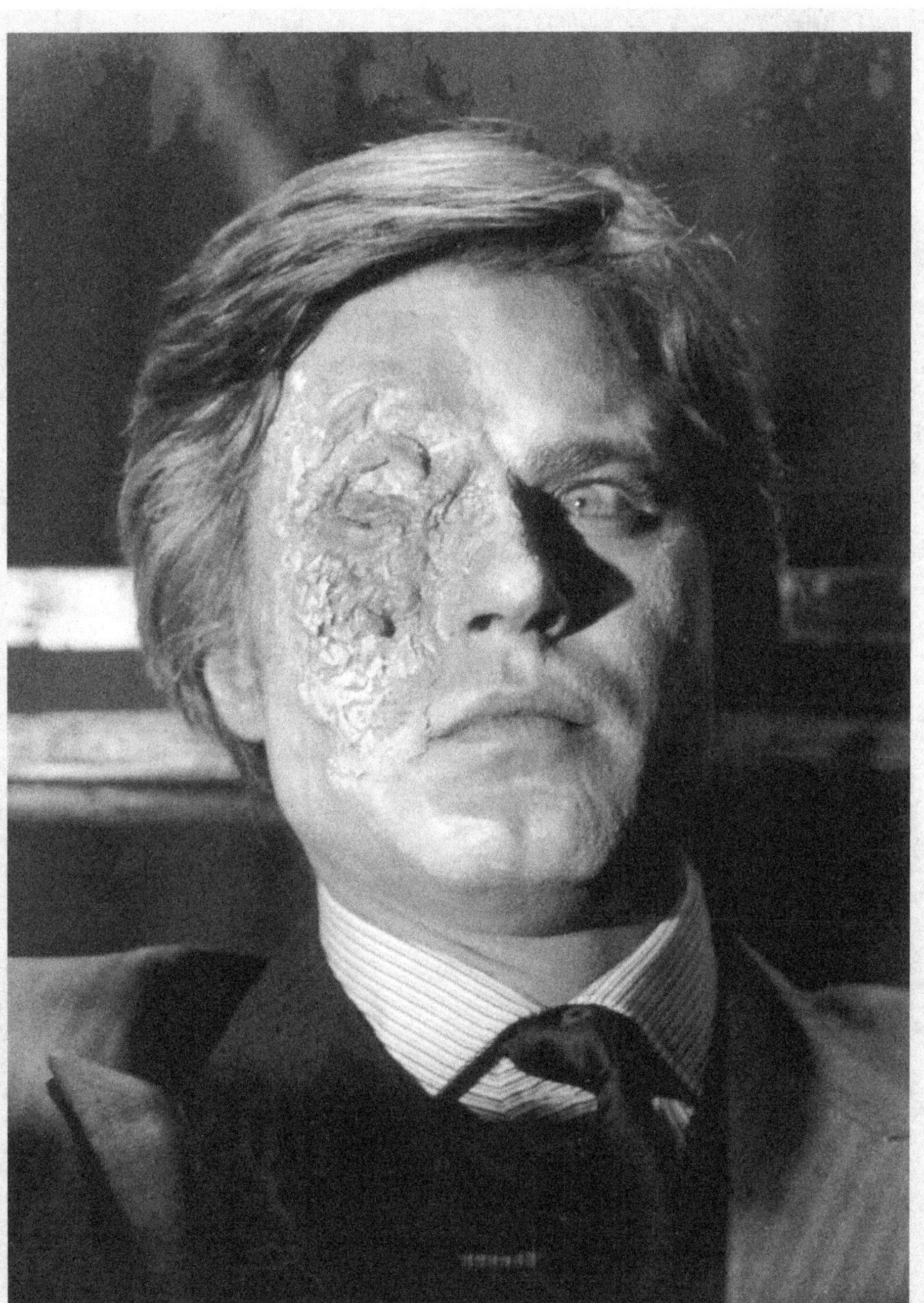

**Frank (Jean Sorel) appears as another mutilated corpse in Carol's dream.**

**MB/KG**: Do you remember much of Franco Di Girolamo's make-up effects? Especially the scene at the table where you are all made up like corpses?
**JS**: Yes, yes, I remember that. But I have not seen Fulci's movies in a very long time. These movies go back to the 1970s. And I think that the films we did came out in France. I saw them in France when I did the French dubbing. I don't have copies on VHS or DVD, so I have not seen them again in so many years.
**MB/KG**: What do you think of the cult following of Fulci and his movies?
**JS**: First of all, Fulci was someone that I liked a lot. And he was a friend of ours, a friend of my wife, and one of my friends, too. And I am very happy that he is being recognized as an important director. That would have been great if he could have been recognized in his lifetime. It's just wonderful that he has made his mark. It's good for his daughter and it's good for the people he was friends with, because back then he was only considered a competent director, but not as a great one. I think he was very brave.
**MB/KG**: Thank you.
**JS**: You're welcome.

# Carlo Rambaldi Interview by Mike Baronas and Kit Gavin

Mike Baronas and Kit Gavin conducted the following interview with Carlo Rambaldi on August 21, 2002. *Maestro* Rambaldi was the long-time protégé of Italian horror legend Mario Bava and would go on to become one of the most accomplished and heavily lauded special effects artists of his day. He won Academy Awards for his work on the box-office hits *Alien* (1979) and *E.T.: The Extra-Terrestrial* (1982). *Maestro* Rambaldi passed away in 2012, at the age of 86. We are very grateful that he took the time to answer these questions about his only collaboration with Lucio Fulci.

**Mike Baronas and Kit Gavin**: Could you tell us about the dog effects in *A Lizard in a Woman's Skin*?
**Carlo Rambaldi**: Yes, the dog effects were in the screenplay. Florinda, the actress, runs desperately; she is being pursued, and is suddenly confronted with these four vivisected dogs. In reality, they were coyotes, not dogs.
**MB/KG**: Why coyotes?
**CR**: Because, of course, I had begun to design these effects by looking for real dog skin, but the Roman *couture* houses did not have dog skin; at the most, they had coyote skin. Therefore, I needed to make it vivisected coyotes. Because of this, the production company had serious problems, because in many cities where the film was shown—especially in Milan, Genoa and Turin—some animal protection people saw the film and thought that we had used real dogs. They filed a complaint against the production company. As you know, each complaint generates its own proceedings, with a different judge for each. And so, I had to show my dogs to four different courts and convince four different judges that they were not real dogs but in actuality were mechanical dogs that had been vivisected with our special effects.
**MB/KG**: Do you remember how you created these effects with the dog that has its eyes closed? It seems difficult to create.
**CR**: No, it wasn't difficult. What matters is that the director must clearly state what he wants, and then we create the effects mechanically. As a matter of fact, for example, E.T. was much more complex because of the articulation in his facial expressions.
**MB/KG**: The rumor is that when Florinda Bolkan, the actress, saw the dogs for the first time, she was shocked …
**CR**: Well, no, because she … had rehearsed earlier, so she knew what the dogs looked like. She had seen them before, it's not as if… I mean, the audience believes that as she runs, she opens the door and is suddenly faced with these dogs for the first time. In reality, that's not how it was, because she had seen them several times before.
**MB/KG**: Another effect in the film is the bat attack; do you remember that episode?
**CR**: Well, yes, we had 35 electrical bats equipped with an invisible mechanism that made them rotate in the room, you know? The most challenging part was creating efficient bats. These were battery-operated. When the board clapped, 10 mechanics would turn 10 bats on so as not to waste too much time. And so, the carousel around Florinda began.
**MB**: Were all the bats fake, electronic bats?
**CR**: Everything was electronic: the rotation, the beating of the wings, everything. There's a tiny motor that drives a cam. The bat was hanging from invisible wires; you could not see this. And the wings were beating all along. At the end of the shot, all we had to do was turn the switch off, thus stopping the wings from beating.

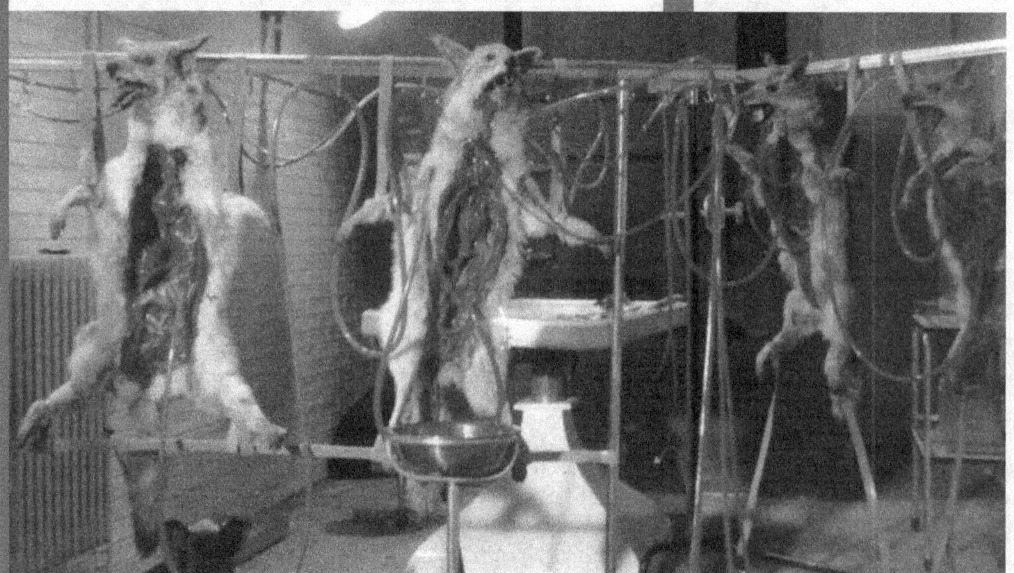

**Carlo Rambaldi's eviscerated dog effects were so realistic that Fulci and producer Edmondo Amati ended up in court on animal cruelty charges!**

# 1972

## The Eroticist (Italy/France)

**Italian *fotobusta* for *The Eroticist.***

Aka *All'onorevole piacciono le donne (Nonostante le apparenze... e purché la nazione non lo sappia); The Senator Likes Women; A su excelencia le gustan las mujeres; Le député plait aux femmes; Der lange Schwarze mit dem Silberblick*

Directed by Lucio Fulci; Produced by Edmondo Amati, Maurizio Amati and Jacques Roitfeld, for Fida Cinematografica, Les Productions Jacques Roitfeld and New Film Production S.r.l.; Story and Screenplay by Alessandro Continenza, Lucio Fulci and Ottavio Jemma; Director of Photography: Sergio D'Offizi; Editor: Vincenzo Tomassi; Music by Fred Bongusto; Song: *Dormi serena*, performed by Bruno Martino

Main Players: Lando Buzzanca (Senator Gianni Puppis); Lionel Stander (Cardinal Maravigli); Laura Antonelli (Sister Hildegarde); Corrado Gaipa (Don Gesualdo); Francis Blanche (Father Scirer); Renzo Palmer (Father Lucion); Agostina Belli (Sister Brunhilde); Arturo Dominici (His Excellency); Eva Czemerys (Fantasy Woman); Anita Strindberg (French Ambassador's Wife); Feodor Chaliapin (Senator Torsello)

*Senator Puppis is in line to become the next President of Italy. It is a position for which he has been groomed since he was a child, under the guidance of power-hungry Cardinal Maravigli. Now that the goal is within his grasp, Puppis begins to crack under pressure. He becomes sexually preoccupied and is observed grabbing a woman's backside in public. Maravigli and his minions take Puppis into hiding and try to exorcise him of these impulses. However, the impulses become more pronounced and eventually Puppis decides that he has had enough of being a puppet in the political landscape ...*

The commercial success of *A Lizard in a Woman's Skin* revived Fulci's career in a big way. Producer Edmondo Amati, a long-time champion of the director's talents, decided to put him to work on a comedy. It was a genre that Fulci was intimately familiar with, after all, so the idea certainly made sense. However, Fulci's desire to push buttons soon created complications for the film.

By way of a little civics lesson, it helps to put things into perspective with regards to the Italian political scene of the period. Following the devastation of World War II and the Fascist regime, the Italian political scene changed dramatically. The Christian Democracy party had been formed in 1942 but did not begin to wield significant power until 1946; bowing to pressure from the Allies, principally the United States, they gradually severed ties with the Communist and Socialist parties and came to control the Italian political scene until the party dissolved in disgrace, amid allegations of corruption, in 1994. For a self-described Marxist like Lucio Fulci, the party's emphasis on competitive practices in the business world was akin to blasphemy; sooner than work towards a society in which everybody (or at least those who are willing to contribute) was on an equal playing ground, the Christian Democracy instituted a social policy which was closer to the "dog-eat-dog" mentality of the Americans. Within the party, there were varying degrees of "left" and "right," but to keep things simple, it must be understood that the party was never so clearly defined as the Democrats and the Republicans in American politics, for example. As the name denotes, however, the party is very closely affiliated with Church and the Vatican, which is a theme that plays a major role in this film—and inevitably, which would land the film in some difficulties with the censors of the period.

*The Eroticist* allowed Fulci to let loose with some harsh satire and commentary on two of his favorite targets: politicians and the Church. *Operations Saint Peter's* and *Beatrice Cenci* had already shown that the two entities were very strange bedfellows and *The Eroticist* allows him to offer his most pointed and witty illustration of this concept.

The action starts as the votes are being tallied as part of the general election. Senator Puppis is established as an uptight, humorless and rather self-important figure. Rumors fly fast and loose that he is a repressed homosexual, but when he is observed pinching a woman's backside, all hell breaks loose. The peculiarly Italian tradition of ass grabbing gets a wonderful send-up in this film, as Puppis attempts to control his "baser" instincts with little or no success. The pressures of politics and the imminent success of his political campaign have caused a schism in his personality. The implication is that the political life was never of his choosing to begin with and now that he is on the verge of becoming an extremely public figure, it is all too much for him. His relationship with his opponents is civil, if distant. Torsello, the veteran opponent who also has his eye on the presidency, is convinced that Puppis and his colleagues are determined to "give him the shaft" and this ultimately proves to be true when an "accident" is arranged which takes him out of the running during a

**Anita Strindberg bares (almost) all as yet another of Senator Puppis' erotic visions.**

delicate period of the race. As played by character actor Feodor Chaliapin (best-remembered for his turn as the architect Varelli in Dario Argento's *Inferno*, 1980), Torsello is emblematic of a man whose life and well-being has been irreparably damaged by the back-stabbing of the political scene; he is a neurotic mess who nevertheless proves to be prophetic where it counts—it is a dog-eat-dog world, after all.

As Puppis' erotic impulses begin to spiral out of control, Fulci has a great deal of fun cataloguing his gradual breakdown. Puppis is susceptible to blackouts, during which time his hand involuntarily convulses and attaches itself to a shapely female posterior. Fulci films these scenes like something out of a *giallo* or a horror film, adopting subjective camerawork, exaggerated lighting effects and dramatic music to simultaneously underline and mock the drama of the situation. This is twisted to a memorably unexpected effect during the scene in which Puppis' friend and confidante, the unorthodox Father Lucion, takes the Senator by car to a cloister where he will be able to grapple with his impulses. They pull over at a rest station, where the sight of numerous shapely tourists in mini-skirts assails Puppis. He tries to control himself, but it is to no avail: Seeing a figure bent over a car, wearing a skirt, he slips into a complete trance, staggers his way over behind the individual and grabs them square on the ass. Fulci zooms out to reveal that the figure is actually a Scotsman in a kilt, who does not take kindly to being groped. He slaps Puppis, which knocks him out of his trance, and the tongue-tied Senator tries to smooth things over by babbling on about Italian-Scottish relations. It's a hysterical sequence, undoubtedly one of the funniest in Fulci's *oeuvre*.

At the cloister, things do not go as planned. Father Lucion entrusts Puppis to the care of the strict (and very German) Father Scirer. Scirer tries his best to instill order in the situation, but the presence of some nuns proves to be too great a distraction. On his first night there, Puppis grabs hold of Sister Brunhilde and holds on tight as he sleeps; Scirer is called to "rescue" the petrified virgin, but he determines that the best course of action is to allow Puppis to wake up gradually in the morning sooner than risk shocking him by removing his hand from the nun's backside. Scirer attempts using psychoanalysis to get to the root of Puppis' problem, thus allowing Fulci another chance to ridicule the profession and to break out some of the dreamy and surrealistic imagery found in *A Lizard in a Woman's Skin*. Puppis' dreams are haunted by naked women, as well as by the chastising comments of his mentor, Cardinal Maravigli. The linkage between sex and sin is deeply enforced in the sexually confused Senator and Scirer is ill-equipped to deal with things properly: His motivation should be to help free Puppis of his loathing of women, but given that this loathing was instilled by the Church in the first place, he is conflicted to say the least. Eventually, Puppis' desires go beyond grabbing bottoms and extend into full-blown sexual escapades. He takes advantage of the various nuns, who comply in the interest of Christian charity, and the sudden burst of amorous activity seems to cure him of his propensity for blackouts.

From there, things become more complicated, due in no small measure to the meddling of Cardinal Maravigli. He is the film's true villain. He is corrupt, insensitive and totally dominated by greed. Maravigli has succeeded in warping Puppis' mind with his fanatical views on women. The Cardinal, anxious to put forth Puppis as a wholesome alternative to the sex-hungry politicians he is up against, controls Puppis like a puppet-master. Puppis accepts this out of loyalty, but his sexual awakening causes him to begin to challenge his mentor. Puppis may be weak and a little bit dim, but he is basically a good man. Maravigli, by contrast, is a borderline psychopath. He is in collusion with the local Mafia, represented by Don Gesualdo (played by Corrado Gaipa, best-known to American viewers for his role as Don Tommasino in Francis Ford Coppola's contemporaneous *The Godfather*), and uses these ties to "canonize" his enemies. This deliciously blasphemous conceit sees the Cardinal ordering hits on his enemies, who are then embalmed in effigy form and put on display as figures of Saints in local churches. Maravigli's desire to run the country through the puppet presidency of Puppis knows no boundaries; he will ultimately destroy numerous lives and warp the mind of his prodigy in the process.

Things appear to be improving for Puppis when Sister Hildegarde approaches him. The latter explains to the Senator that she was the only nun in the cloister whom he did not molest; this troubles her greatly and had awakened her lustful side, so she demands satisfaction. In a film loaded with male authority figures, Hildegarde is the only female who is allowed to develop much beyond a sexual object. She is presented in a sympathetic and endearing fashion as she wrestles with her Earthly desires and the sexual relationship she engages upon with Puppis seems poised to present the latter with some measure of redemption. Unfortunately, the corrupt Cardinal sees to it that this, too, does not come to fruition. She is eventually abducted and canonized like the rest of his enemies.

The film ends with Puppis, newly elected as president, addressing the public on television. He is a broken shell of a man; his opportunity to redeem his humanity has been stolen from him and he is in the pocket of a dangerous psychotic who is determined to wield power through him. As a final biting irony, Fulci has the presidential address interrupted by the finale of a lame Italian game show—the simpleton answering the question correctly succumbing to glee bordering on mania when it is announced that he is going to win a prize. The implication seems to be that the Italian public gets the leadership it deserves.

Compared to Fulci's earlier comedies, *The Eroticist* is a revelation. Fulci's flair for absurd, manic situations is still much in evidence, but the more genteel nature of his comedy has been replaced with a more acerbic kind of wit. The film is relentlessly grim and nasty in its visualization of the Italian public. Fulci's vitriol is not limited to the politicians and the representatives of the Church. The police, the *carabinieri*, indeed the public at large is equally deserving of condemnation and ridicule in his eyes. It is the film of a man who has become disillusioned with the society he is living in; Fulci uses comedy to underline the absurdities of it all, but it does not dilute the potency of his message. The finale is particularly bleak, especially in a comic context. If Fulci pulled his punches a bit in films like *Operation Saint Peter's*, the same is not true of this film: *The Eroticist* is his nastiest comedy, and also his funniest.

Predictably, the film's pointed satire would land it in some hot water. Fulci decided to forego subtlety and have Lando Buzzanca (in his second of three films for Fulci, following *Operation Saint Peter's*) made up to resemble

**Senator Puppis (Lando Buzzanca) prays for guidance while Sister Hildegarde (Laura Antonelli) embraces a new way of life.**

Christian Democrat minister Emilio Colombo. Colombo (1920-2013), who served in the Italian parliament from 1948 onwards before being elected Prime Minister from 1970 to 1972. He went on to become the President of the European Parliament from 1977 to 1979 and then worked as a Foreign Minister of Italy, serving two terms from 1980 to 1983 and from 1992 to 1993. Colombo was also a deeply closeted homosexual and the fact that Puppis is also rumored to be gay surely hit a little too close to home. Fulci's decision to openly deride the active Prime Minister was courageous, to say the least, and the joke was not lost on its intended target. Cinematographer Sergio D'Offizi later recalled: It wasn't the idea of the make-up man, Giannetto De Rossi. Fulci was the one who wanted him to look like that minister."[1] De Rossi confirmed, "Fulci wanted that kind of character because he felt he represented the political scene of the time."

Star Lando Buzzanca was also in on the joke and applauded Fulci for his courage:

> They made me up to look like Colombo, who was a minister at the time. This Colombo—I have an anecdote about that. Almost 30 years later [...] I met Colombo in Ischia. He was greeting lots of people, including me, but hadn't realized who I was. Someone said, "Buzzanca, here!" He said, "Where? Where?" "You just shook hands with me." "Ah, Buzzanca!" He hadn't even looked at me. "Hello Buzzanca, we share a problem." I said, "We were young!"

*The Eroticist* opened in Italy in the middle of March of 1972 and did very good box-office, its popularity helped in no

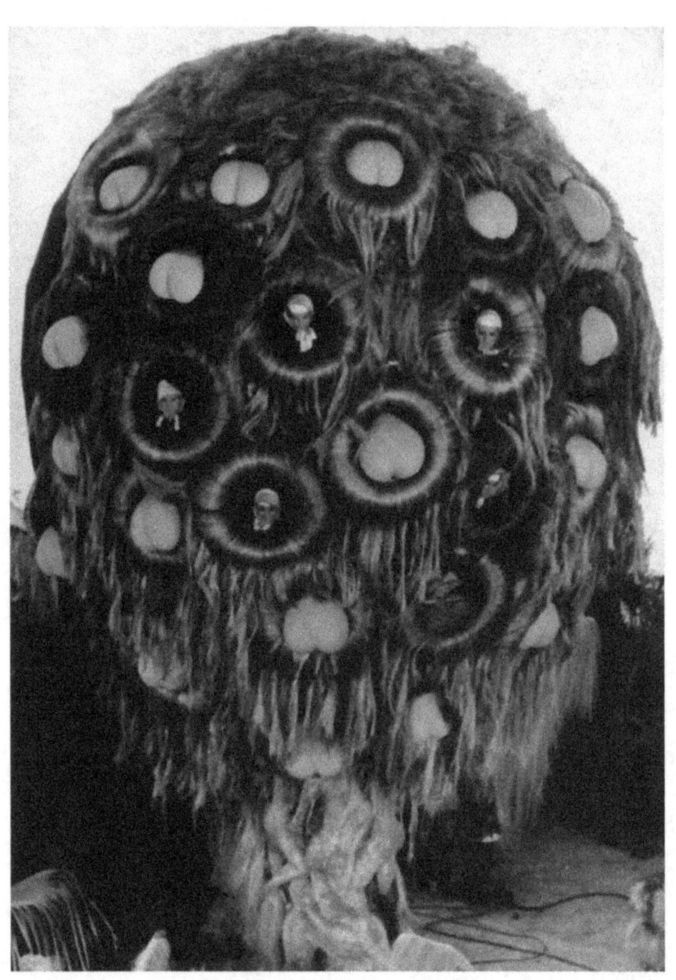

**A tree of asses; one of the stranger sights to be found in *The Eroticist*.**

small measure by the various newspaper articles and critiques which played up its scandalous nature. According to Buzzanca, however, it very nearly never saw the light of day:

> The movie had been blocked. The Christian Democrats tried to buy it—or perhaps the government, but I think it was the Christian Democrats. They offered to cover the costs of the filming, but the producer was obviously hoping to make a lot more money by having it promoted.

The movie did well at the box-office. Indeed, the film was initially blocked from release, with an official justification of "obscenity." Producer Amati appealed the decision and made six minutes worth of cuts to the picture; it was ultimately released in early 1972 ... by which point Colombo had resigned as Prime Minister.[2]

The film marked the first time that cinematographer Sergio D'Offizi worked with Fulci and it also allowed make-up artist Giannetto De Rossi (who had worked on *The Maniacs*) to finally demonstrate his considerable talents. D'Offizi (born in Rome in 1934) had mixed feelings about his relationship with Fulci, noting: "I didn't have the feeling one should have when going to work—that going to work is pleasurable." Even so, the gifted cinematographer brought his tremendous skills to bear on the film, giving it a slick and stylish look. He would go on to collaborate again with Fulci on *Don't Torture a Duckling* and would later photograph Ruggero Deodato's notorious *Cannibal Holocaust* (1980). De Rossi (born in Rome in 1942) would become a much more significant part of Fulci's personal "Repertory Company," lending his talents to such films as *Zombie*, *The Beyond* and *The House by the Cemetery*. De Rossi created some striking effects during the various hallucination sequences and found working with Fulci to be a great pleasure:

> I had a lot of fun working with him. As a director, on the set, he had a great deal of energy. He swore a lot, but in a witty way, like the Romans and the Tuscans. And since he was very professional, he went wild when he came across some amateur who only pretended to know what he was doing. He'd yell like a madman, but quickly forgot about it.

Unfortunately, the filming was not without its problems and Fulci created a minor drama when his "inner Puppis" got the better of him. Sergio D'Offizi later claimed:

> Lucio had a disagreement with Laura [Antonelli] at one point, and it didn't reflect well on him. Because Laura had to show her breasts in a particular scene and he spoke to her in a way that women don't appreciate, particularly in front of the crew. He said something like, "Bring out the boobs!" Naturally, Laura didn't like it because it was an unpleasant thing to say in front of everyone. [...] Lucio sometimes behaved in a way that really didn't appeal to the actors.

By contrast, Lando Buzzanca was extremely impressed with his director:

> He was an immensely cultured, immensely intelligent man. [...] That's why I respected and loved him.

That said, Buzzanca had a different recollection of what happened that led to the falling out between Fulci and Antonelli: According to him, Fulci couldn't resist the urge to grab the actress' bare bottom in one scene and she was understandably nonplussed.

Fortunately, the tensions on set do not manifest themselves negatively in the finished picture. Fulci's sense of pacing and framing is as keen as ever. Vincenzo Tomassi's editing and D'Offizi's cinematography are absolutely first-class. And the actors all perform with tremendous aplomb. Buzzanca is particularly effective as the conflicted Puppis, while Antonelli manages to be both sexy and moving as Hildegarde. Anita Strindberg reappears from *A Lizard in a Woman's Skin* and is put to similar use as a fetish object that excites Puppis' imagination; he envisions her wearing silver coins over her nipples and *lire* over her crotch, and the eye-catching ensemble certainly rivals her black boots and panties outfit in *Lizard*. Among the supporting cast, American actor Lionel Stander is particularly good as the vile Cardinal. Stander (1908-1994) enjoyed some success as a character actor in Hollywood—in such classic films as Frank Capra's *Mr. Deeds Goes to Town* (1936), William A. Wellman's *A Star is Born* (1937) and Preston Sturges' *Unfaithfully Yours* (1948)—before running afoul of Senator Joseph McCarthy's Communist witch-hunt of the 1950s; he then relocated to Europe and worked with such maverick filmmakers as Roman Polanski (*Cul-de-sac*, 1966) and Sergio Leone (*Once Upon a Time in the West*, 1968) before making his one and only film with Fulci, though in all he did over 30 movies in Italy. He later found renewed fame back in the U.S. as the chauffeur Max on the popular TV series *Hart to Hart* (1979-1984).

Controversy to one side, *The Eroticist* (and it must be noted, the American title is utterly senseless and appears to have been utilized in a desperate attempt to evoke William Friedkin's blockbuster *The Exorcist*, 1973; the original Italian title, *The Senator Likes Women … Despite Appearances and Provided the Public Doesn't Know*, is much more appropriate) performed well at the Italian box-office; from there, Fulci would go on to direct the film he was proudest of.

Notes:
1. All quotes in this review are from the documentary *Nel supremo interesse della nazione – A History of Censorship* (2007), written and directed by Federico Caddeo, and included on the Severin DVD release of *The Eroticist*.
2. Based on censorship information retrieved from, http://www.italiataglia.it

## *Don't Torture a Duckling (Italy)*

Aka *Non si sevizia un paperino; Angustia de silencio; La longue nuit de l'exorcisme; Fanatismo*

Directed by Lucio Fulci; Produced by Edmondo Amati (uncredited[1]), for Medusa; Screenplay by Gianfranco Clerici, Lucio Fulci and Roberto Gianviti; Director of Photography: Sergio D'Offizi; Editor: Ornella Micheli; Music by Riz Ortolani; Songs: *Quei giorni insieme a te*, performed by Ornella Vanoni; *Crazy*, performed by Wess and the Airedales; *Rhythm*, performed by Riccardo Cocciante

Main Players: Florinda Bolkan (Maciara); Tomas Milian (Andrea); Barbara Bouchet (Patrizia); Marc Porel (Don Alberto); Irene Papas (Aurelia); Georges Wilson (Francesco); Virgilio Gazzolo (Commissioner); Ugo D'Alessio (Modesti); Antonio Campodifiori (Lieutenant); Vito Passeri (Giuseppe Barra)

*A small Italian village is shocked by a series of child murders. Local outcast Maciara comes under suspicion by the superstitious locals, but the police are not convinced of her guilt. As the murders continue, a reporter from the city, Andrea, begins to investigate and uncovers other leads. He teams up with a girl from the city, Patrizia, who is staying in the village trying to kick her drug habit. The police mark Patrizia as a possible suspect, as well …*

*Don't Torture a Duckling* is an angry film. It presents a decidedly jaundiced view of humanity and it does not spare the viewer's delicate sensibilities by downplaying its horrors. It is a *giallo*, but it is much more than that. It is also Lucio Fulci's finest work; this is an opinion which Fulci shared, as he would later refer to it as his personal favorite of all the films he directed.[2]

Fulci developed the story with his old writing partner Roberto Gianviti, but when it came to the screenwriting phase the duo reached out to a third collaborator. Gianfranco Clerici began writing screenplays in the mid-1960s and had dabbled in everything from Spaghetti Westerns (*Zorro the Rebel*, 1966) and comedies (*Seven Times Seven*, 1967) to adventures (*Samoa, Queen of the Jungle*, 1969) and *gialli* (*The Bloodstained Butterfly*, 1971). Clerici proved to be a strong collaborator and he would go on to work with Fulci on such films as *The New York Ripper*, *Murder-Rock: Dancing Death* and *The House of Clocks*. He also contributed to the screenplay for Ruggero Deodato's *Cannibal Holocaust* (1980). The three writers outdid themselves on *Duckling*, constructing a screenplay that is both suspenseful and rigidly logical. There are no "cheats" to complain of in the film and the content goes beyond just trying to surprise the viewer into making some deeply personal socio-political commentary, as well.

One of the striking elements of the film is the way it flies in the face of convention by embracing its Italian roots. This is especially unusual in the context of the *giallo*, which is an irony worth considering. In the interests of securing a wider international release, many Italian filmmakers downplayed the nationality of their films by adopting pseudonyms and setting their films in "English friendly" locales like London or the United States. It was a ploy Fulci already adopted in *A Lizard in a Woman's Skin* and which he would later embrace in many of his 1980s

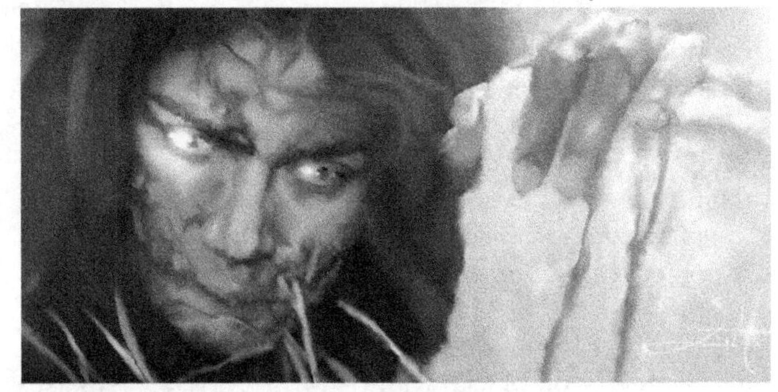

**Don't Torture a Duckling*; original artwork by Scott Hoffman.**

genre films, but for this film he threw caution to the wind and went for a very specifically *regional* Italian setting. Not only is the film openly set in Italy, it is set in a part of Italy that is seldom depicted in the more "picturesque" portraits of the country. The film depicts an Italy of superstition and bigotry, of backward thinking and hate-crimes; it was a presentation that landed Fulci in hot water in some circles, as it was tantamount to airing one's dirty laundry in public. However, this was nothing compared to the ire the film would generate over its jaundiced view of that most inviolable of sacred cows: religion.

*Don't Torture a Duckling* has often been described as anti-Catholic. But is it really? Fulci's impatience with the closed-minded mentality of the superstitious mountain community is evident, but he does not seem to be suggesting that the religion is, in itself, completely to blame in this scenario. Fulci's iconoclastic stance made him fond of taking on windmills and it certainly can be seen as an aspect of his character which would ultimately derail, or at least inhibit, his career. As such, it would be a mistake to read the film simply as an anti-Catholic diatribe. Fulci is interested in exploring the more outdated aspects of religion, or perhaps, more accurately, the way these elements have been twisted and misinterpreted by backward-thinking cultures, but at the end of the day the Church is not the true monster in this film.

**Italian *locandina* for *Don't Torture a Duckling*; artist unknown.**

The film deals with a spate of murders involving children in a small mountain village. The local police force is not up to the task, so police are imported from the city. The locals view any outsiders with suspicion and this extends to the barrage of reporters who have also swarmed in on the village in search of the next big story. In the film's cynical *milieu*, just about everybody is on the make for something: Patrizia is in exile while she awaits a drugs trial, Andrea is looking to capitalize on the sensational story even as he looks down upon his colleagues for doing the same thing, and so forth. Amid this hard-bitten environment, the characters of Maciara and the priest, Don Alberto, stand out. Maciara is an outcast because of her involvement in the black arts; she is also marked as being "different" because she is mentally unstable. By contrast, Don Alberto represents a sort of time-suspended innocence that evokes the Peter Pan complex. He is portrayed as kindly, caring and compassionate, but he is unusually removed from "adult" concerns. He spends his time playing soccer with the local boys and reacts awkwardly when the worldly Patrizia expresses interest in him. As the story unfolds, these two characters deepen with regards to their relation to the mystery. Maciara inevitably falls under suspicion: she is "weird" and doesn't fit in, so she must inevitably be guilty of the crimes. The logical but ineffectual police commissioner from the city (played by Virgilio Gazzolo, who had already appeared as a papal emissary in *Operation Saint Peter's*) correctly asserts that the evidence does not support the notion that Maciara is to blame, but he is unable to avert the inevitable violence that erupts. The locals band together and attack Maciara, mercilessly beating her to death. In the meantime, Don Alberto coasts through the village without ever attracting the slightest hint of suspicion; as a priest, he is surely above suspicion. Inevitably, this being a *giallo*, the true culprit is the one everybody least suspects. Andrea eventually corners Don Alberto and their ensuing dialogue provides insight into his twisted pathology: He was simply looking to spare the children from the evils of the world. Don Alberto is ultimately punished for his sins when he takes a falling dive off of a cliff, but it does not follow that safety and normality has been restored.

The movie is one of the relatively few *gialli* that works on an emotional level as much as a visceral one. Fulci's celebrated/reviled propensity for indulging in protracted scenes of shocking violence is in evidence, but here it is bolstered by a genuine sense of emotional involvement in the characters. The sequence depicting the chain-whipping of a major character by the inbred locals is justly celebrated as the finest individual set piece of Fulci's career, but it is not just because of the skill and polish of its editing, cinematography and make-up effects; it works because the audience is genuinely sorry to see the character being killed off in such a truly horrid and unjust fashion. The climax is similarly stunning, and if Fulci arguably overdoes it with a few too many lingering close-ups of a prop body being pretty much torn to shreds, it is easy to overlook his zeal in light of the overall impact. One is again reminded of Fulci's love for the playwright Antonin Artaud; the major "spectacle" scenes involving bodily mutilation would not be out of place in the so-called Theatre of Cruelty.

The story is gripping from beginning to end. While some have faulted the police procedural scenes for being dry, they are executed with style and are well integrated into the film. Fulci's desire to retain a logical progression of events in his *gialli* is evident throughout; the film never goes off on a tangent or relies on hokey contrivance in order to get from point A to point B. The contrast between the "enlightened" city officials and the superstitious villagers may be a little obvious, but Fulci does not spare the former characters any punches either. In the film's slightly bitter landscape, ignorance and misunderstanding comes in many forms. In this respect, the figure of the Commissioner is particularly interesting. He is not presented as a bad person; indeed, he seems genuinely committed to finding the culprit and ending the series of killings. However, his use of psychology draws sneers from his colleagues in the local police force and he is ultimately unable to make much headway into the matter. His intentions might be honorable, but in presuming to condescend to the "superstitious" locals, he is unable to see the forest for the trees.

The concept of a series of child killings immediately puts the film on a different level than the average *giallo*, while inevitably opening it up to more than the usual run of criticism. The child murders are handled in a—dare one say it—comparatively tasteful and restrained fashion, but they are disturbing by their very nature. Fulci does not sensationalize the killings in a tacky way, but it is hard to deny that the whole "destruction of innocence" theme is different and more inherently affecting than the usual run of killings one may normally find in films of this nature.

The director's theme of intolerance and bigotry is powerfully addressed in the picture. The small village is the sort of place where everybody knows everybody—and what they are up to. Fulci clearly has no patience for this kind of in-bred *milieu*. The outsider figures are regarded with suspicion for no better reason than being perceived as different. Nowhere is this more evident than in the character of Maciara. The latter is one of Fulci's most memorable "misfit" characters. She is spurned and rejected by the locals owing to her beliefs and has adopted an anti-social attitude as a result. When the locals gang up on her, they do so in the belief that she is responsible for the murders; given her association with black magic and her status as an outsider, this makes perfect sense to them. Sooner than allow the police to complete their investigation, they decide to take matters into their own hands. Maciara is similar to the character of Bob (played by Giovanni Lombardo Radice) in his later horror film *City of the Living Dead*. Both characters exist separately from society and both are viewed with contempt and distrust because they do not fit into the established norms. Fulci's sympathies clearly lie with these oddball characters; for him, they represent a level of purity that is preferable to the hypocrisy and violence of the townspeople.

**Maciara (Florinda Bolkan) is brutally attacked in one of Fulci's most vivid and heartbreaking set pieces.**

The relationship between Don Alberto and his victims has been the source of much speculation among fans. Given the recent spate of allegations of molestation leveled against Catholic priests, one can be forgiven for assuming the worst—but truly, looking at the film in a more objective fashion, nothing supports the hypothesis that Don Alberto is a pedophile. The image of him frolicking with the children at the end of the picture—intercut with images of his face being shredded by the jagged cliffs as he falls to his demise—may appear a little suggestive, but in this instance it seems likely that the most obvious interpretation is the correct one: Don Alberto is merely a victim of arrested development. In his twisted mind, he sees the boys' growing interest in sex as indicative of moral decay. He is trying to save their souls before it is too late, so he goes about it the only way he knows how; by killing them. Don Alberto's actions may be horrible, but he still comes off better than the ignorant city people who callously continue driving even after catching sight of poor Maciara bleeding to death on the side of the road. Alberto is insane; the city people are simply indifferent and self-absorbed.

Fulci's command of the medium is evident throughout the film. Together with cinematographer Sergio D'Offizi, he creates some of the most striking and memorable imagery in the genre. The contrast between the wide-open spaces, often seen in broad daylight, and the claustrophobic, slightly shabby interiors helps to give the film tremendous mood and atmosphere. The editing is skillful and precise and Riz Ortolani's soundtrack is one of his very finest. The use of music during the aforementioned chain-whipping scene is particularly inspired, as the use of diegetic music on a radio helps to drown out the cries and screams. Ortolani's achingly beautiful "*Quei giorni insieme a te*," performed by Ornella Vanoni, underscores the majority of the scene and its aftermath, but the initial songs which set a more jarring tone were not the work of Ortolani at all: "Rhythm" was composed by Luis Bacalov and performed by Riccardo Cocciante and "Crazy" was written and performed by the group Wess & The Airedales ... a band which, incidentally, had previously supplied the insanely catchy song used to drive Carroll Baker insane in Umberto Lenzi's ground-breaking *giallo*, *Orgasmo* (1969).

**Andrea (Tomas Milian) and Patrizia (Barbara Bouchet) comfort the injured Aurelia (Irene Papas).**

The cast performs exceptionally well. Florinda Bolkan rejoins Fulci following her leading role in *A Lizard in a Woman's Skin*; while the character of Maciara is not a main part, *per se*, it is arguably a more memorable characterization on the whole. Maciara belongs to a line of sad outcast figures seen in Fulci's work. Her principal crime is in being different, and for the local townspeople this is reason enough to view her as the likely perpetrator of the violence. Bolkan does not have a great deal of screen time, but she manages to be frightening, even feral, in some of her scenes and heartbreaking in others. Bolkan enjoyed working with Fulci but recalled that filming her death scene was unpleasant:

> I had to stay for hours on the floor, waiting for the actors and everything to be ready to start again when they kill me—that long scene, and he would come and talk to me and say silly things to me and promised it wouldn't take long and then it would take another day and another day ... But he was very sweet. He would come and say, "Now, Florinda, don't worry, [...] and don't get upset, it's just one scene." I think he knew I was that patient ... he was just very sweet and gave me that marvelous feeling of being with me.

Tomas Milian also makes his second Fulci appearance, and this is indeed an unusually restrained and ordinary role for the gifted actor. Milian sensibly does not try to overburden the character with tics and plays the role in a naturalistic fashion. He is all the more effective because of it.[3] Andrea is not an entirely sympathetic character, but he proves more efficient at uncovering the culprit than the police, even if his motivations are somewhat sketchy: Is he truly concerned about the people of the village or is he just looking for the ultimate scoop for his newspaper?

Barbara Bouchet plays one of her most memorable roles as the drug-addicted "big city" girl, Patrizia, who lands on the list of suspects simply because she is another outsider. It is also strongly implied that she is a total deviant, and the scene in which she openly seduces a young boy and offers to deflower him would prove to be so controversial with the censors that Fulci would have to prove that the boy and the naked actress were never in the same shot together, and the image of the boy in the foreground being tempted by Bouchet was accomplished with an adult midget stand-in![4] The scene in question is definitely shocking and remains so to this day. Here again the viewer is left to ponder its implications, as Patrizia is interrupted before anything can happen. Was she truly going to have sex with the boy or was it just one big tease? No matter how one reads it, however, it certainly puts her in a position of moral ambiguity, which is unusual for a "heroine" in a genre picture. Bouchet is impressive in the role, and once again proves that she was a very capable performer when given a chance to do something beyond adding to the scenery. She was born as Barbara Goutscher in what is now part of the Czech Republic in 1943 and immigrated with her family to America when she was a child. She made an inauspicious start in films in the early 1960s, usually cast as window-dressing in mostly forgettable teen-oriented comedies of the period. She was then cast as Moneypenny in the big-budget James Bond spoof *Casino Royale* (1967) and appeared opposite future Fulci *alumnus* Richard Johnson in Seth Holt's stylish spy thriller *Danger Route* (1967). She made her way to Italy in the 1970s and starred in a number of *gialli*, *poliziottteschi* and horror films, including Paolo Cavara's *The Black Belly of the Tarantula* (1971), Emilio Miraglia's *The Red Queen Kills Seven Times* (1972), Fernando Di Leo's *Caliber 9* (1972) and Andrea Bianchi's notorious *Cry of a Prostitute* (1974), in which she is repeatedly brutalized by hit man Henry Silva—and likes it! In more recent years, she also appeared in a small role as the wife of David Hemmings' character in Martin Scorsese's epic *Gangs of New York* (2002). Bouchet never worked again for Fulci, but at least her one appearance for him proved to be a memorable one.

The supporting cast includes yet another actor making a second appearance for Fulci: Georges Wilson, who plays the local warlock, Uncle Francesco. Wilson does not get a lot of screen time compared to his flashy role as Francesco Cenci in *Beatrice Cenci*, but he brings some welcome dark humor to the proceedings. Distinguished Greek actress Irene Papas is very good as Aurelia, the taciturn mother of the misguided priest, while Marc Porel is outstanding as Don Alberto. Porel was born in Switzerland in 1949. He broke into films in the late '60s, making early appearances in Costa-Gavras' *Shock Troops* (1967) and Henri Verneuil's *The Sicilian Clan* (1969), but found his true *métier* in Italian genre films of the 1970s. He would appear in Luchino Visconti's *Ludwig* (1972) and *L'innocente* (1976) and Mario Bava's swansong *La Venere d'Ille* (1978). Fulci was impressed with Porel and cast him again in *The Psychic*, but the two men reportedly clashed on that picture and did not work together again. Following an appearance in Cesare Canevari's sleazy *giallo Killing of the Flesh* (1983), Porel died at the age of 34; some sources indicate that he died from meningitis, while others point to his long-standing issues with heroin abuse as the cause.

Despite its problems with the censors (which Fulci ascribed to a delayed fall-out from *The Eroticist*[5]), *Don't Torture a Duckling* proved sufficiently successful to allow Fulci to continue working at a steady pace. Undoubtedly the film's unsavory subject matter and its regional setting hurt its chances of securing the same kind of international exposure as *A Lizard in a Woman's Skin* and it never did secure a theatrical release in the States. His next films would not be so personal or passionately committed as this one, but then again *Don't Torture a Duckling* would be a very difficult act to follow up at the best of times.

Notes:

1. Amati is not credited on the prints or any of the advertising, but Fulci would later claim that he produced the film in Michele Romagnoli's book, *L'occhio del testimone*, (Bologna: Granata Press 1992, p. 35).
2. Thrower, Stephen, *Beyond Terror: The Films of Lucio Fulci* (Guildford: FAB Press, 1999), p. 98.
3. Milian is dubbed on the English track by veteran actor/vocal artist Michael Forrest, best known to Italian genre fans for providing the English voice of *poliziottesco* superstar Maurizio Merli in many films.
4. Thrower, Stephen, *Beyond Terror: The Films of Lucio Fulci* (Guildford: FAB Press, 1999), p. 70.
5. Audio interview with Lucio Fulci, conducted by Pier Maria Bocchi and Andrea Bruni, included on the Shriek Show DVD release of *Touch of Death*.

## Florinda Bolkan interview by Mike Baronas

Mike Baronas conducted the following interview with Florinda Bolkan via fax on September 14, 2000. Ms. Bolkan's long and distinguished career encompassed two major roles in two of Lucio Fulci's finest films: *A Lizard in a Woman's Skin*, in which she plays the duplicitous Carol Hammond, and *Don't Torture a Duckling*, in which she plays the village outcast, Maciara. Fulci held Ms. Bolkan in high esteem and we are very grateful to her for taking the time to answer these questions.

**Mike Baronas**: When was the last time you watched either *A Lizard in a Woman's Skin* or *Don't Torture a Duckling*?
**Florinda Bolkan**: A long time ago, as I don't have copies.
**MB**: I believe that the films, and the themes they contain, hold up very well all these years later. What are your thoughts on them after so long?
**FB**: As far as my friends tell me, you are right. They have held up well.
**MB**: How did you come to be cast in these roles?
**FB**: Through my agent, Carol Levi, who was with the William Morris Agency.
**MB**: What was your initial impression of Lucio Fulci?
**FB**: I found him extremely disagreeable and almost decided not to do it, but was convinced by Carol that he was talented. Later on, I began to like him extremely and I did the second film with him with great pleasure.
**MB**: What was your experience like working with Fulci?
**FB**: The first day we were like cats and dogs. The following days, we began to like each other enormously. Lucio only respected people who had guts.
**MB**: Fulci utilized you as the "strong but scorned (and often brutalized) woman" in both these films. Was this a role you were comfortable in playing?
**FB**: With his films, yes; I don't know about others.
**MB**: *Lizard* is a beautifully made film, but it encountered some controversy when it was released in 1971. The lesbian sequences were surely considered more "taboo" at the time then they would be today.
**FB**: It is true that at the time, it was a big scandal; nowadays it would seem banal!
**MB**: Speaking of the film's controversy, I have read that Fulci was taken to court over the "eviscerated dogs" sequence. Do you have any memories of this?
**FB**: I only recall reading about what a scandal the film was causing.
**MB**: Are there any other experiences related to *Lizard* that you would like to share?
**FB**: I liked Lucio very much and he respected me, which wasn't always the case with the other actors; I noticed that particularly on *Lizard*. Lucio could be quite critical of the other actresses on the picture.

**Lucio Fulci confers with Florinda Bolkan on the set of *Don't Torture a Duckling.***

**MB**: You wouldn't still happen to have the fur coat you wore in that film?

**FB**: Unfortunately I don't, otherwise I would still be wearing it!

**MB**: What about some of the props, like the paper knife?

**FB**: All that belonged to the wardrobe.

**MB**: Tell me about the make-up process you had to undergo for your death scene in *Duckling*…

**FB**: It was interesting. I had the best make-up man and make-up woman in Italy and they did nice work. I enjoyed doing that a lot.

**MB**: Was your death scene difficult to film?

**FB**: It was long and tiresome, with many hours under the sun, making the same horror face. The interesting thing was that I used to eat at a very nice restaurant and I would go there with the make-up still on. The first day, the people there were really shocked; they thought it was for real!

**MB**: Do you have any other experiences you'd like to share about making *Duckling*?

**FB**: The amazing thing is that I never met any other actors during the shooting of my scenes. Every scene was prepared as if the other actors would not be performing with me; interesting, no?

**MB**: You continue to be active in films, I believe?

**FB**: I have done fewer films lately. I still do some TV and my last film appearance is in a film I wrote and directed in Brazil titled, *I Didn't Know Tururu*. It is going to the San Sebastian Film Festival next week and will be released in Brazil next November.

**MB**: Do you remember hearing about Lucio Fulci's passing?

**FB**: I was not in Rome at the time, unfortunately; I often go abroad to Brazil.

**MB**: How did Fulci compare with some of the other directors you worked with?

**FB**: Lucio was very nice and easy with me, but he was different with other people. He liked to joke, but sometimes his jokes could be very offensive. Fortunately, he liked me!

**MB**: Lastly, do you have a favorite horror film?

**FB**: A French film called *Les Diaboliques* by Clouzot.

# 1973

## *White Fang (Italy/Spain/France)*

Aka *Zanna bianca; Colmillo Blanco; Croc-blanc; Wolfsblut*

Directed by Lucio Fulci; Produced by Harry Alan Towers and Ermanno Donati, for In-Cine Compañía Industrial Cinematografica, Les Productions Fox Europa and Oceania Produzioni Internazionali Cinematografiche; Screenplay by Guy Elmes, Roberto Gianviti, Thom Keyes, Piero Regnoli, Guillaume Roux and Harry Alan Towers [as Peter Welbeck], from the novel by Jack London; Director of Photography: Erico Menczer and Pablo Ripoll; Editor: Ornella Micheli; Music by Carlo Rustichelli

Main Players: Franco Nero (Jason Scott); Virna Lisi (Sister Evangelina); Fernando Rey (Father Oatley); John Steiner (Charles 'Beauty' Smith); Missaele (Mitsah); Raimund Harmstorf (Kurt Jansen); Carole Andre (Krista); Daniel Martín (Charlie); Maurice Poli (Mountie)

*Charlie, a Native American fur trapper, is out with his son Mitsah when they come upon a wild dog and its pup. Mitsah bonds with the pup, which alarms Charlie, but the animal proves to be a loyal companion. The boy names the dog White Fang and the two become inseparable. When Mitsah is nearly killed falling through the ice, Charlie is forced to take him to a nearby mining camp for medical attention; White Fang shadows them every step of the way. The boy is nursed back to health, but Charlie is killed when he refuses to sell White Fang to a corrupt businessman named Charles 'Beauty' Smith. A reporter named Jason Scott takes the boy under his wing and attempts to protect him, but Smith's treachery knows no bounds and soon endangers the entire community …*

In 1973, Lucio Fulci was riding high on a string of successful films. His renewed reputation in the business put him in line for a prestigious assignment that originated from the most unlikely of sources. The previous year, producer Harry Alan Towers had scored a success with the release of *The Call of the Wild* starring Charlton Heston and directed by Ken Annakin. It was an uncommonly mainstream picture for producer Towers, who was better known for his low-budget exploitation fare, including the *Fu Manchu* series starring Christopher Lee and a string of films directed by Spanish maverick Jess Franco, which included such fusions of horror and eroticism as *Eugenie—The Story of Her Journey into Perversion* and *Venus in Furs* (both 1969). The presence of Heston top-lining the film no doubt helped, but the star was none too impressed with the picture and made a point of avoiding Towers-backed projects for the remainder of his career. Even so, *The Call of the Wild* was a popular success and Towers was not about to pass up milking the property completely dry. Looking into the catalogue of author Jack London's stories, he decided that *White Fang* was an ideal picture to bankroll. The international co-production would attract financing from Italy, Spain and France—and with a disgruntled Annakin following in Heston's footsteps, there was certainly no question of hiring him to take control of the film. Towers was looking to save money wherever possible, anyway, and the Italian co-producers put forth Fulci's name as a viable candidate. A deal was struck and Fulci was set with the task of directing one of his most ambitious pictures to date.

Towers adapted the story himself under his usual *nom de plume* of Peter Welbeck, but Fulci was not entirely satisfied with his efforts and drafted his friend and collaborator Roberto Gianviti to work on the script. Veteran screenwriter and director Piero Regnoli also had a hand in the writing process and the size and scope of the material determined that a second unit would have to be created to deal with some of the more action-oriented sequences set in the snowy Yukon wilderness. Location filming in America was out of the question, so the mountains of Austria were utilized instead. To head up the second unit, Fulci reached out to his old friend Tonino Ricci, who was rewarded for his efforts by being promoted to director on one of the film's sequels, *White Fang to the Rescue* (1974). The process of making a film with so much rugged location filming, combined with the added stressors of having to rely on animal performers, pushed Fulci's patience to its limits, but the end result was worth it: *White Fang* would become a sizable box-office hit.

The story plays fast and loose with London's 1906 novel. The book, of course, is a reliable standby in high school English literature classes and it remains a compelling portrait of nature for many young readers. Film versions started to appear in 1925 and the story has been adapted as recently as the late 1990s. Fulci's take on the story dispenses with much of the background of White Fang and introduces him as a fully developed—and very wild—animal. The basic outline of the story is more or less the same, but new characters are introduced, others are rechristened and the film builds to a very different finale compared to that of the book. The changes do not improve upon what London wrote, but they do hang together well enough and make for a compelling screen narrative.

Fulci's pragmatic approach is very much in evidence. On the face of it, this was a very unusual assignment for the director; his flair for the violent and the bizarre should not have put him on the short list of sensible directors for what was ultimately intended to be a family-friendly movie. Even so, he rises to the occasion and handles the material with great flair. In many respects, the film is akin to his Spaghetti Westerns; there's plenty of horseback action and the mining camp community is reminiscent of the settlements found in the typical Western of the period. The presence of Franco Nero also solidifies this, though his characterization as Jason Scott is considerably softer around the edges compared to his stoic hero in *Massacre Time*, to say nothing of his more amoral anti-heroes for director Sergio Corbucci in the likes of *Django* (1966) and *The Mercenary* (1968).

**Italian *locandina* for *White Fang*; artist uknown.**

Viewers accustomed to the excesses of Fulci's later horror films may find the action in *White Fang* a little too genteel, but there are a few deeply uncomfortable moments to be found in the picture. It would ultimately be released in the United States with a PG rating, but don't let that fool you: There's a little bit of violence here which would surely prove unsettling for younger viewers. One of the most disturbing sequences occurs when White Fang fights one of "Beauty" Smith's dogs. The scene is intense and very drawn-out. The animals are remarkably well trained and perform very convincingly and the use of squeals and cries on the soundtrack implies some pretty strong brutal-

**French lobby card for *White Fang*.**

ity. The sequence ends, predictably enough, with White Fang as the victor. For a period of time, however, it looks as if the wounds sustained in the fight will prove fatal—and this, too, is pretty strong stuff for a younger viewer to process.

The human characters are not immune to the brutality of the setting, either. One of Smith's minions stabs Charlie, Mitsah's kindly father, in the gut for refusing to sell him the dog. Later on, Krista, a performer in Smith's saloon, is accidentally killed when she refuses to give in to her employer's romantic overtures; she falls and hits her head against the sharp edge of his desk and the nasty wound on her temple gives the scene an added jolt. Later, her father, a disgraced priest named Father Oatley, defends Mitsah to the death; he is shot in the head for his troubles. Fulci does not go in for the sort of lurid detail he is known for staging in his other films, but he doesn't exactly downplay the violence, either. Even in a subject such as this, he cannot be bothered to trivialize violence and its consequences; this may perhaps make the film a little tough on some of the younger viewers, but it helps to give the movie a dramatic punch, which many other versions of the story fail to equal.

Production values are excellent throughout. This is Fulci's last collaboration with the gifted cinematographer Erico Menczer (Spanish cinematographer Pablo Ripoll is also credited, but this is likely for quota purposes) and the two men create some striking imagery. The snowy landscapes and harsh terrain give the film a sense of gritty reality, while the massive Dawson City set created by Enzo Bulgarelli is impressively detailed and rendered. The bursts of violence help to make the drama all the more involving: This is not a "safe" sort of family film where all the good people will survive and the wicked will be punished, so the film never falls into that kind of a dramatic rut. Fulci's flair for staging action scenes is evident throughout, but he knows, where appropriate, how to play on the heartstrings as well. His work is not renowned for its tearjerking abilities, but the ending of this film is genuinely moving, as Jason, Mitsah and White Fang are reunited after having endured many hardships; Carlo Rustichelli's melodramatic but effective score beautifully underscores the finale's dramatic effect.

The impressive cast certainly helps. Franco Nero gives a sturdy performance as Jason Scott. Nero brings his considerable charm to bear on the role and provides the film with a strong dramatic center, but the narrative focus is not honed in on him. Nero has spoken well of his collaborations with Fulci, but the sentiment was not mutual. As the acerbic director would later recall:

> Another one with whom I did not go along at all was Franco Nero, when we were shooting *White Fang*. He was already famous and did everything to be insufferable, perhaps forgetting that Sergio Corbucci and I had made him a star in 1966, after a period of being an absolute nonentity. [...] During filming he was pissed off since he had to pass on *The Devil Is a Woman* (1974), with Glenda Jackson, because he was busy on our picture, and always said that he did not like the idea of making such a "shitty movie." He kept repeating that he wanted to do *The Devil Is a Woman* and kept biting the hand that fed him. Then I started speaking to Nero through my assistant, who was [Francesco] Cinieri: "Talk to this gentleman ..." and Cinieri obliged. "Tell him to stay with his back to the camera ..." And yet he always tried to get a good close-up, so I said: "Well, let's do this close-up, since we need the actor's face ..." On *White Fang* there were other very good actors: Fernando Rey, the great Buñuel actor, Virna Lisi, John Steiner—still, only Franco Nero was a constant pain in the ass. Until one day the producer Ermanno Donati showed up on the set, asking us to make peace, otherwise shooting would never end (it lasted nine weeks, whereas I usually make a film in four or five weeks). So I called a break and gathered all the cast. The dog, Buck, was scratching about nearby ... I asked for their attention and said: "Ladies and gentlemen, do you know who is the real star of this film?" And Buck kept scratching about. "There he is! The dog. You all count for nothing!" I remember the detail of Virna Lisi laughing out loud, when I said that."[1]

The dog hired to play White Fang is remarkably effective; in truth there were at least two dogs cast in the role, with one responsible for the various fight scenes. Child actor Missaele, about whom precious little is known, played the role of Mitsah. The character is sidelined for a large chunk of the narrative as he recuperates from his early near-death experience, but the child is very effective in his dramatic scenes and remains an endearing presence throughout. The supporting cast includes two standouts: Fernando Rey and John Steiner. Rey (1917-1994) was born in Spain and began working in films in the mid-1930s. He became a favorite of director Luis Buñuel, who cast him in such films as *Viridiana* (1961) and *Tristana* (1970), the latter also co-starring Franco Nero. He found his biggest success in America when William Friedkin cast him in the Oscar-winning blockbuster *The French Connection* (1971); he reprised his role as the suave Alain Charnier in John Frankenheimer's *French Connection II* (1975). Rey vacillated between art house and commercial assignments for much of his career. *White Fang* provided him with his only opportunity to work with Fulci, but he certainly makes the most of the role he is given. He gives Father Oatley a real dignity that makes his fate all the more moving and tragic. John Steiner pretty much steals the show as the sadistic "Beauty" Smith. It's one of those wonderful Snidely Whiplash villains that allows for rampant overacting, but Steiner does not lay the melodramatics on too thick. He is a credible villain, one without the slightest redeeming value: Even his appearance (pencil-thin mustache, greasy hair, permanent sneer) marks him out as somebody to be avoided. Steiner was born in England in 1941 and started acting on the stage and television before making his film debut in Peter Brook's celebrated *Marat/Sade* (1966). His performance as one of the inmates marked him out as an actor with a flair for eccentric characterizations, and he ultimately made his way to Italy in the late 1960s. *White Fang* elevated his stock considerably and he became a big star in Italian cinema thanks to his role as the villain in Marino Girolami's *Violent Rome* (1975). He and Fulci would reunite on *Challenge to White Fang* and *Young Dracula*, and he would also go on to work with Mario Bava (*Shock*, 1977), Antonio Margheriti (*The Last Hunter*, 1980), Dario Argento (*Tenebrae*, 1982) and others before retiring from films and going into the real estate business in California. Steiner took an instant liking to Fulci:

> He actually really was a very vulnerable and interesting man. Of course I think his private life was not a particularly happy one. But I think maybe he was shortened in the amount of work he actually did partly because of his personality, which was difficult. A lot of people didn't understand or took it too seriously. But he was an interesting man.

The admiration was mutual: Fulci would later refer to him as a "very good friend" and a fine actor whose career should have gone further.[2]

*White Fang*'s success at the box-office lead to a series of sequels, the first of which—*Challenge to White Fang*—was directed by Fulci himself. After that, the franchise disintegrated quickly as other filmmakers cranked out the likes of *I figli di Zanna Bianca* (1974), *White Fang to the Rescue* (1974, starring Nero's "rival" Maurizio Merli), *Zanna Bianca e il cacciatore solitario* (1975, with Spaghetti Western star Robert Woods) and *Zanna Bianca e il grande Kid* (1977) in rapid succession; with the exception of Fulci's first sequel, none of these later efforts were even given a theatrical release in the United States.

Notes:

1. Romagnoli, Michele, *L'occhio del testimone*, (Bologna: Granata Press 1992), p. 40.
2. Audio interview with Lucio Fulci, conducted by Pier Maria Bocchi and Andrea Bruni, included on the Shriek Show DVD release of *Touch of Death*.

# Roberto Sbarigia Interviewed by Lionel Grenier

Lionel Grenier conducted the following interview with Roberto Sbarigia on June 3, 2013. The interview can also be accessed on Lionel's website, which can be found at www.luciofulci.fr. Roberto worked as the production manager on *White Fang*, *Challenge to White Fang* and *Four of the Apocalypse* before being promoted to producer on *La pretora*. He is also the son of producer Giulio Sbarigia, who produced *Young Dracula* and *The Black Cat*. Roberto has our thanks for sharing his thoughts on working with Lucio Fulci.

**Lionel Grenier**: How did Lucio Fulci join the *White Fang* project?
**Roberto Sbarigia**: He arrived as a director with vast experience, as a great professional who was still buzzing from the success of his previous movie released the year before: *Don't Torture a Duckling*.
**LG**: Can you remember the length and budget of the shoot?
**RS**: I can't remember exactly the budget but we had about 10 weeks for the shoot.
**LG**: If I am right, *Four of the Apocalypse* and *White Fang* were both partly shot in Austria. Where was the location exactly and why was it chosen?
**RS**: It was in the village of Bad Mittendorf in Austria, about an hour's drive from Salzburg, and decorator Giovanni Natalucci built the Western town there on land rented by the production company. It is in this village that *White Fang*, *Challenge to White Fang*, *Four of the Apocalypse* and *Killers of the Savage North* [Note: directed by Aristide Massaccesi and starring two of the leads from *Four of the Apocalypse*: Fabio Testi and Lynne Frederick] were successively shot. This choice was made as much because of the sets as for, I suppose, co-production imperatives. Some scenes where shot in the nearby mountain, Tauplitz Alm. I can't really remember if it was in the first or second movie, but there was a lake on which a paddleboat was operating and this is where the opening scene was shot. Again, [I am] not sure if it was in the first or second installment, but a team left for Manitoba to shoot a few scenes of Husky-led sleds racing.

**German lobby card: Kurt (Raimund Harmstorf) during *Challenge to White Fang*'s climax.**

**LG**: It was for *Challenge to White Fang* ...
**RS**: That was it ... Nevertheless, for *Four of the Apocalypse*, the shoot was carried out in Almeria, near Rome in Manziana, at Cinecittà studios and in Elios studios in Rome and in Austria.
**LG**: Lots of different screenwriters are in the credits. How did the writing process go?
**RS**: I remember the presence of Roberto Gianviti, Alberto Silvestri and Fulci ... [I'm not sure] whether it was on *White Fang* or *Challenge to White Fang*. For *Four of the Apocalypse* collaboration existed with Ennio de Concini
**LG**: It is often very complicated to shoot with animals ... Was White Fang "played" by the same animal?
**RS**: Yes, it is really difficult to shoot scenes with dogs. After long research in Germany and Italy, the two animals chosen belonged to Sebastiano Arcifa's kennel in Rome. One of them was more gifted for the main shots, while the other was much better for the long running scenes in the fields, whitened by the snow (he was also the one in the "swimming scene"). The second shooting team, ran by Tonino Ricci with Sergio Salvati as DP, made a huge effort. Carlo Rambaldi was getting the fake dog heads ready (the ones used in the main shots of the dog fights) as and when they were needed. This was to avoid the dogs actually getting hurt and secondly to counter any potential criticism from the animal protection groups. So no two dogs actually came into physical contact.
**LG**: The other difficulty was to shoot with children. How did Fulci behave with Missaele and then Renato Cestiè?
**RS**: Missaele was the son of an Indian nation's diplomat and Lucio didn't get on very well with him, showing very little patience. On the other hand, he was very friendly with Renato Cestiè and the feeling was mutual.
**LG**: Can you remember how the scene of the avalanche in *Challenge to White Fang* was shot?
**RS**: I was not there but it was the very talented Emilio Ruiz who built the model that was then integrated into shots already made not far from Rome (but I could be wrong).
**LG**: How did *Four of the Apocalypse* come to be?
**RS**: After the success of *White Fang*, the producers offered Cineriz the possibility of shooting another Western with Lucio Fulci. One of the two producers, Emanno Donati, had the idea to write a script inspired by the stories of Bret Harte. It is also he who involved Ennio De Concini in the writing process.
**LG**: This Western is important for Fulci as he works for the first time with Sergio Salvati as his main director of photography. Tell us about how they worked together?
**RS**: Sergio Salvati came from a publicity background and turned out to be a superb discovery for us as well as for Fulci. Both of them were consummate professionals.

**LG**: Fulci was not happy with De Concini's script. Did he modify it to put his signature on it? Fabio Testi says that Fulci made its ending darker.
**RS**: As far as I can remember, Fulci wanted his two usual co-writers, Gianviti and Silvestri, for this Western. Donati forced the collaboration with De Concini. I also remember that while working he was taunting him on his dialogue and that he was making changes with Giandalia, his faithful assistant director in whom he had total confidence.

***White Fang*; original artwork by Scott Hoffman.**

**LG**: Can you talk to us about Roberto Giandalia, who was script then assistant director for Lucio Fulci for a long time?
**RS**: Roberto was Lucio's shadow: script, assistant director ... Sometimes he helped Lucio with reworking a few dialogue exchanges. He was a great professional who knew Lucio's personality really well and could anticipate almost every time how he would react. He was a real friend.
**LG**: You have witnessed Fulci working with Fabio Testi, Franco Nero and Tomas Milian, three actors with very different personalities. Can you say whom he got on with the best?
**RS**: In my opinion, the actor to whom he was the closest was Tomas Milian in *Four of the Apocalypse*. He got along pretty well with Fabio Testi. But with Franco, with whom he shot for the longest period, it was a real love/hate relationship, but one always backed by a mutual respect.
**LG**: Is it true that there were problems with Michael J. Pollard and Harry Baird during the shoot of *Four of the Apocalypse*?
**RS**: Yes, during the shoot in Almeria, we were forced to use a body double constantly because the production sent Michael to a rehab clinic. Most of the first main shots had to be redone with him at the end of the shoot. The choice of Harry Baird must have been a hard one during pre-production, as during the shooting period, we never managed to find another actor who could replace him for Fulci. During the shoot, I think there was another issue concerning the nude scene in the cemetery.
**LG**: What do you mean?
**RS**: Harry Baird was very unnerved by the idea of getting entirely naked. I am almost sure we had to call his agent in Rome.
**LG**: Fulci then shot *La pretora*. How was he implicated in this production?
**RS**: *La pretora* happened right after Buzzanca's movie [*Young Dracula*]: at the time, Edwige Fenech's films always had great success at the box-office. So after the not-so-engaging results of *Four of the Apocalypse* and *Young Dracula*, we were hoping that this movie would work better than the others.
**LG**: It is obvious that *La pretora* was conceived as a vehicle for Edwige Fenech ... Fulci's personality is less recognizable. Was he more constrained on this film than he had been on the others?
**RS**: Of course, the movie was created for Edwige Fenech. In my humble opinion, Fulci was not pressured to do this film. At that time, it [sexy comedies with Fenech] was the new fad. The main male actor, Raf Luca, who was recommended by Donati, did not contribute a bit to the success of the movie.
**LG**: Why is that?
**RS**: Maybe that came out wrong: Rather than be recommended, Donati chose him. At that time, Raf Luca had started being successful on TV and in a few comedies.
**LG**: The movie is notable for its many nude scenes with Edwige Fenech. For *The Eroticist*, Fulci was not very considerate with his lead actress [Laura Antonelli] when she had to appear in the nude. How did it go with Edwige Fenech?
**RS**: When the production called Edwige Fenech for the movie, she had just finished shooting *Cattivi pensieri* with Ugo Tognazzi and Luc Meranda. She was then adamant that she was bored with that kind of movie, as she didn't have to keep getting naked. She was invited to the production's office and was surprised when Ermanno Donati showed her—right in the middle of the conversation—a copy of *Playmen* where which she was nude in every shot. Then she signed the contract and there never was any issue with the nude scenes. She simply requested, which was more than fair, that on the stage only the minimum required number of technicians would be present. Everything went very well between Fulci and her: They were both from the same agency.
**LG**: We often talk about the relationships between Fulci and the producers or the actors. But how did he behave with the rest of the team?
**RS**: I was lucky enough to have had the pleasure to work with Lucio on four of the six movies produced by my dad, Giulio's, company, and we always had a nice and loyal relationship. (I was not part of the shoot of *Young Dracula* and *The Black Cat*). If he had any remarks to make about the production, he always did it in a constructive manner with the producers and on another level he also kept me in the loop as I started to learn the producer's job on his movies. Then for the two *White Fangs*, he was always discussing the production with Ermanno Donati, with whom he was making all the most important decisions after the projection of the rushes of the day. At that time I didn't have enough experience to be involved in such important decisions.

The work was being done in a serene manner and, apart from a few episodes, Lucio was always keeping our spirits up with his jokes. I have very fond memories of Fulci and I am very pleased he is still talked about today: He was a consummate professional and a great artisan of Italian cinema.

## 1974

# *Challenge to White Fang* (Italy/Spain/France)

Aka *Il ritorno di Zanna Bianca; The Return of White Fang; Le Retour de Croc Blanc; La Carrera del Oro*

Directed by Lucio Fulci; Produced by I.C.I., Les Productions Fox Europa and Oceania Produzioni Cinematografiche; Screenplay by Lucio Fulci, Roberto Gianviti and Alberto Silvestri, from a story by Roberto Gianviti and Alberto Silvestri, based on characters created by Jack London; Director of Photography: Silvano Ippoliti and Aristide Massaccesi [uncredited]; Editor: Ornella Micheli; Music by Carlo Rustichelli

Main Players: Franco Nero (Jason Scott); Virna Lisi (Sister Evangelina); John Steiner ('Beauty' Smith/Charles Forth); Renato Cestiè (Bill Tarwater); Harry Carey, Jr. (John Tarwater); Raimund Harmstorf (Kurt Jansen); Werner Pochath (Harvey); Donald O'Brien (Liverpool); Missaele (Mitsah) [uncredited]

*After the death of his beloved Mitsah, a fur trapper named John Tarwater rescues White Fang, who gives the dog to his grandson Bill. The dog adapts well to its new masters, but their idyll is not destined to last long. Dastardly "Beauty" Smith has established himself in a mining community under an assumed name, and when he gets word that Tarwater has access to a potentially gold-rich piece of property, he sets about trying to take control of it. Jason Scott, also in the area, shows up to protect the Tarwaters, but his efforts will not prevent further bloodshed before "Beauty" and his minions get their comeuppance ...*

The success of *White Fang* inspired a series of sequels. Harry Alan Towers did not involve himself in any of these subsequent ventures, but the other co-producers responsible for the 1973 smash hit were not about to let go of a profitable franchise. Lucio Fulci had risen to the challenge of making a stylish and enjoyable film suitable for the whole family (more or less!), so he was inevitably asked to come back and try to recapture the same lightning in another bottle. *Challenge to White Fang* is therefore his first official sequel, though arguably *Operation Saint Peter's* can be viewed as a sequel of sorts to *The Treasure of San Gennaro*. In any event, for a director who was so often criticized for copying the trends established by other filmmakers, the movie allowed Fulci to mine the riches of his own personal success.

The film starts off with the rather shocking murder of Mitsah, again played by the child actor Missaele, who goes without credit this time. It isn't that the set piece is terribly graphic, but something is doubly upsetting about seeing a charismatic child performer such as this being killed off, to say nothing of the way the character had endeared himself to the audience in the previous adventure. Fulci makes it clear right off the bat that he is not going to coddle the viewer; the characters inhabit a harsh terrain and the specter of death is never very far removed from the action.

Fulci does not shy away from the harsh realities of living in such an unforgiving terrain. Characters are shown suffering dismally from the cold and a few even die from the extreme conditions. Another character suffers from such a severe case of frostbite that he loses his legs. The film doesn't go in for graphic gore or lingering close-ups, but neither does it paint an unrealistically sunny picture of life in such a setting.

The movie alternates good-humored set pieces with comparatively grim ones. This is a slippery slope to explore, dramatically speaking, but Fulci and his collaborators (including Roberto Gianviti) are more than equal to the task. One early scene of slapstick in the mining town is a bit out of place, but beyond that the film manages to work effectively as a drama and as an action adventure. Fulci depicts the characters in a more positive light than usual, making it all the more appalling and unsettling when bad things happen to them. Sister Evangelina, for example, returns from the first film only to be shockingly killed off when she attempts to rescue Bill from a conflagration. It's a dark and disturbing sequence in what is nominally intended to be a piece of light family entertainment. Similarly, the fate of poor old John Tarwater is also a grim reminder of the unpleasant realities of life in the unforgiving wilderness: He is left to freeze to death after being betrayed by "Beauty" and his minions.

White Fang comes to occupy the role of the misunderstood outsider. This character archetype is familiar throughout Fulci's work: Maciara in *Don't Torture a Duckling* comes to mind, as does Bob in *City of the Living Dead*. Fulci's sympathies typically lie with these marginalized characters. They are condemned and treated poorly by the so-called "enlightened" people simply because they exist outside of the norms of society. White Fang is similarly marked as being "different" because the animal is part wolf. The bigoted settlers therefore believe that it is predisposed to violence and are only too quick to turn on it when another settler is killed by a pack of dogs. The death, of course, is engineered by "Beauty" for precisely this purpose. His lack of empathy gives him tremendous insight into the bigotry and bloodlust of the other settlers and it proves to be an effective plan: The people band together and come to kill White Fang, although Bill and Jason do their best to defend the dog. The sequence of the townspeople hitting the dog with sticks and stones is harrowing to watch and carries a similar emotional charge compared to the chain whipping of poor Maciara in *Duckling*.

The ironically named "Beauty" is even more vile and debased than he had been in the first film. Having been disgraced and unmasked in the earlier film, he is now hiding in plain sight under an assumed name. His arrogance allows him to believe that he has escaped his past and that nobody will recognize him for who he really is, but Sister

Evangelina and Jason spoil his plans. "Beauty" even goes to the extremes of pretending to be a helpless cripple in order to rise above all suspicion. His tactics remain much the same, however: He uses bribery and blackmail to get what he wants and takes advantage of the gullible in order to line his pockets. He is first seen taking advantage of some Native Americans. When they refuse to sell him their canoe so that he can use it to get to safety, he calmly and callously shoots them in cold blood. When Mitsah arrives on the scene and recognizes him, he doesn't think twice about murdering him as well. If the film has a major flaw, it is in failing to give this sniveling bastard a proper comeuppance. Instead, he dies far too quicky and conveniently in an avalanche. While a properly gory demise would have been out of place in such a film, there are more satisfying ends meted out to some of his accomplices: For example, the duplicitous Harvey (played by wild-eyed Werner Pochath, a sort of kinder, gentler version of Klaus Kinski) is thrown from his sled and then run over by it, the metal rails slicing his throat. One spends so much of the film waiting for "Beauty" to finally get his, it just seems a wasted opportunity to dispense with him so quickly and neatly.

In any event, Fulci's direction is rock-solid as usual. He makes good use of the wintry landscapes and the cinematography by Silvano Ippoliti is attractive without being too picture-postcard pretty. Ippoliti's hard-edged style was put to great use in Sergio Corbucci's wintry Spaghetti Western masterpiece *The Great Silence* (1968), which was an ideal warm-up for this assignment. As Fulci later revealed, his old friend Aristide Massaccesi, who goes uncredited on the finished prints, did the second unit location work.

**American one-sheet for *Challenge to White Fang*.**

> Massaccesi is an excellent cameraman. We set up the scenes thanks to well-planned storyboarding and he filmed everything from high up. Massaccesi is a born professional.[1]

The location work is actually somewhat more impressive than it had been in the first film and the end result benefits from the lack of faked studio exteriors, which marred some of the early scenes in its predecessor.

Once again, Fulci proves adept at wringing out the emotional content of the material. Viewers only familiar with his later horror films may find this hard to believe, but his empathetic treatment of the characters in this film is frequently very touching. There are some legitimately heart-rending moments along the way, especially in its depiction of the relationship between Bill and White Fang. The tone of the film is more sympathetic, but that does

**A behind-the-scenes snapshot of Franco Nero and make-up artist Gino De Rossi.**

not come at the expense of dramatic tension: After killing off the juvenile lead of the last picture in its opening reel, Fulci announces quite clearly that this is a film where unpleasantness is not going to be avoided altogether!

The actors do a commendable job: Nero, Steiner and Lisi are all excellent, reprising their roles from *White Fang*, while Renato Cestiè proves to be a likable new juvenile lead. His performance as Bill is ingratiating and unaffected and he more than holds his own against the incredibly charismatic Nero; his earlier credits included an unbilled appearance as one of the murderous tykes in Mario Bava's *Twitch of the Death Nerve* (1971) and he would go on to be something of a teen idol-type in various films and television appearances. His drunken grandfather is played by Hollywood Western veteran Harry Carey, Jr., who followed in the footsteps of many of his contemporaries by making a brief foray into the world of Italian moviemaking at this time; he also appeared in Antonio Margheriti's *Take a Hard Ride* (1975), but inevitably he is best-remembered for his appearances in such classics as John Ford's *She Wore a Yellow Ribbon* (1949) and *The Searchers* (1956). Minor roles are filled by the likes of Donald O'Brien, John Bartha and Ezio Marano, all of whom had either already appeared in films for Fulci or would subsequently make more with him: O'Brien would go on to appear in *Four of the Apocalypse*, *Silver Saddle* and *Rome, 2072 A.D.: The New Gladiators*, and Marano had already played a memorable role as a quirky, giggly policeman in *A Lizard in a Woman's Skin*. Hungarian-born character actor Bartha (born 1920) is one of the more recurring presences in Fulci's films, though he seldom plays roles that really allow him to stand out. He can also be seen in *The Maniacs*, *Oh! Those Most Secret Agents*, *Massacre Time*, *Operation Saint Peter's*, *Beatrice Cenci*, *The Eroticist*, *Don't Torture a Duckling*, *White Fang* and *Young Dracula*. Bartha is one of those hard-working "familiar faces" that dots the landscape of European cult cinema, along with the likes of fellow Hungarian Tom Felleghy and native-born talent like Fulvio Mingozzi. Not many viewers are able to identify them by name, but their presence is almost invariably greeted by fans with the sentiment, "Hey, it's that guy!" Bartha's last known film appearance was in Umberto Lenzi's *Cannibal Ferox* (1981), but it is not known if he is still among the living.

The special make-up effects are the work of Gino De Rossi (not to be confused with another make-up wizard affiliated with Fulci's work—Giannetto De Rossi, who is no relation). Gino De Rossi would go on to work with the director on *Zombie* (on which his contributions were uncredited), *City of the Living Dead* and *The House by the Cemetery*. The fact that Giannetto De Rossi also worked on *Zombie* and *The House by the Cemetery* has provided some confusion for some writers, but suffice it to say they are two different people who have enjoyed separate and prolific careers. Gino De Rossi would later recall:

> Lucio Fulci left a very strong impression on me. I was certainly impressed [...] because, besides the problems he had because of the death of his wife and later with his kids, and the industry people who ranted that he was a pain [...], he had problems. I have wonderful memories of Lucio because he was a director that knew what he wanted.

*Challenge to White Fang* was not quite as profitable as Fulci's first Jack London adventure, but it did well enough to keep the franchise running for several more entries. Fulci would bring some of its pathos and its wintry atmosphere to bear on his next film and the end result was one of his finest films.

Notes:

1. Palmerini, Luca M. and Gaetano Mistretta, *Spaghetti Nightmares* (Florida: Fantasma Books, 1996), p. 59.

# 1975

## *Four of the Apocalypse (Italy)*

Aka *I quattro dell'apocalisse; Los Cuatro del Apocalipsis; 4 de l'apocalypse*

Directed by Lucio Fulci; Produced by Edmondo Amati (uncredited), for Coralto Cinematografica; Screenplay by Ennio De Concini, based on the stories of Bret Harte; Director of Photography: Sergio Salvati; Editor: Ornella Micheli; Music by Franco Bixio (as Bixio), Fabio Frizzi (as Frizzi) and Vince Tempera (as Tempera); Songs: *Movin' On, Stubby (You're Down and Out), Was it All in Vain?, Bunny (Let's Stay Together)* and *Let Us Pray*, performed by Greenfield Cook and Benjamin Franklin Group

Main Players: Fabio Testi (Stubby Preston); Lynne Frederick (Emanuelle 'Bunny' O'Neill); Tomas Milian (Chaco); Michael J. Pollard (Clem); Harry Baird (Bud); Adolfo Lastretti (Reverend Sullivan); Donald O'Brien (Sheriff); Bruno Corazzari (Lemmy); Giorgio Trestini (Saul)

*Professional gambler Stubby Preston is thrown in jail upon his arrival in Salt Flat. There, he makes the acquaintance of a pregnant prostitute known as Bunny, a crazed African-American named Bud and an alcoholic named Clem. The sheriff sits idly by while a lynch mob kills off most of the prisoners, but knowing that Stubby has money, he spares his life and the lives of his new friends. Now penniless, the four friends are given a wagon and allowed to leave. They run into an outlaw named Chaco who turns out to be a ruthless sadist; he drugs the group with peyote and rapes Bunny before making his escape. Clem tries to stop him, but loses his life for his troubles. Stubby vows revenge, but must first see Bunny through her pregnancy …*

Bret Harte (1836-1902), sometimes known as Francis Bret Harte, was a prolific author who specialized in the Old West. His stories on the topic were very popular in their day and they have gone on to inspire several films and operas. Probably his best-remembered—and most referenced—story is "The Outcasts of Poker Flats," which is also the inspiration for Lucio Fulci's second Western.

According to Fulci:

> It's a story that was badly scripted by Ennio De Concini in which I again tried to establish a timeless relationship between the three characters. In the end, they devour each other out of an excess of love … the idea behind it being a sense of possessing what the other has inside. It's a particularly odd film, which didn't make a penny anywhere, but that was partly because it was a wandering Western and also, De Concini wrote a script, which I didn't like at all.[1]

Fulci had already collaborated in a rather contentious manner with De Concini on *Operation Saint Peter's*, but on that film he argued that he was restricted in what he was allowed to do because the writer was the "pet" of producer Edmondo Amati; on this film, however, he was given a free hand to overhaul the script to his satisfaction. It's inevitably impossible to determine where De Concini's work ends and Fulci's begins, but De Concini's decision to reach back to the larger-than-life tales of Harte for inspiration proved to be a fertile starting point.

The film establishes its main characters neatly and efficiently in the opening scenes: Stubby is a gentleman gambler similar to John Carradine in John Ford's *Stagecoach* (1939). He is immaculately dressed, always ready

**Italian *locandina* for *Four of the Apocalypse*; artwork by Mauro.**

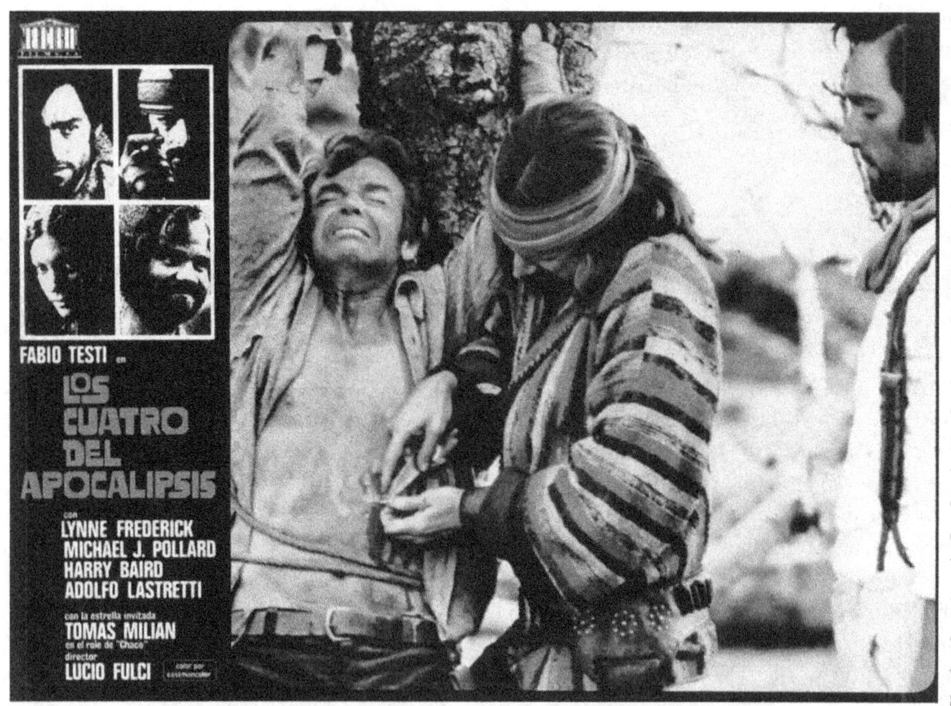


**Spanish lobby card: Chaco's sadistic streak comes out when he tortures the deputy (Lorenzo Robledo).**

with a witty aside and is more than a little self-involved and narcissistic. Bunny puts on airs and tries to present herself as a lady, but Stubby sees right through her; despite her classy exterior, she is an experienced prostitute. She is not presented in an unfavorable light, however: As Fulci recognizes, the West was a difficult terrain for young women and she is merely doing what she can in order to survive. Her livelihood has been complicated, however, by her pregnancy—which she does her best to conceal from Stubby until her morning sickness gives the game away. Bud, the African-American, is lost in a world of fantasy and imagination; he believes that there are spirits surrounding them at all times and is in close contact with them. Interestingly, Bud's skin color is never made into an issue; he is a man of compassion at heart, even if his delusions eventually send him over the edge into out-and-out insanity. Clem, on the other hand, is a sad sack wallowing in his alcoholism. None of these people are presented as unpleasant or unsympathetic; they simply all have their vices and their problems, but they possess enough empathy to be able to work together as a sort of familial unit.

Their idyll is eventually disrupted by the arrival of Chaco, a terrifying bandit whose sadism and cruelty throws everything off-kilter. Chaco is completely self-absorbed and is only interested in playing people so that he can get what he wants to survive. Compared to Stubby, who is a cardsharp with a conscience, Chaco is utterly irredeemable. This becomes evident early on when he kills a deputy who takes the group by surprise; sooner than humanely dispose of the threat, Chaco ties the man to a tree, carves out a hunk of his flesh and pierces his breast with his rusty tin star. The pleasure Chaco derives from this puts him in the same category as so many of Fulci's sadistic villains, including Nino Castelnuovo in *Massacre Time* and Georges Wilson in *Beatrice Cenci*. Stubby is horrified by his violent excesses but is unable to get the upper hand; Chaco subdues and drugs him, then proceeds to brutalize the similarly-dazed Bunny in one of the director's most difficult-to-stomach set pieces. The scene isn't eroticized in the least, thank goodness, but it is protracted and made all the more unbearable due to the knowledge that Chaco is raping a pregnant woman. On top of that, the viewer can't help but like Bunny: she is a sweet natured, slightly naïve young woman and she never does anything to harm anybody. For Chaco, she commits the sin of being desirable; in his twisted, machismo point of view, she is ripe for the picking because she excites his curiosity. Having taken everything that caught his eye—and fatally wounding Clem for good measure—Chaco makes off into the sunset, but there's little doubt that he will return at some point.

The gang makes tits way to a deserted ghost town, which allows Fulci and cinematographer Sergio Salvati to create some truly stunning visuals. Clem succumbs to his injuries while Bunny and Stubby fall in love with each other. Bud, on the other hand, is driven to madness as his fantasies about the spirits of the dead become more and more pronounced. The gloomy town, devoid of people but with a very prominent cemetery, is the ideal setting for Bud's psychosis to take root. At one point, he comes in from the rain and claims to have killed an animal, thus providing the three survivors with some food. They dig into the meat without thinking anything of it, but the next day Stubby makes a horrific discovery: Bud has not buried Clem as instructed and has actually hacked off part of the corpse's backside. Thus, this becomes the first "taste" of cannibalism to be found in Fulci's filmography; he had no way of knowing it at the time, but this theme would become very prominent in his biggest worldwide box-office hit just a few years later.

Stubby and Bunny press on alone; Bud disappears into the recesses of the town and appears to be happy to have found a monument to the dead that he can call home. The rambling structure alluded to by Fulci is very apparent, but the episodic nature of the screenplay does not work against the movie. The characters are well delineated and Fulci's control of mood and atmosphere is absolutely faultless. Crucially, too, each episode builds effectively on what comes before it and none of the segments feel gratuitous or thoughtlessly tacked-on. In some respects, the film sees Fulci at his most inspired and poetic: This is certainly evident in the ghost town sequence, and it is also very much in evidence in the following episode. Bunny is on the verge of giving birth when they run into Reverend Sullivan, a kindly man of the cloth whom Stubby has known for several years. The Reverend escorts them to the snow-bound mountain village of Alphaville, which is so named because it is comprised entirely of men. The misogynist inhabitants have all sworn off women for one reason or another and live a peaceful if sterile existence in the mountains. The arrival of the three strangers throws things into a tizzy, but they eventually welcome the distraction. Excitement builds as Bunny prepares to give birth and the grizzled inhabitants begin to place bets on everything from the child's sex to its birth manner to the size of its manhood—if it turns out to be a boy, of course. There is ample charm and warmth in this segment of the film as the men flutter about and become excited over the prospect of helping to bring a new life into the world. The baby is eventually born, but Bunny dies soon thereafter. This scene is one of the most heart-breaking in all of Fulci's filmography: It unfolds with very little dialogue, but the depth of emotion in the filmmaking and in the performances of Fabio Testi as Stubby and Lynne Frederick as Bunny is really remarkable. Stubby decides to leave the child in the care of the town, so that he can go off and hopefully get his revenge on Chaco.

The last act is devoted to this act of vengeance. Stubby tracks Chaco down to an abandoned farmhouse and takes his time tormenting the psychopath, seeing as how he has the upper hand this time. The casual sadism dished out by Stubby is fully deserved and does not cost him the viewer's sympathy. The ferocious, animalistic Chaco is like a rabid dog—and when Stubby finally pulls the trigger and ends his life, one has no doubt that it was for the best. The ending sees Stubby alone and riding into the sunset.

*Four of the Apocalypse* is without a doubt one of Fulci's finest films. It represents a significant improvement over his *White Fang* adventures and shows him developing his propensity for screen violence. Characters are no longer shot and fall quietly to their deaths; Fulci goes all out for Sam Peckinpah-levels of blood and gore, with squibs exploding and bright red blood splattering the scenery as people meet their demise. Chaco's brutality allows for some moments that can truly be seen as outtakes from Artaud's Theatre of Cruelty, making him an even more despicable and horrific presence than the killers in Fulci's early *gialli* like *A Lizard in a Woman's Skin* and *Don't Torture a Duckling*. At least Don Alberto in the latter truly believed he was doing a good deed by killing the village children; Chaco has no such scruples and indulges in sadism for the simple reason that he gets off on it. In addition to this greater intensity in the violence, the film also fulfills the signs of poetry and lyricism hinted at in earlier works. The imagery is consistently gorgeous and there is a real depth of feeling to the characters and their relationships. With the exception of Chaco and the corrupt sheriff in the opening scenes, most of the characters are presented rather warmly. Certainly the group of misfits—Stubby, Bunny, Bud and Clem—is a likable one, while stray characters like the Reverend or the inhabitants of Alphaville are shown in a very positive light. For Fulci, however, even a handful of people like Chaco are enough to disrupt the balance and send things crashing down; the threat of violence and death looms around every corner and the group of four is ultimately reduced to one lonely outlaw making his way through a barren landscape.

The film represented the first collaboration between Fulci and two of his most invaluable colleagues. Cinematographer Sergio Salvati was born in Rome in 1938. The son of a key grip named Adolfo Salvati, he started off working among the crew of such films as Sergio Leone's *The Good, The Bad and The Ugly* (1966) and Pier Paolo Pasolini's *Medea* (1969), then made the transition to becoming a cinematographer in the early 1970s. *Four of the Apocalypse* was one of his first assignments as a director of photography and he and Fulci found that they worked remarkably well together.[2] It has been claimed by those who knew them that they complemented each other. Fulci was aggressive and bombastic, while Salvati was soft-spoken and courteous. The two had very similar aesthetic tastes, however, and they would bring out the best in each other as a result. Salvati would go on to photograph *Young Dracula*, *The Psychic*, *Silver Saddle*, *Zombie*, *City of the Living Dead*, *The Black Cat*, *The Beyond* and *The House by the Cemetery* for Fulci, after which the two men parted ways; they were due to reunite on the Dario Argento-produced *Wax Mask*, but fate had other plans. Salvati remains sporadically active in Italian films. His camerawork on *Four of the Apocalypse* is luminous and remains some of his very best work; the sequences in the ghost town and in Alphaville, in particular, have a tremendous feel for texture and atmosphere. Salvati later recalled his collaboration with Fulci:

> What I realized about Lucio Fulci is that beyond the movie-making scene, he certainly was a generous man, friendly, untidy, fun to be around. Because we worked on these 10 movies, we had many opportunities to share meals together at dinnertime or with the catering lunch box. He could be something else, he even gave me anxiety, because he'd raise his voice in the hotel restaurant and put on this director act [...] It wasn't bothering me, but it gave me some anxiety. He had this agitation going, his strong character, he was always playing the director. He loved telling stories. He was a skilled director. He was the same in his everyday life. We'd go out and he was a lot of fun to be with, always telling stories. [...] He was a volcano. He was a volcano who ran us down, but he was so capable.

**Spanish pressbook still: Chaco (Tomas Milian), 'Bunny' (Lynne Frederick) and 'Stubby' (Fabio Testi), three of the Four of the Apocalypse.**

The film's impact is greatly aided by a marvelous soundtrack by the composing trio of Franco Bixio, Fabio Frizzi and Vince Tempera. Robert Altman's *McCabe & Mrs. Miller* (1971, set to the music of Leonard Cohen) and Sam Peckinpah's *Pat Garrett and Billy the Kid* (1973, scored by Bob Dylan) influenced undoubtedly the use of ballads here, but the device still feels fresh.[3] Some viewers have taken exception to the songs, feeling they hit the nail a little too squarely on the head, but they work very well in the context of the movie and offer a fine, gentle counterbalance to the sometimes shocking imagery. The three composers would work again with Fulci on *Young Dracula* and *Silver Saddle*, but it was Frizzi who would become particularly identified with Fulci's work. Born in Bologna in 1951, he started off working in films while still in his teens. His music greatly impressed Fulci, who brought him back to score *Zombie*, *Contraband*, *City of the Living Dead*, *The Beyond*, *Manhattan Baby* and *Nightmare Concert (A Cat in the Brain)*. During his lengthy career, Fulci had the good fortune to work with such stellar composers as Ennio Morricone, Riz Ortolani and Pino Donaggio, but arguably Frizzi stands above the rest for providing the most memorable musical accompaniment to his shocking imagery. The composer later recalled:

> Like any true friend, he came with huge flaws, but because he was a friend, you got to appreciate those flaws as well. […] The most beautiful flaw, the one I envy because I don't have it myself, was his blasphemies. That was his most absurd characteristic and the funniest one, as well.

Frizzi's association with Fulci continues to this day, as he continues to tour the globe and perform musical tributes to his late friend before enthusiastic audiences.

The cast is one of the sturdiest Fulci was ever fortunate to work with. Fabio Testi gives a strong performance as Stubby; he is initially superficial and flippant, but as the story develops, the character deepens and Testi proves more than adequate to meeting its demands. He was born in Verona in 1941 and got his start as a bit player and stunt man, usually in Italian Westerns. He can be seen as one of Henry Fonda's thugs in *Once Upon a Time in the West* (1968), for example. In the early 1970s, his career took off: he worked with Vittorio De Sica on the Oscar-winning *The Garden of the Finzi-Continis* (1970) and graduated to playing leads in such films as Aldo Florio's *Dead Men Ride* (1971) and Massimo Dallamano's *What Have You Done to Solange?* (1972). He would also hold his own against Oliver Reed in Sergio Sollima's excellent *poliziottesco Revolver* (1973) and would appear in three films for maverick American filmmaker Monte Hellman: *China 9, Liberty 37* (1978), *Iguana* (1988) and *Road to Nowhere* (2010). Testi would also work again with Fulci on the violent *Contraband*. Fulci would later describe Testi as "A wonderful man—not a good actor, but a wonderful man."[4] Truth be told, his assessment of Testi is a little unfair: While he was often cast in roles that relied upon his chiseled good looks, when given the opportunity—as he is in both of his films for Fulci—he could be counted upon to deliver the goods. Testi later recalled that things got off to a rocky start with Fulci:

> He hated actors. I remember on the first day, in a village in Austria, it was 12 degrees below zero and it was snowing. He put me 50 meters away from the camera, stationary on a horse. […] He said, "You stay there." […] It was his way of challenging me on the first day of shooting. At the time, I was involved with Ursula Andress and she was on the set, so she was part of this strange situation. No

> actor should have to remain absolutely still for so long. We finished the day and I got sick. [...] Then we became friends and continued on with the film, and the rest was collaboration. But at the beginning he practically violated me.[5]

Chaco is played to icy perfection by Tomas Milian, in the last—and far away, the flashiest—of his three roles for Fulci. Chaco is an irredeemable sadist and psychopath and Milian plays the character's psychosis for all it is worth, without tipping the character into pantomime theatrics. He is truly one of the most frightening figures to be found in a Fulci film. Milian later claimed that he devised the character's unusual look:

> The two crosses under the eyes kind of defined it, because I remembered the swastika on Charles Manson's forehead. So I thought the evil inside this man was very close to Manson.[6]

Milian had nothing but praise for his co-star Michael J. Pollard, who plays the pathetic Clem—at least up to a point:

> He's a magnificent actor, the best one there—better than me. (*Pause*) Nah, I don't think he's better than me. I was trying to be nice. (*Laughs*) But he is a big talent. There is a case of letting the talent take you over and letting yourself get identified with playing the crazy little character and that's it—you're finished.[7]

Pollard gives a good performance, but Milian is on point in the sense that the role is typical of the "type" with which he was identified. Thanks to his Oscar-nominated role in *Bonnie and Clyde* (1967), Pollard (born in New Jersey in 1939) became typecast in movies as weirdoes and outsiders, usually of a very twitchy variety. It is a role he had reprised again and again, in everything from Jonathan Demme's *Melvin and Howard* (1980) to Rob Zombie's *House of 1000 Corpses* (2003). British actress Lynne Frederick played Bunny. Frederick (1954-1994) is best known today for being the last wife of British comedy legend Peter Sellers, but she appeared in a number of interesting cult films in the 1970s, including Hammer Films' *Vampire Circus* (1971) and Saul Bass' *Phase IV* (1974). *Four of the Apocalypse* was part of her brief foray into Italian cinema in the mid-1970s and it remains arguably her most heart-felt and moving performance. Harry Baird (1931-2005), a native of British Guyana who enjoyed a reasonably prolific career from 1955 to 1975, played the crazed Bud; he also appeared in Gordon Hessler's *The Oblong Box* and Peter Collinson's *The Italian Job*, both released in 1969. *Four of the Apocalypse* was his last film. Cast in smaller roles were familiar character actors like Adolfo Lastretti (Jess Franco's *Venus in Furs*, 1969) as the kindly Reverend Sullivan, Donald O'Brien (*White Fang*) as the corrupt sheriff and Bruno Corazzari as the grizzled but kindly Lemmy, who serves as a "midwife" during the delivery of Bunny's child; he would go on to appear in Fulci's *The Psychic* and *The Black Cat*.

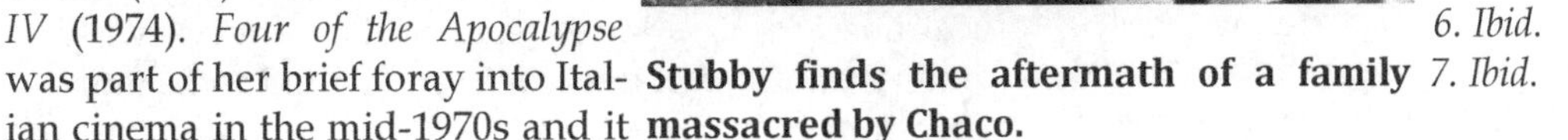

**Stubby finds the aftermath of a family massacred by Chaco.**

*Four of the Apocalypse* was an artistic success for Fulci, but on a commercial level it did not meet expectations. Producer Edmondo Amati would later re-unite with Fulci for *Rome, 2072 A.D.: The New Gladiators*, but this film satisfied the end of their three-picture agreement. Fulci would retreat to the world of horror and comedy, again inching ever closer to an association with the genre that would take over the last stage of his career.

Notes:

1. Palmerini, Luca M. and Gaetano Mistretta, *Spaghetti Nightmares* (Florida: Fantasma Books, 1996), p. 60.
2. In fact, Salvati had previously worked as director of photography on the second unit headed by Tonino Ricci on *A Challenge to White Fang*. In an interview included on the French DVD release of *The Beyond* from Neo Publishing, Salvati recalled that he had no interaction with Fulci on that film, as the director was not interested in what the second unit was filming.
3. In a 2008 interview with Lionel Grenier, http://www.luciofulci.fr/interviews/interview-exclusive-avec-fabio-frizzi, Frizzi recalled that the film was "temp tracked" with Dylan's song *Knockin' on Heaven's Door*, which had been written for *Pat Garrett and Billy the Kid*. "Temp tracking" denotes the use of music as placeholders or suggestions for the composer, etc. to help guide them in the scoring process.
4. Audio interview with Lucio Fulci, conducted by Pier Maria Bocchi and Andrea Bruni, included on the Shriek Show DVD release of *Touch of Death*.
5. Quoted from "Fulci of the Apocalypse" (2001) featurette included on the Anchor Bay DVD release of *Four of the Apocalypse*, directed by Gary Hertz.
6. *Ibid.*
7. *Ibid.*

**Italian *locandina* for *Young Dracula*; artwork by Averardo Ciriello.**

## *Young Dracula (Italy)*

Aka *Il cav. Costante Nicosia demoniaco, ovvero: Dracula in Brianza; The Demonic Womanizer Costante Nicosia, or: Dracula in Brianza* (literal English-language translation); *Dracula in the Provinces; Muérdame, señor conde*

Directed by Lucio Fulci; Produced by Giulio Sbarigia, for Coralta Cinematografica; Story and Screenplay by Mario Amendola, Pupi Avati, Bruno Corbucci, from a story by Lucio Fulci, with additional dialogue by Enzo Jannacci and Giuseppe Viola; Director of Photography: Sergio Salvati; Editor: Ornella Micheli; Music by Franco Bixio (as Bixio), Fabiro Frizzi (as Frizzi) and Vince Tempera (as Tempera)

Main Players: Lando Buzzanca (Costante Nicosia); Rossano Brazzi (Dr. Paluzzi); Sylva Koscina (Mariù); Moira Orfei (Bestia Assatanta); John Steiner (Count Dragelescu); Ciccio Ingrassia (Salvatore, the Wizard of Noto); Valentina Cortese (Olghina Franchetti); Christa Linder (Liù Pederzoli)

*Industrialist Costante Nicosia is concerned with only one thing, making money. He ignores his beautiful wife, Mariu, and is cruel and condescending towards his employees. After insulting an old witch named Great Aunt Maria, Costante is cursed with the evil eye. He goes to Romania to close a business deal and meets the enigmatic Count Dragelescu. The Count promises Costante all manner of depraved entertainments if he comes to visit him at his castle, but Costante finds him creepy and does not accept the offer. A night of boredom in his tacky hotel changes his tune, however, and Costante makes his way to the castle. True to his word, the Count provides several beautiful women who seem game for anything. Costante gets drunk and has a good time, but the next morning when he awakens he finds himself in bed with the Count. In addition to finding some puncture marks on his neck, he also worries that he has been molested by the Count and begins to fear for his manhood. Back in Italy, he goes about trying to prove his heterosexuality and notices that he has developed a peculiar fixation on human blood …*

Fulci leapt into his next assignment before *Four of the Apocalypse* died at the box-office. Tellingly, the resulting film managed to bridge his past specialty with that of a new genre that would become his focal point in just a few years. *Young Dracula* is therefore his one and only true send-up of the horror genre. Some of Fulci's later genre work would incorporate ample doses of dark comedy—*Aenigma* and *Touch of Death* come to mind—but this is the only one that plays out as a proper spoof.

Fulci devised the scenario, but initially entrusted the writing to the gifted Pupi Avati. Born in Bologna in 1938, Avati got his start working as an assistant director before branching out to writing and directing in the early 1970s. Often working with his younger brother Antonio, he has crafted a rich, diverse and imaginative body of work, which encompasses everything from art house erotica (*House of Pleasure for Women*, 1976) and genteel nostalgia-driven drama (*Jazz Band*, 1978) to *gialli* (*The House with Laughing Windows*, 1976) and horror films (*Zeder*, 1983). As Fulci later explained:

> Pupi Avati wrote some very amusing parts and then went off to make a film with [Ugo] Tognazzi [Note: *La mazurka del barone, della santa e del fico fiorone*, 1975] and was substituted by the duo of [Bruno] Corbucci and [Mario] Amendola, who cleverly interpreted some of my ideas and added some more comic gags.[1]

The film is one of Fulci's more overtly political comedies and is arguably the only one to really address his Marxist political views. Fulci seldom discussed his political beliefs in interviews and was also prone to rejecting attempts at reading sociological commentary into his work,[2] but it is difficult to get around the topic in the context of this film. Costante is a spoiled, self-centered egomaniac who lives for the thrill of making money. He has no real passion for anything beyond this, though he is fashionable enough to keep a mistress on the side. Costante's desire to be seen as a typically macho Italian male is telling: He seems to be more concerned with this for the sake of appearances than anything else. In his relations with his workers, he is cruel and unyielding. He treats them like serfs and expects them to bow and scrape to him in return. When he is ultimately infected with vampirism, the satire is taken to another level as he literally bleeds his workers dry. The metaphor is obvious, perhaps, but it is still amusing: In order to feed his need for blood and also ensure ample productivity from his employees, he sets up a blood bank complete with financial incentives. The poor workers fall for the ploy without hesitation and the exploitation of the working class continues as before. Fulci and his co-writers are also careful to stress that Costante is a self-made man who left the south of Italy and found success in the north.

The political commentary is tempered with an exploration of the Italian male psyche. Costante, as already established, is not a particularly sexual man. He has his needs like anybody else, but he does not seem to be driven by his libido. Amusingly, it is his encounter with the effete Count Dragelescu—the name evoking both Dracula and the notion of the "drag queen"—which throws his neatly ordered universe into a tizzy. Fulci never reveals just what happens between the two men: The only thing Costante and the viewer knows is simply that the two men wake up in bed together, stark naked. Fulci teases the comedy by making Costante blissfully unaware of who he is sharing a bed with until the last second; the casting of John Steiner as Dragelescu, with his slight and boyish frame, is key to the illusion, as when his back is turned, he is almost able to pass for a slender female. When Costante realizes what has happened, he freaks out and runs back to the safety of his regular daily grind in Italy. The fact that he awakens with fang marks on his neck doesn't seem to trouble him much—it's the notion that he was possibly "tainted" by homosexuality that troubles him. He turns to his trusted physician, Dr. Paluzzi, for advice and the doctor advises him to try screwing his mistress to make sure he is still capable of being aroused by women. The notion of going home and making love to his wife never really occurs to him: As is so often the case, Italian men love to treat their wives like plaster saints and reserve the kinky stuff for the mistresses. When the encounter with the mistress proves unsuccessful, Costante suffers a major crisis of identity. He then consults a wizard—played by Ciccio Ingrassia, in his first film with Fulci since *Il lungo, il corto, il gatto* in 1967—in the hopes of escaping the "curse" affecting his manhood. The wizard is a fraud, however, and Costante has been encouraged to go to him by his family because they have arranged for him to advise Costante to rehire a bungling relative who has recently been let go from the factory. Costante continues to slide deeper and deeper into depression and eventually lashes out, trying to re-establish himself as an insatiable sex machine. He visits some prostitutes with comically unsatisfying results—the set piece involving S/M dominatrix Moira Orfei is particularly amusing—and is unable to deal with the possibility that he is no longer the man he once believed himself to be. When he finally unleashes his frustration on his wife, he ends up baring his fangs and biting her on the ass; the exchange leaves the woman pregnant and this seems to restore Costante's self-confidence. The film ends with a predictable but effective sight gag, as Costante's bouncing baby heir opens his mouth to reveal a set of fangs. Throughout it all, Costante seems far less concerned with having been transformed into a vampire; the affliction will continue through his son, but he nevertheless ends up in a position of power and control which seems to make him feel happy again. Costante may be a vampire, but he can still make money and has proven his prowess by siring a son of his own. And yet, for all of that, none of his problems have been properly resolved: he will simply go on draining his workers dry (literally, now!) while continuing to build his empire, but his homophobia and his basic lack of empathy and compassion remains blissfully unaffected.

Fulci displays very little sympathy for his protagonist, preferring to make him look ridiculous instead. The film does not endorse negative gay stereotypes, but it does use them to underline Costante's ridiculously parochial views. Costante is a hypocrite and a fraud and his relationships

**A behind-the-scenes glimpse of Fulci (right) directing Buzzanca in his visit with dominatrix Moira Orfei.**

with women are purely superficial; the notion of becoming "infected" with homosexuality is a typical mentality shared by many closed-minded bigots, as if being in close proximity with a gay man or woman could potentially "rub off" and threaten one's "normal" way of life. For Costante, the appearance of rugged virility is all-important—therefore, to risk being seen as a "sissy" is a fate worse than death. His sex life is as dysfunctional as ever when the film ends, but the important thing for him is that he has a child—a living testimony to his ability to "get it up" with a woman. Beyond his sexual hang-ups, Costante is ridiculous in many other ways: he never comes across as being terribly bright or cultured, and his pompous, condescending attitude marks him out as a fool from the start. He is the type of man who only does a good deed if something is profitable in it for him; thus, he drops product placement hints for his toothpaste company wherever possible. Costante is always on the make and Fulci and his co-writers exorcise their frustration for what he represents by ridiculing him at every turn.

**Moira Orfei as the dominatrix.**

Lando Buzzanca gives an amusing performance as the pompous and cretinous Costante. He is a rare talent who seems to be unafraid of playing unsympathetic characters: He does not attempt to make Costante into anything more than a bigoted weasel. He is slyly amusing in his early scenes as he pompously denounces the people around him, then really comes into his own as he begins to struggle with his "issues." One of the funniest scenes involves his return from Romania. His wife and various employees greet him, all vying for his attention. He is so preoccupied with his fears over what happened between him and Count Dragelescu; however, that all he can manage is to repeat "Up yours!" to every person who tries speaking to him. It would prove to be Buzzanca's final collaboration with Fulci; had their collaboration developed under different circumstances, during a period in which Fulci was making more comedies, he may well have become as much of a staple in the director's work as Franchi and Ingrassia.

John Steiner and Ciccio Ingrassia also make their final appearance in Fulci'a filmography. Ingrassia had already more-or-less split from his long-time partner, Franco Franchi, and was earning accolades for his work in considerably more highbrow fare like Federico Fellini's *Amarcord* (1973) and Elio Petri's *Todo Modo* (1976). He is very amusing as the phony wizard, though his appearance is limited to only one scene. Steiner already proved his adroitness with playing villains in the *White Fang* films, so this movie allows him a chance to try his hand at camp comedy. He is wonderfully perverse as Count Dragelescu, eyeing up Costante like a Thanksgiving turkey and conveying a boundless capacity for the joys of the flesh. Steiner looks to be having a blast in his scenes and it's only a shame that he doesn't have more screen time. Fulci's relationship with actors could be strained—to say the least—but for Steiner, there was real warmth and vulnerability in the man. He later recalled that filming the orgy scene left the normally volatile filmmaker at a loss for words:

> I was always very touched when I could see him totally out of his element, as it were. My first day on *Dracula*, I was totally naked and surrounded by all these beautiful naked girls. And he walked in at 7 o'clock in the morning, as we all did, and was at a total loss as to what he should do or where he should put the camera. We would always think that he always had everything so under control, but that's not the case.

One of the naked girls alluded to by Steiner is none other than Hungarian-born Ilona Staller. Born in 1951, Staller worked a bit as a spy for the Hungarian Communist Party and also established herself as a model, before making her way to Italy. She appeared in some films in the 1970s under her own name, then adopted the pseudonym of Cicciolina and began a career as a major star of Italian-made porn films in the 1980s. While acting in the adult movie scene, she also had a somewhat successful career in Italian politics—and she would infamously offer to have sex with the likes of Saddam Hussein and Osama bin Laden in exchange for a peaceful end to the conflicts in the Middle East; sadly, they did not take her up on the offer. It's true what they say: Sometimes truth is stranger than fiction!

Fulci's next film would also push the comedy-erotica angle and would benefit from the presence of one of Italian cinema's most beloved sex icons of the period.

Notes:

1. Palmerini, Luca M. and Gaetano Mistretta, *Spaghetti Nightmares* (Florida: Fantasma Books, 1996), p. 59.
2. "Social comments are always out of place in a fantasy film, which should be all the more enjoyable for having nothing in common with the masses of films made by amateurs who take up social standpoints [...]" (*Ibid.*)

# 1976

## *La Pretora (Italy)*

Aka *My Sister in Law; La juez y su erotica hermana; On a demandé la main de ma soeur*

Directed by Lucio Fulci; Produced by Roberto Sbarigia, for Coralto Cinematografica; Story and Screenplay by Franco Marotta, Laura Toscano and Franco Mercuri; Director of Photography: Luciano Trasatti; Editor: Ornella Micheli; Music by Nico Fidenco

Main Players: Edwige Fenech (Judge Viola Orlando/ Rosa Orlando); Raf Luca (Raffaele Esposito); Giancarlo Dettori (Count Renato Altero); Mario Maranzana (Bortolon); Carlo Sposito (Prosecutor); Walter Valdi (Zaganella); Gianni Agus (Angelo Scotti); Oreste Lionello (Francesco Lo Presti)

Cameo Appearance: Lucio Fulci (Second Gas Station Attendant)

*Judge Viola Orlando presides over the legal system of her village with an iron fist and puritanical principles. Her exacting standards make her unpopular with many people, including a con man named Raffaele who is due for sentencing. When it transpires that she has a twin sister named Rosa who is anything but puritanical, Roberto and his lawyer, Bortolon, do their best to create a scandal that will cause Viola to leave office. Meanwhile, Viola's frustrated lover, Count Renato, is most taken by the sexually liberated Rosa and begins to wonder about exploring the possibilities of enjoying a sexual liaison with her …*

*La Pretora* finds Lucio Fulci working with a very different group of collaborators. He is not credited with working on the screenplay—though its social satire surely appealed to him—and apart from assistant director Roberto Giandalia (making his debut as Fulci's assistant; he would go on to serve in the same capacity on most of Fulci's films over the next eight years, culminating with *Murder-Rock: Dancing Death*) and editor Ornella Micheli, the crew does not include many of his regular collaborators.

The screenplay is the work of husband-and-wife team of Franco Marotta and Laura Toscano, with additional dialogue contributed by Franco Mercuri. Marotta and Toscano's other credits include Massimo Dallamano's *The Night Child* (1974) and Enzo G. Castellari's *Inglorious Bastards* (1978). *La Pretora* anticipated much of their later output, which is largely comprised of comedies. Mercuri's work was basically confined to the sexy comedy films—several of which starred *La Pretora*'s Edwige Fenech, including Sergio Martino's *Giovanna Long-Thigh* (1973) and Mariano Laurenti's *The Schoolteacher Goes to Boys' High* (1978), and he was likely drafted in on the actress' request to give the dialogue a little extra sparkle. The script is heavy on incident and farce and Fulci handles the material with the casual ease one would expect of an old hand well versed in

**Italian *locandina* for *La Pretora*; artist unknown.**

comedy. It doesn't really rank among his more remarkable or interesting works, but it succeeds where it should and gets a lot of mileage out of the director's flair for visualizing absurd situations.

The film opens with a reprise of a gag Fulci had already used at the beginning of *Gli imbroglioni*. In the earlier film, Spianelli (Claudio Gora) gets into an altercation with a man in the court parking lot; he is shocked when he goes to court and finds that the man is actually the presiding judge. Here, the sleazy Raffaele sees Viola walking and ac-

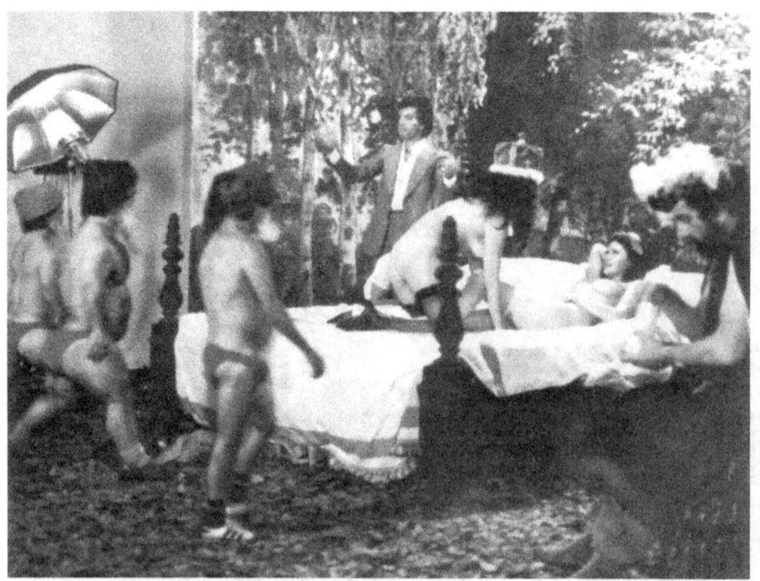

**Raffaele (Raf Luca) stages his cheerfully tacky porno version of Snow White, with Edwige Fenech as the title character.**

costs her; subsequently he is humiliated when she comes into the courtroom and is revealed to be the fierce judge whom everybody fears. Raffaele is plainly established in this opening scene: He is a sexist pig who sees women as pieces of meat. He does his best to win Viola over with his charm and is evidently shocked when she doesn't reciprocate; clearly he is used to getting what he wants. Fulci and his screenwriters go out of their way to make Raffaele look ridiculous throughout. He is not a likable character, nor is he meant to be. In his sexist mentality, Viola should be "easy pickings," but she stymies him by not conforming to what he has come to expect out of women. His oily charm holds no meaning for her and this not only confuses him, it offends his fragile ego.

Viola is initially depicted as a bitch and an ice queen. She runs a tight ship in court and has inflexible moral standards. Fulci has fun detailing her piousness; she objects to sexy comic books (*fumetti*), sees to it that pornography is confiscated and withheld from the local populace and downplays her own Earthy allure by hiding her fantastic figure in conservative clothing. One of the best sequences involves her screening an erotic film so that she can have her minions take notes about its objectionable contents. The humor is smutty and not exactly subtle, but it doesn't need to be. The projectionist charges patrons to cram into the projection booth to watch the film as it is being screened, knowing that it will never be approved for public consumption by the uptight Judge. Viola watches the film dispassionately, noting unacceptable depictions of sodomy and fellatio; her chancellor does not understand these terms and when they are explained to him, he speaks for the public at large by exclaiming, "Oh, she takes it in the ass!" and "Ah, a blowjob!" Viola is unfazed by these outbursts, but in her world sex is something to be kept behind closed doors and should never be reduced to a public spectacle; she believes that she is doing a public service, but in fact all she is doing is imposing her own blinkered morality on the public at large.

By contrast, her sister Rosa is not affected by these hang-ups. Indeed, she is not very much like her sister at all—with the obvious exception of the superficial elements. Rosa is sexually promiscuous and uses her physique to take advantage of wealthy men. When she drains her men dry—in more ways that one—she invariably falls back on calling Viola for monetary assistance. Rosa is also as dim as Viola is bright. It's therefore telling that the two women are able to so effectively pass off as the other at different points; the implication is that the superficial is all that matters to the various men they encounter and so they are not able to see beyond this level. Rosa is not an entirely unsympathetic character, but she does not represent a preferable alternative to the stiff-necked Viola, either. The ideal rests somewhere in between the two extremes.

As the story unfolds, Viola begins to soften. She does not lose sight of her principles or reduce herself to a brainless sex object, but she does come to understand the need to be more flexible in her attitudes. She uses the similarity between herself and Rosa to test the fidelity of her lover, Count Renato; the Count is obviously attracted to Rosa's freewheeling sexuality, but his heart belongs to Viola and she comes to realize that he is a man worth keeping in her life. Fulci and company are to be congratulated for not falling back on negative sexist stereotypes; the director may have cultivated a reputation for being something of a misogynist, but films like *La Pretora* show that he is willing to present interesting, layered female characters with positive attributes beyond their surface glamour and sex appeal.

The allure of Viola/Rosa leads to some extremely funny set pieces. In one sequence, Raffaele stages a pornographic version of *Snow White and the Seven Dwarfs*, with Rosa as Snow White; as Rosa enacts some lewd situations as part of a *fumetti* spread, the bashful and sexually frustrated Count Renato looks on from the sidelines. The idea is to use these pictures to try and embarrass Viola, but Renato tries to do the decent thing and buys the negatives with the intention of destroying them. Raffaele objects that the images have "cultural significance" and Renato cannot resist stealing a stray pair of Rosa's sexy underwear for his own personal pleasure. Fulci has a lot of fun with this scene, exploiting the obvious sexual imagery while playing up its absurdity for comic effect. Similarly, the later scene in which Viola attempts to resign by showing her superior the scandalous pictures—which Raffaele has managed to publish anyway—is beautifully realized. The staff superior is obviously enticed by the pictures and when Viola assures him that she is nothing like her sister—except when it comes to their looks—he begins inspecting the pictures closely, trying to get a sense of what she must look like beneath her conservative garb. He then begins picturing the young woman sitting there stark naked, which causes him no small amount of consternation. Fulci plays up the superficial, chauvinist attitudes of the male characters while maintaining a sympathetic disposition towards Viola and her desire to be seen as something more than a shapely figure.

*La Pretora* is undoubtedly one of the more interesting sexy comedies for its star, Edwige Fenech. The gorgeous Fenech is renowned by fans of Italian cult cinema for good reason: Not only is she a veritable feast for the eyes, she is also a legitimately talented actress. She plays two very different sides of the same coin in this film and manages to create two separate and clearly defined characterizations. She was born as Edwige Sfenek in France in 1948. After gaining attention as a model, she started appearing in films in the late 1960s. With her fabulous physique and elegant looks, it didn't take her long to make a name for herself. She was initially confined to comic films, usually with a sexy bent, but in the 1970s she became affiliated with the *giallo*, starring in the likes of Ottavio Alessi's *Top Sensation* (1969, virtually burning a hole in the screen in her scenes with the equally beautiful Rosalba Neri), Mario Bava's *Five Dolls for an August Moon* (1970), Sergio Martino's *The Strange Vice of Mrs. Wardh* (1971) and Giuliano Carnimeo's *The Case of the Bloody Iris* (1972), among many others. The latter half of the '70s saw her swinging back more towards comedy, this time with an even more erotic bent, top-lining the popular *Schoolteacher* and *Policewoman* films. She remained prolific throughout the '80s and early '90s but has been seen only sporadically on screen in more recent years; still radiant, she appeared in a small role in Eli Roth's Euro horror homage *Hostel: Part II* (2007). Fulci and cinematographer Luciano Trasatti ensure that Fenech looks her best throughout and they capture her ethereal beauty from almost every angle imaginable; she strips off quite frequently as well, and doesn't hold anything back in that department either. Her presence helps to make the film Fulci's most openly and unabashedly sexual to date.

Fulci would later recall the film and its star with affection:

> The film is a cute little sketch, which Edwige was happy about as she had two roles: the slutty sister and a puritanical magistrate. Give an actress two roles and she will dutifully make the movie, even enthusiastically. [...] My rule is that if we ask an actor to play a priest or a homosexual, he will always accept. Whereas an actress always agrees to play a whore or a dual role! She obliged scrupulously, since she's a good actress, obedient, extraordinary on the human side ... she was a little modest when it came to do the nude scenes: "But why, you took your clothes off for the other films?" But eventually she gave up. And this is one of the few films that feature Edwige's full frontal [...]. It's the typical onan-film [Note: Fulci's witty wordplay on onanism]. She did it because she thought it was a correct and serious thing to do ... It's a good film, anyway.[1]

Unfortunately, it would seem that Fulci's attempt to cash-in on Fenech's popularity fell victim to bad timing. As producer Roberto Sbarigia later explained:

> *La Pretora* was born out of the need to make a film starring Fenech, who at that time was a box-office star. Alas, we made it at the wrong time, as when we decided to try our hand at the genre Fenech's moment had already passed and her name was not so much of an asset as before. In fact the film did not go too well at the box-office.[2]

The film was never given an English-language theatrical release and an English dub does not seem to be available. U.K. editions reportedly bear the nonsensical title *My Sister in Law*, but surely a more accurate title would have

***La Pretora;* original artwork by Scott Hoffman.**

been *My Sister and I*? In any event, Fulci would next find himself at work on one of his personal favorite films—and like so many of his favorites, it would carry its own share of heartache for the director.

Notes:
1. Fulci interviewed in the documentary *La notte americana del dott. Lucio Fulci*, directed by Antonietta De Lillo.
2. Albiero, Paolo and Giacomo Cacciatore, *Il terrorista dei generi. Tutto il cinema di Lucio Fulci* (Rome: Un Mondo a Parte, 2004), p. 165.

# 1977

## *The Psychic (Italy)*

Aka *Sette note in nero; Siete notas en negro; L'emmurée vivante; Murder to the Tune of Seven Black Notes*

Directed by Lucio Fulci; Produced by Franco Cuccu, for Cinecompany s.r.l.; Screenplay by Lucio Fulci, Roberto Gianviti and Dardano Sacchetti; Director of Photography: Sergio Salvati; Editor: Ornella Micheli; Music by Franco Bixio (as Bixio), Fabio Frizzi (as Frizzi) and Vince Tempera (as Tempera); Song: *With You*, performed by Linda Lee

Main Players: Jennifer O'Neill (Virginia Ducci); Gianni Garko (Francesco Ducci); Marc Porel (Luca Fattori); Gabriele Ferzetti (Emilio Rospini); Ida Galli (Gloria Ducci); Jenny Tamburi (Bruna); Fabrizio Jovine (Commissario D'Elia); Bruno Corazzari (Canevari); Luigi Diberti (Judge)

*Virginia Ducci has the gift of extrasensory perception. One day, she is assailed with the vision of a woman being walled-up alive. She believes it to be the memory of a crime that has already occurred and tries to convince her skeptical husband, Francesco, but he refuses to believe her. It transpires that the vision is connected to the disappearance of a young woman who used to be Francesco's lover, and when the woman's corpse is found walled-up in his cottage, he comes under suspicion of murder. Virginia tries desperately to clear his name, but it soon becomes apparent that the vision also entails another crime which has yet to occur ...*

*The Psychic* marked another step for Fulci towards the horror genre. It's definitely a *giallo*, no question about it, but it contains elements of the paranormal, which would become a hallmark of his later macabre works. For Fulci, it was a film that inspired strong feelings:

> It's one of my most beautiful, and at the same time, unsuccessful films and it cost me a lot of grief for personal reasons ... As a film, it's extremely mechanical and I'd gladly do it again tomorrow; I just adore mechanical scripts.[1]

The film marked the first of several important collaborations between Fulci and screenwriter Dardano Sacchetti. Sacchetti was born in 1944 and established himself as a major force in genre filmmaking in the 1970s. He collaborated with Dario Argento on the screenplay for *The Cat O'Nine Tails* (1971), but a later collaboration on *Inferno* (1980) proved to be more contentious, with Sacchetti not receiving any credit on the final release print. After his initial collaboration with Argento, he went on to collaborate on the screenplay for Mario Bava's *Twitch of the Death Nerve* (1971), which proved to be a more fulfilling experience; he would work with Bava again on the director's final film, the ghost story *Shock* (1977). Sacchetti's credits encompass collaborations with some of the most significant directors in the field of Italian horror, suspense and fantasy, including Lamberto Bava (*Demons*, 1985), Sergio Martino (*Hands of Steel*, 1986), Damiano Damiani (*Amityville II: The Possession*, 1982), Antonio Margheriti (*Cannibal Apocalypse*, 1980), Enzo G. Castellari (*1990: The Bronx Warriors*, 1982), Michele Soavi (*The Church*, 1989) and Umberto Lenzi (*Ironmaster*, 1983). Sacchetti continued working with Fulci on some of the director's most significant films, including *Zombie*, *City of the Living Dead*, *The Beyond*, *The House by the Cemetery* and *The New York Ripper*. The collaboration between the two men was sometimes complicated, as Sacchetti explained in an interview:

> Fulci has always suffered from the knowledge that I was the one who wrote the stories, which has made him extremely jealous of me, and this has led him to systematically disparage my work in order to give himself importance.[2]

Even so, their relationship began on a positive note with *The Psychic*. Sacchetti put it thus:

> [T]hat was a period of great harmony, a creative time which was extremely valid and enjoyable. We began with [*The Psychic*], a film I love dearly but which was not really understood.[3]

The story deals with the concept of fate. Virginia is blessed (or cursed) with the gift of second sight, which enables her to see fractured glimpses of events which have either occurred in the distant past or which have not yet come to pass. In trying to avert a potential tragedy, Virginia merely fights against the inevitable. No matter how hard she struggles, the fact remains that these glimpses must be played-out in reality. The paranormal component of the narrative points towards the gradual shift of the *giallo* into the horror film; indeed, the *giallo*'s significance in Italian pop culture would gradually diminish in large part due to films made by two of its most significant practitioners: Dario Argento's *Suspiria* (1977) and Fulci's *Zombie*, itself inspired by the tremendous box-office success of George A. Romero's *Dawn of the Dead* (1978), would open the floodgates of horror and gore in the Italian popular film scene.

Virginia is an interesting protagonist. She is stubborn and determined, yet paradoxically she is not in control of her own fate. No matter how hard she tries, she is unable to alter the course of events as they have been "revealed" to her. Fulci, Gianviti and Sacchetti leave the viewer in no doubt that her psychic abilities are real. This is evident from the opening of the film and is never called into doubt. Horror films and thrillers are awash with phony mediums—many of whom ultimately are revealed to actually have genuine abilities by way of a plot twist—but *The Psychic* does not go down this well-traveled road. Virginia does not utilize her gifts for commercial gain; indeed, she would much rather not have this gift at all. Her frustration over being burdened with second sight leads her to a parapsychologist named Luca, who does his best to assuage her fears and assure her that she is in control of her own life. Fulci's distrust of the psychiatric profession is evident here, as Luca is ultimately just dispensing platitudes, but the character is presented in a sympathetic, even humorous fashion. Virginia's relationship with Luca is fraught with double meaning and one could easily see them being involved as a couple, but she is devoted to her husband Francesco. Francesco, for his part, is revealed to be a fraud; unbeknownst to Virginia, he has been involved in a past crime and her visions gradually begin to bring this to light. When it becomes apparent that she is in danger of learning too much, Francesco determines that it is time to eliminate his collaborators—and Virginia, as well.

The finale is wonderfully ambiguous. Virginia has her final showdown with Francesco, at which point his role in a robbery that turned into a murder is revealed. Francesco claims to be saddened that he has to take extreme measures, but he certainly doesn't flinch when the time comes to subdue Virginia. Sooner than give this woman, whom he supposedly loves, a pain-free and quick demise, he determines to wall her up alive; the evidence of her murder will therefore disappear into ashes, just as the remains of his former lover have also dwindled in the same makeshift tomb located in his abandoned family villa. Francesco takes his time walling Virginia in, while Luca gradually comes to realize what is going on and leads the police to the location. The last we see of Virginia is of her gasping for air as Francesco puts the last brick into place, thus sealing her in without oxygen. Luca arrives on the scene with the authorities, but he has no proof and Francesco has already covered his tracks. Only the chiming of Virginia's charm—the seven black notes alluded to in the title—reveal her whereabouts just as Francesco is about to make his escape. One is reminded of the final, fateful sneeze by robber Martin Balsam which tips off cop Walter Matthau at the end of Joseph Sargent's *The Taking of Pelham One Two Three* (1974); but whereas that final shot was played for chuckles, the final shots of *The Psychic* are much more portentous. The viewer is denied the comfort and closure of seeing Virginia rescued by her knight in shining armor, Luca. We have no way of knowing whether she has survived this traumatic experience or if she has effectively predicted her own demise. Francesco, at the very least, has been caught red-handed; but whether it is all too late for the heroine, we will never know.

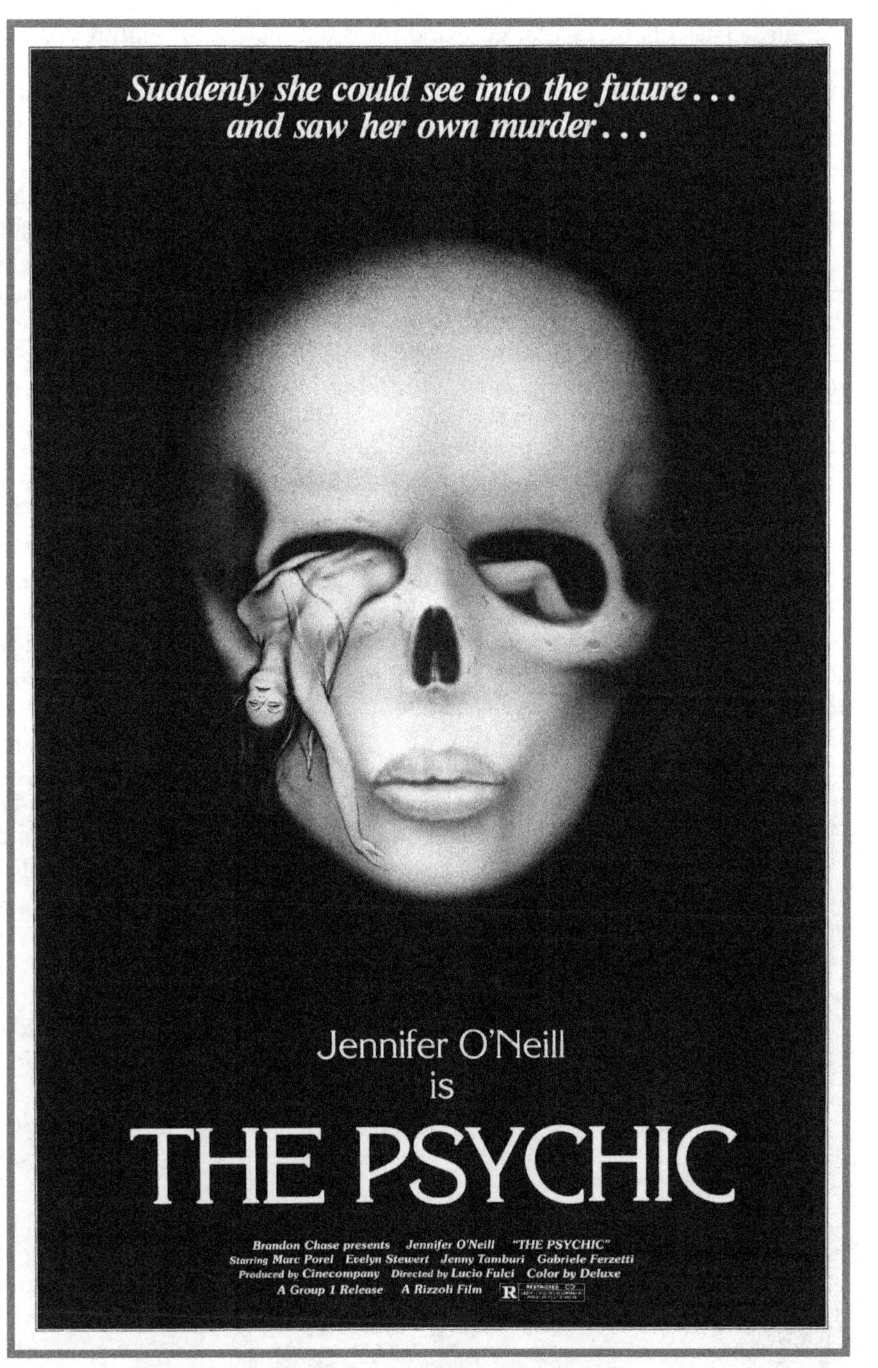

**American poster for *The Psychic*; artist unknown.**

Despite Fulci's criticism that it suffers from a mechanical narrative, the story and structure of the film is immensely satisfying. The use of fragmented visions assailing the heroine harkens back to the traumatic event that haunts the deranged killer in Mario Bava's *Hatchet for the Honeymoon* (1970), and Fulci's stylistic use of sharp zoom-ins to her eyes conveys a sense of entering into the character's frame-of-mind. Fulci would soon find himself staging scenes of spectacular gore and sadism, thus earning the appellation of "Godfather of Gore" among adoring horror fans, but this film is notable for its restraint. The violence is quick and sudden and the overall approach is stately and measured. Fulci seems to take great pleasure in putting his heroine through the paces as she attempts to solve a puzzle, which is almost certain to end in tragedy.

*The Psychic* compares well to Fulci's previous *gialli*, but sadly it proved to be a box-office disappointment. The producers invested a sizable sum in the movie, which certainly shows on screen, but for whatever reason it failed to connect with audiences. Fulci always bristled at being compared with Argento, but it seems obvious that *Deep Red* (1975) was his inspiration to some extent. The sequence of Virginia hacking into the wall, uncovering a body, recalls a similar scene involving David Hemmings in the Argento movie, while elements of the score seem to be directly impacted by the success of Goblin's prog-rock soundtrack.[4] That a commercially successful model inspired the film is hardly surprising however; indeed, this is the basic backbone of the Italian film industry. Fulci takes a little bit from Argento's movie, but in so doing, he delivers his own unique take on the material. Fulci's approach is far more logical and plot-driven, in its own way, versus the more baroque and fanciful approach of Argento. The irony in this is that Fulci would soon eclipse Argento as Italy's most cheerfully over-the-top director of horror films, many of which were truly unconcerned with plot or narrative. For the time being, however, the film's

**Italian poster for *The Psychic*; artist unknown.**

failure cost Fulci dearly and put him in an awkward position for the next couple of years. His fortunes would only revive when he found himself at the helm of *Zombie*, a project he ultimately lucked into directing fairly late in the game. From that moment on, Fulci's own destiny as a filmmaker would undergo a radical change: The former director of comedies, thrillers and Spaghetti Westerns would be reborn as a "Master of Horror."

As indicated above, the production was granted a generous budget, and this is obvious while watching the film. The cinematography by Sergio Salvati is elegant and loaded with memorable images. Salvati had already worked with Fulci on *Four of the Apocalypse* and *Young Dracula*, and he would become one of the director's most loyal and reliable collaborators. His work on films like *Zombie*, *The Beyond* and *The Black Cat* provided Fulci with some of the most striking images of his career. Salvati is justifiably proud of his work on *The Psychic*: "From the point of view of photography, it is one of my favorite films."[5] The settings and costumes are appropriately classy, as befits the upper-crust environs in which the story is set, and special make-up effects are generally very good; the opening flashback scene even quotes a remarkable demise from *Don't Torture a Duckling*, as Virginia's mother plunges to hear death off the cliffs of Dover and her face is shredded by the jagged cliffs. The music score by the trio of Fabio Frizzi, Vince Tempera and Franco Bixio also deserves a nod. The three had already scored *Young Dracula* and *Four of the Apocalypse* and would go on to score the director's next film, *Silver Saddle*. Their music for *The Psychic* ranges from sub-Goblin compositions during some of the more hysterical sequences to a haunting title theme which seems indebted to Ennio Morricone's "pocket watch chime" theme from *For a Few Dollars More* (1965) and was subsequently sampled by Quentin Tarantino in *Kill Bill Vol. 1* (2003). The use of a saccharine song over the opening titles may well draw sneers from some viewers, but the lyrics have a certain thematic weight and the song itself makes for a nice contrast between the generally grim goings-on.

Unfortunately, the film is burdened with a rather wooden central performance from Jennifer O'Neill. O'Neill's one-note interpretation of Virginia grates early on and does not improve much as the story unfolds. She was born in Brazil in 1948, but was raised in New York. She started off as a model and began appearing in films in the late 1960s. After appearing in Howard Hawks' *Rio Lobo* (1970), she scored her most iconic role in Robert Mulligan's sweetly romantic *Summer of '42* (1971), but her subsequent film work has been spotty at best. She did play a memorable supporting role in Luchino Visconti's swan-song *The Innocent* (1976), on which she met the actor Marc Porel, with whom she had a tumultuous relationship. O'Neill's career was rumored to have been compromised by issues with substance abuse, and allegations abound that she introduced Porel to narcotics as well. In any event, she would continue appearing in films, including David

Cronenberg's *Scanners* (1981), but much of her subsequent work would be on the small screen. O'Neill's performance is the film's Achilles heel, but she is supported by a number of fine actors, including her off-screen lover of the time, Marc Porel. Porel is marvelous as the slyly humorous parapsychologist, Luca. It's a very different character from the one he had played in *Don't Torture a Duckling*, and he appears relaxed and engaged throughout. According to Salvati, the two were professional on their own but were difficult to be around when they were together: "They argued constantly. [...] They were jealous and threw their defects in each other's faces."[6] Gianni Garko is in fine form as Virginia's husband, Francesco. Garko is required to convey an air of moral ambiguity, and he does this with great skill. The distinguished Gabriele Ferzetti is also on hand to play Emilio Rospini, a chief suspect in the mystery. Ferzetti doesn't have a lot of screen time, but his charismatic presence adds some gravitas to the proceedings. The supporting cast also includes the first appearance in a Fulci film by character actor Fabrizio Jovine, who plays the role of Commissario D'Elia. Jovine would go on to play another police figure in *Contraband,* as well as the damned Father Thomas in *City of the Living Dead*. Jovine's slightly ironic presence brings shading and nuance to a role that could have been eminently forgettable and he makes for a brighter-than-usual police commissioner. Fulci didn't endear himself to many actors, but Jovine would become a close friend and confidante. He later recalled Fulci with warmth and affection:

> My fondest memory of Lucio was his wit—his cruel wit. He had an absolutely rude, cruel but *incredible* wit. His sense of humor was so sinister but so enjoyable. It was an absolutely rewarding experience because he was keeping your brain alert—and obviously, you didn't want to be one of his targets, so you better be his friend and try to outsmart him! [...] I was more of a friend than an actor to him. As a friend, I knew he was frustrated because he could have been one of the great names in Italian cinema.

The film continued Fulci's happy association with cinematographer Sergio Salvati. His camera operator on this film was Franco Bruni, another individual who would go on to work on a number of Fulci's films; he would operate for Salvati on *Zombie*, *Contraband*, *The Black Cat*, *The Beyond* and *The House by the Cemetery* and also assisted cinematographer Guglielmo Mancori on *Manhattan Baby*. Bruni remembers Fulci as a friend and a teacher:

> He was someone that taught me a lot. He had an incredible technique. On the human level, although on the outside he didn't show it, he was a good one. He was a person who often injured himself by his own actions. [...] He would lean on me. I was like his "eye." He trusted my capabilities. [...] He was a filmmaking giant.

**Jennifer O'Neill (right) makes a gruesome discovery; Japanese video ad.**

Fulci would revisit the *giallo* with his most controversial film, *The New York Ripper*, and by that stage in the game his reputation as a purveyor of gory thrills preceded him. His earlier thrillers like this, however, show a very different side of the man and his work. *The Psychic* is a well-plotted and beautifully crafted thriller and it remains one of the director's most satisfying pictures.

Notes:

1. Palmerini, Luca M. and Gaetano Mistretta, *Spaghetti Nightmares* (Florida: Fantasma Books, 1996), p. 59.
2, *Ibid*, p. 59.
3. *Ibid*, p. 125.
4. One should also make note of the premature burial/walled-up-alive motif of Edgar Allan Poe, one of Fulci's favorite writers; Fulci's later Poe homage *The Black Cat* (1981) would reprise this internment set piece, and it is also evoked in the justifiably famous sequence of Catriona MacColl being buried alive in *City of the Living Dead* (1980).
5. Audio commentary with Sergio Salvati moderated by Federico Caddeo on the French DVD edition of *The Psychic*.
6. *Ibid*.

# 1978

## *Silver Saddle (Italy)*

Aka *Sella d'argento; Silbersattel; They Died With Their Boots On*

Directed by Lucio Fulci; Produced by Piero Donati, for Rizzoli Film; Story and Screenplay by Adriano Bolzoni; Director of Photography: Sergio Salvati; Editor: Ornella Micheli; Music by Franco Bixio (as Bixio), Fabio Frizzi (as Frizzi) and Vince Tempera (as Tempera); Song: *Silver Saddle*, performed by Ken Tobias

Main Players: Giuliano Gemma (Roy Blood); Sven Valsecchi (Thomas Barrett, Jr.); Ettore Manni (Thomas Barrett); Cinzia Monreale (Margaret Barrett); Geoffrey Lewis ("Two Strike Snake"); Gianni De Luigi (Turner); Aldo Sambrell (Garrincha); Donald O'Brien (Fletcher)

*As a child, Roy Blood sees his father ruthlessly murdered by a gunman. Roy takes his father's gun and shoots his father's murderer dead; he also takes the outlaw's horse, which is adorned with an ornate silver saddle. Years later, Roy establishes a fearsome reputation as a bounty hunter. He rescues a young boy from being killed, only to discover that the child is the son of a man named Barrett – the same man who betrayed Roy's father and sent the gunman to kill him. He initially rejects the child, but his better instincts take over and he begins to serve as his protector. Roy is accused of kidnapping the child, but is ultimately enlisted by the boy's uncle, Thomas Barrett, Sr., to rescue him from a Mexican bandit named Garrincha. Roy rescues the child, but little Thomas is still not out of harm's way …*

Fulci's third and final Western – the *White Fang* duo is sometimes referred to as Westerns as well, but that is stretching the definition a bit thin – is a more family-oriented affair compared to *Massacre Time* and *Four of the Apocalypse*. It doesn't reach the same heights as those earlier films, but neither is it the total disappointment it is often painted to be.

The film admittedly suffers from a weak and uninspired screenplay by Adriano Bolzoni, but Fulci handles the material with customary flair. Bolzoni (1919-2005) previously worked with Fulci on *Operation Saint Peter's* and also had ample background working in the Spaghetti Western, thanks to the likes of Sergio Leone's *A Fistful of Dollars* (1964), Sergio Corbucci's *Minnesota Clay* (1964) and *The Mercenary* (1968) and Giuseppe Vari's *Shoot the Living and Pray for the Dead* (1971), among many others. The project was not written with Fulci in mind, but following the failure of *The Psychic* he was scrambling for work and the project seemed appealing.

**Silver Saddle*; original artwork by Scott Hoffman.**

The opening scenes promise much; the betrayal and murder of Roy's father, followed up by the boy taking arms and committing his first murder is a vivid start. Fulci risks alienating the audience by showing a young boy pulling the trigger and taking a man's life, but there's little doubt that the action is justified in context. From there, the action flashes forward a number of years: Roy is now a grown man and working as a bounty hunter. He befriends a colorful vagabond known as "Two Strike Snake" and initially it seems as if more is going to be made of their friendship. Snake is certainly an endearing character – a magpie of sorts, he cleans up after blood has been shed by retrieving money and valuables that are no longer going to serve the owners any practical purpose. Unfortunately, Snake is only present sporadically in the action and Roy carries out much of the narrative. This is problematic for the simple reason that Roy is so sketchily developed as a character. He lacks the grit and moral ambiguity of the best Western anti-heroes. He is virtuous to the point of boredom, seems disinterested in sex and can stubbornly be relied upon to always do the right thing.

Unfortunately, the villains are every bit as loosely depicted. The Mexican bandit, Garrincha, is only a few steps removed from comic stereotype: He is properly hissable, but he never establishes himself as a really vile or disturbing presence, especially compared to the deranged villains of *Massacre Time* and *Four of the Apocalypse*. Similarly, the revelation of Thomas Sr.'s role in the plot as the principle villain is poorly timed and lacks sufficient dramatic impact. Here again, the character is much too vaguely defined and so the surprise factor doesn't follow suit.

The relationship between Roy and the young Thomas sets the tone for the film. Roy is an orphan who channels his anger over the death of his father into a life of catching villains; Thomas is an orphan desperately looking for a father figure. They start off on rocky ground, but ultimately Roy's moral compass ensures that he will do the right thing by the boy. The characters are not nearly as interesting as one might like, but there is warmth in their scenes that is relatively unusual in Fulci's work of this period. Given that Fulci grew up without a father, perhaps he latched on to this idea and invested a bit more emotional resonance into it as a result.

The director's flair for action is evident in the various shootouts, though the comeuppance for both Garrincha and the elder Thomas seems arbitrary and thoughtlessly executed. The operatic violence of *Four of the Apocalypse* is nowhere to be seen, though there is a rather distressing sequence depicting the aftermath of carnage at a monastery. The images of the monks' bloodied and lifeless bodies littering the clean white landscape evokes Alexandro Jodorowsky's *El Topo* (1970) and points to the kind of inspired mayhem Fulci is capable of, but this being a Western for the whole family, such imagery is in short supply.

The family angle also ensures that sex is only vaguely alluded to. Roy is established as having had a relationship with the beautiful brothel madam, Sheba, but their days as lovers are in the past and Roy cannot be bothered with rekindling things. The patrons who populate the brothel seem curiously genteel and the prostitutes themselves are presented in an unrealistically glamorous fashion. Even so, by de-sexualizing this aspect of the plot, Fulci and Bolzoni ensure that the material remains suitable for a general audience.

*Silver Saddle* may be the least of Fulci's Westerns, but it is still a well-made and entertaining movie. Sergio Salvati's widescreen cinematography is up to his usual standards and the soundtrack by Franco Bixio, Fabio Frizzi and Vince Tempera is appropriately jangly—even the mellow theme song works very well in context. The crisp editing is by Ornella Micheli, in her final collaboration with Fulci. The two had worked together off-and-on since *Le massaggiatrici* in 1962 and she was responsible for the editing of some of Fulci's best films. She would continue working as an editor until 1981, at which point her filmography stops cold. Fulci would begin utilizing Franco Fraticelli as his primary editor after this film and fortunately he would prove to be a more than adequate successor.

Giuliano Gemma heads the cast in the role of Roy Blood. It isn't Gemma's fault that the character is poorly delineated; within the obvious deficiencies of what he is given to work with, he gives a compelling performance. Gemma is impossibly rugged, handsome and virtuous and seems more akin to the homespun heroes of 1930s and '40s serial Westerns from America; he doesn't possess any of the moral ambiguity that marks out the protagonists in Fulci's other Westerns or the Spaghetti Western at large. Born in Rome in 1938, Gemma was a movie buff from a young age. He also excelled in sports and did very well in everything from boxing to gymnastics. With his handsome features and chiseled physique, he had little difficulty in catching the attention of casting agents. He initially worked as an uncredited stunt man (he is rumored to have worked on William Wyler's Oscar-winning epic *Ben-Hur*, 1959), afterwards he began securing more substantial assignments in the 1960s. He appeared in Luchino Visconti's *The Leopard* (1963), but shot to stardom as the star of Duccio Tessari's *A Pistol for Ringo* and *The Return of Ringo* (both 1965). The success of these films established him as a viable alternative to Clint Eastwood, Lee Van Cleef and Franco Nero in the pantheon of Spaghetti Western anti-

**Italian *locandina* for *Silver Saddle*; artist unknown.**

heroes and he would go on to appear in Tonino Valerii's *The Price of Power* (1969) and Michele Lupo's *Amigo, Stay Away* (1972), among others. Gemma also broadened his horizon by appearing in everything from Valerio Zurlini's *The Desert of the Tartars* (1976) to Dario Argento's *Tenebrae* (1982); and he appeared in a small role for Woody Allen in *To Rome with Love* (2012), but much of his later years were devoted to his passion for sculpting. The Allen film would prove to be his swansong; he was killed in a car crash in 2013, at the age of 75. Among the supporting players, the real standout is American actor Geoffrey Lewis. Lewis is splendid as the slimy but endearing "Two Strike Snake" and the film would have benefitted enormously if he had been given more screen time. Lewis easily steals every scene he is in and makes for a wonderful comic sidekick

**Fulci (right, in hat) with director of photography Sergio Salvati (with mustache).**

to the straight-laced Roy. Born in 1931, he started cropping up on American TV in the 1970s, doing guest stints on everything from *Along Came Bronson* and *Mission: Impossible* to *Barnaby Jones* and *The Amazing Spider-Man*. He became a favorite of Clint Eastwood, who cast him as the villain in *High Plains Drifter* (1973) and then used him in such films as *Thunderbolt and Lightfoot* (1974) and *Every Which Way You Can* (1978). Horror buffs also remember him for his appearances in Tobe Hooper's *Salem's Lot* (1979) and Rob Zombie's *The Devil's Rejects* (2005). *Silver Saddle* was part of a brief foray he made into European Westerns, which also included the Sergio Leone-produced, Tonino Valerii-directed *My Name is Nobody* (1973). Lewis' daughter, Juliette Lewis, is also a popular actress, best known for her appearances in Martin Scorsese's *Cape Fear* (1991, for which she was nominated for an Oscar as Best Supporting Actress) and Oliver Stone's *Natural Born Killers* (1994). Lewis would later recall Fulci with fondness:

> When I think of Lucio Fulci, I think of a smallish guy … maybe five foot eight, five foot nine … with his arms outstretched and screaming some wonderful Italian aria. He was a wonderful fellow, a dear little guy—you know, a dear man. But he would explode daily, like Vesuvius. One day he was expounding, screaming and everybody, all the crew, was looking down as he was thundering over them. He happened to look over at me and I was looking at him and he winked. So the whole thing became a put-on after that.

Geoffrey Lewis passed away on April 7, 2015, at the age of 79.

*Silver Saddle* was not only the end of Fulci's affiliation with the Western genre, it was also the last true Spaghetti Western of the golden age, which is usually classified as taking place between 1964, with the release of *A Fistful of Dollars*, and 1978. The genre's popularity waned throughout the '70s, a trend borne out by the increasing popularity in Spaghetti Westerns spoofs, typified by the raucous Terence Hill/Bud Spencer *Trinity* series. That Fulci was able to make a film as dark and poetic as *Four of the Apocalypse* during this period of decline is something of a miracle. *Silver Saddle* didn't allow him to bottle that magic again, but it is a respectable swansong for a genre that overflowed the market place for over a decade. At this time, extreme horror was becoming the new flavor of the month—and Fulci would find his career re-energized and refocused when he (somewhat inadvertently) helped to put this trend over-the-top with his next picture. In the meantime, he reteamed with Franco Franchi for a foray into the Italian TV series *Buonasera con* (more about that later, in the review for the Fulci-directed mini-series *Un uomo da ridere*) and was absolutely in the dark about where his career would take him next.

# 1979

## *Zombie (Italy)*

Aka *Zombi 2; Zombie Flesh Eaters; Zombies 2; Nuevo York bajo el terror de los zombie; Woodoo*

Directed by Lucio Fulci; Produced by Gianfranco Couyoumdjian, Fabrizio De Angelis and Ugo Tucci, for Variety Film; Story and Screenplay by Elisa Briganti and Dardano Sacchetti (uncredited); Director of Photography: Sergio Salvati; Editor: Vincenzo Tomassi; Music by Fabrio Frizzi and Giorgio Tucci [actually Giorgio Cascio]

Main Players: Ian McCulloch (Peter West); Tisa Farrow (Anne Bowles); Richard Johnson (Dr. David Menard); Pierluigi Conti [as Al Cliver] (Brian Hull); Auretta Gay (Susan Barrett); Olga Karlatos (Mrs. Paola Menard); Stefania D'Amario (Menard's nurse); Dakar (Lucas)

Cameo appearance: Lucio Fulci (News editor)

*When an abandoned boat shows up in a New York harbor, the police investigate. A freakish man attacks the investigating officers and tears the throat out of one officer before being shot to death. The story attracts the attention of reporter Peter West, who discovers that the boat belongs to the father of Anne Bowles; Anne is concerned because her father appears to have disappeared and was last heard from in the Lesser Antilles. Peter and Anne fly to the Antilles to investigate and discover that there is a strange epidemic afflicting the island and the natives are convinced that voodoo is bringing the dead back to life. Dr. Menard is investigating the phenomenon scientifically, but appears to be hiding a secret …*

Prior to 1968, the zombie was a somewhat marginalized presence in the pantheon of screen monsters. Probably the first really noteworthy instance of a zombie-oriented horror film was the independently produced low-budget gem *White Zombie* (1932), directed by Victor Halperin and starring Bela Lugosi as a mysterious man who controls people, including the recently deceased, via telepathic means. *I Walked With a Zombie* (1943) is a famous instance of a producer—in this case, the gifted Val Lewton—being saddled with a hokey title and making cinematic art out of it: A variation on *Jane Eyre*, it deals with a nurse (Frances Dee) who encounters voodoo and the undead in Haiti. In England, Hammer Films released *The Plague of the Zombies* (1966), directed by John Gilling, which deals with a voodoo-practicing Squire (a marvelous John Carson) who is using the recently departed to work his tin mine. There were certainly many other entries in the subgenre, but these were arguably the most significant before Pittsburgh-based filmmaker George A. Romero arrived on the scene. Romero's *Night of the Living Dead* (1968) helped to transform the modern horror film: His movie dealt with the bodies of the dead returning to life in order to attack and eat the living. The zombies now became equated with cannibalism, and Romero did not shy away from showing their flesh-ripping activities. The genre would never be the same. Unfortunately for Romero and his associates—including co-writer/bit player John Russo and producers/actors Karl Hardman and Russell Streiner—the film was bedeviled by bad luck which arose out of their lack of business savvy; originally titled *The Flesh Eaters* and copyrighted under that name, the filmmakers neglected to put a copyright credit under the new title when it was hurriedly changed; the end result was a morass of legal red tape which saw the filmmakers sitting impotently on the sidelines as the film generated huge profits—for everybody but them. Life moves on, however, and it was only a matter of time before the film's influence was felt on an international scale. Undoubtedly the most significant of the films to be influenced by Romero's initial success was Jorge Grau's Spanish-Italian *Let Sleeping Corpses Lie* (1974), produced by Fulci's erstwhile associate Edmondo Amati. A richly atmospheric and genuinely scary gem, it took the social commentary offered by Romero and amped-up the violence with the addition of lurid color; the special effects were by Giannetto De Rossi, who would eventually become irrevocably associated with the subgenre thanks to his work on Fulci's efforts. Romero himself was slow to revisit the subgenre for fear of being seen as a one-trick pony, but he received added incentive when fan and fellow genre titan Dario Argento offered to provide some financial backing for a sequel in exchange for the right of final cut on European prints. Romero shot *Dawn of the Dead* over a period of approximately four months, beginning in late 1977 and finishing in early 1978. True to form, he shot a lot of footage—ideally he should have had a year or more to work on the editing, but in order to complete the film in time for the 1978 Cannes Film Festival, he and his collaborators worked around the clock. The initial edit was further finessed by Romero and the film was ultimately released—unrated, as the MPAA was intent on slapping an "X" rating on the picture—in April 1979 in the U.S. Argento, however, wasted no time in releasing

**The iconic American poster for *Zombie*; artist unknown.**

his edit in Italy—the upside being that his version, titled *Zombi* (or *Zombies*, in the U.K.), was released in Italy in September of 1978. The film's success was immense: critics adored its mixture of slapstick, social commentary and savage violence, and audiences responded in kind. True to form, the Italians were not about to let the film's success slip by without unleashing some homegrown zombie films of their own.

*Zombie* originated from a screenplay written by the husband and wife team of Elisa Briganti and Dardano Sacchetti. Sacchetti has long claimed that the film was written long before Romero's, but his timeline is a little at fault: It was definitely written before the film was released in Italy, but by the time he and his wife were developing the script, Romero's film was already in production in the United States. Whether they were influenced by the news of Romero's new production or not is open to speculation, but the scenario they developed is a far cry from Romero's splashy social satire. Sacchetti has claimed that the original source of inspiration was a comic strip called "Tex Willer in the Land of the Living Dead," which producer

**Greek poster for *Zombie*—the bare-chested cannibal does not appear in the film, and the background action is from Fulci's later *The Black Cat*! Artist unknown.**

Gianfranco Couyoumdjian had brought to the writer in the hopes of making a film adaptation. Sacchetti rejected the material as unfilmable, but he and Briganti offered to write another zombie adventure from scratch.[1] Originally titled *Island of the Living Dead*, the script was finished and submitted and producer Ugo Tucci approached Enzo G. Castellari to direct. Castellari was not impressed, however:

> The producer wanted me to do it, but I don't like horror. [...] I said, "Hire Lucio Fulci. He hasn't worked in a long time."

Castellari's suggestion of Fulci proved to be an artistic inspiration and a lifesaver (and game-changer) for the older filmmaker. Fulci had spent some time in the wilderness and was reaching a point of desperation, fearing that his opportunity to establish a name for himself as a filmmaker may have passed him by. *Zombie* would provide him with just such an opportunity.

*Zombie*'s reputation as a "rip-off" of Romero's film has long obscured its many qualities as a piece of filmmaking. First things first: It is not a rip-off of *Dawn of the Dead*. Briganti and Sacchetti (though only the former is credited on screen) undoubtedly appropriated elements of *Night of the Living Dead*—cannibalism, the need to shoot the creatures in the head in order to kill them—but they also reached back to the old days of zombie lore by bringing in Voodooism. Romero also threw in passing reference to voodoo in *Dawn*, but nothing much was made of it in the context of his film; in Romero's films, it doesn't really matter where the phenomenon sprang from, it merely matters that it is happening. Briganti and Sacchetti are much more concerned with how and why it is happening, and it is the contrast between belief in voodoo and the stoic efforts of Dr. Menard to explain the phenomenon scientifically which provides the narrative with its backbone. Romero's film was played for laughs and gasps; the contrast between the absurd humor and the shocking doses of blood and gore provided a very giddy mixture indeed. *Zombie* is played deadly seriously. There are traces of dark humor in some set pieces—the bickering coroners oblivious to the fact that the dead body on the slab is beginning to stir, for example—but overall the emphasis is on suspense, mood—and in-your-face violence. On the latter point, Romero had certainly pushed things as far as he could in *Night*, but *Zombie* outdid everything else that came before it. Tom Savini's make-up effects in *Dawn* look positively cartoony in comparison. But again, the conception of the gore sequences as defined in the screenplay came before Sacchetti and Briganti had an opportunity to see a single frame of *Dawn*; they were therefore pushing the envelope doubly further, as they had no way of knowing just how far Romero and Savini were going in their latest effort. Ultimately, it cannot be denied that *Zombie* is a cash-in on the Romero picture, but to call it a rip-off is shortsighted in the extreme.

If the film ultimately owes anything to Romero's *Dawn*, it is in the marketing of the picture. Producers Ugo Tucci and Fabrizio De Angelis saw the money Romero's picture was raking in at the Italian box-office and decided that a change of title was in order: It would be changed from *Island of the Living Dead* to *Zombi 2*, which aligned it as a sequel of sorts to the American film. Argento was furious and a lawsuit was brought against Variety Film (the production company responsible for Fulci's film), but a judge decreed that the word "Zombie" was too generic to fall under copyright laws. Fulci felt the entire ordeal was ridiculous:

> When Argento wrote that *Dawn of the Dead* was his creation, I wrote him a letter listing 12 films which demonstrated that zombies were around even before Tourneur's day, before *I Walked With a Zombie*. Zombies belong to Haiti and Cuba, not to Dario Argento.[2]

Tucci and De Angelis proceeded to laugh all the way to the bank, as the film became an unexpected box-office smash.

*Zombie* became Lucio Fulci's defining film, yet it has to be admitted that he was involved in the film purely as a hired gun. He had no hand in developing the screenplay, nor did he feel that it needed to be reworked during filming. He would deviate from the script in the normal fashion, whenever he decided changes needed to be made, but overall he remained true to what Briganti and Sacchetti had written. There is no indication that Fulci was even overly enamored with the genre prior to making this film. He would later indicate that he decided that the film required an atmosphere-driven approach and that he reached back to films like *I Walked With a Zombie* for inspiration, but it is unlikely that Jacques Tourneur, who directed the earlier film, would have seen many traces of his work in the finished product. As he would later claim in an interview:

> The zombies in my movies derive from Jacques Tourneur's *I Walked With a Zombie*, they're born of pure fantasy and horror traditions, zombies with no political inclination or social meaning.[3]

Fulci's comment about social commentary is well taken: for Romero, zombies are metaphors for the mindless consumerism of American society; for Fulci, they evoke a sense of horror and dread rooted in tradition. Romero's zombies are symbols; Fulci's are monsters. Truth be told, Fulci's approach is a perfect synthesis of the old and the new: The film's atmosphere is rich and overpowering, but it does not pull any punches when it comes to graphic violence. Fulci's pragmatic approach is perfectly in tune with the demands of the screenplay: Sooner than soft-pedal the violence or rely on the hoary cliché of what the audiences imagines is far worse than anything any film can show, he goes for the gut and succeeds every time. A comparison between the screenplay and the finished picture is nevertheless helpful in this context as it illustrates the changes made during production, many of which would have been made at Fulci's behest, either to facilitate the production or to add a little extra punch to the proceedings.[4]

The film opens with a close-up of a gun, which turns towards the camera. A cut shows a shrouded body rising into frame. Drum music swells on the soundtrack. The gun points right at the camera and fires—the shrouded figure is hit square in the head and blood splatters all over the white sheet and clean white wall. A silhouetted figure grimly intones, "The boat can leave now. Tell the crew." We cue the opening credits. *Wow!* What an opening! Fulci dispenses with subtlety right from the get-go; it is going to be one of "those" movies, and he makes sure the audience knows it. Up until this point, the film follows the suggested screen directions more or less as provided. There are some minor alterations to the dialogue and Fulci elected to go in for a gory close-up of the bullet hitting the cadaver in the head, but beyond that, it is more-or-less filmed as written. After the credits, we are treated to a bit of mood and suspense as the camera roams the decimated interior of a boat drifting into the New York City harbor. Two cops, played for goofy comedy, board the boat and investigate. Fulci and cinematographer Sergio Salvati caress the shabby interior of the craft, which is littered with maggots and rotting food. The atmosphere is palpable and the suspense builds as one of the cops goes below deck. After milking the situation for all it is worth, suspense gives way to shock horror as a rotting cadaver assails the hapless cop and proceeds to tear his throat out. The zombie then sets his eyes on the cop's partner, who fills the creature full of lead and it plops into the water, apparently now "really" dead. This section varies a little more dramatically, with some chatter between helicopter police added in to allow for some added production value in the form of aerial helicopter views of the harbor. The attack on the policeman in the below-deck cabin also plays out rather differently. Briganti and Sacchetti specify that the zombie is black, and, after bursting through the door, he goes for the cop's legs, tearing a chunk of flesh out of

**Scandinavian poster for *Zombie*; artist unknown.**

his thigh. The zombie then goes for his throat and tears out another chunk of flesh as the poor cop expires from his blood loss. Fulci ignores the specifics with the biting of the thigh and instead adds in a nice detail with the cop struggling with the zombie, inadvertently pulling a piece of flesh from its arm, revealing it to be rotting and suffering from advanced gangrene. From there the scene plays out basically as written, again with the exception of some minor tweaks to the dialogue.

Fulci handles these opening scenes with an immaculate eye for detail. He uses the widescreen frame to its full effectiveness and the pacing and gradual ratcheting of suspense is faultless. This is particularly important because the subsequent half-hour or so is more or less free of incident and is devoted to the burdensome business of establishing the plot and characters. Without this double-punch of activity bracketing the opening titles, *Zombie* would be off to a very slow start; but with them, the audience can then use the next half-hour to decompress and relax a bit before the next big burst of activity.

The characters are not a particularly inspiring lot: Peter West is a cliché big city newspaperman looking to make it big. He is cocky and condescending and doesn't make for the most engaging of heroes in this context. Anne is all wide-eyed and confused, but she never has a chance to really register as a strong presence. In short, they are pawns—but they are necessary pawns, as it is the disappearance of Anne's father that prompts the action to move to the Antilles. The scenes in New York are functional: they move the plot from point A to point B, but following the rich opening set pieces, they feel a bit arbitrary and clunky.

Once the action moves to the Caribbean, however, it regains its footing and never loses track. The audience is introduced to a much more interesting figure: Dr. Menard. The doctor is ambiguous, to say the least. He seems devoted to finding a cure for the outbreak of disease on the island, but is his interest motivated by a desire to help people or is he simply driven by curiosity? His relationship with his emotionally fragile wife is unsteady, to say the least: she curses him as a cruel sadist and implies that he is partially to blame for the outbreak, an accusation he flatly rejects. Unfortunately, the two are only allowed one big scene together: It is never clear if the wife is succumbing to madness or if there is some truth to her accusations. The lack of closure is not a defect, however; it simply adds to the movie's sense of mystery.

The next big set piece is probably the film's most spectacular: Peter and Anne persuade fellow Americans Brian and Susan to take them by boat on a tour of the islands, hoping to locate Anne's father. The crew stops for a little break, allowing Susan to do some deep-sea photography. While submerged in the water, she sees a shark approaching; panic-stricken as she is, she is ill-prepared when things go from bad to worse when a zombie, apparently existing underneath the water, makes an attack on her. She escapes his moldering clutches and the zombie then gets involved in a little underwater mayhem with the shark. The zombie-versus-shark scene is rightly revered; it's absurd enough to pass for surrealism and it is so beautifully realized by underwater cameraman Ramon Bravo that it remains one of the film's signature sequences. That said, it must be noted that it has been rumored that Fulci had nothing to do with its execution, as he felt it was an absurd last-minute digression; the scene was reportedly overseen by producer Ugo Tucci and an uncredited René Cardona, Jr.; Cardona's experience directing the *Jaws* (1975) knock-off *Tintorera* (1977), also photographed by Bravo, reportedly got him the job. In any event, the scene is present in the 1978 English-language screenplay translation and that the underwater portion of the screenplay was farmed-out to another director on another unit is hardly surprising.

The next big scene is the most infamous: Mrs. Menard, alone in her cottage, has a slow, sensual shower as a voyeuristic zombie spies on her. The zombie, of course, is not motivated by carnal lust so much as a desire to get a bite to eat, but Fulci allows the scene to play out in a seductive manner before introducing the element of danger. The tension builds quickly when Mrs. Menard realizes that she is not alone and attempts to barricade herself in her room. Just when it appears that she has saved herself, a rotting hand thrusts through the door, splintering the wood. Mrs. Menard finds herself pulled by the hair toward the shattered door and a very nasty wooden splinter begins to loom large—terrified and unable to escape, she is eventually pulled onto the splinter, which penetrates her eye in graphic close-up. The scene continues Fulci's fascination with eye trauma, which first manifested itself in the murder of Francesco in *Beatrice Cenci*. Amazingly, the screenplay is a little more graphic, adding in the unsavory detail of the zombie tearing away the flesh from Mrs. Menard's scalp as he pulls her towards him, but Fulci and his crew elected to disregard this idea. It could be that it was simply another time-consuming effect that would slow the production down, but it is also entirely logical to suppose that the touch was deemed gratuitous, since nothing—and I do mean *nothing*—could top the eventual climax of the sequence as Mrs. Menard's eye is ruthlessly destroyed in graphic close-up. It can be argued that Fulci simply filmed the scene as written, but his attention to detail is paramount to the scene's effectiveness. For one thing, the way he and Salvati emphasize the expressive green eyes of actress Olga Karlatos in her earlier scene is a marvelously understated form of foreshadowing. The juxtaposition of objective and subjective camerawork maximizes the effectiveness of the scene, as well: Fulci and editor Vincenzo Tomassi cut back and forth from Mrs. Menard's point of view as the splinter comes closer and closer. Horror fans, long conditioned to being set up for a big payoff only to be disappointed when the filmmakers coyly cut away to something else, no doubt expected more of the same here; when the splinter punctures the eyeball in graphic close-

**This German lobby card features an atmospheric view of the zombies congregating on the island of Matoul.**

up, however, the payoff is more than sufficient—and Fulci goes even further by showing the piece of wood breaking off and damaging the eye even further as the zombie continues to pull Mrs. Menard even closer. It's a gruesome, even nauseating moment that helps to take the film to the next level of graphic violence, which even Romero could not top in his own zombie epics. Fulci's matter-of-fact approach to sequences such as this demonstrates plainly that he was the ideal director for the assignment; hired gun or not, he displays a tremendous flair for atmosphere and is not afraid to go where other filmmakers would never dare to tread.

After that, a brief period of respite ensues as the four travelers barricade themselves with Dr. Menard inside his clinic; once the zombies descend upon the place, the action turns into a melee of action and gore as they do their best to fend off the shambling creatures. The gore flows plentifully and Fulci's expertise in staging complicated action set pieces comes through as the survivors use bullets and fire to try and rescue themselves. The finale sees Peter and Anne left alone, as the infected Brian is locked into the ship's hull (ironic given that his last name is Hull!), and they sail back to civilization. The final capper—again, apparently a bit of last-minute inspiration, as it was not included in the original script—sees them turning on a radio and realizing that the zombie phenomenon has spread to the city as well. A radio announcer excitedly announces the developments before thoughtfully narrating to the eager listeners that the zombies have broken into the studio ... that they are coming closer ... *Ahhhhh*! It's a marvelously inspired bit of EC Comics lunacy, even if it threatens to tip the action into overt farce. The final shots of the zombies shuffling across Brooklyn Bridge are spoiled only by the presence of traffic moving in and out of the city; even the zombie apocalypse won't keep the Big Apple from booming! The screenplay is actually more subtle and effective, as it does not include the radio announcer's demise nor does it go back to New York to show the zombies shuffling their way into the city. In this particular instance, Fulci would have done better adapting a "less is more" approach, as the script specified that Peter and Anne should turn off the radio in disgust after hearing the news of the spreading epidemic. Anne turns to Peter and asks what they should do now, but Peter has no reply. Then, from below, they hear the sounds of the reanimated Brian beating at the door of the cabin where his body has been

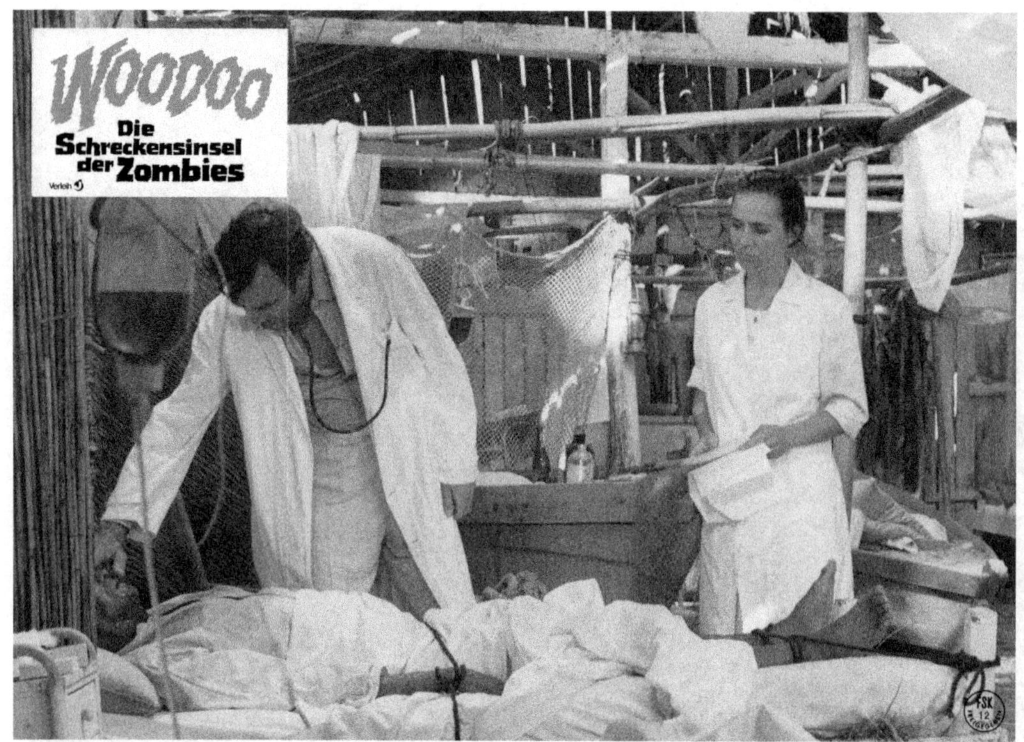


**German lobby card: Dr. Menard (Richard Johnson) tends to his patients as his assistant (Stefania D'Amario) looks on.**

stored. The End. It's a striking ending and it accomplishes the same basic purpose, leaving the protagonists stranded and their fate unclear (but not looking promising), but the added shots of the zombies marching on the city are arguably a little too literal.

*Zombie*'s success helped to push Fulci's career into a completely different direction. The director would later reveal that he felt that the screenplay was too mechanical and indeed his complaints are justified: there's a little too much interplay between the uninteresting leads in the early scenes, but once the action starts to flow, Fulci displays a complete mastery of his craft and never lets up on the tension and suspense. For all of its gory excesses, the film deserves to be remembered as much for its thoughtful attention to mood and atmosphere. Romero's films are aggressively modern: cleanly lit, free of cobwebs and Gothic trappings, with a rich vein of social commentary and comedy. Fulci's approach is comparatively old-fashioned, in the best sense of the term. He takes the time to establish a sense of mood, but his refusal to soft-pedal the violence takes the film in shocking directions. Fulci would overcome the structural defects in his subsequent horror films, which he tended to have a stronger hand in developing, but his work on this film is virtually impeccable. Despite some narrative hiccups, *Zombie* remains one of his most purely enjoyable pictures; it also remains his watershed achievement, the "moment" which helped to define him for a new generation of viewers.

The cast is headed by Scottish actor Ian McCulloch, who parlayed his success as the star of the U.K. TV series *Survivors* (1975-1977) into a brief foray into the world of Italian genre cinema. Born in Glasgow in 1939, he started appearing in films and TV in the late 1960s, notably appearing in the Richard Burton/Clint Eastwood WWII thriller *Where Eagles Dare* (1969). He played the juvenile lead in the Freddie Francis-directed horror film *The Ghoul* (1974), starring Peter Cushing, before landing the lead on *Survivors*. *Zombie* was the first of several Italian horror films he made in the late '70s and early '80s—and it is far and away the best. He would follow it up with Marino Girolami's *Zombie Holocaust* and Luigi Cozzi's *Contamination* (both 1980). McCulloch would display an ambivalent attitude towards his Italian genre films for years, but ultimately came down on the side of praising Fulci for his ability in making the most out of very little. In a commentary with journalist Jason Slater recorded for the Roan Group laser disc of *Zombie*, he recalled how the low budget did not extend to securing location-filming permits for the scenes shot in New York City. During his introductory scenes set in the offices of a New York newspaper office, for example—which allows him to share a scene with Fulci, playing the no-nonsense news editor who calls him a "limey"—the crew descended upon a boardroom and opened the door. As McCulloch recalls, a man with a fiery temper yelled out, "Who the *fuck* are you? Get the fuck out!!" and had the door closed in their faces. "I'm not entirely sure, but I think it was Rupert Murdoch," he mused. McCulloch brings a lot of charm to his rather flatly written character and is to be commended for not walking through the film with an air of disdain.

Tisa Farrow plays the role of Anne. The lesser-known sister of Mia Farrow, she was born in Los Angeles in 1951. She started appearing in films in 1970 and made memorable appearances in Alberto De Martino's *Blazing Magnums* (1976) and James Toback's *Fingers* (1978) prior to working with Fulci. Like McCulloch, she went on to do some more Italian genre cinema, notably Aristide Massaccesi's notorious *Anthropophagus* (1980), after which her career cooled-off. She has since left the business and is reluctant to talk about her film work, preferring to focus on the present instead of dwelling in the past. Farrow's performance is rather flat and listless and she has no real chemistry with McCulloch, unfortunately. Even so, she would later tell

Mike Baronas that she enjoyed her time working with Fulci on the film:

> He adored me and called me "Tisa, my Queen." He taught me many colorful Italian curses, a few of which I enjoy pulling out of my hat to this day. He perhaps was not so kind to Auretta Gay. He also was prone to ridiculous temper tantrums, which in turn made me giggle. He was a dreadful, extreme little man who I found quite amusing.

The real standout in the cast is the wonderful Richard Johnson, who gives a splendid performance as Dr. Menard. Johnson approaches his role seriously and provides the character with shading that far eclipses the sketchy characterization on the page; he also rewrote much of his own dialogue, which really benefits as a result. Johnson was born in Essex in 1927 and made his film debut in 1959. An accomplished stage actor with a background appearing in the classics, he proved to be ideally suited to film work and soon established himself as a handsome and charming leading man. He was reportedly considered for the role of James Bond and later played a Bond-inspired version of Bulldog Drummond in *Deadlier Than the Male* (1967) and *Some Girls Do* (1969). He also appeared alongside his friend Charlton Heston in such films as *Khartoum* (1965), *Julius Caesar* (1970) and *Treasure Island* (1989). Johnson attained immortality with horror buffs thanks to his appearance in Robert Wise's classic *The Haunting* (1963) and would also rack up quite a few genre appearances in films made in the U.K. and in Italy. In the latter category, he also appeared in the likes of Damiano Damiani's *The Witch* (1966), Massimo Dallamano's *The Night Child* (1974) and Sergio Martino's *Island of the Fish Men* (1978). Johnson also worked extensively in the dubbing industry and has also racked up some credits as a producer, including John Irvin's *Turtle Diary* (1985), starring Ben Kingsley, and Nicolas Roeg's *Castaway* (1986) with Oliver Reed. His more recent credits include the blockbuster *Lara Croft: Tomb Raider* (2001) and the critically acclaimed holocaust drama *The Boy in the Striped Pajamas* (2008). His performance is crucial to *Zombie*'s effectiveness: He plays the role without a hint of parody and helps to convince the viewer that the situation is to be taken very seriously. It is only a pity that he never worked again with Fulci, as the two men reportedly got along very well and appreciated each other for their professionalism. Richard Johnson passed away at the age of 87 on June 5, 2015.

The supporting cast includes the first appearance by Al Cliver in one of Fulci's films. Born Pierluigi Conti in Alexandria, Egypt in 1951, he changed his name to Al Cliver at the behest of his agent. He made a brief, uncredited appearance as a Nazi in Luchino Visconti's scandalous *The Damned* (1969) and became a more prominent face in *poliziotteschi* like Fernando Di Leo's *Rulers of the City* (1976). *Zombie* made him into a popular cult figure among genre fans and he would go on to appear in such Fulci films as *The Black Cat, The Beyond, Rome, 2072 A.D.: The New Gladiators, Murder-Rock: Dancing Death, Touch of Death, The Ghosts of Sodom, The House of Clocks* and *Demonia.* He gives a solid performance as the doomed Brian; it isn't a terribly well developed character, but Cliver's natural charisma shines through anyway. Olga Karlatos also impresses with her brief but iconic appearance as Mrs. Menard. Karlatos plays well off of Johnson in their big dramatic scene together and certainly rises to the challenge during her big set piece scene with the zombie and the splinter of wood. Karlatos conveys the character's growing sense of terror very nicely and her expressive features suit the material well. She would go on to play a much larger role in *Murder-Rock: Dancing Death.*

**Mrs. Menard (Olga Karlatos) is about to have her infamous meeting with a nasty splinter.**

The technical crew is at the top of their game, as well. Fulci's harmonious working relationship with Sergio Salvati made him the director's go-to cinematographer for the next few years. The two work in tandem to create some magnificent images, often finding a vein of visual poetry in even the most horrific of imagery. Fabio Frizzi's music score is catchy and infectious while perfectly underlining the film's grim subject matter.[5] Vincenzo Tomassi's crisp editing confirmed that he would be an ideal "replacement" for Ornella Micheli in Fulci's stable of valued collaborators. And the special make-up effects by Giannetto De

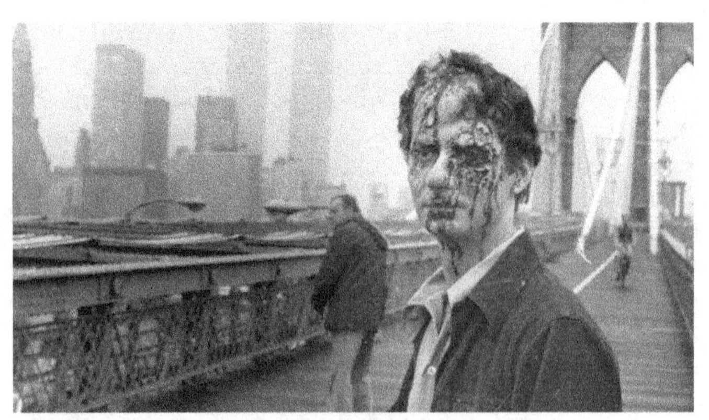

**Lucio Fulci (in the background) gets ready to film the march of the living dead in New York City.**

Rossi and Rosario Prestopino are absolutely amazing, especially when considering the low budget and inadequate resources. Ignoring the pasty-faced ghouls of Romero's films, De Rossi and Prestopino emphasize their deterioration by showing varying levels of rot and decay. The film's iconic "worm-face zombie," so prominently utilized in the film's ad campaign, is representative of their approach: Barely recognizable as human, it is a visage straight out of a nightmare. He would later explain that, as he felt the film was imitative of *Dawn of the Dead*, he decided to go for something different, "[R]ealizing that our film was going to be a low budget imitation, I decided to try and give the special effects a touch of originality [...]"[6] De Rossi would continue to work with Fulci on many of his subsequent "living dead" films, but arguably he would never top the impact of his work on this picture.

*Zombie* became the source of considerable controversy when it was released from 1979 into 1980. In the U.K., skittish censors subjected the film to numerous cuts. When the home video boom of the early 1980s took off, it became one of the infamous "Video Nasties." Readers interested in learning the full, convoluted back story of the "Video Nasty" debate and the films affected by it are encouraged to check out Jake West's exhaustive and definitive documentary *Video Nasties: The Definitive Guide* (2010) and its follow-up *Video Nasties: The Definitive Guide, Part 2* (2014). To recap the basics, however, here is a rundown of some salient points made in the documentaries: the whole sorry mess got underway thanks to staunchly conservative moral crusader Mary Whitehouse, who campaigned relentlessly against the availability of violent and sexually explicit videos on the grounds that they could warp impressionable minds. In 1982, Vipco Video, a U.K.-based outfit, brought a lot of heat on itself by taking out lurid, full-page ads for their release of Abel Ferrara's controversial *Driller Killer* (1979) on VHS. A short time later, another video outfit, Go Video, inflicted even further self-injury by bringing Mary Whitehouse's attention to their release of Ruggero Deodato's *Cannibal Holocaust* (1980); they had hoped that the ensuing controversy would help sell copies, but instead it led to a crackdown on the sale of films deemed unfit by the British Board of Film Censors (BBFC). James Ferman, director of the BBFC from 1975-1999, decided to back Whitehouse, bowed to pressure from various special interest groups and devised the *Video Recordings Act 1984*, which decreed that all films for sale on cassette must be approved by the BBFC; films released without this classification would be impounded as obscene, and people who broke the law could face stiff financial penalties or even jail time. *Zombie* had secured an official "X" certificate for distribution in British theaters under the name *Zombie Flesh Eaters*, but nearly two minutes of gory thrills were removed in the bargain. When Vipco decided to play slick and release it on video in its fully uncut form, the film found itself on the list of "Video Nasty" targets. As censorship began to soften a bit, the film was ultimately released on video in the U.K. in 1992—but this, too, was the version passed for exhibition by the BBFC. The film was eventually removed from the official "Nasties" list sometime in 2005, at which point it cropped up on video in its intended form. Ultimately, the *Video Recordings Act 1984* was repealed and replaced by the comparatively liberal *Video Recordings Act 2010*. *Zombie* was the first of Fulci's films to encounter this kind of difficulty in the U.K., but it would not be the last: *The Beyond* and *The House by the Cemetery* would also land on the list, after having been cut for theatrical exhibition, while *The New York Ripper* found itself banned in *any* form for many years. Absurd as the furor over these so-called morally indecent films may have been, it seems likely that the moral finger-painting helped make the films more desirable among thrill-hungry genre buffs. Elsewhere, the film was subjected to varying cuts, but it played uncut in

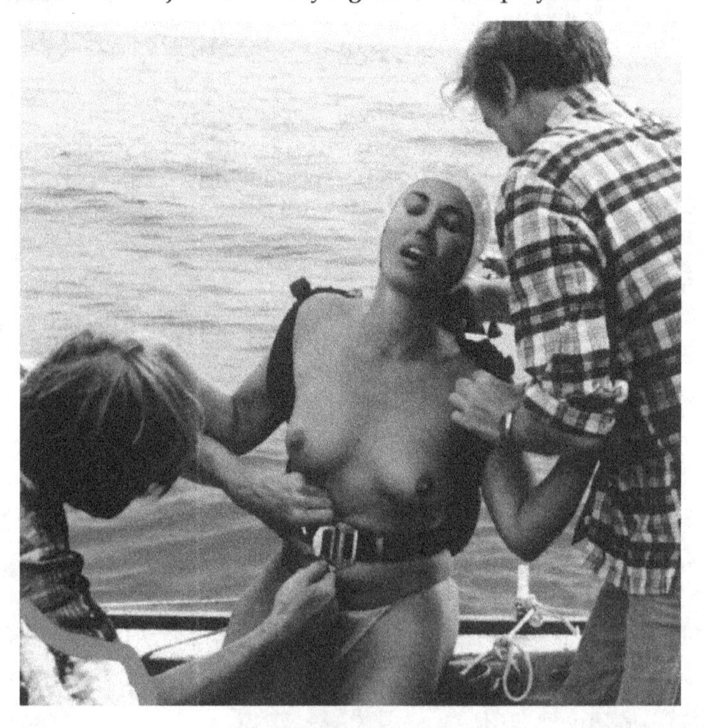

**Auretta Gay provides *Zombie* with a little exploitative nudity.**

the United States, where the Jerry Gross Organization launched an aggressive ad campaign (with the irresistible tag line: "We Are Going To Eat You!") and reaped plenty of profits.

Fulci did not benefit financially from the film's success, but it did announce him as "the new kid on the block" in the genre of Italian horror. Of course, the fact that he had already been in the business for over 30 years did not register with many genre fans, most of whom were unaware of his previous credits. With Mario Bava more or less in retirement mode (he would die in 1980) and Dario Argento straddling the line between horror (*Suspiria*, 1977) and thrillers (*Deep Red*, 1975), Fulci would offer stiff competition as the new King of Italian Horror. It was a source of competition that Argento did not welcome, but even so it provided Fulci with a steady stream of employment following a fallow period. From this point on, whether he liked it or not (and it seems he was generally quite content with it, truth be told), he would be known as The Godfather of Gore for an adoring fanbase; to the unconvinced, however, he would be damned as an imitative hack and a pornographer of violence. His next picture would see him bringing this flair for violence to a different genre.

Notes:

1. Interview with Dardano Sacchetti included in the Arrow Video Blu-ray release of *Zombie Flesh Eaters*.
2. Palmerini, Luca M. and Gaetano Mistretta, *Spaghetti Nightmares* (Florida: Fantasma Books, 1996), p. 59.
3. Curci, Loris, *Shock Masters of the Cinema*, (Florida: Fantasma Books, 1996), pp. 69-70.
4. All references to the screenplay are derived from a copy of the English-language translation of the script, prepared by Chuck Smith; the script, titled *Nightmare Island (Island of the Living Dead)* is copyrighted 1978 and was donated to journalist Jason Slater by Nick Alexander, who directed the English-language track of the film. My thanks to Jason for donating this for me to read.
5. There has been some confusion over the soundtrack for this film. The titles credit Frizzi and Giorgio Tucci with composing the score, but according to Frizzi, this is not so. In an interview with Lionel Grenier, http://www.luciofulci.fr/interviews/interview-exclusive-avec-fabio-frizzi, Frizzi is quoted as saying: "Actually, it was not Giorgio Tucci but Giorgio Cascio. We said Tucci because he was Ugo Tucci's nephew, one of the producers. When Lucio called me, I had just broken up with Bixio and Tempera. So they wanted us to form a duo. Giorgio was a nice fellow who worked for Alitalia; he didn't have much experience in soundtrack music. Our "duet" didn't continue and we lost sight of each other. As for the division of roles, let's say that I was the one who drove the car."
6. Palmerini, Luca M. and Gaetano Mistretta, *Spaghetti Nightmares* (Florida: Fantasma Books, 1996), p. 119.

# Richard Johnson interview by Troy Howarth

The following interview with actor Richard Johnson was conducted via email on September 5, 2014. Mr. Johnson's lengthy and distinguished film career is recounted in detail in the preceding pages. Suffice it to say, his participation in *Zombie* helped lend the film some much-needed gravitas. I am extremely grateful to Mr. Johnson for taking the time to answer these questions.

**Troy Howarth**: How did you come to be cast in *Zombie*?
**Richard Johnson**: I think Franz de Blasi, my Italian agent, put me up for it.
**TH**: What were your initial impressions of the script? Did you tinker with your dialogue at all? It sounds much more natural than some of the other lines, I have to say.
**RJ**: People who didn't speak English very well translated all Italian low-budget scripts—they couldn't afford a proper writer. So, I always rewrote my own dialogue. I wrote the doctor's explanation of "The Science of Zombie Phenomena" myself, on set, for example … and had a lot of fun doing it! But I didn't like to tinker with my fellow actors' parts.
**TH**: What was Lucio Fulci like to work with?
**RJ**: *A blast!* Passionate, committed, knew what he wanted and went a bit crazy when he didn't get it.
**TH**: Do you have any particularly favorite memories of the shoot?
**RJ**: The producers hired a model to play the part of the lady who got eaten by the shark (*Author's Note*: Mr. Johnson is alluding to Auretta Gay, who comes close to being devoured, but survives): She had certain attributes they thought were important commercially, I think. She was a nice girl, but I think it's fair to say that acting wasn't one of her strongest suits. Lucio struggled to get emotion out of her. One day he became so exasperated that he flung himself on the ground and started eating the turf. Eventually regaining his composure, he apologized and, by way of explanation, added: "If I don' eat-a the grass, I eat-a you."
**TH**: When did you first see the film? And what did you think of the ensuing controversy it "enjoyed" in the U.K.?
**RJ**: I saw some of it in the dubbing theater, of course, but I didn't see the whole thing until years later. It was banned in Britain as a "video nasty," presumably on the grounds that the population would start digging up graves to check that the bodies were still in them, and not roaming the streets chewing on their fellow citizens. *Absurd!* But I was proud to be in a banned horror film, of course. The authorities must have been really frightened by it, at least ...
**TH**: You worked on a number of other Italian genre productions. How did you think Fulci compared to Damiano Damiani or Sergio Martino or Massimo Dallamano, for example?

**Dr. Menard falls victim to the zombies.**

**RJ**: I absolutely loved working in Italy. Italians adore moviemaking! The enthusiasm and emotion among *"la famiglia,"* as the crew consider themselves, is electric. Completely different from the class system that often permeates British and American films, where the actors are segregated. We're usually housed in different hotels on location from the crew, often hardly getting to speak to many of them. In Italy, the actors eat with the crew, stay in the same places and become part of their family. I got on well with all the directors I worked with in Italy—I think they appreciated whatever help I could give with making their films acceptable to a wider audience.

**TH**: Are you surprised by the popularity the film continues to enjoy?

**RJ**: Frankly, I'm astonished! It is a tribute to Lucio, of course, that this film and others in his oeuvre remain highly popular around the world. I guess it is his passion and commitment shining through them.

**TH**: Did you ever feel at all embarrassed doing these low-budget films, considering some of the more high-profile projects you were involved in?

**RJ**: No. I love to act—it's what I do. You are required to act just as well in a low-budget film as a Hollywood epic. Possibly more so, because the work relies more on the performers than the special effects ...

**TH**: Your best-known horror films are *The Haunting* (1963) and *Zombie*—two very different approaches: one very subtle, one very in your face. Do you have a preference between the two styles?

**RJ**: No.

**TH**: And finally, do you have a favorite film or role of all the films you have made?

**RJ**: No. All were such a pleasure to make. I have the best job in the world.

**TH**: Mr. Johnson—thanks again for your time!

**RJ**: Good luck with your book!

# Al Cliver Interview by Troy Howarth

The following interview with Al Cliver was conducted via email on October 6, 2014. Al began working with Fulci on *Zombie* and he would come back to appear in a number of films, including some made at the very end of the director's career. Al has also recently completed his memoirs, which will hopefully be published in English in the very near future. He has my thanks for taking the time to share some of his memories of working with Lucio Fulci.

**Troy Howarth**: You've been appearing in films since the late 1960s. How did you come to change your name from Pierluigi Conti to Al Cliver?

**Al Cliver**: At that time they produced many Spaghetti Westerns. For more international audiences, each actor adopted an American or English name. I came along after that period, but I was still obliged to use a "Western" name.

**TH**: You first worked with Lucio Fulci in 1979 on the film *Zombie*. How did you come to be cast in that picture?

**AC**: I was with the William Morris agency, but I am not sure if Lucio was one of their clients. However, the offer came to me through William Morris.

**TH**: Were you familiar with Fulci's work prior to making this film?

**AC**: Sure! Even though he was not internationally famous yet, I knew of his work; quite rightly, he became more famous after *Zombie*.

**TH**: What were your initial impressions of Fulci as a director and a person?

**AC**: For this answer, it is best that I quote from my newly written memoirs: Fulci was ugly, he used to get dirty at every opportunity like a child with *Nutella* (Note: a popular Italian hazelnut cream); he was ironic, brilliant, sadistic with women, a single parent, naïve, exasperating, difficult; he had the need to blow off steam, to give nicknames and laugh at everyone—only a few among the producers, colleagues and actors escaped his jokes and his biting nicknames, and throughout the shooting he was like a constantly boiling pot, an uninterrupted muttering bout of thoughts. He immediately called me "Tufus," because, whereas Michelangelo was given Carrara marble to sculpt his masterpieces, Fulci had been given a piece of tuff from the outskirts of Rome to be shaped like an actor. (Note: Tuff is a cheap material often used in Italy; it is considerably cheaper to afford than marble.)

**TH**: Fulci had the reputation of being very tough and short-tempered on set; did he ever lose his temper with you?

**AC**: Here again, I will quote from my memoirs: In Santa Domingo we hired an offshore powerboat. Our location was a village in the middle of nowhere, made up of 10 or so straw huts. The pride of the village was a bridge made of twisted, worn branches. Docking the boat there wasn't easy, as the ropes twisted round the propeller, and we had to wait for a team of divers to untangle them. While we waited, Fulci would sit on his director's chair smoking, or chewing on his pipe, and watch the goings-on. Then suddenly, he would get impatient, or get hit by sudden inspiration, and shout out: "Where's Tufus?" This wasn't aimed at anyone in particular, as everyone present could hear him, after all.

"He's underwater. One of the ropes got twisted and he's helping to untie it."

"What's Tufus doing?!" he screamed, nonplussed.

Again, the reply: "He's holding the boat still underwater."

"Shit, we've got a crew of 30 people and we have to send down the leading man?! Get him back! Hoist him up with a winch if you have to. We're here to film, not conduct underwater explorations."

At that moment I emerged.

"Where the fuck were you? There are 30 people waiting to get on with their work here, and you're off scuba diving!"

"Lucio, the boat was going adrift, so I went to have a look. I was just following my seafaring spirit," I smiled.

"Your *what*? Seafaring spirit?!" He addressed the crew sarcastically: "Did you hear that?! His *seafaring* spirit! Don't make me laugh, you don't even know what a buoy looks like."

"Lucio, what d'you mean? I even had a Piver Trimaran (Note: State-of-the-art sailboats based on the designs of amateur sailor Arthur Piver) that was 7.5 meters (Note: Approximately 25 feet) long."

"Really?" he asked dubiously. "So where did you keep it?"

"At Fiumara."

"I've had some boats moored there too ... okay ... now, come up to the captain's deck and don't move from there."

We finally managed to moor the stern, with me watching from the wheelhouse. The cameras were positioned on the pier in order to film me from below. The cameraman, his assistant and another of the crew were also down on the pier. Then there was the script supervisor sitting in her chair, and Lucio in his chair, which had two legs resting on terra firma and two on the pier.

"Stand with your back to us and make out you're turning a key. Your hand will be out of shot, so no one will know. Then take a step back, turn towards us and say your line."

"Where am I looking?"

"Down here, on a level with the camera."

A crewmember slaps the clapperboard; clap!

"And ... Action!"

I smile: "We should be in sight of the coast in about ..."

"*Stop!* What the hell are you smiling about?! You're supposed to be worried. You're sailing towards a mysterious island. There are zombies on it! You think that's funny?!"

"I want to come across as a nice guy."

"Fuck you, Tufus! Concentrate, goddammit! Ready?"

"Yeah. "

I went to the Captain's deck.

Crewmember with clapboard: "Scene 3, take 2." Clap!

"And ... Action!"

I opened my eyes, inserted the key in the dashboard, turned it, stepped back and looked towards the pier, as a *nightmare* unfolded before me. Twin hundred-horsepower engines fired up all at once, as I had forgotten that the gear shift was in 3rd – *instead* of neutral, thus the engines kicked into life and the boat surged with tremendous force, tearing the mooring lines and wooden pier stilts right out of the ground.

**German lobby card: Anne (Tisa Farrow), Peter (Ian McCulloch) and Brian (Al Cliver) prepare to embark on their journey.**

Instant chaos: The cameraman grabbed the camera and held it above his head as if it were his own child, while he tried his best to stay with his head above the water. The camera assistant, loyal to the end, tried to hold their equipment in the air, although by that point they

**Brian and Anne attend to the injured Peter.**

were pretty much submerged. Powerful arms had lifted the *Maestro* out of the water when he was on his way down, but the Script Supervisor had been submerged by the giant waves created by the motor. Our *Maestro* sat there dauntless, with his pipe gone out and his glasses halfway down his nose, waiting for whoever had saved him to take him to shore. Everyone else was retrieved from the sea.

We managed to moor the boat again, in the place where the village-landing pier had once stood, and I got off, completely mortified.

"Um … sorry, I uh … I forgot to put it in neutral."

A chorus of "*Fuck you, Tufus!*" arose from the crew. However, after that, no one said anything further about it. The shoot resumed as normal. These unexpected things happened almost daily.

That was the kind of relationship that we had. Lucio could say whatever he liked about me, but if anyone tried to attack me, he defended me like a lion. On the other hand, I understood how our relationship worked, and was always ready with some joke or trick to play on him that would cause him to despair. We were like a pair of comic actors; I was his sidekick.

**TH**: What do you remember of your costars on the film, including Richard Johnson and Ian McCulloch?

**AC**: I have to say that we became a lot more friendly 30 years later, when we met each other at a few conventions for the anniversary of *Zombie*. Then we were finally able to share our feelings and memories that we had of that time … For example, we discovered that Richard Johnson and I had been sharing the same girlfriend during the making of the film!

**TH**: And what about Tisa Farrow?

**AC**: Tisa was the most anti-diva-like actress I have ever met in my film career. During the many long breaks during filming, she sat facing East under the scorching sun, protecting herself with a handkerchief or a polystyrene panel that someone would offer to her. She ate with the crew, her boyfriend was an electrician, and she never complained about or demanded anything.

**TH**: Were you surprised by the film's popularity?

**AC**: The film was an old project that for one reason or another never saw the light of day. After a certain point, they hired Fulci to direct it. Fulci thought he was just making another film. None of us could ever have imagined the success that it achieved.

**TH**: You went on to work with Fulci on *The Black Cat* and *The Beyond* in 1981. Did Fulci specifically request you for those roles?

**AC**: After *Zombie* I became a kind of lucky charm for Fulci. He tried to put me in all of his films.

**TH**: Your next film for Fulci was *Rome, 2072 A.D.: The New Gladiators*, an action/science fiction movie … was the experience of doing a film with so much action different than making the horror films?

**AC**: In my opinion *Zombie* had lots of action … so I don't think there was much difference.

**TH**: You also played rather small, uncredited roles in Fulci's *Murder Rock* and *Ghosts of Sodom* … do you remember much about making those films?

**AC**: Yes … what I remember is that when I saw Fulci again, he seemed older … aged. And the films were super-low-budget.

**TH**: Did you get to know Fulci personally during all these films, or was your relationship strictly professional?

**AC**: It depends on how you define "personally." For a few years, we lived on the same street, one in front of the other. It sometimes happened that we would run into each other at the coffee shop and I would say hello. He would either completely ignore me, or he would start to speak for a long time about his sailboat. He had two contradictory personalities.

**TH**: Do you have a favorite of the films you made with Fulci?

**AC**: Sure: *Zombie*. I had a lot of fun during the shoot.

**TH**: And lastly, are you surprised by the enduring popularity of Fulci and his movies?

**AC**: I remember once when he was old and sick he told me, you cannot imagine how well known I am in other countries. He had just returned from a convention in England. And he was sincerely surprised. If he was surprised, just imagine how I feel!

**TH**: Thank you for your time.

**AC**: You're welcome.

# 1980

## *Un uomo da ridere (Italy)*

Aka *Make 'Em Laugh* (unofficial English-language translation)

Directed by Lucio Fulci; Produced by Fabrizio Centamori, for RAI Radiotelevisione Italiana; Scripted by Lucio Fulci and Giorgio Mariuzzo; Director of Photography: Salvator Occhipinti and Massimo Sallusti; Editor: Maria Di Mauro; Music by Marcello De Martino; Song: *Un uomo da ridere*, performed by Franco Franchi

Main Players: Franco Franchi (Bianco Bianchi); Dino Valdi (Totò); Carlo Croccolo (Totò's voice); Gloria Paul (Annarita); Silvio Spaccesi (Adamo Amleti); Maurizia Camilli (Nora Noris); Mario Merola (Himself); Antonio Sabato (Himself); Duccio Tessari (Himself)

Cameo appearance: Lucio Fulci (Usher)

*The great comedian Totò narrates the story of Bianco Bianchi from heaven: Bianco is a former superstar of vaudeville who has since fallen on hard times, owing to the changing audience tastes in comedy. Bianco undergoes many humiliations as he attempts to launch a comeback ...*

***Un uomo da ridere*; original artwork by Scott Hoffman.**

## Un uomo da ridere: comedy, television and the critics ... Fulci-style
## A Guest Review by Roberto Curti

[Note: Given that *Un uomo da ridere* has never been made available in English and exists only in un-subtitled versions, it made sense to entrust its critique to a native Italian who could better appreciate its subtleties as well as its complex network of reference points.]

Broadcast on RAI 2, Italy's second public television channel, starting from March 30, 1980, the six-part miniseries *Un uomo da ridere* was in many ways a pivotal moment in Fulci's career. For one thing, it marked the end of his working experience for the small screen, which had started in 1978, out of necessity: After the work-for-hire Western *Silver Saddle*, Fulci was finding it difficult to make another film, and had to turn his head towards cinema's main competitor.

He was not the only one who contemplated such a move. In late 1970s the constant decrease in grossing figures had made it evident that Italian cinema was heading headfirst towards an unprecedented crisis, which coincided with the irresistible rise of local broadcasting channels, legitimated in 1976 by a sentence of the Constitutional Court, thus breaking the monopoly of RAI-TV.[1] Audiences soon lost interest in going to the movies (especially since the rise of crime and violence prevented many from going out in the evening in big cities) and savored the newfound possibilities in owning a remote-controlled TV set.

Fulci's partner in this venture on the small screen was Franco Franchi. The director had been trying to mount another project starring Franchi and Ingrassia, in the vein of their 1960s spoofs: *I due figli di King Kong* (*The Two Sons of King Kong*) was conceived as a hit-and-run parody of John Guillermin's *King Kong* (1976), but the time for such ventures had long gone, and the prospect of having Franco and Ciccio beg for laughter in such an unlikely comeback was distressing. However, the project was shelved for good, but Fulci and Franchi considered the idea of a more fruitful collaboration. Broadcast from November 1, 1977 to June 1982, the show *Buonasera con ...* had proven a successful formula. Each month it was hosted by a different personality—actors, singers, comedians, even the illusionist Silvan—and consisted of two parts: In the first one, the show host went through his own routine, with sketches, songs, etc., while the second featured either a TV series or cartoons, aimed primarily at kids.

For the occasion, Fulci teamed up with Giorgio Mariuzzo, an assistant director-turned-scriptwriter who had been his assistant director in a 1960 TV commercial. Working at a frantic pace, with Mariuzzo writing sketch after sketch and the director shooting in a nearby Milan TV studio, the show was ready for a spring broadcasting: *Buonasera con ...* debuted on May 16 and went on until

**A candid shot of Fulci (back right) dining with Franco Franchi (back left) and company during the filming of *Un uomo da ridere.***

June 16, 1978, in the 6:45 p.m. slot, paired with Go Nagai's anime TV series *UFO Robot Grendizer* (known in Italy as *Goldrake*). It proved a great showcase for the Sicilian comedian, whose career had gone downhill since the mid-1970s, after the split with Ciccio Ingrassia and the commercial failure of his most recent pictures, such as *Il sogno di Zorro* (1975) and the *Death Wish* spoof *Il giustiziere di mezzogiorno* (1975).

The experience of collaborating on *Buonasera con ... Franco Franchi* was so satisfying that Fulci and Mariuzzo started working on another much more ambitious project centered on the Sicilian actor, *Risate a crepapelle*, which eventually became *Un uomo da ridere*. Fulci and Mariuzzo—with the uncredited contribution of Marcello Marchesi (1912-1978), an eclectic figure of comedian-scriptwriter-songwriter-director whose work indelibly marked Italian showbiz in the postWWII years—concocted an ambitious scenario in the vein of the great examples of the *commedia all'italiana*, by using a peripheral figure as a prism through which to tell the story of the country and its changes in society and morals throughout the years; a bit like Dino Risi had done with Alberto Sordi in *A Difficult Life* (*Una vita difficile*, 1961) and Ettore Scola with Nino Manfredi and Vittorio Gassman in *We All Loved Each Other So Much* (*C'eravamo tanto amati*, 1974). This time, though, a more specific scenario was envisioned, one that took full advantage of Franchi's own screen persona and career and delved deep into the world of Italian show business, tracing its evolution and decline over the years and up to the present, through the story of Bianco Bianchi, a smalltime comedian who becomes a movie star, modeled—as the name gives away—upon Franchi himself.

It was a bold move, given television's tight budgets, limited technical means and thematic demands. As was customary in the period, Fulci shot *Un uomo da ridere* partly on film (for the exterior scenes) and mostly on tape. Even though he experimented with blue-back and electronics, the result was a bit rough around the edges. What is more, the main storyline was interspersed with musical interludes, in the spirit of Italian vaudeville that it evoked, most of them featuring the female lead, dancer-and-singer Gloria Paul. Overlong and sometimes annoying, these numbers—usually inserted into the narrative as Bianco's daydreams—come off as *Un uomo da ridere*'s least interesting part by far, paying tribute less to vaudeville than to the typical format of TV shows of the period, which featured lots of such interludes ... even a surreal fantasy ballet which somehow recalls the final number in Bob Fosse's contemporaneous *All That Jazz* (1979) will make the director's fans raise their eyebrows, as the set piece is dominated by a gigantic eye, to and from which the camera zooms with wild abandon, as well as huge props in the shape of Rolling Stones-like lips.

Even though it was born as a barely-fictionalized rendition of Franchi's own story, *Un uomo da ridere* has a lot of Fulci in it, starting with the choice of its tutelary deity. The whole narration is punctuated by the presence of the late Prince Antonio De Curtis, that is Totò, who comments on the proceedings from atop a cloud—an image made even more striking by the casting of Totò's own stand-in Dino Valdi, who had often replaced the elderly comedian in later films whenever the shooting proved to be too demanding for Totò's health conditions, and who makes an almost perfect replica of Totò's trademark gestures and body tics.[2] What is more, Totò's voice is provided by Carlo Croccolo (who also plays a key role in the show), who used to dub the comedian in most of his later films, given that Totò's very bad eyesight (since the late 1950s an illness left him almost completely blind) did not allow him to do his own dubbing during post-production.

In the opening scenes Totò makes it clear that, through Bianco Bianchi, *Un uomo da ridere* is going to narrate "the story of a cinema perhaps unjustly labeled as 'minor'," and, along its six installments, Fulci paints an ambitious portrait of Italian postwar popular cinema as seen through the eyes of an insider. It all starts in 1953, at the Teatro Jovinelli, one of the key places in the history of Italian *avanspettacolo* (vaudeville). Inaugurated in 1909, it was the stage on which Italy's most famous comedians took their first steps, from Ettore Petrolini (who was given his first important break in 1910 by the theater's impresario Giuseppe Jovinelli) to Totò, who debuted there in 1919 and immediately became a favorite amid the audience. Fulci charts its transformation into a movie theater, where the screenings were interspersed with live sketches and musical numbers. Soon a TV set would be placed onstage for the audience to follow *Lascia o raddoppia?*, the immensely popular quiz show hosted by Mike Bongiorno since late 1955, which brought a vital contribution to the medium's popularity.

Fulci's intent goes so far as to including excerpts from several of Totò's best films, such as *Il medico dei pazzi* (1953) and the celebrated spaghetti-eating scene in *Miseria e nobiltà* (1955), as well as a scene from a tearjerking drama with Amedeo Nazzari and the iconic Trevi Fountain scene of Fellini's *La Dolce Vita* (1960), plus a myriad of cinephile references, from *Samson and Delilah* to *Rio Bravo*. Then there are the film-within-a-film scenes from Bianco Bianchi's own movies, most of them alluding to Franchi's own works, whose titles are often just slightly retouched.[3] Here, Fulci manages to recreate a small story of Italian genres, from *peplum* to Spaghetti Western, from spy flicks to Decamerotics—going for laughter but in the process analyzing the process of filmmaking, the mechanisms of comedy and, most of all, giving the audience a priceless behind-the-scenes view.

Many of the episodes are based on real-life anecdotes: Fulci drew on many of Cinecittà's oft-told stories as well as his own memories that he had recently freshened-up when interviewed, together with dozens of other insiders, by Franca Faldini and Goffredo Fofi for their mammoth oral history of Italian cinema, *L'avventurosa storia del cinema italiano raccontata dai suoi protagonisti*, whose first volumes were published in 1979 and 1981. Several of the most amusing bits feature Carlo Croccolo as the hack film director Tony Boccea, a transparent dead ringer for the notorious Tanio Boccia (alias Amerigo Anton, 1912-1982), a mediocre genre filmmaker who would go from sword-and-sandal epics to Westerns without batting an eyelid, and who was known for his habit of nonchalantly improvising under the direst budgetary circumstances in order to get the film done, no matter what. Boccia's reputation in Cinecittà was nothing short of legendary, even if not in the way the term is usually employed: "He was a negative myth at Cinecittà, where they used to say, 'Worse than that, there is only Tanio Boccia.'"[4] A well-known anecdote has it that, immediately after winning his fourth Academy Award for *Amarcord* (1973), Federico Fellini received a prank phone call from Alberto Sordi, who yelled at him: "Federico, they didn't give you the award, they gave it to Tanio Boccia!"[5] Croccolo is even given one notorious line attributed to Boccia: During lunch break, when the crew members are given their lunch baskets, he claims: "Two for me—I'm the director!"

As a celebration of the underbelly of the Italian showbiz, *Un uomo da ridere* features a parade of character actors and extras whose faces popped-up regularly throughout the years, from Memmo Carotenuto to Pietro Torrisi (as a bodybuilder doing exercises on the beach who is cast as Hercules in a peplum), from the skinny Fernando Cerulli to the flamboyant Giò Stajano (in one of his usual "queer" roles), from Silvio Spaccesi (as Bianco's greedy scoundrel of an agent) to actor/dancer Paolo Gozlino. Other cast members play themselves, like Enzo Andronico, a former member of the "Trio Sgambetta" (which also featured Ciccio Ingrassia) and a recurring presence in many Franco & Ciccio films. Mario Merola is the most important guest star of the show: he first shows up in the second episode, sweating under a fur coat as he enters a bar where the penniless Bianco is hopelessly trying to find someone who will treat him to breakfast. When his old friend Bianco asks him why he is keeping that heavy coat on even if he is dripping sweat, Merola shows that underneath he is wearing only his underwear, having sold all his possessions for food. Later on, in an amusing duet with Franchi, the two—hired for cheap by a shady impresario—are distracted by the smell of food coming from a nearby restaurant kitchen, thus ruining their stage act. Eventually, Fulci allows Merola to celebrate himself by recreating one of his favorite showpieces, *L'emigrante*, a bit from one of his most popular *sceneggiate*. Antonio Sabàto also shows up as himself, re-enacting with gusto his own beginnings as a faceless body double in Westerns ("I did 12 films, all with my back to the camera," he quips) before his sudden rise to fame after being chosen for John Frankenheimer's *Grand Prix* (1966), while Duccio Tessari pops up as a film director who is shooting an apparently very bad Western called *Due dollari d'argento* (*Two Silver Dollars*) starring a perpetually drunk Donald O'Brien.

However, Fulci and Mariuzzo build up their own chronology of events, stretching and mixing periods: A scene is set during a prize ceremony where awards are copiously given to either *La Dolce Vita* or *A Fistful of Dollars*, as if the two films were made in the same year, which was not actually the case. Instead of mere carelessness, the authors' choice is most likely caused in equal parts by the will to soften the pill a bit and give the story that bit of

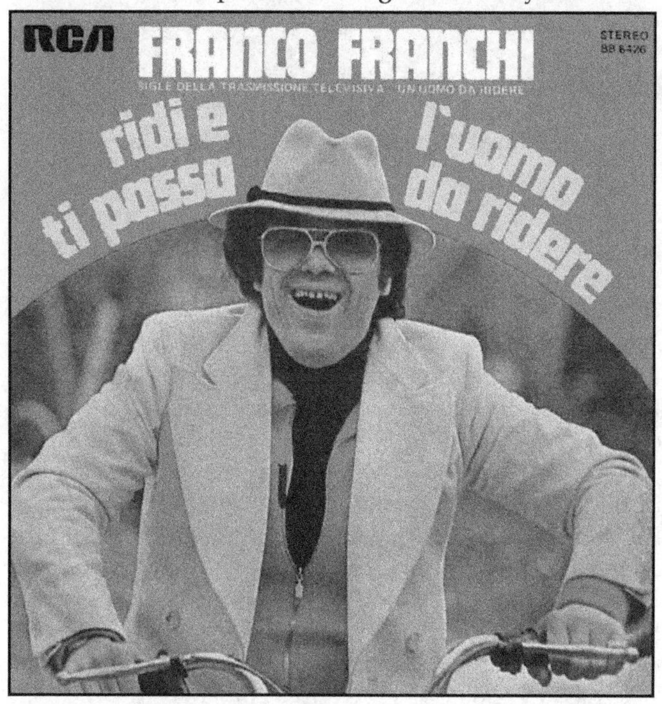


**Sleeve for the soundtrack 45 single of *Un uomo da ridere*, released by RCA.**

fairy tale-like quality that would hurt less all the people involved: After all, the events recalled were still fresh in many people's minds, and so were the scars.

Indeed, for all its humorous interludes, the core of the tale is profoundly bitter. Totò's comments, conveyed by the comedian's characteristic interludes and wordplays, are packed full of observations about the art of comedy and its importance within Italian postwar culture: "In all periods of crisis, either laughter or tears will do," he notices, pointing out the two ruling genres—comedy and melodrama—of Italian cinema in the 1950s. Equally frank is the view on the death of vaudeville and the dismantling of many stage companies in the late 1950s; in the following years, most actors would recycle themselves in the movies, whereas dancers would move on to striptease or prostitution, a bitter note that Fulci's film does not overlook.

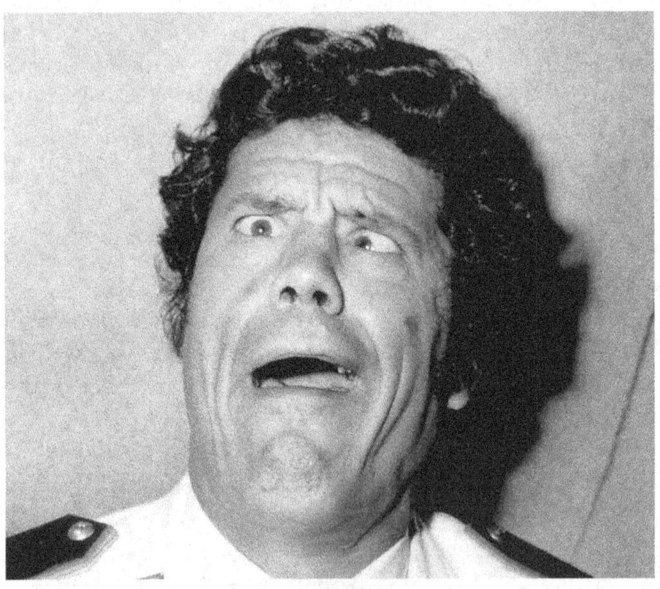

**Franco Franchi mugs for the camera.**

Franchi's portrayal, as self-satisfied as can be, hits just the right notes. When, near the end, Merola invites Bianchi on stage during a celebratory show and the two friends evoke their early days, Franchi's words sound sincere and heartfelt: "You know how much we fought in life to succeed. Every one of us, in life, tries to. Some are lucky; some are not. We were." But there are also a number of motifs that seem to belong to Fulci rather than to his star. Bianco's relationship with women is always troubled, as he is divided between the girl of his dreams, Annarita (played by the statuesque but insipid Gloria Paul) and the actress Renatina (Marina Marfoglia), who goes all the way from smalltime *striptiseuse* to sex starlet and eventually has an unwilling part in sinking Bianco's career when the comedian's simple, family-friendly films are being overwhelmed by the new wave of sex comedies in which she is starring. There is more than a hint of misogyny in here, and if Bianco goes through the usual routine of the unhappy clown who makes women laugh but cannot have them fall for him ("We comics are never handsome-looking"), one senses that the director was putting on the screen some of his own ghosts here.

What is more, the portrayal of Bianco Bianchi's rise to fame, even though somehow simplified (and deprived of the vital presence of Franchi's partner, Ciccio Ingrassia), is no less sweetened. On the contrary, Fulci and Mariuzzo make a few pointedly cynical remarks about the attitude and practices in Italian popular cinema of the period, from the liberal use of IOUs instead of real money on the part of producers to the willingness to improvise with small budgets, with results often bordering on the ridiculous. For instance, before shooting a massive battle scene between the Romans, the Greeks and the Macedonians for his sword-and-sandal epic, Boccea is told that the budget allows for only 12 extras. Not the least worried, he tells his assistant that he'll just have the extras change their costumes again and again after each shot, so as to make them look like they are three real armies. Later on, while Boccea is shooting a scene, the furniture on the set is taken away, since the production did not pay for its hire; an episode inspired by an incident that happened to Fulci during the filming of *I ladri*: Having to shoot on a completely empty set, Boccea simply opts for close-ups of the hero. Actors do not even have to learn their lines; the notorious habit of them saying numbers instead is well documented too.

Lack of originality is also mercilessly underlined: Like surfers riding a wave, producers and filmmakers jump on the bandwagon of the latest box-office hit, were it *A Fistful of Dollars* or a James Bond film, shamelessly churning out clone after clone. Similarly, once an actor becomes popular, he is squeezed like a lemon: In one scene, Bianco is seen shooting three films at once, jumping from one set to the next, becoming in turn a musketeer, a Tarzan-like hero and a kung fu practitioner (is this a nod to Nando Cicero's 1973 chopsocky spoof *Ku Fu Dalla Sicilia con furore*, one of Franchi's last box-office hits?). Franchi, Fulci and Mariuzzo are very candid about it; it is just a matter of money, as Bianco's empty house is seen filling up with furniture, film after film. And when he timidly tells his agent that he would like to make a committed film for once, he is laughed at, and given yet another simpleton comic role.

Equally candid is the author's view on the flood of naked female flesh on the screens, which characterized Italian cinema in the 1970s and practically sank old-style comedy. This changeover is first hinted at when Bianco sees a poster for his latest film being covered by another depicting a naked woman (Renatina). In the film's most revealing episode, Bianco is summoned for a meeting by his agent, who offers him a film (to be directed by the omnipresent Tony Boccea) called *Il Decamerotico comico* (*The Comic Decamerotic*)[6], a sex farce which demands him to abandon his usual audience for a stab at the adult market. ("She's lying naked, you jump on her and the coupling takes place," as each scene ends in Boccea's explanation of the film's story.) The anecdote hints at Franchi's refusal to star in erotic comedies, which marked a sudden decline in his career: The actor even regretted having starred in the amusing *Last Tango in Paris* spoof *Ultimo tango a Zagarol* (1973, Nando Cicero).

Somehow, despite *Un uomo da ridere*'s shortcomings, Fulci captures the dichotomy between *auteur* and genre cinema, which always characterized the industry. A biting example is the scene (shot at Villa Miani, one of the most recognizable settings in Italian cinema of the 1960s and 1970s) of the award ceremony, where Bianco and Antonio Sabàto are invited but given a table far from the main room where the personalities are gathered, and eventually Bianchi is even mistaken for a waiter by some of the staff. On the other hand, the director (who pops up as the Cinecittà usher who does not want to let Bianco Bianchi in; an in-joke about Fulci often not being recognized because of his shabby appearance) has several pebbles in his shoe to remove, the most conspicuous being embodied by Trentapenne (Armando Bandini), a film critic who epitomizes the director's contempt for the type, which was just as strong as Franchi's grudge towards them. "Now he must fight with a character in the shadows: the critic," Totò's narration comments. "His greatest pleasure is to find a nasty joke that serves him to slate. What's important to him is to criticize—otherwise, what kind of critic would he be?" The critic's essence is synthesized through this biting percentage: "70% is wanting to be a director, 20% is hatred towards successful movies, 9% is a love for boring yet austere films and 1% is critical intuition."

The unpleasant-looking, almost caricatured Trentapenne, with his round glasses, thin mustache and bowtie, reappears in the last episode, set in the present, during a talk show populated by critics coming up with abstruse, obscure, stiff-upper-lipped analyses about Italian comedy. Time for critical re-evaluation, indeed! Still, the director is patently disenchanted, even mocking towards this attitude: Trentapenne is openly portrayed as an opportunistic, empty subject whose "critical" opinions come out of sheer pose and sound as shallow and insignificant as can be. One cannot but remember Totò's own words on the subject matter: "My funeral will be very beautiful because there will be words, big words, and praise, and I'll be remembered as a great actor: because this is a beautiful country, where, however, you have to die to be recognized for something."

Eventually, though, Bianco savors his newfound notoriety and re-appreciation. When he objects that he belongs in the past, Trentapenne replies, "You will always make them laugh ... you are mass culture! Your work must be studied, analyzed, taken into universities" (which, incidentally, is what would happen with Franchi as well as others, including Fulci), yet he warns that cinema is no longer a place for him. A new means of fruition must be used—that is, television. Eventually, then, *Un uomo da ridere* ends with a reflection on the end of Italian popular cinema and the ultimate victory of the small screen. Bianco and his friends seem to be optimistic about it, but the critics definitely did not think the same way. Reviewers panned *Un uomo da ridere*. One, commenting on the broadcasting of the sixth and last installment, titled his piece *È finita la noia* ("The bore is over"), calling the mini-series "one of the most mediocre shows ever broadcast on Sunday primetime."[7] Never mind: Franchi's rediscovery was just starting to happen on the part of the younger generations of critics, which led him to act for the Taviani brothers in the Luigi Pirandello-inspired anthology *Kaos* (1984), together with Ciccio—with whom he finally reconciled during the broadcasting of *Un uomo da ridere*[8]—and Fulci's was about to come.

Fulci saves some of his mordant humor for his peers too. The ex-sexy starlette Renatina is now starring in a film based on Borges and directed by Jancsó ... where, nevertheless, what she has to do is take off her clothes ("Miklós is so demanding ... it is not one of the usual nude scenes, you know; it is an intimate, suffering nudity, seen from the inside ..." and Franco: "So you're not making a movie, but taking an X-ray"), and even the incompetent Tony Boccea finally receives praises on the part of the critics.[9] Fulci seems to imply that sooner or later everybody's going to meet a similar fate, whether he deserves it or not. Ultimately, he was long-sighted.

Even more, by showing the pathetic elderly filmmaker swaggering and pretending he had always been the *auteur* he is now being celebrated as, to the point of switching from genre to experimental films, Fulci proved to know his peers very well: Boccea's airs of self-importance would be often mimicked in real life by countless hacks who seized the opportunity of taking their own vengeance against years and years of derision and sufficiency by starting to behave as if they really were those masters the younger (and often blissfully ignorant) cinephiles believed them to be. The final song-and-dance number underlines the film's disenchanted moral: success, the lyrics say, is like "a cloud in April," and despite talent, luck is the necessary ingredient to fame.

If Fulci was then already waiting to be rediscovered, one wonders whether he was expecting that such a reevaluation would not be propelled by his work in comedy (21 films out of 59, a third of his output, which included the whole first decade of his career, starting with his first forays as a scriptwriter) but because of his resurrection as a horror film specialist—which incidentally happened just between the filming of *Un uomo da ridere* and its broadcasting, with *Zombie* another work-for-hire assignment which soon became much, much more.

In 1981, Italy's most renowned film critic Tullio Kezich penned a notoriously condescending review of *The Beyond* for the popular weekly magazine *Panorama*, which ended as follows:

> Nevertheless, one notes that amidst the banality of the contents and the gory bad taste, an effective

and even elegant film style manages to make room for itself. Credit goes to Lucio Fulci, an unknown soldier of popular cinema, active for more than 20 years with an output of over 40 titles: You can bet that Matarazzo's fans will soon rediscover him.[10]

That same year, another film critic, Claudio Carabba, saw *The Beyond* in an empty theater in Milan, at the midnight show, and by the end credits he was utterly amazed. Three years later he supervised a retrospective on the director for Cattolica's Mystfest, perhaps the first official step at recognizing Fulci as an *auteur* of sorts. The French had beaten Fulci's compatriots, however: By the time of the 1984 Mystfest retrospective the director had been interviewed *twice* by Robert Schlockoff on *L'Ecran fantastique*, in 1980 and 1982.

Soon, the new wave of critics would dig into the deepest recesses of Italian cinema and come out with rough diamonds, hidden jewels or just plain junk which nevertheless would be polished-up and exposed as if it were the eighth wonder of the world. Would it be a fair retribution for a man who often said he had ruined his life for the movies, to be championed the same way as all the Tony Bocceas around, or would it be the umpteenth bitter irony? Even though he savored this newfound popularity, in his later interviews Fulci was often openly sarcastic about his re-evaluation *in articulo mortis*, as he loved to underline, in a perhaps not unwilling reference to Totò's earlier quote about being critically rediscovered at one's own funeral: "Perhaps I am a zombie too," he quipped.[11] Having started out with comedies, he always knew when to tell a good joke.

**Franco Franchi in another comedy, *Stasera mi butto* (1967).**

Notes:
1. "1976 saw enormous amounts of money being invested in the broadcasting field, with the illusion that owning the hardware was enough to produce profit [...]. However, soon the other editorial entrepreneurs (Rusconi, Rizzoli, Mondadori) allowed the predatory Berlusconi to subject to his power the Wild West of Italian private broadcasting." (Angelo Zaccone Teodosi, "Ipotesi di riscatto per una provincia dell'impero audiovisivo," in Enrico Magrelli's (edited by), *Sull'industria cinematografica Italiana*, Venice: Marsilio 1986, p. 55). By taking advantage of the lack of laws on the subject, Finivest and other smaller companies bought as many films as they could from small distributors, often at ridiculously low prices, and started offering a wide array of movies throughout the day. Compared to RAI's more timid and serious palimpsests, they represented a succulent alternative, but they also opened a new world for average moviegoers, who used to go to the movies because of alluring titles and posters that promised excess and forbidden transgressions. Of course, those titles offering sex and violence were privileged; what's more, many local broadcasters offered stripteases and assorted erotic shows.
2. For instance, Valdi replaced the Neapolitan comedian during the shooting of Pier Paolo Pasolini's *The Hawks and the Sparrows* (*Uccellacci e uccellini*, 1966), in the scenes where Totò and Ninetto Davoli are seen walking or running in the fields in the distance.
3. Examples: *Il buono il cattivo il maleducato*, *Il sanculotto*, *Per un pugno sul naso*, *Il segno di Zozzo*, *L'evaso di notte*. There is even a Western named *Le colt cantarono ...*, which refers to Fulci's own *Massacre Time*.
4. Farassino, Alberto, "Tanio Boccia chi è e perché si parla di lui," *La Repubblica*, 11.20.1996.
5. Federico Fellini, Paquito Del Bosco, *Le favole di Fellini*, Rome: Rai ERI 2000, p. 85.
6. Mariuzzo was not new to the subject matter, having written 1972's *Decameroticus*, directed by Giuliano Biagetti under the alias Pier Giorgio Ferretti.
7. a.vald., "È finita la noia," *La Stampa*, 5.5.1980.
8. p.per, "Franchi e Ingrassia sono di nuovo insieme," *La Stampa*, 4.21.1980. The piece reports Franchi's claim to his partner, "Now, I don't know whether you've seen me on TV in *Un uomo da ridere*. I am a dramatic actor, not a moron."
9. Not unlike the real Boccia, who in the 1990s was championed by several Italian critics as "the Italian Ed Wood," after the notoriety attained in Italy by the director of *Plan 9 From Outer Space*, thanks to Tim Burton's film.
10. Kezich, Tullio, *Il nuovissimo millefilm. Cinque anni al cinema: 1977-1982*, (Milano: Mondadori, 1983), p. 148. The reference to the discovery of Raffaello Matarazzo, whose sensational melodramas were being championed by the younger generations of critics, was supposed to be mordant, but Matarazzo was indeed an excellent filmmaker. On the other hand, in an ill-advised attempt at showing himself to be up-to-date, Kezich had praised Umberto Lenzi's *Nightmare City* (1980); surely not one of Lenzi's best, and definitely not on a par with *The Beyond*, by a mile.
11. Romagnoli, Michele, *L'occhio del testimone*, (Bologna: Granata Press 1992), p. 26.

## *Contraband (Italy)*

Aka *Luca il contrabbandiere; The Smuggler; Das Syndikat des Grauens*

Directed by Lucio Fulci; Produced by Sandra Infascelli, for Primex Italiana c.m.r. Cinematografica; Screenplay by Ettore Sanzò, Gianni De Chiara, Lucio Fulci and Giorgio Mariuzzo, from a story by Ettore Sanzò and Gianni De Chiara; Director of Photography: Sergio Salvati; Editor: Vincenzo Tomassi; Music by Fabio Frizzi; Songs: *You Are Not the Same* and *New York Dash*, performed by Cricket

Main Players: Fabio Testi (Luca Ajello); Ivana Monti (Adele Ajello); Marcel Bozzuffi (Francois Jacquin, aka The Marsigliese); Saverio Marconi (Luigi Perlante); Guido Alberti (Don Morrone); Fabrizio Jovine (Chief of Police); Venantino Venantini (Captain Tarantino); Ajita Wilson (Luisa); Giordano Falzoni (Charlie, the doctor); Enrico Maisto (Michele Ajello); Ofelia Meyer (Ingrid); Luciano Rossi (Drug expert)

Cameo appearance: Lucio Fulci (Old boss with machine gun)

*Luca and his brother Michele run a successful smuggling operation out of the bay of Naples. Things take a grim turn when they realize that somebody is setting up conflict among the various outfits in the hopes of taking control of the entire operation. When Michele is murdered, Luca vows to find the culprit. Eventually it is revealed that the ambitious Luigi Perlante is in league with a Frenchman known as The Marsigliese, who is looking to establish a crime empire in Naples. Perlante and The Marsigliese have Luca's wife kidnapped and raped as a warning, but the stubborn Luca will not give up. It is up to the aged Don Morrone, a former crime boss, to reunite his old friends and try to restore order among the criminals …*

Following the completion of *Zombie*, Lucio Fulci found himself somewhat adrift for a period of time. He put Franco Franchi through his paces one final time on the mini-series *Un uomo da ridere* and found himself directing his first—and last—*poliziottesco*: *Contraband*. One would think that the success of *Zombie* would have catapulted Fulci to the forefront of Italian genre directors, but there was a lag between the film's completion and its worldwide box-office triumph. Screenwriter Dardano Sacchetti would later complain:

> If you think that even after the success obtained by *Zombie*, neither Fulci nor I worked for a year, you can see the sadness of the situation very clearly. It's very difficult to work in the Italian cinema, especially if you do horror films and often you find yourself on the breadline.[1]

In fact, Sacchetti is misrepresenting Fulci's situation. The filmmaker did find further work, but beyond that the point is well taken—it would take a little while for Fulci to be able to follow up on the promise of that first huge success.

*Contraband* originated from a screen story by Ettore Sanzò and Gianni De Chiara. When Fulci became involved, he decided to rework the script with the assistance of his friend Giorgio Mariuzzo. The two men first met in 1960, with Mariuzzo assisting Fulci on a television commercial; by the time of *Contraband*, the younger man had a number of credits under his belt as a screenwriter, including the unusual *giallo*, *Interrabang* (1969), directed by Giuliano Biagetti. Born in Venice in 1939, Mariuzzo also tried his hand at directing, helming several films throughout the 1970s. He had greater longevity as a screenwriter, however, and would go on to work with Fulci on *The Beyond* and *Aenigma*, as well. He later recalled his first meeting with Fulci:

> The first time I met him, I was still very, very young and working as an assistant director and he was already a well-known director. And I asked him, "Excuse me, sir, where do you want the camera?" He flipped a coin and said, "There!" He said, "It's not important where you put the camera; it's important what you put in front of the camera!" It was a real lesson for a young assistant director.

**Cover sleeve for the U.S. DVD release of *Contraband*, from Blue Underground; artist unknown.**

**Luca (Fabio Testi) will stop at nothing to get back at those who have wronged him and his family.**

the brutality and depravity all the more horrifying. Indeed, until his next properly "realistic" thriller, *The New York Ripper, Contraband* would remain Fulci's most squirm-inducing and unpleasant view of humanity.

Filming did not proceed without hiccups, however. The budget was on the low side to begin with, but the entire enterprise nearly stalled out altogether when the production ran out of cash. As Lionel Grenier reports in his liner notes for the collector's edition DVD release of the film from The Ecstasy of Films in France, "Tensions arose and Fabio Testi threatened to leave if he didn't get paid. But while shooting the river burial, Fulci received an invitation from strangers to join them at a night club. Upon his arrival, he was taken to a large room occupied by four men surrounding a fifth, who went by the name of Gianni Bilcream. Bilcream, very polite, offered financial help so that the production could continue. Fulci accepted and a couple of days later, money from Neapolitan merchants started to flow in. In exchange, the "good samaritans"—who turned out to be smugglers—demanded that the title *Violenza/Violence*, chosen by Fulci be abandoned because of its negative connotations and imposed a new one, *Luca Il contrabbandiere/Luca The Smuggler*. They also demanded that the anti-drug aspect of the movie be reinforced so as to diminish the impact that smuggling cigarettes had on the general public." So there you have it: Lucio Fulci, the so-called Godfather of Gore, being made an offer even he couldn't refuse! Assuming that there is nothing apocryphal about this incident, there is something oddly endearing about the notion of a vicious mob thriller made with the assistance—indeed, the blessing!—of the Mafia. That the film turned out as provocative as it did is a testimony to the overall mission statement to play up the violence to its fullest, all the while playing on the notion of petty smuggling and racketeering looking like the sport of gentlemen compared to the ruthless, cut-throat tactics of the drug peddlers.

The film belongs to the trend of police thrillers known as *poliziottesco* films—or *poliziotteschi*, in its plural form. The genre got its start in the tumultuous year of 1968, a time of great political upheaval and unrest in Italy. As the country was shocked by kidnappings, bombings, demonstrations turned violent and nightly displays of violence on the local news, filmmakers began to transpose this unease and violence to their films. The Spaghetti Western

Fulci had enjoyed collaborating with him on *Un uomo da ridere*, so when the need presented itself to overhaul what Sanzò and De Chiara had written, Mariuzzo proved to be the ideal go-to person:

> The project originated with [producer] Sandra Infascelli [...] but the story just didn't work. Lucio called me to reshape it, so I did. [...] I basically "restructured" the story, giving it the right rhythm and pacing: first, second and third act, which at the time was something rather new. [...] I also added a number of violent scenes: Lucio loved these kinds of things, even though in real life he was a good sport. Fulci got bored during the screenwriting phase. He used to get started and put three or four ideas on paper, some of them really brilliant, but he just didn't have the patience to go on and write the script scene by scene. [...] It was a very good movie, too bad the title was awful.[2]

Mariuzzo is hardly exaggerating when it comes to the film's violent content: Even compared to *Zombie*, this is a spectacularly cruel movie. Fulci's love of Artaud's Theatre of Cruelty manifests itself as he catalogues the various atrocities committed by the criminals, ranging from torture and mutilation to rape and murder. *Zombie*'s status as a fantasy had helped to take some of the edge off of the violent imagery; *Contraband* restores the balance by setting the action firmly in the real world, which serves to make was beginning to veer into self-parody, the *giallo* had yet to really catch on and horror films were still a way off from attaining acceptance, so the *poliziottesco* would become the genre of choice for the next decade. Spaghetti Western superstars like Franco Nero and Tomas Milian would hang up their spurs and put on civilian gear to top-line a series of brutal crime films throughout the '70s, while new stars would emerge in the form of actors like Maurizio Merli (often unfairly dismissed as "the poor man's Franco Nero," but a charismatic performer in his own right; sadly, he never collaborated on any of Fulci's movies) and Luc Merenda. As had been the case in the Spaghetti Western, some fading American talent would also find renewed popularity working in the *poliziottesco*; stone-faced Henry Silva proved to be the ideal hitman in the genre's amoral universe, for example. In a way, it is surprising that it took Lucio Fulci so long to participate in the genre. He was a filmmaker who courted public favor by working in popular genres, after all, so one can only assume that he was perhaps put off by the more "fascist" undertones of the genre. *Contraband*, his sole contribution to the genre, does not glorify the police as they use sadistic violence to combat the criminal class; instead, the film focuses on the Neapolitan Camorra underworld and depicts it in varying shades of gray—and *red*, as in blood.

The story focuses on the character of Luca, a smuggler with a strong sense of family loyalty. Despite Luca's criminal activities, he is presented as a basically decent man. Fulci and Mariuzzo also take a page from *The Godfather* (the film and the book) in earning him audience sympathy by establishing him as a man of ethics. Smuggling cigarettes and other comparatively "harmless" items is one thing, but he is not in favor of the importing of hard narcotics. It's a romanticized notion—the ethical thief—but it works well enough in the context of the movie. Luca is not a man prone to violence as a rule, but when his family is threatened, all bets are off. Luca goes through the same kind of grueling ordeal that Tom Corbett was forced to endure in *Massacre Time*: He sees his loved ones being killed and maimed and is then beaten to the point of death himself before he can finally get his well-deserved revenge.

The film is loaded with scenes of blood and gore, but the most uncomfortable sequence is one of sexual violence. Luca takes his wife, Adele, and his little boy, Francuccio, to stay with his father-in-law, the former mob boss Don Merrone. The villainous Marsigliese manages to kidnap Adele, however, and establishes his superiority as the new boss by having his thugs pin Luca down and force him to listen by phone as Adele is beaten and brutalized. The scene builds to a frenzy as the Marsigliese instructs his minion to rape the woman—but sooner than simply rape her, he decides to make the point even stronger by having the thug sodomize her. Fulci does not sexualize the action: It's ugly and unpleasant in the extreme, which is as it should be. Much of the action is played off of the devastated reaction of Luca as he is forced to listen and can do nothing to protect her. It's a powerful scene that has nevertheless predictably drawn accusations of misogyny from some quarters. Fulci's complicated relationship with women is well documented and can be traced to his strained relationship with his mother. The director's treatment of some of the actresses on his films is also very well-known, but it also deserves to be noticed that for every actress who recalled him being a sadist on set, an equal number recalled that he simply liked to provoke—and that if they stood up to him, they would earn his lasting respect. No matter how one views his attitude towards women, however, there are quite a few strong, resourceful women depicted throughout his filmography; one need think no further than *Beatrice Cenci* as a good example. Fulci does not imply that Adele deserves the violence that is inflicted upon her, nor does he encourage the audience to side with the thugs who are raping her. Instead, the scene is vital in establishing the lengths to which the Marsigliese will go in order to attain his goal; he is a twisted and cruel character, so the fact that he supervises such a vile act is completely in character. The scene is not gratuitous, nor is it undone by bad-taste eroticism. It packs a genuine punch and it is disturbing to watch, but that is not the same thing as implying that it somehow celebrates brutality against women; as is so often the case in Fulci's work, the kneejerk reaction may be the convenient one, but it is not well-informed, nor does it fairly characterize the man and his motivations.

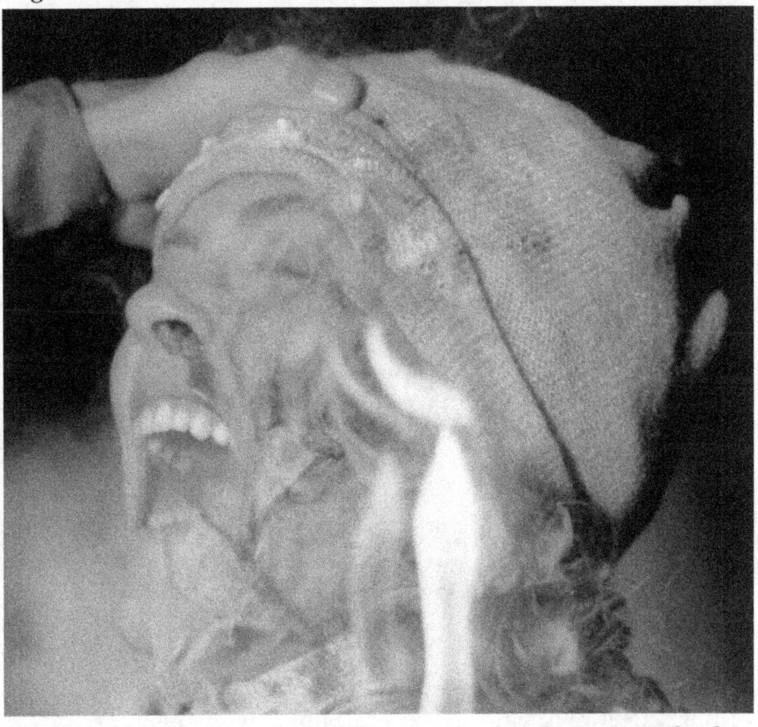

**In one of the film's most sadistic set pieces, a drug smuggler has her face charred by a Bunsen burner.**

*Contraband* is frequently exciting and tells an engrossing story. It also has genuine human interest, thanks to the thoughtful attention paid to Luca and his relationship with his family. In a way, it is also a rather somber and introspective movie; as such, it doesn't have quite the same exhilarating celebration of spectacle that marks many *poliziotteschi*. As such, many viewers tend to find it a bit disappointing compared to the flashier, splashier examples of the genre, notably the more comic book-like efforts by Umberto Lenzi, for example. In terms of violence, it's hard to beat: Heads are blown away, knives are twisted into bellies, a face is even melted off via blow torch but the movie never celebrates this brutality, instead adopting a position of horror at the excesses indulged in by these criminal lowlifes. Even at the end, when Luca is reunited with his family and the wicked Marsigliese has been properly dealt with, there is not much sense of celebration; as Fulci and his collaborators know only too well, there is more where that came from, so the victory is merely a temporary one, to be savored until the next Marsigliese tries to muscle his way into town.

**German pressbook ad for *Contraband*; artist unknown.**

The cast includes several familiar faces from Fulci's other works: Fabio Testi gives a commendable performance as Luca. He makes the character into a hero worth rooting for, but is not afraid to show vulnerability either. The scene in which he is forced to listen to Adele's rape works in large part because of his wonderfully expressive eyes, which convey the appropriate mixture of horror, sadness and rage. Fulci's friend Fabrizio Jovine makes his second appearance for the director, following *The Psychic*, and he shares several scenes with another actor who would become part of Fulci's inner circle: Venantino Venantini. Venantini was born in Fabriano in 1930 and made his film debut in 1954, with a minor role in Steno's *Un giorno in pretura*—on which Fulci worked as a cowriter and assistant director. He started appearing in more prominent roles in the 1960s, including Jacques Besnard's *The Big Restaurant* (1966) and Massimo Dallamano's *Bandidos* (1967). He would go on to appear in *City of the Living Dead*, which also featured Jovine. He later recalled Fulci in glowing terms:

> Lucio was the wildest cat in the movie business that I ever met. He was sincere. Some people play schizo, but he really was. That is why I found him interesting. He was honest. [...] He was very nervous. He always had problems—with life, with women, but his spirit was ... He was a fabulous guy.

Marcel Bozzuffi and Saverio Marconi play the main villains. Bozzuffi is properly terrifying as the Marsigliese; Bozzuffi does not allow even a glimmer of humanity in his performance and makes for a wonderful contrast to Testi's soulful hero. Bozzuffi (1928-1988) enjoyed a distinguished screen career, working for such directors as Jean-Pierre Melville (*La Deuxieme Souffle*, 1966), Costa-Gavras (*Z*, 1969), William Friedkin (*The French Connection*, 1971), Robert Altman (*Images*, 1972) and Michelangelo Antonioni (*Identification of a Woman*, 1982). He wasn't afraid to get down and dirty in exploitation fare, however, and also appeared in everything from Massimo Dallamano's *Colt 38 Special Squad* (1976) to Mario Landi's *Patrick Lives Again* (1980). Marconi is also very effective as the slimy and duplicitous Perlante. He was a virtual newcomer compared to Bozzuffi when he made *Contraband*, but he recalled a strong bond with his director:

> He didn't even ask me to read for it. I felt honored because he trusted me with it. I immediately appreciated him. He was a very intelligent man; very detail-oriented, cynical, ill mannered, but very creative.

Unfortunately, *Contraband* is saddled with one of the worst English dubs to ever be inflicted on an Italian genre film. The quality of the vocal performances is on par with an episode of *Speed Racer*, and this only serves to undercut the film's many merits when viewed in that form. Seen in Italian (and it appears that the film was shot in Italian for once, whereas most genre cinema was filmed in English to facilitate the dubbing), it seems much more sober and impressive. In any event, the film didn't do much to alter the course of Fulci's career—but the popularity of *Zombie* finally started to work in Fulci's favor and from here on out he would work primarily in the horror genre.

Notes:
1. Palmerini, Luca M. and Gaetano Mistretta, *Spaghetti Nightmares* (Florida: Fantasma Books, 1996), p. 124.
2. Albiero, Paolo and Giacomo Cacciatore, *Il terrorista dei generi. Tutto il cinema di Lucio Fulci* (Rome: Un Mondo a Parte, 2004), p. 195.

# Venantino Venantini Interview by Troy Howarth

The following interview with Venantino Venantini was conducted by phone on November 28, 2014. In addition to appearing in two films directed by Lucio Fulci—*Contraband* and *City of the Living Dead*—Venantino also made his debut in *Un giorno in pretura*, on which Fulci served as an assistant director and cowriter. He also became a good friend of Fulci's, and he has our thanks for taking the time to answer our questions.

**Troy Howarth**: First things first: What made you want to become an actor?
**Venantino Venantini**: Actually, I am a painter. I'm 84 now. But in the beginning, when I was at school, to make some money, I went to Cinecittà—this was the time when the Americans came to make movies there, like *Quo Vadis* and *Ben-Hur*. I started to play extra parts; they told me I was a tall, good-looking guy, so I should give it a try. I don't know, I was 21, 22, 23 and I also worked in the offices there as a messenger boy, too. I took messages from office to office. Then I met the assistant of Alberto Lattuada, a very famous Italian director. I was talking to him and I told him that I was trying to be a painter, so I ended up getting a scholarship and went to Paris. When I came back, I saw Lattuada's assistant again and he told me that I should do a screen test. I said, "Thank you very much, but I am happy being a painter." He said that it was for a big movie that was being made in Tahiti. I said, "Hold on, OK." (laughs) So they flew me out to Tahiti to do a screen test and I stayed there for about four months. They were making *Mutiny on the Bounty* (1962). Marlon Brando was in it; he loved being among the Tahitians so much, he decided to marry a Tahitian.
**TH**: Do you remember your first meeting with Lucio Fulci?
**VV**: Lucio Fulci was crazy! (*laughs*) He was always screaming and he would drink tomato juice and get it all over himself. (*laughs*) He was a very bright guy, but very difficult. He was always going against what everybody wanted; if somebody said it was good, he would say it was bad. He was very, very bright. But you know, he didn't like actors very much. I can agree with him on that. Actors are a bunch of shits. (*laughs*) I did two movies with Marcello Mastroianni, and I remember him saying to me that actors are the only people in the world who enjoy suffering and who are always thinking about themselves. And yet, they treat you like you were a God. In movies, you meet the most beautiful women and you live in great comfort. You travel all over and everything is first class—planes, trains and so forth.
**TH**: Lucio Fulci directed you for the first time in 1980, in two movies: *Contraband* and *City of the Living Dead* …
**VV**: Yes, 1980. My son Luca was also with him.
**TH**: He was in *City of the Living Dead*.
**VV**: Yes, in Georgia. I remember one day (*laughs*) he was putting worms on the face of my son … he was only 12 or so. And Lucio was screaming at him to stop whining. Luca came to me crying, "Papa!" And he had worms all over his face, getting into his mouth (*laughs*). And Lucio was yelling at him to shut up and do the scene.

I know he had some very bad times in his life. I remember hearing that Lucio's wife had killed herself—she put her head in an oven. But anyway, Lucio was a very interesting man. He was a loner. He was always fighting against something. I thought he was a very interesting guy.
**TH**: He had a reputation for being very tough on his actors—was he like this with you?
**VV**: Yes—well, remember what he was like with my son! (*laughs*) I think he liked me because I was a painter, not a real actor, so he saw me differently. He was very tough on his actors. In his own way, though, he was a real genius.
**TH**: Did you get to spend time with him away from the set?
**VV**: Yes, a couple of times. We had dinner. He was always messy and he would spill things on his shirt and he didn't

**Mike Baronas with Venantino Venantini.**

**Venantino Venantini poses with his son Luca on location for *City of the Living Dead.***

care. But in a way, he was very fragile. I was always very impressed with him because he was so bright.

**TH**: Do you remember much about the first film you did with him, *Contraband*? It starred Fabio Testi ...

**VV**: No, I don't remember it well. It's been so long—but thank you so much for reminding me! (*laughs*)

**TH**: You shared some scenes with an actor named Fabrizio Jovine in that film ...

**VV**: Yes, I remember him. I ran into him again later. Actually, he was supposed to come to the one horror movie festival that Mike [Baronas] did. I liked him very much. He played a priest in the second film.

**TH**: That's right, he is the priest in *City of the Living Dead.*

**VV**: Bravo, yes! He was the priest. I liked him very, very much.

**TH**: Was it your idea to cast your son Luca in *City of the Living Dead*?

**VV**: No, no—I didn't push him. It was his agent in Rome with William Morris; they asked for him and Fulci was happy to have him, I suppose. It helped that he spoke English as well as Italian. I just remember (*laughs*) him crying and Lucio yelling at him to shut up.

**TH**: I heard Fulci gave him a slap?

**VV**: Yeah, but you know, he was right! (*laughs*)

**TH**: Did you ever meet Fulci's daughters?

**VV**: No, unfortunately but I know that he was a good father. He was always talking about them. To me, he was a man who was outside of the pack. You know what I mean? He was always off by himself and he liked to sail, too, I remember. He had a boat. But he was a very valuable talent. You know, he assisted people like Steno before he became a director.

**TH**: One of your first movies was directed by Steno—it was called *Un giorno in pretura* and Fulci was actually the assistant director and cowriter on that film ...

**VV**: Yes, I remember that film. I did another one with him later called *Dio li fa e poi li accoppia*, but that was many years later [1981].

**TH**: Do you remember meeting Fulci on *Un giorno in pretura*?

**VV**: I remember seeing him there, but we didn't talk much. I was a little shy. When we met again years later, we spoke about remembering seeing each other before.

**TH**: Did you keep in touch with Fulci in the years after *Contraband* and *City of the Living Dead*?

**VV**: A couple of times. Our paths didn't cross too much, though, no.

**TH**: He had a lot of health problems.

**VV**: Yes, he was very sick. I remember he was a diabetic, because he couldn't eat or drink certain things because of his sugar. I know that used to bother him sometimes; he missed having certain things.

**TH**: Would you agree that Fulci was underrated, especially in Italy?

**VV**: Well, he was considered a crazy director, but I think he was seen as talented. In Italy, we class directors as A-Class and B-Class, you know? Fulci was classed as a B-director. And I was fortunate enough to work with a lot of directors who had great talent, like Antonio Margheriti, who is also known as Anthony Dawson—because people thought the movies would sell better if they changed their names, so he became known as Anthony Dawson.

**TH**: What are your memories of Antonio Margheriti?

**VV**: I did a couple of movies with him. He was another bright guy—a very bright guy, very intelligent, very quiet. He was another one classed as a B-director. But like so many so-called B-directors, he knew how to use the camera. The A-directors, though ... nobody seems to really care much about Fellini anymore or Visconti, but people like Margheriti or ... I did a Western called *Bandidos*, directed by Massimo Dallamano ... and these were the Italian movies that sold all over the world. People still talk about them. These guys knew how to shoot! Just think of somebody like Mario Bava, for example. These guys were very, very important.

**TH**: How about Umberto Lenzi?

**VV**: Umberto Lenzi? He's crazy, my *God*! (laughs) I mean, he shouts—and he *cries*! He would carry on! But you know, he is a big authority on the Spanish Civil War. He knows everything about that—even the songs of the Republic and the Fascists. He knows it all. I did two or three films with him. But I don't like him all that much as a person—I preferred Fulci. Fulci was a very good director.

**TH**: How about Pupi Avati, who directed you in *The Hideout*?
**VV**: I worked with him only once; he took me to Iowa. It was only about four or five days of work.
**TH**: Did you like working with Avati?
**VV**: Yes. He is another one who shouts and everybody jumps, but he knows his job very, very well.
**TH**: Do you have any final thoughts on Lucio Fulci?
**VV**: He was a fatalist. He was kind of a philosophical guy. I think he felt like life was against him, like every day could be his last. I noticed this, whether it was a cigarette or a piece of chocolate or whatever, it was like it could be his last one. He was waiting for something bad to happen to him.
**TH**: Did you ever see the two films you made with him?
**VV**: I saw them both when we did the dubbing, of course, but I saw *City of the Living Dead* again later. I remember them both being good movies. I enjoyed making them. In Italy now, there are no movies being made. You know the film that won the Oscar recently?
**TH**: *The Great Beauty*?
**VV**: Yes, that's it. What did you think of it?
**TH**: I liked it.
**VV**: I didn't like it. I think it's a movie made to win prizes. It was a long time since we won the Oscar, so they set out to make a film to win an Oscar. I think the so-called B-movies we did were better.
**TH**: They certainly have had a long shelf life; people still enjoy them and talk about them, as you say.
**VV**: Exactly!
**TH**: Well, I just want to close this up by thanking you again for taking the time to talk with me.
**VV**: You're welcome. When you see Mike, tell him I say hello—and if you ever come to Rome, give me a call, OK?
**TH**: Absolutely!
**VV**: OK, *ciao*! Take care!

## *City of the Living Dead (Italy)*

Aka *Paura nella città dei morti viventi*; *The Gates of Hell*; *Miedo en la ciudad de los muertos vivientes*; *Frayeurs*; *Ein Zombie hing am Glockenseil*

Directed by Lucio Fulci; Produced by Giovanni Masini, for Dania Film, Medusa Distribuzione and National Cinematografica; Story and Screenplay by Lucio Fulci and Dardano Sacchetti; Director of Photography: Sergio Salvati; Editor: Vincenzo Tomassi; Music by Fabio Frizzi

Main Players: Christopher George (Peter Bell); Catriona MacColl [as Katherine MacColl] (Mary Woodhouse); Carlo De Mejo (Gerry); Janet Agren (Sandra); Giovanni Lombardo Radice (Bob); Antonella Interlenghi (Emily Robbins); Luca Venantini (John-John Robbins); Venantino Venantini (Mr. Ross); Fabrizio Jovine (Father Thomas); Daniela Doria (Rosie Kelvin); Michele Soavi (Tommy Ross); Adelaide Aste (Tersesa, the medium)

**Italian *locandina* for *City of the Living Dead*; artwork by Enzo Sciotti.**

Cameo appearance: Lucio Fulci (Dr. Joe Thompson)

*The village of Dunwich is beset by strange happenings following the suicide of Father Thomas. Mary Woodhouse, a psychic, believes that the suicide has opened the gates of hell—and that the only hope for humanity is to reach Dunwich in time to undo the damage that has been done. She enlists the help of a journalist named Peter Bell and together they head to Dunwich to try and avert disaster. Along the way a therapist named Gerry, who has also been witness to some strange goings on, joins them. In the meantime, the dead begin to rise from their tombs and claim more victims …*

*City of the Living Dead* finally allowed Fulci to fulfill the promise shown by *Zombie*. The film made it clear that the previous film was no happy accident and it also enabled him to be involved in the project from the word go. *Zombie* may have been a gun-for-hire assignment that just happened to fall into the director's lap at an opportune

**Above: A behind-the-scenes glimpse of filming: Lucio Fulci (back to the camera) directs Janet Agren, Luca Venantini and Catriona MacColl.**
**Below: Behind-the-scenes high jinx with Christopher George, Luca Venantini and Catriona MacColl.**

moment, but *City of the Living Dead* would be a project he could nurture and develop to his own specifications. He later said that he wanted to make a film that captured the feeling and logic of a nightmare, the type of film "where horror is ubiquitous, even in apparently innocuous forms."[1] The end result marked the first time Fulci would throw logic out the window in one of his films; it would not, however, be the last.

Surprisingly, the same team that had backed *Zombie* did not produce this film. Producer Fabrizio De Angelis would soon come calling on Fulci again, but in the meantime he backed a much-inferior zombie film directed by Marino Girolami, which is alternately known as *Zombie Holocaust* or *Dr. Butcher, M.D.* Instead, Fulci had to seek out his own financing and finally found a sympathetic ally in the form of producer Giovanni Masini, an exploitation veteran who principally worked as a production manager; his other credits include Ruggero Deodato's *Cannibal Holocaust* (1980) and Umberto Lenzi's *Eaten Alive!* (1981). The present film came together quickly, much to the chagrin of cowriter Dardano Sacchetti:

> Well, Fulci, in the long run, managed to persuade the Medusa people to finance *City of the Living Dead*, which I consider one of our least successful films, in as much as it was thought out and shot in an atmosphere of sheer desperation. I received four million [*lire*] and I think Fulci got 15 million. The moral of the story: I had to live for a year and a half on six million *lire*. That's the Italian cinema for you![2]

*Zombie*, of course, had been written independently of Fulci; he came to the film fairly late in the game and was sufficiently impressed with its content not to insist upon any major changes. Even so, he felt that the film was a little mechanical in its structure and decided to avoid this problem by encouraging Sacchetti to take the story for *City* in a different direction. Sacchetti would later contest this, arguing that he wrote the screenplays on his own:

> I've never seen Fulci at a single script sitting! I was always the one who structured his stories and then Lucio read and approved them.[3]

The contentious nature of their collaboration would later result in a full-fledged falling-out between the two men, but for the time being they were able to channel their energies into creating something new and unique.

Fulci and Sacchetti turned to the works of American writer H.P. Lovecraft for inspiration. Born Howard Phillips Lovecraft in Providence, Rhode Island in 1890, he was a psychologically fragile individual who channeled his morbid fantasies into extraordinary works of literature. Much of his work focuses on horrors too ghastly to visualize, with an intricate mythology of "old Gods" providing a rich backdrop. Lovecraft virtually created his own universe, with obsessively recurring character names and locations providing a sense of loose continuity through his work. On the downside, a definite strain of racism can be detected in his writing, but if one can see past this unfortunate part of his character, much can be savored in his rich descriptions and in his uncanny ability to evoke a creepy sense of atmosphere. Lovecraft was not taken seriously in his time and barely made enough money to make ends meet; he died in 1937. Fulci and Sacchetti specifically allude to the writer's beloved village of Dunwich—as in his 1928 story, *The Dunwich Horror*—and a more elliptical evocation of his writing comes in the emphasis on a horrific sense of evil and foreboding. Lovecraft never really went in for the kind of graphic shock effects favored by Fulci, of course, but the sense of something horrible slithering into

**Behind-the-scenes shot of the filming of *City of the Living Dead*: Fulci is seated, reading a magazine, with cinematographer Sergio Salvati seated beside him; photo courtesy of camera operator Roberto Forges.**

reality through a portal to the great beyond is very much in the spirit of Lovecraft and helps to make the film more successful in evoking a sense of his flair for atmosphere than many of the "official" screen adaptations—notably the 1969 adaptation of *The Dunwich Horror*, directed by Daniel Haller. The film—and its "spiritual cousin" *The Beyond*—also make use of Lovecraft's favorite theme of a book which contains the key to another dimension; in his stories, it is the fabled *Necronomincon*, while in *City* it is the book of Enoch—and in *The Beyond*, later on, it is the book of Eibon. In all three instances, possession of the book allows one the opportunity to gain insight into contacting the other dimension—but this power comes with a terrifying price.

The film begins with a scream underneath a plain black screen; then the title comes up, timed to the sinister strains of Fabio Frizzi's remarkable music score. As had been the case with the "gunshot" opening of *Zombie*, Fulci is careful to grab the viewer right off the bat—and this time, he doesn't let go. The credits play over a sequence of a priest (Fabrizio Jovine, returning from *The Psychic* and *Contraband*) walking amid the tombstones in a misty graveyard. Fulci and cinematographer bust out the entire classic Gothic horror film imagery they can muster, and the scene ultimately climaxes when the priest—for reasons known only to him—hangs himself. It's a strong opening; moody and atmospheric, with a minimum of fuss as to who the priest is or why he does what he does. In the film's narrative landscape, cause and effect are of little importance; it doesn't matter why somebody does something—it only matters that they *do*.

From here, the film proceeds to introduce its main characters; a young psychic named Mary Woodhouse, a hard-bitten crime reporter named Peter Bell and a caring but basically ineffectual therapist named Gerry. The film doesn't dwell a lot on character and motivation, but Fulci and Sacchetti earn points in a crucial area: The characters are likable, so we actually care about what happens to them. Mary apparently dies of heart failure during a séance—she sees the priest hanging himself and foretells the opening of the gates of Hell, triggered by his blasphemy—and is promptly buried. Peter is in the cemetery sniffing out a story when he hears cries coming from the young woman's coffin: He realizes that she has been buried alive and proceeds to free her from her coffin with the aid of a pickaxe. Pedantic viewers will question why Mary wasn't embalmed or why Peter resorts to using a dangerous weapon, which could easily kill off the very woman he is trying to rescue. The fact of the matter is, it doesn't really matter: The coffin set piece is there for show, and Fulci is not about to pass up an opportunity to show off his flair for creating tension and suspense. The use of the pickaxe is a bit of self-referential dark humor, as its sharp point comes very close to gouging Mary's eye out; Fulci is counting on viewers remembering his big set piece in *Zombie* and, coyly, he denies us the spectacle of a follow-up: Peter frees Mary from her grave and the two form an alliance to find the village of Dunwich and close the gates

**Spanish lobby card: The suicide of Father Thomas (Fabrizio Jovine) kicks off the action in *City of the Living Dead.***

of Hell before it is too late. Fulci's staging of the premature burial sequence is masterful and would later inspire Quentin Tarantino, who quoted the sequence in his film *Kill Bill, Volume 2* (2004). From there, we meet Gerry, who is introduced trying to restore a sense of calm and order to his patient Sandra. Sandra is neurotic and fixated on some childhood horror she cannot bring to light, but her problems are about to become pretty insignificant compared to the horrors that are going to engulf their town. Gerry is empathetic and rational, but his Freudian analyses don't really accomplish much; once again, the director's distrust of the psychiatric profession is evident, and Gerry will only be promoted to the role of hero by pure chance.

The heroes (if one can use such a word in this context) having been established, Fulci and Sacchetti introduce the most significant—and tragic—of their supporting players. Bob is the village outcast. He lives by himself in a drafty, abandoned house in the middle of nowhere. He has no friends, save for Gerry's girlfriend, Emily. Emily is the only person in town who takes pity on the poor outcast—even the ultra-liberal Gerry seems wary of him. Bob is one of Fulci's classic outsider figures—and like Maciara in *Don't Torture a Duckling*, his being marked as "different" will have devastating repercussions. Fulci and Sacchetti introduce him in an admittedly bizarre fashion: The young man busts out a blow-up sex doll and is about to pleasure himself with it, when he catches a glimpse of something horrible; a corpse rotting on the floor. Why the corpse is there is never established; it is simply part of the unusual chain of events that signals the growing breakdown of logic and order in the town. Bob flees in terror—abandoning Emily at one point, when she tries to help him, thus making her another victim of the zombiefied Father Thomas—but is later caught by the bigoted and hotheaded Mr. Ross. Ross blames Bob for what is going on and decides to take matters into his own hands—he skewers Bob's head with an electrical drill. If *Zombie*'s sequence of eye-mutilation is Fulci's most infamous set piece, then the murder of Bob by Mr. Ross is probably a very close second. The make-up and special effects work by Rosario Prestopino and Gino De Rossi is first class, and Vincenzo Tomassi's precision editing ensures that the illusion is never shattered; Bob may be a strange character, but the audience can't help but feel sorry for him as he is put to death for crimes he had no hand in committing. Here again, Fulci makes it clear that he has no patience for the bigoted, closed-minded mentality of small town communities.

Another memorable set piece occurs when Fulci and Sacchetti reference the hoariest of slasher movie clichés: horny teenagers! A young couple is found making love inside of a parked jeep, but their idyll does not last for long: Father Thomas appears like an avenging angel and exacts a horrific punishment on them, presumably for daring to engage in premarital sex. The girl is fixated by Thomas' baleful gaze and begins crying tears of blood; she then proceeds to puke her guts out—literally. The panic-stricken boy tries to escape to no avail; Father Thomas ultimately tears the boy's brain right out of his skull. Fulci's ongoing critique of the Catholic Church manifests itself in the figure of the zombie priest. It is his suicide that sets the plot into motion; he disregards one of the cardinal rules of the church and a vengeful God responds by allowing the bowels of Hell to open. If Father Thomas can be viewed as a sort of moral avenger, striking down the wicked, it is not a moral judgment that Fulci and Sacchetti happen to be siding with; the two young people do not deserve their horrific deaths, but in the nightmarish scheme of things such spectacular demises almost seem to be inevitable. Fulci amps-up the gross-out factor in this scene, and one can't help but feel for actress Daniela Doria, as she gamely spits out a number of animal innards before the effects boys take over and utilize a prosthetic head instead; Doria's guts apparently impressed Fulci, who would also put her into some sticky situations in *The Black Cat, The House by the Cemetery* and—most spectacularly—*The New York Ripper*.

Ultimately, the three protagonists come together and attempt to undo the damage inflicted by Father Thomas—

unfortunately for them, it's too late: They arrive at the cemetery on All Saints Day, and this is the day that it has been foretold that the dead would come forth from their tombs. Peter is killed for his troubles, leaving Mary and Gerry to face Father Thomas. The priest's gaze nearly claims Mary, as well, but Gerry thinks fast and grabs a large wooden cross—and proceeds to thrust it into the priest's crotch. *Zombie* (and George A. Romero before it!) had established that only a head-wound would kill off the zombies, but of course Gerry is not aware of this bit of folklore. His decision to attack the priest in that specific spot is loaded with subtext, but Fulci and Sacchetti do not dwell on the action for long: It appears to be successful, sending Father Thomas and his minions up in flames. Mary and Gerry then emerge from the underworld—literally, finding their way out through one of the burial plots—and are about to be reunited with the little boy, John-John, whose parents and sister have been savagely killed by the undead. And then, something inexplicable happens: As the boy runs towards them, they recoil in horror ... Mary shrieks and Fulci ends on a freeze-frame, which disintegrates into all-consuming blackness. The apocalypse, as it happens, has not been averted after all. The ending is controversial, to say the least: Many viewers find it an arbitrary and clumsy final shock effect, but it actually does seem to work fairly well in context. *City of the Living Dead* is gloriously illogical from beginning to end: It is, ultimately, a nightmare on film. Fulci would later reveal that the ending was something of a fluke, however:

> It was the editor's idea. The child started running and laughing and then, at a particular moment, who knows what he saw ... and the editor got the idea of splitting up the frame, which works very well. All credit to the editor.[4]

Would the film have been spoiled by a final assertion of good winning out over evil? No, it wouldn't have been spoiled—but it would have seemed inconsistent with the dark perspective offered by Fulci in so many of his films. As it stands, this final happy accident merely serves to underline his pessimism and allows the film to end on a disquieting note.

*City of the Living Dead* is almost certainly Fulci's most richly atmospheric movie. From the first frame to the last, it creates and sustains an atmosphere of overwhelming dread. Even the functional scenes establishing the relationships between the characters do not break the spell. Fulci loads the movie with weird touches: Characters behave in an odd manner, locations are presented in a skewed and subtly surreal fashion and even sequences set in the daylight have a hazy texture to them that makes one feel as if they are trapped inside of a waking dream or nightmare.

For example, consider the scenes set in the funeral home. This is undoubtedly the grungiest and most unpleasant funeral home ever depicted on celluloid. The décor is drab. The walls seem to be slimy with decay. The undertaker looks like a ghoul who could pass for being a zombie. And even his basic job skills are called into question, as he makes the bodies up in a way that borders on caricature. Only the implication of necrophilia could have pushed this setting even further into the realm of a freakish sideshow, but Fulci makes do by showing the undertaker to be a common thief as he loots the bodies for their precious valuables.

Early on in the film, Mary is introduced in the midst of a séance overseen by a medium named Teresa. Teresa is a wonderfully idiosyncratic figure: overtly, almost comically, creepy and over-the-top and living amid a dark and dingy environment straight out of an Expressionist horror movie. The cops who interview her after Mary's "death" are condescending and rude, but the viewer never has any doubt as to her abilities: She is the real deal, and it is her insight which provides the heroes with the knowledge needed to defeat the forces of evil. The scenes with Teresa are wonderfully arch and loaded with interesting stylistic flourishes, from the seductive circular camera movement used to introduce the members of the séance (a technique Fulci would reprise later in *Demonia*) to the tight eye close-ups, which also refer back to the traumatizing moment of horror in *Zombie*.

Fulci milks ample suspense and tension out of the material. There are no dull sequences designed to advance the plot: "Plot," in this context, is a slippery concept, anyway. The story has elements of a detective thriller—à la *Zombie*, which is structured around two mysteries: Primarily, why are the dead returning to life? And what has happened to Anne's father? But Fulci underplays this aspect of the scenario. It is pretty obvious from the get-go that Peter, Mary and Gerry are not going to be successful in their quest. Try as they may, they are up against forces which are much too powerful for them to overcome; whether they know it or not, we are reasonably certain that they are doomed from the start. The nihilism of this approach does not deprive the film of suspense value, however: Given that the characters are depicted in a sympathetic light, we still hold out hope that they may prove successful. The introduction of other characters like Sandra and Bob add to the film's nightmarish sense of fatality; these characters wrestle with inner demons which the film doesn't have time enough to delve into, but they engage our interest and the feeling of loss which accompanies their demise is genuine.

Many critics have complained that Fulci's fixation on shock effects comes at the expense of characterization and logic. While there is some truth to this with regards to his horror films, this only tells part of the story. Yes, the characters in *City of the Living Dead* are a sketchy lot—but as emphasized above, they are still sympathetic and recognizably human. Simply because Fulci and Sacchetti don't take the time to establish a three-dimensional background for them is not the same as saying that they are simply there to move the plot forward. There is wit and charm

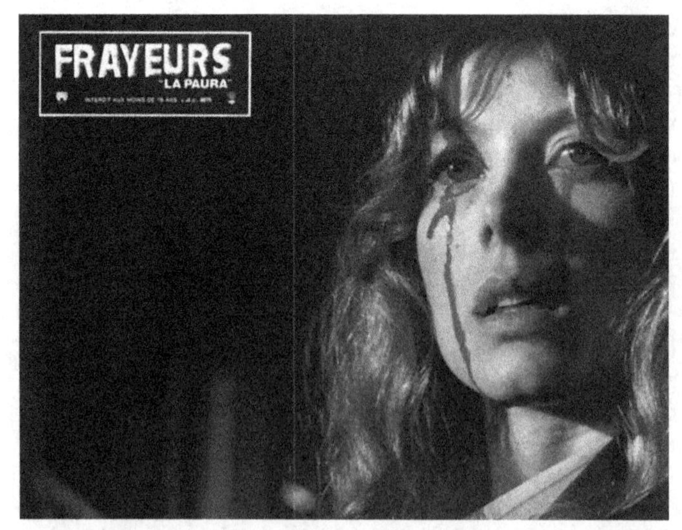


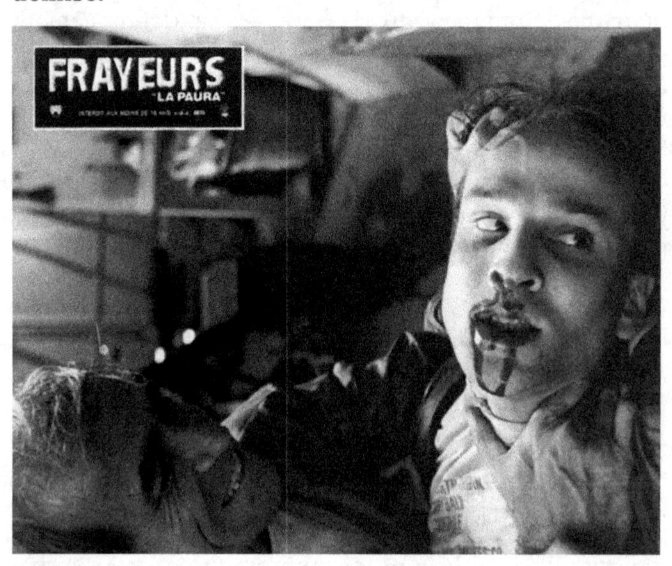


**Above: French lobby card: Daniela Doria is about to lose her lunch—and much more—in *City of the Living Dead*. Below: Giovanni Lombardo Radice meets a gruesome demise.**

to the interplay between Peter and Mary, for example, though Fulci is wise not to burden the film with a gratuitous love subplot; in a story such as this, there simply isn't time for that kind of diversion. As for logic, it is true that the film disregards it at every turn—but this is a relatively new development in Fulci's cinema. His *gialli* are rigidly logical, for example, and other films like *Beatrice Cenci* plainly demonstrate that the director is capable of telling a complex, emotionally involving story when he chooses to do so. To harp on character and logic in the context of a film like *City of the Living Dead* is to miss the point entirely: Fulci makes it clear from the start that he is interested in capturing the disorientation of a nightmare on celluloid, and he accomplishes this with considerable flair and style.

The film is also a very unusual example of the zombie subgenre, truth be told. Not many critics have picked up on this, but the flesh-eating angle is downplayed here—and the living dead are in possession of unusual powers, which make them rather more threatening than the usual shambling corpse. These ghouls are able to teleport from one spot to another! John-John runs away from one zombie, yet the ghoul always manages to stay one step ahead by materializing before the child's disbelieving eyes. Later on, Peter is taken by surprise when the reanimated Sandra appears before him and his cohorts, then suddenly appears behind him, allowing her to take him off-guard and kill him. If Fulci worried that the over-reliance on people frozen in fright as the zombies move ever so slowly toward them might become played-out, he certainly found a novel way of overcoming this in this picture; it's a touch he would never revisit in other living dead films and, unless another example has passed this writer by, it doesn't appear to have been taken up by any other followers either. Similarly, *Zombie* basked in sequences of characters being devoured by the living dead. *City of the Living Dead* skirts past this almost entirely; only the aftermath of the carnage in Junie's Bar shows anything in the way of cannibalism—and that instance is so brief, it could conceivably have been added in late in the day as an afterthought or as a concession to box-office demands.

In an interview included on the Blue Underground Blu-ray edition of *City of the Living Dead*, Sergio Salvati explains his approach to the film's lighting: "The color that best represented fear was black—solid black with white slashing lights."[5] True to his description, the visual scheme of the film is a deliberate play on jarring contrasts between light and dark. It's a very dark film indeed; much of the action is set at night and even the daytime scenes avoid a conventionally sunny aesthetic. Amid the deep blacks and clean whites, Salvati employs splashes of colored lighting that would have made Mario Bava proud. The use of red, blue, green and purple spotlighting to vary the frame is beautifully done. The style is rigidly employed throughout the film; here again, it outdoes its predecessor by sticking to a very specific style and not bowing to the demands of imposing a more orderly and realistic approach.

Fulci was able to reassemble a number of the same artisans who had helped to make *Zombie* a success: cinematographer Sergio Salvati, composer Fabio Frizzi, make-up artist Rosario Prestopino, editor Vincenzo Tomassi, etc. To handle the special effects, Fulci turned to Gino De Rossi, who had also worked on *Zombie*, albeit in a subservient capacity to primary make-up effects guru Giannetto De Rossi. Gino De Rossi's work on *City of the Living Dead* is generally very good and provides the film with some memorably gruesome highlights. Salvati's cameraman on the film would not be Franco Bruni, however; instead the job went to Roberto Forges Davanzati. Davanzati's previous credits included Sergio Leone's *Once Upon a Time in the West* (1968) and *Duck You Sucker* (1972), Dario Argento's *Four Flies on Grey Velvet* (1971) and Fernando Di Leo's *Nick the Sting* (1976). He came to the film hot off of working with Sergio D'Offizi on Ruggero Deodato's *Cannibal*

*Holocaust* (1980) and would go on to work on Fulci's next picture, *The Black Cat*, as well. In an interview included on the Blue Underground Blu-ray of the film, he recalled:

> With Lucio Fulci, we had—don't get the wrong idea—a love relationship. This mutual love existed with all the crew, not just with me. [...] He had a great technique and, to me, he was a brilliant director. He had been underestimated all his life; every single crew he worked with just ended up loving him. Not quite the same things happened with the actors, because sometimes he would get rather severe with them.[6]

The sets and costumes were the work of the gifted Massimo Antonello Geleng, who would go on to work on Fulci's *The Black Cat* and *The Sweet House of Horrors*. He later recalled approaching the assignment with trepidation:

> When I met [Fulci], he had a reputation as being a nasty man. People knew him as mean and as a cynic, and at times an aggressive sadist. What I noticed instead was, beyond it all, he carried a demon inside and he needed to exorcise it through such behavior. A sense of profound worry, profound pain embedded his whole existence. And the series of personal problems that were very serious [...] He used all this material for self-mockery, because I can recall some incredibly heavy things he said, sometimes in front of his daughter, as well, who was working by his side. However, it wasn't just plain nasty expression for the sake of it, but his way of trying to exorcise his specific personal issues.

Production was split between DePaolis Studios in Rome and location work in Savannah, Georgia, with a brief stopover in New York for some quick location shots. Once again, the location work in America was done without securing proper permits, but the "flying by the seat of your pants" nature of the production seemed to inspire a sense of creativity and quick thinking between Fulci and the crew. As Geleng recalled,

> The production chose Savannah because of its beauty. It's a historic city, with old fancy buildings just perfect for my idea of set designing.[7]

The mixture of American exteriors and Roman interiors is artfully achieved, and the unity of style extends beyond the cinematography to the overall design scheme of the film as well.

Fulci and Salvati photographed their other horror films of the period in the wide 2.35 aspect ratio, but *City of the Living Dead* made use of the smaller, more intimate 1.85 format. Indeed, some viewers have wondered if the film was actually intended for 2.35. The fact of that matter is, attempting to matte the film to that ratio would be unrealistic and would completely sabotage the artfully rendered compositions. Precisely why Fulci and Salvati elected to go for the smaller ratio is open to speculation, but it does seem to be particularly well suited to the film's more claustrophobic aesthetic.

American actor Christopher George, who gives a winning performance as Peter Bell, heads the cast. George brings in a number of charming touches and character tics that help to fill-out an otherwise one-dimensional characterization. One would be hard-pressed to imagine Fulci or Sacchetti making a crack about Arlington cemetery, for example, whereas George would certainly have thought to introduce such a touch himself. Born in Michigan in 1931, he did a tour of duty in the Marines before making his film debut with an uncredited bit part in Otto Preminger's epic *In Harm's Way* (1965), starring John Wayne. George became friendly with Wayne and the two men shared similarly right-leaning political views, which made them somewhat unfashionable in the decidedly leftist film industry of the period. Even so, George managed to snag some good roles in films like Howard Hawks' *El Dorado* (1966) and William Castle's *Project X* (1968), in addition to snagging the lead role on the popular TV adventure show *The Rat Patrol*, which aired from 1966 to 1968. The 1970s saw him top-lining more B-movies, including William Girdler's nature-run-amok flicks *Grizzly* (1976) and *Day of the Animals* (1977), both of which also starred his wife, actress Lynda Day George. In the 1980s, he appeared in a number of low-budget horror films, of which *City of the Living Dead* was certainly the best. He died in 1983 from a heart attack that many believe was due to an untreated mishap he suffered on the set of *The Rat Patrol*. It seems that Fulci and George did not get along very well. Make-up artist Rosario Prestopino later recalled that:

> I remember the very first day of filming, [George] and Fulci had an argument. He wanted to smoke a cigar in the church and Fulci didn't agree. But George said, "We are in America, we do things differently here. You can do it!"[8]

The tension eventually boiled over when George got his revenge after the filming of the infamous "storm of maggots" scene, in which he and several of the other actors were required to have live maggots crawl all over their bodies. Camera operator Roberto Forges Davanzati later recalled that Fulci was in the habit of carrying a bag which contained his pipe and smoking tobacco; George got hold of the bag and stuffed it full of maggots, so that when Fulci reached in for a smoke he got a fistful of worms instead. The director was furious, but nobody would own up to it. "It was the lead actor, who hated him," Davanzati claimed. "They hated each other."[9] The tensions between Fulci and George are not evident on screen, however: George commands the screen with charm and charisma.

Catriona MacColl, who would become a significant part of the "Fulci universe," played Mary. MacColl plays the role with absolute conviction, and she has excellent chemistry with George. Fulci was never known for his warm and fuzzy feelings towards actors, but MacColl—along with Florinda Bolkan—appears to have been his favorite. He would later say, "Catriona was one of the actresses I got on best with. She was a very brave one."[10] MacColl, who was born in London in 1954, started off as a ballet dancer before making the transition to film. She appeared in small roles in some minor films before landing her first lead in Jacques Demy's *Lady Oscar* (1979). She recalls her work with Fulci in an interview included later in this book, but by her own admission she approached *City of the Living Dead* with trepidation; she soon realized that she had better bring her "A-game" to the picture, however, and the film benefits from her sincere performance. She would go on to star in *The Beyond* and *The House by the Cemetery*, making her a favorite with fans of the director.

The supporting cast includes Carlo De Mejo, who gives a good performance as Gerry.[11] De Mejo's slightly bemused and deadpan presence is put to good effect in the film, and he would rejoin Fulci on *The House by the Cemetery* and *Manhattan Baby*. The son of actress Alida Valli and painter/composer Oscar De Mejo, he was born in 1945 and began appearing in films in the late 1960s. His other credits include Pier Paolo Pasolini's *Teorema* (1968) and Armando Crispino's *The Dead Are Alive* (1972). He and Fulci got along harmoniously, and he later recalled with great amusement:

> I thought he was adorable because when he got angry, he had everybody running around. [...] I owe a lot to Lucio. I loved him.

The gifted stage and screen actor Giovanni Lombardo Radice played the ill-fated Bob. Lombardo Radice gives the character great weight and sympathy, and he is to be lauded for not reducing him to a freakish caricature. He was born in Rome in 1954 and built up a good theatrical résumé before making his film debut in Ruggero Deodato's *The House on the Edge of the Park* (1980). *City of the Living Dead* was only his third film, but it helped to make him into a European Cult Cinema icon; his later credits include everything from Michele Soavi's *Stage Fright* (1987) and *The Church* (1989) to Martin Scorsese's *Gangs of New York* (2002) and the rather gratuitous remake of *The Omen* (2006). Lombardo Radice also remains very active in the theater and embraces his legacy as a fan favorite for his roles in gory Italian horror films. The aforementioned Michele Soavi (born 1957) also makes a brief appearance as the boy who is killed while making out with girlfriend Daniela Doria. Soavi began appearing in films in the mid-'70s, but ultimately decided that he was more interested in working behind the camera. He made the transition to directing with *Stage Fright* and would go on to direct some of the most imaginative and visually stunning Italian horror films of the 1980s and '90s, including *The Sect* (1991) and *Dellamorte Dellamore* (1994). While working on location on *City of the Living Dead*, he impressed Fulci by asking to work as part of the crew. The director was notoriously volatile with actors, but respected people who were willing to pitch in and do manual labor. Soavi later recalled:

**Left: American poster for *City of the Living Dead*, under the title *The Gates of Hell*; artist unknown.**

> Lucio kind of scared me a lot, but I saw this guy was a hell of a worker. He could fix a scene in a matter of minutes and everything was so clear in his mind. All right, he had this dictatorial tone, but everybody followed his orders in silence.[12]

Fulci's friends Venantino Venantini and Fabrizio Jovine also make their final appearances in one of the director's films: Venantini is properly imposing as the violent Mr. Ross, while Jovine is positively haunting without ever uttering a word as the ghostly Father Thomas.

*City of the Living Dead* helped to cement Fulci's reputation as one of Italy's primary purveyors of the macabre. Other directors dabbled in the genre with middling results, but with Mario Bava's passing in 1980, only Dario Argento and Lucio Fulci were firmly established as masters of this kind of material, at least until the later emergence of Soavi towards the end of the decade. Fulci wasted no time in taking advantage of his renewed popularity: He would continue to jump from project to project and the results were all the more impressive considering the speed with which they were conceived and executed.

Notes:

1. Thrower, Stephen, *Beyond Terror: The Films of Lucio Fulci* (Guildford: FAB Press, 1999), p. 163.
2. Palmerini, Luca M. and Gaetano Mistretta, *Spaghetti Nightmares* (Florida: Fantasma Books, 1996), p. 124.
3. *Ibid*, p. 125.
4. *Ibid*, p. 60.
5. Quoted from the featurette "The Making of *City of the Living Dead*," included on the Blue Underground Blu-ray release of *City of the Living Dead*.
6. Quoted from the featurette "Memories of the *Maestro*," included on the Blue Underground Blu-ray release of *City of the Living Dead*.
7. Quoted from the featurette "The Making of *City of the Living Dead*," included on the Blue Underground Blu-ray release of *City of the Living Dead*.
8. Quoted from the featurette "The Making of *City of the Living Dead*," included on the Blue Underground Blu-ray release of *City of the Living Dead*.
9. *Ibid*.
10. Palmerini, Luca M. and Gaetano Mistretta, *Spaghetti Nightmares* (Florida: Fantasma Books, 1996), p. 60.
11. On the English track vocal actor Frank von Kuegelgen dubbed De Mejo; he also dubbed De Mejo in *Manhattan Baby*. He also did the English dubbing for Marc Porel in *Don't Torture a Duckling*, Paolo Malco in *The House by the Cemetery* and *The New York Ripper* and for Giuseppe Mannajuolo in *Murder-Rock: Dancing Death*, among many others.
12. Quoted from the featurette "The Making of *City of the Living Dead*," included on the Blue Underground Blu-ray release of *City of the Living Dead*.

## Giovanni Lombardo Radice Interview by Troy Howarth

The following interview with actor Giovanni Lombardo Radice was conducted via Skype on August 31, 2014. *Signor* Lombardo Radice—sometimes known as John Morghen, and known to his friends and fans simply as "Johnny"—is an accomplished stage actor whose film career happens to have encompassed appearances in some of the most notoriously violent Italian genre films. The contradiction is amusing, for he is truly one of the mildest and most kindhearted men you could hope to meet. "Johnny" has my sincere thanks for taking the time to talk with me about his career and about his feelings regarding Lucio Fulci, in particular.

**Troy Howarth**: Do you recall how you came to be cast in *City of the Living Dead*?
**Giovanni Lombardo Radice**: It was my third movie, after *House on the Edge of the Park* and *Cannibal Apocalypse* (both 1980). And the horror crowd in Rome was a little one, so they all knew each other and exchanged information. So I guess either [Ruggero] Deodato or [Antonio] Margheriti—or maybe both—recommended me to Fulci. Plus, we knew each other a little socially because we were both friends of director Duccio Tessari, who, with his wife Lorella De Luca, had a sort of open house at night—showbiz people would go there and have drinks and chat and gossip or whatever, so I had met him there … but not talking much, because he was rather gloomy and by himself, so I didn't pay much attention to him. But I guess he did pay attention to me. So I am sure I did not audition—I was just called … and as I learned, I was stealing a role for the second time from Michele Soavi, who had been Deodato's original choice for Ricky in *House on the Edge of the Park* and had been Fulci's first choice for Bob. Then he wanted me. So that was how it happened.
**TH**: Had you ever seen any of his films?
**GLR**: No. Well, I don't recall if it was before or after I worked with him, I saw one that was called … what was the title? Florinda Bolkan was in it. It wasn't a horror—it was a thriller, and quite a good one.
**TH**: *Don't Torture a Duckling*?
**GLR**: No, no … *not* that one.
**TH**: *Lizard in a Woman's Skin*?
**GLR**: Yes, maybe that one. I don't recall anything about it except that I liked it a lot. I don't like horror movies, but I do like thrillers.
**TH**: What were your initial impressions of Fulci?
**GLR**: Before working with him, I was told when friends knew that I was going to work with him, I was told that he was terrible—that he was mistreating people and that he

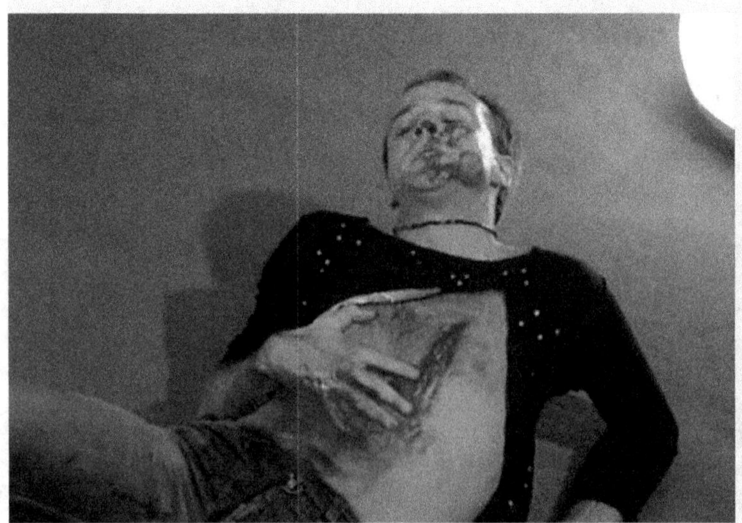

**Giovanni Lombardo Radice under attack in *The House on the Edge of the Park* (1980).**

was a "shouting" director ... My impression was entirely different because, with me, he was always very respectful and polite—even complimentary, at times. I was the only actor he was having dinner with at nighttime after shooting. We chatted. He respected my being a theater person. So I had an entirely different impression. He wasn't very likable or social—of course, he was a difficult man, and I would say a suffering man ... maybe due to some tragedies that happened to his family, and he suffered a lot because he would have liked to have been recognized in Italy, not as a B-director, but just as a great director, as he was known in France. He wasn't jolly. He did make scenes, mostly with production—at times with actors, but I must say that with the production he explained that it was a technique he was using because he said maybe one day you will want to direct a movie, being a theater director, so he gave me this tip: With production you always have to have them almost on edge, otherwise they get sloppy and you don't get what you want. So you must every two or three days make a scene out of nothing, just to keep them going. With actors, as far as I know, when he made a scene he was generally right, because they were assholes or conceited. All in all, I had a wonderful relationship with him.

**TH**: You did not share any scenes with the film's stars, Catriona MacColl and Christopher George, but did you get to meet and know them during filming?

**GLR**: During filming, no, I never met them. I am sure we were in the same hotel, but I never met him. I met Catriona some 10 years ago when we started doing conventions together. She's enchanting, a nice lady, and we have had some great times together. But at the moment I was spending time with Michele Soavi, who played a minor role and also acted as an assistant director. I was spending time with Antonella Interlenghi—I had a big crush on her.

**TH**: How about Venantino Venantini? He was an old friend of Fulci's and his son was also in the movie.

**GLR**: Yes. The big drilling scene with him was done in Rome. As a matter of fact, I think he was on location in Savannah also because of his child, who later became an actor himself. He was a quiet child, very professional. Not an annoying child. Venantino ... you know, we were very young: Michele, Antonella, myself, so Venantino was many years our senior ...

**TH**: You had a funny experience with Antonella Interlenghi, I believe ... could you talk about that?

**GLR**: You mean the zombie make-up and smoking joints?

**TH**: Yes!

**GLR**: (Laughter) Well, Antonella was really a fan of grass ... I've never been, I must say. But at that time, if there were pot to smoke, I would smoke it. But I was never in a mad search for it, as she was. She wanted to smoke every day, and always managed to find it. She met with the most incredible people, like *huge* black guys out of a gangster movie, who circled the set like vultures in search of her. Anyway, that day we had the zombie scene, so make-up started at six in the morning and went on for hours and hours. The final touch was applying marmalade to our faces to give the idea that we were decomposing, which meant that if there was a wasp or bee around, you had a hard time. We were devastated—we couldn't eat or drink, we had all this stuff on our faces. Our clothes smelled because they had been covered with dirt to give the idea of coming back from the dead. So we just shut ourselves in a van and we waited and waited ... They weren't calling us. So, Antonella said, "*I'm bored. Why don't we make a joint?*" I said, "*Okay, do it.*" She prepared a joint: It was the most incredible grass I ever smoked. It was like LSD. We flipped-out completely, and we were watching ourselves in zombie make-up and shouting. It went on and then we calmed down, and I said, "*They can't have us waiting here for hours, it's not professional; I'm going to make a scene.*" So I opened the door of the van, ready to shout, "*What the fuck are you doing?!*" or something, and there was a lady with a five or six-year-old boy. He started shouting, "*Mommy! Mommy! The creature!*" (*laughs*) He was absolutely enthusiastic about it. He wanted to be photographed with me, in my arms, so that was the end of it.

**TH**: Do you recall how long you filmed for on the movie?

**GLR**: I would say a couple of months in Savannah, and some other days in Rome. I think the only thing I shot in Rome was the drill scene. I may be wrong. Most of it was in Savannah.

**TH**: What is your opinion of *City of the Living Dead* as a film? And what do you think of your performance in it?

**GLR**: Well, you must bear in mind that those films, in general, are not my cup of tea, so what can I say? I have watched it many times, even recently because of conventions and commentaries. There's the scene of Daniela Doria puking up her entrails, and I can never watch it. I have to divert my glance, because it's too much. I must

say it has a certain atmosphere, a certain Lovecraftian atmosphere, good photography—but for me, I'm not very interested in zombies and horror and blood. It's not for me. I think I am mighty good in it as far as the roles in those movies are more like comic books than the stage, so it's very roughly sketched. But I think I was good in it.
**TH**: You definitely stand out in the cast—you get a real sense of a character that goes beyond what is written on the page.
**GLR**: Well, I am a theater person, so even if I didn't like those movies—I prepare for my role exactly as if I was doing Shakespeare, so I went through the animal technique, where I study an animal who reminds me of the character and how the animal moves and behaves. I apply it to the character I am playing. Bob was a rat, of course, a sewer rat. I must say I was always very professional, so maybe it shows. (*Laughs*)
**TH**: Did you get the impression anybody was treating the film as a joke?
**GLR**: You mean the other actors?
**TH**: Yes
**GLR**: No, not as a joke, but maybe they were taking it more lightly than I was. Maybe they didn't prepare so much. But I wouldn't say they treated it as a joke.
**TH**: You are well known for your love of acting in the theater ... Do you feel that your film career has helped your stage career, or has it hindered it in any way?
**GLR**: They didn't meet. They just didn't meet. The theater crowd in Italy either ignores that I was in horror movies, or if they know they think it is one of my many extravaganzas ... (*laughs*) I am considered an extravagant person. But they never met. If you look at my website [Note: www.giovannilombardoradice.com], it's divided into two halves—the nice side and the horror side. Anybody who is interested in my horror movie career doesn't give a shit about theater, and vice versa ... The two sides never met.
**TH**: I would certainly love to see you performing Shakespeare, etc.—but obviously, since I live in the U.S. that would be difficult!
**GLR**: Well, yes, I would like to do some theater in English—in the United Kingdom or the U.S. I don't know, I guess I should move. I often think, not of the U.S., but I often think of moving to London. But at my age it's not that easy to change. But I would like to.
**TH**: What do you think of the cult that exists around these low-budget horror films you made?
**GLR**: Well, I got used to it. Not sharing this affinity, it's difficult for me to say why people like these movies. I think it's either because they are a projection of hidden sides of one's personality or just because they are the modern rendition of fairy tales, which are quite horrific in their original versions—not the Disney cartoons, but the *Grimm's Fairy Tales* are pretty horrific. Like birds pecking at Sisyphus' eyes or legs cut off or heads being chopped off. So, yes, I think they appeal to a dark side. I sincerely don't understand the love for blood and all that stuff. I was really shocked because before the Internet, I had received some requests for interviews, but I thought it was just a little group of bizarre people worshiping this stuff. But then when I got on the Internet I realized how *huge*, how incredibly *huge* it was, and how many fans I had—and now I am doing conventions and so on ... It's just a side of humanity.
**TH**: Did you keep in touch with Fulci after the filming was finished? He was quite sick in later years, struggled with diabetes and so forth?
**GLR**: No, in later years I lost track of him. Right after the movie, we kept seeing each other at the Tessaris. I used to have a very big house, and I invited him to a party. While the theater posters were proudly displayed in the living room, as a joke, the horror posters were in the bathroom. So Fulci went to the bathroom and when he came out, he shouted, "*People! People! I am in the loo!*" (*laughs*) So he had a sense of humor about it. But in the last years, I am afraid I lost track of him.
**TH**: How do you think Fulci compares with other Italian genre directors like Michele Soavi or Lamberto Bava or Umberto Lenzi?
**GLR**: You know—each one is different. I don't want to talk about Lenzi. I can't really say anything about Bava because I made only one movie with him, but it was only a little role and I can only say that he is very professional. Michele is the one who is really different from the rest. You know, people tend to think that Deodato and Fulci and Margheriti were fans of these movies—this not true. They were just professionals who were shooting what was fashionable at that time. They did ancient Rome epics,

**Giovanni Lombardo Radice as the Vietnam veteran-turned-cannibal in *Cannibal Apocalypse*.**

*gialli,* Westerns, and when zombies and cannibals became fashionable, they went with the wave and were asked to do these movies. But it wasn't a personal passion for it, whereas Soavi was a real fan of Lovecraft and the Gothic and horror. So he had a passion which I think shows in his movies. As for Fulci, he was a great professional and he was very good along with Sergio Salvati, the director of photography, in creating atmosphere.

**TH**: Dario Argento never directed you, but you were in some films he produced … What do you think of him?

**GLR**: Oh, I love Dario! He is so funny. You wouldn't think it to look at him, but he has a great sense of humor. He has a real passion for movies. He was always on the set—not as a producer who wanted to control things, he was just helping the grips with building things and doing special effects. I respect that. I liked a few of his first movies. *Deep Red* (1975) was one of the last horrors I saw before I decided I just didn't like to get scared; but he is a very nice person.

**TH**: Did your association with these films ever embarrass you? And if so, has your attitude towards them softened in recent years?

**GLR**: The word *embarrassment* is not in my vocabulary. If I do something, I do it and am open about it. So, no, [I never felt] embarrassment. I must say that at the time I was making them I considered them shit. I was doing them professionally, but I thought that they weren't B—but Z-movies. But looking back in recent years I have changed my mind. For example, I think both *House on the Edge of the Park* and *Cannibal Apocalypse* are both quite good movies.

**TH**: You worked with John Saxon on *Cannibal Apocalypse* …

**GLR**: Yes. But I didn't have any kind of private relationship with him. I think he hated the movie and hated being in it. So he stayed by himself. He was very professional and I think he's *very* good in the movie, but I can't say …

**TH**: That is a film he seems to be embarrassed by—though he liked Margheriti.

**GLR**: Yes! He didn't like the movie. And he is not a very amiable man. I met him recently at a convention, and you know at these conventions you see people that you haven't seen in years. For example, I met Bo Svenson; he was really warm and pleasant … Well, John just nodded his head. He always gave me the impression of being cold—a cold person, but professional.

**TH**: Do you have any film projects on the horizon? And how is your theater work going?

**GLR**: As for the theater, I recently produced this Scottish thing by Shakespeare. And I also had a role in it as King Duncan. Oh, one should not name the characters [Note: The play was obviously *Macbeth*]. Knock on wood. (*Laughs*) It's an English superstition. In Italy, it is not seen as this curse, but I stick to the idea of not naming it. When you are doing it, that's one thing, but now it's over. I translated some plays from English to Italian. I recently translated the Christopher Durang play *Vanya and Sonia and Masha and Spike*, a pastiche about Chekhov. But I have no projects on stage now. As for movies, I keep doing little independent productions abroad, or even in Italy. I will start a movie in a couple of weeks that is a remake of a German horror film with a very romantic title: *Violent Shit.* (*laughs*) And I am going to be the Devil in it, which is interesting because I have been God in an English movie called *The Reverend*. So I keep doing what they offer, which isn't much.

**TH**: You had a small role in *Gangs of New York* (2002), which is a film I love.

**GLR**: It wasn't a role, really. I didn't even include it in my credits. The thing is, [Martin] Scorsese wanted to have a staged scene of *Uncle Tom's Cabin* in the movie and there were some lines, and so he wanted real actors. I was hired, then he realized before shooting the movie that it was going to be too long. So he cut the lines from the play. At that point, my agent told me to quit, but the money hadn't changed and it was very good money—and I was very curious about the set, which was *incredible* … I had never seen such a thing in my life. The whole of New York built in Cinecittà. You could get lost in all the streets and alleys and the harbor and whatever. It was amazing. It was bigger than life. We were explicitly told not to go off on our own because people had already gotten lost. I think it was a very good movie, but I can't say it was a significant role for me.

**TH**: Did you get to meet Daniel Day-Lewis? He is amazing in the film.

**GLR**: Yes, he was in the scene with me. I can't say I got to know him, however. I think he is the best living actor. He and Jeremy Irons are the best living actors. But he is a little bit better. He is number one, I think.

**TH**: Absolutely. Daniel Day-Lewis is always different in every role.

**GLR**: Yes, that's it. That is what acting is about. Not being himself, but changing to the point where at the beginning—I first saw him in *A Room with a View* (1985), where he was the dandy, stupid aristocrat … then, not long after, I saw *My Beautiful Laundrette* (1985), where he was the punk, with blonde hair. And only at the end did I realize it was the same actor! That is what acting is about, in my opinion.

**TH**: Okay, well I think that covers all the questions I have … do you have any final thoughts on Fulci and his legacy?

**GLR**: What else can I say? I am sorry that he is not here to witness all the love and recognition he is getting now. I am sure he would be very happy to see how many people like his movies and love him. He died before the Internet was big and he didn't have time to realize how much he was loved all over the world. As for legacy, as we know it's a poor time for horror—not because of the director, it's just a poor time for production in Italy.

**TH**: Thank you for your time, Johnny.

**GLR**: No problem. Good luck with your book!

# Antonella Interlenghi Interview by Troy Howarth

The following interview with Antonella Interlenghi was conducted via email on September 11, 2014. Ms. Interlenghi played the role of the ill-fated "nice girl next door" Emily Robbins in *City of the Living Dead;* she was also one of the few Fulci actresses to come back from the grave as one of the living dead. Ms. Interlenghi has my thanks for agreeing to answer these questions.

**A glamorous shot of Antonella Interlenghi.**

**Troy Howarth**: You began making films in the late 1970s ... what made you want to become an actress?

**Antonella Interlenghi**: I wanted to become an actress because my parents are both actors, they seemed very pleased with their profession. I realized I was attractive, so I tried for it.

**TH**: *City of the Living Dead* was one of your earlier film roles ... how did you come to be cast in the picture?

**AI**: I was cast in Fulci's picture because I had very good newspaper coverage at the time. And Fulci really wanted me. He felt I was a very commercial figure, which could bring money.

**TH**: What did you think of Lucio Fulci as a person and as a director?

**AI**: I felt Lucio Fulci was a very warm and interesting person as a director; when I saw the film I thought "bravo," really.

**TH**: You shared your scenes with Janet Agren, Carlo DeMejo and Giovanni Lombardo Radice... do you have any memories of them?

**AI**: I have good memories of them; nice people and good professionals. I had one scene with Giovanni Lombardo and we were supposed to be both terrified. Well, I thought he was so good I tried my best, the scene worked.

**TH**: Fulci had a reputation for being very tough on the set; was he ever like that with you?

**AI**: On the contrary, he had a soft spot for me. Once I arrived late for make-up and he was very sweet about it, perhaps because I was young and pretty.

**TH**: What is your favorite memory of making the film?

**AI**: My favorite memory is when I die by hand of the demon. They squished ground meat and worms on my face. I felt sick for a week.

**TH**: Was it unpleasant being underneath the make-up for your scenes as a zombie?

**AI**: Yes, it was unpleasant to be under the make-up as a zombie, and extremely laborious to put it on. It took two to three hours. Plus the finishing touches were marmalade, so the bees would try to reach my face to eat ... a problem!

**TH**: The film was made on location in Georgia and in a studio in Rome ... Did you get to go to America to film any of your scenes?

**AI**: Yes, I was In America a month; I shot numerous scenes there, even the ones in the casket, I don't know why. And the ones filmed outside the window, where I was made up as a zombie.

**TH**: As a film, were you impressed with *City of the Living Dead*?

**AI**: Yes, I saw the film and liked it. For a precise target, people who like the horror genre certainly.

**TH**: Did you ever encounter Lucio Fulci again after the filming was finished?

**AI**: No, I never saw Lucio Fulci again.

**TH**: And lastly, are you surprised by the enduring popularity of Fulci and his films?

**AI**: No, I was not surprised by the enduring popularity of the film. It's a good product!

**TH**: That is all the questions I have for you. Thank you for your time.

**AI**: Thank you.

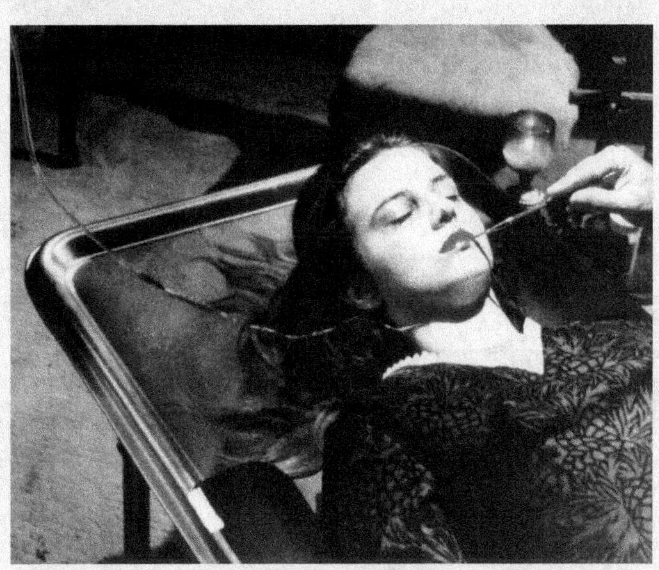

**A less-glamorous shot of Antonella Interlenghi, laid out for the embalmer in *City of the Living Dead.***

# 1981

## *The Black Cat (Italy)*

Aka *Il gatto nero; Le chat noir*

Directed by Lucio Fulci; Produced by Giulio Sbarigia, for Italian International Film and Selenia Cinematografica; Screenplay by Lucio Fulci and Biagio Proietti, adapated by Biagio Proietti from the story "The Black Cat" by Edgar Allan Poe; Director of Photography: Sergio Salvati; Editor: Vincenzo Tomassi; Music by Pino Donaggio

Main Players: Patrick Magee (Robert Miles); Mimsy Farmer (Jill Trevers); David Warbeck (Inspector Gorley); Pierluigi Conti [as Al Cliver] (Sergeant Wilson); Dagmar Lassander (Lillian Grayson); Bruno Corazzari (Ferguson); Geoffrey Copleston (Inspector Flynn); Daniela Doria [as Daniela Dorio] (Maureen Grayson)

*An English village is beset by a number of mysterious murders. Sergeant Wilson is nonplussed and calls in a Scotland Yard detective, Inspector Gorley, to help investigate. Meanwhile, an American tourist named Jill Trevers is in the area taking photographs of the old ruins and cemeteries. Jill encounters the mysterious Robert Miles, a psychic whom the villagers tend to avoid. Miles reveals that he is in a life-and-death struggle with his pet black cat, which he believes will inevitably be the cause of his destruction. Could there be a connection between Miles and the cat and the series of murders?*

Somewhat surprisingly, Fulci elected to follow up the gory excesses of *City of the Living Dead* with a horror film in a considerably lower key. *The Black Cat* continues the director's referencing of Edgar Allan Poe, which was properly initiated in *The Psychic*, but the finished film owes only a small debt to the writer's original story. Truth be told, Poe adaptations that are actually faithful to Poe are very few and far between. The reasons for this are many and varied, but the key reason rests in the stories themselves, which are generally much too short in length and long on mood versus incident to make for adequate screenplay material.

Edgar Allan Poe (1809-1849) lived a short and tragic life, but he left behind a treasure trove of short stories, poetry and essays. *The Black Cat*, first published in 1843 in *The Saturday Evening Post*, tells of a man who lives a charmed life with his beloved wife and their many pets. When the man descends into alcoholism, his relationship with his companions begins to sour. One night, he attacks his black cat, named Pluto, and gouges its eye out with a knife. The cat, understandably, becomes frightened of its master and begins avoiding him. The man feels guilt over what he has done, but in time his guilt turns into annoyance and paranoia. He gets hold of the cat and hangs it in his garden. Later that night, the house catches fire and the man and his wife are forced to flee the premises. The house is almost entirely destroyed, save for a single wall—the next day, the man surveys the damage and sees that the image of the cat hanging from a tree has been crudely drawn onto this wall. The man rationalizes this as a prank by a neighbor who saw him killing the cat and eventually falls back into feeling remorseful for his actions. He finds and rescues another black cat, this one emblazoned with a patch of white fur on its chest; to his horror he realizes that the white patch is shaped eerily like a gallows. He grows to fear the cat, believing it to be a feline avenger, and when he tries to kill it, his wife intervenes; he kills her in a fit of fury and walls the body up in the cellar of their new home. The police come to investigate her "disappearance," and the cocky protagonist tips his hand when he raps on the wall containing the body, causing the cat—which, unknown to him, has also been entombed with its mistress—to let loose an ear-piercing howl. The police tear down the wall and find the wife's rotting corpse; the cat is perched atop her head.

Veteran screenwriter and director Biagio Proietti adapted *The Black Cat* for the screen. Proietti (born in 1940) had been active in films since the late 1960s, but much of his work was in Italian television. Prior to *The Black Cat*, he had gained an intimate knowledge of Poe's *oeuvre* by writing the mini-series *I racconti fantastici di Edgar Allan Poe* (1979); among the stories he adapted for the series were *The Fall of the House of Usher*, *William Wilson* and *Ligeia*. It seems a safe bet that the experience of working on this project inspired Proietti to expand his horizons by bringing Poe back to the big screen. Poe adaptations can be traced all the way back to the silent era, and *The Black Cat* has certainly been the subject of a number of different adaptations. There is some solid reasoning for this: it's one of the few Poe stories that really offers a conventional three act structure, thus making it easier for scenarists to adapt it without having to rely on too many wild inventions. Amazingly, with this in mind, very few adaptations have hewed particularly closely to the source material. In 1934, director Edgar G. Ulmer crafted one of the most stylish and disturbing horror films of the golden age with his version of *The Black Cat*; its pairing of horror icons Boris Karloff and Bela Lugosi made it a smash at the box-office, but truth be told, it had virtually nothing to do with Poe. Even so, the atmosphere of morbid sexuality and obsession is very much in the spirit of Poe, and it certainly doesn't suffer because of its lack of fidelity to the text. Universal produced the film, and they were also responsible for another "Poe-in-name-only" adaptation in 1941; despite an impressive cast headed by Basil Rathbone and some stylish cinematography courtesy of Stanley Cortez, it's a rather tired old dark house comedy. In the 1960s, producer/director Roger Corman struck pay dirt with his series of baroque Edgar Allan Poe adaptations, many penned by either Richard Matheson or Charles Beaumont. The films varied from the faithful (*House of Usher*, 1960) to the fanciful (*The Raven*, 1963), and he worked on the segment of *The Black Cat* into the anthology *Tales of Terror* (1962). In it, Peter Lorre gives a scene-stealing performance as a drunkard who kills his wife (Joyce Jameson) and her lover (series star Vincent Price) and walls them up in the basement; the segment is played for laughs and it is certainly successful on that level. After Corman bid adieu to the series in 1965, the producers at American International Pictures (AIP) tried to keep the franchise going by shoe-horning films which had nothing to do with Poe into the cycle by imposing Poe titles upon them (for example, releasing Michael Reeves' powerful historical horror movie *Witchfinder General*, 1968, as *The Conqueror Worm*) or by producing further, rather anemic entries (Gordon Hessler's *The Oblong Box*, 1969). In the 1970s, as horror films began to escape the confines of Gothic crypts and misty cemeteries, Poe fell out of favor with audiences and there was a general slowing down of pictures based on his writings. Fulci, of course, had worked in elements of the writer's obsession with premature burial into *The Psychic*, but *The Black Cat* would fly in the face of convention by retreating to a more genteel form of horror during a period in which gory excesses were in full swing.

The film is the closest Fulci ever came to directing an old school Gothic horror in the style of England's Hammer Film Productions. Hammer, of course, spearheaded a revived interest in the Gothic in the late 1950s, thanks to the worldwide success of *The Curse of Frankenstein* (1957) and *Dracula* (1958). Their success also inspired Fulci's old friend and colleague Mario Bava, whose "official" directorial debut, *Black Sunday* (1960), was conceived in light of the renewed interest in horror movies. Fulci was certainly aware of the horror films that came before his, but he never gave much indication of being a genre enthusiast in interviews; it was the success of *Zombie* that shifted his career in this direction, though he certainly threw himself into the macabre with wicked abandon. Interestingly, Fulci would later admit that he was not a fan of Hammer's horror films, finding their approach too staid and classically British, though he did admit admiration for one of Hammer's most iconic performers, Christopher Lee.[1] It's quite possible that the excesses of *Zombie* and *City of the Living Dead* had him chomping at the bit to prove that he could make a horror picture with a greater emphasis on mood and suspense as opposed to blood and gore, but the film's disappointing box-office take would send him scrambling back to the drawing board to continue with the winning formula of blood and the living dead. Fulci would later

**American poster for *The Black Cat*; artist unknown.**

**Irish actor Patrick Magee gives a compelling performance in *The Black Cat*.**

claim—perhaps in light of the film's box-office failure—that he only directed the film as a favor to producer Giulio Sbarigia, who had earlier produced *Young Dracula*.[2] In any event, the film remains something of a curio in this stage of the director's career; a proper, old-fashioned English Gothic viewed through an Italian lens. For many viewers, the mixture of styles is an uncomfortable one. Taken on its own terms, however, *The Black Cat* has plenty to offer—and its status as something of a thorn between the two roses of *City of the Living Dead* and *The Beyond* among some fans seems based more in an inability to accept a more low-key approach than on any major shortcomings within the film itself.

Bearing in mind that there is a bit of narrative confusion at the heart of the film, Fulci nevertheless manages to create and sustain an appropriate air of doom and gloom. The use of the English countryside locations certainly helps, while Sergio Salvati creates some of his most beautiful imagery since *Four of the Apocalypse*. The end result does not quite cohere in narrative terms, but its execution can hardly be faulted.

Part of the problem with the script is its inability to reconcile the precise nature of the central conflict: Is Robert Miles the real villain of the piece, or is it the cat? The cat seems to be acting under Miles' malefic influence, but after a certain point he is unable to control the creature. He attempts to dispose of it—in a long sequence that works in some explicit quotations from Poe's story—but the kitty seems to be in possession of nine lives and refuses to stay dead. Miles tries to rebel against the cat, but to no avail. Like Virginia in *The Psychic*, his extrasensory perception has allowed him to foresee his own death, and nothing is going to prevent the inevitable. The more Miles rebels against this inevitability, the stronger the cat's hold becomes over him. The end result is another meditation on the futility of trying to escape one's personal destiny, but Fulci and Proietti seem unclear—maybe even undecided—on whether or not Miles is a tragic antihero or a flat-out villain. Similarly, his vendetta against the villagers is muddled. He speaks of being ostracized by them, but he doesn't seem particularly welcoming to people who invade his well-ordered universe, either; on the face of it, he appears to be a lone wolf, but could it be that he secretly yearns for acceptance? Even so, if his desire is to get back at the villagers, he seems to be going about it in a terribly arbitrary manner. For example, sooner than go after his estranged lover, Lillian, he gets to her by killing off her daughter and the girl's boyfriend. Miles seems horrified by the outcome, which again raises the question: Is he in control of the cat, or is the cat twisting his bitterness into a means of engaging in wanton bloodlust? Only the film's inability to clarify this central theme prevents it from joining the ranks of Fulci's finest horror films.

Even so, the film offers up some tremendous mood and atmosphere. Visually it is among the most beautiful of Fulci's films, and a gorgeous soundtrack by Pino Donaggio underlines the pastoral ambience. Donaggio (born in Veneto in 1941) is best known for his collaborations with American director Brian De Palma, who often utilizes his Bernard Herrmann-inspired approach to highlight the thread of Alfred Hitchcock worship which runs throughout his thrillers, like *Dressed to Kill* (1980) and *Body Double* (1984). Donaggio made an impressive cinema debut with his music for Nicolas Roeg's arty horror film *Don't Look Now* (1973) and he has also worked on several films directed by Fulci's genre "rival" Dario Argento, including *Two Evil Eyes* (1990) and *Trauma* (1993). This is the only time Fulci and Donaggio collaborated, which is a shame; his beautiful themes suit the film perfectly and create a sense of melancholy in some scenes, while accentuating the frantic horror of others.

Fulci is also well served by a strong cast. Patrick Magee gives a wonderful performance as the ambiguous Robert Miles. Magee's striking eyes are put to particularly good effect as Fulci and Salvati often zero in on them for tight close-ups; these close-ups have been derided by many viewers (often due to the fact that prior to the advent of DVD, the film was often shown in brutally panned-and-scanned editions which made them look very strange indeed), but they are a perfectly legitimate way of underlining Miles' psychic and hypnotic abilities. Certainly, unlike many actors, Magee possesses the presence and character to really pull off the notion of mind-control, and he provides the film with a solidity it desperately needs in light of its sometimes-slippery screenplay. Born in Ireland in 1922, Magee was principally a theater actor at heart—it is well known that the playwright Samuel Beckett regarded him as his favorite actor—but he started appearing in films in the late 1950s. His unusual voice and penetrating eyes made him a natural for villainous roles, and he attained fame for his performance as the Marquis de Sade in Peter Weiss' *Marat/Sade*, a role he reprised in Peter Brooks' well-regarded 1967 film of the same name. Magee appeared in two films for the mercurial *auteur* Stanley Kubrick—as the memorably deranged Mr. Alexander in *A Clockwork Orange* (1971) and as the Chevalier de Balibari, who teaches Ryan O'Neill how to cheat at cards, in *Barry Lyndon* (1975)—and he also appeared in films by William Friedkin (*The Birthday Party*, 1968), Don Siegel (*Telefon*, 1977), Joseph Losey (*The Servant*, 1963) and others, but he found that low-budget horror films were often his port of call. Magee willingly lent his talent to such films as *Asylum* (1972), *Demons of the Mind* (1972) and *The Sleep of Death* (1980), as the money he earned from them enabled him to finance work in his primary love; the stage. Magee came to be cast in the role of Robert Miles after two other genre super stars passed on the offer. Peter Cushing was first approached to play the role and went so far as to annotate his copy of the script with notes as to the character and the wardrobe. Just why he dropped out of the picture is unknown, but it is possible that Fulci's new-found reputation for making gory horror films may have played a role; alternatively, the actor may have feared that the Italian filmmaker would be inclined to animal cruelty, as he made a special point of noting in the margins of his script, "No cruelty to cats ... vet must be standing by."[3] The mind still reels at the prospect of Cushing, the "gentleman of horror," collaborating with the rough and blasphemous Lucio Fulci; in any event, Cushing ultimately withdrew from the project. The part was then offered to Donald Pleasence, but when the filming of David Hemmings' *The Treasure of the Yankee Zephyr* (1981) went over schedule, he was forced to withdraw. Magee was then offered and accepted the part. Unfortunately, it did not prove to be a smooth collaboration for Fulci and him. In an interview with Robert Schlockoff in *L'Ecran fantastique*, later translated into English and reprinted in the U.K. magazine *Starburst*, Fulci recalled his star:

> He is a marvelous actor, but shooting with him was extremely exhausting, as he has a lot of personal problems. He didn't actually collaborate much, I even had incredible difficulties with him, but his acting talent is beyond criticism. I think Patrick Magee was the perfect choice for a film I wanted to do as an atmosphere film, not as a horror film.[4]

Co-star David Warbeck was in awe of the Irish actor's talent, as well:

> He was one of the megas—trying to work opposite that guy, with those eyes and everything, you had to come up with a whole bag of tricks [...] No, Patrick had a problem, but he was lovely ... his daughter was there, trying to help him through his last days. His was such a very sad story: an extraordinary talent ... brought down by the bottle.[5]

*The Black Cat* would prove to be Magee's last starring role; he died on August 14, 1982, at the age of 60.

The aforementioned David Warbeck is cast in the somewhat thankless role of Inspector Gorley, the nominal romantic interest. Warbeck does not have the benefit of an interesting character to play, but he brings his considerable charm and sardonic wit to the role. He would go on to top-line Fulci's next film, *The Beyond*, and became a favorite among European Cult Cinema aficionados in the process. Warbeck was born in New Zealand in 1941. He started appearing in uncredited bit roles and on British television in the 1960s, then gradually began attracting more attention in the 1970s. He played the hero in Hammer Film Productions' *Twins of Evil* (1971), opposite mooted star, Peter Cushing, and also starred in Russ Meyer's *Blacksnake* (1973). He secured a small role in Sergio Leone's *Duck You Sucker* (1972), playing the IRA informant whose murder haunts James Coburn throughout the movie, and loved working in Italy so much that he determined to make it his base of operation. Rumor has it that he was seriously considered as the replacement for Sean Connery in the James Bond franchise, but nothing ever came of it. *The Black Cat* marked his first association with Fulci, for whom he felt tremendous warmth and respect:

> I adored, liked him immensely, though everyone regards him as completely barking mad. He was a raving madman on set, but always to the correct purpose, and he was always very good with me. Totally mad, though ...[6]

**French lobby card: Inspector Gorley (David Warbeck) and Jill (Mimsy Farmer) deal with a crime scene.**

Warbeck embraced his genre cinema legacy and endeared himself to fans at various convention appearances, before succumbing to cancer in 1997 at the age of just 55.

American actress Mimsy Farmer plays Jill. The waif-like actress displayed genuine acting chops in a number of other films, but she seems a bit adrift here. She was born in Chicago in 1945 and came to prominence thanks to her role in Barbet Schroeder's counterculture cult favorite *More* (1969). She started appearing in Italian films in the 1970s, notably appearing in Dario Argento's *Four Flies on Grey Velvet* (1971) and Armando Crispino's *Autopsy* (1975). Farmer and Fulci got on well enough during the filming, with Fulci later saying,

> Mimsy Farmer [...] is terrific: She is both a very friendly person and a very good actress for this type of film. Producers tried to launch her as the "leading American woman in Italy" a few years ago, but, as films like *The Black Cat* are very rare in Italy, I don't think she has played in any films since then.[8]

**The Black Cat is none-too-pleased—no wonder with a crew member's hand visible to keep him in place!**

Warbeck would later tell fellow Englishman abroad Mark Thompson Ashworth of how focused Fulci would be on set, sometimes to comic effect. During the filming of one scene:

> The camera was on a dolly and moving backwards. Fulci was perched on an elevated seat on the dolly and giving instructions to David as he walked forwards, following the camera. Suddenly he heard: "*AAAAARGGGGH!*" and saw that Fulci had banged his head very hard on the low ceiling.[7]

Farmer reciprocated the sentiment:

> I have a good opinion of him because, although he is sometimes tactless, I think he is a very straightforward and intelligent person. Another thing I like about him is that he doesn't take himself too seriously. [...] It was interesting to work with Patrick Magee.[9]

David Warbeck was less enthused about his leading lady, however:

> Mimsy ... frankly, I thought she was a bit odd ... I remember we were doing one scene of potential intimacy, sitting on a couch and I was delivering my lines for all I was worth and when the time came to take break, she turned to me and said, "You call that acting?" I thought she was joking at first, but she hadn't shown much of a sense of humor up to that point; she never said very much at all, and I realized that she meant it. So when I saw her later on this bed, bouncing up and down with the special effects and everything, I thought, "Do you call that acting?"[10]

The supporting cast includes a couple of faces familiar from Fulci's earlier films: Bruno Corazzari, so memorable as the "midwife" in *Four of the Apocalypse*, returns as the unfortunate drunk who falls afoul of the titular kitty. Vito Passeri, who played the prominent role of the mentally unstable Giuseppe in *Don't Torture a Duckling* and a smaller role in *The Psychic*, appears briefly in one scene; this would be the final time both actors would work with Fulci. On the other hand, Al Cliver returns from *Zombie*—and would go on to appear in quite a few more Fulci films. He gives a solid performance as the befuddled Sergeant Wilson and contributes some nicely understated humor in his scenes with Warbeck.

*The Black Cat* is one of Fulci's most underappreciated films. Despite its narrative obscurity, it has style to burn, offers up some nicely staged sequences of suspense and manages to capture something of the obsessive nature of Poe's writing. Fans would be well advised to revisit it if they haven't done so already.

Notes:

1. From the article "Effetti speciali," originally written by Lucio Fulci for an Italian magazine in 1992, then republished in the book *Miei mostri adorati* (Bologna: Edizioni Pendragon, 1995).
2. Thrower, Stephen, *Beyond Terror: The Films of Lucio Fulci* (Guildford: FAB Press, 1999), p. 189.
3. Gullo, Christopher, *In All Sincerity, Peter Cushing* (Xlibris Corporation, 2004), p. 318.
4. Retrieved from, http://www.shockingimages.com/fulci/interview2.html
5. Palmerini, Luca M. and Gaetano Mistretta, *Spaghetti Nightmares* (Florida: Fantasma Books, 1996), p. 152.
6. *Ibid.*
7. Personal correspondence with Mark Thompson Ashworth.
8. Retrieved from, http://www.shockingimages.com/fulci/interview2.html
9. Palmerini, Luca M. and Gaetano Mistretta, *Spaghetti Nightmares* (Florida: Fantasma Books, 1996), p. 48.
10. *Ibid*, p. 152.

## The Beyond (Italy)

Aka ...*E tu vivrai nel terrore! L'aldilà; El más allá; L'au-delà; Geisterstadt der Zombies; Seven Doors of Death*

Directed by Lucio Fulci; Produced by Fabrizio De Angelis, for Fulvia Film; Screenplay by Lucio Fulci, Giorgio Mariuzzo and Dardano Sacchetti, from a story by Dardano Sacchetti; Director of Photography: Sergio Salvati; Editor: Vincenzo Tomassi; Music by Fabio Frizzi [rescored for the US release by Walter E. Sear]

Main Players: Catriona MacColl [as Katherine MacColl] (Liza Merril); David Warbeck (Dr. John McCabe); Cinzia Monreale [as Sarah Keller] (Emily); Antoine Saint-John (Schweick); Veronica Lazar (Martha); Michele Mirabella (Martin Avery); Pierluigi Conti [as Al Cliver] (Harris); Tonino Pulci [as Anthony Flees] (Joe, the plumber); Maria Pia Marsalla (Jill)

Cameo appearance: Lucio Fulci (Town clerk)

*New Orleans, 1927: a lynch mob attacks a reclusive painter named Schweick in his hotel room at the Seven Doors Hotel; they believe him to be a warlock, and that he is trying to bring evil upon the area. Schweick condemns his attackers and warns them that the hotel is built atop one of the seven gateways to hell; their actions have the potential to open the door, and only Schweick knows how to save them. They carry out their execution, anyway. Decades later, Liza Merril inherits the Seven Doors Hotel from her uncle and sets about trying to restore the place. Strange events conspire to keep the hotel closed and Liza turns to a local doctor, John McCabe, for assistance. The two of them will soon face an onslaught of horrors as Schweick's prediction begins to finally come true ...*

For his next film, Fulci again turned to H.P. Lovecraft for inspiration. He decided to take the experiment of *City of the Living Dead* even further by de-emphasizing plot even more. Dardano Sacchetti drafted a story that adhered to the basic concept Fulci expounded upon in a later interview with Robert Schlokoff:

**_The Beyond_; original artwork by Scott Hoffman.**

**Italian *locandina* for *The Beyond*; artwork by Enzo Sciotti.**

> My idea was to make an *absolute* film, with all the horrors of our world. It's a plotless film; a house, people, and dead men coming from the beyond. There's no logic to it, just a succession of images. The Sea of Darkness, for instance, is an absolute world, an immobile world where every horizon is similar. I think each man chooses his own inner hell, corresponding to his hidden vices. So I am not afraid of Hell, since Hell is already in us. Curiously enough, I can't imagine a Paradise exists, though I am a Catholic—but perhaps God has left me?—yet I have often envisaged Hell, since we live in a society where only Hell can be perceived. Finally, I realize that *Paradise* is indescribable. Imagination is much stronger when it is pressed by the terrors of Hell.[1]

Fulci's ambivalence over religion to one side, it seems he never quite shook loose of his faith completely:

> This may seem strange, but I am happier than somebody like Buñuel, who says he is looking for God. I have found Him in the others' misery, and my torment is greater than Buñuel's. For I have realized that God is a God of suffering. I envy atheists; they don't have all these difficulties.[2]

Theological concerns aside, Fulci determined to make *The Beyond* his most surreal film to date; its willful lack of structure and logic would prove jarring for many viewers, but it has also made it into his most celebrated and beloved film. *The Beyond* may not be his finest work, but it is certainly his most popular.

The Fulci/Sacchetti dynamic was mixed up by the addition of Giorgio Mariuzzo to the mix. Mariuzzo had already earned Fulci's respect on such diverse projects as *Un uomo da ridere* and *Contraband*, but *The Beyond* would prove his facility with working in the horror genre as well. He would go on to work with Fulci and Sacchetti one more time on *The House by the Cemetery*, but Sacchetti remains adamant in interviews that he wrote these films primarily on his own. According to Sacchetti, he had to work hard to push Fulci toward accepting the lack of logic in these scenarios:

> I had tiring discussions with Lucio, and perhaps succeeded in demolishing the perfect mechanisms his cinema was made of. I am the one responsible for all those illogical mishaps our zombie films outlined. Lucio really struggled with his desire for logic, which was threatening his genial instinct to surface.[3]

Fulci establishes the right mood in the opening prologue sequence. The photography sets up the basic plot in purely visual terms, presented in moody sepia-tinted black-and-white. Very little dialogue is included, nor does it need to be included. The locals (played mostly by members of the crew, according to David Warbeck and Catriona MacColl's audio commentary for the Anchor Bay DVD release of the film) band together and decide to kill off the painter, Schweick. Here again, Fulci highlights the danger of herd mentality by demonstrating what can happen when ignorant people gang up on an innocent outsider. Schweick, like Bob in *City of the Living Dead* or Maciara in *Don't Torture a Duckling*, is condemned for no better reason than being "different." He lives as a recluse, does not bother anybody, but his inability to fit in with the crowd disturbs the locals. They justify their actions by branding him as a warlock, but it is unclear whether he was planning anything "evil," anyway. He passes his time painting impressionistic portraits of a strange landscape and possesses a deep understanding of the occult, but neither of these things justifies the horrific "justice" which the locals dole out on him. In a scene that recalls the tragic death of Maciara in *Duckling*, they corner the frightened man and beat him mercilessly with chains. He is then hauled down to the basement, where his body is dissolved by quicklime. The remains are then hidden in the very foundation of the hotel, but the sins committed will not stay buried indefinitely.

**Behind-the-scenes on *The Beyond*: David Warbeck strikes a smile, while Al Cliver smokes in the background.**

From there, Fulci, Sacchetti and Mariuzzo take a little time to establish Liza and her role in the proceedings. Liza is an engaging protagonist. Bearing in mind that precious little time is devoted to something as trivial as characterization, she is established as a positive and resourceful presence. She is warned-off from the hotel by the locals and is genuinely disquieted by the eccentric workers who appear to have "come with" the hotel, but she is not one to be cowed or discouraged very easily. She needs to make the hotel work as a thriving business in order to get her head above water financially, and she is prepared to fight in order to make that happen. Liza is a forceful presence in a milieu that is mostly inhabited with ciphers and freaks. She will provide the film with its dramatic core, even if the powerful forces she finds herself running up against limit her.

Liza's plans to renovate and reopen the hotel do not go as planned. Accidents occur among the workers and before long an ancient evil begins to rear its head. A plumber tries to trace the source of a leak that has flooded the basement and inadvertently opens the portal leading to another world; he loses his eyes as punishment and will eventually return as a shambling zombie. The other workers employed at the hotel are a strange lot: The maid, Martha, is clearly hiding something and her assistant, Arthur, seems a short sidestep removed from total mania. As the dark forces begin to take hold, any semblance of normality is gradually erased. Liza finds herself living in a nightmare from which there appears to be no escape.

Her main contacts in the area are a mysterious blind girl named Emily and the rugged local doctor, John McCabe. Emily appears otherworldly and for good reason; she was first introduced in the prologue and is now seen looking much the same, save for the fact that she has gone completely blind. Emily tries warning Liza not to stay at the hotel, but Liza will not be put off. McCabe means well and does his best to provide a source of comfort, but his macho posturing cannot conceal his basic inability to deal effectively with the situation. McCabe is something of a parody of horror film heroic figures: He is rigidly logical and tries to solve problems in an assertive manner, but he bungles his way through much of the film. His inability to accept the supernatural marks him out as arrogant, and even his attempts to play the action hero backfire. Liza remains the only one who truly seems to understand what is going on, even if she is basically powerless to do anything about it; even so, she never comes off as arrogant and hopelessly inept as McCabe. In short, she is yet another strong female protagonist for Fulci, and helps to disprove the kneejerk criticism that Fulci hated women.

Once the characters are established, there really isn't anything in the way of a plot. The film moves from one set piece to the next. Some sequences are designed to shock, while others are geared more toward mood and atmosphere. Fulci's direction is elegant and assured throughout. He makes excellent use of the New Orleans locations, and the lighting by Sergio Salvati and camerawork by Franco Bruni is some of the most eye-catching to be found in the director's filmography. Giannetto De Rossi again contributes some memorable special make-up effects, as well. Fulci's determination to shock the viewer results in some truly spectacular sequences. One of these depicts the re-emergence of Joe, the plumber; last seen mutilated and dead in the waterlogged basement, he shows up—quite illogically—in one of the hotel's bathtubs. One can't help but wonder if Fulci and his cowriters were inspired by Stanley Kubrick's *The Shining* (1980), which also tells the story of a haunted hotel; both films share in common a scene of a rotting body rising from the bathtub, though the two films play the scene out in different styles. Kubrick teases the viewer—and his psychologically unstable protagonist, played by Jack Nicholson—by showing us the beautiful and inviting figure of a naked woman emerging from the bath; the protagonist responds by embracing and kissing her, at which point an expertly timed shock-cut re-

**Behind-the-scenes on *The Beyond:* Rita Agostini, David Warbeck, Lucio Fulci and Catriona MacColl smile for the still photographer.**

veals that the figure is actually a decaying old crone. Fulci doesn't go for the erotic; he goes for the visceral. The body of Joe emerges from the tub and backs the terrified Martha against the wall, before smashing her skull into a nasty looking, rusty nail; the nail penetrates her skull and forces her eyeball out of its socket. Fulci's longstanding fixation on eye trauma gets ample screen time in *The Beyond*. Joe loses his eye, as well, and there is more still to come.

One of the film's most celebrated sequences involves the demise of Liza's architect friend, Martin. Martin goes to look up the hotel's ground plans at a local library—that's Fulci himself playing the clerk who is determined to leave Martin alone so that he can get his lunch break—and when he realizes that something is amiss, he is suddenly struck down by a gust of wind. At this point, dozens of tarantulas appear and set about devouring the poor man, who is paralyzed and unable to fight back. The scene has been derided for its sometime obvious fake spiders, but there are plenty of real ones in there as well. The scene is indicative of Fulci's dark humor: He knows only too well that the jerky fake spiders look phony as hell, and he seems to be inviting the viewer to succumb to mocking the film by lingering on the shots of them for a little too long. He then pulls the rug out from under us by lingering on truly horrific shots of the spiders tearing the man's flesh from his bones; it goes so far over-the-top as to border on the ridiculous, but it is truly gross and truly effective. Before all is said and done, Martin will suffer some eye trauma, as well, as a spider chews away one of his eyelids in nauseating detail.

The finale of the film sees Liza and McCabe fighting for their lives as logic and reason break down even further. They find themselves besieged by a horde of the living dead at the hospital, before escaping down a flight of stairs—which lead, bizarrely, to the flooded basement of the hotel itself. McCabe is reduced to protesting, *"Impossible! Impossible!"* but Liza is not about to argue with her senses; impossible or not, it is a reality, and they must react accordingly. The two make their way through the mist and end up in the impressionistic landscape pained by Schweick at the start of the film. They find themselves surrounded by death and decay and attempt to escape, but it is too late; they lose their sight and eventually disappear into the sea of darkness.

If *City of the Living Dead* can be criticized for a bit of clumsiness in its final, hastily improvised sequence, no such qualms can be voiced with *The Beyond*. The ending is striking; downbeat yet poetic, grim but beautiful. Fulci would later claim that the zombie action was added in on the insistence of the German distributor, but those scenes do not feel like an afterthought. *The Beyond*, like *City of the Living Dead*, is not a conventional zombie movie: The living dead do not feature prominently in the movie, and, as in the earlier film, the spectacle of flesh-munching is downplayed in favor of creating an atmosphere of fear and dread. To suggest that *The Beyond* is a sequel of any kind to *City of the Living Dead* is inaccurate, but the two films are unified by a bracing disregard for logic and a palpable flair for Gothic atmosphere.

Ultimately, *The Beyond* does not match the sheer poetry and mood of *City of the Living Dead*, but it is renowned by Italian horror buffs for good reason: It is a wonderfully imaginative movie and, stylistically, it can hardly be faulted. Fulci was working at the top of his game at this time, supported by a crack team of technicians and exploring new ideas and terrain with enthusiasm. The tremendous energy and flair he brought to the films he made during this period is all the more impressive when one considers the speed with which these projects were assembled. *The Beyond* was filmed on a low budget and didn't have the luxury of a long schedule, but very little suggests this onscreen—only the odd gaffe like a sign written in English as "Do Not Entry" betrays any of the haste with which the film was produced. Unfortunately, some critics—including the late Roger Ebert—used this minor but rather charming *faux pas* as an excuse to attack the film; sooner than admire the efforts of Fulci and his crew for overcoming tremendous odds and delivering a film of style and atmosphere, picking on mistakes such as this only goes to show the contempt with which some viewers view this sort of material.

Like *City of the Living Dead*, *The Beyond* is steeped in the creepy atmospherics of H.P. Lovecraft. However, it seems likely that Fulci, Sacchetti and Mariuzzo were equally influenced by several other sources. *The Shining* has already been alluded to, of course. The book by Stephen King was a bestseller upon its original release in 1977, and the fact that a major *auteur* like Kubrick decided to bring it to the screen made the film an eagerly anticipated happening in 1980. Many viewers were disappointed by the film's measured pace and long running time, including Fulci himself:

> I didn't like the film because, in my opinion, although Kubrick is a great director, he deals with things that don't concern him at all, and so, he expands it and drags it out until it becomes implausible. [...] I do find the film fantastically shameless [...] But I think Mr. Kubrick is too good for horror films.[4]

Another likely source of inspiration is Michael Winner's *The Sentinel* (1977), the story of a cursed hotel that contains a portal to another dimension. Despite glossy production values and some genuine scares, the film's use of handicapped extras as freaks upset some critics. Even so, it was the type of film that Italian filmmakers loved to quote from: Its stylish and trippy imagery made it ripe for the picking, indeed. In addition, there are also the first two entries in the so-called "Three Mothers" trilogy by director Dario Argento: *Suspiria* (1977) contains a scene in which a blind man is savaged to death by his possessed seeing-eye dog; *The Beyond* includes a similar fate for poor Emily. *Inferno* (1980) focuses on yet another cursed hotel setting and is similarly unconcerned with maintaining a conventional structure or logic; Dardano Sacchetti has long insisted that he contributed to the writing of that film and that Argento deprived him of a credit, so *The Beyond* allows him to revise some of the same atmospherics.

**Behind-the-scenes on *The Beyond*; preparing the final desolate vision of the beyond ...**

Inevitably, many critics missed the point of what Fulci and his collaborators were trying to achieve and took the film to task for being nonsensical. It's a shame that so many literal-minded viewers have a difficult time turning off the logical component of their brain when viewing films such as this; Fulci demonstrated repeatedly throughout his career that he was capable of telling a coherent story in a perfectly capable manner, but *The Beyond* sees him building on the thesis of *City of the Living Dead* by detailing a story completely devoid of logic. This is not due to bad writing or carelessness; on the contrary, it's a very deliberate tactic. Fulci would later comment on this:

> People who blame *The Beyond* for its lack of story have not understood that it's a film of *images*, which must be received without any reflection. They say it is very difficult to interpret such a film, but it is *very easy* to interpret a film with threads: Any idiot can understand Molinaro's *La Cage aux Folles*, or even Carpenter's *Escape from New York*, while *The Beyond* or Argento's *Inferno* are *absolute* films.[5]

This is a point worth considering: In American film criticism, in particular, there is a stubborn tendency to rely upon narrative cohesion as an indicator of thoughtful filmmaking. Directors like Michelangelo Antonioni and Joseph Losey spent their careers trying to break down some of these prejudices by demonstrating that it is possible to avoid narrative cliché by unfolding their narratives in a more elliptical fashion; sooner than explicitly spell out every single plot point, even major incidents could be alluded to or conveyed in a way that could become alienating for viewers more accustomed to "classical" Hollywood storytelling. Fulci's aim in *The Beyond* is explicit: He wants to create an atmosphere akin to a nightmare. The story itself is secondary. The fact that things happen which make no literal sense—for example, the spiders suddenly appearing in the library—is not indicative of sloppy filmmaking; it's all part of the grand design. Those viewers who can appreciate this and accept it without fighting the

**Liza and Dr. McCabe enter the beyond ... and will never be the same.**

film every step of the way are in for a treat. *The Beyond* is one of the relatively few horror films—along with the likes of Carl Theodore Dreyer's *Vampyr* (1932), Mario Bava's *Lisa and the Devil* (1973), Argento's *Inferno* and Fulci's *City of the Living Dead*—which truly does justice to that hoary old cliché; the horror film as a celluloid nightmare.

Technically speaking, *The Beyond* is beautifully rendered. Sergio Salvati's cinematography is consistently superb, Vincenzo Tomassi's editing respects the very particular rhythm of the material and the production design and art direction by Massimo Lentini is top notch. Special note should also be made of the superb soundtrack composed by Fabio Frizzi. It's undoubtedly his most popular film score, and for good reason: The mixture of eerie chorales and themes, which range from the elegant to the funky, suits the visuals perfectly.

Catriona MacColl is back aboard for her second of three Fulci performances; Liza is her favorite of the three roles, and there are elements of her own life to be found in the character: She explains that she is a former model and dancer, for example. MacColl's winning personality and ability to sell even the most unbelievable of lines makes Liza into a character worth caring about. David Warbeck has his work cut out for him in the role of McCabe. The character is deliberately obtuse, and one can't help but get the feeling that Fulci is undercutting him as a means of turning genre conventions on their head; McCabe is the type of character one would normally expect to see rescuing Liza from danger, but his inability to grasp the simple concept that the zombies are vulnerable to being shot in the head makes it clear that he is no knight in shining armor. Warbeck is very good in the role and he and MacColl play off of each other very well. He would recall working with MacColl with great affection:

> She was a wonderful girl, a pleasure to work with … an English girl, and, like myself, she was a bit mystified as to why we were being whisked off all over the world to do these films. Also, like myself, she was quite delighted about it all. She was great to work with, we used to deliberately send each other up on set.[6]

The fun-loving actor decided to have a joke on his director at one point by reloading his gun by putting the bullets down the barrel; this bit of levity makes its way into the film, apparently having never been noticed by Fulci or Tomassi, and Catriona MacColl can briefly be seen breaking character by grinning broadly at the action. Warbeck was also on his second time working with Fulci, but unlike MacColl, he would not repeat it a third time. Even so, he would regard the film as a career highlight and never seemed to tire talking about it with fans. He later recalled the tumultuous relationship between Fulci and producer Fabrizio De Angelis:

> There were some amazing fights between Fulci and Fabrizio, and one time, though I don't think Fulci exactly pushed him, but I know Fabrizio fell into the cesspool in the cellar, the one the warlock comes out of … I remember everyone was in great glee, because Fabrizio is always very dapperly turned-out […][7]

Warbeck and MacColl would reunite to do a commentary track for the eventual Anchor Bay DVD release of the film,

**Italian lobby card for *The Beyond*.**

and it would prove to be his last work; he died a couple of weeks later. Up until the end of his life, Warbeck entertained the notion of making a sequel to *The Beyond*; during the course of the commentary track, he even notes with hopeful optimism that the project is soon to get off the ground—but sadly, it never came to pass. Even so, the track is tremendous fun to listen to and the enthusiasm the two show for the film and for Fulci in general is infectious and sincere.

*The Beyond* encountered difficulties with the censors, especially in England. The BBFC passed the film with an "X" rating, demanding numerous cuts. The film would later end up on the infamous "Video Nasties" list, but was ultimately released fully uncut to video in 2001. The film did not enjoy the same kind of theatrical exposure in the U.S. as *Zombie* did, for example: It was eventually acquired by distributor Terry Levene, who gave the film a release in 1983 under the title *Seven Doors to Death*. Levene decided to anglicize the credits, making Fulci into "Louis Fuller," for example, and also decided to jettison Frizzi's haunting soundtrack in favor of a synthesizer score by Walter E. Sear; Sear also rescored the American release of Marino Girolami's *Zombie Holocaust* (1980), memorably retitled as *Dr. Butcher, M.D*. The fully uncut version did not officially surface in the U.S. until after Fulci's death, by which time it had already developed into a major cult item. Grindhouse Releasing—a company run by Bob Murawski and Sage Stallone, the late son of action film icon Sylvester Stallone—put the film out in a limited theatrical run, where it drew cheers from adoring fans and sneering notices from critics who knew nothing of Fulci and his legacy. The film was eventually put out on DVD by Anchor Bay in the U.S., with a Blu-ray release following in the U.K. through Arrow Video; an American Blu-ray release is also planned from Grindhouse.

Censorship woes and distribution issues to one side, *The Beyond* proved to be another winner for Fulci and producer Fabrizio De Angelis, and the association would continue with another foray into the realm of gory horror.

Notes:

1. Retrieved from, http://www.shockingimages.com/fulci/interview2.html
2. *Ibid.*
3. Curci, Loris, *Shock Masters of the Cinema*, (Key West: Fantasma Books, 1996), p. 129.
4. Palmerini, Luca M. and Gaetano Mistretta, *Spaghetti Nightmares* (Florida: Fantasma Books, 1996), p. 61.
5. Retrieved from, http://www.shockingimages.com/fulci/interview2.html
6. Palmerini, Luca M. and Gaetano Mistretta, *Spaghetti Nightmares* (Florida: Fantasma Books, 1996), p. 153.
7. *Ibid.*

# Catriona MacColl Interview by Troy Howarth

The following interview with Catriona MacColl was conducted by phone on September 28, 2014. She is the only actress who was allowed to carry three of Fulci's horror films—and the association could have gone on even longer, but life had other plans. Catriona was delightful to talk to, and she has my thanks for giving so much of her time to discuss her life and career with me.

**Troy Howarth**: What made you want to become an actress?

**Catriona MacColl**: Well, actually acting, so to speak, was my second love because I wanted, from a very early age, to be a ballerina. I decided at age five that was what I wanted to be and I set out trying to become one. It was a hard slog, I would say. I went to one of the top schools for ballet dancers in Britain and I came out when I was 18. Then I set out doing auditions trying to get into a European ballet company. It took me a while, but I did achieve that. That's what brought me to France, where I now live. In fact, that audition changed my life in many respects and had a long-lasting effect on my life, in fact. And I remained with this stock company, which is still known as "The Ballets de Marseille," and in fact I still live relatively close to that city. And I remained with that company for a couple of years, until sadly I got a rather classic complaint for people who are exerting themselves in physical activities like dancing—an injury that put paid to any pleasure that I got before from following that path, so I decided to turn to my second love, which was acting.

So it was through dance, I suppose, to cut a long story short. I found that when I became an actress, that was also a chance encounter—I kind of wanted to become an actress but didn't know how to go about it, but I had a chance encounter with one of the then "wild childs" of French theater. It was in Marseille and he was looking for somebody who could dance, but not on point, which was where I was suffering the most, and so he offered me a small part in a play in which I also had to dance. And that was the beginning of my second passion, which is now my first passion since I gave up dancing many years ago.

**TH**: Your first major role was in *Lady Oscar* (1979) ... how did you get that role?

**CM**: That's correct, yes. I got that part because—how old was I then? Twenty-three, I think. I got that part because I was playing the young heroine in a period drama TV film and the director of this TV film had been, many years before, the first assistant director to the director of *Lady Oscar* and they were still very close friends. One day, the director of *Lady Oscar*, Jacques Demy, was talking to the TV director complaining about the fact that he couldn't

**Catriona MacColl suffers for her art in *The City of the Living Dead*.**

find the heroine for this Japanese-French co-production and the TV director asked him on the phone what he was looking for, and Demy told him, and the TV director said, "Well she is standing right beside me, so I will send her to you when she has a day off." So I was sent by train to Paris and probably didn't quite realize it at the time, but I think I almost certainly had the part before I walked into Jacques Demy's office, because I came with such strong recommendation from his ex-assistant director. So considering the circumstances, they worked in my favor. Also, and this is absolutely true, I was the last of a long line of actresses that they had seen for that part, because the producers and Jacques Demy simply couldn't agree on who was to play this part, and I guess I had all the right qualities and I turned up at the right time. But having been a dancer, I had a physical ability which fit the part, because you had to be able to fence—it was 18th century France and I was supposed to be a woman dressed as a man and I had to be able to sword fight and ride a horse, etc., etc. So the fact that I had been a dancer meant that I had certain ease with my body, which possibly other young actresses in those days didn't have.

**TH**: How was working with the film's director, Jacques Demy?

**CM**: Oh, he was absolutely extraordinary. He didn't take to fools gladly, so he kind of put you through your paces, but with an immense amount of Gallic charm, and he really nurtured me and looked after me and I really wanted not to disappoint him. He was fantastic. He knew so many people from a certain era of French filmmaking, from a long time back, and he never hesitated to introduce me to them and to sing my praises. So he gave me a lot of confidence. He gave me enough confidence to be able to play this lead role; despite the fact that I had performed eight roles on French television by then, I had not done a film of that ilk, with that kind of responsibility. I got on with it, I guess.

**TH**: I imagine that kind of pressure could have been very unpleasant.

**CM**: Yes, it could have been but it was so exciting and everybody was so supportive that my memories are all very positive. What was not easy was riding; I had ridden a horse as a child, but the classical ballet dancing and riding do not go together; they use contradictory muscles, and so I hadn't ridden in a long time. So that was not particularly easy, stopping a horse on a mark and getting off elegantly and getting back on elegantly ... but other than that (laughs) the rest was wonderful, really wonderful.

**TH**: How did you come to be cast in *City of the Living Dead*?

**CM**: Well, they were equally extraordinary circumstances, really ... by that stage I was a young actress living mainly in Paris and sometimes in London. I had an agent in London that I acquired as a result of my role in *Lady Oscar*, and one day the agent showed my photograph to an Italian agent called Giuseppe Perrone, who was a rather large figure in the Italian film industry in the early '80s. He took my photo back to Rome; he didn't meet me at that particular point, but he took my photo and the next thing I heard, my London agent called up and said, "They want to fly you over to Rome." I said, "Great, I'll go." Who wouldn't? When I got there, I knew it was to meet a director called Lucio Fulci. I didn't know who he was in those days, because I hadn't had much chance to see those kinds of movies. And I wasn't a horror film fan then. I'm still not really, though my attitude towards horror and fantasy filmmaking has completely changed. So Lucio Fulci was there in Giuseppe Perrone's office and it was very impressive because we were in an Italian palace. Giuseppe Perrone was a relatively wealthy man and lived in this gorgeous palace in the most chic area of Rome, and it was quite impressive and slightly daunting, in a way. Lucio was not particularly eloquent, which turned out to be pretty much Lucio, but I didn't know that then. But he was very serious and said everything that was relevant. What was slightly awkward was that I was supposed to be doing a very small part in a well-respected Swiss film that was to be shot in France. It was going to cross with Lucio's film, but Lucio and Giuseppe Perrone kept saying, "Don't you realize we are offering you a lead part? It's completely different." I was trying to work out which would be the best for my career, which of course you never know as you prepare to pick. Anyway, at the end of the meeting with Lucio, he said—this is relatively unheard of; it had never happened to me before—he said, "Here is the script. Take it back to your hotel. Read it. And I want your answer if you are going to do it tomorrow morning before you get back on the plane." So I took myself out to dinner at an Italian restaurant and I read this script, which I realized I had never read anything quite like it before, because the way it was translated made me come to the wrong conclusion. I made some rather unfavorable comments about Dardano Sacchetti, who is actually a very charming, intelligent and elegant man, who wrote it with Lucio ... I can't remember, was it just the two of them, or was there somebody else?

**TH**: It was just the two of them.

**CM**: That's what I thought, yeah. So I had made some rather unkind remarks about the script since, but on reflection, well I didn't read the Italian version and it was also partly to do with the style in which those kinds of films were written. Plus it was translated into English and probably didn't read quite as well as it might have done in Italian. So anyway, mortified is the word (laughs), so I thought about it and said, nevertheless, it's three weeks in America and however many weeks in Rome—that's nice. I need the money. So I read through it again and focused on the scenes I was in and realized that I didn't really, compared to most of the others, have anything too horrific to do. I had to run and scream and be terrified and all of that, and there was the awkward scene in the coffin, and the worm blasting scene, but compared to what other people had to go through, it appeared relatively minor. I didn't have to have eyes gouged out or things like that. So I thought, "Oh well, what's the harm." So I rung up my English agent and said, "What have you got me into here? What should I do? Is this a good career move or not?" And of course, he hadn't actually read it himself and had no idea who Lucio Fulci was. He just knew this Italian agent. So he said, "Well, do you have any other projects?" I said, "Well, just a small part in a French film. It's only a couple of days filming, so I can't really compare it to a lead role in an eight to ten-week shoot." He said, "Do you need the money?" I said, "Well, yes I do." He said, "Do you want to go to America?" I said, "Of course I do. I've never been." And he said, "Do you want to spend seven or eight weeks in Rome?" Then he literally said, "Oh darling, do it—no one will ever see it!" (*laughs*) Those words were engraved in my brain and have been ever since in light of the cult they have become. Of course, nothing could have been further from the truth, but that's what I based my decision on. I said to myself, "I suppose he's right. I can go to Rome; I need the money and everything else. I suppose if nobody's ever going to see it, then it's all right to do it, and it won't have too much effect on my career." So I did it and then I did the others in that trilogy, and in fact I didn't put any of them on my CV for years. And then, one after the other, they crept on when I realized how adored these films were and—this may sound strange to say—how fond of them people are all around the world, and so many different types of people—not just geeky fans (*laughs*) but all kinds of people of all walks of life I have met in different countries when I do these festivals.

**TH**: What did your friends and family think of you making these types of films? Were you married to Jon Finch at this stage?

**CM**: No, I wasn't. I can't quite remember. I think possibly I had a boyfriend, a French lighting cameraman, and I think he was still around when I did the first one. Well basically, I was living in France, I was a young actress, I had an agent in London and I would occasionally go over to England. My family were always incredibly supportive—my parents, that is; it was never up to my younger brother or sister to tell me what to do. They supported me but they had no idea what I was going to do; they knew I was going to make a movie, a horror movie, but that didn't really mean anything to them because they had never seen any. I decided nobody was ever going to see it and I wouldn't put it on my CV. It was more about practicing my craft. I always tried to believe that no matter what one did—and I still try to practice this—one should try to do it to the best of one's ability, otherwise there's not much point in doing it. I think that factor paid off and has something to do ... although, I said about this for many years, I think it's kind of a magical recipe as to why these films worked so well. It's down to Lucio's talent, it's his vision, apocalyptic or whatever term one likes, but there is something in his choice of me to play these parts. There was some kind of magic working between—and I don't want to sound pretentious—him and myself. It just worked. I think he made the right choice. I have often wondered, "Did I make the

**David Warbeck and Catriona MacColl face *The Beyond*.**

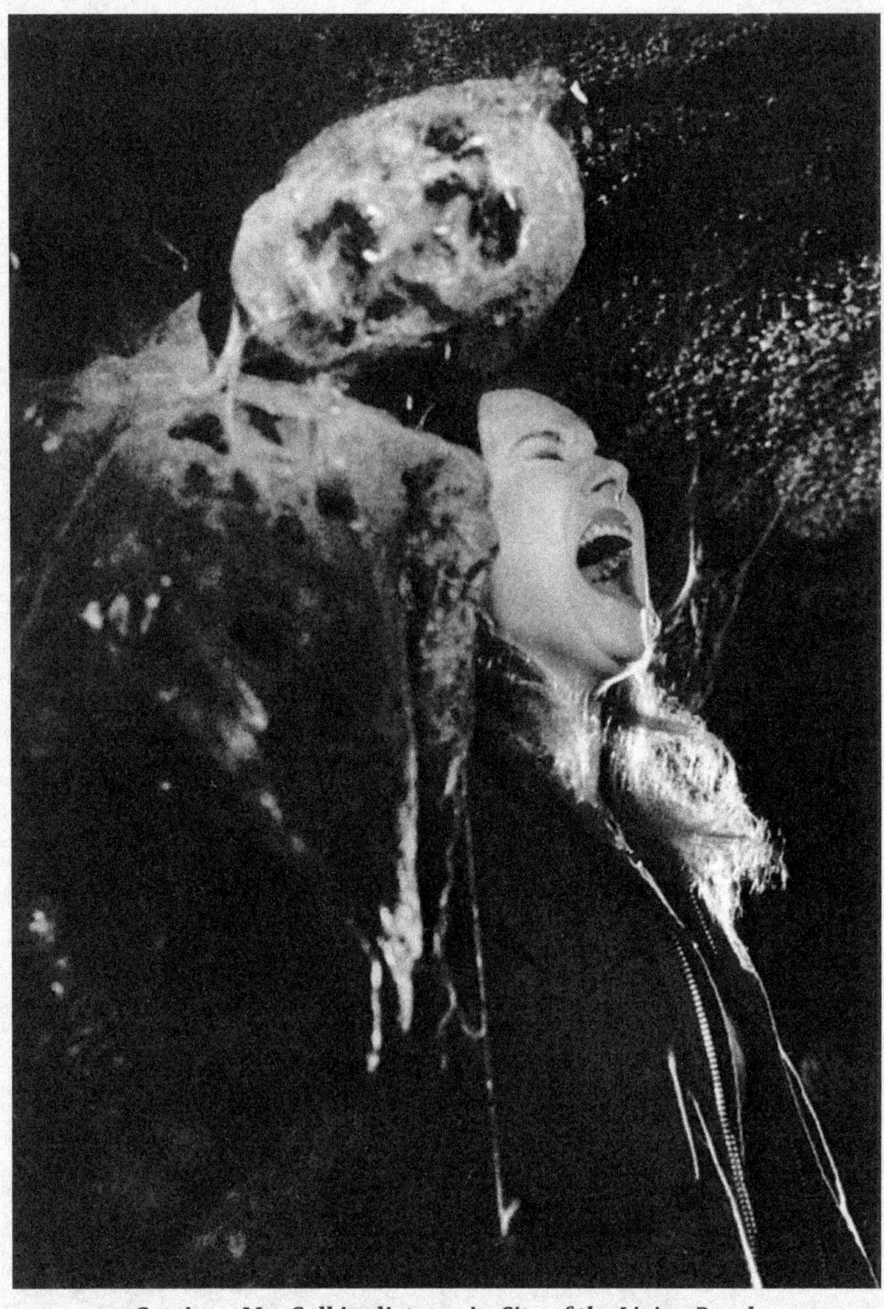

**Catriona MacColl in distress in *City of the Living Dead.***

right choice?" Obviously I don't know what would have happened had I not done them; maybe nothing would have happened. Now, obviously, I am known for being very much a part of that kind of film, but I preferred to see myself as part of the more fantastic side of those films, because I prefer the term fantasy filmmaking to horror filmmaking, because I am not a gore or horror fan as such, myself, but I have become extremely interested in fantasy. That covers a much larger thing. I have been invited to be president on various film juries and I love going to these things because you can see such a large spectrum of talented people in what is today such a fashionable genre.

**TH**: Fulci had a reputation for being very rough on actors—did you find him to be so?

**CM**: And he very rough especially on his actresses, no? (*laughs*) Well, yes, I saw that side of him on many occasions. He was another one who didn't suffer fools gladly and he couldn't put up with whining or moaning or perhaps some of the younger Italian actresses who were more concerned with looking beautiful than what they were actually playing. It wasn't really their fault, because I think the attitude toward women in those days was far more sexual, so really the fact that they were so concerned with their appearance ... I know most actresses are very concerned with their appearance all over the world, but it seemed to me that in countries like France and England, certainly, we have come a long way from that even in those days and it seemed to me that they weren't completely away from that in Italy. I'm not talking about all of them. I'm just talking about some of them, so I want to stress that. Like, there was an actress called Veronica Lazar who played for Dario Argento, and she was a real actress. She didn't care what she looked like; she just got on with it and did a really good job as well and was very talented. When Lucio was disrespectful or mocking towards actresses or actors, it was usually because they were behaving in a way that he didn't like. He was an intelligent man and if you kind of gave him as good as he gave you, it kind of worked. He had an incredibly amicable, even more than amicable, relationship with Paolo Malco. They adored each other on an intellectual, philosophical level. So Lucio could be extraordinarily interesting. After all, he was part of the whole *Dolce Vita* movement, so he was complex, for sure (*laughs*), but extremely entertaining and interesting at times; at other times, he could not say anything on a social occasion and then you didn't know what exactly was going on in his mind. But I think he did like strong women with personalities. He just didn't like, you know ... bimbos (*laughs*). I know that sometimes he had actors imposed on him, so he had to sometimes just get on with it whether they were right for the part or not.

**TH**: Some have indicated that Fulci was—and I'm trying to put this delicately—a little less than concerned with his appearance ... do you agree?

**CM**: Oh yes, Lucio was quite the opposite. He probably should have been a little more concerned! (*laughs*) That might have been a very good idea, but that was part of the Lucio complexity. A little pathetic on the one side and probably, as he went downhill and became ill, sadly I had no interaction with him then, I had kind of removed myself from that whole scene, so I slightly regret that I didn't see Lucio more, when I take into consideration what has now happened with these films, people like yourself contacting me and how often I am invited to the States, but I slightly regret that I didn't know him later. I am sure his appearance became more and more pathetic in the sense we were talking about, but it was a kind of basis of jokes among us in those days (*laughs*).

**TH**: What do you remember about Christopher George?

**CM**: Christopher George was my first partner, obviously, and I was probably not quite as relaxed as I became on the two later films because I knew everybody by then and I knew what to expect, so I was probably a little more distant with Christopher George. I do remember that he was incredibly professional as an actor and extremely amusing and handsome, but always a very professional man. He was charming off set, but we didn't get to know each other as well as I got to know David Warbeck or Paolo Malco. That is said with all due respect, and I was very saddened when I heard that he passed away, not long afterwards it seems to me.

**TH**: He died three years later. How did Christopher George seem to regard the film and Fulci? Did they ever seem to clash?

**CM**: No, they didn't. Possibly they would have clashed more if Christopher had spoken Italian. I'm trying to remember ... I mean, Christopher didn't have spiders over him, did he? No, that was an Italian actor in *The Beyond*.

**TH**: He was in the scene with you and the worms.

**CM**: Yes! He didn't seem to mind the worms nearly as much as I did. I had the worst time with that scene, because I had established a relationship of mutual respect with Lucio and I knew that he was in accord with what I was doing and he liked how I was portraying the character. I always have a problem with worms. It's one of my neuroses. I think my brother and his friends used to throw worms at me and they used to get stuck in my hair and I was traumatized. Probably those memories were rekindled during that scene. The long shot was okay because the wind machine was blowing mainly rice, so that was fine. It was the close-ups that were so difficult to do, and I was not looking forward to doing it. They put everybody else through their paces, and as time went on the producer was on the set and it was getting late, so they wanted to get on with it. In the end, the make-up man came and put this special transparent cream on my face and told me that way the worms were not actually touching me. They stuck my t-shirt down around my neck and arms, so they couldn't get in. Anyway, the show must go on; I had to go through with it. The difficult moment was not so much having the worms put on me, because I knew it was coming. It was Lucio's reaction that really disappointed me and annoyed me; I got pretty angry. I wasn't acting in that scene; I was doing it for real. Lucio let the camera roll and kept letting it roll and I kept thinking, "You've got *enough*!" He's actually *enjoying* watching me suffer! So that was the more perverse side of Lucio's sadistic side, which I saw aimed at myself. I was not too pleased. I don't think he kept it in the film, but I actually ended up in tears because I was thinking, "Why don't they stop the *fucking* camera?!" (*laughs*) "You've got enough!" And he wouldn't stop it. So that was the more unpleasant side of his character coming out.

**TH**: *City of the Living Dead* isn't exactly noted for its sparkling dialogue, but your scenes with Christopher George have a more natural sound ... did you two improvise much?

**CM**: Not really, no, but we could have done that—but even though Lucio's English was not that fantastic, by any means, I'm not sure he really knew what we were saying—he kind of insisted that we stuck to the script. But thank you for the compliment, and, yes, Christopher, as I said before, was an extraordinary professional and we kind of matched each other. We did work well together, but then I think I worked well with the other two as well.

**TH**: Absolutely. Were you aware that *City of the Living Dead* encountered censorship problems in the U.K.?

**CM**: No. I mean, I went to see it incognito, so to speak, because in those days we didn't have VHS cassettes, or if they were available, they were only just around, so I knew I would never be able to get hold of a VHS of it and I wasn't sure I wanted one anyway (*laughs*). So I went alone the day the film came out; I went to a 2 o'clock performance in Leicester Square and went with my brother and my very brave mother. I just remember knowing what was coming and nudging them on occasion, saying, "Don't look now!" I spent half the film peeking out from behind my hand, and I closed my hand when the really gory sequences came on. I had no notion of it having any problems at the time. I knew it was a sort of an underground film, it wasn't getting a general release.

It was actually a few years later—I had done the other two—it was about six or seven years later, when my brother was reading an entertainment magazine, a much respected, weekly magazine. And he said there was a conference hosted by the very infamous English censor, whose name was strangely like Mary Woodhouse—in fact, I kind of wondered if Lucio had done that on purpose—but her name was Mary Whitehouse. She was a socially conservative woman, an upright, moral woman ... supposedly. Anyway, he said, "Oh there's a huge conference chaired by Mary Whitehouse discussing 10 video nasties. And, oh look, you are in *three* of them!" (*laughs*) I was horrified, absolutely horrified. He thought it was terribly funny, but I was horrified. I thought it was all going to come out, you know, "Famous Shakespearian actress about to be ruined." But, I wasn't. That was when I came to realize that this was perhaps more serious than I had originally reckoned.

**TH**: Your next film with Fulci was *The Beyond* ... did he specifically request you for the film?

**CM**: Yes, he did. And to be honest, I had so enjoyed being in Rome for that length of time and I had made quite a few friends in Rome ... the Roman way of life really appealed to me. So much so that after the first one I contemplated maybe leaving Paris and going to live in Rome. In fact, I'm glad I didn't because it was the end of an era, and as a foreign actress—though of course there are foreign actors living in Rome to this day—but we don't see them very much. I thought after the third film that as an actress living out of Paris, that is complicated enough. I was well known among people in the business in Paris in those days and I had contacts in London, so I thought it might be a stupid move to go and live in Rome and cut myself off from everything I had already set up.

So the idea of going and discovering an appealing area of the United States—this was all pre-Hurricane Katrina in New Orleans—was appealing and the idea of spending another 10 weeks in Rome ... And I guess by that stage, to be honest, the script of *The Beyond*, the character appealed to me and is probably the character I played in the three films that I liked the best. So, I liked the character and I have always been drawn to adventure, so this was embarking on another mad Italian adventure and I knew how Lucio worked, and we had a great time.

**TH**: This was your first meeting with David Warbeck, I would assume?

**CM**: Yes. Absolutely. The wonderful, lovely, hugely amusing David Warbeck ... the man we all miss. In fact, my friendship with David ... you know, the days were long and the scenes were tough, but all the scenes towards the end of the movie that we shot at DePaolis Studios, walking around in the water of the so-called cellar of the hotel that had been rebuilt at DePaolis ... It was just before Christmas and it was kind of damp and wet, and so David and I didn't really socialize when we were working, but I did keep in touch with him until the end, really, when he passed away. So the friendship continued with David after the filming. He was such a warm, fun-loving person. It was virtually impossible not to be friends with David once you met him.

**TH**: You and David both had already done films with Fulci and seemed to get along well with him and with each other ... did you feel that you were making something special this time around?

**CM**: I did feel ... Well, I mean, of the trilogy of films that I made with Lucio, everybody has their favorite, and it's not always the same one. I do think *The Beyond* does come quite high up on the list of everybody's favorites. But some people prefer *City of the Living Dead*, while others prefer *House by the Cemetery*, for various different reasons. But *The Beyond* is my favorite and I think it was better, or seemed better, than the others. Of course, it's very personal what I'm saying, I am not putting down the quality of the others; it's just that, for me, probably again because the character I played appealed to me the most. Although I do like the character that I played ... I think the one with the least substance that I played was in the first one. I tried to make her into something. I think I achieved that, but she was probably the one [least developed]—also because it was my first venture with Lucio—it seemed to me that the other two have a bit more substance. I don't know if they were written with me in mind, I never asked that question, but maybe they were—because he immediately offered it to me, and the same with *House by the Cemetery*.

**TH**: I would agree that the character in *City* has less of a sense of a backstory compared to the other two.

**CM**: Exactly. So, obviously they were more interesting to play. By that stage, I was kind of enjoying the exploration of my own personal, emotional fear. I actually quite enjoyed seeing where I could go with that, and I then began to realize how therapeutic screaming was (*laughs*). And the crew was great, they all got on incredibly well, and the fact that they were all such serious film technicians, that they had worked with all the different film greats in that era of Italian film history ... One knew that when doing these films, no matter what one may have thought of them back in Britain, the fact that this standard of technician was working on these films, as they would be if they had been doing a period Visconti film or something like that, told me that it must be okay to do these films. I kind of relaxed into the idea of making them. Plus they had very good actors, the sons and daughters—like Carlo De Mejo and Antonella Interlenghi—sons and daughters of renowned stage and film Italian actors and actresses, so you kind of thought, "Well, if their sons and daughters are in this kind of movie, coming from stage or TV or whatever, they have to be okay."

**TH**: Right. Well, for example, the make-up artist Giannetto De Rosi had worked with Fellini and Bertolucci ...

**CM**: Exactly. That's exactly what I mean. So I thought, "It's all in a day's work for them, whether they were doing a Fulci movie or a Fellini movie." So I felt it was just a matter of them practicing their profession.

**TH**: What do you remember of cinematographer Sergio Salvati?

**CM**: Oh, lovely, lovely man. Fairly typical of directors of photography in so much as they are not particularly forthcoming. They watch you, but don't speak. My experience with cinematographers is that they are very discreet observers as opposed to eloquent shouters like Lucio. But a very great contrast to Lucio, I remember him as—I mean, I didn't know him that well—but he always seemed to be in a state of serenity, which was highly necessary, I would imagine, if you were Lucio's lighting cameraman. He was a very discreet, charming, quiet, nice man.

**TH**: It's rumored that Fulci rounded-up some homeless drunks to play the bodies at the end of the film ... any truth to this?

CM: (*Laughs*) Well, I heard that many years later. I wasn't involved in the casting of the extras and quite frankly I had my own problems that day with the filming—again, it was just before Christmas, it was very cold and my problems were with having to wear these bloody contact lenses that, in those days, were made to measure—but my *God*, were they painful! They were horrendous to wear and we really couldn't keep them in for any longer than was necessary, so for a start I didn't *see* anything. I was led to the set and I couldn't see anything at all. That's a fairly anxiety-ridden experience, and so I basically wasn't very involved in how they got that extraordinary set and look together, but all I can say is it is an extremely powerful and a beautiful sequence. In hindsight, I like it a lot now. Whoever they were, poor things (*laughs*), they behaved in the scene. And it's part of the Lucio legend and is rather wonderful in a way, and I'm sure it probably is true.

**Catriona MacColl (left) poses with the crew on the set of *The Beyond*.**

TH: Did you ever get to meet the composer, Fabio Frizzi?

CM: The lovely Fabio Frizzi. I didn't get to meet him, so far as I can remember; I don't remember him coming to the set. Possibly I shook his hand. But he looms in my life now, because all the contacts I have in the fantasy world, whether they are journalists or fans or filmmakers, a lot of them have met Fabio Frizzi, so there is a kind of idea running around, as we have been talking via Facebook ... and he really is a most lovely man. So we have this idea that it would be nice if I could present one of these concerts that he does; he likes that idea, and I like it, too. We haven't got it together yet, but I am sure we will meet eventually.

TH: That would put a lot of people in the seats, I'm sure!

CM: I think so. He did a concert in London, I think last year, and it did incredibly well. I didn't know anything about it, and so far as the States is concerned, normally Mike [Baronas] is the one who normally sets this kind of thing up, but now Mike isn't really doing that anymore, but ... We are working on it, let's just put it that way.

TH: Do you have any favorite memories of making these films?

CM: Obviously, the scene with the worms we already talked about; I wouldn't say it's still a trauma but it's a memorable scene. And the coffin scene, which again in hindsight I find it macabre but extraordinarily poetic. I really love that scene. I can't believe that I had the guts to actually get into that coffin, but I was so young and the idea of actually passing away seemed so far down the track. I saw it as a challenge and I had to do it, so I went with the concept of "You read the script, you know what you are going to be asked to do, so just do it." It's not the same thing as something that's not written in the script that you don't want to do. That's a different story. So that coffin scene, which [was filmed] in the actual cemetery in New York went as well as it could have gone, despite their needing to close the lid on the coffin—that's something you don't forget—for a couple of seconds. And then Christopher George starts hitting the top of it. I wasn't in it all of the time (*laughs*) but I was in it part of the time. But the main difficulty was when we shot the inside of the coffin, which really looks fantastic, and we did that weeks later in DePaolis Studios. When we did the close-up of my face, I had this kind of anxious physical reaction; I knew I was supposed to be playing dead, but my eyes started to twitch. I had a whole film crew looking at me, and Lucio was there. The whole idea was I needed to be still and suddenly my eyelid started twitching, a nervous reaction, and then Lucio started getting cross. The whole thing took forever because my eye wouldn't stop twitching and the crosser he got, the more my eyelid twitched. Then he sort of pulled me out of the coffin and he got in it, and that was quite the occasion (*laughs*), and he tried to mimic me in the coffin to show me how easy it was to play dead.

So that was a difficult scene, but I tried to explain that there was nothing I could do about it, apart from deep breathing—and of course, if I did deep breathing, you would see that I was moving ... so that's a memory. But I think it was all worth it because it's a fairly extraordinary sequence. I'm rather proud of it, all these years later. There's something Edgar Allan Poe-esque about it. It's a beautiful sequence.

And then the other films ... In *The Beyond*, there is a mixture of Bourbon Street and New Orleans and jazz clubs and Pontchartrain Bridge; driving across that every morning was an experience, and the extraordinary house that had been in Louis Malle's *Pretty Baby* (1978) ... The house was extraordinary, even though the interior was rebuilt in the studio. I also remember lots of laughter with David Warbeck, which was always a kind of necessary light relief. I also remember the anecdote in the DePaolis canteen where we would eat, one of the days with the zombies in make-up—some of whom, I believe, had careers as zombies in those days—they were extremely disgusting and the canteen was in a basement and there were these windows that were street-level. There were people passing outside and the zombies would frighten people. It was very amusing. So, lots of laughter ... I don't think there were any particularly tricky scenes, apart from that week of being in that damp DePaolis studio doing the last sequence in the flooded cellar, but it was a bonding experience. We were all in the water, and everybody got on with his or her job. Nobody seemed to complain much, which was fairly extraordinary (*laughs*).

In *House by the Cemetery*, I have very fond memories of the beautiful countryside around Concorde, where we filmed, and of course the lovely town of Boston. But nothing really comes to mind as far as scenes go. Everybody always asks me about that last scene where I am being dragged down the ladder; in fact, I used to really enjoy those scenes. Having trained as a dancer, I was attracted to the physicality of acting, and that sequence was set up as a stunt in so far as they put down a sort of finish on the steps, a thin layer that meant I wouldn't hurt myself. But that also meant I could accept the challenge of doing the stunt myself and doing it as real as possible. That appealed to me. I also remember the little boy, Giovanni Frezza, whom I later re-met and it was very emotional, more emotional than I would have guessed, a few years ago when Mike took us to "Chiller" with the Italian Invasion—it was the 30-year anniversary of the film. (Note: Actually, the show in question was the Horrorhound Weekend, in March of 2011). Giovanni is an extraordinarily successful engineer, he lives in Chicago, and he was incredibly touched to be invited to this event. He took the time to come out of his work schedule. And he seemed to be as amazed as everybody else there, like Carlo De Mejo, Silvia Collatini, who is adorable ... Everybody seemed [so kind] to me—some of them have continued in the profession, others have gone on to do other things, like Giovanni, but everybody seemed incredibly grounded. These films have not affected any of them in a negative way; on the contrary, everybody was extremely happy to be reunited. That was a nice completion of the circle, that meeting at "Chiller."

**TH**: I was able to interview Silvia; unlike you, she is actually a horror movie junkie, so this was heaven sent ...

**CM**: Indeed she is. (*laughs*) But you have to remember, she has a totally different background than me as far as horror movies were concerned. I probably saw *Dr. Who*, which isn't horror anyway. And I saw *Hammer House of Horror* or *Frankenstein*, or a few vampire films or movies with Vincent Price or whoever. That was the extent of my viewing. In Italy, of course, at least up until today, I'm not sure what is happening in that genre there now—not terribly much, I wouldn't think ...

But you know, I mustn't forget to say this, I have just done another fantasy film that I just filmed. It's going to be coming out in February in France, but we just had a world premiere in Paris a couple of weeks ago ... It's called *Horsehead*. And I am going to a festival in November with it as well. It's a young director, his first movie. He is a very talented and highly intelligent and passionate young man. I have been encouraging him for a number of years, and I first met him through a kind of Fulci connection at a festival, so Lucio's legacy lives on—not only with directors, but what is happening to me now, occasionally being contacted by young European film directors who are huge fans of Lucio's work. I would never have believed that these films would live on and continue to live on. Life is full of surprises. (*laughs*)

**TH**: Yes, it is. The first two films you did with Fulci were more mood and atmosphere driven, whereas *House by the Cemetery* seems a little more coherent in terms of plot. Would you agree?

**CM**: Yes, totally. When I read the script, the first one, in that restaurant in Rome, it seemed to me—which is why, again, I may have been slightly condescending to Sacchetti—that the script was an excuse in that film for stringing together a lot of special effects. Whereas, *House by the Cemetery* seemed a bit deeper and more coherent, as you say.

**TH**: That said, do you have any explanation for the scene with the maid cleaning up all the blood while you look on without even noticing?

**CM**: (*laughs*) Every time I watch it, I notice that. I guess again because we didn't shoot it in chronological order, but someone should have ... Well, I certainly should have picked up on that; I'm not blaming the script or the wonderful script lady, Rita Agostini ... wonderful character, I adored her. She was also very reassuring to have around because she had Lucio's ear and could get to him and ask him things and sometimes make him agree. But that's something somebody should have picked up on—possibly me, even, but it kind of works because I am having a semi-nervous breakdown anyway, so we may get away with it because of that, but people do laugh at that point, yes. (*laughs*) It's ridiculous, yes.

**TH**: You mentioned that Fulci got on very well with Paolo Malco; how was he to work with?
**CM**: Oh he was a gentleman. He's highly intelligent, very sensitive. I seem to recall that at the time he was involved in antiques. He was a pleasure to work with. We socialized a bit, usually at his house. He used to throw dinner parties, not too many people, but Lucio was invited as well. Sadly, I was hoping afterwards that other things might have developed out of these parties. But I wasn't there, and I sort of hoped that if they needed a British actress who knew Italian that they would come and look for me outside of Italy; but also the bottom sort of fell out of the Italian film industry. I don't doubt that there are still great talents there today, and occasionally one gets to see it… I don't know if you saw it, it's not a horror movie, but a film called *La grande bellezza* (2013), that won the …
**TH**: Yes, it won the Oscar. Wonderful film.
**CM**: There's a talent for you. That film was brilliant. But on the whole, one doesn't get to see many Italian movies today, but hopefully Paolo is still going strong. He probably is.
**TH**: The rumor is, Fulci offered you other films, which you turned down. Do you remember that?
**CM**: Oh yes, I remember that quite clearly. It's more than true. By that stage, I think I felt that sometimes you can have too much of a good thing; enough is enough. I felt it was time to try and do other things. Of course, at the time I had no idea that the films would become a cult thing like they became. I had no idea anybody would ever see them, because my agent told me they wouldn't. *City* had this very sort of undercover release in the British Isles, but I wasn't going to spread the word because I was ashamed of them at the time. I was not ashamed of anybody's performance, I was just ashamed of the content and of being involved. I decided it was time to do other things, and from what I have heard, I hadn't even read the script because I had turned it down before, but I was told I was right to turn it down. I think it was extremely violent, which I wouldn't have liked. Also, I am told it just wasn't that good. I think maybe from what I am told by critics, that he had peaked by then. I don't know if you would agree?
**TH**: Well, his later films were done under very harsh conditions, even lower budgets—plus his health deteriorated badly.
**CM**: So it wasn't really his fault, and I'm not saying it was, but perhaps he had peaked or perhaps it was a collection of different reasons, but I think perhaps if I had been involved—and again I want to underline that I'm glad I wasn't—maybe that would have taken away from the magic of the trilogy that I did with him.
**TH**: You also appeared in the cult fantasy film *Hawk the Slayer* (1980) … what was it like to make that film?
**CM**: Of course I remember … that also became kind of a cult movie, as you say. It was part of the sword and sorcery genre with, I think, one of the first of its kind to have this kind of special effects with laser swords and everything like that. It's kind of funny when you think of everything that came after that movie, you know things like *Harry Potter*. But yes, it was a charming film to work on. It had some extremely good actors … I have lots of good memories about that film.
**TH**: Did you get to know Jack Palance?
**CM**: Oh yes, I did, because I was responsible for Jack Palance's death in the movie. He was a very impressive but slightly daunting man. Not only was he extremely tall and well built, but also he was also quite a shy man. So he didn't communicate that deeply, and people were frightened of him.

**Catriona MacColl in *City of the Living Dead.***

**Catriona MacColl and Lucio Fulci join journalists Robert and Alain Schlockoff at a French film festival in 1983; photo courtesy of Lionel Grenier.**

I was going to be responsible for thrusting a torch in his face, more or less, so I decided to try and break the ice beforehand. So I went up to him and—mind you, once you have worked with Lucio Fulci and made an attempt to tame Lucio Fulci, and possibly have succeeded—nothing was that daunting after that. Everybody else was fairly easygoing. (*laughs*) So I think I broke the ice with Jack Palance, and, I mean, I didn't have that many days filming with him, but I was delighted to be able to say that I worked with him and he was extremely charming to me. But he had to wear this kind of Darth Vader-like suit and he didn't say very much, but he had a daunting presence. But he seemed to me quite a docile man, really.

**TH**: You appeared in an all-star mini-series called *The Last Days of Pompeii* (1984) ... did you find that to be a memorable experience?

**CM**: Oh God, do I remember ... It went on for weeks during one long sunny summer. It was great fun. It was great fun. There were so many well-known actors in it, and for me it was a whole new experience because I was practicing my craft surrounded by great British actors. With all due respect to foreign actors—you know what I mean when I say that ... European actors—but it was nice to be part of the crowd that I came from.

**TH**: You have been more active in films in recent years ... how was making *A Good Year* (2006) for Ridley Scott?

**CM**: Oh, really that was such a small role; hardly worth talking about. In fact that came about because the film was shot in and around the area where I live. In fact, a lot of it was shot in the actual village that I live beside. So I knew a lot of people working on it. Also, my best friend happens to be married to Albert Finney, who starred in it. So I was delighted when I heard that Albert was coming down for about three weeks to this wonderful part of the world, and he was delighted, too, so we met up a number of times and had meals together. He said we have to try and get you into this movie, despite the fact there really isn't anything you can play. There really wasn't anything for me. So he went to Ridley Scott and Ridley Scott had me play this British wife who was looking to buy an apartment. But if you happen to blink at the wrong spot, you miss me. My husband is in it, too, playing the piano on the stage of a lake behind a romantic encounter between Russell Crowe and Marion Cotillard. So that's what that entailed: two nights' shooting, so I sort of hung around the set but I couldn't really say that I did anything extraordinary in that movie.

**TH**: And you worked with Richard Stanley on *The Theatre Bizarre* (2011) ...

**CM**: That's true. Now *that* was an experience. He was of the Lucio ilk; I have to say. (*laughs*) That was great. I loved playing that role. For a start, it was filmed in the historically soaked area of the southwest of France. It was shot around the village where Richard Stanley had lived.

And Richard certainly is a larger-than-life character. He was another one that needed some icebreaking. He is also quite shy. It's funny, that's what they all have in common—even Lucio, you know; they compensate in other ways. Richard is deeply entrenched in the esoteric, so he would talk a great deal about that, which was extraordinary. He doesn't stop, he has so much knowledge about that, but you can't even follow him.

But Richard and I got on very well and I would like to work with Richard again, since I greatly enjoyed playing this role. I'm at an age now where I can play interesting older parts, like witches, which I never would have been offered before. It was lots of fun. (*laughs*)

**TH**: He is a big Fulci fan, I believe. Did he ever grill you about working with Lucio?

**CM**: Oh, he's a *huge* fan of Fulci. He rang me up before—I don't remember if he offered me the part or it might have been the producer, actually—and then Richard rang me up in great reverence talking about Fulci and how honored he would be if I played this witch. And I said, "Yes of course I will do it." Yeah, he is a huge Fulci fan.

**TH**: You talked about doing some of these horror conventions. Obviously they attract all kinds of people. Have you ever had any unpleasant experiences dealing with the fans?

**CM**: Well, before I came out of the wardrobe, if you like, and decided to take on all of this and what these films began to represent, that really was my first concern. Am I going to meet weird people? But I would say that of all the people I have met at these festivals and conventions—not that I have done that many, but I have done a few now—they are so well organized, especially the ones on your side (*laughs*) I mean. Mike did such a fantastic job of looking after people—honestly I was more than reassured that the people one met came up to me having seen these movies since they were kids or adolescents ... I mean I was *horrified* at the ages they were seeing these movies ... but honestly these films have such fond memories for them, it was really very touching; they were delightful, most of them. I mean, occasionally you do get one [odd ball] at these things; I went to a festival in France and towards the end of the evening, there was a person who was obviously slightly deranged and wouldn't leave me alone, but I was well-surrounded and they managed to get him out of the cinema. I think if I met a lot of strange people, I probably wouldn't keep doing these festivals and conventions. I mean, at "Chiller," the whole family comes: granddad, grandma and the cousins (*laughs*). So it's very often a family event. I mean, I'm sure these films do attract some slightly strange people, but I haven't had too much experience that way, I'm pleased to say. Quite frankly, there are other films in mainstream cinema that are extremely violent, probably more so than these films, and I expect they attract some strange people, as well. I'm not sure if you would agree with me?

**TH**: Probably so. I have only attended a few of these things, myself, but what always strikes me is that you see all walks of life and all ages.

**CM**: You do. I can say Mike was always particularly good at looking after his guests, so I could never say that I was particularly bothered. One meets some quite simple folk at times, but nothing unpleasant.

**TH**: And lastly, a question I am sure you have been asked a thousand times: Are you surprised by the continued popularity of Fulci and these films?

**CM**: Well, I have known about it now for quite a long time. Now I am not surprised, because there is something timeless and universal about these movies. I mean, I don't know how long they are going to go on being popular, but they certainly continue to survive. Now we're on to the second generation and the sons and daughters of my generation who grew up with them, so we'll see how long it continues. But I guess they have already taken their position in the genre and history. And despite the fact that my relationship to them is still slightly ambivalent because I am not an admirer of downright violence on the screen, but I am aware that mainstream cinema is in many cases even more frightening because that deals with real violence, so the times have changed. I don't know. Did I answer that question? (*laughs*)

**TH**: You did. You did, indeed. I just want to thank you—it's been very enjoyable talking to you.

**CM**: Likewise. I would love to read the book when it comes out. Thank you, Troy. It's been very interesting going back down memory lane!

## Cinzia Monreale Interview by Troy Howarth

The following interview with actress Cinzia Monreale was conducted via email on November 12, 2014. Cinzia worked with Fulci on *Silver Saddle*, *The Beyond* and *The Sweet House of Horrors* and is a fan favorite for her role as the blind Emily in *The Beyond*. Cinzia has my thanks for taking the time to answer these questions.

**Troy Howarth**: How did you come to be part of Lucio Fulci's films?

**Cinzia Monreale**: I worked with Lucio on *Silver Saddle*, a Spaghetti Western with Giuliano Gemma; about two years after that, he cast me in *The Beyond*.

**TH**: Do you recall your first meeting with Lucio Fulci? What impression did you form of him?

**CM**: I remember being so excited about being directed by him in a Western; it's funny, but I just knew that we would have fun on set and get along.

**TH**: Fulci had a reputation for being tough on the set. Was he ever that way with you?

**CM**: I know that many found him to be that way, but I never saw that side of him, personally. He was never tough with me, ever. He could be very blunt, even childlike, but never mean—certainly not ever with me.

**TH**: On *The Beyond*, what did you think of the script and the character of Emily?

**CM**: The script is beautiful. I could even envision writing my own script around Emily, a fantastic ghost story without all the blood and splatter. I'm not a horror movie fan, I admit, but I think *The Beyond* is a great film.

**TH**: Were the contact lenses unpleasant to wear?

**Cinzia Monreale (right) warns Catriona MacColl of the dangers of *The Beyond*.**

**Cinzia Monreale meets a gruesome demise in *The Beyond.***

**CM**: They were terribly unpleasant to wear! They were horrible. I was completely blind with them on. They made little holes for me to see through, but every time I moved my eyes, the lenses would move, too, so I was back to being blind again.
**TH**: Do you have any favorite memories of the filming?
**CM**: Yes, above all I remember the locations: New Orleans was fabulous! In fact, I think I filmed more in New Orelans than I did in Rome, which is where we filmed the interiors.
**TH**: You next had a small, uncredited role in *Rome, 2072 A.D.: The New Gladiators* ... do you recall if Fulci specifically requested you for that film?
**CM**: I believe that Lucio often kept me in his mind, in his imagination; he often involved me in his projects.
**TH**: What did you think of *New Gladiators* as a film?
**CM**: I never saw *New Gladiators*; for me, it was a little diversion: one day on set for my friend.
**TH**: Your last film with Fulci was the TV movie *The Sweet House of Horrors* ... Fulci was in ill health by this time ... had he changed noticeably?
**CM**: His health was bad, but that had not changed his sarcastic humor, or his enthusiasm for life.
**TH**: What did you think of Fulci as a director and as a person?
**CM**: I already mentioned several adjectives about him; now I will add that I think he was a visionary. He was so intelligent and cultured. Above all, he was a mercurial personality who was in perpetual motion. Lucio was also a very generous man, and also very opinionated. He had a temper and would throw tantrums, but he was never violent. He had a tough life and he suffered a lot. As a director, he was always very clear and very precise. We understood each other. I understood what he wanted without much discussion.
**TH**: Did you keep in touch with Fulci in his later years?
**CM**: I did not see him in the last years of his life, unfortunately.
**TH**: Are you surprised by the cult that surrounds these films?
**CM**: I'm not surprised, simply because Lucio was always so ahead of his times; now he is finally coming up to date.
**TH**: Do you have any favorites among the films you have made?
**CM**: *The Beyond* is my favorite; it is a very special movie to me. Emily is my favorite character. I truly loved playing this character and felt I was right for the part; I made the part my own.
**TH**: Cinizia, thank you for your answers.
**CM**: You're welcome!

## *The House by the Cemetery (Italy)*

Aka *Quella villa accanto al cimitero; Aquella casa al lado del cementerio; La maison près du cimetière; Das Haus an der Friedhofsmauer*

Directed by Lucio Fulci; Produced by Fabrizio De Angelis, for Fulvia Film; Screenplay by Lucio Fulci, Giorgio Mariuzzo and Dardano Sacchetti, from a story by Elisa Briganti; Director of Photography: Sergio Salvati; Editor: Vincenzo Tomassi; Music by Walter Rizzati and Alessandro Blonksteiner (uncredited)

Main Players: Catriona MacColl [as Katherine MacColl] (Lucy Boyle); Paolo Malco (Dr. Norman Boyle); Giovanni Frezza (Bob Boyle); Silvia Collatina (Mae Freudstein); Dagmar Lassander (Laura Gittleson); Ania Pieroni (Ann, the babysitter); Carlo De Mejo (Mr. Wheatley); Gianpaolo Saccarola (Daniel Douglas); Giovanni De Nava (Dr. Jacob Tess Freudstein); Daniela Doria (First female victim)

Cameo appearance: Lucio Fulci (Professor Muller)

*Dr. Norman Boyle brings his family to stay with him at a creepy old house in New England as he continues the research of a late colleague. While at the house, Norman's wife, Lucy, begins to fear that something is not right. Their son Bob begins talking with a little girl named Mae, whom his parents cannot see. Norman thinks it is all just a childhood fantasy, but Lucy is not so sure. In time, it is revealed that the topic Norman's predecessor was investigating may have contributed to his breakdown and eventual suicide. Mysterious events begin to transpire and some people die violently, then Norman is forced to act to defend his family from an ancient evil hiding in the bowels of the house ...*

Following *The Beyond*, producer Fabrizio De Angelis was keen to continue exploiting a winning formula. He reassembled much of the same team to make another modern Gothic. This time Elisa Briganti, the wife of Dardano Sacchetti, conceived the story. As Briganti later explained,

> The plot of *The House by the Cemetery* comes from my interest in child psychology. [...] And so the story was born from a very simple starting point:

the cellar, dark places, unexplored locations in our lives and the places we live in as children.[1]

To bring the finished screenplay into shape, Fulci collaborated again with Dardano Sacchetti and Giorgio Mariuzzo. Sacchetti claims:

> The story reflects my childhood and Elisa's experience as a child psychologist. [...] When I was 10 years old, I had to do a test of courage and walk around the graves in a cemetery with a lit torch. [...] For me, kids have always been the key, the password between the adult world and the rest between reality and metaphysics.[2]

The screenplay for *The House by the Cemetery* is considerably more plot-heavy than the ones for *City of the Living Dead* and *The Beyond*. Fulci does not aim for quite the same air of dream logic this time out, though the attention to logic and incident is still deliberately slippery. Compared to the characters in the earlier two horrors, there is much more "meat" to the protagonists of this film. Norman and Lucy are both very interesting characters. Norman is the nominal hero—though, this being a Fulci film, the concept of a hero is disposable at best. He is established as a serious academic with a strong sardonic streak. He fusses over Lucy, yet their relationship seems strained. It is strongly implied that Lucy is recovering from a nervous breakdown, and it appears that this has caused some problems between the two of them. Fulci deliberately throws suspicion in Norman's direction: Could he be manipulating Lucy for his own sinister purposes? Ultimately, of course, it is merely a cheat designed to add a layer of ambiguity to Norman's character. Like John McCabe in *The Beyond* or Dr. Menard in *Zombie*, Norman is a strict rationalist who refuses to accept the presence of the supernatural. He tries to explore the mysteries of the house and its previous occupants scientifically, but it is all for naught: The key to the mystery lies outside of his well-ordered view of things. Norman is eventually punished for his arrogance when he is killed off in the chaotic finale. As for Lucy, she is mentally and emotionally fragile—but she still has an independent streak. She is not a quivering victim who needs to be rescued at every turn, but her ability to effectively deal with the situation she has been placed in is compromised by her weakened mental state. As the film unfolds, she becomes more and more incapacitated, even as she tries to defend her family from harm; the strain is too much for her, and she, too, will ultimately lose her life in the final struggle.

The villain or "monster" of the piece is the mysterious—and irresistibly named—Dr. Jacob Tess Freudstein. As Sacchetti later explained:

> [Producer] Luciano Martino created the name Freudstein. I hadn't given a name to the character, to leave him in a metaphysical state. But Luciano Martino called him Freudstein, which I didn't like, but, from a certain point of view, he was right.[3]

Briganti is quick to admit that:

> The main author of Dr. Freudstein is Dardano. As often happens, he took the reins of the story. He created, molded, elaborated the character of Dr. Freudstein, and I have to say that he did a great job.[4]

The name in itself is suggestive, to say the least, making the character the bastard offspring of Sigmund Freud and Dr. Frankenstein. Fulci's distaste for psychiatry is well represented in other films, so he must have been posi-

**Spanish pressbook cover for *The House by the Cemetery;* artwork by Enzo Sciotti.**

**Ann (Ania Pieroni) is gruesomely disposed of.**

tively tickled by the name. Here, finally, he could take a proper potshot at the founder of modern psychology and psychoanalysis! The character is cut off from the action proper and is not really introduced until the very end of the picture. He lives in squalor, secluded in the rambling recesses of the cobweb and bat-infested basement. As Norman eventually realizes, he is a sort of mad scientist who has uncovered the secret of immortality: By claiming innocent victims, he uses his surgical skill to remove body parts and cells to regenerate his own moldering carcass. Dr. Freudstein is truly a figure out of a nightmare; his moral regression is symbolized by his rotting appearance, and he takes the lives of others for no better reason than to continue existing—he doesn't even have the benefit of being able to enjoy his prolonged existence, cut off as he is in the confines of the spooky basement setting.

Fulci always understood the value of grabbing the audience in the opening scene, and, true to form, he opens *The House by the Cemetery* on a high note. The camera caresses the exterior of the house, the foreground of the frame dominated by a weathered gravestone. Once inside, he plays up the Gothic ambience with the use of shadowy lighting and skillful art direction. The house is more than a house: It has real character and it's obvious from the get-go that it is not the type of place one would wish to visit for a vacation. Fulci introduces a young woman getting dressed after a sexual assignation—pretty, doe-eyed Daniela Doria, who had already suffered grisly demises in *City of the Living Dead* and *The Black Cat*, plays her. For the initiated Fulci fan, her presence denotes that something bad is about to happen. The director skillfully builds tension and suspense as she realizes that her boyfriend appears to have disappeared. She begins looking for him, and her search leads her to the basement. The atmosphere and buildup in this sequence is absolutely flawless in its execution. The tone changes from the spooky to the horrific when the girl finds her boyfriend, thoroughly the worse for wear, at which point she lets out a scream; the knife-wielding killer, who we later realize is Dr. Freudstein, silences her for good by stabbing her through the skull with a nasty-looking blade. Fulci demonstrates flair for suspense and also for shock horror in this little *tour de force* set piece. The scene starts the film off on the right note, and the placement of a good, grisly shock effect allows Fulci to satiate the target audience before settling into a slower, more introspective approach.

The emphasis on mood and atmosphere is not significantly different from Fulci's previous horror films, but the overall tone is far closer to something like *The Black Cat*. The shocks are well engineered and appropriately splattery, but there are less of them. It could be that Fulci and his collaborators were growing tired of making films that relied too heavily on such shock tactics, but whatever the reason they are certainly successful in playing *The House by the Cemetery* on a lower key.

Here again, the film draws heavily upon the writing of H.P. Lovecraft—and there is also another significant dose of Stephen King by way of *The Shining*. The Lovecraftian flavor is evident in the New England setting and the growing sense of *something* hiding in the dark, while the use of a child character with a particular sensitivity to the spirit world is straight out of King's book and the ensuing Stanley Kubrick film adaptation. The impact of popular successes on Italian filmmakers really cannot be overestimated: The flood of imitations which greeted the success of films like *Zombie* or *The Bird with the Crystal Plumage* (1970) or *Cannibal Holocaust* (1980) or *A Fistful of Dollars* (1964), or any of the other watershed genre films, is a testament to this. Kubrick's film encountered ample criticism in genre circles—and King himself was certainly quick to condemn it—but money talks, and the film made plenty of it. Fulci may not have been overly enamored by it, but elements of the film find its way into the film's visual language. The sequences of Bob staring off into space, carrying out conversations with people who only he can see, or wandering through the maze-like house, playing with his toys carry more than a slight air of familiarity to anybody who has seen Kubrick's film. That said, the similarities are not terribly heavy-handed, and it would be a mistake to suggest that Fulci and his collaborators were simply copying an American model. *The House by the Cemetery* is its own entity, and it remains one of Fulci's most legitimately frightening films.

One of the things the film does remarkably well is to convey the special world of children. All too often, children are represented as symbols of purity and innocence, but Fulci and his cowriters recognize that they have a special insight, which is born out of their lack of prejudice. As they have not been conditioned to view the world through a rigidly logical lens, they are more open to the possibility of the supernatural. Bob is a happy-go-lucky little boy who loves playing with his toy cars, but he has a special sensitivity to the supernatural that allows him to see and correctly interpret things that his parents are too self-absorbed to notice. Bob enjoys a rather touching friendship with the enigmatic Mae, who flits in and out of the narrative without ever appearing to interact with the other characters. Mae warns Bob not to come to the Freudstein house, but the decision is not his to make: He voices his concerns to his parents, but they predictably brush them off with a laugh. Unbeknown to Bob, Mae exists on a different plane: She is the deceased daughter of the horrible Dr. Freudstein, and, as such, she knows only too well how dangerous the house truly is. Fulci and his cowriters do not get into particulars, but it seems likely that Mae and her mother—also glimpsed, albeit even more obliquely than Mae—were among the first victims of Freudstein's obsessive quest for immortality. Mae does her best to protect Bob, but she can only do so much. At the end of the film, after Bob bears witness to the shocking murders of his parents, it is Mae who rescues Bob by pulling him away from her father's clutches. However, his "escape" is not exactly what it initially appears to be: Instead, he joins Mae and her mother on another plane of existence. He, too, has crossed over to the great beyond. Fulci handles this potentially upsetting plot development with great tact and sensitivity: Bob may be dead, but he has found a companion in the form of Mae, and the reassuring presence of Mae's mother suggests a sense of familial stability which stands in contrast to the dysfunctional family life of his earthly existence.

The film also touches upon childhood fears, as Bob is put through various unpleasant situations. One of the gorier bits involves Norman being attacked by a bat, which latches onto his hand. In order to kill the creature, Norman stabs it with a pair of scissors; the bat refuses to die, however, and he has to keep stabbing it over and over, before trying to shake it off of his hand. As he jerks his hand and attempts to free himself from its fangs, Norman inadvertently splatters the horrified Bob with blood. Bob's reaction suggests a significant trauma, but Norman seems curiously unconcerned about comforting the child or addressing how such a potentially psychologically traumatizing incident may affect him; it is consistent with the film's point of view that the adults live in a world of their own, while the needs of the children are frequently ignored and pushed aside as a result. As such, Bob and his parents almost seem to exist in separate narratives: Lucy and Norman are too focused on their own respective problems (that is, Lucy's deteriorating mental state and Norman's tunnel-visioned obsession with unraveling the Freudstein mystery) to provide much guidance in the child's life, and so he reverts to his world of imagination and the paranormal, instead. Bob's interactions with Mae are charming and provide brief moments of levity and lightness in what is otherwise a pretty bleak movie. Later in the film, when Bob goes to investigate the basement on his own, Fulci creates the film's most indelible moment: As children, we have all experienced the fear of going to a darkened basement or attic; many of us had to sleep with a nightlight for fear of a monster emerging from underneath the bed or out of the closet. Our parents assuage these fears by assuring us that there is nothing hiding in the dark. Fulci twists this conceit by demonstrating that there *is* something in the dark—and, as such, Bob has every reason to be fearful. As the child descends into the clammy basement, Fulci cuts to a close-up of a pair of yellow eyes staring out of the darkness. It's a truly frightening moment; it may seem a relatively minor flourish, especially compared to the other scenes of bodily mutilation on display, yet it lingers in the mind. The image of the eyes recalls similar moments in Mario Bava's *Baron Blood* (1972) and Dario Argento's *Inferno* (1980), but Fulci arguably outdoes his predecessors by virtue of putting a child at risk: This allows the film to broach something archetypal as Bob's "irrational" fears are validated in the most

**Lucio Fulci (behind the camera) lines up a shot in *The House by the Cemetery*.**

traumatic of ways. His subsequent attempt to escape is stymied when the door slams shut and locks him into the basement. Norman attempts to save the boy by hacking at the door with an axe, but Freudstein takes perverse glee in pinning the boy's head against the door; in a typical Hollywood film, this wouldn't generate nearly so much suspense, but in Fulci's world anything is possible and the viewer watches with bated breath, fearing for the worst but hoping for the best. Norman manages to narrowly avoid splitting the boy's head in two, but as already discussed, things will not end happily for them anyway.

*The House by the Cemetery* continues Fulci's remarkably strong run of horror films. By the time the film went into production, the director and his collaborators had scarcely had an opportunity to relax for over a year. For Fulci, the hectic workload meant a steady source of income, something he was particularly grateful for following a comparatively lean period at the end of the 1970s. His enthusiasm never wavered, and he found himself working in perfect harmony with collaborators like Sacchetti and cinematographer Sergio Salvati. The Sacchetti relationship would soon turn sour, but they were still on good terms at this stage in the game. The writer would later explain why he felt that Fulci stood apart from the rest of the pack:

> Technically speaking, he's on par with established American colleagues like John Carpenter, the substantial difference being that Fulci makes his films with low budgets.[5]

**Catriona MacColl and Paolo Malco begin to wonder if they were wise to move in to *The House by the Cemetery*.**

Catriona MacColl, making her final appearance for the director, heads the strong cast. MacColl plays a very different role here compared to her earlier work on *City of the Living Dead* and *The Beyond*: Lucy is very fragile psychologically, and her inability to cope with the stress of her situation pushes her to the breaking point. She is still a positive presence, however, which makes her final demise all the more upsetting. Norman is played by Paolo Malco, making the first of his two films for Fulci; he would go on to appear in *The New York Ripper*. Born in Liguria in 1947, Malco began appearing in films in the early 1970s. Prior to working with Fulci he appeared in such films as Damiano Damiani's *I Am Afraid* (1977) and he also played the title role in the biopic *Masoch* (1980), which dealt with the writer Leopold von Sacher-Masoch. Malco recalled that things got off to a rocky start between himself and Fulci:

> The first days of filming in Concord weren't easy for me, because he had a way of filming—an approach with actors—that I had never experienced before. I mean, he yelled all the time. In fact, the first two days I told myself it wasn't going to work. Instead, a great love and friendship came out of it.[6]

Malco would join the likes of Venantino Venantini and Fabrizio Jovine by becoming one of the few actors that the director became friendly with; the two men shared a similar outlook and sense of humor, and they bonded throughout filming. Malco would even serve as Fulci's best man for the director's third and final marriage to American actress Violet Jean. He would later reflect on his friendship with Fulci and say:

> Lucio was, like they are discovering now, a great, great director. [...] For me he was a life-teacher and a companion on great adventures. We practically lived together. Without him, I feel much more lonely.

Silvia Collatina and Giovanni Frezza fill the difficult roles of Mae and Bob. Collatina (born in Rome in 1972) made her film debut in Sergio Martino's *The Great Alligator* (1979), and she brings the right mixture of innocence and creepiness to her role as Mae. The character is deliberately ambiguous throughout much of the film, but it is ultimately revealed that her intentions are honorable; she is a tragic figure, trapped in the past thanks to the horrific actions of her father, searching for a "normal" friendship, which is truthfully outside of her grasp. Frezza (born in Basilicata in 1972) was also at the beginning of his short-lived career when Fulci cast him in this film. Bob is a tricky character to bring to life, and unfortunately English-speaking viewers have long underestimated Frezza's performance. The

**Dr. Freudstein remains one of Fulci's most disturbing monsters**

reason for this is simple: The dubbing of his character is truly wretched. Most of Fulci's films that were dubbed into English play perfectly well this way; truth be told, the overall quality of the dub on this film is also very high—but the dubbing artists dropped the ball in a big way when it came to Bob. Instead of hiring a little boy to dub the part, it almost sounds as if a middle-aged woman was utilized; try as she might, she simply doesn't sound convincing, and the effect is truly grating. Seen in Italian, the performance comes off much better—but the English vocal performance does him no favors and the character has become something of a pariah among Fulci cultists as a result. If one can get past this admitted distraction, however, it is possible to appreciate what a genuinely fine job Frezza does in the role. He is required to carry some important scenes, and he does not let the movie down. Fulci would go on to work with both actors again, casting Collatina as the wheelchair-bound murder witness in *Murder-Rock: Dancing Death* and Frezza as one of Christopher Connelly's kids in *Manhattan Baby*, but stories vary as to his feelings about dealing with the two kids on set. Catriona MacColl would later recall that:

> It seemed to me that he was really sweet with them. He got down to their level and joked around and tried to explain what he wanted them to do.[7]

Paolo Malco, on the other hand, has a less rosy recollection:

> Lucio wasn't fond of the kids too much. He would say, "What a pain in the ass. We're working with the children today." Sometimes he would get a kick out of scaring them.[8]

Collatina, a major horror movie buff in her own right, recalls her experiences working with Fulci in an interview included in this book, while Frezza, who has gone on to a successful career as an architect in the United States, would later comment:

> Lucio Fulci, most of the time, was upset. So everybody was hoping he was having a good day. When it was a good day, he was pretty nice. He had an aggressive attitude. I'm not sure if it was because he wanted to create a kind of emotional state or if it was because he was just like that. [...] I cried a couple of times.[9]

The supporting cast includes appearances by Dagmar Lassander (previously seen in *The Black Cat*), Carlo De Mejo (*City of the Living Dead*), Gianpaolo Saccarola (*The Beyond*) and the aforementioned Daniela Doria. Doria would go on to have her most spectacular death scene in *The New York Ripper*, while De Mejo would also appear in *Manhattan Baby*. De Mejo recalls:

> I was happy to work with him again right away. And to me just working with him was pleasant—I had so much fun on the adventure of *City of the Living Dead*. [...] It was a pleasant collaboration where he called me and asked me to come down. It was nice just to go down and have a cup of coffee with him. I would have done that, too.[10]

The beautiful Ania Pieroni makes one of the more striking impressions, in her only film for Fulci. She plays the character of Ann, a mysterious babysitter established as a potential menace who ultimately loses her head (literally!) to Dr. Freudstein. Fulci and cinematographer Sergio Salvati highlight Pieroni's striking eyes: They have the capacity to make her appear seductive one minute and morally suspect the next. Pieroni (born in Rome in 1957) first made a significant impression as the mysterious music student who is implied to be one of the mythical "Three Mothers" in Dario Argento's *Inferno* (1980), and she would go on to appear as the shoplifter who is slashed to death in Argento's *Tenebrae* (1982). She got married and walked away from films in the mid-1980s. Giovanni De Nava (born in Rome in 1944), who had previously played the zombie version of Schweick in *The Beyond*, plays Dr. Freudstein.

Speaking of zombies, many viewers are insistent upon bracketing *The House by the Cemetery* with *City of the Living Dead* and *The Beyond* as a sort of loose-fitting zombie trilogy. *City of the Living Dead* and *The Beyond* are hardly conventional examples of the living dead genre, as has been expounded upon in their respective chapters, but

***The House by the Cemetery*; original artwork by Scott Hoffman.**

there is even less reason to include *The House by the Cemetery* in this context. Truth be told, there are no zombies in this film. There are ghosts, certainly, but Dr. Freudstein, despite his alarming appearance, is not a reanimated cadaver—instead he is a very human villain who has sustained his life artificially. He may not have the appearance of a living person, but that does not make him a zombie. If the films are united at all, it's more by virtue of their rich atmosphere and their ability to evoke something of the flavor of Lovecraft and his writing, to say nothing of their technical sheen as related to the recurring presence of key artisans like cinematographer Sergio Salvati and make-up wizard Giannetto De Rossi. Sadly, this would prove to be the end of the line for Fulci's collaboration with both men. Salvati and De Rossi would go on to fresh pastures, and their presence was certainly missed in a big way when Fulci made a late-period attempt to revisit his former glories with the notoriously troubled production of *Zombie 3*. Fortunately, however, there were still some good times ahead before that particular ignominy reared its ugly head.

Notes:

1. Quoted from the featurette "A Haunted House Story" included on the Blue Underground Blu-ray release of *The House by the Cemetery*.
2. *Ibid.*
3. *Ibid.*
4. *Ibid.*
5. Palmerini, Luca M. and Gaetano Mistretta, *Spaghetti Nightmares* (Florida: Fantasma Books, 1996), p. 123.
6. Quoted from the featurette "Meet the Boyles," included on the Blue Underground Blu-ray release of *The House by the Cemetery*.
7. *Ibid.*
8. *Ibid.*
9. Quoted from the featurette "Children of the Night," included on the Blue Underground Blu-ray release of *The House by the Cemetery*.
10. Quoted from the featurette "My Time With Terror," included on the Blue Underground Blu-ray release of *The House by the Cemetery*.

# Paolo Malco Interview by Troy Howarth and Mike Baronas

The following interview with Paolo Malco was conducted via fax on November 18, 2014 Troy Howarth and Mike Baronas prepared the questions, and Silvia Collatina has our thanks for connecting with *signor* Malco and making the interview possible. *Signor* Malco has our sincere thanks for taking the time to answer these questions.

**Troy Howarth and Mike Baronas**: What made you want to become an actor?

**Paolo Malco**: In 1969, I attended the Political Sciences faculty at the State University of Milan, and I thought my future lay in a diplomatic career. But, prodded by a female friend, I enrolled in Milan's "School of the Little Theatre" … out of curiosity and in jest. But then, in 1970 Luca Ronconi signed me to feature in the great "Orlando Furioso." That's how it all began and, show after show, I became an actor!!!

**TH/MB**: One of your earliest films was *Io Ho Paura* (1977), directed by Damiano Damiani … any particular memories of that film?

**PM**: I don't recall much about *Io Ho Paura*, since I only had a small role.

**TH/MB**: Any memories of Gian Maria Volontè, who starred in the film?

**PM**: I have a lovely recollection of Gian Maria Volontè. In the film *Tre colonne in cronaca* (1990), directed by Carlo Vanzina, and produced by a very good friend of mine, Fernando Ghia (an Oscar-nominee for *The Mission*, 1986), playing alongside Volontè was very thrilling. He was the silent type, and severe-looking, but all that was needed to make you feel at home was a smile! In *Tre colonne in cronaca*, I had co-star status, so the work was enormous!

**TH/MB**: Did you enjoy working with Antonio Bido on *Watch Me When I Kill! / Il gatto dagli occhi di Giada* (1977)?

**PM**: Antonio Bido was a very amiable person and, besides, during the shooting of the film I met the love of my life, Paola Tedesco, my partner.

**TH/MB**: You played Leopold von Sacher-Masoch in *Masoch* … did you find that to be a memorable film to make?

**PM**: *Masoch* was perhaps the most thrilling experience of my career. It was like sitting down for a psychoanalytic session with director Franco Taviani. On the last day of shooting at Cinecittà's Studio 5, I shut myself in the studio of my reconstructed house and wept for a whole hour!!! It was similarly extraordinary at the Venice Film Festival, where we were in competition.

**TH/MB**: You first worked with Lucio Fulci on *The House by the Cemetery* … what was your very first meeting with him like?

**PM**: Lucio didn't like actors very much, and he was right!!! The first day's work in New York, he was aggressive and sarcastic in my regards. I replied, "If you start out like this, I'll take the first flight out and quit!"
**TH/MB**: How long did it take you to become close to Fulci? Was yours a gradual friendship or did you take to each other right away?
**PM**: Our friendship was born at that precise moment—we became inseparable. Our circle of friends used to call us "The Couple"! We dined together every night in various Roman restaurants or I cooked dinner at my house. Then the evening was spent in various salons in Rome and, during summer, on his yacht. Lucio had a very nice sailing boat, "Lele Oui"—Lele was his grandson, the son of his daughter Antonella. Those were memorable, unforgettable days.
**TH/MB**: Fulci had a reputation for being very volatile on set. Did you ever see this side of him?
**PM**: On the set, Fulci often shouted and took it out on some actress, but, at the end of the day, it was all a bluff—he tried in this way to conceal his timidity. On *The House by the Cemetery*, after a shouting and growling match, he turned the character played by Ania Pieroni into a mute. However, he adored the crew, who had great respect for him, and which he reciprocated. He gave nicknames to everybody—producer Fabrizio De Angelis was "The Cobra."
**TH/MB**: Any memories of your *House* costars, including Catriona MacColl?
**PM**: Catriona was a wonderful costar and a very good actress—even Fulci liked her a lot.
**TH/MB**: After this, you worked with Fulci on *The New York Ripper* … did he make any specific requests of you for this red herring role?
**PM**: No, he made no specific request—with Lucio, by then, there was a perfect understanding.
**TH/MB**: Are you a fan of horror films and *gialli*?
**PM**: I love horror very much—but, alas, they don't make them anymore.
**TH/MB**: Do you have a preference between *The House by the Cemetery* and *The New York Ripper* as films? Did you prefer one character to the other?
**PM**: I prefer *The House by the Cemetery*—I find it neater, more rigorous.
**TH/MB**: After *The New York Ripper* you never worked with Fulci again, but you were considered to be one of his closest friends. How often did you keep in touch with him?
**PM**: No, it's true, I never worked with Lucio again—also because I was very often busy in the theater and with Lamberto Bava and Enzo Castellari—he was very jealous of that—but we were always together, and I absorbed his great culture and refined intelligence.
**TH/MB**: How would you describe Fulci as a person? Was he a difficult person to get to know?
**PM**: Fulci was a very fascinating man.

**French poster for Damiano Damiani's *I Am Afraid* (1977); artwork by Arnstam.**

**TH/MB**: Fulci was very ill in later years; did he ever confide to you about his medical problems?
**PM**: Fulci underwent heart surgery, and I was by his side every day. He managed to joke even about the state of his health.
**TH/MB**: How did Lucio's death impact you?
**PM**: Lucio's death was a great blow—it left a great void inside me.
**TH/MB**: Are you still in touch with Fulci's children?
**PM**: No—it's been many years since I last saw Camilla and Antonella.
**TH/MB**: Would you agree that Lucio deserves to be mentioned among the best Italian directors of all time?
**PM**: Lucio was truly one of Italy's greatest directors—but, also, often underrated.
**TH/MB**: And lastly, are you surprised by the continued popularity of Fulci and his films?
**PM**: I'm surprised, but happy that, thanks to you, he is remembered and re-evaluated.
**TH/MB**: Thank you once again for your time—we hope you will be pleased with our tribute to Lucio.
**PM**: Thank you both—and a big thanks to Mr. Baronas, for his efforts and the passion with which he keeps alive and validates the memory of Lucio Fulci!!! Thanks.

# Silvia Collatina Interview by Troy Howarth

The following interview with actress Silvia Collatini was conducted via email on September 26, 2014. In addition to appearing as Mae Freudstein in *The House by the Cemetery*, Silvia also made an unbilled appearance as the wheelchair-bound Molly in Fulci's *Murder-Rock: Dancing Death*. Silvia not only appeared in horror films; she is also a genuine fan. She has my thanks for taking the time to speak with me about her film work.

**Troy Howarth**: You made your film debut when you were very young ... was acting something that you were passionately interested in from such a young age?
**Silvia Collatina**: Frankly speaking, I did not have a real vocation for acting. A friend of my mother introduced me to the profession when I was 5 years old (together with my sister) and I did not consider that opportunity a job or an achievement of a personal desire. Acting was so easy to me and I had fun, like a pastime, even though I was very responsible and I did it with all the possible commitment.
**TH**: Your film debut was in Sergio Martino's *The Great Alligator* ... do you have any memories of making that film?
**SC**: I still have vivid memories of all the movies I did. I remember the journey to Ceylon: a totally different country from Italy, and everything caused me strong emotions. I remember Claudio Cassinelli, Barbara Bach and Mel Ferrer. They were all very kind to me. I remember the strange and big insects, the snakes, the lagoon and the wild nature of that place ... nothing can be canceled from my mind; they are very precious memories.
**TH**: You first appeared for Lucio Fulci in *The House by the Cemetery*. How did you come to be cast on that film?
**SC**: Frankly speaking, it was very simple: My agent proposed me for the audition. I just did it and I got the part!!! I was very happy to fly to New York. I still remember the phone call my mother received from my agent. She was on the phone and mimed "the airplane," so I understood what it meant. I could not wait to fly and to shoot the movie!
**TH**: What were your impressions of Lucio Fulci as a person and a director?
**SC**: I cannot judge him from a personal point of view, because I only knew him as a director. He was a very bizarre person, but surely very charming in his way of directing. I know that he had a bad reputation about treating actors, and, yes, I can say that he was not particularly polite or gentle to us—but neither was he a jailer!
**TH**: Fulci had the reputation of being very tough on actors ... was he like that with you and your costar Giovanni Frezza?
**SC**: Shooting *House by the Cemetery* did not cause me any problems, except for some crying, but nothing shocking! Yes, he used to shout more than normal, but I followed every advice he gave me, as I considered him a teacher.

**Silvia Collatina and Giovanna Frezza flank Teresa Rossi Passante, who plays the ghostly Mary Freudstein.**

**TH**: Did your parents ever worry about your appearing in such a bloody horror film?
**SC**: Oh no, my parents were not upset at all. We were all fans of horror, my brothers and sister included. We used to see horror movies all together in the evening, and from there comes my passion for horror in general.
**TH**: Do you have any particularly strong memories of the filming?
**SC**: Of course, many! For example, the scene where the babysitter's mannequin loses its head in the shop window really worried me, because I was very shy and I did not want people wandering around there and staring at me. The staff told me not to worry: American people would not pay attention to me; they minded their business. When the scene was finished, I turned my head and I realized that behind me there was a curious crowd! Oh my God, what an embarrassment!
Besides, what impressed me a lot were the worms coming out from Dr. Freudstein's body after Paolo Malco stabbed him in the stomach, and when the former consequently tore off a piece of Paolo Malco's throat. Everything looked so real, and Fulci said with satisfaction: "Good first take." I was totally fascinated by this scene.

As a side note, Nicoletta Elmi (the redheaded girl in Dario Argento's *Deep Red*) and I have lots in common; the same color of the hair, having shot a horror movie, and, most importantly, my family and hers were friends because we were neighbors. They lived in the apartment under mine! That's an incredible coincidence!

**Silvia Collatina (left) is reunited with Catriona MacColl and Giovanni Frezza in 2011; image courtesy of Mark Jason Murray.**

**TH**: What do you remember about your costars, including Catriona MacColl and Giovanni Frezza?

**SC**: Catriona was very kind to me. [She was a] very sweet person and an extraordinary actress. Giovanni was a friend. We used to play together, and spent most of the day together as well when in New York. I thought he was very good at acting, even if he was very young. He was so spontaneous and real!

**TH**: You next worked for Fulci with a small, unbilled role in *Murder-Rock: Dancing Death* ... do you think Fulci specifically requested you for this role?

**SC**: Yes, I think so ... perhaps he thought I could play the part of a cunning girl with a passion for the macabre. I was not and I am still not a sly person, but surely I love the macabre and horror!!!

**TH**: Do you have any particular memories of the making of that film?

**SC**: I had a very short, but remarkable, role in that movie, which I shot in one day in Italy. I remember the wheelchair and me exercising on the corridors of the house. Compared to *House by the Cemetery*, it was easier for me to portray Molly than Mae. Perhaps because I already knew Fulci!

**TH**: After *Murder-Rock*, you were apparently not active in films for approximately 30 years ... what happened during that time frame?

**SC**: I was an anti-conventional actress: I was very shy, and being an actress caused me a lot of embarrassment; I wanted to be like the other "normal" girls and boys, so I decided to keep on studying and abandoned this career. At the time I did not know how lucky I was. Later on I tried to again enter this "field," but had no success. Unfortunately, here in Italy you must be a model to make it...

**TH**: You recently made your first film appearance in many years—did you find it to be enjoyable?

**SC**: Do you mean *Lust Murders*? Yes, I really, really enjoyed appearing in that teaser trailer, and a special thank goes to Bérangère Soustre de Condat Rabourdin and David Marchand, who gave me that opportunity—but I also realized that I love being behind the scenes, participating as a scriptwriter or giving my point of view while shooting. I have lots of ideas ... I am also writing a horror novel; I would like it to be a movie ... I know it's a hard dream to realize, but I am hopeful! I would like to give my contribution to horror. We all need something to scare us again, but, unfortunately, as far as I am concerned, I think that there is nothing new on the market that is able to frighten us fans again...

**TH**: Do you plan to continue acting?

**SC**: At the moment, I prefer taking part in the horror conventions abroad as a representative of the actors and actresses who did Italian horror movies in the '70s and '80s, but who knows ... I do not close any doors!!! Why not!

**TH**: How old were you when you first saw the films you made for Fulci? What did you think of them?

**SC**: When I saw the *House by the Cemetery* I was 10, I think. I saw the preview with my family. I was very excited, while my sister was completely scared. On the contrary, as *Murder-Rock* had some particular scenes, I saw it later. I really must say that Molly in *Murder-Rock* was cruel and ugly!!!

**TH**: And lastly, are you surprised by the enduring popularity of Fulci and his films?

**SC**: I think he really deserves this popularity, even though he is not alive ... He was a genius, an odd person full of ideas. It's a pity that in Italy the majority of people do not know him, while abroad he is "The Master of Horror." Here in Italy the only name known in connection with horror movies, respectfully speaking, is Dario Argento.

**TH**: Thanks for answering these questions!

**SC**: You're welcome!

# 1982

## The New York Ripper (Italy)

Aka *Lo squartatore di New York; L'éventreur de New York; El descuartizador de Nueva York; El destripador de Nueva York; Der New York Ripper*

Directed by Lucio Fulci; Produced by Fabrizio De Angelis, for Fulvia Film; Screenplay by Gianfranco Clerici, Lucio Fulci, Vincenzo Mannino and Dardano Sacchetti, from a story by Gianfranco Clerici, Lucio Fulci and Vincenzo Mannino; Director of Photography: Luigi Kuveiller; Editor: Vincenzo Tomassi; Music by Francesco De Masi

**Italian *locandina* for *The New York Ripper*; artwork by Enzo Sciotti.**

Main Players: Jack Hedley (Lieutenant Williams); Paolo Malco (Dr. Davis); Almanta Suska [as Almanta Keller] (Fay Majors); Alexandra Delli Colli (Jane Forrester Lodge); Andrea Occhipinti [as Andrew Painter] (Peter Bunch); Renato Rossini [as Howard Ross] (Mikis Scellenda); Cosimo Cinieri [as Laurence Welles] (Dr. Lodge); Cinzia de Ponti (Rosie); Zora Kerova [as Zora Kerowa] (Eva); Daniela Doria (Kitty); Barbara Cupisti (Heather)

Cameo appearance: Lucio Fulci (Chief of Police)

*A maniac is slashing-up young women in New York, and embittered Lieutenant Williams doesn't have any leads to follow. He enlists the aid of a brilliant young psychologist, Dr. Davis, in the hopes of generating a profile that may help to trap the killer. Meanwhile, the killer begins calling Williams and taunting him on the phone ...*

The early 1980s witnessed the death of the *giallo* as an especially viable commercial commodity, but it was not a genre that went quietly into that good night; films like *The New York Ripper* demonstrated that there were still ample buttons to be pushed within the genre.

Lucio Fulci undertook this project during a period of heated creativity; he had just finished making several of his most beloved horror films in the form of *City of the Living Dead, The Beyond* and *The House by the Cemetery*, and the sudden burst of activity emboldened him and compelled him to push the envelope of excess further and further. *The New York Ripper* would transpose this emphasis on blood and gore into a more realistic context; what played out as over-the-top and operatic in the context of the supernatural would now seem sadistic and cruel. The critics tore the film to shreds, censors sought to hack it to bits (the British would ban it outright for many years before passing it with cuts for home video release in 2002), and bewildered fans didn't quite know what to make of it. No doubt many of these fans were unfamiliar with Fulci's prolific output prior to *Zombie*, however, and failed to realize that the film built upon groundwork already established by the filmmaker in his *gialli* of the late '60s and 1970s. *The New York Ripper* wouldn't prove to be his final word on the subject in the literal sense—he would helm one more *giallo*, *Murder-Rock: Dancing Death*—but it may as well have been.

In a sense, the film can be seen as Fulci's reaction to the enthusiastic reception of his gory horror films. So many of the fans and critics alike spent so much time going on about the excessive violence in these films (in a positive and negative way, inevitably) that very often the other aspects of the films went unappreciated. Fulci's artful use of framing, the luscious cinematography by Sergio Salvati, the crisp and efficient editing of Vincenzo Tomassi or the inventive soundtracks by Fabio Frizzi received little ink; instead, one review after another dwelled on the films' assorted gory highlights. This was surely not unexpected, but by the same token it must have amused Fulci no end to realize that, at the end of the day, so much of the re-

**Behind-the-scenes on *The New York Ripper:* Fulci (left) supervises the filming of a scene on location in New York City.**

sponse these films generated was down to their elaborately choreographed scenes of cannibalism and mutilation. By removing this action from the realm of the "fantastic," where they were somehow more palatable (pardon the expression), Fulci succeeded in pushing the envelope further than ever before. His *gialli* of the 1970s had moments of potent violence (think no further than the vicious chain-whipping in *Don't Torture a Duckling*), but such sequences were more along the lines of punctuation points. In *The New York Ripper*, they would become far more central to the film's gritty and seedy ambience. By pairing the realistic presentation of violent death with sleazy doses of sex and perversion, he concocted a heady cocktail that proved to be a little too potent for its intended audience. Avid gorehounds didn't appreciate having their fetish thrown in their face, and many rejected the film outright. On the other end of the spectrum, the apoplectic critics who had long complained that Fulci's work showed a misogynist streak had a field day, as they felt this film provided the final and absolute validation of their thesis that Fulci was little more than a vile pornographer who traded on "money shots" of women being brutalized in nauseating detail. In any event, if Fulci's intention was to confront his fans and critics alike on the topic of violence, it was not a discussion people were necessarily prepared to have at the time of the film's original release; time and plenty of weak, watered-down *gialli* and Italian horror films have done much to rehabilitate the film's reputation, though it still remains something of a hot-button topic among fans of the genre in general and of Fulci's work in particular.

That said, Fulci approached the film first and foremost as a psychological thriller. Having spent the better part of two years making films about zombies and the supernatural, *The New York Ripper* would allow him to restore logic to his cinema. His desire to strive for a dream-like state of consciousness in his horror films had flown contrary to his belief in logic and story structure, so reverting to his old methods on this picture must have seemed like a relief by comparison. Prior to the film's release and subsequent firestorm of criticism, he played up its suspense factor to interviewer Robert Schlockoff:

> It's the story of a mad killer committing terrible murders in New York, but to some extent it's a fantastic film, if only because the police have to spot this madman among 20 million New Yorkers. Much less horror than my previous films, no zombies, but a human killer working in the dark. The setting is deliberately conventional: Though I aim at making a new style of thriller, I want to pay a tribute to Hitchcock. *The New York Ripper* is in a way a Hitchcock revisited, a fantastic film with a plot, violence, and sexuality.[1]

Fulci's allusion to Hitchcock may seem slightly facetious, but in fact the film is rather cleverly plotted and explores a theme the famed British *auteur* knew only too well; the banality of evil. Fulci and his cowriters sprinkle the film with a number of credible red herrings, but the final reveal that the murderer is blandly handsome Peter Bunch comes out of left field; he is so very straight-laced and so completely uninteresting, it simply never occurs to the viewer to ever consider him as a realistic candidate. Peter is the sort of psychopath people always speak about on the evening news: "Oh, he seemed so nice ... so normal." Beneath his surface of placid serenity, however, Peter is driven by feelings of rage, guilt and self-loathing: His little girl is wasting away in a hospital, suffering from a degenerative disease, which is ravaging her body. Peter cannot deal with the thought that she will never grow up to become a "normal" woman, so he takes out his frustration on women who appear to be enjoying their lives—and naturally, in his twisted psychopathology, he equates an aura of comfortable sexuality with abnormality. The murders he commits are nasty and pointedly sexual.

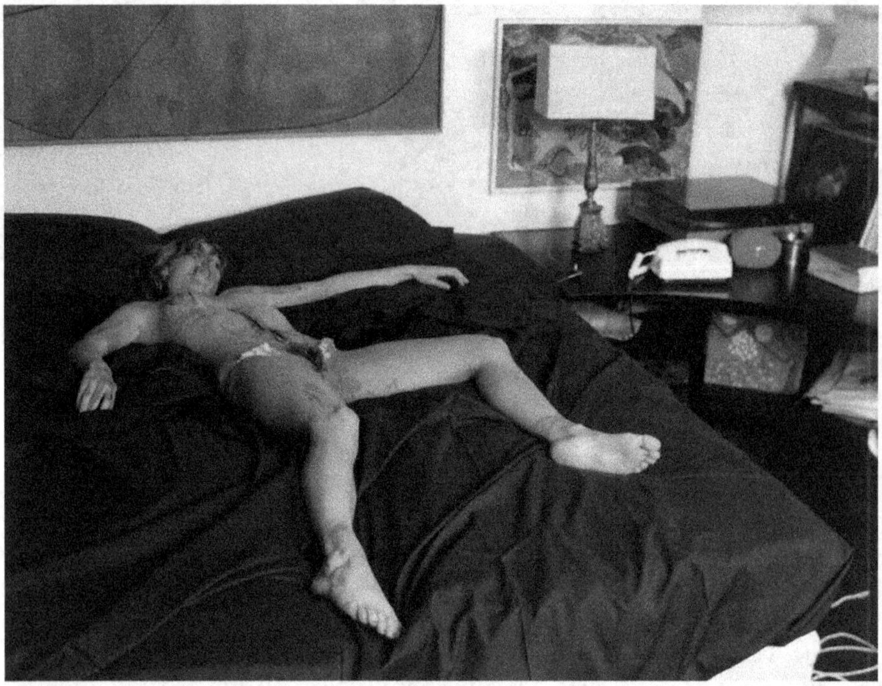

Much has been written about *The New York Ripper* down through the years, and a good chunk of it is negative. Stephen Thrower's fine book on the director, *Beyond Terror: The Films of Lucio Fulci*, made a valiant attempt at evening the scales somewhat, but little of any real thought or sensitivity has ever been attempted on this most misunderstood of *gialli*. In a way, it's easy to see why: To put it bluntly, this is one mean *bastard* of a movie. It opens with a golden retriever finding a severed hand amid the trash of New York City and it closes with a pathetic little girl, lonely and parentless, crying her eyes out as the police prepare to rest on their laurels now that their latest psychopath has been put out of commission. It wallows in scenes of kinky sex: Live sex shows in the city's Times Square district (this was long before Mayor Bloomberg turned it into a far-less-atmospheric tourist trap), illicit motel room hookups and more are detailed in an appropriately sordid manner. On top of that, it presents a cast of characters that can charitably be described as dysfunctional. In the film's embittered milieu, innocence is no guarantee of happiness, and the representatives of "justice" are just a hair's-breadth removed from the criminals they are seeking to apprehend and punish. The question becomes, was Fulci really seeking to provoke his critics into a fit of sputtering rage? If so, he certainly succeeded beyond his wildest dreams.

**Daniela Doria meets *The New York Ripper* in Fulci's most notorious scene of violent excess.**

Even those connected to the film don't all have positive things to say about it. Dardano Sacchetti was one of Fulci's key creative collaborators during this period, and he has often spoken with enthusiasm of the work they did together. When it comes to titles beloved by the fans like *City of the Living Dead* or *The Beyond*, Sacchetti is quick to point out that he had a major hand in developing some of the more outré and outrageous ideas present in those films; when the topic of *The New York Ripper* comes up, however, his response is somewhat different. When asked where the film's scenes of kinky sex sprang from, Sacchetti responded:

> From Fulci's perverse mind! He nurtures a profound sadism towards women. However, he's not an

aggressive person—he works it all off in his films! [...] He's had such a wretched life that, in the end, he's turned nasty himself.[2]

These are strong words, pregnant with a none-too-subtle suggestion that Fulci's so-called misogyny was deeply etched into his character and therefore spilled out into his art. Even if we ignore the notion of Sacchetti eagerly looking to take credit for the things that the fans liked while distancing himself from those that they didn't, it is still dangerous to accept these allegations at face value. *The New York Ripper* is often classified as a textbook example of cinematic misogyny and, in fairness, it's easy to understand why: The victims tend to be female, and the nature of the violence is often directed towards mutilating their beautiful visages or, worse, toward attacking their very sexuality itself. Matters aren't helped by the presence of a "hero" figure, Lieutenant Williams, who smugly passes moral judgment on the victims while trying to apprehend their murderer. Fulci is banking on his critics forming a kneejerk reaction, but might he have been hoping that his fans may have been willing to look beneath the surface and examine things more clearly? It's hard to know for sure just what he was thinking, but it seems hard to reconcile the idea of Fulci, with his "liberal" social conscience (as evidenced in his earlier works), truly embracing the notion of punishing his female characters for simply exploring their sexual fantasies. In essence, Fulci's intentions here are to provoke the viewer while also telling a tightly plotted and mostly logical thriller scenario. As Stephen Thrower posits in his analysis of the picture, this is a very sophisticated game of cat and mouse, with Fulci losing out in the end by virtue of the fact that so much genre criticism is so superficial and reactionary; again, however, time and reflection are beginning to make the film's more sophisticated elements more evident.

The characters are a deliberately cold and unfeeling lot. Lieutenant Williams is a variation on the tough, cynical detective figures associated with the *noir* genre; he even wears a raincoat with an upturned collar. He may occupy much of the film's narrative space, but he is not a conventional hero by any means. Williams is crass, crude and downright inhuman in his dealings with other people and in his reactions to the carnage that is taking place around him; one can argue that he's been hardened by his work, such is the nature of the job, but he's deliberately shown in a very abrupt and unsympathetic fashion. Even worse, he's a bigot and a hypocrite. He has no problem implying to the grieving husband of one victim that the woman brought about her own death by fooling around, yet his only real relationship outside of his "office" is with the prostitute he beds on a semi-regular basis. There's something rather sad and lonely in this, serving to make him a little pathetic, but the cold, arrogant and condescending attitude he displays throughout the picture makes the audience keep him at arm's length. Still, if one accepts the notion that he is the hero and that this therefore makes him the film's "moral compass," then his allegations against the victims would indeed be very troubling. This is, again, one of the subtle elements that Fulci and his collaborators (including Sacchetti, whether he likes the film or not) worked into the picture, which has generated so much confused criticism down through the years. To assist in his investigation, Williams enlists the aid of a psychologist/teacher Dr. Davis. Davis is one of the film's most interesting characters. He is defined by a morbid, ironic sense of humor. This, in itself, sets him apart from Williams, who is presented as completely humorless. Davis also displays a smug, self-satisfied quality, with a healthy ego, yet he has a measure of compassion and empathy that sets him apart from the lieutenant. Interestingly, he is also revealed to be gay. Critics who have argued that Fulci was displaying an overzealous Catholic attitude to sex and sexuality tend to conveniently overlook this aspect; if this were really true, Davis would be marked as aberrant because of his sexuality. True, he hides it from people, and the audience only discovers it by virtue of a brief scene where he is seen picking up a copy of *Blueboy* magazine from a local newsstand, but it's a telling moment and it's included for good reason. Part of it is to play on the conventions of the genre, which often conflates the "different" with the aberrant; as Fulci demonstrated in earlier works like *Don't Torture a Duckling* and *City of the Living Dead*, however, it is not the "other" figures who are predisposed to violence and hatred, but rather the bigoted, so-called "normal" characters. *The New York Ripper* remains true to this thesis by presenting Davis as a basically affable and likable character who uses his intellect to help trap the killer. In the film's chilly environment, Dr. Davis is one of the few characters who shows any real humanity. Similarly, the nominal heroine, Fay, is not really all that interesting. Indeed, she is rather a dense and irritating presence overall; she may embody the "Catholic" ideal of the sexually conservative woman (she may even be a virgin, though this is not dealt with in any meaningful detail), but she consistently displays poor judgment and never really engages audience sympathy. By contrast, many of the Earthy" victims have real spunk and are considerably more lively and interesting. For example, Jane Forrester Lodge may fit the profile of the "affluent pervert" one is accustomed to seeing in so many *gialli*, but she still has real humanity and comes across as a sympathetic presence. She is married to a successful doctor, but their relationship seems chilly and distant. She gets off on having sex with random men; he gets his kicks by listening to the audio recordings and masturbating to them in his study instead of simply having sex with her. Fulci does not pass moral judgment on this character, even if Lieutenant Williams does. Indeed, the scene where she is trying to escape from the Ripper's clutches is one of the most suspenseful in the picture—and it's suspenseful for the best of reasons, because we want to see her escape from his clutches. Here again, if Fulci were really intending to condemn this character, the emphasis and execution of this sequence would be very different; there's no doubt that he's on her side, rather than that of the killer, but this again would prove to be a distinction that was too subtle for many reviewers.

In addition to the film's seedy ambience and graphic sadism, the other controversial element is the killer's duck-like voice. Believe it or not, there is actually a somewhat compelling psychological reason provided for this at the end of the picture, but it understandably threw viewers for a loop, and continues to do so to this day. Proceeding on the assumption that Fulci was intelligent enough to realize that this would draw snickers from some viewers, it seems safe to conclude that he was having a little bit of fun with genre convention: Dario Argento had popularized the use of breathless, whispering, vaguely androgynous voices for his killers (largely to keep their identity shrouded in mystery until the end of the film), and Fulci takes things a step further by adopting an even more ludicrous form of subterfuge. Whether the decision was a wise one or not is open to debate, but there's no denying that it is a memorable touch, and the final explanation goes a long way towards validating it in context.

*The New York Ripper* seldom gets its due as a piece of filmmaking, but it is definitely one of Fulci's best, most assured pictures. He directs the film with energy, style and conviction. The pace is steady throughout and the mixture of police procedural sequences and shocking sensationalism is nicely balanced. The film benefits from its location shooting in New York (with interiors filmed in Rome; the old Italian tradition of transforming a setting into something overtly "American" by plastering the Stars and Stripes on a wall as set dressing is in evidence in at least one scene), and Luigi Kuveiller's lighting is superb. This was Kuveiller's first experience working with Fulci since *A Lizard in a Woman's Skin*, and his presence helps to take the sting away from the absence of Sergio Salvati; sadly, Kuveiller, too, would then leave the fold for good, and cinematographers of the same skill would become harder and harder to come by over time. The second unit work is by the veteran Guglielmo Mancori, who had last worked with Fulci on *Il lungo, il corto, ill gatto*; he would return to photograph the director's next movie, *Manhattan Baby*. The use of color is more naturalistic than in some of Fulci's more stylized '70s thrillers, but there's a marvelous, Mario Bava-like moment when one victim is killed in a room suffused with green light; when the killer leaves the room, the red light from the hallway filters in and highlights his gory handiwork in an almost Expressionistic flourish. The Bava connection is strengthened by the presence of Kuveiller's camera operator, Ubaldo Terzano, who worked as Bava's chief camera operator for a number of years. Francesco De Masi's funky score[3] is alternately thrilling and mournful, while Germano Natali's special make-up effects are notable for their queasy realism.

The cast includes a number of familiar faces. English actor Jack Hedley may seem odd casting as the gruff New York cop, but he gives an excellent performance.[4] Hedley resists the urge to soften the character and is admirably committed in showing him as the cold-hearted son-of-a-bitch that he really is. Hedley was born in London in 1930 under the name Jack Hawkins; he changed the name later on to avoid confusion with the star of British films of the same name, best-known for his appearances in such films as David Lean's *The Bridge on the River Kwai* (1957) and William Wyler's *Ben-Hur* (1959). Under the pseudonym of Jack Hedley, he began appearing on British television in the late 1950s and made his film debut in 1958. He played an uncredited bit role in David Lean's *Lawrence of Arabia* (1962, which featured his namesake in a much larger role, with proper billing!) before landing meaty, starring roles in Don Sharp's *Witchcraft* (1964) and John Gilling's *The Scarlet Blade* (1964). He popped up in everything from Roy Ward Baker's *The Anniversary* (1967) to John Glen's James Bond adventure *For Your Eyes Only* (1981) before making his only foray into the world of Italian exploitation cinema with *The New York Ripper*. Hedley spent the rest of the decade into the early 2000s working predominantly in television, before retiring from acting; he is reportedly now living in South Africa. Paolo Malco plays Dr. Davis quite effectively. Malco's mixture of charm and cynicism helps to make the character a likable one, and he and Hedley have excellent chemistry together. Andrea Occhipinti (born in Milan in 1957) plays Peter Bunch, in the first of his two appearances for Fulci; he would return for *Conquest*. Occhipinti's handsome looks and buttoned-down demeanor are ideal for the role; he barely registers as a character for much of the film, which is exactly as it should be, but secondary viewings reveal little tics and details which point to the character's paranoia. He would go on to appear in Lamberto Bava's *giallo A Blade in the Dark* (1983), and in recent years has become a prolific and well-regarded film producer in his own right; among his credits in this area is the documentary *How We Got the Italian Movie Business Into Trouble: The True Story of Franco and Ciccio* (2004), which features some archival interview clips with Fulci. Fay, the film's somewhat boring heroine, is played by Almanta Suska. Suska (born in Rome in 1961) brings a blank quality to the part, which may or may not have been deliberate on her part, but it certainly makes the character difficult to read; she does not engender much audience interest or empathy, but her relationship with the twisted Peter is fittingly ambiguous. Suska made her film debut with the film, and she would go on to appear opposite Fulci's former leading man David Warbeck in Antonio Margheriti's *Hunters of the Golden Cobra* (1982). Alexandra Delli Colli plays Jane Forrester Lodge, who manages to convey great depth of character in her relatively few scenes. Delli Colli was born in 1957 and began appearing in films in the mid-'70s. Her statuesque build and elegant looks made her a natural for exploitation cinema, and she bared all in quite a few films, including Marino Girolami's demented *Zombie Holocaust* (1980). She disappeared from films in the late 1980s and was married for a time to the great cinematographer Tonino Delli Colli, whose lengthy career included a few early collaborations with Fulci back when the latter was still working as an assistant director. Character actor Cosimo Cinieri plays her husband herein. Cinieri (born in Puglia in 1938) is appropriately ambiguous as the wealthy pervert with a fetish for voyeurism; his sinister looks and repressed demeanor suit the role beautifully, and Fulci would go on to use him in such films as *Manhattan Baby*, *Rome, 2072 A.D.: The New Gladiators* and *Murder-Rock: Dancing Death.* Cinieri would later recall his work with Fulci with enthusiasm:

**German lobby card: Zora Kerova bares all to play the doomed sex show performer in *The New York Ripper*.**

> Lucio Fulci touched me personally because he was fundamentally a kind man. He was a very sensitive human being. He suffered from a lack of affection, not from the Italian public, but in the movie machinery; from the production staff who didn't give him the credit he deserved. [...] I met him once and he was working as a sailboat distributor to make ends meet. He was a little embarrassed. [...] He was a director of the highest standards; technically extraordinary. [...] With me he was always passionately affectionate. [...] When we were on the set, he continuously applauded my work."

Renato Rossini played the role of Mikis, the Greek immigrant whose taste for kinky sex lands him on the suspect list, under his usual *nom de plume* of Howard Ross. Rossini gives a good performance, despite having virtually no dialogue. His imposing build and slightly seedy appearance make him a credible red herring, and he easily dominates his scenes. Born in Rome in 1941, Rossini got his start working in *pepla* like *Esther and the King* (1960, directed by Raoul Walsh, with uncredited assistance from his cinematographer Mario Bava) and *Hercules Against the Mongols* (1963); from there he went on to appear in a number of Spaghetti Westerns (Bava's *Savage Gringo*, 1966; Giovanni Grimaldi's *Johnny Colt*, 1968) and *gialli* (Bava's *Five Dolls for an August Moon*, 1970; Giuseppe Bennati's *The Killer Reserved Nine Seats*, 1974). He would reunite with Fulci on *Rome, 2072 A.D.: The New Gladiators.* Daniela Doria (born in Rome in 1956) makes her final bow for Fulci; and what a note she goes out on! She is sweetly endearing as Lieutenant Williams' favorite prostitute; she does not allow the gruff policeman to push her around, and makes it clear that she is a professional who deserves to be treated as such. When the ripper kills her off to get back at him, the scene works on several levels: For one, Williams delays acting out of embarrassment over revealing how he knows where to find the girl (the ripper has evaded a phone trace, knowing that Williams will be reluctant to tip his hand to his colleagues), for another, the way in which she is killed is particularly vile and nasty and for another, she has been established—however briefly—as a character worth caring about. Her death scene allows Fulci to push his penchant for violence to its all-time high: A razor bisects her nipple, with her eye shortly following suit. It's a rough scene, but it is not structured or executed in a way that celebrates the sadism; instead, it shows violence in an unflattering way. A similar approach can be found in the demise of the sex show performer played by Czech actress Zora Kerova. Kerova (born in Prague in 1950) does not have much of an opportunity to show off her acting skills, but she throws herself into what the role demands of her with enviable professionalism. She had already impressed with her starring role in Bruno Mattei's *The True Story of the Nun of Monza* (1980) and had appeared in such gory shockers as Aristide Massaccesi's *Anthropophagus* (1980, where she is cannibalized by the film's "monster," Luigi Montefiori, who memorably rips the fetus from her womb and eats it!) and Umberto Lenzi's *Cannibal Ferox* (1981, where she is hung from a pair of nasty looking meat-hooks, impaling her breasts), so her demise by vaginal mutilation here was not exactly shocking for her. She would go on to appear in *Touch of Death* and *The Ghosts of Sodom*, as well as one of the films "supervised" by Fulci: *Hansel and Gretel.* The lovely Barbara Cupisti plays Dr. Davis' wiseass assistant. It is not a large role, but the actress (born in Tuscany in 1952) does a capable job in it. This is actually Cupisti's first film; she would go on to appear in such films as Tinto Brass' *The Key* (1984) and Dario Argento's *Opera* (1987), as well as several

**English character actor Jack Hedley plays the memorably callous protagonist, Lieutenant Williams.**

pictures by Michele Soavi: *Stage Fright* (1987), *The Church* (1989) and *Dellamorte Dellamore* (1994); in recent years, she has also directed several documentaries.

To say *The New York Ripper* was greeted with controversy would be a major understatement. The British had already developed a queasy relationship with Fulci based on his recent horror films; it is probably fair to say that the BBFC held their breath every time a copy of his latest film came into their office. *Zombie*, *The Beyond* and *The House by the Cemetery* were all subjected to heavy-duty cuts for theatrical release and would end up on the "Video Nasty" list, but *The New York Ripper* proved to be too much for them to stomach. In the documentary *Video Nasties: The Definitive Guide, Part 2* (2014), Carol Topolski, a former examiner with the BBFC from 1983 to 1995, recalled seeing the film for the first time:

> I saw a film with [BBFC director] Jim Ferman and two other senior colleagues, both of whom were women, called *The New York Ripper*. And it is simply the most damaging film I have ever seen in my whole life. It was simply a relentless catalogue of the eponymous antihero/villain cutting women up. And the filmmakers were feasting on what women's bodies looked like when they were cut up. At the end of that film, which was clearly never, *ever* going to be passed—there was no way that that level of unremitting sadistic attacks on women was ever going to be passed—at the end of the film, all four of us sat in the cinema, and three of us were quite quietly weeping, as we ... actually, all of us went into Jim's office just to recover, because it was the most—it was being in the presence of a film which was gratifying a particular desire. I always thought that the difficulty for censors ... the *question*, not difficulty, for censors is the dispiriting thing about seeing a film of that nature is not that it was made, because it could have been made and left in a cupboard, but that there was an audience for it. I think that says something about the viewing audience."

Wow—quite a statement, no? Leaving aside Topolski's obvious right to hold and express her own opinion, the extreme sensitivity of her reaction to Fulci's film is indicative of the slippery slope of film censorship. Simply put, censors are human beings and they are in the position of passing a form of moral judgment over the films they are assessing. Ideally, people who do this job should possess the intelligence to be able to see past their own kneejerk reactions and understand the point the filmmaker is trying to make; even if they don't like the film, they should hopefully be able to comprehend that there is a place for confrontational cinema. *The New York Ripper* shows Fulci at his most abrasive. It's an unpleasant film. This is deliberate, not accidental. As such, to criticize it for being too unpleasant or by jumping to the conclusion that it is inherently misogynistic for depicting the crimes of a misogynist is to completely miss the point; indeed, the fact that the film proved to be so upsetting to the censors is proof of its effectiveness. There is a time and a place for restraint and good manners, but *The New York Ripper* is not that type of film. Sadly, Topolski and her cohorts at the BBFC used their position and power to ban the film outright in the U.K. for many years; it would not be permissible to sell or own a copy of the film in England until 2002, and even then its release would come with the built-in caveat of some edits in the murder of Daniela Doria. In the U.S., the film was granted only a very limited theatrical release in 1984; it garnered wider exposure on VHS in 1987, though the panned-and-scanned (and slightly edited) release by Vidmark Home Entertainment made the film look seedy and removed the gloss and craftsmanship of its widescreen cinematography. In more recent years, the film has been presented fully uncut and restored to its proper 2.35 aspect ratio, but its status among Fulci fans remains problematic. For many, it is just too nasty and too brutal to embrace; perhaps that is as it should be, given its pragmatic approach to a nasty piece of subject matter.

Those viewers who can accept this and appreciate the film for its stylish execution and its dark wit are in for a treat, however: *The New York Ripper* is one of the director's best films, and it remains a high watermark in the latter period of the *giallo*, which would continue to wind down into a stream of indifferent (not-so-) erotic thrillers throughout the '80s and '90s.

Notes:
1. Retrieved from http://www.shockingimages.com/fulci/interview2.html
2. Palmerini, Luca M. and Gaetano Mistretta, *Spaghetti Nightmares* (Florida: Fantasma Books, 1996), p. 125.
3. At least one cue is not by De Masi, however; during the scene in which Alexandra Delli Colli is frantically trying to escape from the binding used during her sexual encounter with Renato Rossini, the piece "Disperazione," written by Alessandro Alessandroni for his album *Angoscia* is heard playing on the radio.
4. Prolific voice actor Edward Mannix dubbed Hedley's voice into English. Mannix is one of those names Euro Cult buffs may not recognize—but his voice is certainly recognizable: Among his many English-language dubbing credits are Mario Bava's *Twitch of the Death Nerve* (where he dubbed Luigi Pistilli), Sergio Martino's *Your Vice is a Locked Room and Only I Have the Key* (again dubbing Pistilli), Massimo Dallamano's *What Have They Done To Your Daughters?* (dubbing supporting player Ferdinando Murolo), Fulci's *Zombie* (as the voice of the cop who busts Ian McCulloch and Tisa Farrow as they snoop around the deserted boat), *The House by the Cemetery* (where he dubs Fulci's character) and *Manhattan Baby* (where he dubs Cosimo Cinieri), Juan Piquer Simón's *Pieces* (dubbing Paul L. Smith) and many, many more.

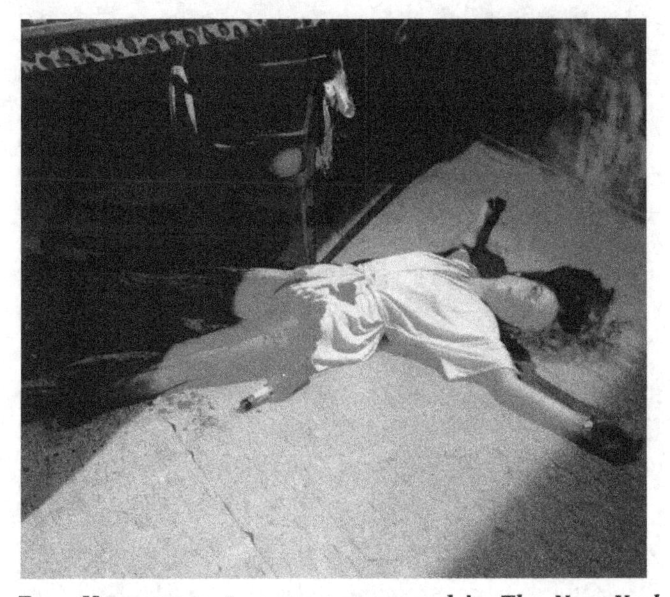

**Zora Kerova meets a gruesome end in *The New York Ripper.***

# Zora Kerova Interviewed by Troy Howarth

The following interview with Zora Kerova was conducted via email on October 16, 2014. Zora played the role of the ill-fated Eva in *The New York Ripper*, and she also appeared in *Touch of Death* and *The Ghosts of Sodom*. She has my sincere thanks for taking the time to talk about her career and her experiences working with Lucio Fulci.

**Troy Howarth**: You were born in Prague; what made you come to Italy?
**Zora Kerova**: I moved to Italy in the spring of 1969, as I wanted to be far away from the first anniversary of the Russian invasion. I was working for a small "Cabaret" theater as a guitarist, dancer and singer, and an Italian manager saw us and engaged us for a tour in Italy. We jumped at the chance!
**TH**: When did you decide you wanted to be an actress?
**ZK**: Everybody always says the same thing, but since I was a little girl, I just knew it was what I wanted to do with my life.
**TH**: You made your film debut in a *giallo* by Pupi Avati titled *The House With Laughing Windows* (1975) ... do you recall how you were cast in that picture?
**ZK**: At the time I used to live in Bologna, where I met Gianni Cavina and both Avati brothers (Note: Pupi and Antonio); and from there, it all happened naturally.
**TH**: What did you think of Pupi Avati?
**ZK**: Pupi was and still is a very, very kind man—calm and gentle. I have met him on other occasions after the movie, but unfortunately no other roles have come up.
**TH**: You played the protagonist in the film *The True Story of the Nun of Monza* (1980), directed by Bruno Mattei. Was that a difficult experience?
**ZK**: *The Nun of Monza* was my favorite role, until someone decided to make the picture more "erotic" and inserted some simulated sex scenes. But it was a very beautiful part, and I think one of my best performances. Naturally, some sequences were difficult, but I always preferred difficult parts.
**TH**: What are your memories of Bruno Mattei?
**ZK**: Bruno was my friend, a very kind man; we did others pictures later and also kept in touch as friends. When he died, I was really upset.
**TH**: You also worked with Aristide Massaccesi on *Anthropophagus* (1981), which remains rather notorious ... what do you remember of that one?
**ZK**: Oh yes, I still remember my role in English! At the time, I still hadn't learned English yet, so I learned my lines phonetically—and I can still remember them! *Anthropophagus* is one of my favorites: the trip to Greece, the

people, the places—everything was fantastic. My only unpleasant memory is of getting seasick, but the sailors were really empathic with me and I was finally able to get on with it.

**TH**: What did you think of Massaccesi?

**ZK**: Aristide? I remember him as a quiet man who told the actors only what was necessary, albeit in an exact and clear way. His brother was also part of the crew, and I loved Tisa Farrow, who was an exceptional colleague.

**TH**: Luigi Montefiori starred in the film and also wrote the script; do you have any memories of him?

**ZK**: Luigi is my friend from a long time ago. I met him when I first moved to Rome; he worked with a producer named Dante Fava and he wrote more films I appeared in, as well. We have come into contact numerous times since then, and we also met up during some little film festivals in Italy—for example, in Livorno. He is a beautiful person.

**DVD sleeve for the Italian DVD release of *The True Story of the Nun of Monza* (1980).**

**ZK**: The scenes in the live sex show were very difficult for my partner and myself. Fulci did everything to make me feel at ease, and there we became friends. Fulci encouraged us to focus on the work and not to feel self-conscious. Lucio must have been impressed, because he always remembered me.

**TH**: You had a very brutal death scene in the film; do you remember much about how it was filmed?

**ZK**: I had many brutal deaths on film, but they never bothered me so long as they seemed to be logical sequences in the film.

**TH**: Was this your first meeting with Fulci?

**ZK**: Yes, the first time we met was on the set of *The New York Ripper*; Fulci's assistant director called me out to the set, and from there we went right to work.

**TH**: Fulci had a reputation for being hard on his actors; did you find this to be the case?

**ZK**: Yes, this was his reputation, but with me he was different, though it took him a while to warm up to me. When we began to speak about literature, especially the Russian classics that I had studied in Prague, he changed and treated me very well.

Only once, while making *Touch of Death*, he gave me the nickname of "dead dog" because I forgot my lines in English and couldn't continue with a scene. Learning the lines in English was very important. The following day I was perfectly prepared and I asked him to acknowledge that in front of the whole crew. He was very kind and did so, which made me very happy. But it's true: He could be very hard on his actors, especially the actresses.

**TH**: How did you think Fulci compared with directors like Mattei and Massaccesi?

**ZK**: It's impossible to compare them. Each of them had such different personalities; with Fulci, I think I probably had a deeper understanding, like friends usually have.

**TH**: Did you ever see *The New York Ripper*? If so, what did you think of it?

**ZK**: I didn't like *The New York Ripper* at all.

**TH**: *Anthropophagus*, *Cannibal Ferox* and *The New York Ripper* were all notoriously violent films; did the content of these films ever bother you?

**TH**: How did you come to be cast in Umberto Lenzi's *Cannibal Ferox* (1981)?

**ZK**: Umberto Lenzi's film came about by luck: I was back in Prague at the time, and suddenly my agent Vitaliano Elia called and said, "Zora, come back today! Or tomorrow, at least! You have a chance to make a film in the Amazon!!!" The next day, I was in Rome, met Lenzi, and, without any problems, the part was really mine!

I have to say that I was worried because I'm horrified of insects, but in a short time I decided to accept the offer and go. And it was a really fantastic experience: not always easy, not without real difficulties, but fantastic. The actors and crew were so professional. Only Lenzi sometimes lost his calm—he is known for this—but with me was special. He wrote a new sequence just for me—the scene in the prison with another girl, when I had my strong monologue.

**TH**: How did you get along with Umberto Lenzi?

**ZK**: Lenzi is a very, very particular man, but if you know how to relate with him, everything is okay; fortunately for me, I knew how to deal with him.

**TH**: After this, you were cast in *The New York Ripper*; your role required you to do some fairly explicit sex scenes—did this bother you at all?

**Zora Kerova is manhandled by the cannibal tribe in Umberto Lenzi's *Cannibal Ferox* (1981).**

**ZK**: I did have some problems with the Czech embassy because of them, but nothing came of it; just some speeches that I prefer to forget.
**TH**: You next worked with Fulci on *Touch of Death* and *The Ghosts of Sodom* in 1988; did Fulci request you for those films?
**ZK**: Yes, and this was typical of Fulci's style. He said, "If you accept to do *Ghosts*, I'll give you a part in *Touch of Death*." Really tricky, isn't it? And I did it.
**TH**: Fulci was very frail by the time he made these films; was he very different on the set?
**ZK**: Lucio changed only physically. His tactics and spirit and intelligence remained the same.
**TH**: Both of these films were made on a very low budget; do you have many memories of making them?
**ZK**: At the time I was going through some financial difficulties; the producers knew this and took advantage of it. Luccherini and Lucidi only paid us a pittance. You know, we actors are able to work while we are hungry and we still do our best!
**TH**: You recently made a film in the Czech Republic titled *Líbás jako dábel* (2012); are you no longer making films in Italy?
**ZK**: Nothing special, unfortunately: just the occasional small role or an appearance on a television series.
**TH**: Are you surprised by the lasting popularity of Fulci and his films?
**ZK**: Sincerely, yes I am; this surprises me. Probably it's because I'm not exactly a big fan of this genre.
**TH**: And lastly, do you have a favorite among the films you have made?
**ZK**: I loved everything where I could play strong roles, both physically and psychologically. My favorites are *The True Story of the Nun of Monza*, *Cannibal Ferox* and a Czech film called *The Chain* (1981).
**TH**: Thank you so much for your time!
**ZK**: Well, Troy, I hope I answered your questions okay. I look forward to seeing your book; thank you for your hard work.

# Barbara Cupisti Interview by Mike Baronas and Kit Gavin

Mike Baronas and Kit Gavin conducted the following interview with Barbara Cupisti on September 19, 2001. Horror fans best know Ms. Cupisti for her appearances in Michele Soavi's *Stage Fright* (1987), *The Church* (1989) and *Dellamorte Dellamore* (1994), but she made her film debut with a small role in *The New York Ripper*. Ms. Cupisti has our gratitude for her willingness to cooperate in this project.

**MB/KG**: When did you first feel you wanted to be an actress?
**Barbara Cupisti**: Ah, that's a nice question. I started off as a dancer; I was a classical dancer. I did an audition for Louise Falco, and I was with him in his company. It was a contemporary dance troupe, and I was with them for probably six months. After *Fame*, the TV series, and after that I worked as a dancer here in Rome for six months. And during rehearsals I broke my ankle, so I had to change my work. During this time, because of my injury, I had to stay in bed. So I went back to my parents, who are not from Rome. My parents are from the north of Italy, from a small village near to Florence.

And I had to go back to my parents, and I didn't really want to go back, so I decided I had to do something else. At the same time as all this was happening I had an audition for the Academy of Dramatic Art here in Rome. And so I passed the audition and I started to work as an actress afterwards, and I preferred that to dancing ...
**MB/KG**: And it's safer as long as you don't break your ankles ...
**BC**: Yes (*smiles*) but I still broke my hand this summer. (*laughs*)
**MB/KG**: Do you come from a big family?
**BC**: Three brothers, one sister and my Mama and Papa. My father was—is—an opera singer, and a painter. And my mother was working in [home] decoration. So I was pushed into this sort of career; better that I do this than be a doctor, for example. Very strange, completely different from a normal family ... My sister Olivia Cupisti is now a dancer, and she appeared with me in one of my films—*The Church*.
**MB/KG**: Did you start off straight away in films or television?
**BC**: When I first started, I started to work in theater. But with Lucio Fulci, I started at the very beginning of my career, in fact before I went to drama school, I think ... when I made that movie (*The New York Ripper*)
**MB/KG**: How did you get the role?
**BC**: I had an agent for dancing, because sometimes, as with some of the other dancers, you are dancing but you are working in movies also. Sometimes I have done the stand-in or doubles in movies, for my abilities with my body,

**Barbara Cupisti with Mike Baronas.**

because I was able to move and maybe do some things that some actresses are unable to do ... to jump or to make specific gymnastic maneuvers, or some action scenes that maybe some actresses don't want to do—such as stunt work or dangerous movies—because I like to live a bit on the edge ...

And my agent called me and told me there was a possibility to meet Lucio Fulci, so I went there and I got the role. Possibly I passed an audition, but I don't remember.

**MB/KG**: Did you know of Fulci's work before?

**BC**: Yeah, sure, sure ... because I liked his kind of movies, because I get scared easily, but I don't look. I went to the cinema to see these kind of movies but I covered my eyes all the time.

**MB/KG**: What was Lucio like to work for, as he had a reputation for being quite hard with young actresses?

**BC:** No (*vehemently*)! I know that with everybody else he was very hard. I remember with the other actors in my scene he was terrible. With me, I don't know why, he was so gentle and so nice and kind. I probably decided to form this career as an actress because of him. He was telling me, "You are better than all the others," and it was my first day on set. And he was spending a lot of time with me and giving me a lot of encouragement and help, so I didn't have this type of relationship with Lucio that normally lots of people did. With me he was so wonderful.

**MB/KG**: You had a scene with Paolo Malco. What was he like to work with?

**BC**: Yes, Paolo, he was nice. He helped me as well, because for me it was my first time. It was my first line ... that's the truth: it's my first line.

**MB/KG**: Do you remember your first line?

**BC**: No, I don't.

**MB/KG**: In the English-language version you come into an office and Paolo Malco creeps up behind you, and your first line is: "Oh Paul, you're such an asshole sometimes!" (*laughs*)

**BC**: (*Bursts out laughing*) What a way to start my career. What a wonderful line ... to start off with. My first line ... Poor Paolo.

**MB/KG**: Was it frightening for you the first time in front of the cameras?

**BC**: Oh no, I really liked it. I had worked in theater too—I prefer to be in front of a camera. I felt and feel natural in front of the camera. The relationship between an actor and a camera is different, and so deep and I like that ...

**MB/KG**: After that you went on to a larger role in *The Key* for Tinto Brass. What was he like as a director?

**BC**: Again, he has a reputation for being terrible with actors and crew, but again, with me he was nice. I don't know why—it's very strange, but I have a wonderful picture in which Tinto is like a father to me. And the movie was very hard to make, and in the film there were many erotic scenes, and I was so young he never wanted me on the set when they were shooting these erotic scenes and also asked the crew that I be off-set when they were shooting the erotic scenes ... And because of this he showed me great respect by not filming these scenes with me around ... So it was like we were shooting two different movies ... It was strange, because the first day I was in make-up and I had my eyes closed while the make-up was being applied. I was only 18 years old at the time—and when I opened my eyes I saw all these casts of men's private parts (*bursts out laughing*). This was because the make-up person organized everything to do with special effects, and there he was showing these to Tinto. So I opened my eyes and there was this great big penis in front of me (*laughs*). Everyone was so lovely with me on the set. I remember reading the script, and it was very different from the movie. The script was more to do with the mind. And after I watched this movie, I was impressed but surprised ...

**MB/KG**: In the film you play Stefania Sandrelli's straight-laced daughter ...

**BC**: Yes, and Frank Finlay's, too. They were both important to me as a young actress.

**MB/KG**: And Tinto Brass?

**BC**: Tinto is wonderful. I think he is one of the best directors we have in Italy. He is a technical wiz. He also likes movies. The problem is the kind of cinema he chooses to make; whether you like them or not, I think he is a very good professional—because he was an editor before. He is very clear in his eyes everything he wants to do. He is a master, I think. I would like to work with him again, but not in a spicy role. I think he could be a very good director of a different sort of genre. All he needs is the right script and the right enthusiasm …

**MB/KG**: After this you appeared in the massively successful *Chateuvallon* for European television; your first foray into television …

**BC:** Yes, that was very nice, and I was working with a lot of very different actors from other countries in Europe. It was strange, because it's not like now … You know all the other films I shot in English. In *Chateauvallon*, each actor was working in his own language. So it was really so strange, because I was talking in Italian and I had my mother—a French actress who was answering me in French, and a friend of my cousin was German and he was talking to me in German, all on the same set in the same scenes—five different languages. So strange, because you would never realize when the project was finally finished and we all had to make some kind of signal to each other when it was our cue. Especially with the German actors, it was very difficult for them. I mean, I speak French, so I understood everything. This was a very special period of my life …

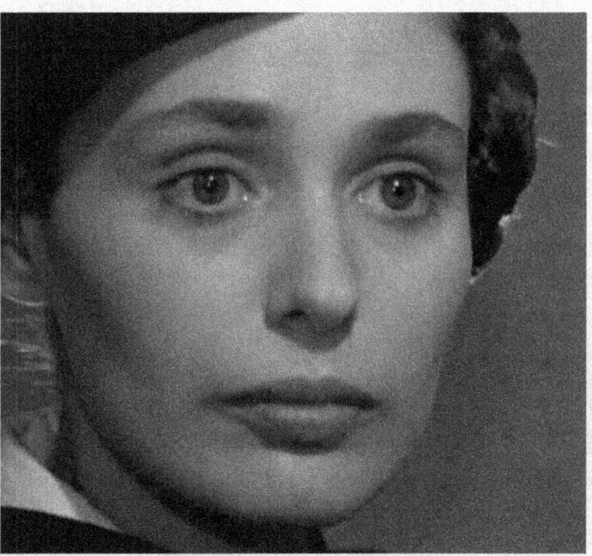

**Barbara Cupisti in Tinto Brass' *The Key* (1983).**

**MB/KG**: It was all shot in wonderful locations, amazing countryside …

**BC**: Yes, a nice house, nice actors, a wonderful ambience …

**MB/KG**: Moving slightly forward, or backward … when did you first meet Michele Soavi?

**BC**: Ah, Michele, Michele has been a friend for years and years. And he was an actor … And I met him during an audition. He had done an audition for a serial, a television serial, and he was so … bad *(laughs)* in that audition; he knows everything, because we are still very close. He was so bad (*laughing*), and at the end of the audition I looked at him I asked him, "Why are you an actor?" *(bursts out laughing)* I was 18, 19 years old, and so everything I thought I told everyone outright. I said to him, "You are so nice, but why are you doing this job? It's not for you …" We did the audition together, and though Michele did not get the role, we decided to go out together and to be friends … So I was near to Michele throughout his evolution, since he made all the steps forward. I mean he has done all the steps—he has been an assistant and he worked in production, he brought cups of coffee to the actors and I was close to him for all of this time. When he made his first movie [as director] it seemed right that we should work together. We worked together as a team.

**MB/KG**: When you first saw the screenplay for *Stage Fright*, did you think that this was going to be the classic it became?

**BC:** Yes, it was clear to me—I'm not sure about the others. For me, because Michele was a lover of these kinds of movies—I don't know now, but at that time I would go to the cinema with him and he would be watching the films and watching scene by scene. He was a lover of this kind of movie. Also, Luigi Montefiori [aka George Eastman] was writing scripts for everybody, and he had worked with Joe D'Amato.

**MB/KG**: Was Aristide Masseccesi [*Joe D'Amato*] on set when you made *Stage Fright*?

**BC**: Aristide, yes, sure … He was a very nice person, and with Michele; he loved Michele … And he was there for him. I remember one day we didn't have a cameraman, and Aristide being a cameraman before he was a director. I don't remember the exact details—perhaps Michele needed another cameraman, and so Aristide took the camera and started to film …

**MB/KG**: The film has a very polished feel, and everybody is very professional in his/her acting … David Haughton, Giovanni Lombardo Radice …

**BC**: I knew David Haughton (aka David Brandon) from before, because he was working previously with Lindsey Kemp, and we were doing the same tour with the same company. In Rome, there was me with Louise Falco and he with Lindsey Kemp, so I had the possibility to meet him before. Michele was also an actor before, and it's very different to work with directors that have been actors before or are used to working with actors, and they give you the greater possibility to work deeper within your craft. It's very different from the others, because Michele is very technically minded in comparison to the others. But Michele is also good with all the actors, not because he is always giving you advice, but because he makes everybody feel at ease, because he knows what it feels like to be an actor. Everybody, we were all so young in that movie, full of emotions and hopes in our minds and on our faces.

**MB/KG**: And Giovanni?

**BC**: He was a very good friend, he was also a very good actor.

**MB/KG**: It seems like you and Giovanni are always in Michele's movies, like lucky charms for Michele.

**BC**: Yes, that's true (smiles)

**MB/KG**: In the film it is a sort of horror musical that is being staged—can you see this ever happening for real?

**BC**: No, no, never … I hope (*laughs*)

**MB/KG**: In the film, you break your ankle—was this a sort of joke referring to your past as dancer and how you became an actress?

**BC**: Probably we used that from my real life experience, yes, sure, because Michele knows everything about me. Also, I am the person who lets the killer into the theater! (*laughs*)

**MB/KG**: Then you made *Testimone oculare* ("Eyewitness") for the *Alta Tensione* television series. What was Lamberto Bava like to work with a director?

**BC**: When I came to make this I had known Lamberto for a long time, because Michele and Lamberto were friends and they had worked together with Dario … Ah, there was something I wanted to tell you: At the very beginning of my career I had done a stand-in job on *Tenebrae*, when the lady [Carole Stagnaro] is dead on the floor. In the last scene, when Anthony Franciosa is killing everyone with the axe. The actress has to lie there, dead on the floor. I was visiting Michele on the set, and he was an assistant director in that movie, and they didn't know how to shoot the scene as they preferred to have a real body on the floor, so they asked me to act as a double for the dead girl. So I was a dead body in that film …

**MB/KG**: In the film Michele has a small acting role and walks by a swimming pool with Eva Robins …

**BC**: I was not on set when they shot this scene, as Michele has asked me never to be on set, because of what I said to him before (*laughs*), when he is acting in a film.

**MB/KG**: Michele also has these little cameos in his films, like Hitchcock; in *Stage Fright* he is playing a policeman.

**BC**: That's right, in this film he is eating all the time.

**MB/KG**: *Testimone oculare* …

**BC**: That's right. As I said, I had known Lamberto for a long time, and he asked me to do that role, and I liked the role. For me it was a challenge, and it was very hard for me to perform the role as a blind girl. In this film with Lamberto and his wife, and I loved to work on these kind of movies, and I liked his and his father's movies. It was such a nice experience … and it was difficult when you have this kind of role in a terror movie and you have to stay blind all the way through. So I went to a school for blind people and I was trying to find the sensitivity and to reach inside to understand blind people, so it was very good training.

**MB/KG**: After *Testimone oculare*, you made *Opera* …

**BC**: But in *Opera* I am only in the film for a few seconds. Originally the role was a much bigger role, but we had problems with Vanessa Redgrave. She was supposed to be in the movie—but I don't remember—something strange happened and she wasn't, and she had to cancel and we had to cut her role. And my role was appearing together with Vanessa Redgrave—in the script we had lots of scenes together. So then she had to cancel due to scheduling problems. Once Vanessa Redgrave canceled, and because my role was so interwoven with hers, my role became much smaller and I was offered another role in France … another big television serial, and I asked Dario, as my role was so small, if I could leave the movie and go and do a serial in France instead. And he told me okay—and I had maybe done two or three small scenes already, and so I only had a small part …

**MB/KG**: Then you appeared in one of the most beautiful recent horror films: *The Church*.

**BC**: It was a very hard and difficult experience, because we were working inside a real church. We were in Budapest; a horror film being shot inside a real church. We were working inside it for two months. We were eating inside it and sleeping there, too (*smiles*). During shooting you have moments when you are doing nothing, so at the end it was so strange, because at the end we had a sort of respect, because you are inside a sacred space, but after two weeks it was like working on a normal set, and sometimes because the church was not closed—sometimes it was closed for the movie, but the priest was there—there were people coming in and praying. The odd thing was that for us it was just a set—we were sleeping and eating on the pews, and there were people smoking and drinking coffee in the church. Also, afterwards he used lots of special effects for this movie, which were hard to achieve, such as the effects on Antonella Vitale. At that time computer graphics were not available. Sergio Stivaletti did all the effects by hand. And afterwards the movie was nice, the ambience was nice, because we were shooting in Budapest, which was still behind the Iron Curtain, and there was a great atmosphere and feeling in the town, which lent something to the film. A very heavy, repressed feeling.

**MB/KG**: In the film you play an art restorer …

**BC**: Do you know why? Michele's sister is an art restorer. I had classes and she taught me how to do it properly.

**MB/KG**: And your costar is Tomas Arana, who is now very popular in the United States with successes such as *L.A. Confidential* …

**BC**: It is strange, I was talking to Michele, because we went to London to make auditions for the role taken by Tomas [Evan the librarian], but Tomas was living in Rome at that time. And we went with the production company to London for four or five days, and Michele was quite sure about an English actor—I don't remember who—and in Rome one of his assistants [Claudio] Lattanzi met Tomas and filmed Tomas during a conversation, and, when we watched that recording, immediately Michele exclaimed that he was the right actor for the role. He has a very powerful face, and when I was working with him, I was sure that he was going to become popular because he was such a good actor.

**MB/KG**: Was Hugh Quarshie discovered while you were in London?

**BC**: Yes, Hugh Quarshie; wonderful actor.

**MB/KG**: *Hell's Gate* was your next project. Umberto Lenzi, who has a reputation for shouting at his actors, made it.

**BC**: Yes, that's right (*laughs*). He is from Tuscany, like me … and the Tuscanians are a very passionate people. And he was shouting all the time. We had a scene with the fire, I don't know if you remember, and he wanted a real fire. And he wanted us to pass through the flames, and he was shouting, "*Perche non intrare?!?* (Why aren't you going through the flames?)" (*laughs*). And the explosion at the start; he was never, never happy. And at a certain moment everybody was so nervous about this explosion—as it was such a big one, and he told everyone not to worry, not to worry. And for those of us, we are in the scene and standing on our marks and the explosion was *so* strong we were (*jolts forward*), you know, by the explosion, and we were only 10 meters away, and he was shouting (*laughs*), "Why aren't you staying in your places? In your marks?" You cannot imagine—this enormous explosion—and we were expected to stay in our places …

**MB/KG**: Then you decided to move forward into sci-fi in *Escape from Paradise*, with Lou Castel and others.

**BC**: Yes (*laughs*) You know everything about my career. With Inés Sastre, [and] a big American actor, I can't remember the name… [Van Johnson] It was strange, because it was a film with a lot of money, a big budget. It was unusual, because in Italy you normally have to work with very low budgets, little money. Like Mario Bava, like Lamberto, like Michele in the beginning. And all the special effects were handmade, and we had to work out the best way to use the camera to create special effects because we didn't have the money. And there was so much money, like an American movie, and for me it was an odd set-up, because during that time I had been working in horror films with very little budgets, very little money, where we had to do everything by and for ourselves, to help with the crew, etc. And in that film you just had to be an actor and nothing more. It was strange for me, because I had to move from one hotel to the next. From inner Spain to Lanzarote, from Lanzarote to Rome, doing a few scenes here, a few scenes there. It was so strange, but pleasant.

**MB/KG**: Then Michele made a film called *The Sect* and I couldn't find you in it …

**BC:** No, I am not in that film. Michele didn't call me for that film. At the time when he was making that film I was in the States, I was in Santa Fe where I lived for a year. I didn't do anything; I just relaxed. At that time I was married to an Italian—and he was shooting in Santa Fe a television series where I didn't work for a year, ten months—something like that.

**MB/KG**: And then you came back to Italy and resumed work as actress?

**BC**: I came back and worked in some television—nothing very exciting.

**MB/KG**: In 1994 you worked in a film directed by Norman Jewison—an American film called *Only You*, with Marisa Tomei.

**Italian *locandina* for Michele Soavi's *The Church* (1989); artist unknown.**

**BC:** You know, I have never seen that film. I missed it at the cinema, but I would love to work again with Norman Jewison. There was so much film shot that was probably never used. It was strange, because I live in Trastevere and I was in a hotel at Piazza Navona because the production wanted all the actors staying in the same hotel, even if I live in Rome and I have my home only a few meters from the set. So it was quite fun. You could bring home towels

**Fan-made artwork for Michele Soavi's *Dellamorte Dellamore* (1993); designed by Silver Ferox.**

and loo paper (*laughs*) and get your pajamas, and when I would arrive on set they showed me what to do and the director would tell me what I had to do. It was a wonderful experience. It was very different, because it was American, it was all scripted, there was no improvisation, because here in Italy we improvise everything and in France even more so than in Italy. If someone has an idea during the rehearsal then you can talk to the director. With the Americans, it was so calm but it is completely different, very professional.

**MB/KG**: In 1994 you worked once again with Michele for *Dellamore Dellamorte*, with Rupert Everett.

**BC**: I used to read the *fumetti* (comic books) when I was young. I loved the comics—also, I told my son that I was meeting you today, and he said to me that I have to ask you everything about *Diabolik*. He has a school bag, a lunch box—everything with *Diabolik* on it …

Rupert Everett was, I don't know, he is so beautiful. The first impression that you have is his appearance, because he is so tall and so beautiful; he is also so charming, and also he is a very good actor, and you know I didn't have the opportunity to work a lot with him, but you know Michele. We shot two different variations of the scenes, and the first one Michele didn't like, and so we reshot it. My scene with Rupert Everett was at first written in a different way. You know I do like to work a lot with English actors. I would like to work more with them because they have a special capacity and their method is so very different from our actors. Our actors are two different people. They are joking all the time on the set, and the clapperboard comes down—*ciak!*—and they change. But English actors have a sense of continuity about them, they bring part of themselves, their lives, from here (*places her hand on her heart*), and they put that into their roles. When you work with them it's like you go inside their soul; it's a different feeling, so it's a different experience. I would like to work in England, but my agents here in Italy are not interested.

**MB/KG**: Since your horror films, you made a number of comedies and popular TV series …

**BC**: *Pah!* I am not interested; I am actress. I need to work, but it is just work. I like to do different sorts of roles, to try to do comedy. But ultimately I like to use my body, because I was a dancer at the start of my career; maybe do an action movie. I don't like to just sit around and do my role—I like adventure. In these films I have to be the lady in the kitchen—I don't like that. They have all been really just a job and because here in Italy these films are very popular.

**MB/KG**: Recently you have been working in Italian television, on RAI3 as the hostess on *Survivor* …

**BC**: Ah yes, *Survivor*. I enjoyed that because it was exactly what I like doing. It was a problem all about extreme situations and conditions of life; it was like a movie. Because we were living and working at each location, each set for 15 days. The first one was in the world's highest hotel—filmed in Lapland. There is a great big hotel where everything inside is made from ice, you even sleep on an ice-bed. And there I had interviews with two explorers, both very well known, who were used to enduring the extremes …

Another we did in an underwater hotel in Miami, so I had to swim underwater, and I liked that, because I have to do a lot of very different things. And I liked that, because it was a very good experience for me. I worked another year in television after that, and I worked for RAI International.

**MB/KG**: Your latest project was *Gialloparma* …

**BC**: Again it was a film, a job. You have to work to survive.

**MB/KG**: What do you see the future as bringing for Barbara Cupisti?

**BC**: Now I have just finished a very well-known TV serial here in Italy—*Distretto di polizia*—and even in this I do not have a big role, because I stopped a little, you know, because at one time in Italy we were doing only movies and serials. My way of working is different because I like to act with emotions, I like thrillers, I like horror films and I like action movies. If I have to work in something like a

**Barbara Cupisti in recent years.**

soap opera it's boring for me. I can live and work there for six months. After six months I feel trapped inside and I feel I have to move on, and I feel bad. I don't want to do something like that.

So I prefer these days to work less and do projects I enjoy more. And this series is nice because it's a police serial and I had a small part in this—the role of a magistrate. It also gives me time to be with my son. Up until two weeks ago I was starring in a French movie based on the books of Jean-Claude Izzo, with Richard Bohringer and Daniel Duval [Note: *Total Kheops*]. In the film I was speaking in French again. We were shooting in Marseilles. It was nice, because I can see that we are doing other kinds of movies again. Italian cinema is dying, and even Michele is now working in television. But in Italy the cinema is dead.

**MB/KG**: Like in England …

**BC**: But at least in England you have all sorts of possibilities. You know the English cinema I love. In England there is a sort of surrealism, even if you do an everyday story there is a different aspect—a different dimension, a different sensation. Here in Italy all cinema we do now is very flat and boring, apart from three or four directors who have a special point of view. But normally it is *so* flat—*flat*—and we talk all the time about the same things, and so ultimately it is boring. Michele is one of the few directors that has this kind of vision.

**MB/KG**: Did you see Dario's new film, *Sleepless*?

**BC**: No, I didn't see it. Dario is not the same director that he was. Not a maverick, like Polanski.

**MB/KG**: In Europe the horror scene is nearly dead, apart from a few directors like Lars Von Trier in Denmark, who made a horror TV series called *The Kingdom* [about zombies living underneath a Copenhagen Hospital!]

**BC:** Yes, I remember. I couldn't watch it (*laughs*); it was too much for me. It was frightening and horrible …

**MB/KG**: And yet you've made horror films with Soavi, Fulci and Argento! (*laughs*)

**BC:** (*Laughs*) I would love to work with Von Trier, I would work immediately—I wouldn't even have to read the script …

## *Manhattan Baby (Italy)*

Aka *Eye of the Evil Dead; Possessed; La malédiction du pharaon; Amulett des Bösen*

Directed by Lucio Fulci; Produced by Fabrizio De Angelis, for Fulvia Film; Story and Screenplay by Elisa Briganti and Dardano Sacchetti; Director of Photography: Guglielmo Mancori; Editor: Vincenzo Tomassi; Music by Fabio Frizzi

Main Players: Christopher Connelly (Professor George Hacker); Laura Lenzi [as Martha Taylor] (Emily Hacker); Brigitta Boccoli (Susie Hacker); Giovanni Frezza (Tommy Hacker); Cosimo Cinieri [as Lawrence Welles] (Adrian Marcato); Cinzia de Ponti (Jamie Lee); Andrea Bosic (Optician); Carlo De Mejo (Luke)

Cameo appearance: Lucio Fulci (Dr. Forrester)

*Professor George Hacker unveils an Egyptian tomb and in the process he unleashes a powerful evil. Hacker's daughter Susie becomes affected by his blasphemy when the spirit of an evil entity inhabits her. Back in New York, her behavior begins to become more and more erratic, and various people disappear without any apparent explanation. Hacker takes her to a doctor in the hopes of finding out what is wrong, but nothing medically can be found. In desperation, he and his wife Emily then enlist the aid of the mysterious Adrian Marcato, a psychic who claims that he can free Susie from her affliction …*

Having distanced himself from *The New York Ripper*, Dardano Sacchetti collaborated with his wife, Elisa Briganti, on a very different type of horror scenario. Originally developed under the much more compelling title of *Il malocchio* (*The Evil Eye*), the project would undergo a torturous birthing process and ended up as a disappointment for pretty much everybody concerned. As Sacchetti would later recall:

> *Manhattan Baby* came as an attempt to disconnect myself from the traditional kind of work. […] In this case, there was an attempt to do a technological piece. I was attempting to approach themes that were no longer classic or traditionally Gothic. I was trying to bring horror in a different direction.[1]

Sacchetti and Briganti may have had the best of intentions, but little of their original concept would end up on the screen.

*Manhattan Baby* plays like something of a grab bag of elements culled from films like *The Exorcist* (1973), *The Omen* (1976) and *The Awakening* (1980). The latter is particularly surprising, as the Charlton Heston-starring adaptation of Bram Stoker's 1903 novel *The Jewel of Seven Stars* (previously filmed to greater effect by Seth Holt as *Blood from the Mummy's Tomb*, 1971) was not anybody's idea of a particularly good horror film. *Manhattan Baby*'s screenplay is littered with in-jokes and references: characters' names like Adrian Marcato and Jamie Lee refer back to *Rosemary's Baby* (1968) and *Halloween* (1978), respectively, and at one point Giovanni Frezza is heard whistling the film's theme music. Fulci works hard to create a mysterious atmosphere, but the material simply isn't there. Given that the project underwent some radical tinkering, one doesn't wish to point the accusing finger in the wrong direction: Sacchetti and Briganti were less than thrilled with the end result, but the fault is not really with them. As Sacchetti explained:

> When the producers decided to cut three-quarters of the budget, some of the special effects could not be realized, and the film was ultimately very poor. So the producers thought they could save the project by making it more classical. And then they worried that they wouldn't be able to sell the film.[2]

**Italian *locandina* for *Manhattan Baby*; artwork by Enzo Sciotti.**

The film validates this criticism, as it can't seem to make up its mind exactly what it wants to be or what effect it is striving for.

The film begins with an extended sequence in Egypt, though Sacchetti would later complain that this was added on as an afterthought: "They decided to shoot an opening sequence in Egypt to give the movie an international feel."[3] Fair enough, but it has to be said that the Egyptian sequence is probably the most atmospheric to be found in the film. Fulci and cinematographer Guglielmo Mancori make excellent use of the locations and create a spooky ambience that borders on the metaphysical. True, the sequence is pretty basic and cliché from a story point of view—Hacker uncovers the tomb of an Egyptian deity, and the locals fear the worst—but in terms of its execution it can hardly be faulted. The sequence climaxes with Hacker being stricken (temporarily) blind as a punishment for his transgressions and with little Susie coming under the spell of a malefic influence.

Back in New York, things settle down to a somewhat sluggish tempo. Not much really happens for a long stretch of time, but Fulci and Mancori do their damnedest to keep things visually dynamic and interesting. There are a few strong sequences along the way: a violent thunderstorm, an obnoxious colleague of Hacker's wife coming to a surprise demise, etc. But for the most part, the film seems to be marking time for much of its running time. Without the benefit of interesting characters or a truly electrifying scenario, there is only so much that can keep the mind and the eye alert and engaged by the material. The scenario again plays on the fears of children, establishing a connection with *The House by the Cemetery*, but even the kids here lack much in the way of depth and conviction.

Compared to Fulci's other horror films of the period, *Manhattan Baby* is uncommonly slack and lacking in interest. It is by no means a complete disaster, however: The good bits are very good, and it builds to a pleasingly demented finale, where Fulci's flair for the absurd really takes hold. The arrival of the mysterious Adrian Marcato certainly helps: Unlike Hacker and his wife, Marcato is a genuinely interesting presence. He starts off in full-blown red herring mode, and the viewer is conditioned to expect the worst, but he emerges as the film's unlikely hero—ultimately saving Susie at the cost of his own life. The big set piece at the end involves his fate; his stuffed birds spring to life and proceed to peck him to death. It's an outrageous conceit and Fulci knows it, but he plays it for all the spectacle it is worth. The special effects are a little ropey, but there is genuine nastiness in the close-ups of the beaks and talons tearing into Marcato's flesh, as he encourages them to "*Consume me!*" If only the film had more sequences like it.

Sadly, the project would mark the end of Fulci's tenure with producer Fabrizio De Angelis. De Angelis (born in Rome in 1940) scored his first major international hit with *Zombie* and provided ample support for Fulci on films like *City of the Living Dead*, *The Beyond*, *The House by the Cemetery* and *The New York Ripper*. So long as the films turned a profit, De Angelis was satisfied. Unfortunately, he seemed to have some difficulty in figuring out exactly what he wanted from *Manhattan Baby*. Applying the rather silly and nondescript title of *Manhattan Baby* certainly didn't help matters either: Sacchetti would later reason that it was his attempt to evoke *Rosemary's Baby*, but the similarities between the two scenarios are tenuous at best. Fulci recalled the film as a disappointing end to an otherwise pleasurable working relationship with his producer:

> *Manhattan Baby* marked the end of the contract with my first-rate producer, De Angelis, and I had no choice but to make that film because he was obsessed with it. I think it's a terrible movie; I'd venture to describe it as one of those setbacks that occur as you go along.[4]

If the film represents an example of Fulci doing a film under duress to satisfy a business arrangement, it at least shows him in a professional light: He does not toss the movie off with indifference, though his efforts are undone by the absence of a strongly realized scenario. Perhaps if he had been able to film the script as originally written—which Sacchetti regards as one of his best efforts[5]—he may have been able to end his tenure with De Angelis on a more triumphant note; as it stands, however, it is one of his less interesting horror pictures.

On the plus side, the film is graced with some good production values. Fulci and De Angelis were able to keep much of the same team responsible for their earlier triumphs, with the notable exception of cinematographer Sergio Salvati. Guglielmo Mancori—a veteran whose earlier credits included three films for Fulci (*Le massaggiatrici*, *Uno strano tipo* and *Il lungo, il corto, il gatto*) as well as films for Sergio Sollima (*Run, Man, Run*, 1968), Umberto Lenzi (*Orgasmo*, 1969) and Mario Bava (*Savage Gringo*, 1966)—proves to be a capable replacement, however. His color scheme tends to be more muted and naturalistic than that of Salvati, but he makes good use of strong, moody shadows and helps to create a sense of atmosphere even when the story is lagging. Vincenzo Tomassi's editing is up to his usual excellent standards, while Massimo Lentini's production design and costuming helps to conceal the low budget. Fabio Frizzi's score includes some marvelous new themes, but much of the soundtrack is admittedly padded-out with themes from his scores for *Zombie*, *City of the Living Dead* and *The Beyond*. It would prove to be his final score for Fulci for the better part of a decade; they would reunite on *Nightmare Concert (A Cat in the Brain)*.

The casting is also problematic. Christopher Connelly walks through his role as Hacker with an air of tired disinterest. His lack of charisma and conviction provides the film with a black hole where a solid lead would have been beneficial; one can easily imagine any number of actors familiar from Fulci's work (be it Paolo Malco, Christopher George, David Warbeck or Richard Johnson) proving much more compelling in his stead. Kansas-born Connelly was born in 1941 and worked most extensively on American television, appearing in such popular shows as *Alfred Hitchcock Presents*, *The Fugitive*, *Mission: Impossible*, *Ironside* and *Night Gallery*; he also starred on a few series of his own, including *Peyton Place* and *Paper Moon*. His film work encompassed family favorites like *Benji* (1974), and like many of his contemporaries he drifted to Italian films in the hopes of finding steady employment. He also appeared in Enzo G. Castellari's *1990: The Bronx Warriors* (1982) and Ruggero Deodato's *The Raiders of Atlantis* (1983), among others. He died in 1988 at the age of 44, from cancer. Laura Lenzi plays his wife, and she gives a similarly listless performance; she did not enjoy a particularly lengthy and varied career, appearing in less than a dozen titles between 1976 and 1995. Giovanni Frezza, in his second and final Fulci appearance, and Brigitta Boccoli play their children. The English dubbing this time does not compromise Frezza's performance nearly as much, but Boccoli appears a bit adrift. Machiavelian character actor Cosimo Cinieri dominates the supporting cast; this is the second of his four films for Fulci. Cinieri makes Marcato into a compelling figure, and one wishes that he be allowed to carry the film instead of Connelly and Lenzi.

For Fulci, *Manhattan Baby* represented little more than another paycheck; he invests the film with as much style and conviction as he can muster, but the flat performances by the lead actors and the front office interference by De Angelis and his cohorts prevent it from attaining full maturity. From here, Fulci would embark on his first sword and sorcery picture.

**Fulci (right) and camera operator Franco Bruni film Brigitta Boccoli's nightmare in *Manhattan Baby*.**

Notes:
1. Quoted from the featurette "Beyond the Living Dead" included on the Anchor Bay DVD release of *Manhattan Baby*.
2. *Ibid.*
3. *Ibid.*
4. Palmerini, Luca M. and Gaetano Mistretta, *Spaghetti Nightmares* (Florida: Fantasma Books, 1996), p. 62.
5. Quoted from the featurette "Beyond the Living Dead" included on the Anchor Bay DVD release of *Manhattan Baby*.

# Carlo De Mejo Interview by Troy Howarth

The following interview with Carlo De Mejo was conducted via email on December 5, 2014. Carlo appeared in three films for Fulci: *City of the Living Dead*, *The House by the Cemetery* and *Manhattan Baby*. My thanks go to Carlo's son, Pierpaolo, who helped to facilitate this interview, and of course to Carlo himself, for taking the time to answer these questions.

**Troy Howarth**: You came from a very artistic background ... did you know from an early age that you wanted to become an actor?

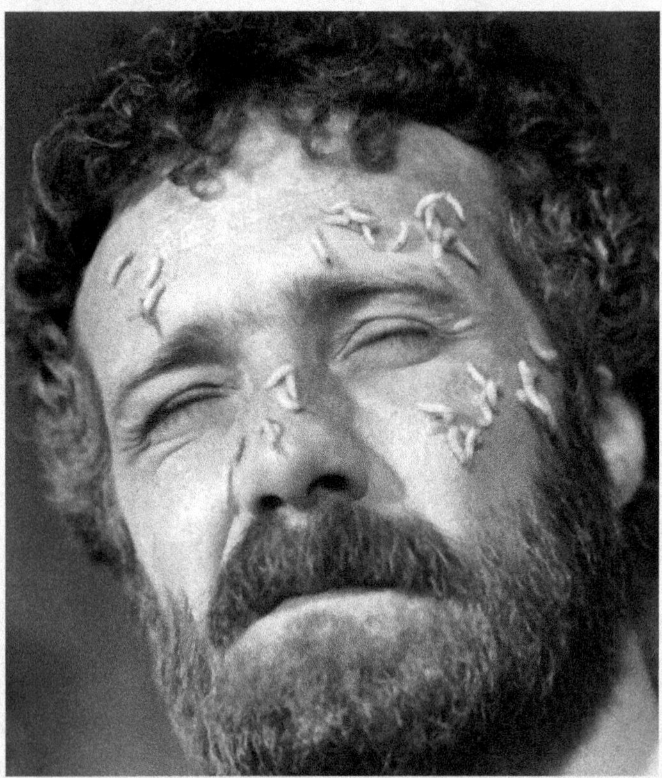

***City of the Living Dead* saw Carlo De Mejo getting a face full of maggots, but the actor remained a fan of Fulci's anyway.**

**Carlo De Mejo**: Not at all, as far as wanting to be an actor, although my mom was the wonderful movie star Alida Valli. I was more into sports: swimming, soccer. Then, one day, my high school history teacher (Mr. Mario Viggiano) started a theater group. I was just 13, and I had my first roles in plays like *Treasure Island* and *Cinderella*. I loved so much the magic of the stage that I said: "Here we are, this is what I want to do in my life."

**TH**: Where did you train as an actor?

**CD**: Stella Adler Acting Studio (I've had the honor to study directly with Stella!) in London and New York.

**TH**: What do you remember of working with Pier Paolo Pasolini on *Teorema*?

**CD**: A fantastic experience. What a fabulous cast! I was just 23 years old, a child; it was my second experience in a movie, and I had to play a passionate love scene with the beautiful Silvana Mangano. I was very excited and afraid at the same time. But Pier Paolo was a very easy director to work with: very calm, gentle, smooth, almost directing in a whisper, as if he was a kind country priest!

**TH**: You appeared in a *giallo* by Armando Crispino titled *The Dead Are Alive*, or *The Etruscan Kills Again* ... what do you remember of working with Crispino?

**CD**: It was very exciting to work with Armando. His film was not just a "genre" film, but an "A" film, very well written, structured and directed, with an international cast: Alex Cord, Samantha Eggar (who had just finished filming *The Collector*, with Terence Stamp, who, by the way, was in *Teorema* with me). Armando was a very experienced director, accurate, careful, sophisticated (in the good way), and a very special and nice person.

**TH**: *Terror Express* was a thriller directed by Ferdinando Baldi ... did you enjoy working with Baldi? Did you enjoy appearing in thrillers like this?

**CD**: Yes, I enjoyed working with Baldi, and with the adorable Werner Pochath. In *Terror Express* I played the role of the bad guy. [It was] very funny. I do enjoy appearing in thrillers.

**TH**: What was Luigi Cozzi like to work with on *Contamination*?

**D**: Luigi Cozzi is a wonderful person and a very prepared director, especially in "*fantascienza*" and horror movies. I've met him several times during later years (we both live in Rome), and it's always a pleasure.

**TH**: You first worked with Lucio Fulci on *City of the Living Dead* ... do you remember how you got the role of Gerry?

**CD**: Yes, I do. It was in an office. He was smoking one of his favorite cigars. He took one glance at me and said: "Interesting face ... how is your English?" I replied: "Reasonable." He replied: "You will be my Gerry!"

**TH**: What were your initial impressions of Fulci as a person?

**CD**: At first glance, he could seem a surly and cynical person. No. The truth is that he had a terrific and extraordinary personal sense of humor. I must say, and I confirm

**Carlo De Mejo gets in on the cast reunion for *The House by the Cemetery* in 2011—with him (from left) are: Silvia Collatina, Giovanni Frezza, Catriona MacColl and Dagmar Lassander; photo courtesy of Mark Jason Murray.**

what I've always said during the years, that we had a beautiful relationship. It was as if I always knew what he wanted from the scene. I know some of the actresses had quarrels with him. For what concerns me, he always put me in a good mood.
TH: Fulci had a reputation for being tough on actors ... was he like this with you?
CD: Never.
TH: What do you remember of your costars, including Christopher George and Catriona MacColl?
CD: Christopher was very easy to work with. He was a very nice guy. And I can say the same about my pal Catriona.
TH: Did you enjoy the experience of filming in Savannah, Georgia?
CD: Yes, I remember I spent a beautiful time with the all cast and crew. When I watched the movie backstage for the first time in my life (thanks to the recent DVD edition), it was a very touching moment. I could see myself playing basketball with the little Luca Venantini (the son of my dear friend Venantino) during the free time! I also had already worked in Georgia, during my experience with the Barn Dinner Theatre in Marietta, just after the Stella Adler acting school.
TH: After that, you played small roles for Fulci in *The House by the Cemetery* and *Manhattan Baby* ... did you enjoy working on those films?
CD: I did. I would always work with that terrific man.
TH: What is your favorite memory of working with Lucio Fulci?
CD: The day Lucio played, in *City of the Living Dead*, his usual cameo. He liked to appear in his own movies, as Hitchcock used to do! I found him very funny playing the role of a serious doctor. Also the scene where I have to give support to the crying and sad John (Luca Venantini): a very touching scene.
TH: Did you keep in touch with Fulci in later years?
CD: I did.
TH: How do you feel Fulci compares with other directors you have worked with?
CD: One of the greats. No doubt.
TH: And lastly, are you surprised by the continued popularity of Fulci and his films?
CD: Surprised, not at all. I knew he was *big*.
TH: Thank you so much for you time!
CD: You are welcome!

# 1983

## *Conquest (Italy/Spain/Mexico)*

Aka *La conquista de la tierra perdida*

Directed by Lucio Fulci; Produced by Giovanni Di Clemente, for Clemi Cinematografica, Clesi Cinematografica, Conquest Productions, Esme and Golden Sun; Screenplay by Gino Capone, Giovanni Di Clemente, Carlos Vasallo and José Antonio de la Loma, from a story by Giovanni Di Clemente; Director of Photography: Alejandro Ulloa (as Alejandro Alonso García); Editor: Vincenzo Tomassi and Emilio Rodriguez Oses; Music by Claudio Simonetti

Main Players: Jorge Rivero [as George Rivero] (Mace); Andrea Occhipinti (Ilias); Sabrina Siani [as Sabrina Sellers] (Ocron); Conrado San Martín (Zora)

*Ilias leaves his home in order to prove his manhood. While on his quest, he encounters another nomad named Mace; the two men become friends and unite to fight off various creatures put in their path by the wicked Ocron. Ilias and Mace set out to destroy Ocron and free the land from her tyranny, but this is no easy task to accomplish ...*

*Conquest* is as close as Fulci ever came to directing a *peplum*. The *pepla* genre took off in the 1950s thanks to the worldwide success of Pietro Francisci's *Hercules* (1958); over the next decade, there were literally hundreds of sequels, rip-offs, homages and the like, but with the exception of co-writing a modern dress send-up of the genre in the form of *Hector the Mighty*—a film he notably went to great lengths to get out of directing, as well—Fulci never made any significant contributions to the genre. All of this changed in 1983, when producer Giovanni Di Clemente talked the director into helming *Conquest*. The film is not a *pepla* proper, however; instead, it belongs to the trend of sword and sorcery movies, which can be viewed as a sort of bastard offspring of the earlier films. The sword and sorcery trend enjoyed a brief upswing in popularity thanks to the success of John Milius' *Conan the Barbarian* (1982) and Jean-Jacques Annaud's *Quest for Fire* (1981), both of

**American poster for *Conquest*; the artist's name is illegible.**

which enjoyed particularly great success in Italy. Other directors threw their hat into the ring, as well, including Umberto Lenzi, who delivered *The Ironmaster* (1982), and Ruggero Deodato, who made *The Barbarians* (1987). Even Luigi Cozzi's *Hercules* films starring Lou Ferrigno owed as much to the sword and sorcery boom as they did to the *pepla* of the 1950s. Inevitably the trend died down in time, but of the films that came about because of the success of Milius and Annaud's model, *Conquest* is certainly one of the more interesting.

The film is something of a "road movie," and as such it has a certain kinship to the director's earlier Western, *Four of the Apocalypse*. In common with both films is the theme of friendship, as people pull together and help each other out as they embark upon a difficult quest. Fulci's cynicism is kept in check as he details the relationship between the youthful and naïve Ilias and the older and more hardened Mace in surprisingly optimistic terms. The optimism is tempered with fatalism, however, and the film will ultimately explore one of the director's favorite themes; the futility of trying to change one's destiny. Earlier films like *The Psychic*, *City of the Living Dead* and *The Black Cat* featured psychic characters who foresee something unpleasant and expend a great deal of energy trying to escape it; *Conquest*, too, deals with a similar theme.

The villain of the piece is the sensual Ocron, who presides over an army of freaks and monsters. Ocron is a petty tyrant who cloaks the countryside in a state of perpetual semi-darkness. During a drug-induced stupor, she sees the figure of a young man coming to her and destroying her. She eventually realizes that the faceless man in her vision is Ilias, so she sends her minions out to destroy him first. Ocron, driven by arrogance, does not reckon on the interference of Mace, who acts as the younger man's protector. As the story unfolds, Ilias also becomes stronger and more assertive; his goal was to establish himself as a man, and, in doing so, he discovers an inner strength that enables him to survive some terrible hardships. Ilias' death is inevitable, but it will not be in vain—Mace will avenge his friend and destroy Ocron, thus freeing the land from her villainy.

According to Fulci, the film was something of a pet project for producer/cowriter Giovanni Di Clemente. Di Clemente (born in Rome in 1948) had earlier produced such films as Mauro Bolognini's *The Murri Affair* (1974) and Stelvio Massi's *Speed Cross* (1980), and he reckoned on the success of Annaud's film, coupled with signing popular Mexican leading man Jorge Rivero to play the lead, to make the film a popular success. As Fulci explained to Massimo F. Lavagnini,

> It was a movie that the producers wanted to do at all costs, because it stars Jorge Rivero, one of the most important Mexican actors. They asked me to do a prehistoric movie. I tried to do a movie based on the friendship, because it's the story of a friendship between Rivero and Occhipinti. You won't find the same old theme of the dinosaurs … I shot it all in back lighting, all with fog, with the help of a great cameraman, a Spanish guy named Alejandro Ulloa. Well, *Conquest* was a flop in Italy, but in Mexico people lined up to buy a ticket! That's because this Jorge Rivero is so popular.[1]

It doesn't appear that Fulci had much of a hand in the writing of the script—his name is not listed among the writers—but, regardless, he latched onto the themes that interested him and approached the film as a stylistic exercise. The story may be thin, but his visualization of a surreal landscape is frequently striking. The use of diffusion and copious amounts of fog makes the film deliberately obtuse—sometimes it's even difficult to get a good grasp of what is going on. This gives the movie something of a drugged-out quality. Some viewers have a hard time with this dreamy ambience, but if one doesn't fight it and just goes with the flow it has a strange effectiveness. The barren landscapes, misty atmosphere and various weird creatures and monsters combine to create a hallucinatory quality, which is consistent with Fulci's approach in his "plotless" horror films like *City of the Living Dead* and *The Beyond*. Here again, logic is of little interest: the goal is to get the action moving from point A to point B, and Fulci uses his considerable skills to sustain a sort of bargain-basement surrealism, which keeps things interesting throughout.

The director's flair for sadistic violence is also much in evidence. Early on, Ocron's minions attack a clan of cave dwellers. One of the men is brutally scalped, then the brutes take a naked woman and appear intent on raping her—instead of doing so, however, they pull her legs apart until she literally splits in two. It's a gruesome image, one that Fulci would revisit later in the horror film *Demonia*. Elsewhere, characters bleed profusely when they are stabbed, and poor Ilias is subjected to a nasty skin condition due to blood poisoning before ultimately losing his head. Fulci doesn't skimp on the gore and the pus one bit, and the contrast between the dreamy, almost fragile atmosphere and the doses of in-your-face violence gives the film an off-kilter charm.

Nevertheless, it is precisely the film's utter weirdness that makes *Conquest* an off-putting experience for many viewers. Fans accustomed to Fulci's horror movies did not react favorably to the film, and the director himself did not find it to be a particularly pleasurable experience:

> *Conquest* was a bit of a strange affair—the producer, Di Clemente, was terrible, even though he's now become important; I was supposed to do two films with him, but when the first one was over I refused to do the second film and he took me to court. I won, though, because the law states that if a person doesn't want to work, he doesn't have to, as he has the freedom to choose.[2]

Even so, the film allowed Fulci to rekindle his relationship with cinematographer Alejandro Ulloa, with whom he had first worked on *Perversion Story*. Ulloa (1926-2002) was born in Madrid and got his start as a camera operator in the late 1940s. By the late 1950s, he was a cinematographer in his own right, and he would go on to work on such pictures as Orson Welles' *Chimes at Midnight* (1965, on which he worked on the second unit battle scenes), Jess Franco's *The Diabolical Dr. Z* (1966), Sergio Corbucci's *The Mercenary* (1968) and Eugenio Martín's *Horror Express* (1972). He would go on to photograph *The Devil's Honey* for Fulci, and then retired from films in the early 1990s. Ulloa's work on *Conquest* is in a very different key from *Perversion Story*, which was incredibly sharp, loaded with deep-focus shots and striking use of primary color; *Conquest* goes for a much more wispy and color-drained approach, save for the occasional burst of vivid red or blue lighting. The film's visual scheme is effective in context, and truly makes the film into an experience like none other.

As already mentioned, the lead role of Mace was entrusted to Mexican actor Jorge Rivero. Born in Mexico City in 1938, the handsome and muscular Rivero made his debut in René Cardona, Sr.'s *Neutron Traps the Invisible Killers* (1965); he spent the entire film with his face concealed behind a mask, but soon he became a major sex symbol in Mexican cinema. Hollywood beckoned in 1970, and he found himself costarring with John Wayne in Howard Hawks' *Rio Lobo*, and with Candice Bergen and Donald Pleasence in Ralph Nelson's *Soldier Blue*. He also appeared in a number of pseudo-Spaghetti Westerns and gained some experience in the Italian genre scene by appearing in the likes of Mario Siciliano's *Evil Eye* (1975). In an interview with Mike Malloy, Rivero recalled working with Fulci:

> Lucio Fulci was a very, very special director. He was so special that even when he shaved, I think he shaved in the morning without looking at himself in the mirror. And you could see from the lines of his beard that he wasn't well shaved. And he had a sweater—because we were doing this movie in the winter, in Sardinia—and he had a white sweater through the whole movie full of soup! Never changing it! [...] He was a very, very special man. In the beginning, when we started the movie, he had his chair as a director, and he wanted nobody at the same level. All the actors had to be behind him. At the end of the movie, the producer wanted to cut the movie; I think he didn't have enough money. So he wanted to cut it short. And Lucio Fulci at one point said, "Jorge, are you going to back me up?" And I say, "I will back you up." And when the producer came, I said, "I'll back Lucio through the whole movie." And fortunately we finished the movie like he wanted. And at the end of the movie, I had my chair at the same level as his chair.[3]

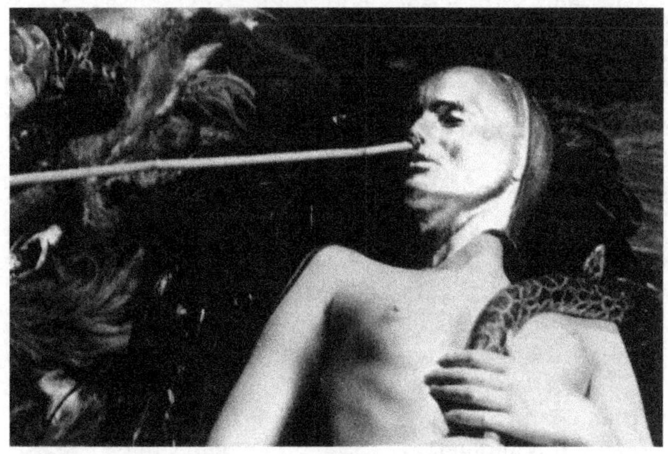

**Sabrina Siani as the masked Ocron.**

**Mace does battle with some odd creatures on his journey.**

Rivero brings his considerable charisma to the role of Mace and helps to give the film a bit of gravitas. Andrea Occhipinti, in his second role for Fulci following *The New York Ripper*, plays Ilias. Occhipinti brings the right level of naïveté to the character, and makes for an endearing presence. The relationship between the two men is sincerely depicted and adds a little depth to what is otherwise essentially a purely stylistic exercise. The beautiful Sabrina Siani, who spends the entire film basically naked, save for a metallic mask that she wears over her head, plays the villainous Ocron. Siani doesn't get much of a chance to really emote, but her mime work is surprisingly effective, and she is to be commended for being such a good sport about her appearance. Siani (born in Rome in 1963) had previously appeared in Jess Franco's *White Cannibal Queen* (1980) and Antonio Margheriti's *Hunters of the Golden Cobra* (1982), and she would go on to appear in another sword and sorcery epic, Franco Prosperi's *Throne of Fire* (1983); she retired from films in the early 1990s.

Beyond its curious presentation and its status as Fulci's only sword and sorcery movie, *Conquest* is also noteworthy as the first of the director's films to be presented in Dolby Stereo—and it is also the only one of his films to be scored by the gifted Claudio Simonetti. Simonetti's score isn't really one of his more outstanding efforts, but it does underline the movie's spacey ambience rather nicely. Simonetti (born in Brazil in 1952) came to prominence as a key member of the Italian progressive rock ensemble Goblin; they achieved overnight success scoring Dario Argento's *Deep Red* (1975) and *Suspiria* (1977), but the group would ultimately dissolve due to infighting among the members. Simonetti remained a key part of Argento's films, regardless, and would contribute to such films as *Tenebrae* (1982), *Phenomena* (1984), *Opera* (1987) and *The Card Player* (2004), as well as such Argento productions as Lamberto Bava's *Demons* (1985) and Michele Soavi's *The Church* (1989). Simonetti was working extensively with just about every major Italian genre filmmaker of the period, so it was only a matter of time before he worked with Fulci. He would later recall, however, that he had no interaction with the director; Fulci explained that he was too busy being sued by Di Clemente to have much time for postproduction duties.[4]

Notes:
1. Retrieved from, http://www.shockingimages.com/fulci/interview.html
2. Palmerini, Luca M. and Gaetano Mistretta, *Spaghetti Nightmares* (Florida: Fantasma Books, 1996), p.62.
3. Malloy, Mike, A Chest Full of Stories: An Interview with Jorge Rivero, *Shock Cinema* #37, p. 36.
4. Retrieved from, http://www.shockingimages.com/fulci/interview.html

## Andrea Occhipinti Interview by Mike Baronas and Kit Garvin

Mike Baronas and Kit Garvin conducted the following interview with actor Andrea Occhipinti (aka Andrew Painter) on September 12, 2001. *Signor* Occhipinti's career includes two films for Lucio Fulci: *The New York Ripper* and *Conquest*. We extend our thanks to *signor* Occhipinti for taking the time to discuss his career and his collaborations with Fulci.

**Mike Baronas**: Let's start at the beginning of your career. You started off working in the theater?

**Andrea Occhipinti**: Yes, I started off in the theater playing Julius Caesar, directed by Maurizio Scarpala, which we did all over Italy. And from that I started doing television and movies as well. I did a big thing with RAI that was called *L'accezza di Palma*, directed by Mauro Bolognini, with Gian Maria Volontè. It was about color. And I did another series before that which was called *Perdono proibito*, with Lea Massari. It was the first thing that gave me a degree of popularity. I think it was after *L'accezza di Palma* that I met Fulci for *The New York Ripper*.

**MB/KG**: What were your first impressions of Fulci?

**AO**: First of all I would like to say that, while I knew about those films, but I was not a fan of that sort of film. So I went around and looked at the posters and noticed that he was a very prolific director, and at the same time I was very curious to know a little better about this kind of movie. And when I met him he was very kind, it was very interesting to meet with him, to talk with him. I mean, meeting someone who has been around for quite a while in this business. I also knew he had been a screenplay writer with many other famous directors.

But, coming to the subject of *The New York Ripper*, when he told me about it, the project, it was really like playing like a kid. Then it is like *(laughs)*, this is not like working, it's like having fun in a film that sounded very unusual and very strange, and also it fueled my ambition. There was the money, and I was eager to work—anything that would come my way I would consider experience. So I started working in this film, and I was very happy with the idea of going to New York. It never happened. I never got to New York.

**MB/KG**: All your scenes were shot here ...

**AO**: My "hands" or somebody else's hands were in New York. But working in the film I was getting to know, and to learn, all the things I didn't already [know] in movies, like the stuntmen, the doubles, heads exploding ... All these kinds of special effects that I was not used to, and it was all very good fun and playful. And at the same time I got to know the aspect of Fulci that was bloody, disgusting (*laughs*). He was always on the lookout for new disgusting things; I remember one scene where we were shooting in a movie theater near here called the Tetorio and where there was this girl in the theater and I was supposed to cut her belly with a knife. And, very interesting this, he [Fulci] wanted to shoot this from the point of view of her belly—from the inside. So he positioned the camera behind this plastic thing that I would cut. And from inside you only could see me with blood leaking down. So I thought at that point, "Wow!" So the special effects guy bought five kilos of, I don't know what, in a butcher's shop—which was bloody, smelly, disgusting stuff. And he brought it in, and everybody was disgusted; the smell, but also the sight of the intestines spilling everywhere. And Fulci went on the set and said, "What is this? Not even my 10-year-old nephew will be horrified; this is nothing. Give me some *real* stuff, some real blood." And everybody said (*smiles*), "My god! This man has got to be a freak." So it was at moments like that where I knew Fulci better. And I knew and understood him better that in a way he had dedicated himself to this kind of genre, and that we wanted to go deeply and fully in that direction. And he knew that his strengths lay in really going down, not really enjoying it, but concentrating specifically on it, deeply, strongly.

I knew him better from other films. I don't know really how he turned in this direction and where he was coming from, but I think that somewhere along the way there was a disillusionment somewhere, and there was a kind of rage that he was expressing in his life and his ability at making films in this genre ... I think he was more than voyeuristic, sadistic; he was expressing his personal rage because he was a very smart man. He was a very cultured man, but at the same time he was really bursting with anger, with rage. When he asked for more blood he was really enraged, so there was something.

**Andrea Occhipinti in *Conquest.***

**MB/KG**: [He possessed] a "dark side," so to speak?

**AO**: A dark side, and something that I said to him, "Okay, I'm doing this, so I'll go for it. And I'll *really* go for it." But to me—and this is my personal opinion—I don't know if it was his first passion to do this kind of film or if he became good at it and he became successful and then he dedicated himself to it. Maybe he hated this genre, even though he didn't create it, but in a way, he was known for it and he was "caught" in it. What else can I say?

**MB/KG**: Do you remember your female costar? "Almanta Keller"—there is some controversy to her identity. Some people say it was Antonella Interlenghi.

**AO**: Her name was Almanta Suska. I knew Antonella at the time, but it was not her who played my girlfriend.

**MB/KG**: Did you know going into the film that you would be the killer?

**AO**: Of course I did. I got the full script, and I knew what the story was. I was also in a way fascinated by the script, but also in his films there were references to many other films. There were bits of scenes from some film that you had already seen, that you had already seen or heard. So in a way it was a kind of mixture of genres. And I also knew about my character: This guy was not the sort that you should suspect, whether he is a freak or whatever.

**MB/KG**: Now, a silly question: Did he ever ask you to talk like a duck like it appears in the final film?

**AO**: *Errr* ... no he didn't. (*laughs*)

**American lobby card: Andrea Occhipinti joins forces with Jorge Rivero in *Conquest.***

**MB/KG**: Now, your death at the end of the film: Did you have to have a life-cast mask made of your face?

**AO**: That was a first time for me. I mean, my face was completely covered with this plastic stuff. I mean, it was pretty claustrophobic for me, because I had to spend 30 minutes without moving or breathing. I wanted to pull it off my face. It was very unpleasant to do. But then it was fun to see when the head came out. It was very interesting to see how the make-up artists were making up this head like I was. And in the end I asked for the head, and I brought it home and put it out to see.

**MB/KG**: Do you still have it?

**AO**: No *(laughs)* sadly.

**MB/KG**: Was the same mold used for *Conquest*, or did you have to go through the same procedure again?

**AO**: No, I only had one life cast—just that one time. Going back to that scene for me, it was very fascinating. There was stuntman rolling down the stairs playing me—it was pretty amazing and interesting to watch. It was also slightly upsetting, because I knew that this explosion of my head was the end of the film for me, my character. Just knowing it was difficult. And because he [Fulci] was so intense, despite all this disgusting subject matter. Work was always very demanding, and he never had had enough.

**MB/KG**: Do they have premieres of those types of films here in Italy?

**AO**: No. The film just comes out.

**MB/KG**: In the film you play a physicist dealing with entropy and absolute zero.

**AO**: Yes (*smiles*). That was always in the script; he was always a physicist, and at the end he was supposed to be a nice guy with a nice profession, a guy every girl would like to marry, and the last one you would suspect. I remember we shot all the exteriors outside the British Academy here in Rome—a nice building with a terrace, and it looked like New York in the film.

**MB/KG**: Did you mix with any of the members of the cast from the film?

**AO**: Not really the cast. I remember I was mostly fascinated by the technicians—mostly by the make-up people. For instance, the make-up artist was Manlio Rocchetti, who has become one of the best make-up artists here in Italy. He has worked with Scorsese and in many other big films, and it was fascinating, because I met them again, later, in other movies. It was interesting to see all this handiwork behind the scenes, and it was interesting to see because everything was done with such little money. Everything was crafted; it was made then and there, made more than with money but with good ideas.

**MB/KG**: Does it surprise you now that these sorts of films are still popular?

**AO**: No, it doesn't really surprise me anymore, because I knew somewhere in the world freaks like you (*laughs*) would be interested in these sorts of films! I still get people asking me about Lucio Fulci and *The New York Ripper*. But yes, it did surprise me, because I did not expect this film at all to become a sort of cult. At the time I was doing a B-movie, and that was the way I was approaching it, having fun and working and learning.

**MB/KG**: Your next film was *A Blade in the Dark*. What was that like as an experience—and what was Lamberto [Bava] like as a director?

**AO**: Completely different from working with Lucio. Lucio was very demanding and very neurotic and Lamberto was very calm and very laidback. I knew Lamberto from before, he had acted as assistant director on other films that I had done. He was very kind, and he was keener on doing this sort of film; easygoing, you know? He was more a coordinator of what was going, and very much relying on the action scenes and on the DP for certain scenes. He was more relaxed in his approach; and even though the film was shot very quickly—I think we shot it in three weeks. The scenes inside were done in 15 days. It was just shot in and around a house—the house of the producer [Martino]. He had just bought this villa, and the house was completely empty, so we could shoot there. It was in Via Flaminia.

**MB/KG**: Did you actually have to learn to play the piano for the film?

**AO**: No, I didn't learn to play the piano. I just had to pretend to play the piano. Again I liked that experience; there were all sorts of inspirations from all kinds of other movies. Like the voices on the tape made me think off *Blow Up* and *The Conversation* by Coppola.

**MB/KG**: Did you know Michele Soavi before or since making the film together?

**AO**: I knew Michele from before, because he and I were in the same acting school and classes when I first started—and he was an actor at the start of his career. And I was surprised to find him in the role of assistant to the director, and he was also playing the killer at the end of the film.

**MB/KG**: It must have been quite strange seeing him dressed up in a dress, and a wig and make-up?

**AO**: That was not foreseen, the fact that he was supposed to play that role. I think they tried to think of somebody and to cast somebody, but then one day Lamberto said, "You are perfect, Michele (*laughs*). Dressed up as a woman you can be feminine enough, you have something *Psycho* about you" (*laughs*).

**MB/KG**: You then moved on to shoot *Conquest* with Fulci. What attracted you to the role?

**AO**: That's right. It was shot in Sardinia. With that film I had a direct inspiration somehow from the Jean-Jacques Annaud film *Quest for Fire*. Fulci told us we had to think like we were in an early world, like the one in *Quest for Fire*. There was this mixture of the past and the future—there was this kind of kitsch mixture of characters, and there it was really like reading and appearing in comic books—with men who had wolves' heads. That was another fascinating experience.

I don't know, but at the beginning we were supposed to either shoot in Mexico or in Spain, as it was a Spanish co-production, and I knew there was this actor who had done this kind of thing in Mexico.

**MB/KG**: Jorge Rivero.

**AO**: That's right, Jorge Rivero, famous for these kind of action films, and also when I met Fulci again, he was there too, so it was interesting to have been playing one of the two leaders of this story. All of the things I remember—the action, the fantasy …

It was, I remember a very hard and fast shoot, because we were in Sardinia in winter and Sardinia is very cold and windy in winter, and we suffered a lot because of the cold and the costumes we had to wear. Also, Fulci was very sadistic in those situations. He didn't care whether you were cold or in the mud. He didn't care (*laughs*). He was also full of tension, as well as was the set, because it was really uncomfortable to shoot those scenes.

I remember there was a scene where I was supposed to have ants on my body, and the ants were in the mood to bite. And then they started to bite me, and Lucio said, "Okay … that's nice, that's really good (*laughs*)." And I was in agony … and he was saying, "One more shot, one more shot." He was really sadistic (*laughs*), and he was enjoying that I was really being bitten, because I could only wear a fleece. That was really tough to shoot, because there were so many problems, and it was cold. And also, like usual, the means were not much. I know I have this incredible scene with this boat at the beginning where I go out … And I have just this big stick, a branch, not even an oar, so I could move this boat … And Lucio wanted to make it very primitive.

It was also a difficult shoot, because there were lots of animals involved, and he was not really interested in the animals involved … I mean there was a big snake, and he didn't care about their welfare, so I put a little bit of distance between myself and him.

**MB/KG**: How did you get along with your costar, Jorge Rivero?

**AO**: Very well, very well. He was very nice. We basically were laughing at what we were shooting, with my sword, etc.—very like *Clash of the Titans*. Basically, we had fun. The best working relationship I had with another actor, because basically we were in the same boat, and we were both in this incredible situation.

It was difficult because of the meteorological situation, because often it was raining and we couldn't shoot, or we had terrible conditions, so it was difficult to reach the locations. We would wake up at dawn, and then it would start raining, and we had no caravans or trailers or anything. It was raining, there was nowhere to take shelter, the sleeping conditions were awful—the beds were full of fleas—it was awful (*laughs*).

**MB/KG**: Off the set, what was it like in Sardinia?

**AO**: Sardinia, basically there is nothing to do, especially in the winter. I remember in a town in the north of Sardinia—I can't remember what it was called—I remember I became friends with the woman who was married to the U.S. Army guy, because there is a NATO base there near Madalena, so there are a lot of American residents there. And there was something unusual with a party, with a turkey [Thanksgiving]. Also the shoot was very, very quick. We didn't shoot over a very long time. It was also shot in some caves here in Rome, where there are these incredible caves under the city, and we also shot there, a little bit, under the city.

**MB/KG**: Did you actually have to learn archery for the film?

**AO**: I remember the stunts master telling me. There were a lot of these stunt specialists, and the producers demanded that we be taught how to use the bow and arrow and how to choreograph all the fights.

**MB/KG**: One of your next films was *Bolero* with Bo Derek…

**AO**: I'm not sure if it was my next film. It was a very difficult set, and it was not pleasant working with John Derek. It was not pleasant working in that production, because they [Bo and John Derek] were really very moody throughout, and also because I was taking the role from somebody else

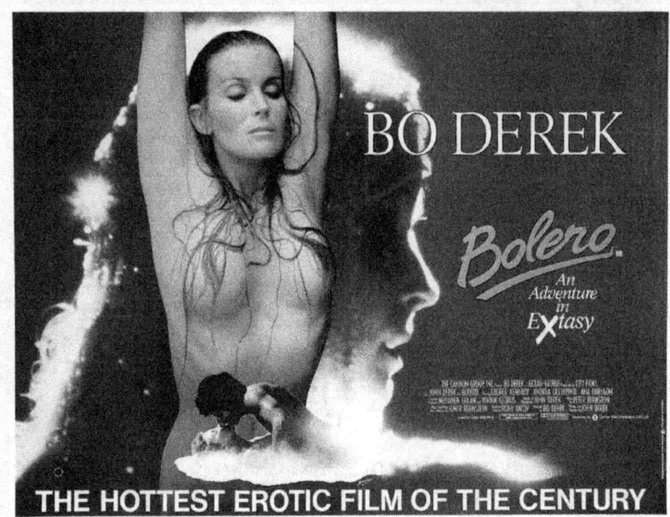


**The advertising for *Bolero* (1984) made much of Bo Derek's nude scenes.**

that they had originally cast. Originally it was supposed to be Fabio Testi, and Fabio Testi was not available, and so instead they called me. It was difficult especially to work with a married couple—both were very egocentric.

**MB/KG**: Another filmmaker you worked with was Ettore Scola in *The Family* ...

**AO**: Yes, that was great. It was really a beautiful experience, because he was a great director and there were a lot of great actors and we had a lot of time—two years—and you could really get into your character, your aspect of the film. Also the film went to Cannes, and it won Best Foreign Film at the Academy Awards, so it was truly a great experience, and also to co-share the role with Vittorio Gassman was great, it was really very challenging.

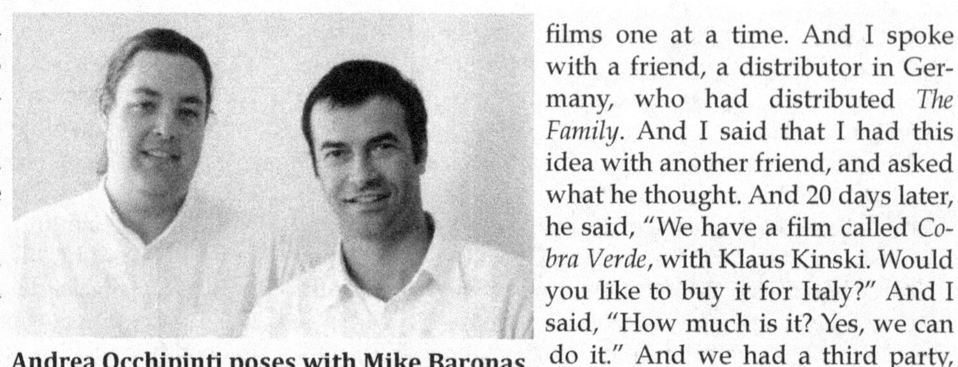

**Andrea Occhipinti poses with Mike Baronas.**

**MB/KG**: What was Ettore Scola like to work with as a director?

**AO**: As I said, what was great was that we had a lot of time on our hands. And we would shoot one scene for days. And you would shoot and approach the scene from different angles, so that allowed you to really get into what you were doing; there was no need to rush. You would have the rehearsal, the *provino*, then and the opportunity to sit and discuss it. There was no rush; the main goal was to get what he wanted. That was one of my best experiences working as an actor, definitely, but there also are other roles where I was very happy, like the remake of *Two Women* that I did with Sophia Loren. I was very happy with the end film, and also the experience of working with Sophia Loren ...

**MB/KG**: And what was Sophia Loren like to work with?

**AO**: Oh, she's great, she was great ... because I was very intimidated by the thought of working with Sophia Loren. She was very formal at the beginning, saying things like, "Sir, would you like to redo your scene," and I would say, "Yes, Madam, I would like to." So, the first day we were kind of Sir / Madam. Then one day we were shooting the scene, and it was first time, second time, and she was hiding down beside me because the Germans were passing in the scene. And at one point she said to me, "My thighs are painful," and it was very funny, and from that point she started to talk Neapolitan with me ... She started to tell me what great cooking she was doing at home, in the hotel, and she would like to invite me over for some Neapolitan *spécialités* she was preparing; so from that point she was very warm. I'm half-Sicilian, but I was born in Rome. My father is Sicilian.

**MB/KG**: So, when did you set up Lucky Red Distribution?

**AO**: I set it up in 1987. Just after I did the film with Ettore Scola while I was doing *The Family*, and I started very slowly. I always had the idea of getting involved in a different aspect of film, not just acting, and I started buying films one at a time. And I spoke with a friend, a distributor in Germany, who had distributed *The Family*. And I said that I had this idea with another friend, and asked what he thought. And 20 days later, he said, "We have a film called *Cobra Verde*, with Klaus Kinski. Would you like to buy it for Italy?" And I said, "How much is it? Yes, we can do it." And we had a third party, because we didn't have the money at the time ...

**MB/KG**: And where did the name come from—i.e. Lucky Red?

**AO**: It was a combination my partner and me trying to work out a name that was recognizable in Italy or abroad. So, naïvely, I said, "Why don't we call it Lucky Strike?" And he said that we couldn't call it that, because it was a brand name, and he suggested, "Let's call it Lucky Red." And he was red-haired as well, and it went from there ...

**MB/KG**: You haven't acted for some time now. Do you miss it at all?

**AO**: No, no. I did my last movie two years ago, and I decided to quit. Also, I split with my former partner, and I had to make the choice. Either, I would fold this company—there are 20 people working here. [Because of the company) I cannot afford to go away for eight weeks. Before I could, now I can't. So I had to make the choice, and I did, and I did it radically. I said, "I don't want to act anymore," and from this [distribution] work I get lots of satisfaction—probably more than I was getting of late from acting, because I was doing mostly television series that aren't really fun.

**MB/KG**: And working in this environment is more like a family?

**AO**: Not really. I mean, working on the set of a film can be like a family, too. But I do not have an industrial view of this kind of work. I mean, the kinds of movies I do and distribute are films that I like and I have a certain type of line. And the kind of work we do—it's not many films. It's all very important, the campaigns we make; the marketing campaigns. And we have to make those films known and famous. With the kind of films I do, it is worth gauging the market. Also we have to be creative here. We also have to work out which films will become famous later.

I got involved with *The Others* [which was being distributed in Italy the following day] because I co-produced *Eyes Wide Shut*, with Tom Cruise. In fact, in the beginning of *The Others*, she [Nicole Kidman] was not supposed to be in it, it was supposed to have a lower budget. It was still set in Spain, but they were looking for someone like Emily Watson. Then Nicole Kidman saw what we doing, and she wanted to play the role. And she's great in the film ...

**MB/KG**: Thank you very much.

**AO**: Thank you.

# 1984

## *Rome, 2072 A.D.: The New Gladiators* (*Italy*)

Aka *Il guerrieri dell'anno 2072; Roma, año 2072 D.C.: los gladiadores; 2072, les mercenaires du future; Die Schlacht der Centurions; Fighting Centurions*

Directed by Lucio Fulci; Produced by Edmondo Amati, Maurizio Amati and Sandro Amati, for Regency Productions; Screenplay by Elisa Briganti, Cesari Frugoni, Lucio Fulci and Dardano Sacchetti, from a story by Elisa Briganti and Dardano Sacchetti; Director of Photography: Giuseppe Pinori [as Joseph Pinori]; Editor: Vincenzo Tomassi [as Vincent Thomas]; Music by Riz Ortolani

Main Players: Jared Martin (Drake); Fred Williamson (Abdul); Renato Rossini [as Howard Ross] (Raven); Eleanor Brigliadori [as Eleanor Gold] (Sarah); Cosimo Cinieri (Professor Towman); Claudio Cassinelli (Cortez); Penny Brown (Sybil); Hal Yamanouchi (Akira); Pierluigi Conti [as Al Cliver] (Kirk); Donal O'Brien (Monk); Cinzia Monreale (Linda) [uncredited]

*In futuristic Rome, barbarism has come back into style: The big television networks push the envelope by broadcasting shows that place their contestants in grave danger. With the ratings starting to flag thanks to public apathy, Cortez comes up with an idea to do a special event program in which gladiators on motorcycles will fight to the death. To populate the show, he pulls some prisoners off of death row—and to provide a bit of human interest, he frames beloved athlete Drake for murder, thus ensuring that he, too, will participate and hopefully send the ratings through the roof ...*

Fulci followed up the bizarre *Conquest* with his first foray into pure science fiction. *Rome, 2072 A.D.: The New Gladiators* (often referred to simply as *The New Gladiators*) is part of a run of dystopian science fiction thrillers inspired by the success of films like George Miller's *Max Max* (1979) and *The Road Warrior* (1981), and John Carpenter's *Escape from New York* (1981). These films present a bleak portrait of an oppressive future society dominated by violence. The concepts behind these films proved that it wasn't always necessary to mount sci-fi on lavish budgets, and this was certainly a relief to Italian filmmakers looking to cash-in on the trend. In the space of a few years, Italian cinemas would be overrun by the likes of Enzo G. Castellari's *1990: The Bronx Warriors* (1982), *The New Barbarians: Warriors of the Wasteland* (1983) and *Escape from the Bronx* (1983), Ruggero Deodato's *The Raiders of Atlantis* (1983), Bruno Mattei's *Rats: Night of Terror* (1984) and many more. Compared to some of the tackier entries in the subgenre, Fulci's sole foray looks pretty impressive.

The husband and wife team of Dardano Sacchetti and Elisa Briganti devised the story. They created a story that

***Rome, 2072 A.D.: The New Gladiators*; original artwork by Scott Hoffman.**

is surprisingly prescient, with its emphasis on reality television and the push to find the next new extreme in broadcasting. In a culture—if such a term can even be applied—saturated with the likes of *Keeping Up With the Kardashians, Here Comes Honey Boo Boo* and *Duck Dynasty*, to say nothing of competition programs like *Survivor* and *Fear Factor*, the concept may no longer appear very novel; when it was written, however, the trend towards so-called reality television had yet to take hold. Sacchetti and Briganti were not the first writers to explore this concept, however; an earlier example that comes to mind is Nigel Kneale's *The Year of the Sex Olympics* (1968), which deals with a future society that is so apathetic that it turns to television for stimulation instead of engaging in the real thing. This has the added effect of keeping the population under control, since most people don't want to bother with procreation and would rather just see other people doing it on TV. Sacchetti and Briganti devised an ambitious scenario that would ideally have required a substantial budget, but inevitably it didn't receive the treatment it really deserved when brought to the screen by producer Edmondo Amati. Amati decided to cut costs wherever possible, but his decision to bring Lucio Fulci onto the project proved inspired. Fulci was already an old hand at making silk purses out of sow's ears, anyway, and he entered the project with enthusiasm. All that being said, it is entirely likely that Sacchetti and Briganti were inspired by the publication of *The Running Man*, a novel originally published in 1982 and credited to Richard Bachman. Bachman, of course, is the pseudonym of Stephen King—and when the book was republished later in the 1985 anthology *The Bachman Books*, King's paternity was inevitably played-up on the cover.

**Drake (Jared Martin), Abdul (Fred Williamson), Sarah (Eleanor Brigliadori) and Kirk (Al Cliver) in *Rome, 2072 A.D.: The New Gladiators.***

The book also deals with a futuristic society that indulges in sadistic reality TV programming, and it would eventually be filmed in 1987, with Arnold Schwarzenegger. Whether Sacchetti and Briganti had read the book by the time they wrote their story is unknown, but the similarities between the two stories are nevertheless striking.

In an interview with Massimo Lavagnini, Fulci spoke of the project:

> I have to say that there's a very good topic by Sacchetti, and it's about the television following us everywhere. Television torments us until we become heroes. This is the reading key of *The New Gladiators.* A great idea for an anticipating movie, but I'm not very satisfied with it. I wanted to do a future Rome in which the ancient monuments were covered by gigantic Plexiglas domes. Amati, the producer, [had]me ... add the skyscrapers. Ridiculous. He's a great producer, but it has his tastes ...[1]

Fulci may have been frustrated by Amati's stipulations, but in other respects he does an honorable job of realizing the story within its low-budget framework. Indeed, the project was conceived as a "two-fer" deal with Amati, with the proposed follow-up, also scripted by Sacchetti, to have been *Blastfighter.* As Sacchetti later explained,

> Unfortunately, Fulci argued with production and the thing ended up in court. They had already sold the film, but, no longer being able to use our script, they kept the title and applied it to a film of a different genre [...][2]

When *Blastfighter* emerged in the summer of 1984, it had undergone a major rewrite by Sacchetti and became something of a clone of John Boorman's *Deliverance* (1972), with Lamberto Bava directing in Fulci's stead.

To assist on the finished shooting script, the production turned to Cesare Frugoni, an experienced screenwriter whose career got underway with Mario Bava's troubled kidnapping thriller *Rabid Dogs* (1974). Frugoni had already dabbled in schlocky adventure horror terrain with the Sergio Martino films *The Mountain of the Cannibal God* (1978), *Island of the Fish Men* (1979) and *The Great Alligator* (1979). Fulci also contributed to the writing process, and the collective team of writers devised a scenario that had ample wit and foresight, even if it inevitably reached further than the budget would allow for.

Fulci begins the film with some impressive model work: The panoramic views of the modern civilization is indeed impressive, and if the camera lingers a little too long, thus spoiling the illusion, one is still left impressed by the detail and craftsmanship that went into creating such an elaborately detailed model. A voice-over explains that the trend towards reality television is currently experiencing a crisis: Viewers are becoming bored with the programs, for the simple reason that they lack an ingredient of real danger. Sacchetti and Briganti's central thesis is a grim but realistic one: Despite years of "culture" and "education," mankind remains pretty bestial at heart. In order to appeal to the lowest common denominator, a decision is reached to put a proper old school gladiator competition on the air—only this time, it will be updated to be on motorcycles!

Drake is introduced as the film's hero, and he is roped into the competition in a particularly vile and cynical fashion: Cortez, the ambitious head of the one TV network, arranges for some men to break into his home and murder Drake's wife; Drake is then sent to death row for murdering the assassins in revenge. The sequence depicting the home invasion is probably the eeriest in the film: The assailants torment Drake's wife by moving in and out of the shadows, whistling a tune in unison, making it clear that they are enjoying the process of playing cat-and-mouse with her. When Drake kills them off, the audience is on his side—and they remain so for the rest of the picture. Drake is a man of integrity and conscience in a world overrun by greed and avarice; as such, he is something of a throwback to another era.

By contrast, Cortez is a petty despot who is driven onwards by his ambition. Cortez doesn't care who he hurts; his only goal is to succeed in creating the "next big thing" in reality television. He has an unnamed ally in this quest: the public. Fulci and his cowriters make it clear that the only reason these shows are proliferating and becoming more and more exploitative and violent is because it's what the public wants. It's tempting to read into this a cynical critique of the movie industry itself, with Fulci wryly reflecting on the thirst for sensationalism, which pushed him to making horror films of an increasingly graphic and gruesome nature. Fulci does not resent this, however: He dives into the work with wicked abandon, but he also recognizes the nature of the beast. Without an enthusiastic public lapping this stuff up, he would never be allowed to cut loose and indulge his flair for the sadistic and the macabre.

Despite the obviously low budget, Fulci and cinematographer Giuseppe Pinori create some striking images—though admittedly they do rely a little too heavily on star filters to create a glittery effect. Pinori would go on to photograph *Murder-Rock: Dancing Death*, and his jarring contrasts of light and shade marked him out as a potential successor to Sergio Salvati, but unfortunately their collaboration ended after only the two films. Pinori does a commendable job of lighting the miniatures, and the film looks very slick and stylish from beginning to end. Fulci's flair for action is evident only sporadically, however: Much of the film is more concerned with cloak-and-dagger shenanigans involving the network, but when the action starts to cut loose in the final section of the movie, Fulci delivers where it counts. The film is well paced, and certainly does not overstay its welcome.

The cast performs quite credibly. American actor Jared Martin gives a good account of himself as the stoic and honorable Drake; he plays the role as a man of great integrity, without draining him of humor and making him come off like a self-righteous prig. Martin works some sly humor into his reactions to the mayhem unfolding around him and makes for a compelling protagonist. Born in New York in 1941, Martin made his debut with a role in Brian De Palma's directing debut, *Murder à la Mod* (1968). He went on to appear in De Palma's *The Wedding Party* (1969) before doing guest stints on such popular shows as *The Partridge Family*, *Night Gallery* and *Columbo*. He found popularity with recurring roles on the soap operas *Dallas* and *One Life to Live*, and would later reteam with Fulci on *Aenigma*. In more recent years, he has transitioned to directing; his most recent credit is the political drama *The Congressman* (2014). The imposing Fred Williamson plays Drake's right-hand man, Abdul. Truth be told, Williamson is chiefly utilized for his intimidating screen persona and doesn't have much of an opportunity to really emote. Born in Indiana in 1938, Williamson played football for The Pittsburgh Steelers, The Oakland Raiders and The Kansas City Chiefs before transitioning to acting. He became a star in the "Blaxploitation" movement of the 1970s, thanks to such films as *Hammer* (1972, Williamson's nickname while playing football was The Hammer), *Black Caesar* (1973) and *Hell Up in Harlem* (1973) and he began appearing in Italian genre films in the late 1970s, racking up appearances for Antonio Margheriti (*Take a Hard Ride*, 1975) and Enzo G. Castellari (*The Inglorious Bastards*, 1978), among others. In more recent years, he has made noteworthy appearances in Robert Rodriguez's *From Dusk Till Dawn* (1996) and Todd Phillips' *Starsky & Hutch* (2004). Renato Rossini played the villainous Raven, in the second of his two Fulci films appearances following *The New York Ripper*. Rossini is properly despicable in the role and is a worthy opponent to Martin's hero. Claudio Cassinelli played the master villain, Cortez. Cassinelli perfectly embodies the kind of slimy corporate villains that were becoming all the rage in the 1980s; he's not exactly Gordon Gekko,

**Enzo Sciotti's stylish promotional artwork for *Rome, 2072 A.D.: The New Gladiators.***

but he's cut from the same cloth. Born in Bologna in 1938, he started acting in films and television in the early 1960s. After playing notable roles for Damiano Damiani in *The Devil is a Woman* and for Massimo Dallamano in *What Have They Done To Your Daughters?* (both 1974), he became a favorite of director Sergio Martino, who cast him in a number of films, including *The Suspicious Death of a Minor* (1975) and the aforementioned *Island of the Fish Men* (1979). He would go on to appear one more time for Fulci, in *Murder-Rock: Dancing Death,* before his tragic death in a helicopter crash during the filming of Martino's *Hands of Steel* in 1985; he was only 46 years old. The supporting cast includes a number of faces familiar from earlier Fulci films, including Donal O'Brien, Cosimo Cinieri, Al Cliver, Penny Brown and an uncredited Cinzia Monreale, who can be seen as a contestant on a virtual reality TV show based around *The Pit and the Pendulum*!

The film marks a couple of significant signposts in Fulci's career. For one thing, it is the first time Fulci would use his daughter Camilla in an official capacity on one of his films. Born on July 6, 1963, Camilla is the younger of Fulci's two daughters, and she would become a significant presence on the set of her father's later works. As Fulci's health began to deteriorate and the conditions imposed on him by penny-pinching producers became more exasperating, he desperately needed the support of somebody close to him to get through the day. Camilla—sometimes billed as Mily—would serve as her father's support system on set and helped him to complete the day's work by attending to details while he focused on dealing with the actors. On this film, she is credited as a second unit script supervisor; in time she would be promoted to assistant director, as well.

On a more unfortunate note, *Rome, 2072 A.D.: The New Gladiators* would mark the end of Fulci's collaboration with Sacchetti (and by extension, Briganti). The two men had equally bullheaded personalities, and clashes were inevitable, but things came to a head over a proposed project titled *Evil Comes Back.* Fulci would later claim that,

> One day I told [Sacchetti] the story of *Evil Comes Back*, a sequel on a fantastic note to [James M. Cain's] *The Postman Always Rings Twice,* and he proposed it several times over with my name on it as director and then, one day, he registered it with his name on it! (*laughs*). I later found out that he'd sold it to a friend of mine—[Luciano] Martino—but in view of our past friendship, I decided not to sue him, I just broke off all relations with him.[3]

These allegations incensed Sacchetti, who fired back,

> That's completely false! When I proposed to him the treatment, which was nothing more than a sequel in fantasy style to *The Postman Always Rings Twice,* in which the dead man returns, he became really enthusiastic and had it read by a producer, who then commissioned me to write the script. Then, for various reasons, problems arose and the film wasn't made. Four years later, [Lamberto] Bava used the script to make *Until Death* (1987), and Fulci, who wasn't working at the time, got angry with me and started hurling these accusations.[4]

Sacchetti would blame the dissolution of his partnership with Fulci on the older man's pride:

> Fulci has always suffered from the knowledge that I was the one who wrote the stories, which has made him extremely jealous of me, and this has led him to systematically disparaging my work in order to give himself importance.[5]

A lot of finger-pointing and accusations surround the collaborations between Fulci and Sacchetti, but it's clear that Sacchetti was Fulci's most significant writing partner, along with Roberto Gianviti; his subsequent films would sometimes suffer from the absence of similarly strong writing partners, which seemed to bring out the best in Fulci's talents. In the meantime, however, he would collaborate one more time with Gianviti on what would turn out to be the director's final *giallo.*

Notes:
1. Retrieved from http://www.shockingimages.com/fulci/interview.html
2. Palmerini, Luca M. and Gaetano Mistretta, *Spaghetti Nightmares* (Florida: Fantasma Books, 1996), p. 125.
3. *Ibid*, p. 63.
4. *Ibid*, p. 125.
5. *Ibid*, pp. 124-125.

# Jared Martin Interview by Troy Howarth

The following interview with actor Jared Martin was conducted via email on September 28, 2014. In addition to appearing in *Rome, 2072 A.D.: The New Gladiators*, Jared also appeared in *Aengima* for Fulci. He is also an accomplished director in his own right. Jared has my thanks for taking the time to answer these questions.

**Troy Howarth**: How did you come to be cast in *The New Gladiators*?
**Jared Martin**: I had been in Rome the previous year working on an American film called *The Lonely Lady* (1983), [when] my Italian agents contacted, or were contacted by, Fulci's producers. And a deal was struck. It didn't hurt that I was a star on *Dallas*, which was extremely popular in Italy at the time.
**TH**: What were your initial impressions of Lucio Fulci?
**JM**: Gruff, distanced, impatient, highly focused, not interested in social skills, wheels always turning, unkempt, explosive, a cornered genius of sorts. We didn't share a language together, but I sensed he saw things in images and may have had problems communicating what he saw in words. Liked to work with actors he knew and trusted.
**TH**: How was Fulci to work with? He had a reputation for being temperamental … did you find this to be the case?
**JM**: It depends on how you define temper. Yes, he shouted, sometimes he waved his arms, and made faces and displayed impatience and disapproval; all of these manifestations were part of a larger creative force that was clearly dedicated, driven, focused, aiming at the highest standards within the limitations he was forced to work with. I didn't mind the temper—I grew up in theater, temper is just one of the brushes theater people paint with. I don't know how he behaved with his other colleagues or subordinates. He was always decent with me. I knew he wanted the absolute best from everyone, and I had to respect that.
**TH**: How did you get along with your costars, including Fred Williamson and Claudio Cassinelli?
**JM**: Never worked with Claudio, who was in the other part of the film. I loved working with Fred, a complete professional, both laidback and intense, with a great sense of humor. He made it fun.
**TH**: How long was the shoot?
**JM**: If memory serves, it was 10 weeks.
**TH**: The script was rather ambitious—did the low budget hurt the film, in your opinion?
**JM**: Yes. It needed a strong infusion of special effects and set design, especially special effects; that spaceship at the end looked silly, and we could have used bigger motorcycles.
**TH**: Do you have any favorite memories of the filming?
**JM**: Living in Rome. *Gladiators* was my second of two features in the city, and I enjoyed living in my small apartment on the Via Sacconi near the Ponte Milvio; shopping and cooking, walking, jogging near the Stadio Olimpico and immersing myself in the epic grandeur of the time-soaked Eternal City. I enjoyed the camaraderie on the set, particularly the prison dormitory where the gladiators lived. We spent much time doing these scenes, and we all got on well.
**TH**: You reunited with Fulci on *Aenigma* in 1987; how did that come about?
**JM**: The same as *New Gladiators*—agents making a deal that produced an offer. I always took advantage of an opportunity to work abroad. I was an easy catch.
**TH**: Fulci was rather ill by the time he made *Aenigma*; did he seem different to you compared to how he was on the first film?
**JM**: *Aenigma* was a smaller film, shot in a smaller city. The crew spoke Serbian, the department heads spoke Italian, only Carlo [Klemencic], the art director, and Lara [Naszinski], my leading lady, spoke English. I spent time alone, not necessarily a bad thing. Sarajevo is a magical city—or was—this was before the civil war that destroyed many areas we filmed in. I'd heard Fulci was sick, something was wrong with his liver; he was on a diet. He seemed quieter and older, and more or less kept to himself.
**TH**: Do you have any particular memories of the shoot? It was filmed, I believe, in Serbia and in Boston?
**JM**: I had friendships with Lara and Carlo. I roamed the city with a new camera when I wasn't working. This was the beginning of a habit of taking pictures that developed into another career as a photographer. I took advantage of the immersion in a foreign culture that working on a film provides. The production chooses interesting places to work in and guarantees entry and complete access. I spent

**Jared Martin strikes a heroic pose in *Rome, 2072 A.D.: The New Gladiators.***

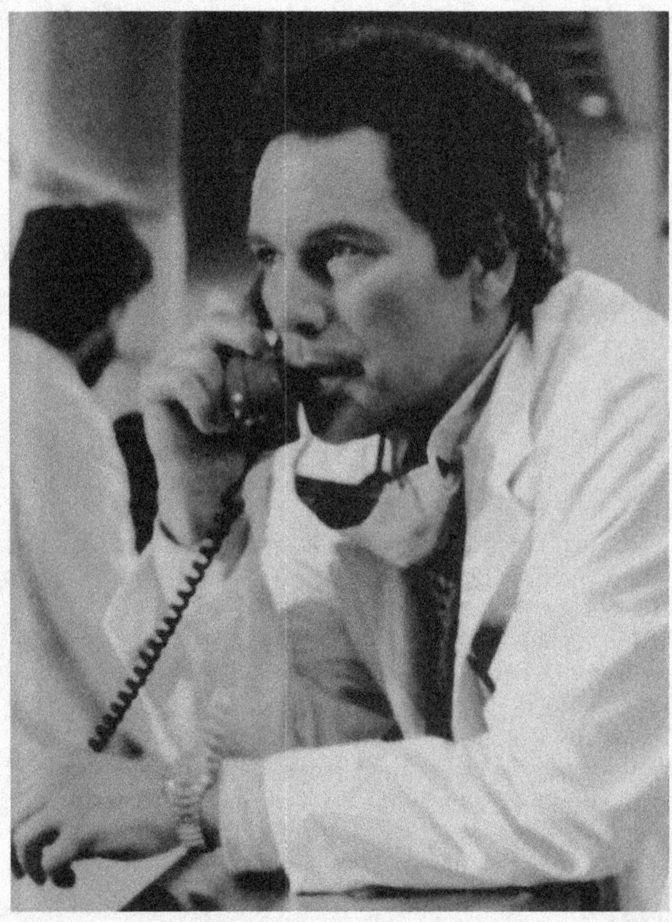

**Jared Martin in *Aenigma.***

time in the *souk* and bought a magic carpet and became an addict of Turkish coffee. Exterior location shots were taken in Boston, but I only worked in Sarajevo.

**TH**: Did you keep in touch with Fulci after this film?

**JM**: No.

**TH**: Did you ever see the two films you made with Fulci? If so, what did you think of them?

**JM**: I liked the energy, audacity and conception of *New Gladiators*; I had problems with *Aenigma*.

**TH**: You have worked most extensively in American TV … how does making films in Italy compare to working in the U.S.?

**JM**: It goes quicker, faster, not necessarily better, in Italian films. Sound is not an issue, as most films are dubbed in post. Same with Hong Kong films, where I also worked. It felt more congenial in Italian films, longer lunches, people were friendlier, more curious. I was invited home to dinner by some of the crew, entering a private household and meeting wives and children was an honor I will always remember.

**TH**: I gather you are now directing a film titled *The Congressman* … can you tell us a little about it?

**JM**: I've actually directed two features and about three-dozen short films before taking on *The Congressman*. In 1995, I cofounded and was creative director of a nonprofit production company that worked with disadvantaged, sometimes troubled, youth in Philadelphia's inner city. We served over 3000 kids and made around 250 films; I've lost count. I did this for 15 years after leaving Hollywood. *Congressman* is not the first, and hopefully, not the last. I enjoy directing. My secret is to hire the absolute best people and let them do their job. *Congressman* was stressful but beautiful. We had a 20-day production shoot schedule; half the film was shot on a rugged island off the coast of Maine. I was climbing on rocks and tramping through forests trying to keep up with younger people. A challenge. We got some beautiful footage. The story was unique and the acting was superb. They made me look good. As I write, we're finishing up and have entered the Sundance Film Festival. Directing a film demands the same attention as falling in love … concentration, energy, emotional commitment, invention, curiosity, patience and deep, deep understanding.

**TH**: What made you want to direct? And do you plan to make more films?

**JM**: At a certain point I realized I knew a lot about how to make a film, and it seemed natural, if people were willing to put up with me; to utilize this knowledge in creating product. I made a choice not to grow old before the camera, yet I didn't want to say goodbye to this business, which has been my true family for so many years. I rarely plan anything except plane and train schedules and trips to the dentist.

**TH**: Jared—thanks again for your time!

**JM**: You're welcome; good luck with the book!

**Jared Martin and Fred Williamson make an unpleasant discovery *Rome, 2072 A.D.: The New Gladiators.***

## *Murder-Rock: Dancing Death (Italy)*

Aka *Murderock – Uccide a passo di danza; Danza mortal; Murderock; Murder Rock; Slashdance*

Directed by Lucio Fulci; Produced by Augusto Caminito, for Scena Film; Screenplay by Gianfranco Clerici, Lucio Fulci, Roberto Gianviti and Vincenzo Mannino; Director of Photography: Giuseppe Pinori; Editor: Vincenzo Tomassi; Music by Keith Emerson; Songs: *Tonight is the Night, Not So Innocent, Are the Streets to Blame* and *You Are Not Alone Tonight*, performed by Doreen Chanter

Main Players: Olga Karlatos (Candice Norman); Ray Lovelock (George Webb); Cosimo Cinieri (Inspector Borges); Claudio Cassinelli (Dick Gibson); Giuseppe Mannajuolo (Professor Davis); Christian Borromeo (Willy Stark); Geretta Geretta [as Geretta Mary Fields] (Margie); Carla Buzzanca (Janice); Pierluigi Conti [as Al Cliver] (Voice Analyst); Giovanni De Nava (Hotel Receptionist); Silvia Collatina (Molly)

Cameo appearance: Lucio Fulci (Phil)

*A student at a New York dance academy is murdered, and the police try to discover who is responsible. Their investigation reveals that there is much competition and jealousy among the students and faculty alike, thus making it harder to pin down a main suspect. The murders continue, while Inspector Borges decides to follow a hunch in the hopes of bringing the chaos to a close ...*

Following the outrage that greeted *The New York Ripper*, Lucio Fulci began making gentler films for a period of time. Perhaps he had been cowed by the backlash against his most extreme film to date, or perhaps he was just bored with all the excess and decided to pursue other options ... whatever the rationale, he was damned if he did, damned if he didn't: critics and audiences may have felt he went too far with *The New York Ripper*, but they were equally vociferous in stating that *Murder-Rock: Dancing Death* didn't go nearly far enough. Fulci himself would later describe the film as representing:

> The end of an era—at that point, I felt the need to renew myself, realizing that such violent, wild horror had had its day.[1]

The film continues the dialogue about America that started with *The New York Ripper*. In the earlier film, the characters speak of the need to be the best at their particular field; similarly, the characters in *Murder-Rock: Dancing Death* are driven by the desire to be the best in their own field. Fulci's theme here is not exactly anti-American as such, but it does critique the way in which people are often pressured to succeed at all costs within the culture. The dog-eat-dog mentality is very much at the core of this film, whereas it was more subtly integrated into the earlier film. Fulci and his cowriters don't hammer the message home too forcefully, but it does add a bit of subtext that adds interest for those who are willing to dig beneath the surface.

Unfortunately, the plot is pretty generic. The characters are mostly ciphers and suspense isn't generated nearly so forcefully as in the director's earlier *gialli*. That said, the film is hardly the disaster some have painted it to be. It is arguably the last really slick, well-crafted film the director would make; shrinking budgets and Fulci's failing health would taint subsequent films. He still appears to have been in robust form when he made this film, and he busts out plenty of stylistic devices to help shore up the shaky narrative. Fulci often spoke of his love of Mario

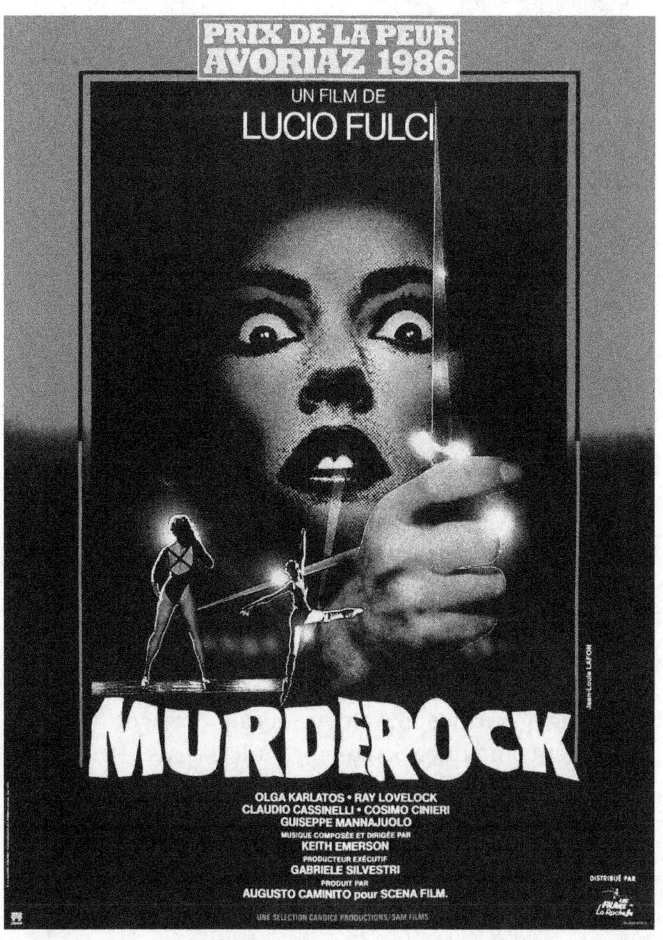


**French poser for *Murder-Rock: Dancing Death*; artwork by Jean-Louis Lafon.**

Bava's work, and *Murder-Rock: Dancing Death* allows him to borrow the Bavaian trope of shooting scenes in half-darkness, with pulsing light illuminating the action from outside the windows. This device was utilized to great effect by Bava in the "Drop of Water" segment of *The Three Faces of Fear* (1963) and in the antique shop murder scene of *Blood and Black Lace* (1964), but Fulci goes it one better: Much of the film is done in this style. The use of exaggerated lighting effects, wide-angle lenses and mobile cam-

**Filmexport Group handbill for *Murder-Rock: Dancing Death*; artwork by Enzo Sciotti.**

erawork gives the film a kinetic quality that helps to make up for its script issues.

If the majority of the characters are noteworthy for being either bland or backstabbing, Fulci seems to find much to love in the character of Inspector Borges. The character would seem to be an extension of Lieutenant Williams in *The New York Ripper*, right down to the shabby raincoat, but while Williams was a hypocrite and a bit of a bastard, Borges is far more humanistic. He even has a family, which Fulci demonstrates in subtle visual terms via the portrait of him with his wife and children shown on his desk; Fulci doesn't dwell on this detail and it would be easy enough to miss it, but as is so often the case in the director's work, nothing is arbitrary within the frame. Borges is a cynic who isn't afraid to resort to rough tactics in order to get the information he needs, but he is also distinguished by a wry sense of humor. When discussing the case with his psychologist colleague Professor Davis (an older, tenured version of the character played by Paolo Malco in *The New York Ripper*, perhaps), Davis states that one suspect is a psychopath; Borges snaps back, "He's not a psycho—he's an *asshole*!" Borges' quips and amusingly unorthodox style go a long way towards redeeming the film's otherwise functional investigation scenes. If only the other characters had been developed with similar wit and sensitivity, the film would surely have benefitted as a result.

Even so, the film looks great thanks to Giuseppe Pinori's lighting and Fulci's interesting use of framing and camera movement. This would be one of the last times that his flair for the visual would be firmly in evidence. Pinori had enjoyed the experience of working with Fulci on *Rome, 2072 A.D.: The New Gladiators*, and jumped at the chance of collaborating with him again. However, as he recalls, their collaboration began even further back:

> I met Lucio Fulci 10 years before [*Murder-Rock: Dancing Death*]. We were doing a commercial for mineral water. [...] I think it was still in black-and-white at the time. He worked on the commercial with the same freedom that he'd do a film, a thriller.[2]

Unlike many collaborators, Pinori recalled Fulci as a calm, even-tempered presence on set and emphasized that the director was very meticulous in his approach:

> Lucio was the type who liked people a lot. If he saw that they were dedicated to him and the project and not just in it for the money, he'd really be affectionate. [...] It's nice when a director tells you to take chances, and when I did it, he let out a shout of joy. That's just wonderful. [...] Lucio didn't ever take himself so seriously; he never made trouble. [...] He was also sick during that time in New York, but he always had things under control [...] He was always decisive, never had any doubt. I've never seen him hesitate about the placement of the actors or the camera.

Pinori's reference to Fulci's health is telling and sets the stage for the problems that would dog the director for the remainder of his life and career. Diabetes and a bout with hepatitis that lead to cirrhosis of the liver would ultimately take a mighty toll on his body, even if his spirit remained as fiery as ever. When summing up his own feelings on *Murder-Rock: Dancing Death*, however, Fulci would maintain that these problems occurred after the filming:

> With *Murder-Rock*, I was attempting to move away from the type of film I'd been making, and what I came up with was a detective story, a decent American-style television film, nothing more. After that, I went down with the illness I told you about earlier, and two years went by without me being able to work.[3]

*Murder-Rock: Dancing Death* does indeed stand apart from the other genre work Fulci had been doing in the '80s: He downplays the violence and focuses instead on putting together an intricately plotted thriller scenario. The various murder scenes are bloodless—the killer uses an ornate hatpin (!) to penetrate their breastplate and stop the victims' hearts from beating—and nudity is on the light side, especially when compared to the excesses of Fulci's previous thriller. The film's use of trippy dream sequences and a female protagonist dreaming of her own demise call to mind *A Lizard in a Woman's Skin*. If the film isn't worthy of that earlier gem, it's still a solid and enjoyable late-period entry in his filmography. Indeed, the film's similarities to *Lizard* go beyond the dream sequences: Candice is a protagonist in the same mold as Carol in the earlier film. Both women use their dreams as an alibi to enable them to carry out a series of murders. Carol's intention is to obfuscate a Sapphic affair, which would cause a scandal and ruin her father's political aspirations, while Candice is driven by self-loathing and a need for revenge. George's presence in her dreams is logically motivated: He is the man who ran her over while driving drunk, thus ending her career as a dancer. Candice, like Peter in *The New York Ripper*, cannot handle seeing young women enjoying themselves or prospering because of this deep-rooted sense of self-loathing; in Peter's case, his hatred is generated by his little girl's degenerative illness, while in Candice's it is motivated by the realization that the girls she is training are going to enjoy the kind of success which has been denied to her. The final revelation of her role in the mystery is surprising and provides the film with its only real narrative punch—but at least it is reserved for where it really counts.

The film's musical milieu calls for a particularly strong music score, and, depending on who one asks, British rock legend Keith Emerson either delivers the good or cripples the film at the starting gate. The popular musician, best known for his work with the progressive rock trio Emerson, Lake and Palmer, had been hired by Dario Argento to score *Inferno* (1980), and he made a very good job of that assignment. However, here he was hired to provide a kitschy sort of soundtrack, which was designed to fit into the breakdancing craze spearheaded by the success of Adrian Lyne's *Flashdance* (1983). The film's similarities to that popular piece of schmaltz led to its being referred to as *Slashdance* in some areas. In any event, the breakdancing scenes are mercifully few and far between, but Emerson's songs are bound to inspire a mixture of groans and derision. His more conventional suspense cues are more in keeping with the genre and its codes, but for many viewers, the presence of songs like "Tonight is the Night" and "Are the Streets to Blame" are hard to forgive, let alone overlook. Fulci would later dismiss the score, while Emerson does not recall meeting with him for the project. In any event, the score is certainly distinctive—and it seems very much part and parcel of the film's offbeat, slightly goofy appeal.

Olga Karlatos gives a rather flat performance as the beleaguered Candice. Candice is the film's nominal heroine, but she is an ambiguous presence and could have been a rather interesting figure if Karlatos had been up to the demands of the role. Unfortunately, her weak performance puts the film on an uneven keel. Born Olga Vlassopulos in Athens in 1947, she changed her name to Karlatos and began acting in Italian films in the mid-1960s. Her beautiful looks went a long way toward getting her roles, but she was seldom more than adequate in her acting. She appeared in Enzo G. Castellari's superior Spaghetti Western *Keoma* (1976) before first working with Fulci on *Zombie*. She would go on to play a very small role in Sergio Leone's final masterpiece, *Once Upon a Time in America* (1984), and snagged her biggest mainstream role, playing the mother (!) of rocker Prince in his vanity project *Purple Rain* (1984). She retired from films in the mid-1980s. Ray Lovelock puts in a good performance as George Webb; he is established early on as a threat by virtue of his presence

**French lobby card: The murderer strikes again.**

in Candice's dreams, but this, of course, is misdirection. Lovelock is very good at conveying the character's ambivalent moral stance and he ultimately becomes a sympathetic presence. Lovelock was born Rome in 1950. He initially pursued a career in music before landing a small role in Guilio Questi's surreal Spaghetti Westerm *Django Kill!* (1966), costarring his good friend (and sometime musical associate) Tomas Milian. Lovelock would make a number of films with Milian, including Carlo Lizzani's *Bandits in Milan* (1968) and Umberto Lenzi's *Almost Human* (1974), and he also landed a supporting role in the hit musical *Fiddler on the Roof* (1971), directed by Norman Jewison. His other credits include Jorge Grau's superior zombie film *Let Sleeping Corpses Lie* (1974) and Ruggero Deodato's violent *polizziotesco Live Like a Cop, Die Like a Man* (1976); *Murder-Rock: Dancing Death* would remain his only film with Fulci. Claudio Cassinelli follows up his appearance in *Rome, 2072 A.D.: The New Gladiators* with a red herring role as Dick Gibson, who is clearly infatuated with Candice; he is very good in the role, and one regrets that he did not work more often with Fulci. A number of Fulci veterans pop up

**Some aerobic action in *Murder-Rock: Dancing Death.***

in small (sometimes uncredited) roles: Silvia Collatina, Al Cliver and Giovanni De Nava. However, Cosimo Cinieri makes the best impression as Inspector Borges; the character name, no doubt, was a tip of the hat to the great Argentine writer Jorge Luis Borges, the father of so-called "magical realism" in literature. Cinieri's offbeat performance gives the film a much-needed injection of humor and humanity, and he effortlessly steals the film from his costars. Borges is certainly the best of his roles for Fulci, allowing him to move on from his collaborations with the director on a high note. He remains active in Italian films and television; he recently played the writer Alberto Moravia in Federico Bruno's docudrama *Pasolini, la verità nascosta* (2013).

*Murder-Rock: Danicing Death* marks the end of Fulci's long working relationship with assistant director Roberto Giandalia; Giandalia had begun working with Fulci as a continuity person on *Beatrice Cenci* (a role he reprised on *Silver Saddle*), before moving on to the role of script supervisor on such films as *A Lizard in a Woman's Skin, Don't Torture a Duckling, Challenge to White Fang* and *Four of the Apocalypse* and then graduating to assistant director on *La Pretora.* Giandalia would assist Fulci on pretty much all of his late '70s/early '80s pictures, but he would eventually be replaced by Fulci's daughter Camilla, who would gradually work her way up to becoming her father's assistant on later films. The film also sees the end of the long and fruitful screenwriting collaboration between Fulci and Roberto Gianviti. Having already parted ways—on less than amicable terms with Dardano Sacchetti—the loss of Gianviti would prove doubly unfortunate. The two men had worked harmoniously on some of the director's best works, and Gianviti, like Sacchetti, seemed especially capable of bringing out the fiery best in Fulci's cinema. *Murder-Rock: Dancing Death* is not one of their more successful screenplay collaborations, perhaps, but it nevertheless displays a solid structure and a penchant for logic which marks Fulci's *giallo* work in general. Gianviti would only work on a handful of other films before his death in 2001.

Sadly, *Murder-Rock: Dancing Death* would also mark the end of Fulci's association with the *giallo.* He is seldom lionized in the same way as Dario Argento, but he definitely should be. His *gialli* are remarkably well done on the whole, and if this one marks a weak finale to his career in the genre, it still stands head and shoulders above much of the genre's subsequent output.

Notes:

1. Palmerini, Luca M. and Gaetano Mistretta, *Spaghetti Nightmares* (Florida: Fantasma Books, 1996), p. 62.
2. Quotes from Giuseppe Pinori are pulled from the audio commentary he recorded with Federico Caddeo for the Shriek Show DVD release of *Murder-Rock: Dancing Death.*
3. Palmerini, Luca M. and Gaetano Mistretta, *Spaghetti Nightmares* (Florida: Fantasma Books, 1996), p. 62.

# Ray Lovelock Interview by Troy Howarth

The following interview with actor Ray Lovelock was conducted via email on September 8, 2014. In addition to appearing in many popular Italian genre films, Mr. Lovelock is an experienced singer and musician. He only worked with Lucio Fulci once, but he had fond memories of the experience. Mr. Lovelock has my gratitude for taking the time to remember his experiences in working with Fulci.

**Troy Howarth**: What made you want to become an actor?
**Ray Lovelock**: I became an actor by chance; my dream was to become a professional soccer player.
**TH**: One of your earliest screen credits was the Spaghetti Western *Django Kill!* directed by Giulio Questi. What do you remember of the film?
**RL**: In that movie I had my first small speaking role. The meeting with Tomas Milian was important, because the year after we made up a musical group to play at the Piper club in Rome, where a well-known agent noticed me and asked me if I wanted to try to become a professional actor. I answered, "Why not?" So I took part in Carlo Lizzani's *Bandits in Milan,* and that was the very beginning of my career.
**TH**: You mentioned wanting to be a professional soccer player ... why did you not pursue that career?
**RL**: After the success of Carlo Lizzani's *Bandits in Milan,* they convinced me to go on a movie career.

**TH**: In the 1970s, you appeared in many popular genre films, including *Let Sleeping Corpses Lie*, directed by Jorge Grau, and *Live Like a Cop, Die Like a Man*, directed by Ruggero Deodato ... What was the Italian film scene like at that time?
**RL**: In that period, *giallo* and *poliziotteschi* actors worked a lot in Italy.
**TH**: You appeared in quite a few *gialli* and horrors ... are you a fan of the genre?
**RL**: I'm not that much of a fan of horror movies, but I loved to make them.
**TH**: You are also an accomplished musician, and your songs can be heard on the soundtrack of Tonino Cervi's *Queens of Evil*, among other films ... do you prefer acting or doing music?
**RL**: Music is my hobby, acting my job. But it's been very rewarding when I had the opportunity to do both.
**TH**: How did you come to be cast in Lucio Fulci's *Murder Rock*?
**RL**: Fulci and the producer called my agent for a meeting, and they offered me the role.
**TH**: Were you familiar with Fulci's work prior to being cast in the film?
**RL**: I was familiar with his films, but I didn't know Lucio personally.
**TH**: What was Fulci like as a person and as a director?
**RL**: I didn't have any kind of problems with him, as a person or as a director.
**TH**: Can you remember any favorite incidents from the filming?
**RL**: Fortunately, I had a nice feeling with all my collaborators, including Lucio.
**TH**: Did you keep in touch with Fulci after the filming was completed?
**RL**: No. However, we met again a few years later, when we both went to receive a festival prize.
**TH**: Do you recall what festival or event that was?
**RL**: I just remember it was in Fabriano (Marche, Italy), and that Lucio Fulci, composer Pino Donaggio and I were honored.
**TH**: Do you have any favorites among the films you have made?
**RL**: For different reasons *Bandits in Milan*, *The Fiddler on the Roof*, *Cassandra Crossing* and the *poliziotteschi* films. But also several movies I made for Italian television.
**TH**: And lastly, are you surprised by the enduring popularity of Fulci and his films? Would you describe your experience with him as positive?
**RL**: Not at all. But I'm a little bit surprised that his popularity in Italy is not like in some other countries. It was a positive experience working with him.
**TH**: Do you think Fulci will ever become better appreciated in Italy?
**RL**: As it so often happens, I'm sure that little by little he will be more popular in his own country.
**TH**: Mr. Lovelock, thank you for your time!
**RL**: Good luck with your book!

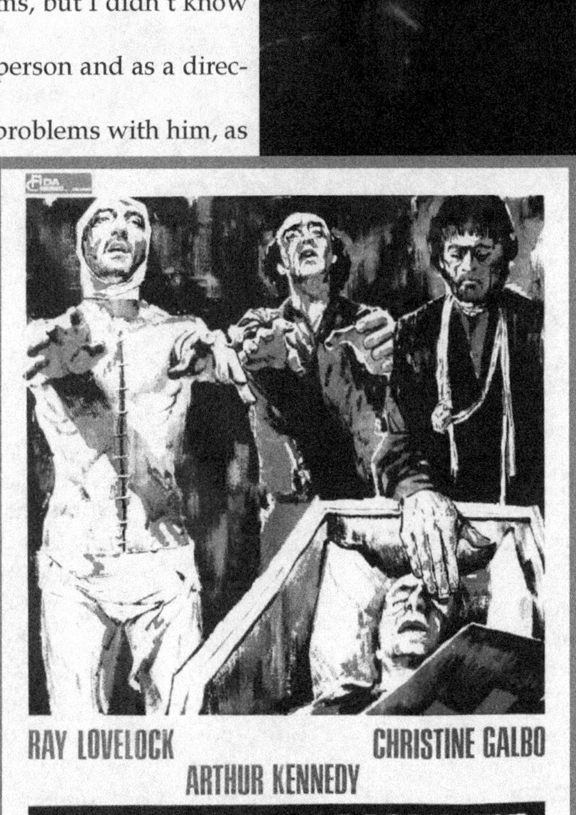


**Above: Ray Lovelock in *Murder-Rock: Dancing Death*.**
**Left: Italian poster for Jorge Grau's *Let Sleeping Corpses Lie* (1974); artist unknown.**

# Geretta Geretta Interview by Troy Howarth

The following interview with actress Geretta Geretta was conducted via email on November 3, 2014. Geretta was born in Portland, Oregon, and got her start acting on stage before making her way to Italy in the 1980s; while there, she worked in a number of cult genre titles, including *Murder-Rock: Dancing Death*, in which she plays the role of Margie. Geretta has my sincere thanks for taking the time to talk about her career in Italian horror and for sharing her memories of working with Lucio Fulci.

**Geretta Geretta (right) in *Murder-Rock: Dancing Death*.**

**Troy Howarth**: How did you come to be cast in *Murder-Rock*?

**Geretta Geretta**: My then-agent, the late Fernando Piazza, who was basically the talent agent to all foreign actors in Rome at that time, sent me over for an interview. In Rome you really didn't audition in the sense of, go in with a monologue, or even read from their script. They just looked at you, talked to you and then—based on what they thought of your photo—you were cast.

**TH**: What were your initial impressions of Lucio Fulci?

**GG**: He seemed straightforward and nice. Of course, he had a reputation even then of being ferocious if crossed, which I had no intention of doing, so it was great.

**TH**: Were you familiar with Fulci's films prior to being cast?

**GG**: No, not at all. Nor did I know he was already a legend in his field.

**TH**: Fulci had a reputation for being tough on actors; did you find this to be the case?

**GG**: Yes, he ripped one of the young male actors a new anus when he questioned Lucio's directions during a certain scene. My agent warned me, so I kept my mouth shut. And I mean, *tight*. The whole shoot!

**TH**: Approximately how long did you film on the movie?

**GG**: I don't really remember, but I doubt it was more than five days.

**TH**: Do you have any memories of your costars, like Olga Karlatos, Ray Lovelock, Cosimo Cinieri or Claudio Cassinelli?

**GG**: Most of my scenes were with Olga. She was very famous then, and was well respected. It was the first time I witnessed an actor getting applause from the crew after a good take. I was awestruck. I said to myself, "Damn, I want that to happen to me one day."

**TH**: When did you first see the finished film, and what did you think of it?

**GG**: I don't think I ever did while I was still in Italy. They barely would tell us release dates back then—and if you weren't the lead, you weren't even invited. I was a costar, but not a lead. So there ya go.

I do recall that I knew my days in Italy were about to come to an end, so I wanted to be in a film with my hair in its natural form, so that's why it's so different from *Demons*, and decidedly different from my big '80s 'do in *Rats: Night of Terror*!

**TH**: What do you think of the cult that exists around these films?

**GG**: *Is* there one?

**TH**: Did you keep in contact with Fulci after the filming?

**GG**: You mean, like, go to his house for dinner? No, of course not. But actually I did go to his house once, and I can't remember for what. I can see it—the room we were talking in—in my mind. But I don't know what we were talking about.

You know, everyone speaks of his *bad temper*. But on set, during one particular take, we were all looking for an "end line" for a scene between Olga and me, and I sort of did a "Black Girl double take" and rolled my eyes, and then I said, *"Well!"* Fulci burst out laughing and said,

Geretta Geretta in Lamberto Bava's *Demons* (1985).

"What is this? Melodrama has been out since the 1800s!" Then he found another solution. Everyone laughed!

**TH**: How do you think Fulci compared with other Italian horror directors like Lamberto Bava, with whom you made *Demons*, or Bruno Mattei, with whom you made *Rats: Night of Terror*?

**GG**: Gee, that's tough ... Ah, for me, I'd say in order: Bava, Fulci, Mattei, but let's let the young'uns fight it out!

**TH**: Are your proud of your association with these Italian genre films?

**GG**: Like, duh ... Of course! What's *not* to be proud of? This is a bit of cinema history, and I'm not sure on this, but I think I am the only person who worked with *all* of the "big five": Argento, Bava, Fulci, Mattei and Massaccesi. You can add Soavi, too, or, shit, for that matter you can add Dino Risi, who was not known for horror but who was definitely a "big gun," and I worked with him, too, on a film called *Good King Dagobert* (1984) with Coluche! And Michele Soavi and I, like, grew up in cinema together: He was something like the third assistant director on *2020 Texas Gladiators* (1982, directed by Massaccesi) and was the man in the mask and first assistant director on *Demons* in less than a few years. Impressive! Now of course, he's a big director in his own right.

**TH**: Geretta, thank you for taking the time to answer these questions!

**GG**: Anytime!

# 1986

## *The Devil's Honey (Spain/Italy)*

Aka *Il miele del diavolo; Dangerous Obsession; La miel del diablo; Le miel du diable; Dämon in Seide*

Directed by Lucio Fulci; Produced by Franco Casati, Sergio Martinelli and Vincenzo Salviani, for Producciones Cinematográficas Balcázar and Selvaggia Film; Story and Screenplay by Jaime Jesús Balcázar, Lucio Fulci, Ludovica Marineo and Vincenzo Salviani, with additional dialogue by Sergio Partou; Director of Photography Alejando Ulloa (as Alessandra Ulloa); Editor: Vincenzo Tomassi; Music by Claudio Natili

Main Players: Brett Halsey (Dr. Wendell Simpson); Blanca Marsillach (Jessica); Corinne Cléry (Carol Simpson); Stefano Madia (Johnny); Bernard Seray (Nicky); Paula Molina (Sandra)

Cameo appearance: Lucio Fulci (Bracelet vendor)

*Jessica and Johnny enjoy a passionate relationship. When Johnny is injured in a motorcycle accident, he is taken to Dr. Simpson for an emergency surgery. Simpson is distracted by his own marital woes, and Johnny dies on the operating table. A vengeful Jessica blames Simpson for Johnny's death and begins persecuting him. Then, she kidnaps the doctor and takes him to her cottage, where she tortures him sexually ...*

Following the completion of *Murder-Rock: Dancing Death*, Fulci's health started to deteriorate. A bout of hepatitis developed into cirrhosis of the liver, and the director found himself bedridden and unable to work. In 1985, he contributed to the screenplay for *The Trap*, but plans for him to direct were scuttled by his ongoing health woes. Finally, he was given the opportunity to get back to work when he was offered a screenplay developed by Ludovica Marineo. The subject matter of sexual revenge bore a certain similarity to the plot of *The Trap*, in fact, and the similarities were surely not lost on Fulci. As he would later explain:

***The Devil's Honey*; original artwork by Scott Hoffman.**

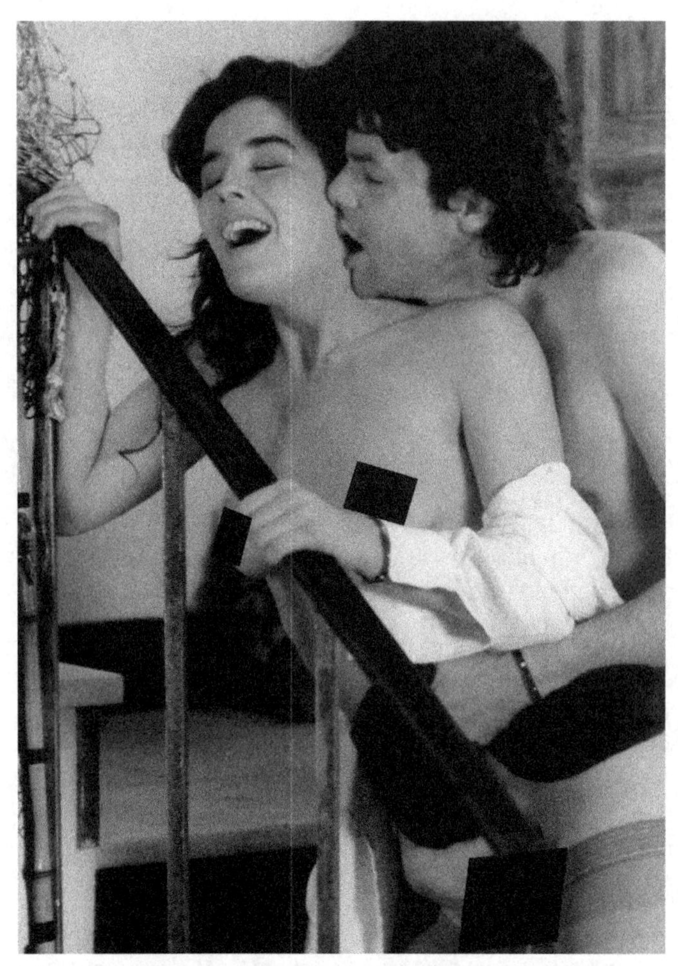

***The Devil's Honey*: Johnny (Stefano Madia) sodomizes an unwilling Jessica (Bianca Marsillach) in the name of love; squeamish distributors elected to censor Marsillach's nipples in this shot.**

> When they offered me *The Devil's Honey*, I considered myself fortunate, even though it meant starting up again on the wrong foot, because, as I pointed out before, rather than being a porno film, it was a desperate "survival" film.[1]

Fulci's implication is that the film was one he undertook out of financial necessity, but he approached the film with energy and vigor. In the same interview, he commented that:

> I tried to make a movie about the misery of sadomasochism, but nobody understood it, though it came out better than the budget should have permitted. I was fairly desperate when I made that film, recovering as I was from an illness which most thought would have seen me off—viral hepatitis, which then became cirrhosis.[2]

His emphasis on the film's sense of melancholy is right on target; in the same way that *Contraband* didn't hew to the usual formula of "fun" violence and brutality in the *poliziottesco* format, *The Devil's Honey* offers up one of the saddest kinky sex films in recent memory.

Fulci establishes the dramatic conflict neatly and economically in the opening scenes. As the opening titles play out to Claudio Natili's sexy jazz score, Fulci treats the audience to a bit of pure cinema as the romantic triangle between Johnny, Jessica and their friend Nicky is established without a word of dialogue. Johnny is a musician recording his first record, while his girlfriend Jessica looks on adoringly; sound technician Nicky is also somehow involved in the mix. As Johnny plays the saxophone, he looks on lustfully at Jessica; she reciprocates, albeit somewhat sheepishly. Fulci then introduces a surprising touch of homoeroticism as Johnny's gaze is met by Nicky, and their eyes also lock. Clearly, there is more going on here than meets the eye, but within the space of a few minutes of footage, Fulci cleverly sets up a major dramatic conflict that will be teased throughout the narrative. Once the recording session is finished, Johnny and Jessica start to make out; Nicky, jealous but not wanting to tip his hand, suggests that they take a 10-minute break and leaves the studio. Johnny takes advantage of the solitude by suggesting a quickie; Jessica is reluctant, and would rather wait until they get home. Johnny is clearly not accustomed to being told "no," and reacts petulantly. Picking up his saxophone, he deliberately places it below Jessica's crotch and begins to play a bit of seductive jazz; the vibrations cause Jessica to get all hot-and-bothered, and an amused Nicky comes back in time to see the tail-end of the action.

From there, Fulci introduces Dr. Wendell Simpson—a seemingly respectable surgeon who is soon revealed to have a kinky streak of his own. He frequents prostitutes, using them to satiate his sexual urges, but his treatment of his long-suffering wife Carol is curiously distant and antiseptic. Like so many chauvinists, Simpson expects his wife to convey the right image of conservative purity, and, as such, she does not excite him sexually; instead, he turns to whores to get his jollies, and his treatment of them underlines his contemptuous attitude. Simpson is not depicted entirely unsympathetically, but there's little doubt that Fulci finds more to like in Carol; she is an attractive woman and she still cares for her husband, but she is determined not to allow him to treat her like a doormat, either. Simpson is a hypocrite, whereas Carol is honest and direct.

The two narrative strands ultimately collide when Johnny is badly injured while horsing around on his motorcycle, trying to endear himself to Jessica for some easy sex. Simpson comes into surgery distracted because he has just been told by Carol that she is leaving him; their attempt at reconciliation has gone poorly and she sees the writing on the wall: The marriage is over, and it's time for her to save her dignity by moving on. Whether it is negligence on Simpson's part or simply a question of Johnny's head injuries being too serious is never openly addressed:

In Jessica's mind, Simpson failed in his duty as a "healer," and she is not about to let him forget it. From there, she begins tormenting him with harassing phone calls and letters, before ultimately taking things to the next level by surprising the doctor in his car and chloroforming him. Once she has Simpson in her secluded cottage, she proceeds to dehumanize him; putting him in a dog collar, tying him to a wall, forcing him to look on at her as she parades around in the nude, scaring him so badly that he pisses his pants, and so forth. The two develop a kinky bond based in a feeling of mutual loss: Simpson's inability to process the loss of his wife, coupled with his difficulties in establishing normal intimate relationships, makes him emotionally vulnerable, while the loss of Johnny coupled with the growing realization that he basically only used her for sex puts Jessica in a very delicate emotional state as well. The film ends with Jessica releasing Simpson from his chains, but sooner than leave, the doctor comes to her and they have sex; as they lie in bed and contemplate their uncertain futures, Fulci pans away to reveal the gun Jessica used while abducting the doctor. As Fulci later explained:

> At the end of the movie you can see a gun in the corner of the room; it means that for me those couples always end up in blood. There's no future for these people."[3]

Fulci had toyed with eroticism as far back as *Le massaggiatrici*, but sex was never really a central concern in his work. Certainly there were flashes of eroticism to be found in the likes of *A Lizard in a Woman's Skin* (Carol's sapphic dream sequences) or the sexy-comedy antics of *The Eroticist* and *Young Dracula*, but prior to *The Devil's Honey* only *The New York Ripper* displayed Fulci's willingness to go for the out-and-out kinky. *The Devil's Honey* ups the ante by virtue of the fact that the eroticism is at the forefront of the narrative, but there is a definite kinship between this film and *The New York Ripper*: The sex in these films is curiously joyous. The reason for this is simple: No matter how hard the characters try to spice the act up with kinky fetish tropes, they are essentially disconnected from one another on an emotional level. This is evident in almost every relationship in *The Devil's Honey*. Jessica and Johnny appear to be ideally suited for one another: They are young, attractive and living high on the excesses of their relationship. But for Johnny, "love" is simply another word for sex. At one point, Jessica cuts him off and says, "You don't love me. You love a *piece* of me." How right she is. In Johnny's emotionally stunted mind, Jessica is little more than a repository for his lurid masturbatory fantasies. He pushes her towards kinky excess, even though she is not comfortable in doing so. He compels her to masturbate him while he's speeding down the highway on his motorcycle, then pressures her into having anal sex—he ignores her protestations that she's not enjoying it, imploring her to let him finish. Sex, for Johnny, is not something to be mutually savored and enjoyed; it's simply a means for him to get his rocks off, pure and simple. Jessica has much more depth of feeling and truly loves Johnny, but her love blinds her to his shortcomings. She confronts Johnny at different points and tries to get him to be genuine with her, but his tunnel vision is always focused on the next lay. The character of Nicky complicates things even further. Late in the film, Fulci confirms what the opening scene hints at; the three friends go to see a movie together, and while Johnny makes out with Jessica, he has Nicky go down on him; when Jessica realizes what is going on, she is aghast. Fulci's point here is not to criticize homosexuality—indeed, in Johnny's case, it doesn't seem accurate to describe him as gay or bisexual: He's *hypersexual*, and, to be blunt, any orifice will do. Nicky is just barely closeted and has a beard in the form of a girl who dotes on him, but he, too, is clearly head over heels for Johnny; unfortunately for him, Johnny isn't interested in anything other than sex. Johnny is pure surface, and his selfishness has a negative impact on the people around him. One of the

**Spanish lobby card: Jessica kidnaps Dr. Simspon and humiliates him sexually.**

**Spanish lobby card: Jessica torments Dr. Simspon.**

film's most striking moments occurs very late in the film, when Jessica is having a flashback to one of their kinky encounters in the bedroom: Johnny thinks it would be fun to photograph Jessica in the nude, with a gun tucked between her legs. She is appalled and lashes out: "Even you weren't like that," she says. "What do you mean?" replies Johnny. Jessica is at a loss for words for a moment. The implication is that Jessica is finally coming to grips with the reality that Johnny was not the man she wanted him to be; in her mind, she is beginning to twist his behavior into something even more lurid and monstrous than he really was. This epiphany allows her to finally let go of the hatred she feels for Simpson. Simpson, of course, is emotionally stunted in his own way: He is all about surface appearance. He and his wife live in a very posh house, they belong to the swankiest country club, they drive an expensive car. As the story unfolds, the surface symbols that are so vital to his existence are gradually stripped away: His wife leaves him, his immaculate clothes are reduced to tattered rags and Jessica even demolishes his car with an axe. Simpson's well-ordered universe does not allow for a genuine sense of being emotionally connected to his wife, Carol, and she rebels by leaving him. Simpson takes the loss hard, but it's entirely possible that he's responding as much to a bruised ego as he is to a genuine sense of remorse. Interestingly, the only real emotional connection happens between him and Jessica. At the end of the film, he is given the opportunity to flee from his captor, but he elects to stay; not only that, he makes love to her willingly, despite—or because of—the many humiliations she has subjected him to. Theirs is not a relationship that will end well—Fulci's final close-up of the gun confirms as much—but for a little while, at least, they are open to each other and communicate like real human beings; a small bit of warmth finally invades what is otherwise a deliberately cold and somber milieu.

*The Devil's Honey* is Fulci's kinkiest film, and it is also one of his most disarming. Viewers going into the film expecting another overheated rip-off of Adrian Lyne's *9½ Weeks* (1986) will surely be disappointed. Far from being Fulci's foray into Zalman King (of *Red Shoe Diaries* infamy) territory, the film continues the melancholy dialogue from his earlier works on man's inability to communicate or empathize with his fellow man. This theme is evident in the many bigoted and violent characters who lash out at the "outsider" figures in movies like *Don't Torture a Duckling* and *City of the Living Dead*, as well as in the symbolic family units of *Four of the Apocalypse*, which are torn apart by the harsh and uncompromising worlds in which they live. Fulci generates sufficient "heat" in the film's various erotic encounters, but he never loses sight of the characters and their feelings. Johnny may lose himself in ecstasy when he is virtually raping Jessica on the staircase, for example, but her reactions make it clear that she is not enjoying herself; her inability to extricate herself from the situation is born out of her misguided love. The sex scenes are kinky and push the envelope in a surprising way, but as Fulci was always careful to emphasize when the topic of the film arose, it never deteriorates into out-and-out porno territory. Fulci's flair for this sort of kinky material stands in stark contrast to the more mechanical and superficial approach common in harder sex films. In his final interview, Fulci would recall his friend and colleague Aristide Massaccesi, a brilliant cinematographer who turned to directing and would later helm many hardcore sex films, often under the name Joe D'Amato:

> It's funny that he directs porno, because women are all the same to him—he is not a noticeably romantic person. He stands over the actors in the sex scenes and just yells, "Fuck fuck fuck fuck!"[4]

Despite the longstanding accusations of misogyny that continue to dog Fulci's legacy, *The Devil's Honey* is just one of many films which makes nonsense of this critique: The characters of Jessica and Carol are painted in a very sympathetic light, while their male counterparts do not come off nearly as well. On top of that, Fulci's ability to create a genuine sense of eroticism in the various kinky encounters points to his ability to convey intimacy on the screen—not just in the sense of an actor and an actress simulating intercourse, but in the way they appear to connect (or not!) in the course of the scene. For these reasons, among many others, *The Devil's Honey* remains one of the director's most striking and underappreciated movies.

The film has a small but very well chosen ensemble. As Dr. Simpson, Brett Halsey makes the first of three official (with one unofficial title thrown in for "good" measure) collaborations with Fulci. He gives an excellent performance in a tricky role; he embraces the character's flaws and does not attempt to make excuses for them. Simpson is a hypocrite, and he pretty much deserves what happens to him, but Halsey's innate likability helps to keep the character interesting. Born in California in 1933 as Charles

Oliver Hand, he secured a contract with Universal-International Pictures in the 1950s following a stint in the Navy. Changing his name to Brett Halsey—the surname was "borrowed" from his famous uncle, Admiral William F. "Bull" Halsey (1882-1959)—he appeared in everything from *Ma and Pa Kettle at Home* (1954) to *The Revenge of the Creature* (1955) before departing to try his luck away from Universal. He appeared opposite Vincent Price in *Return of the Fly* (1959) and eventually made his way to Italy, working for such directors as Riccardo Freda (*The Magnificent Adventurer*, 1963) and Mario Bava (*Four Times That Night*, 1969). In addition to being a prolific actor, Halsey is an accomplished novelist and has also dabbled in screenwriting. Following *The Devil's Honey*, Halsey would reunite with Fulci on *Touch of Death* and *Demonia*; Fulci would also smuggle him into *Nightmare Concert (A Cat in the Brain)*, but more on that later. Halsey later recalled his first meeting with Fulci:

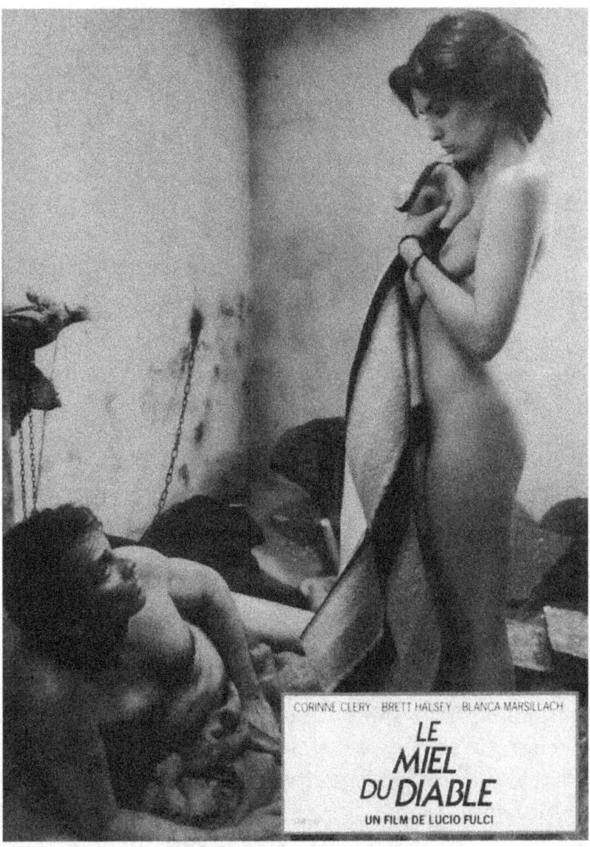


**Spanish lobby card.**

> My first film with Fulci was in 1986, called *The Devil's Honey*. We shot it in Spain. I met him there. He was ill … had been very ill, but it didn't affect his energy in shooting. He was a very nice, kind man if he liked you; he had little patience for incompetence. I remember many times he would come to work raving and yelling in the morning. He would go down a line of people, seemingly angry, and got to me and he'd smile and say, "Hi Brett!" Then he would go on and resume his tirade. He had a good sense of humor. He loved to laugh.

Corinne Cléry, who creates a vivid impression in relatively little screen time, plays Halsey's screen wife. Far from being the martyred spouse who suffers in silence, Carol is an outspoken and independent woman who finally decides to end the marriage when she gets proof of her husband's infidelities; the scene in which she tries to recapture his love by encouraging him to treat her like one of his hookers, only to be rejected when the phone rings and breaks his concentration, is heartbreaking. Cléry is so effective in the role, one wishes that she could have had more to do in the picture. Cléry was born in Paris in 1950 and made her film debut in 1967. She first attracted international recognition with her role in Just Jaeckin's popular slice of erotica, *The Story of O* (1975), and she would go on to provide ample sex appeal in everything from the gritty borderline *giallo Hitch Hike* (1977) to the James Bond adventure *Moonraker* (1979). Blanca Marsillach, who also played a significant role in the aforementioned *The Trap*, played Jessica. Fulci was presumably impressed by her performance in that film and cast her here for that reason. She and Halsey are very good in their scenes together, which is remarkable when one considers how strained their relationship was on set; Halsey goes into some detail on this issue in the interview included after this critique. Born in Barcelona in 1966, Marsillach started appearing in films in the mid-1980s; *The Devil's Honey* is arguably her best screen role, though she remained sporadically active in Spanish films until the early 2000s. She has also worked as a producer in recent years. Stefano Madia played Johnny. Madia is very good in the role and really taps into the character's moral ambivalence; he isn't particularly likable, nor should he be. Madia was born in Rome in 1954 and made an auspicious big screen debut as Vittorio Gassman's son in Dino Risi's *Caro papà* (1979); Madia won Best Supporting Actor at the Cannes Film Festival for his performance. He remained active until his tragically premature demise in 2004, at the age of 49.

*The Devil's Honey* is seldom enthused over in the same way as Fulci's *gialli* and horror films are, and this is indeed a pity. It manages to work as a piece of exploitation erotica, but its darker, more serious undercurrent marks it out as something more than the "survival" movie Fulci later dismissed it as. Unfortunately for the director, he was not out of the woods just yet; he would continue to be dogged by health problems, and his work would begin to suffer accordingly.

Notes:
1. Palmerini, Luca M. and Gaetano Mistretta, *Spaghetti Nightmares*, (Key West: Fantasma Books, 1996), p. 63.
2. *Ibid*, p. 62.
3. Retrieved from, http://www.shockingimages.com/fulci/interview.html
4. Berger, Howard, "The Prince of Italian Terror," *Fangoria*, #154, July 1997, p.82.

# Brett Halsey
## Interview by Steve Fenton and Dennis Capicik

The following interview with Brett Halsey was conducted by Steve Fenton and Dennis Capicik at Mr. Halsey's residence in Toronto on Sunday, April 30, 1995 and was originally published in the British fanzine *Giallo Pages* (Volume 1, Procrustes Press, 1999; edited by John Martin). It is reprinted here with the interviewers' permission. Brett composed a brand-new foreword for this book, but this rare interview provides an excellent insight into his relationship with Fulci, as well as many of the other significant cult filmmakers he has worked with.

**Steve Fenton and Dennis Capicik**: It must have taken a lot of balls to go to Europe in search of success.

**Brett Halsey**: Well, not really. I was doing this American TV series, *Follow the Sun* (1961-1962), and Riccardo Freda had offered me a film, and I couldn't do it. The day the series was dropped, another offer had come from Freda, so I went over and did the picture. Then I went back to Hollywood and did another picture there, and while I was working in Hollywood I got another offer to do six pictures.

**SF/DC**: What are the main differences between working in Hollywood and in Europe?

**BH**: Language is a problem. I remember my first picture there, *The Seventh Sword* (1962) ... I didn't know any Italian then. And one of the first scenes I had, there were five actors in the scene, each one acting in his own language: *five* different languages *[Italian, Spanish, French, German and English]*. So you had to learn ... what you do is, when you learn your lines, you'd learn everyone else's lines as well. In the beginning, I would count: he talks, he talks, he talks, I talk, he talks, I talk, he talks, he talks, I talk.

**SF/DC**: It was just another thing to cope with.

**BH**: Yeah! It was difficult. It took a while to get used to. European actors were used to it. I remember once, Wayde *[Preston]* and I were in a scene. We finished the scene, and we just kept talking. The director didn't speak English. Finally it got to the point where we said, "Y'know, if he doesn't say cut pretty soon, they're probably gonna run out of film!" The director, he didn't know we were finished, because he didn't know we were finished, because he didn't understand what we were saying. Finally, he said, "Are you finished?" in Italian. We said, "Oh yeah, we finished a long time ago" ... "Oh—*cut!*" It was okay, he could just cut the tail off it; we'd played the scene. That passed very quickly, those barriers, if you got used to the system. The hardest thing with language in the early days was when they weren't recording direct sound, so there's all these other noises, and American actors aren't used to that. Many, many, many times there'd be conversations going on, and I'd stop. I'd say, "Who we gonna listen to? We gonna listen to *them*, or we gonna listen to *me*? But I'm not gonna keep talking as long as they talk." Often they would think I was being difficult; I just wasn't used to it.

**Brett Halsey was required to get intimate with Bianca Marsillach in *The Devil's Honey*, but according to him it was no walk in the park.**

**SF/DC**: All your later films were done with direct sound, weren't they?

**BH**: Pretty much, but still there was lots of looping.

**SF/DC**: In *The Black Cat* (1989), for example ... that's not your real voice they used. Clearly you're speaking English, but it's not your voice. That's why I thought they don't still shoot direct sound. Maybe you weren't available for dubbing at the time?

**BH**: It wasn't my voice? May be not. I don't remember whether I had or had not done it. If there's a problem, like getting a microphone placed, they say, "Aww, to hell with it! We'll fix it in the dubbing." They do a lot of that in Hollywood anyway. But the reverse of this was when I came back to Hollywood after almost 10 years over there. My first job was in *Alias Smith and Jones*, the Western TV series. We'd start the scene, and something was wrong; I stopped. The director said, "What's wrong?" I said, "I don't know ..." After the second time, I realized: I couldn't hear the camera! In Italy they don't cover the camera for sound, most of the time. So, when I couldn't hear that camera going *"brrrrrrr,"* I thought something was wrong. Because we could be acting sometimes and you could hear the camera motor running, and sometimes the motor would slow down or speed up, and you could hear a variation in the sound. Well, I stopped because I thought that something was wrong with the camera; it was strange to act without that camera noise ...

I never got used to working with a lot of noise. People talking means they aren't paying attention. When the actors are acting, when the camera's on, that should be everyone's focus. When the camera's stopped, then other things can go on. It only bothered me depending on what I was playing. If I was playing something that took concentration, thinking about what I was saying, then I didn't want any noise. Camera noise was something else, because that was there; it was just there. Like you have five fingers, you don't need six. It was *there*.

**SF/DC**: Like Freda's howling mutts on *The Magnificent Adventurer* (1963)?

**BH**: Oh yeah. I used that in my novel. These dogs would howl: *"Oooo-oooooh!"* Then, you'd complain about it, but those are *Freda's* dogs. No, you can't complain, it'd be like sending his *wife* away or something! His wife was Gianna Maria Canale *[star of her husband's* I vampiri, *1957]*; he was married to her for a long time. He was divorced though before we worked together. She was very nice. But by this time they were already divorced, and I don't think he was married to his present wife, but they were living together. I saw them last year.

**SF/DC**: The last movie he directed was in 1980 *[Murder Obsession]*...

**BH**: Well, he said he wants to direct another movie. He said he's in preparation. That's *bullshit*! Billy Wilder's the same way ... Freda was interested in the mechanics of moviemaking. He liked, I think, setting up shots. I remember once—I don't remember which picture—but he didn't like shooting close-ups. So we'd get to the end of the picture and spend two days shooting close-ups: change costumes ... against the sky ... against the wall. He liked the big picture, the panorama. He'd shoot beautiful masters, but for the close-ups: "Aww, do it later." Unless he really had to, I mean, if he needed something. But if it was a neutral background: "What the hell; shoot it *later*!" I remember, at the end of the picture we had two days of close-ups. Never mind costumes, how about just remembering what you *did*?! Then, continuity ... I remember when doing *Godfather III* (1990), there was an argument about continuity, and I heard [Francis] Coppola say, "Continuity is the hobgoblin of small minds." He said it to the script girl or something: "It just doesn't matter" ... *I* think it matters!

**Halsey reunited with Freda for *The Magnificent Adventurer* (1963); artist unknown.**

**SF/DC**: Gianna Maria Canale costarred with you in *The Avenger of Venice* (*La ponte di sosperi*/*The Bridge of Sighs*, 1964), which was shot in Venice. How did that shoot go?

**BH**: Venice is like a broken toilet! A friend of mine—Burt Nelson—was playing the "heavy." And it was late, it was just before Christmas, late at night, about two or three o'clock in the morning. We had this dueling scene in this wharf in Venice. [Carlo] Campogalliani was the director, I think. And this scene—we had a swordfight, and I didn't wanna kill him because he becomes my pal later. So, my cape somehow is on the ground, and he steps on it, I pull the cape and he trips and falls into the canal. And I was kidding him all the time. I said, "Burt, you dumb son-of-a-bitch, you should never have been a character actor, you shoulda been a *star*. You shoulda been a leading man, like me! Leading men never go into the water; it's only assholes like you who go in the water!" I'm kidding him like this all the time. And then ... they only had one costume, the costume people had forgotten. So, if he went in and if they didn't get it, he'd have to do it again with a wet costume. And it was *cold*! So, we start the scene and get all to the point where he goes in the water, and the cameraman says, *"STOP!* Stop! Stop!"—in the water, this bloated corpse of a dog came drifting into the shot,

**British lobby card for Riccardo Freda's *The Seventh Sword* (1962), the first of many films Halsey would make in Italy; artist unknown.**

right where Burt had to go! Well, I laughed. We were all so tired, giggly. Then they got poles and push this carcass outta the shot. Well, then we start the scene again, he steps on the cape, I pull the thing and he starts to fall, and he gets just to the point of no return—y'know, where your balance is gone—and the cameraman says, "*Stop!* Stop!" So, now Burt knows he's going in the water, there's no dry costume. He's going in the water, he's gonna have to do it again ... and there's *nothing* he can do about it! And he goes—*SLAP!*—into the water. What had happened was that where he was going to fall was out of the camera shot. Well, he had to do it again, poor bastard! Oh, it's just *filthy*.

"The Bridge of Sighs"—it's a little bridge between two buildings, where the prisoners go from the court to the prison. They call it "The Bridge of Sighs" because there are little windows; their last look out before they go up. It's all a museum, now. But we had a shot in the picture where the same actor and I were escaping from the prison—by now I guess our characters were "friends." So we had to jump into the canal and then swim away. Well, the height of the jump was maybe twice this room. Naturally, I wouldn't do it, and neither would Burt, because who would jump into this filthy canal? (I don't know why Burt did it later.) Anyway, the stuntmen had to do it. Well, the stuntmen wanted more money, because it turned out that the water was only shallow, and then it was muck—not just mud—down to ... God knows. So the stuntmen wouldn't do it. Instead, a couple of gondoliers offered to do it for about eight dollars apiece: 5,000 *lire*. Well, the stuntmen were really pissed! (There are unions, but they're so damn ineffectual.)

**SF/DC**: Because of the language barriers, did you run into communication problems ... say, when you would argue with other actors?

**BH**: I never argued with other actors; nothing really serious. The only arguments I can remember were with directors.

**SF/DC**: What was Freda like to work with?

**BH**: Freda's a madman! He was a genius in his own way. He's still alive. I saw him about six months ago, and he's been talking about doing another picture. I don't think he'll ever do another picture. He was crazy.

**SF/DC**: Everything you read about Freda makes him seem like a difficult man to work with. Very quick ...

**BH**: Oh, *quick*! He once made a substantial bet that he could make a picture in 10 days! Now, it wasn't just that he could make a picture in 10 days—he could have a picture made in 10 days from *right now*! No script! *Nothing!*

**SF/DC**: You mean edited and everything, including post-production work?

**BH**: *Everything!* It's like we're sitting here right now, and I could make a movie—10 days from now I'll show you the finished movie! He became famous making spectacle pictures. He would do these films with these great crowds with a few people ... evidence of his genius.

**SF/DC**: What about Gianfranco Baldanello (aka "Frank G. Carrol"), who directed you in your first Spaghetti Western, *Kill Johnny Ringo* (1966)?

**BH**: I found him kind of nice, but ineffectual. He wasn't very inventive. He was okay. I would never put him in the class of any of the other people we were talking about. Nice person, but I just didn't find that he had any original ideas. Mediocre's a good word. I was surprised when I saw his name later; it just surprised me that he continued. I was surprised that he ever worked again after our picture, because he just didn't ... He'd come to work empty-handed.

**SF/DC**: Julio Buchs' *Trumpets of the Apocalypse*/aka *Perversion Story* sure is a strange film!

**BH**: Julio Buchs was a very nice man. Very quiet. Kind of withdrawn, actually. Maybe he wasn't well at that time. *Trumpets* was a very difficult film to make, because we shot so much at night. I did enjoy making it, even though I didn't think the script was very good.

**SF/DC**: Were there any directors you disliked working with?

**BH**: Yeah, there was one. I can tell this story, because I didn't like him, and I still don't like him. The director was Aldo Florio. He was after the leading lady, and he hired her so he could sleep with her, but she wouldn't. So he cornered her one day and said, "I know why you don't want to sleep with me, because you're sleeping with Brett." She said, "Yeah, I am sleeping with Brett. But I'm also sleeping with *John*, *Pete*, *Joe*; this one and that one ... I'm sleeping with *everyone* on this film except you, you son-of-a-bitch, because you're a pig!" (*laughs*)

**SF/DC**: I guess that would keep his ego in check! Did he hit on every actress he worked with?

**BH**: No, he was just hitting on her ... when you say "it's hot" in Italian, the expression is "*fa caldo*." We were shooting the film in the dead of winter, and used to walk around saying, "*Fa caldo*" *[as in "Fuck Aldo"]*, and the crew never did figure it out!

**SF/DC**: You have done a lot of script revisions on your films.

**BH**: That's where I started writing. They would usually give an English translation of an Italian script, and it just didn't work. You can't do it. So, I would rewrite and adapt it until it made sense. They use a lot more words than we do. The way I describe it best is, in an American script, if I say "I love you," that being said, you believe it and we go on to the next scene. In an Italian film, if I say, "I love you," I have to give you 10 reasons why! (*laughs*) So, in our market, for it to make sense, we just cut and cut and cut.

**SF/DC**: I've read that you did a lot of rewriting on Lucio Fulci's *Demonia*, because your costar Grady Thomas Clarkson said the script was virtually impossible to comprehend.

**BH**: The script was pretty bad, but Fulci has never been too big on scripts. He doesn't care too much about continuity. Yeah, I did a lot of rewriting on that film. Grady had a character to play, an Irish drunk, I think. It was barely indicated in the script, though. It said something like "The Irish Drunk" (*laughs*), and he would have some things to say that had nothing to do with the character!

Funny thing happened with that picture: They ran out of money, and they had some problems shooting in Sicily. Apparently there was some Mafia financing involved. There was a time when the producer was concerned for his life, because we were shooting way down there in Mafia territory!

**SF/DC**: They were beautiful locations.

**BH**: Oh yeah! I've never seen anything like it! We were living along the coast, but if you went up into the mountains, there were these little towns where the people looked like mongoloids, because no one ever leaves the town, so they just inbreed and inbreed and inbreed. We shot a lot of the film in this mausoleum in the basement of this church. I believe this part of the story involved naked witches or something.

**SF/DC**: Naked *nuns*, actually!

**BH**: So, we're shooting in this church and we're down in this vault that's about the size of a small warehouse, and there are bodies up on these shelves in the wall at least a couple of hundred years old.

**SF/DC**: *Real* bodies?!

**BH**: Oh yeah! Real bodies! The smell was something awful. Then they opened another vault in the floor that had even more bodies! You could only stand it for a little while. I figured the poor priest who let us in was going to be sent off to Hell or something when the picture came out if some of his bosses were to see this!

**SF/DC**: Maybe that's where the Mafia dumped their fresh kills!

**BH**: There was another story about the prop man and the crucifix he wore around his neck. He'd go to bed at night and wake up in the morning, and his cross would be on the other side of the room, and then another and another. He finally quit! It was really, really *weird*!

**SF/DC**: I guess it was those Roman Catholics messing around with the foundations of the universe, with religion and good and evil ...

**BH**: I'm sure the priest never saw the naked nuns! *I* didn't see 'em! He probably would have loved it (*laughs*), but he wouldn't have done it in order to protect his job. Imagine if the bishop had seen this?!

**SF/DC**: The Italians understandably made more nudie nun films than anybody else. How about heroine Meg Register?

**BH**: Well, she was doing very well until her boyfriend showed up. For some reason or another it seemed her boyfriend—an actor—was out to ruin her, and her acting just slumped. I think he didn't like the fact that she was working and he wasn't. I don't think he's ever acted. I don't think *she* has acted since!

**SF/DC**: Was she pleasant?

**BH**: Yeah. That is until her boyfriend showed up. No one liked her boyfriend, and she always took his side. It was too bad, because it was a good role for a young actress.

**SF/DC**: It's actually a pretty good Fulci film. Was that your idea to set the beginning of the film in Toronto?

**BH**: Yeah, that was my idea. Didn't I have a Roots jacket on? *[Note: Roots is a national Canadian casualwear franchise.]*

**SF/DC**: Yeah. You were already living in Toronto at that time, weren't you?

**BH**: I must have just moved here. Especially if I had a Roots jacket on, because I sure as hell didn't buy that in Rome!

**SF/DC**: *Right!* Like, I'm sure the president of Roots Canada phoned up and said, "Mr. Fulci, we would like a product placement in your upcoming gore film!" (*laughs*)

**BH**: Fulci was okay on that picture, but on *The Devil's Honey* he was very ill. He almost died; it was something to do with his stomach. When we were making *Devil*, he could only eat rice ... Fulci is a tough old bird.

**SF/DC**: Blanca Marsillach—Cristina's sister—was your female costar on *The Devil's Honey*.

**BH**: She was very difficult to work with. We had a big fight one day. I don't remember exactly what we were doing; it was something on the beach. I think I was chained or something, and she's dragging me into the ocean, and then she decides to revive me ... so she gives me this kiss ... and she *stuck her tongue in my mouth*! Well, I thought maybe she had AIDS or something, so I slapped her and I said, "Don't you *ever* do that again! If you kiss me, you close your goddamn mouth!" I wasn't about to have her slobbering in my mouth!

**SF/DC**: So, you weren't attracted to her?

**BH**: Oh no. God, no ... the *dog* would have been better! As a matter of fact, the producer hated her by the end of the picture; she was so difficult. She was always a problem. She had to go to Rome, I think, for dubbing. Anyway, the producer, Vincenzo Salviani, last thing he does—she's at the airport and she's demanding something—and the picture was over, and dubbing was finished. He turned

**Dr. Simpson and Jessica develop a powerful (onscreen) bond.**

around and *socked* her! Knocked her right down, then walked away. She called the cops and stuff, but, uh ... she was out of control, just *out of control*!

**SF/DC**: Didn't *Touch of Death* get bogged down in legal red tape with the distributors ... copyright problems or something?

**BH**: I was going to tell you the story behind *Touch of Death*. The production company was given two million dollars to make that movie. They gave one million to Fulci to make the movie, and he made it for $500,000: so that's your "copyright problem!" The distributors really felt like they got screwed, so they wouldn't release it.

**SF/DC**: How about beating a woman over the head with a baseball bat? That was a really brutal scene!

**BH**: Yeah, my wife was on the set when we shot that, too. And when I stuck her head in a microwave! And then grinding her up and feeding her to the pigs ...

**SF/DC**: It must have been great fun shooting these scenes, eh? A real laugh ...

**BH**: Oh, it was great fun!

**SF/DC**: So you didn't have any qualms about doing the ultra-violence?

**BH**: I didn't *really* hurt her! I guess it was crazy, but I don't think we did anything too bad ... There's some pretty brutal stuff, though. To me it's like a comic book—if you take it seriously, you're a fool.

**SF/DC**: Fulci turned around and reused a lot of footage from his other horror films of that period for *Cat in the Brain*, in whose credits you're identified as "*Il Mostro*" ("The Monster")!

**BH**: It's funny, as we used to be good friends. He used to come to my house for dinner sometimes. Kinda weird. I invited him over during a screening with Clint Eastwood. Then I went to Rome and called him and he never called me back. I called him three or four times, and I couldn't understand why he never called me back! Then I heard about a problem from certain actors: That no one was paid for this film! He used these clips and never paid anyone. You can't do that! (I guess he got away with it ...)

**SF/DC**: On the whole, what was Fulci like to work for?

**BH**: Well, he's a "screamer"—everybody's "a dumb son-of-a-bitch." He's never happy about anything ... always yelling! He was very vicious with some people, but I got along with him very well. We never had any problems. He'd be off screaming at somebody and I'd be having problems with the script, so I'd go up to him and say, "Lucio, what's this about here?" and he'd say quietly, "Okay, okay." Then I would walk away and he would go back to his screaming! (*laughs*) What's also funny about Fulci is that he has a lot of money, and his daughter Camilla (who works as his assistant) has terrible teeth ... which is also true of Fulci: all these rotted stumps! It's too bad, because she is potentially a very pretty girl, who with a few thousand dollars' worth of dental work would be really presentable (*laughs*). When he met Eastwood, Fulci was very subdued, very quiet, very polite.

**SF/DC**: One last Fulci question, about *Demonia*: Was the film ever finished? Initially it wasn't completed, deemed unreleasable, then all of a sudden it showed up on video.

**BH**: I finished my part, but the film was not finished at that point. Then we had to suddenly leave Sicily—I can't remember the exact reason—so we shot more stuff in Rome. Then there was still stuff to be shot with Register, and I don't know whether or not they completely finished it. I went directly from this to *Godfather III*, so I couldn't hang around.

**SF/DC**: From Fulci to Francis Ford Coppola! Did you get the part in *Godfather III* because of your Italian connections?

**BH**: That's funny, because before we started *Demonia*, I got a call from the producer of *Godfather*, who said, "I've got this part for you that I'd like to talk to you about." Everything was settled and I went off to Sicily to shoot the Fulci movie. I came back from the shoot and I talked to somebody at the production, and didn't hear anything. So I was ready to go home and phoned my wife to pick me up at the airport. Then all of a sudden I get a call from the producer: "I heard you're going home! You can't go home, you're in the movie!" Well, I said, "Thanks for telling me!" "Didn't casting call you?" asked the producer. So I phoned my wife and told her not to pick me up at the airport, and to come on over, because I'm staying another three months! You certainly don't see it on the screen.

**SF/DC**: You obviously had dialogue scenes in the film originally …

**BH**: Oh yeah! There were all these stories … it was really embarrassing, because I went to New York and spent the whole day doing ADR. Then I came back here to Toronto a month later when the picture came out, and I was the only actor invited to the Toronto screening, but I didn't even say anything! (*laughs*) There was this whole story that Coppola didn't use about this New Hampshire judge (who I played) and this mobster. The original cut ran like five-and-a-half hours or something!

**SF/DC**: How about Luigi Cozzi's *The Black Cat*?

**BH**: That was a funny picture! They had this script that had nothing to do with Poe's story, but the distributor had sold the film under the title "Edgar Allan Poe's The Black Cat," so they shot all this additional footage with a black cat that had nothing to do with the story!

**SF/DC**: You had a pretty funny role as madman producer Leonard Levin …

**BH**: My character was nuts! It's interesting to know that the film worked out all right, because the stuff Cozzi was doing had me thinking that it wasn't going to work.

**SF/DC**: Caroline Munro complained that she never got paid.

**BH**: *I* got paid!

**SF/DC**: Tell us your memories of Mario Bava.

**BH**: Bava was another very, very nice man. We did two pictures together … my memories of Bava? Just that I enjoyed working with him, even under difficult circumstances. *Four Times That Night* was shot in English. Was it released here?

**SF/DC**: It played a few dates in Toronto in July-August of 1971, in a dubbed print.

**BH**: When we did *Four Times;* we shot it at De Laurentiis studios, and it was winter. It was colder than hell. There was a shower scene, but the controls for the shower were, like, over in that corner, and the shower was over here. And they never could get it right; it was either too hot or too cold. Things like that would drive a director nuts, but Bava just wanted to get on with the shooting. But, if the actors can't get in the shower, whaddaya gonna do? If it's "make-out" or if you're there alone, it doesn't matter—if it's scalding, you can't get in and if it's freezing you can't get in! But Bava was as nice a man as you would ever meet. Good director. A good director is a director who gives his actors confidence. I liked most of the directors. There were some that I didn't like. Aldo Florio I certainly didn't like.

**SF/DC**: You also worked with Jesús Franco, on *Esmeralda Bay* (1989) …

**BH**: Jess Franco's the same way. Everything is under control. They don't get excited about it. They know what they want. And they keep everyone calm. *Esmeralda Bay*, that was funny; with one of the Sheen brothers—God, he was *awful*!

**SF/DC**: Daniela Giordano, "Miss Italy 1967," co-starred with you in *Four Times That Night* …

**Halsey loved working with Mario Bava on such films as *Roy Colt & Winchester Jack* (1970); artwork by Rodolfo Gasparri.**

**BH**: Oh yeah. At first I turned the picture down. I met her, and I said, "Either you buy her a new wardrobe, or give her a bath, or I won't do the picture … she *stinks*." She *did*! She had this terrible body odor: old, dirty sweat. I said, "Goddamn, buy her some clothes … anything! Change her underwear!" and it was really tough to be around her. The only time—I think we were in the shower together—I think that was the only time I could get close to her! Finally I told her, "You stink!"

**SF/DC**: Pascale Petit didn't have a B.O. problem though, right?
**BH**: *No!* Pascale Petit didn't. She was a beautiful girl. Pascale Petit knew her way around. Pascale Petit was a professional actress.
**SF/DC**: How about Marilù Tolo? She was your costar in three films.
**BH**: We didn't get along too well. On the first picture we were shooting a scene in a taxicab with the director and cameraman in the front seat, and Marilù and I were in the back. I didn't know what she was saying to me. The camera was rolling and I turned to her and said, "Marilù, why don't you go fuck yourself!" (*laughs*) She gave this big reaction and the director said, "*Cut!* What did you say to her? That was great! I've never seen her give such a good reaction!"
**SF/DC**: Although you didn't actually work with her, what do you remember about Erika Blanc?
**BH**: She was just a nice little girl. She was pretty; she was blonde. Italians like blondes. And she was around ...
**SF/DC**: Speaking of blondes, tell us about another guy you knew: Klaus Kinski.
**BH**: Kinski ... I knew him pretty well, yeah. He used to come over to my house. I never worked with him. But he was crazier'n hell. He'd do whatever he wanted. I remember once he invited us over for lunch, my wife and I, to his house. He had this butler who would follow him around. The butler would come in and serve him something in a glass or pick up a knife, and Kinski would say, "I'm going to kill you, you faggot son-of-a-bitch! I'm going to cut your throat!" all during lunch. The poor butler! But this "lunch" was amazing. There were only the four of us—his wife and him, my wife and me. He had this big bowl of cut crystal with gold trimming, full of caviar, Dom Perignon—and *that* was lunch! I mean, there must have been over a thousand dollars' worth of caviar! That was lunch. He used to buy new cars all the time. I met him at the garage once. He had a lot of money. He made a lot of money, but he spent it: he'd buy a new Rolls and get tired of it.
**SF/DC**: Are you aware of his autobiography, *All I Need Is Love*/aka *Kinski Uncut*? He wrote about committing incest with his whole family, how he wants ants to crawl up Werner Herzog's ass ... It was so scabrous that the publisher yanked it out of circulation!
**BH**: He wrote that himself?! Maybe it was a put-on. We would have parties and he and his wife would come. He'd sit on the sofa with his wife—very quiet, just meek and quiet. When he was out of his personal element, he was totally subdued. But he was a wild man. Last time I saw him, I think it was at an airport; this must have been shortly before he died. He was all dressed in pink, and he was with this young, young girl of—I dunno—maybe 15, and he was all dressed in this pink. She was tall, whereas he wasn't very tall. She was a big, tall child. I think—I don't know if he said—she was his wife or something.

# 1987

## *Aenigma (Italy/Yugoslavia)*

Directed by Lucio Fulci; Produced by Boro Banjac, Walter Brandi and Ettore Spagnuolo, for A.M. Trading International S.r.l and Sutjeska Film; Story and Screenplay by Lucio Fulci and Giorgio Mariuzzo; Director of Photography: Luigi Ciccarese; Editor: Vanio Amici; Music by Carlo Maria Cordio; Song: *Head Over Heels* (misidentified as *Head Over Meels* (!) in the credits), performed by Douglas Meakin (as A.D. Meakin)

Main Players: Jared Martin (Dr. Robert Anderson); Lara Naszinski (Eva Gordon); Ulli Reinthaler (Jenny Clark); Sophie d'Aulan (Kim); Jennifer Naud (Grace O'Neill); Riccardo Acerbi (Fred Vernon); Milijana Zirojevic (Kathy)

Cameo appearance: Lucio Fulci (Police Inspector)

*Kathy, an awkward outsider at a posh girl's boarding school in Boston, is set up as the butt of a cruel practical joke. The gym instructor, knowing of her infatuation with him, agrees to take her out on a date; it is all a set-up, however, and Kathy is humiliated in front of her classmates. Fleeing from the scene, Kathy is struck down by a car and goes into a coma; while in her coma, she appears to be willing revenge to strike the people who persecuted her, with the aid of a mysterious woman named Eva Gordon, who appears to be acting on her orders ...*

Fulci may have felt a little ambivalent about his brush with soft-core porn, but *The Devil's Honey* enabled him to get back into the swing of things. When the opportunity presented itself for him to make an Italian-Yugoslavian co-production on location in Sarajevo[1], he jumped at the chance. Working with his old friend Giorgio Mariuzzo—in what would prove to be their final collaboration—Fulci devised a scenario which seems indebted to Brian De Palma's film of Stephen King's *Carrie* (1976), Richard Franklin's *Patrick* (1978), Dario Argento's *Phenomena* (1985), with a little dash of Argento's *Suspiria* (1977) tossed in for good measure. Fulci acknowledged the debt to *Carrie* explicitly when discussing the film in an interview:

> *Aenigma* is one of my best films of recent years. It was made on a medium budget and tells the story of a woman in a college—a sort of *Carrie* in which there are two characters—and describes how an ugly-looking woman takes revenge when her karma enters the body of a beautiful woman.[2]

*Aenigma* can be interpreted as the start of Fulci's ongoing dialogue with death, a topic that dominates his final works. No doubt his recent brushes with illness had the director contemplating his own mortality, and a rather somber and introspective quality would begin to seep into his work as a result. The story deals with a woman who is trapped between life and death, lingering in a coma while her body continues to rot in a hospital bed. Early on, Fulci indulges in a bit of cinematic poetry, as the girl's spirit seems to leave her body; the camera takes the point of view of the spirit as it raises through the roof and looks down from above in the heavens. It's a lovely bit of filmmaking that displays a flair for the lyrical that is only sporadically evident in Fulci's work, notably in some of the Alphaville section of *Four of the Apocalypse* and the finale of *The Beyond*. Fulci's complicated relationship with the Church to one side, it seems that in his declining years he was desperately pursuing the idea of consciousness after death; the notion of the consciousness continuing to thrive after the body breaks down and dies is particularly appetizing when one is undergoing just such a gradual decline, and Fulci would continue to pursue the theme in many of his subsequent films. This level of personal involvement helps to give these later works an unexpectedly poignant dimension, even if the filmmaking is a bit rough around the edges compared to the glory days of his earlier works.

**Italian poster for *Aenigma;* artist unknown.**

The film also continues Fulci's fixation on outsider characters. Fellow classmates persecute Kathy because she is awkward and does not fit in. She tries to court their friendship, but they have no patience for her: Not only is she the daughter of the school's slow-witted cleaning woman, she is also lacking in the surface beauty and social graces which would mark her as being part of their class. The bulk of her peers conspire against her, but the most despicable character of all is the gym instructor, Fred Vernon, who, by virtue of his age and position, should know better than to indulge in such childish cruelty. Instead, Vernon instigates the cruel prank and, by extension, is chiefly responsible for Kathy's slow and lingering death. Vernon is a thoroughly loathsome presence: He abuses his authority and he treats the girls in his care as if they are pieces of meat to be used for his amusement. Of course, the snobby classmates are little better. Fulci ensures that the audience is on Kathy's side by stressing that she has never done anything to justify their hatred, and by making the catty classmates into obnoxious characters whom the audience can't wait to see get their comeuppance.

Curiously, Fulci and Mariuzzo start off with an interesting concept but soon lose sight of it: The first couple of revenge killings are based in the concept of Kathy—operating through the mysterious Eva— using the weak spots of her intended targets as a way of tormenting them at their moment of death. For example, Fred is a terrible narcissist—he preens in front of mirrors, flexes his muscles and shows off for anybody who will look, including himself. His self-love is therefore twisted in an inspired way when his mirror image comes crashing out of the looking glass and strangles him to death. It's a very clever variation on the doppelgänger theme, in which an exact double serves as an ill omen; in Fred's case, his fixation on his appearance has literally become deadly. Later, one of the students reacts poorly when snails are served at dinner; she tells Eva that she can't stand the sight of the creatures and that they terrify her. Sure enough, later on she finds herself literally covered in the slimy creatures in the film's most "celebrated" sequence. Viewed logically, it's easy to understand why so many viewers find the notion of a woman being smothered to death by snails so ludicrous; snails are not exactly noted for their speed and ferocity, after all. But in the context of the film, it's a wonderfully audacious moment that plays into this notion of Kathy using vulnerable weak spots as a way of getting back at the people who tormented her. The scene also can't help but remind one of a similar sequence in *The Beyond*, wherein tarantulas devour Michele Mirabella. Granted, there's a world of difference between tarantulas and snails—but the sheer audacity of the scene is disarming, just the same. Sadly, after this, the theme is abandoned; the remaining murders seem to happen by more arbitrary means, suggesting that Fulci and Mariuzzo either grew bored with the concept or didn't have sufficient time to follow it through logically. As such, the remaining kills are comparatively flat and unimaginative—though a

**Dr. Anderson (Jared Martin) gets a little close to the student body at St. Mary's College.**

nighttime museum sequence, in which the sculptures and artwork seem to come to life, is clever and effective.

*Aenigma* is an uneven film—Fulci's direction shows style and flair, but the lighting by cinematographer Luigi Ciccarese (who would also make a mess of *Demonia*) mawkishly copies the blue tint of Romano Albani's work on *Phenomena* without adding much in the way of atmosphere. The score by Carlo Maria Cordio is efficient if unremarkable; the presence of a mawkish theme song over the opening titles (irresistibly mislabeled as "Head Over Meels" [*sic*] in the credits!) is a tough obstacle for many viewers to overcome. Born in Rome in 1952, Cordio started scoring films in 1980; he would go on to write the scores for Fulci's *Touch of Death* and *The Ghosts of Sodom*, making him the de facto successor to Fabio Frizzi in Fulci's *oeuvre* for a brief window of time. The characters are a bit stiff and superficial and the actors are not the most inspiring lot. Jared Martin (in his second and final film for Fulci, following *Rome, 2072 A.D.: The New Gladiators*) gives a good performance as the neurologist who ends up bedding two of the students—would you trust this man to be your doctor? Lara Naszinski (also known as Lara Lamberti) is appropriately enigmatic as Eva. The niece of legendary *enfant terrible* Klaus Kinski, Naszinski was born in France in 1967. She made her Italian film debut as Andrea Occhipinti's girlfriend in Lamberto Bava's *giallo A Blade in the Dark* (1983) and also appeared in Richard Fleischer's *Red Sonja* (1985) with Brigitte Nielsen and Arnold Schwarzenegger. In recent years, she has worked mostly in German television and has also gone into the production end of the business, forming her own production company—Alshain Film—in Spain. Interestingly, the film was originally announced in the trades with a different cast in place, including Andy J. Forrest (presumably in the role inherited by Martin; Forrest was seen in a number of Italian genre films of the period, including Umberto Lenzi's *The House of Witchcraft*, 1989), Sabrina Siani (more than likely in the Naszinski role; she had already appeared in *Conquest* and is still listed as having appeared in the present film by some sources) and Mimsy Farmer (perhaps in the role of the school's severe head mistress?). Fulci also makes an appearance as a police inspector, complete with a *Columbo*-style trenchcoat; the once-imposing filmmaker looks rather gaunt and tired in his brief scene—and sadly, his health problems would only get worse before things would begin to improve somewhat.

For all of its faults, however, *Aenigma* is a worthier film than it is typically given credit for. Compared to some of the more compromised work that lay ahead, it is at least recognizably Fulci's work—and at its best, it displays the finer attributes one associates with the director's better films.

Notes:

1. Some sources claim that location work was done in Boston, Massachusetts, but the lead actors insist that everything was done in Sarajevo; a viewing of the film seems to confirm this, as there was no real need for the production to make a costly move to Boston for location shots.

2. Palmerini, Luca M. and Gaetano Mistretta, *Spaghetti Nightmares*, (Key West: Fantasma Books, 1996), p. 63.

# Lara Naszinksi
# Interview by Lionel Grenier

Lionel Grenier conducted the following interview with Lara Naszinski (or Lara Lamberti, as she is sometimes known) on April 4, 2014. The interview can also be viewed on Lionel's website, which can be found at www.luciofulci.fr. Lara played the role of Eva in *Aenigma* and we thank her for taking the time to discuss her memories of Lucio Fulci.

**Lionel Grenier**: I've heard that you first wanted to be a documentary filmmaker. Why (and how) did you become an actress instead? Your first part was in *A Blade in the Dark*, directed by Lamberto Bava...

**Lara Naszinski**: My very first part was a historical movie in Germany, *Josef Süß Oppenheimer* (1983), directed by Rainer Wolffhardt. I was still in acting school. Then I got my first part in Italy in the movie *Il ras del quartiere* [1983], with Diego Abatantuono. I think *A Blade in the Dark* was my third movie, but I'm not even sure.

Yes, I wanted to become a documentary filmmaker, I wanted to film animals. But there were no real film schools at that time in West Berlin where I grew up for part of my childhood. So I thought I might start with acting, then leave the country and do what was my dream somewhere else, already being in the movie business. It worked out and I went to Italy, but my career took off and I had no time to do anything else. I would have come back to that original plan much later in my life.

**LG**: Why did you use your real name? It would have been easier for you to use the stage name Kinski chosen by your uncle and cousin, who were already famous in the business in the early '80s.

**LN**: I didn't want people to have the impression that I made my career using my famous uncle and cousin. I also felt kind of unauthorized to use the name Kinski because I didn't know anybody of that family. In fact, Kinski is not the real name. The real name is Nakszynsky. But I told my agent about the connection to the Kinski family and of course—little time passed and I was "the cousin of Nastassja Kinski" in every press release. I became the "Polish girl, Nastassja's cousin," while a great part of my family is Mediterranean. I didn't want all this at all, so I decided to give up on the name Nakszynsky and I started working under the name of my Italian family.

**LG**: How did you end up playing Eva in *Aenigma*?

**LN**: I was already known in Italy, and the production company of Ettore Spagnuolo called my agency to offer me the part … very unspectacular.

**LG**: Lucio Fulci had … personality. What was your first impression of him?

**LN**: I don't remember, really. I remember him being kind of shy with me. He held me in high esteem, as he did Jared.

**LG**: Were you familiar with his body of work before working with him?

**LN**: No, honestly not. I have never been too much into the horror genre.

**LG**: Did Lucio Fulci tell you things about your character or the story to prepare you for your part? It is known that he was usually more involved in the technical aspects.

**LN**: I don't think that he gave us much support with the characters. He was in fact more technical. However, we had some talk about the characters before we started shooting. When we were shooting, he usually would tell us what to do, rather than talking about the emotions behind the actions. It drove him crazy when people didn't function technically the way he wanted it. He had the scene in his mind and it had to be done that way. Inside the frames created by his technical imagination, we had a lot of freedom though. Some actors didn't feel comfortable with this way of working. I remember a young girl with a small role who had her own ideas about the way she wanted to work. She was looking for the expression that comes out of the emotions, while Lucio just wanted to see her actions the way he had designed them. He didn't care whether she found the real emotions inside herself or not. Their encounter ended up every day with Lucio screaming and the girl crying. Her character ended up being almost completely cut out.

**Lara Naszinski as Eva in *Aenigma*.**

**LG**: Fulci hated the camera operator, Danijel Sukalo. He once said that because of him, you had to do 36 takes for the same shot. Did you feel some tension between them on the set?

**LN**: Honestly, I don't remember. There were lots of tensions on the set. Jealousy and strange intrigues were part of this set from day one. There was always tension—because of Lucio himself and the way he treated a lot of people, because of the jealousy that those people felt towards others who got along well with everything and with Lucio, and because there were tensions within the crew.

**LG**: Was Fulci more lenient with his own daughter, Camilla, who worked as a script supervisor with him?

**Lara Naszinski**

**LN**: I would definitely say yes. Absolutely.

**LG**: Did the producers interfere and try to make changes during the shooting?

**LN**: We were [shooting] all the time in Yugoslavia, with no break at all. The producers were in Rome and didn't visit. So there was no interference on the set. But I know that the footage was regularly sent to Rome where the producers watched it.

**LG**: The production started November 3, 1986, in Boston. You then went to Sarajevo, Yugoslavia ...

**LN**: I wasn't in Boston. I was only in Yugoslavia.

**LG**: Do you remember what the different locations in Sarajevo were? The ones that became the hall of the school, the cafeteria, the classroom, the gymnasium ...

**LN**: I don't remember the names. We mostly worked in a big house, which was the school building. Almost everything that we were shooting was done there, with a few exceptions like the scene with Dr. Anderson at the car and the garden scene. I don't know whose house the school building was.

**LG**: How hard was it to act/work with actors speaking different languages?

**LN**: I remember that we mostly worked in English, whether people spoke it well or not. I had already been in several productions of this sort and was used to this situation. The fact that I speak six languages fluently was always a welcome option to have the dialogues played in the same language instead of two different languages. However, I have to say that part of the concentration that should go into the acting goes into the languages issues if you do this. It is certainly a lot more complicated than acting just in one language—also because every language somehow changes the character that you're interpreting.

**LG**: What was the most difficult scene to shoot? For instance, the nightmarish love scene with Jared Martin? Or, your nervous breakdown?

**LN**: The nervous breakdown was technically complicated. I had only one try—because I basically had to destroy the whole room. The production didn't have everything available a second time. So Lucio warned me before that if something in the action went wrong, that would have been a disaster. There was a certain tension when we tried. I had to perform the action without hitting the objects. Then we did the real thing—and the camera failed. I remember Lucio being furious. However, the second time it all worked out.

The nightmarish scene was difficult for other things. I've never liked to be naked in front of the camera, and I didn't like it then. I also didn't like the meaning of the scene, and the bloody picture painted in the scene. It was a very technical scene again—and I couldn't find the emotion for it. I was helped a lot by our director of photography, who thoroughly explained to me what they would do, what the intention was and what the audience would actually see. He had the sensitivity that Lucio definitely lacked.

**LG**: Is it true that someone wrote a sequel in the 2010s?

**LN**: In 2011, painter and author José Da Silveira wrote a follow up of *Aenigma*, entitled *Aenigma – The Return*, with Jared Martin and me attached. The project is still awaiting realization.

**LG**: When you think of Fulci today, what first comes to mind?

**LN**: Lucio was bitter and lonely. He had a very rare form of hepatitis—today I would think it was Hepatitis C—and he couldn't really eat. He sat at his table with his daughter and swallowed down his rice without any condiment, while we all had fun; [we] were eating good stuff and were sitting together at other tables. I don't know whether his being alone was a choice or an unwanted and already sadly accepted side effect of his way of being. I don't know if I ever saw him laugh. But I also remember Lucio as a very professional director, a hard worker and someone who was extremely respectful and polite once he was convinced of someone's talent and experience. I had no problem with him at all. For me it was a pleasure to work with him, and many of his extremely rare smiles went to me. I was so very young at that time. Looking back, I have to say that maybe it would have been worth a try to crack his seemingly harsh surface and know more of him and his life. I wish I had done it.

# 1988

## Zombie 3 (Italy)

Aka *Zombi 3; Zombie Flesh Eaters 2; Zombi 3 – Ein neur Anfang*

Directed by Lucio Fulci and Bruno Mattei (uncredited); Produced by Franco Gaudenzi, for Flora Film; Story and Screenplay by Rossella Drudi (uncredited) and Claudio Fragasso; Director of Photography: Riccardo Grassetti; Editor: Alberto Moriani and Bruno Mattei (uncredited); Music by Stefano Mainetti; Songs: *The Sound of Fear*, *Tumble Down*, *Nature* and *Slow Think*, performed by Clue in the Crew

Main Players: Deran Sarafian (Ken); Beatrice Ring (Patricia); Ottaviano Dell'Acqua [as Richard Raymond] (Roger); Massimo Vanni [as Alex McBride] (Bo); Marina Loi (Carole); Deborah Bergamini (Lia); Mike Monty (General Morton); Luciano Pigozzi [as Alan Collins] (Plant Director; Scenes deleted)

*The military devises a new chemical agent as part of their top-secret germ warfare program; the chemical has the unforeseen side effect of bringing the dead back to life and transmitting a terrible contagion that leads to violence and cannibalism. When the chemical is stolen, they track down the thief, but by then the damage is already done – he has become infected and has already spread the contagion. A group of people must then find a way to survive as the contagion spreads …*

Following the completion of *Aenigma*, Fulci was hired by producer Ovidio Assonitis to do some second unit work on his production *The Curse* (1987). Filmed on location in Atlanta, Georgia by actor-turned-director David Keith (who also starred in Donald Cammell's extraordinary thriller *The White of the Eye* that same year), *The Curse* is a very loose adaptation of H.P. Lovecraft's 1927 short story *The Colour Out of Space*, which had already been adapted by director Daniel Haller for the American International horror film *Die Monster Die* (1966), with Boris Karloff. The film represented Keith's first time in the director's chair, and Assonitis worried that the many special effects sequences might be beyond his grasp, so he turned to Fulci to take care of these sequences in Rome. As Fulci later explained:

> In that film I got on extraordinarily well with Assonitis, filmed almost all the special effects, got well paid and was rewarded by the director, David Keith – who was one of the protagonists in *An Officer and a Gentleman* (1982) – who thanked me, saying that he wouldn't have been able to create certain effects without me. Assonitis' only mistake was to name me as an associate producer, which, in America, is the title given to a creative colleague who uses a pseudonym. He anglicized all the names of the technicians and *Variety* magazine wrote, "What ever for? We deliberately choose Italian technicians because they're the best in the world […]" and then they referred to "the veteran Fulci," … hold on … I'm much less veteran than their magazine! (*laughs*)[1]

Fulci's next assignment, however, would prove to be far less pleasurable.

*Zombie 3* was devised by producer Franco Gaudenzi as a throwback to the glory days of Italian horror. The Italian film industry was in very bad shape by this time, and most filmmakers were forced to retreat to the no man's land of television or make films in cheaper locales like the Philippines in order to survive. Fulci had no way of knowing it at the time, but his career was about to take him down both paths. Gaudenzi hired Rossella Drudi to devise a new zombie scenario. Born in Rome in 1963, Drudi started off working in the comic book industry before breaking into films as a screenwriter in 1980. She worked on the screenplays of numerous films credited solely to her husband Claudio Fragasso, including Bruno Mattei's *Dawn of the Dead* rip-off *Hell of the Living Dead* (1980), before establishing a solo reputation thanks to Aristide Mas-

**Early promotional material for *Zombie 3*.**

**Lucio Fulci (right) appears very ill as he tries to get through filming *Zombie 3* on location in the Philippines; his daughter Camilla is seated to the left of the frame.**

saccesi's popular soft-core sex film *Eleven Days, Eleven Nights* (1987). Like a number of her other scripts, Drudi did the lion's share of the work on developing *Zombie 3* and received no credit for doing so; instead, the credit went to her husband, who coauthored the screenplay and would play a fairly significant role in how the project would develop. More on that will be forthcoming in a bit. As for Fragasso, he was born in Rome in 1951. He started off as an assistant director and screenwriter before making his debut as a director in the 1980s. Fragasso's genre work is renowned among connoisseurs of bad cinema and includes the likes of *Monster Dog* (1984), *Zombie 4: After Death* (1989) and, most infamously, *Troll 2* (1990), which ranks high on the list of the most beloved bad films of all time. His partner in crime on the film (and many others) is Bruno Mattei, another man revered for his contributions to the world of bad moviemaking. Born in Rome in 1931, he started off as an editor in the 1950s. He started directing in the 1970s, and would helm films such as *Women's Camp 119* (1977), *Rats: Night of Terror* (1983) and *Robowar* (1988); he finished off directing direct-to-video erotica and horror, including *Zombies: The Beginning* and *Island of the Living Dead* (both 2007). He died in 2007. Fragasso and Mattei both make cameo appearances in the film; they can be seen as the soldiers who put a corpse into the incinerator to be cremated.

The script placed the action in the Philippines for the simple reason that it was a cheap and convenient location for filming. Ever since Francis Ford Coppola had brought attention to the area when he went there to film his Vietnam War epic *Apocalypse Now* (1979), the area experienced a major upswing in international production; much like Canada, it was an area that offered more bang for the buck. The sets constructed for Coppola's film remained standing and filmmakers could go there and make use of them, or construct new ones for next to nothing. The mission statement was clear: *Zombie 3* would be a "fly by the seat of your pants" operation.

Gaudenzi realized early on that the ideal man to direct—in theory, anyway—was Lucio Fulci. Fulci was in the throes of some of the worst days of his illness, but medical treatment did not come cheap and it was necessary for him to continue working. With the assistance of his trusted daughter Camilla, he went to the Philippines for the first and only time to direct the picture. It would prove to be one of the most frustrating and dispiriting experiences of his professional career. He filmed for six weeks in the sweltering heat and humidity, taking time off as needed to have the fluid drained from his swollen and distended belly as he endured the ravages inflicted by cirrhosis, and entrusting second unit material to Bruno Mattei. When all was said and done, he submitted his rough assembly to Gaudenzi, who was less than enthused. The picture needed a lot of work, and it was also way too short. Fulci had already tired of the project, however, and decided to cut his losses. As he later explained:

> I didn't finish making *Zombie 3*, but the reason wasn't anything to do with illness. These things can happen when you're an independent sort of person, as I am. […] As for *Zombie 3*, there were arguments and so, I finished off an hour and a quarter of the film … also, we were working with a dreadful script, which we couldn't get changed because the second-rate scriptwriter was the producer's trusted man. […] Consequently, I had to modify the script as I went along, assisted by my daughter, and we were working in the heat of the Philippines.[2]

Claudio Fragasso agrees with Fulci's version of events:

> After the final cutting and editing, the film was one hour and 10 minutes long, but it was a slow montage—the film was very slow, and so, at the end, it was cut down to 50 minutes.[3]

At this point, Gaudenzi set about trying to rescue the project, failing to realize that it was stillborn to begin with. Bruno Mattei, who had worked on the second unit in an uncredited capacity (since at the time he was also directing his own film in the Philippines [*Strike Commando 2*, 1988]), was brought in by Gaudenzi to work with Fragasso on completing the picture. By this stage, Fulci had washed his hands of the film; surprisingly, he allowed the production to credit him as director, since he would spend the rest of his life more or less excusing himself from blame, saying it wasn't really his film. Mattei and Fragasso developed some new scenes and went back to the Philippines; since the lead actors had already moved on and had other commitments, they were not able to figure into these new sequences, and so Mattei and Fragasso developed some new subplots instead. As Mattei explains:

> I did all of the beginning scenes—and the scenes where the man runs away with the briefcase [containing the chemical agent] and is pursued by the helicopter. That's all me. I also did the scenes with the men dressed in white anti-contamination suits. [...] Let's say I did about 40 percent of the film.[4]

When pressed on the issue of paternity, however, both Fragasso and Mattei agree on one thing: Lucio Fulci should be considered the true director of *Zombie 3*. It is a point of view that Fulci did not share:

> I don't repudiate any of my movies, except *Zombie 3*. But that movie's not mine. It's the most foolish of my productions. It has been done by a group of idiots, which are Claudio Fragasso—natural born cretin—and Bruno Mattei, who before becoming a "director" was a house painter, and a guy named Mimmo Scavia, the director of production, who arrived in the Philippines and his first thought was to just fuck some Oriental girls.[5]

With all of this in mind, it's hardly surprising to find that *Zombie 3* is a mess. It's difficult to reconcile the notion of Fulci ever making anything really presentable out of this makeshift material, but coupled with his serious health woes and the behind-the-scenes tensions, the film was truly doomed from the start. The added scenes shot by Mattei are truly laughable; they add nothing to the film beyond dragging out the running time, and they have absolutely no sense of style or conviction. The acting in these scenes is ghastly, and Mattei's approach generally consists of locking down the camera and zooming in and out as needed.

Fulci's material, however, is not entirely without interest. No, it doesn't begin to compare with his exemplary work on *Zombie*, for example, but it does create some creepy frissons amid the tacky spit-and-polish nature of the production. Consider the long, drawn-out sequence of Patricia exploring the abandoned gas station: Fulci piles on the Gothic flourishes, with cobwebs strewn all over the place and some moody color play à la Mario Bava, designed to create a sense of menace and unease. The eventual attack on the frightened girl by one of the zombies is energetically staged, and, somewhat surprisingly, Fulci forsakes the shambling ghouls of his earlier films in favor of the more energetic living dead featured in the likes of Umberto Lenzi's *Nightmare City* (1980) or Zach Snyder's remake of *Dawn of the Dead* (2004). The fast zombie angle is not utilized consistently, however: For much of the film, they revert to the more familiar slow-moving ghouls, which are familiar from earlier efforts. Later on, there's a pretty effective and suspenseful sequence depicting Carole's fate as she is tossed into a lagoon and attacked from below by some submerged zombies; the scene recalls the famous underwater attack of *Zombie*, but Fulci adds on a new twist: As her boyfriend Bo rescues her from the water, it is revealed the zombies have already severed the poor girl's legs, so she sets about trying to *eat* her would-be protector! The ensuing sequence of Bo running for his life while being pursued by an army of ghouls is actually quite suspenseful and well directed. There is also a sequence depicting a severed head found rotting in a refrigerator which springs to life and latches onto a victim's throat; it's an out of left field moment, and it definitely lingers in the mind as an audacious flight of fancy. If only the film had more scenes like this! Not surprisingly, Fulci would later praise this bit as the only part he was really proud of in the entire picture.[6]

Ultimately, one doesn't wish to give Fulci a free pass—he did direct the bulk of the material, after all—but it is truly difficult to fairly assess a patchwork film such as this. Mattei's new footage rears its ugly head much too frequently, and any mood Fulci may have been able to create in his sequences is constantly interrupted as a result. Make no mistake, even if the film had been left entirely in his hands, *Zombie 3* would likely still represent one of his worst films—but with the added baggage of so much

**Behind the scenes on *Zombie 3*; preparing the underwater zombies.**

**The living dead on the prowl; the atmosphere of this still is not present in the film itself.**

amateurish padding, it makes the film a very difficult slog indeed.

The cast does what it can, but there's only so much to be done with material such as this. Deran Sarafian and Beatrice Ring were a real-life couple at the time of filming, so it's not surprising that they have good chemistry onscreen. Sarafian was born in Los Angeles in 1958 and made his debut in a small role in the Charles Bronson film *10 to Midnight* (1983). After that, he teamed up with Fragasso to direct *Interzone* (1987), which is also where he first met Beatrice Ring. Sarafian took to directing and has amassed an impressive résumé in recent years, thanks to his work on such high-profile TV shows as *Lost*, *House M.D.* and *The Strain*. Ring was born in France in 1965. She started off as a model, but then ended up in Italy, where she pursued a career in films. She had already appeared for Lamberto Bava in the made-for-TV horror film *Graveyeard Disturbance* (1987) and had netted a more high profile job as one of the protagonists in Tonino Valerii's *Sicilian Connection* (1988). Disappointed by the quality of her assignments, Ring eventually abandoned acting in the early 1990s. Sarafian and Ring are to be commended for managing to keep a straight face through it all, and they prove to be appealing leads. Ring did not enjoy her experience working with Fulci—she discusses this at length in her accompanying interview—but Sarafian recalls the experience more favorably. On the commentary track included on the Shriek Show DVD release of the film, he remembers Fulci as treating him with respect; however, even he was not spared the director's withering sense of humor, as he discovered when he balked at doing a stunt: "He said, 'Does your pussy hurt?' He actually said that!"

***Zombie 3*; original artwork by Scott Hoffman.**

The gruesome make-up effects are the work of the talented Franco Di Girolamo, who had already worked on such Fulci films as *Don't Torture a Duckling*, *Contraband*, *The Black Cat*, *The New York Ripper* and *Rome, 2072 A.D.: The New Gladiators*. This would prove to be his final collaboration with Fulci; it's to be regretted that they parted ways under such ignominious circumstances. Even so, Di Girolamo creates some memorably nasty effects, especially when one considers the inadequate resources at his disposal. Unfortunately, the flat and ugly lighting by Riccardo Grassetti undermines the film. Grassetti spent much of his career working on films directed by Mattei, and this was undoubtedly his "in" to the production. This would remain his only collaboration with Fulci.

*Zombie 3* opened to withering reviews and plenty of disenchanted comments from fans, many of which began to wonder if Fulci had somehow "lost" his magic touch. What many of them failed to realize at the time was how compromised the film had become in Fulci's absence; truly, he would have done himself a big favor by insisting upon removing his name from the credits. Why he didn't do so remains a mystery, but perhaps it was an issue of pride: Whether he liked the film or not, he still directed the better part of it, and while the final assembly was completed without him, he could only hope that it would attract enough attention to ensure the opportunity of further work. Happily for him, that opportunity would present itself in short order.

A final note about *Zombie 3* is in order in the hopes of clearing up some long-standing confusion over the film and its origins. Some sources persist in claiming that *Zombie 3* was intended to be filmed in 3D and point to the scene in which the severed zombie head flies at the camera as "proof" of this assertion. In fact, this is erroneous. *Zombie 3* was never intended to be filmed in the costly and time-consuming 3D process; as this review should hopefully have made clear, the film was cash-strapped enough as it was! This confusion stems from the fact that, in 1983, there had been discussions over making a film titled *Zombie 3D*, which would have tied into the (then) burgeoning fad for 3D movies. In *L'occhio del testimone: Il cinema di Lucio Fulci*, Fulci is quoted as saying that he had developed a script for this project with the collaboration of Gianfranco Clerici and Vincenzo Mannino. Fulci claimed that:

> I had proposed it to foreign producers: at first they were very enthusiastic, the project seemed to be on the right track, then they became perplexed because of the difficulties of filming in 3D. At the time, another horror film in 3D, *Friday the 13th Part 3*, was not a success, so the producers threw in the towel.[7]

Notes:

1. Palmerini, Luca M. and Gaetano Mistretta, *Spaghetti Nightmares*, (Key West: Fantasma Books, 1996), p. 63.
2. *Ibid.*
3. Interview with Claudio Fragasso, included on the Shriek Show DVD release of *Zombie 3.*
4. Interview with Bruno Mattei, included on the Shriek Show DVD release of *Zombie 3.*
5. Retrieved from, http://www.shockingimages.com/fulci/interview.html
6. *Ibid.*
7. Romagnoli, Michele, *L'occhio del testimone*, (Bologna: Granata Press 1992), p. 32.

# Beatrice Ring Interview by Troy Howarth

The following interview with actress Beatrice Ring was conducted by phone on November 6, 2014. Beatrice played the role of Patricia in *Zombie 3*. She did not have a pleasurable experience working with Lucio Fulci, but she proved to be a warm and forthcoming interview subject. She has my thanks for agreeing to answer my questions.

**Troy Howarth**: What made you want to become an actress?

**Beatrice Ring**: What made me want to? I *didn't*. My mother was married to a man who worked in film distribution through United Artists in Italy. And when I was little, they were telling me that I should work in films. I was actually interested in computer science; this was the early days of computers. But when I turned 19, I had done some modeling, and I ended up leaving my parents' house and I needed to find a way of making money quickly. So, I had some friends who told me that I should model, and one of them hooked me up with an agent, who told me that there was an American director in town looking for a young actress of your type. I said, "Yes, yes," but I didn't pay any attention. Then I was sent to another agent, and she said the same thing: "Oh there's an American director in town and he is looking for an actress of your type." So I finally went to my first interview and I met Deran Sarafian. Deran Sarafian has worked non-stop for the last 30 years. He is a very prominent director now, and he also works as a producer. He produced and directed some episodes of *House*, for example, and *CSI: Miami*. But back then he was 28 and I was 19 and we met on his second film, and he hired me on this American production in Italy with [Aristide] Massaccesi—they were doing this spoof, a sort of low-budget *Mad Max* comedy/action film called *Interzone* (1987), and we connected on this movie. That was my first movie; I didn't get paid a lot, but thanks to that I also connected with Claudio Fragasso and his wife Rossella, who became my friend. She is still writing screenplays, I believe. Anyway, she wrote the script for *Zombie 3*—but I don't think she got the credit. Her husband got the credit. But I know for a fact that she wrote the script, because the way she wrote, she would go out of town and get a small hotel room outside of Rome, spend the weekend there and get her writing done. But at the time it was harder for women to get established as filmmakers and producers. It's a bit like how Donatella was behind Massaccesi; she was the brain and money behind his work.

Anyway, after *Interzone*, my agent called me and said that they were offering me a zombie movie. He told me, "It's a terrible script and it's just a cheap horror film, but if you have nothing better to do, why don't you go and read

**For Beatrice Ring, working with Lucio Fulci was a grueling and unpleasant experience.**

for it?" So Deran and I went to do it for fun in between bigger things. And Marina was originally cast in the lead, but she said to me, "I really don't want to work this hard. Why don't we switch parts?" I said, "Sure—I'd like to work with my boyfriend." Marina and I were friends since church days. We were together in the choir in church, in Rome. So for us, it wasn't difficult. And we used to be in competition with each other because we are similar types, though we are different personalities. You would go to casting calls and you would see a roomful of people you have seen over and over again.

**TH**: How long did the filming of *Zombie 3* last?

**BR**: We shot for five or six weeks in the Philippines, then I think the movie was too short. Also, Fulci was very sick and the script kept getting changed as they went. So the six weeks in the Philippines finished and later I remember getting word that there was a need to film some more, and I didn't want to know anything about it. So then Fragasso and Mattei went back to the Philippines and shot more scenes to make the story work, so they would have an adequate hour and a half running time for the distributor.

**TH**: Do you remember your first meeting with Lucio Fulci?

**BR**: Yes, actually, it was when I was much younger. It was a very a traumatic experience. He was casting a movie, something about a crime in New York. They were looking for a young dancer who would get killed. I went to this interview and they put me in a strange costume—it was like a nude leotard that made me look naked. So I went into this room full of people wearing this outfit. And Lucio was a grouch. (*Laughs*) He was not somebody you could hold a conversation with. He was brutal. He was incredibly mean. He was vulgar. I really didn't like being around him. I felt sorry on the set of *Zombie 3*, because he really was very sick. He had this giant belly and he was very funny—he would invite people to touch his belly. (*Laughs*) He wanted to see their reaction to it. He used to like to create fear and make an impression. So he'd make you tap his belly, and it was hard. He had a liver disease. Every week during shooting he would go to get his stomach drained; they would remove about 2 liters of liquid. So he was in a lot of pain. This comes up when people interview me … they want to know who directed the movie. The story is that he was on the set three out of five days, then he would take off when he was sick and there were two friends who did the stunt work—Ottavio and Massimo—and they would make their scenes very long and say to Lucio, "Let us do this or let us do that," and it became like a wild fire. Everybody was kind of doing whatever he or she wanted.

**TH**: So Fulci was often absent because of his illness?

**BR**: Not often—I mean, he would try to take care of the day's business, but sometimes he would be ill or he'd have to disappear for a longer period over the lunch break to get medication or go back to the hotel. He was very sick. He was irritable, and he was cursing more than usual. He took a delight in shocking people. He liked to get a reaction. If he saw that it affected you, he would get even worse. So for example, I was raised with a traditional religious background, and in Italy the biggest offense is to curse the Virgin Mary or God. But the gratuity of his vulgarity was just like a performance. So, he was on a power trip. He would just curse all day long and I would say nothing. There was nothing about the project that held any appeal. I know that when I did the interview with Mike Baronas, other people interviewed would claim that he was a genius and a master. With all my apologies, it's just my opinion, but Fulci was not this genius. What is so genius about making scary movies? I don't get it. (*Laughs*)

**TH**: Well, I don't think that *Zombie 3* was a career highlight for anybody involved. (*Laughs*)

**BR**: Yeah, it was an embarrassment. You know, I worked in film and distribution and I tried to establish myself with a career and a family, and people would say, "Why don't you change your name? When you Google your name, all these zombie pictures pop up." And I would say, "But it's been 30 years!" I mean, I am very happy if people like it got something positive out of it, but the experience in the Philippines was extremely painful. I got very sick on the set. I ended up with 36 mosquito bites. I developed a fever of 104; I was hallucinating and was very ill. I was rushed to the Philippines without the proper vaccinations. I was cast on a Thursday, and the following Monday we were to be on the set. I didn't even have a Visa, so when I got to Manila, they wouldn't let me in. I didn't have a Visa, the production company didn't look into any of these details. So I was detained for five days. And besides getting sick, I also lost 10 pounds, which for me was a lot. It made me look skinny, like a skeleton. (*Laughs*) The only good thing about *Zombie 3* was the really nice people I have met because of it. Over the years I have done horror conventions and have met the nicest people from Florida to Pennsylvania. A lot of people come from all over to do these conventions, and that is very nice.

**TH**: Well at least something positive came out of the experience, even if making the film was miserable.

**BR**: Yes, it was hard. They didn't even have any water on the set. They were extremely cheap. They would bring us soda. I remember one day, I lost my mind and I opened a can of Fanta and I spilled it all over my head. Somebody on the crew yelled, "No, don't do that!" And everything got sticky and that drew the insects.

I don't know if you remember the scene where I go inside the gas station?

**TH**: I do, yes.

**BR**: We shot that scene 24 times, because Lucio wanted me to look very scared. And I fought with him over that. I said, "Why would she be scared? I am just looking around a garage." And he said, "No!" Curse, curse, curse—I'm not gonna repeat what he said. And said, "Beatrice, don't be so American! You have to be an actress! You have to look scared! Don't make me waste my film!" You know, he was very vulgar. So we did it 24 times, and it didn't change, and I'm very proud of myself that I didn't give in and overact. He wanted me to do this exaggerated sort of thing, and if you look at the scene, I am walking through this garage covered in cobwebs and I'm saying, "Hello, hello?" And he wanted me to look scared doing that, so he got very angry with me.

In another scene, there is a zombie who chokes me with the chain I wear around my neck. You remember that scene?

**TH**: Yes.

**BR**: We shot that scene four or five times. The fifth time—and this is where when people say he is a great director, I say, I don't think so—he treated the actors like animals. He went to the stunt man playing the zombie and talked to him. Now, I don't know what he said, but I do know that the last time we did the take he *really* choked me! I was actually choking and gasping for air. And I would not be surprised if he went and bribed that Filipino stuntman to really choke me for real. He wanted the choking to look real. And then when the scene was finished, the stuntman stood up and looked at Lucio and they exchanged a glance. It was a terrible thing to do! The nice part after that was, emotionally I was very shaken: I was in the middle of freaking nowhere and I felt terrorized, like I was working with a criminal who would do whatever he needed to get what he wanted. I went to the back of the set, and everybody else went to go focus on the next scene. I had marks on my neck, I felt alone and terrorized and I had this terrible pain in my head. I was crying, and some of the local people came over and said, "Are you okay, are you okay?" And they were trying to make me feel better and make me feel safe. I was crying, because I felt like I had almost died—just for a movie.

**TH**: What was Fulci's reaction to all of this?

**BR**: He didn't care! He was … a lowlife.

**TH**: I believe Fulci had his daughter Camilla with him on the film, right?

**BR**: Yes, Camilla was there. I really felt sorry for her. She was a very nice young lady, and I felt like she was another victim of his.

**TH**: When did you finally see the film?

**BR**: Marina and I went to the premiere. We were very excited and also terrified, because we knew it was low budget and that people were going to laugh and throw things at the screen.

**TH**: And what did you think of it?

**BR**: Oh, I knew it was bad. (*Laughs*) We hid in the back and then we ran out. But Marina has fonder memories, because she is better than me. She is more spirited. She looks back and is able to focus on the positive. She made a lot of friends; she made a film that some people seem to like and which people know because of Lucio and his other films. I just look at it with disappointment, because we spent six weeks of our life on it, we made no money, we were abused, we got sick and then it took me a while to recover from the whole experience. I mean, if I had gone to work as a missionary in Africa or if I had gone off and helped some place rebuild after a catastrophe … but this movie was completely useless. It was a production that was held together with spit. (*Laughs*)

**TH**: It certainly sounds that way! So you had nothing to do with the added scenes by Fragasso and Mattei?

**BR**: No, I wasn't around for that. I mean, Fragasso was not on the set when I was there. Fulci would have stunt people jumping off of roofs and things. And these kids — I call them kids, but they were young men — would always get hurt, so every week there was a new group of people. It was sad how these people were starving, they were so desperate for money; they would do what was asked of them for absolutely little money. They would jump off of roofs — I mean, real high roofs. And when they jumped down on to the street, they would hurt their ankles. I would see these guys jump and then limp away because they hurt themselves. It was crazy. They were treated like animals.

**TH**: In 1987, you also worked with Lamberto Bava on a made-for-TV movie called *Graveyard Disturbance*.

**BR**: Yes, he is a professional and a gentleman; there were absolutely no problems on that. He had a very good director of photography. For a young actress, that is so important, having such a good director of photography. Every time they did a close-up or when they lit the scenes, they created production value and they made everything look more interesting. That helps the actors, too, because it makes them look their best, which helps them to get more work and make more money. I really liked making that film. *Graveyard Disturbance* was an interesting project, and I liked the fact that they gave me the part of the psychic, because, as I'm sure you know, women think they are psychic. (*Laughs*)

**TH**: So obviously, that was a much more positive experience than working with Fulci!

**BR**: Yes, well really most of my experiences have been positive apart from working with Lucio Fulci.

**TH**: Also in 1987, you made a film for Tonino Valerii called *Sicilian Connection* …

**BR**: Oh I see you have done your homework! Very nice! (*Laughs*) I'm so pleased you know these other movies I worked on, thank you so much!

**TH**: You're welcome! (*Laughs*)

**BR**: Well, Tonino Valerii and his wife were there and we shot in Sicily. It was probably the most amazing project I worked on. I got cast as an afterthought. My agent called and said that the actress they had cast wanted too much money. It was an Italian-Japanese co-production with a big budget, so for me to work on it was a beautiful experience. When you have bigger budgets, you have better accommodations and work with more professional people. We filmed in Sicily. I remember filming the scene on the beach. It was supposed to be set in the summer, but it was actually the winter. The director wanted to shoot the scene like the scene in *A Man and a Woman* (1966), the beautiful movie by Lelouch, and there is a scene where the couple meets on the beach and the camera circles around them. It's a very powerful technique; you can really see the passion of the emotion. And we did the scene the same way, with me and a Japanese actor — except it was incredibly cold. So the wardrobe mistress would put a jacket over my shoulder in between takes, then she said, "I have another way to keep you warm." So she gave me some liquor, something sweet, and every time we shot the scene I would go back to the point where I had to start running towards this Japanese actor, and each time she gave me some liquor. I ended up having too much to drink. (*Laughs*) I would run and get a drink and run and get a drink. (*Laughs*) But it was extremely cold. I think the scene came out very nice, actually. In Italy, they have this wonderful care with photography, and they make you look your best.

**TH**: You also made a film for Aldo Lado in 1990, the English title was *Ritual of Love* …

**BR**: They changed the title, yes. The story was about the principle of the human soul, which is divided into two parts: one is the man, one is the woman, and they spend their lives trying to find each other to reunite. I thought the movie had a beautiful concept.

A cute story about Aldo Lado has to do with the casting: I was going back and forth a lot from Italy to the States. I broke off my engagement with Deran Sarafian. We had worked together a lot on a number of films, then around 1989 I started to feel like this business was a lot of nonsense, I should get a real job. So I went to this interview with the attitude I don't care if I get the job, I will show no fear. I felt I deserved an opportunity. I got to where the casting was held and there were no spots, so I just parked the car and went in. The casting director was a young man who was very intellectual, and he kept provoking me. He was being obnoxious. And I felt this security and confidence about not allowing anyone to intimidate me, because I had worked on a number of movies, and felt I deserved a better opportunity. And this man was very offensive, so we fought. I told the guy off. I said to him, "Who do you think you are? I'm out of here!" So I picked up my portfolio and was leaving, then I saw a little man with a long beard and a big smile on his face. He came up to me and he said, "My Valerie! Finally!" And he hugged me! Then I looked at the casting director and he was smiling, too. So it was actually a test; his job was to provoke the actresses to find the actress with the right personality for the part. And that's how I got the job — because I got into a fight.

**TH**: So if you hadn't fought back, you wouldn't have got it.

**BR**: If I had been a little more shy or insecure, I wouldn't have got it, no.

**Is it over yet?! Beatrice Ring and Deran Sarafian attempt to escape from the insanity of *Zombie 3*.**

**TH**: You stopped acting in the 1990s—had you lost interest in acting?

**BR**: You really *did* your homework! (*Laughs*) I started a family, and I decided I didn't want to do it. The main reason was because I felt really betrayed on the Aldo Lado film. There was an incident when my double was working on a scene, which I will not discuss since I dislike the memory, but let's say it was inappropriate on so many levels. She showed up and I said, "Why are you here today?" Then I realized that she was showing her body and they were shooting it so that it looked like it was me. So I freaked-out, I went home, I called my stepfather, who had been in the business for years. He said, "Well, you wanted to be an actress, right?" Then he hung up the phone. That was like twisting the knife even deeper in the wound. And so, I got an attorney and the attorney said, "Listen, if you sue the production company, no one will ever work with you again. We have to find a compromise." But I had signed a waiver allowing them to use a double, which was a huge mistake. Once you sign such a waiver, the production company can do what they like. I should have known better, but when I signed that early on in my career I was only 21, and I didn't have enough experience. So this allowed them to change the script without my approval. The attorney suggested asking them to credit me under another name. So we agreed that the movie would be released with me credited as Valerie Bosch. And the movie was released with my name: They were very mischievous. They wanted to use my name because I had gained some popularity, as I had worked on some films and TV shows; I worked for three years non-stop and was building a name in Italy. And they wanted to use that to help with the distribution, so they used my name up front, then in the end titles they credited Valerie Bosch. So it was kind of like they were mocking me behind their back. The movie was supposed to be a sort of intellectual piece and intended to be shown at Cannes. Then I ran into the actor, a Japanese actor, and he told me he has been invited to promote the film in Japan. I didn't understand why I wasn't invited, too. He said, "I don't know why." Then I found out that they had arranged a special screening of the film with the real-life criminal whom the film was based on. The story deals with a woman who is murdered, then eaten. The man who did it was from Japan, and he was a surgeon. A model had gone missing and they connected her to the surgeon, and the police eventually found the woman in his apartment—cut up into bite-sized pieces. When he ended up in front of the judge, he requested to be extradited to Japan

to be charged. And they only sentenced him to five years. They called it a crime of passion. It was a very scary story, because after meeting the man who did this, I worried he might come after me, too. (*Laughs*)
**TH**: Well, let's hope not!
**BR**: Anyway, we made the film in about six weeks and I gave it my all. I was really happy and felt it was a beautiful opportunity getting to star in a movie that focused on me from the beginning to the end. And this opportunity ended in betrayal, because they changed the script and changed the story that was vulgar—a story of a sexual relationship. Then they invited the actor without even telling me that it was being released in Japan, where it was almost glorifying this criminal. I mean, this wasn't a typical criminal. It was incredibly disturbing.
**TH**: I'm sorry it turned out that way.
**BR**: It's been a long time now, so I am over that anxiety now.
**TH**: At what point did you realize that *Zombie 3* had a cult following? I would imagine you figured the film was done and would never be heard of again.
**BR**: Yes, it was so surprising. I remember I found a store online that was selling it in Florida. So I called and I ordered a copy of the VHS—back then it was still VHS. And this very dull person on the other end of the line said, "Okay, fine, we need your credit card information." So I told him my name for the credit card information and he said, "*The* Beatrice Ring?!" I said, "What?! I don't know!" And he went crazy and was so sweet and adorable. He was just so cute! I had a fan! I didn't know I had any fans! I had no idea! He said, "You know, they are looking for you everywhere?" I said, "They are?!" They thought I had died. He said, "There is a journalist in London you have to speak to." His name was Jason Slater. What a wonderful man. He said, "Can I do an interview?" I said, "Sure, shoot me the questions and I will answer." And you know, between one setback and another, it took me about four months to complete that five-page interview! When it was done, I told him, "Now take all this information and make me sound smart." (*Laughs*)
**TH**: Do you have any final thoughts you'd like to share about working with Lucio Fulci?
**BR**: Well, you know, I have said a lot of bad things about him over the years, and I do regret it. At the end of the day, our main purpose should be to focus on improving ourselves. And the idea that he suffered so badly is sad. I don't know how he spent his last weeks, but knowing how badly he suffered, I do hope he found a place of comfort and peace before he died.
**TH**: I just want to thank you for taking the time to answer these questions.
**BR**: You are very welcome, Troy. I'm happy to contribute and I plan to buy your book, and I wish you every success with it.

## Marina Loi Interview by Troy Howarth

The following interview with Marina Loi was conducted by email on October 22, 2014. Marina played the role of Carole in *Zombie 3*. She was already a fan of Fulci's work by the time she was cast in the film. Marina has my thanks for taking the time to talk with me about her career and her memories of Fulci, in particular.

**Troy Howarth**: What made you want to become an actress?
**Marina Loi**: I started acting as a child in the theater, because my primary school teacher had been involved in show business—for example, he directed the horror movie *Metempsychosis* (NOTE: Antonio Boccaci; the film is known in the U.S. as *Tomb of Torture*, 1965). Then at 16 I acted in a short film and decided I wanted to be a director. At 18 I enrolled at a course on filmmaking, but when I volunteered as an assistant director, they asked me to act. So, in order to enter the movie business, I began doing screen tests, commercials, photo shoots and then movies.
**TH**: You made your film debut in *Demons* 2 … how did you get that role?
**ML**: I got the part through a casting call. I was happy to work in a horror movie; I had already seen the first *Demons* (1985) and I was so happy to be in its sequel. I was aware of the success of *Demons*, but I had no idea it was also distributed in the U.S.A. I found out about that only when I went to New York
**TH**: What do you remember of Lamberto Bava, who directed *Demons 2*?
**ML**: I remember that he was good and kind. Unfortunately, during the making of the movie I was injured, so I had to stay home and skip some scenes, and I was not able to work with him as much as I would have liked. I met him again a few years ago, at the party for the 100th issue of the magazine *Nocturno*. We were both among the guests of honor, along with other people associated with the horror genre, and it was very nice seeing him again.
**TH**: You appeared in a TV movie directed by Sergio Sollima, *Uomo contro uomo* … do you have any memories of doing that film?
**ML**: I knew Sollima for his movies, which are a big part of Italian cinema history. He also did a very successful TV series in Italy, *Sandokan*, which I loved so much. Sollima is a great director, he knows his job and he is a man with lots of irony. So, I liked to work with him. After that experience I became friends with him and his family—the daughter Samanta and the son, Stefano, who is, for me, the best contemporary director in Italy. Sergio, Stefano and I also collaborated on a screenplay for a film, but, unfortunately, we didn't shoot it.

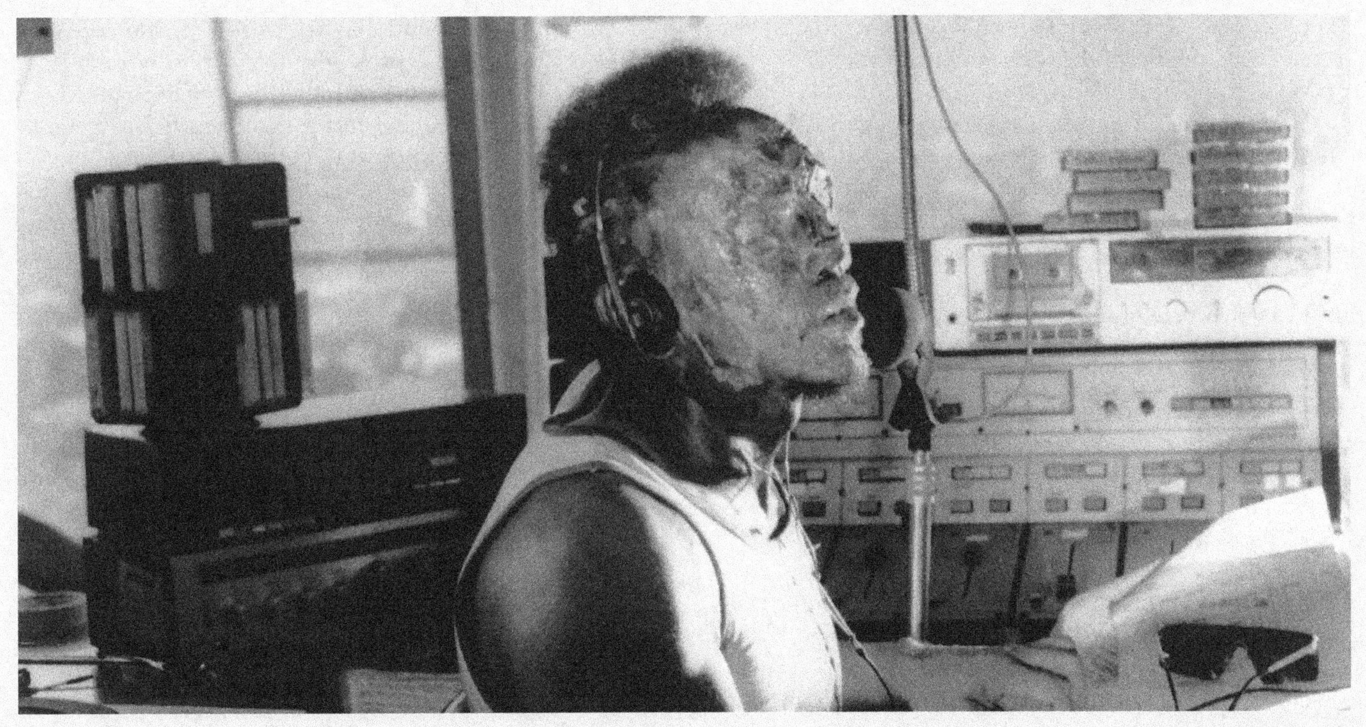

**A zombie DJ—surely one of the dafter inventions in *Zombie 3.***

*Uomo contro uomo* is a TV movie split into two episodes; it was very successful. The story deals with the *'Ndrangheta,* the Italian Mafia in Calabria. I played a 13-year-old controlled by the boss of the organization. I remember Sollima's sense of irony and humor made every moment on the set enjoyable. He was calm, clever and ironic, three good traits. And he was a man of culture, not only cinematographically, but a man with history and experience. Anyway, he was the most amusing director I have ever met.

**TH**: How did you get cast in *Zombie 3*?

**ML**: I got the part after a couple of auditions with Claudio Fragasso—as the first one was not that good, he called me back and I did a better job of it. After that, I met Lucio Fulci. He paid me a lot of compliments, saying he was sure I was going to become a star, and in fact he chose me for the main role, but I swapped with Beatrice Ring because she was the girlfriend of Deran Sarafian. Since Bea and I had been friends since we were children, we decided to exchange the roles ... so she could stay with Deran and I could work a little less and study for my American literature exam.

**TH**: What are you memories of Lucio Fulci?

**ML**: I have so many memories of Fulci ... I loved him, but I had had mixed feelings at times. On the one hand I hated what he had to say at times, but on the other, he said it with such wit, it made me laugh. He was intelligent, with a sharp sense of humor. I loved to hear his stories at the dinner table, always cynical in a pure Roman's style. He was also a man of culture. I could have stayed for hours and hours listening to his tales.

**TH**: Was Fulci difficult to work with?

**ML**: It depends ... sometimes he was sarcastic; sometimes he was great. He could be quite severe on the set. After we did our first scene with him, he referred to us as "amateur hour," which was a reference to a popular TV program in Italy at that time. He was not always very kind, especially with Beatrice Ring. But I remember that during a particularly rough scene (the one in the swimming pool), he was very kind to me. I liked his sense of humor and the nicknames he was giving to everyone. He gave me several nicknames, in fact, and he was famous for the nicknames he used to give to everyone.

**TH**: Fulci was ill during the filming, and Bruno Mattei later took over the film ... did you work only with Fulci, or were you involved in the scenes Mattei and Claudio Fragasso filmed as well?

**ML**: During the time I spent in the Philippines, Lucio Fulci was with us, even though his health was in very bad condition. I shot only some parts of one scene with Bruno Mattei, who was directing the second unit, the one [scene] where I was in the car with Massimo Vanni. Claudio Fragasso wasn't in the Philippines when we shot the film. When I came back to Rome, I got a call from the producers and I was asked to go back to the Philippines to shoot more scenes, but I turned them down because I had to take some exams at my University, and I could not postpone that. I think Claudio Fragasso went to the Philippines that second time. All the footage with Bea, Deran, the girls in the bus and I was directed by Fulci. Fragasso and Mattei then shot new scenes that were not in the original script. I suppose this was because Bea, Deran and I did not accept the offer to come back to the Philippines a second time.

**TH**: Are you a fan of horror movies?

**ML**: Of course! Ever since I was a kid, I have liked Dario Argento, Lucio Fulci and American horror movies.
**TH**: What did you think of *Zombie 3* as a film?
**ML**: I have seen *Zombie 3*. The first time I saw it was at the Fantafestival in Rome. I was with Beatrice Ring. The theater was packed, and the audience was making loud comments on the funniest scenes. Sometimes they were clapping during the goriest scenes. I got two applauses! One was when Massimo Vanni asked me if I want to go with him to look for help and I said yes, with an involuntary mischievous glance. Not to mention the line that Beatrice and I delivered several times in the movie, "Is there anybody here?" ... the audience in the theater was continuously repeating it ... Beatrice and I were desperately trying to hide in order not to be recognized; you know, wearing scarves and sunglasses ... But I must say that watching *Zombie 3* was a lot of fun.

The phrase "is anybody here" remained engraved in the memory of those who were there that night. Years later, when I was making a film in Eastern Europe, the assistant director, who had been present at that Fantafestival screening, got me to inscribe postcards for his friends signed with "Is anybody here?" under which he wrote, "It's her!" Many years later I received the DVD, so I have watched the movie with friends, and they have thanked me for all the laughs and for my ridiculous performance!
**TH**: You apparently stopped making movies around 1990—do you ever miss making films?
**ML**: I stopped because I wanted to do other things with my life ... first, to get my degree. Once I attained that, I became a teacher of communication, cinema and television in different universities in Italy for many years. During the time I was working as a teacher I always declined all offers to act in movies or TV serials ... when I decided to stop teaching I went back into show business on TV as a correspondent, anchorwoman and writer. But I'm still busy in the movie world on different levels, and I don't dismiss going back to the horror field! I wrote some horror scripts, hoping to make them. I also wrote a zombie movie, but in Italy it is not usual to produce that kind of film anymore, so is difficult to get the funding.

Recently I decided to resume my acting career. And so, in April of 2015 I will be playing the protagonist in an "on the road" thriller movie, which will be an "all-female" subject and production.
**TH**: And lastly, are you surprised by the lasting popularity of Fulci and his movies?
**ML**: No, I'm not surprised, absolutely not. Fulci's success grows from year to year—I'm thinking about Tarantino's "declarations of love" towards him, but also about all those who took inspiration from his films. I believe it is right to consider Fulci a great director, even a duty, since his cinema is brilliant, full of contaminations, and he is not afraid to dare. At first I was a little surprised by *Zombie 3*'s popularity. In the 2000s people started calling from all over the world to interview me. Even in Italy I was a guest of several talk shows and magazines as a "scream queen." Last year I starred in a short film in support of blood donation: the biggest names of Italian horror took part in it, including Dario Argento, and a shot recalled a scene of one of Fulci's films. I was interviewed for books, special editions of DVDs and several times I was the protagonist of dossiers about Fulci on magazines such as *Nocturno*. Not to mention all the fans writing to me on Facebook. Last year I was recognized by a group of fans at Rome's Fantafestival, who wanted to take a pic with me. Incredible! I'm sure that even if I won the Nobel Prize for peace, I would always be remembered for *Zombie 3*!!! *Zombie 3*'s popularity grew exponentially over the years and now it is a cult movie. Its weaknesses have become its strength. It's a funny film, weird, different from the others. Even today when I see myself in it I laugh, because I'm rather ridiculous, but luckily I'm self-deprecating. I have a funny story about *Zombie 3*: When I taught at university I kept my past as an actress hidden, of course. I did not want people to know about it, and for this reason I refused to show up at auditions that my agent offered to me. One day a student came over with a mag and pointing at my name in the cast of *Zombie 3*, asked me if I was the same one. After some hesitation I told him, "Yes, but don't tell anyone," and he replied, "Too late." Only then I realized that the whole class (over 100 students) looked at me, smiling. Then I turned back and read a line on the blackboard: "Marina Loi for president."
**TH**: Marina, thank you for your time.
**ML**: Thank you so much!

## *Touch of Death (Italy)*

Aka *Quando Alice ruppe lo specchio; When Alice Broke the Mirror*

Directed by Lucio Fulci; Produced by Antonio Lucidi and Luigi Nannerini, for Alpha Cinematografica; Story and Screenplay by Lucio Fulci; Director of Photography: Silvano Tessicini; Editor: Vincenzo Tomassi; Music by Carlo Maria Cordio

Main Players: Brett Halsey (Lester Parsons); Ria De Simone (Alice Shogun); Zora Kerova [as Zora Ulla Kesler] (Virginia Field); Pierlugi Conti [as Al Cliver] (Randy); Sacha Maria Darwin [as Sasha Darwin] (Margie MacDonald); Marco Di Stefano (The Tramp); Maurice Poli (Newscaster)

*Lester Parsons is a* bon vivant *with a passion for the finer things in life. Unfortunately, he is also an inveterate gambler with an aversion to hard work. In order to finance his extravagances, Lester targets rich, lonely widows and seduces them before convincing them to sign over their money to him; at that point, he kills them and grinds them into hamburger for his pet pigs. Mysteriously, every time Lester commits a murder and covers his tracks, another murder is committed in a similar but far less cautious way; Lester is convinced there is a copycat at work who is trying to drive him insane ...*

After *Zombie 3*, Fulci was at something of a low ebb: He hated the experience of working in the Philippines, he hated the film that resulted out of it and he did damage control to try to minimize his involvement in the picture. As he set about licking his wounds, producers Antonio Lucidi and Luigi Nannerini approached him and offered him a seemingly desirable deal:

> I signed a contract to make a series of films for the Alpha Cinematografica company, of which, in the end, I made [directed] only two: *The Ghosts of Sodom* and *Touch of Death*, which is, in my opinion, a small, low-cost masterpiece. [...] I'm very fond of the film.[1]

What Fulci would not be fond of, however, was the penny-pinching and cost cutting that would dominate these two productions, prompting him to break off his association with Alpha just as it was getting under way. In addition to directing two films for them, he would also lend his name to a series of films produced by Lucidi and Nannerini under the banner of "Lucio Fulci Presents"; Fulci's involvement in these films was more or less in name only, but he would end up using clips from most of them in his self-reflexive *Nightmare Concert (A Cat in the Brain)*, a film apparently made to satisfy the end of his agreement with the two producers following his abrupt departure from Alpha. More on that, however, in the review for *Nightmare Concert (A Cat in the Brain)*—and in the later section devoted to these "Lucio Fulci Presents" titles.

*Touch of Death* is one of only two films for which Fulci is credited as the sole screenwriter; his final film, *Door to Silence*, is the other. In truth, the credit is a bit of a misnomer, as the scenario changed radically due to the collaboration of actor Brett Halsey. As Halsey explained to me in conversation at the 2011 Monster Bash in Butler, Pennsylvania, when Fulci first offered him the role of Lester Parsons, the script was a straightforward *giallo*. Halsey thought it might be fun to switch things up a bit and encouraged Fulci to add in more and more humor. Together, the two of them transformed *Touch of Death* into a dark comedy with some broad touches of slapstick—or perhaps "splatterstick" would be more apt in this context.

The film owes much to Charles Chaplin's classic dark comedy *Monsieur Verdoux* (1947), in which Chaplin's titular protagonist marries rich widows and kills them off for their money. Chaplin's film—reportedly based on an idea by Orson Welles—garnered a good deal of controversy in its day, and time has not really taken the edge off of its biting cynicism. Compared to *Touch of Death*, however, it is positively staid. Fulci's friend and colleague Mario Bava also delivered a *giallo* much-inspired by Chaplin's classic: *Hatchet for the Honeymoon* (1970) tells of a fashion designer who is compelled to kill women in wedding dresses in order to remember a traumatic childhood incident. The thread of dark humor running through these films helps to unite them thematically, even if they play their scenarios out in a very different way. In Fulci's case, the scenario also refers back to *Piccola posta*, one of the films he wrote for Steno in the 1950s. *Piccola posta*'s most impressive segment stars Alberto Sordi as the slick and loathsome head of a nursing home for elderly females; he schmoozes the old ladies into signing over their money to him, then treats them abysmally and drives some of them to their deaths. The director's passion for dark comedy is evident in so many of his films, but of all his horror films, *Touch of Death* is far and away the most overtly comical. For this reason, it tends to put off some viewers who prefer the more straight-laced approach of his classic zombie films, for example.

**One of the more gruesome deaths in *Touch of Death*.**

In a sense, the scenario is a little more ambitious than the budget can sustain: Lester lives an affluent life, but must periodically seek out another naïve woman in the hopes of killing her off and collecting on her insurance money. All the while this is going on, an apparent copycat commits another string of murders. It eventually transpires that the copycat is Lester's alter ego, thus bringing back the doppelgänger theme from *Aenigma*. The twin in this instance is Lester's *shadow*: the two become separated and engage in a struggle for supremacy, but the outcome is inevitable: One cannot kill the other without literally committing suicide. The theme of the shadow taking on a life of its own has great promise, but the threadbare production and indifferent cinematography by Silvano Tessicini fails to thoroughly deliver on it. Even so, the idea is a good one, and Fulci and Halsey are to be commended for milking the material for all the shock value and grim humor it is worth.

Critics who insist upon seeing Fulci as a misogynist have had a field day with this film: Lester's victims are middle-aged, ugly and, above all, incredibly dim-witted. It's true that Fulci and Halsey do not go out of their way to

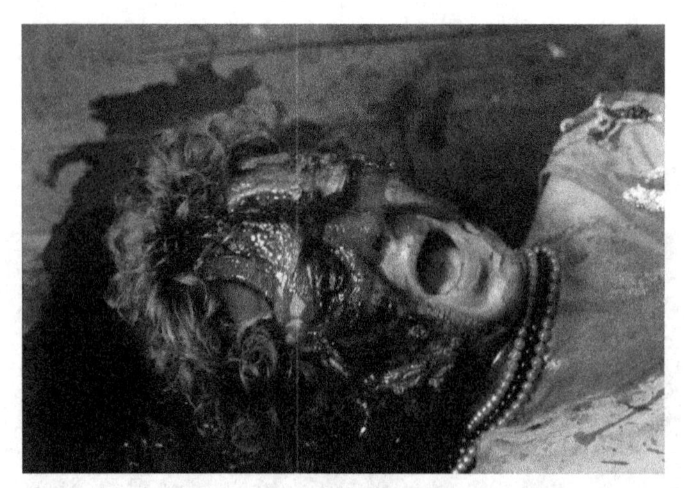

**Another gory death in *Touch of Death*.**

delineate these characters in a meaningful way, but Lester ultimately meets his match in the form of Virginia, played by Zora Kerova, in her second appearance for Fulci following her brief role as the ill-fated sex show performer in *The New York Ripper*. As played by Kerova, Virginia is not the usual naïve pushover: Like the others, she is distinguished by a physical infirmity (in her case, a large scar on her upper lip) and as such, she does not measure up to Lester's standards of beauty, but she gets the upper hand on him and helps to speed him towards his well-earned demise. Like *The New York Ripper*, *Touch of Death* invites charges of misogyny by virtue of its depiction of violence against women. But is Fulci endorsing such violence? In *The New York Ripper*, a close viewing reveals a sympathy towards some of the victims, but *Touch of Death* is a little more ambivalent: The victims here are generally a pretty off-putting lot. However, it would be a mistake to assume that Fulci is suggesting that they are getting what they deserve—or that, more to the point, this is indicative of an attitude towards women as a whole. Lester is a buffoon: Fulci does not encourage us to feel sympathy for him. In the film's rather glib and cynical landscape, there are very few people of any worth—only Virginia emerges as somebody worthy of compassion, and this, in itself, is enough to diffuse the misogyny argument. Had Lester been depicted as a good guy who is doing the world a service by killing off these annoying middle-aged women, then perhaps the thesis would have some real merit; as it stands, the film is simply having a bit of fun by sending up genre conventions. Whether that fun is in good taste is a matter of personal opinion, however.

Brett Halsey gives a delightful performance as Lester. The American actor enjoyed his collaborations with Fulci and has pointed to this one as his favorite for the simple reason that it allowed him a chance to really collaborate on the creative end of things. If the film had played out as a straightforward thriller, it would have been very different indeed; but with Halsey along for the ride to push things into the absurd, it develops a unique character among Fulci's horror films. Lester's victims are played by a trio of actresses who gamely go along with the joke: Sacha Maria Darwin's face is covered with patches of hair, Ria De Simone bursts into operatic arias when she is nearing orgasm and Kerova proves to be far more resourceful than Lester himself. Darwin, born in Austria in 1947, would go on to work with Fulci on *Voices from Beyond*, and later recalled the director as a complex personality:

> He was Dr. Jekyll and Mr. Hyde, because when he was working, he was a terrible man. [...] If you'd wanted to know the other side of Lucio Fulci, like I did, you'd see that he was a very human man, very kind ... a man that had gone through a lot of suffering throughout his life. [...] To avoid that fear of suffering, he put up a wall.

Darwin's broadly humorous performance is put to good use in the scene where Lester attempts to poison her character, as every attempt goes horribly wrong; one is reminded of Chaplin's attempts to kill Martha Raye in *Monsieur Verdoux*. Darwin eventually is subjected to the nastiest death scene in the present film, as Lester beats the woman with a stick, gouging her eye out, before putting her head in the microwave and zapping it to a putrid mess. In addition to Halsey and Kerova, other Fulci veterans are present in the form of Al Cliver (wonderfully slimy as Lester's bookie) and Maurice Poli, who is wasted in a brief appearance as a newscaster.

The film's comic tone in no way diminishes its gruesome imagery: Fulci's passion for eye violence is again on display, and there are some really ghastly images of Parsons butchering his victims; he even indulges in a little cannibalism and cooks a steak from the thigh meat of one of his victims (shades of Bud in *Four of the Apocalypse!*). The make-up effects are by Giuseppe Ferranti, who is sometimes billed as Pino Ferranti, and they are generally of a very good caliber. His work never approaches the inspired lunacy of Giannetto De Rossi and Rosario Prestopino in Fulci's golden era work, but as successors go he proves to be quite adequate; he had already worked on *Aenigma* and would go on to do *The Ghosts of Sodom, Demonia, Nightmare Concert (A Cat in the Brain)* and *Voices from Beyond*.

*Touch of Death* may not be the "masterpiece" Fulci played it up to be, but neither is it the train wreck some critics have depicted it as, either. It shows Fulci melding the broad comedy of his earlier works with the shocking gore of his peak period, and the end results are interesting, especially if one is familiar with the full sweep of his directorial career. Its deficiencies are almost all due to the threadbare production values, and unfortunately these deficiencies would be even more readily apparent in his next picture.

Notes:

1. Palmerini, Luca M. and Gaetano Mistretta, *Spaghetti Nightmares*, (Key West: Fantasma Books, 1996), p. 63.

# Michele de Angelis Interview by Adrien Clerc

Adrien Clerc conducted the following interview with assistant director Michele de Angelis on April 3, 2012. The interview was originally published on the website, which can be found at www.luciofulci.fr. It is reprinted here with the kind permission of Lionel Grenier, who runs the Fulci website. Michele de Angelis was Fulci's assistant on *Touch of Death*, *The Ghosts of Sodom*, *The House of Clocks* and *The Sweet House of Horrors*. He also worked on several of the films "presented" by Fulci around this same time.

**Adrien Clerc**: You were very young when you first met Lucio Fulci. That must have been an unforgettable experience! Can you tell our readers how you first encountered him?

**Michele de Angelis**: I had been hired as assistant director on some movies that Fulci was supposed to "present." He was going to direct 2 of them, but we had trouble with a director shooting one; the movie was turning out pretty bad and most of all it was too short! Fulci was asked to take over and put things in order. I offered myself to go and get him at 6.30 a.m., driving 45 km from my house and then bringing him to the set. Nobody wanted to do it since it was too long of a trip, but I wanted to meet the guy so badly. I remember asking him all sorts of questions about how he shot a sequence there, how he did this and that. He got out of the car once we arrived and went to the producers asking, "Who the fuck is that guy?" Since that day he asked the production to send me every morning to pick him up and then bring him back at night. For me it was kind of hell, working 15 to 18 hours a day, but it was too interesting to give up. We had incredible conversations on films, art and even football!

**AC**: Do you remember the film Fulci finished shooting?

**MdA**: Of course. It was *Hansel e Gretel*, by Giovanni Simonelli. The film was too short. I don't know what the director and producers had in mind, but they didn't take the time to know how long the film would be from the screenplay. This one was way too short. Lucio Fulci worked on some additional scenes during one week of shooting, if I remember it well; some shots featured special effects. Simonelli was an old man at the time, and he was not very interested in his own film. Actually, he didn't give a fuck! I remember one day we were on the set, ready to shoot, everything set up, and we were just waiting for the instructions of the director … who had disappeared. After some investigation, he was found in the basement of the villa where we shot, admiring old bottles of wine. His son, the production manager, just appeared and disappeared too … it was funny.

**AC**: By the way, this is the same Giovanni Simonelli that Fulci later wrote the first treatment for *Nightmare Concert (A Cat in the Brain)*? What was the relationship between these two veterans of popular Italian cinema?

**MdA**: I think that Simonelli has nothing in common with Fulci. He had a privileged relationship with the producers. I think he was there to make sure Fulci did his job and remained under control. But in my opinion, most of the good ideas in *A Cat in the Brain* come from the rewrite done by Antonio Tentori.

**AC**: You were assistant director on *Touch of Death*, even if you're uncredited. Why aren't you on the credits?

**MdA**: I was assistant director at the beginning, but in the end I had some fights with the production company—since I sided with Fulci; they hated me. I remember the production manager saying to me on the last day of shooting, "Congrats for the all the movies you're going to work on in the future with Fulci … definitely not with us!" And I answered, "Thank God."

**AC**: *Touch of Death* was a low-budget movie, but it's still quite impressive, even if it's very different from the horror movies Fulci became famous with—it has a strange mix of humor and realism in it. Did Fulci explain to the team what his aims were with *Touch of Death*?

**MdA**: No, he didn't, just me, the cast, his script girl (Note: daughter Camilla Fulci). It was so much better on paper, along with another one we unfortunately never made: *NHF (No Human Factor)*, but the production … you can't call it cheap, call it miserable. They weren't giving us anything … the mix of black humor was part of Lucio's personality. He was funny, but always with a bitter, sardonic side.

**AC**: Do you remember how long the shooting took? Was it an easy experience?

**MdA**: Easy because he was good, even without any means. He knew exactly what he wanted, and when we

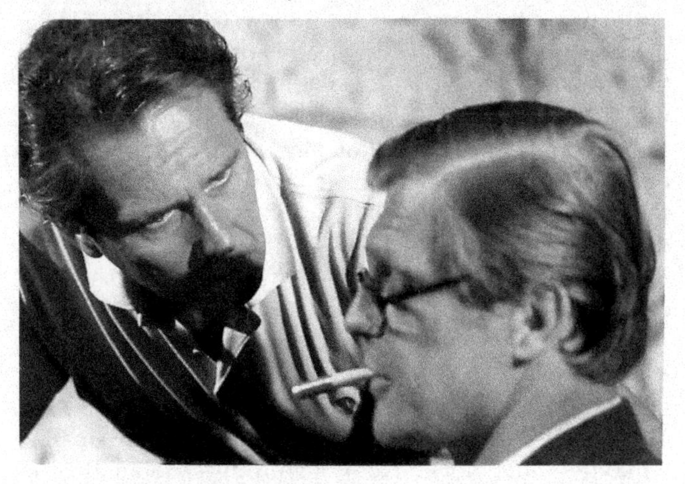

**Candid shot taken on the set of *Touch of Death* for continuity purposes; courtesy of Michele de Angelis.**

had nothing he was always able to improvise something interesting. The shooting was less than three weeks, let's say two-and-a-half.

**AC**: The same year, you worked on *Ghosts of Sodom*, which is, in my humble opinion, one of Fulci's less effective horror movies. Was this experience different from *Touch of Death*? Did you feel Fulci was less interested in that movie?

**MdA**: Same production, same problems; maybe less because they spent a little more money. We shot this before *Touch of Death*. But from one film to another, things were going worse and worse …

**Two more candid photos from the set of *Touch of Death*; courtesy of Michele de Angelis.**

**AC**: Some of the images in *The Ghosts of Sodom*, the mansion, the confrontation between youngsters and Nazis, recall a masterpiece of Italian cinema, Pasolini's last movie: *Salò*. Did Fulci speak about a link between *The Ghosts of Sodom* and *Salò*?

**MdA**: Not at all, never mentioned it. He just wanted to depict the perversion of a declining power.

**AC**: Can you tell more about *NHF*, the unmade project that you've mentioned?

**MdA**: *NHF (No Human Factor)* should have been another film in the "Lucio Fulci Presents" series. Lucio would have directed the film; the shooting was to be in a strange side of Rome called Laurentino 28. It's a hideous recent district built in the '60s, with big monolithic buildings. The story took place in the future, a kind of *Blade Runner* with characters that were not human but synthetic. I remember that the project was really attractive. But with all the problems that we've had with the production company, Alfa Cinematografica, it would have been impossible to make a good science-fiction movie without a significant budget. Because of *NHF*, Lucio broke his contract for the series. He had to make four or five films, but he would direct only two of them. I think that then they agreed that Fulci would direct *Cat in the Brain* with some scenes from other films of the series to avoid a trial.

**AC**: When you talk of production problems, was it just about budgets? Were they supposed to be more important when they signed the contract?

**MdA**: Actually, the budgets were smaller and smaller, while the films moved from one producer to another, to another … Scena Films moved the project to Alfa Cinematografica—and they hired two producers that we nicknamed "the cat and the fox." When they arrived on the

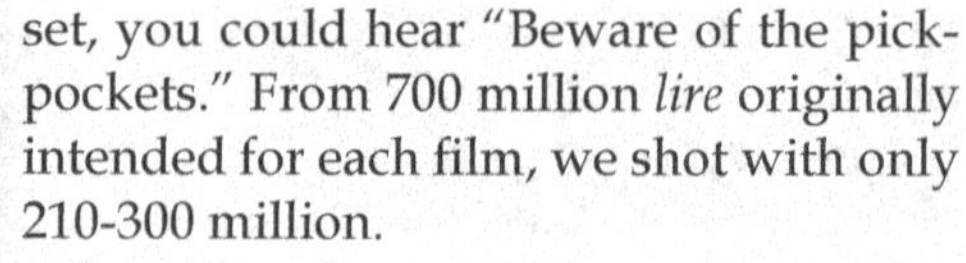

set, you could hear "Beware of the pickpockets." From 700 million *lire* originally intended for each film, we shot with only 210-300 million.

**AC**: You've also worked on other movies from the "Lucio Fulci Presents" series for Alfa Cinematografica. Was the shooting of Andrea and Mario Bianchi different from Fulci's, and if so, in what ways?

**MdA**: The directors were different. They really didn't care too much for the movies. I got along very well with Andrea Bianchi, since he was the one to bring me in, giving me the chance to work in the film industry. Mario was a nice man, who didn't really give a shit about the movie, I believe. He just wanted to put the thing in the can as soon as possible. That was the only movie where I was going home every day at 3 p.m. sharp.

**AC**: How was Fulci with the actors? Was he different with people like Al Cliver or Brett Halsey, with whom he established a strong work relation, than with other actors? He said a few times he got along better with actresses than with actors.

**MdA**: He was wonderful with talented people. He was impressed by Jessica Moore, who at that time was trying to get out of the cliché image she had after doing *Eleven Days, Eleven Nights* (1987). She was kind of good, and he was encouraging her to study and don't give up. With others, especially the bad ones, that are often the most arrogant, he was a nightmare. He hated people with no talent that also pretended to have some. So often he was saying something like, "Good take, you just won a golden bone," implying the actor was a dog, a term in Italy we use to define bad talents.

**AC**: You worked on Fulci's next projects, the two *House* television movies he made for Reteitalia [Note: *The House of Clocks* and *The Sweet House of Horrors*]. This time you're credited as assistant director, alongside Camilla Fulci. How did you decide who was doing what with Camilla?

**MdA**: Camilla wanted to be a director at that time, so she got that credit, but she was still a script girl. Lucio wanted her to become the first European female horror director.

**AC**: How was Camilla?

**MdA**: Actually, I got along well with Camilla. She was ... I don't know, she was like tormented inside. I don't know what happened next, but she broke off all ties with her family and the cinema and I never saw her again after the films we made together. At the time, in any case, she got along very well with her father.

**AC**: Which *House* film was shot first? Did you notice differences between the two shoots?

**MdA**: Not really; they had much bigger budgets and a better production company. Shot back to back, if I'm not wrong, *The House of Clocks* was second. The order doesn't really matter, since we were stopping one day and beginning the new one immediately.

**AC**: *The House of Clocks* is a very beautiful movie. It gets close to the metaphysical feelings conveyed by Fulci's masterpieces. It almost looks like Chirico's paintings from time to time. How did Fulci explain what he wanted with *The House of Clocks*?

**MdA**: Lucio was a huge art lover. He had been part of an elite group of intellectuals that dominated the scene in the '50s and '60s. Most of the famous Italian painters were his friends, probably De Chirico as well. He wanted to do something metaphysical since he was fascinated by the flowing of time and [he wanted] to destroy conventions in narrative filmmaking. As you probably know he was always quoting Artaud as one of the sources of inspirations for structures of the story—an apparent nonsense with no guideline—that when edited together made a whole piece of art.

**AC**: I really love *The House of Clocks*, but every time I watch the DVD I wonder if the movie looked better the first time it was released. I'm talking about the photography quality, the color, the definition—now I can ask someone who might know! Is there a big difference between the movie as it was made and the DVD? Would it be possible to have a better copy, do you know if that exists somewhere?

**MdA**: The movies were made for TV, so the video master probably was brightened up when aired. It would be good to go back to the original 16mm materials to do new high-definition transfers with new color grading and correction. 16mm is softer than 35mm because of the format; when transferred to analogue standard definition DVD, it is going to look so-so.

**AC**: *The Sweet House of Horrors* is not as good as *The House of Clocks*, mostly because of special effects and pacing problems. Do you know if Fulci was happy with it, and if he tried to rewrite the movie on the set?

**MdA**: No dramatic changes occurred. He liked *House of Clocks* more, but was kind of happy with both of them, especially after what he experienced with previous productions.

**AC**: How was Fulci's general attitude towards screenplays and shooting schedules: Did he improvise a lot, or was he following the visual ideas he had before the shooting? On the movies you worked on, was he "editing in the camera," like Hitchcock, or was he covering every sequence with different scales and angles, in a more traditional way?

**MdA**: I don't know. He always knew where to place the camera; if he were improvising, I wish I could do it that well! He was editing in camera, to avoid producers putting their hands on the product. He favored long tracking shots and cranes, which were beautiful to watch. He wasn't covering at all, as I told you he knew exactly what to do and how to achieve it. No need to waste time with many angles, just in case. Everything matched to perfection.

**AC**: *The Sweet House of Horrors* and *The House of Clocks* seem to share the same structure, with very realistic, almost crude beginnings followed by a sudden jump into fantasy. Did Fulci talk about this?

**MdA**: Well, I believe he was very interested in this change. Even in other movies, like *Touch of Death* for instance, you believe what is a realistic serial killer film then turns into surrealism. This is very interesting and leaves the viewer puzzled and surprised.

**AC**: The director of photography on these films was Nino Celeste, a man who worked for TV but had experiences with Bava and Martino. How did he and Fulci work together?

**MdA**: Good. Celeste was actually a good director of photography, fast and doing nice things.

**AC**: Why did you stop working with Fulci after the *House* films?

**MdA**: I started to do some other projects, and Lucio was kind of upset. He had this dominating persona: Once you work with him, you work with him, full stop. For a while we didn't speak to each other that much, but then we were on good terms again. He came to a retrospective I did on Italian horror films and was very pleased; he was running a column in a famous newspaper, and wrote about the festival in excellent terms.

**AC**: You are a true cinema lover, obviously—what do you think of these movies and their place in Italian popular cinema?

**MdA**: I like them, even if they don't match the previous stuff he did. Unfortunately ... because of the budget limits and production restrictions.

**AC**: Do you have another memory about these movies you would like to share?

**MdA**: They were my film school. I learned things that you would never learn in a classroom. The best film school is to work on movies with some professionals and watch them. Then watch all that you can from silent [film days] until now. Some young people now don't realize there's film history before Tarantino or John Woo.

**AC**: Do you have a favorite film of Lucio Fulci?

**MdA**: That's a difficult question. Probably *Don't Torture a Duckling*, then *The Psychic*, *Lizard in a Woman's Skin*, *City of the Living Dead*, *The Beyond* and *House by the Cemetery*; those latter ones are more-or-less on the same level.

## *The Ghosts of Sodom (Italy)*

Aka *Il fantasma di Sodom; Los fantasmas de Sodoma; Les fantômes de Sodome; Sodoma's tödliche Rache*

Directed by Lucio Fulci; Produced by Antonio Lucidi and Luigi Nannerini, for Alpha Cinematografica; Screenplay by Lucio Fulci and Carlo Alberto Alfieri, from a story by Lucio Fulci; Director of Photography: Silvano Tessicini; Editor: Vincenzo Tomassi; Music by Carlo Maria Cordio

Main Players: Claudio Aliotti (Paul); Maria Concetta Salieri (Celine); Robert Egon (Willy); Luciana Ottaviani (Marie); Teresa Razzaudi (Annie); Sebastian Harrison (Jean); Joseph Alan Johnson [as Alan Johnson] (Marc); Pierluigi Conti [Al Cliver] (Drunken Nazi) [uncredited]

*A group of teenagers on their way to the beach stumble upon an abandoned villa in the country. They take refuge and make use of its amenities, not realizing that the S.S. formerly used it for their debauched orgies. The kids start seeing various strange sights, but refuse to believe their senses. It soon becomes apparent that the ghosts of the Nazis are still in the house and they are looking to claim the kids as their victims …*

Fulci followed *Touch of Death* in rapid succession with *The Ghosts of Sodom*. The film represents Fulci's only foray into one of the more questionable subgenres in Italian exploitation: the Nazisploitation film. Inspired by the success of films like Luchino Visconti's *The Damned* (1969), Liliana Cavani's *The Night Porter* (1974) and Pier Paolo Pasolini's *Salò, or the 120 Days of Sodom* (1975), Italian directors on the lower end of the industry responded with a series of lurid, politically incorrect sleaze epics which wallowed in depravity for the sake of depravity: titles like *SS Experiment Camp* (1976), *The Beast in Heat* (1977) and *The Gestapo's Last Orgy* (1977) made it plain that these films were looking to inspire public interest through sheer sensationalism. If filmmakers like Pasolini were looking to make a serious comment on man's inhumanity towards his fellow man, directors like Sergio Garrone were not concerned with such sentiments: These films were designed to be as outrageous as possible, and, truth be told, they often were informed by a streak of impish dark humor, which acknowledged the absurdity of their scenarios.

*The Ghosts of Sodom* name-checks Pasolini's notorious example, but the similarities between the two films are superficial at best. Pasolini's film caused a sensation when it was released, and for good reason: It is two hours of non-stop depravity, in which the excesses of Fascism and Nazism are linked to the philosophy of the Marquis de Sade. Man's boundless capacity for cruelty is laid bare in a deliberately sterile way: Pasolini does not glorify or sidestep his horrific imagery, but rather puts it out there for people to see it for what it really is. The end effect may be a little deadening after a certain point, but its impact is difficult to shake: Images of the youthful victims being sexually tortured or forced to eat shit by their elder oppressors have lost none of their potency down through the years. Sadly, by contrast, *The Ghosts of Sodom* is the kind of film one tends to forget just a few minutes after finishing with it. If Fulci was genuinely interested in exploring the nature of evil, somehow he got lost in a morass of bad horror film clichés as an obnoxious group of teenagers get trapped in a house in the middle of nowhere and find themselves being tormented by the ghosts of the house's former Nazi occupants.

**Japanese VHS cover for *The Ghosts of Sodom.***

Fulci begins the film with a cocaine-fueled orgy sequence. Set during the final days of World War II, as the Allies are beginning to finally eradicate the Nazi presence, it features a group of Nazi soldiers clicking heels with some topless bimbos. The actors bump and grind on top of each other, but the men continue to wear their trousers—one never knows when one is going to be called back to duty, after all—and the women look as though they have wandered in from 1988. A gramophone helps to set the tone of antiquity, but the synth-based muzak emitting from the speaker only succeeds in pushing the action into the realm of farce. The fun and frivolity is ended when the Allies—in the form of black-and-white stock footage—bomb the house and its occupants.

From there, the story enters full-blown *Scooby Doo* terrain as the teenagers are shown driving around the countryside without a care in the world. Sooner than you can say "Scrappy Doo," the kids find themselves in front of the old villa; this being a horror film, they can't resist the urge to poke around inside, and decide to spend the night. Any attempt at suspense or tension is undone by the fact that these kids are so utterly banal and interchangeable; it's literally impossible to tell one of them from the other—perhaps this was part of Fulci's master plan by way of a commentary on contemporary horror film tropes, but if so it doesn't add anything to the experience of watching the movie. The kids squabble and try to bed one another, but nothing much happens until the spirit of a Nazi named Willy (the name seems pregnant with symbolism, but it is perhaps best not to go there) emerges through the mirror and taps into the sadomasochistic fantasies of Marie; he slaps her around and rubs blood all over her, but all is forgotten the next morning and the kids attempt an escape, only to realize that they are now imprisoned. The next big supernatural "happening" occurs when Marc gets drunk and wanders in on a card game between the ghostly Nazis. Willy tempts the horny Marc with the promise of some sex from an unnamed but quite voluptuous naked woman; in order to win her favors, however, he must first complete a card game with a little Russian roulette tossed in for good measure. Fulci manages to create a little suspense in this drawn-out encounter, which is all the more surprising given that Marc is arguably the most irritating of the young characters. Having survived his test, Marc goes to the nameless woman and begins to make love to her; when he grabs at her breasts, however, her chest collapses into an ugly mess of green slime and bile. It's a well-done shock effect, but unfortunately there isn't much else to equal it from here on in. Marc is eventually killed when he falls down a flight of stairs, and the unnaturally quick progression of his decomposition provides a few icky moments of body horror. The story limps along to a lame finale—only to undo itself even further with that most hoary of horror film clichés: It turns out, it was all just a dream. Indeed …

*The Ghosts of Sodom* sees Fulci working on autopilot, with nary a flourish of inspiration to be found. *Touch of Death* was a flawed but interesting film, and it contained some genuinely effective shock sequences; by contrast, *The Ghosts of Sodom* is as flaccid as they come. Even the doses of erotica feel halfhearted—truly surprising in light of the full-blooded kinkiness and energy that fueled *The Devil's Honey*, for example. There are elements of a good movie to be found here, but they are few and far between. Despite the presence of Fulci veterans like Zora Kerova (in her last role for the director) and Al Cliver, both in unbilled roles, the film is saddled with the least appealing cast to be found in the director's filmography; the actors are every bit as vapid and annoying as their characters and that is no easy feat. Silvano Tessicini's cinematography is as flat and uninteresting as it had been in *Touch of Death*, and Fulci mainstay Vincenzo Tomassi does what he can to give the film some sense of rhythm in his editing. Carlo Maria Cordio's score—his last for the director—ranges from the cliché to the comically inappropriate, with his wildly anachronistic synth Vitrola music taking the proverbial cake. Fulci's direction occasionally hits upon a nice stylistic flourish—the shadow of a Swastika flashing across the wall during a thunderstorm, for example—but in general he seems unconvinced by the material and doesn't invest it with the required tension or sense of menace. The director would later sum up *The Ghosts of Sodom* as "a very bad movie"[1]—and, really, who are we to disagree with him?

Notes:

1. Retrieved from, http://www.shockingimages.com/fulci/interview.html

# 1989

## The Sweet House of Horrors (Italy)

Aka *La dolce casa degli orrori*

Directed by Lucio Fulci; Produced by Massimo Manasse and Marco Grilla Spina, for Reteitalia and Dania Film; Screenplay by Gigliola Battaglini and Vincenzo Mannino, from a story by Lucio Fulci; Director of Photography: Sebastiano Celeste [as Nino Celeste]; Editor: Alberto Moriani [as Albert Morris]; Music by Vince Tempera

Main Players: Jean-Christophe Brétigniere (Carlo); Cinzia Monreale (Marcia); Giuliano Gensini (Marco); Ilari Blasi (Sarah); Lino Salemme (Guido); Franco Diogene (Mr. Coby); Vernon Dobtcheff [as Alexander Vernon Dobtcheff] (The Exorcist); Pascal Persiano (Roberto Valdi); Lubka Lenzi [as Lubka Cibulova] (Mary Valdi)

*Roberto and Mary are gruesomely murdered when they return home and surprise a burglar. The burglar places the corpses in their car and makes it look like an accident. Mary's sister, Marcia, and her husband Carlo are then obliged to take charge of their niece and nephew, Sarah and Marco. The children behave strangely and appear to be carrying on conversations with people they cannot see. It is eventually revealed that the ghosts of Roberto and Mary are still in the house and they are doing everything they can to carry on a relationship with their children—and also to prevent Marcia and Carlo from selling the house …*

After breaking his contract with Alpha Cinematografica, Lucio Fulci did not find many producers banging on the door asking for his services. He hadn't directed a particularly successful film in quite a few years, and, while his health was on the rebound, he was still a far cry from his formerly robust self. Thus, when a he received an offer from the Reteitalia Company, he leapt at the chance.

Reteitalia, established in 1979, became a prime producer of television shows and made-for-TV movies in the 1980s, and they had begun to dabble in the production of horror films for the small screen when they produced the series *Brivido giallo*. The series was comprised of feature-length films directed by Lamberto Bava: *Graveyard Disturbance*, *Until Death* (based on the screenplay which caused the final falling-out between Fulci and Dardano Sacchetti), *The Ogre* and *Dinner with a Vampire*. Broadcast between 1987 and 1988, these four films garnered middling ratings, but Reitalia decided to forge ahead with a new series based around the theme of haunted houses, under the umbrella title of *Le case maldette*, or *Doomed Houses*. Fulci's *The Sweet House of Horrors* was the first of this new batch, and it would be followed in rapid succession by Fulci's *The House of Clocks* and Umberto Lenzi's *The House of Witchcraft* and *The House of Lost Souls*, all produced in 1989. The films would remain unreleased in their intended medium, however. Fulci and Lenzi both found the situation frustrating, but for Fulci at least his two entries provided him with access to better production values and collaborators. He would later enthuse that the experience was:

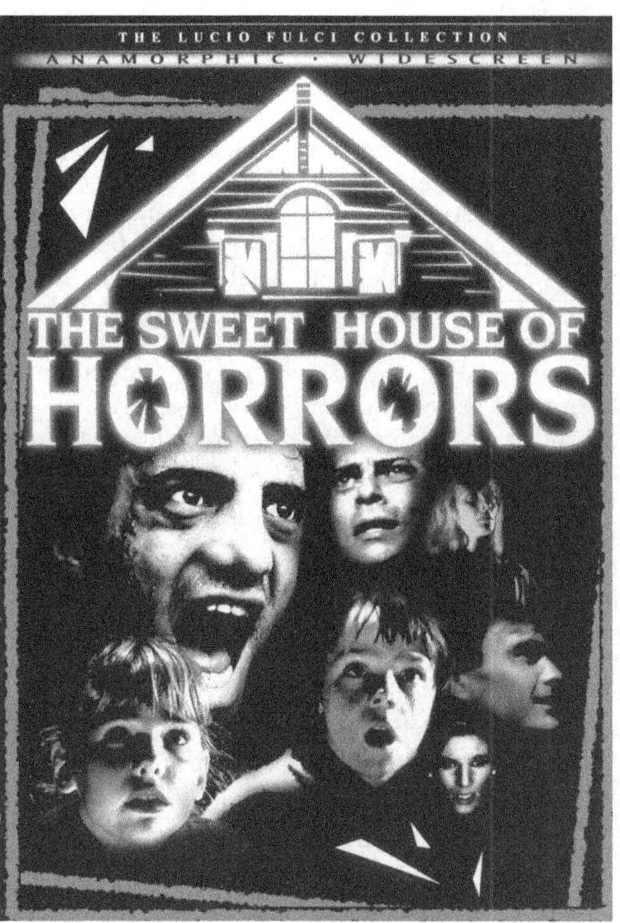


**DVD sleeve for the Shriek Show release of *The Sweet House of Horrors*; artist unknown.**

> Fantastic! Excellent filmmaking! Nino Celeste is a splendid cameraman. They're two of the best films I've made.[1]

Fulci's enthusiasm is not entirely supported by the end results, but both films are a marked improvement over the likes of *The Ghosts of Sodom* and *Zombie 3*.

The film starts off with a set piece of classic Fulci violence: A mother and father surprise a burglar and find themselves fighting for their lives. The ensuing fight between Roberto and the burglar—obviously performed by actors Pascal Persiano and Lino Salemme without the aid of stunt people—is well staged and culminates with Robert getting his head bashed against a wall. The burglar chases the panic-stricken Mary into the kitchen, where he proceeds to brutalize her, smashing her eyes out and crushing her skull. Fulci dwells on the brutality of this scene in clinical detail, and the special make-up effects by Giuseppe Ferranti are definitely up to snuff. The sequence is brutal as hell and it sets the viewer up for expecting much more of the same—however, Fulci stymies expectations from this moment onward.

The bulk of the film is much more genteel than this brutal opening would suggest. The film continues the theme of children interacting with the spirit world from *The House by the Cemetery* and *Manhattan Baby*, but the overall theme is one of melancholia as the child protagonists—Marco and Sarah—yearn to be reunited with their dead parents. Fulci introduces the kids with a marvelous, sustained point of view shot as they are shepherded to their parents' funeral. The kids do not entirely comprehend the gravity of the situation, however, and they laugh at the priest as he struggles to retain composure while a fly insists on crawling across his nose. The scene establishes the schizophrenic tone of the film, which vacillates between the somber and the comic. As the story unfolds, it becomes apparent that Marco and Sarah have little interest in establishing a relationship with their aunt and uncle. Marcia and Carlo mean well and have the kids' best interests at heart, but they are ill equipped to deal with the demands of dealing with two emotionally traumatized children. Their solution is to take the kids out of their environment and move to the city, but this does not sit well with the children because the spirits of their late parents continue to visit them in the house. As is so often the case, the inability for adults to communicate with children is pronounced in this context, and their relationship is strained as a result; Marcia and Carlo are not depicted unfavorably, however; they simply do not know how to deal with the kids and are ignorant to their wants and needs.

The contrast between the comic and the serious gives the film an offbeat flavor. In a way, it's closer in tone to *Touch of Death*, but it's nowhere near so grotesque. Late in the film, an exorcist is called in to lay rest to the spirits haunting the house. The pompous exorcist attempts to assert control, but in the eyes of the children—and the audience—he is frankly ridiculous. His attempts to free the children from the influence of the spirits is ill-conceived, anyway: The spirits mean no harm and are only there to look over their children. Ultimately, he proves to be unsuccessful in his mission, and the children continue to interact with their parents. In a sense, one can read this as a continuation of the themes Fulci began to explore in *Aenigma*: Faced with his own mortality, the director continues to explore the notions of death and the afterlife. Could his refusal to "cure" the children of their continued interaction with their deceased parents speak to Fulci's own desire to continue a relationship with his own family beyond the grave?

*The Sweet House of Horrors* suffers from some ill-advised touches of broad comedy and some generally cheap-looking optical effects. Flames superimposed on the image represent the spirits, but beyond that it offers up considerably richer production values than the films Fulci made immediately prior. The cinematography is by Nino Celeste, who provides Fulci with some of his most attractive lighting among his later films. Born in Santa Croce in 1940, Celeste started off as a camera operator in the mid-'60s, then established himself as a cinematographer in the early '70s. He worked with such directors as Umberto Lenzi (*Violent Naples*, 1976), Mario Bava (*La venere d'Ille*, 1978) and Damiano Damiani (the TV series *The Octopus*, 1984) prior to working with Fulci, and he continues to remain active in films. Celeste's elegant lighting belies the film's TV origins, and he would do a similarly stellar job on *The House of Clocks*; if only Fulci had been able to continue retaining his services.

Fulci devised the story himself but entrusted the writing to the husband and wife team of Gigliola Battaglini and Vincenzo Mannino. Battaglini worked sporadically with her husband, but she was only formally credited on two scripts: Ruggero Deodato's *The Phantom of Death* (1988) and this film. Mannino amassed a much larger filmography and worked in most of the popular Italian genres: *pepla* (*The Revolt of the Seven*, 1964), *gialli* (*Five Women for the Killer*, 1974), horror (*The Antichrist*, 1974), *poliziotteschi* (*Violent Naples*, 1976), etc. He also collaborated with Fulci on the screenplays for *The New York Ripper* and *Murder-Rock: Dancing Death*; this would mark the end of their working relationship.

The cast performs quite capably. Cinzia Monreale is effective as the neurotic Marcia; this was her last role for Fulci and fittingly it is also the largest, though inevitably nothing can quite compare with her wonderfully ambiguous turn as the ghostly Emily in *The Beyond*. Jean-Christophe Brétigniere, who also puts in a good performance, plays her husband Carlo. The roles are somewhat superficial, but the two actors play well off of each other and aptly convey the characters' perplexed attitude towards the children. Brétigniere would later recall Fulci in colorful terms:

> He could be terrifying and then he could be sweet [...] He would eat onions like I could eat an apple.[2]

The imposing Lino Salemme played Guido, the gardener eventually revealed to be the burglar from the beginning of the film. Salemme doesn't have a lot to do in the film, but he would go on to appear in Fulci's *Demonia*. After making his debut as a coke-snorting hoodlum in Lamberto Bava's *Demons* (1985), Salemme went on to become a semi-regular in Bava's work, appearing in the likes of *Demons 2* (1986), *Delirium: Photos of Gioia* (1987) and *The Man Who Didn't Want to Die* (1988), among others. As he later recalled, the experience of working with the laidback Bava did not prepare him for Fulci:

> Lucio Fulci treated us awfully, both Pascal [Persiano] and myself, especially Pascal. We were young at the time [...] It was the first time that a director treated us like that, and it made us nervous. [...] Fulci was always mad, he was always screaming, he treated everyone very poorly.[3]

Salemme would eventually win the director over, however, and they would go on to a more mutually satisfying collaboration on *Demonia*. He later summed Fulci up thus:

> The memory I have of him is as a suffering man. One could see that he was already quite ill ... a very lonely, grumpy, very dark man, especially while working; but I think that was also a cover-up to all that uneasiness and suffering. [...] Looking back, I feel sorry for him, although we had a rough start together.

Veteran French character actor Vernon Dobtcheff plays the role of the exorcist; it's not a terribly well developed character, but Dobtcheff gives him the right mixture of dignity and foolishness. Born in 1934, he started off acting in England and has amassed a ridiculously eclectic array of credits, including several appearances on the cult TV series

**The exorcist (Vernon Dobtcheff, center) tries to help Marcia and Carlo to reach the restless spirits of Roberto and Mary.**

*The Avengers*, as well as roles in everything from Franco Zeffirelli's *The Taming of the Shrew* (1967) and Pier Paolo Pasolini's *The Canterbury Tales* (1972) to Sidney Lumet's *Murder on the Orient Express* (1974) and Steven Spielberg's *Indiana Jones and the Last Crusade* (1989); he remains very active in the international film scene. Pascal Persiano, who plays the role of Roberto, would go on to appear in Fulci's *Voices from Beyond*. He doesn't have a lot to do in this film beyond his impressive fight to the death with Salemme, but he does a credible job. He would later describe Fulci as a very complex character:

> He was a serious professional, compulsive, precise, nothing left to chance. [...] When filming was done, he was like someone else. He'd turn into an adorable person, caring, affectionate, with a large appetite, because he ate tons. He especially loved to talk about sex and women. He'd ask, "Say, what do you got going on with her? Did you shag her? Did you? What did she do?" He was on seventh heaven, like we say in Italy. He'd get a high from these stories. [...] He was also very kind.

*The Sweet House of Horrors* is a minor entry in Fulci's body of work, but it is not without interest. His follow-up for Reteitalia would prove to be even more rewarding, however.

Notes:
1. Palmerini, Luca M. and Gaetano Mistretta, *Spaghetti Nightmares*, (Key West: Fantasma Books, 1996), p. 63.
2. Interview with Jean-Christophe Brétigniere, included on the Shriek Show DVD release of *The Sweet House of Horrors*.
3. Interview with Pascal Persiano, included on the Shriek Show DVD release of *The Sweet House of Horrors*.

**Above and Opposite page: Japanese video pressbook art for *The House of Clocks*; artist unknown.**

## *The House of Clocks* (Italy)

Aka *La casa nel tempo; Die Uhr des Grauens*

Directed by Lucio Fulci; Produced by Massimo Manasse and Marco Grilla Spina, for Reteitalia and Dania Film; Screenplay by Gianfranco Clerici and Daniele Stroppa, from a story by Lucio Fulci; Director of Photography: Sebastiano Celeste [as Nino Celeste]; Editor: Alberto Moriani [as Albert Morris]; Music by Vince Tempera

Main Players: Keith van Hoven (Tony); Karina Huff (Sandra); Peter Hintz (Paul); Paolo Paoloni (Vittorio Corsini); Bettine Milne (Sara Corsini); Pieluigi Conti [as Al Cliver] (Peter); Carla Cassola (Maria); Paolo Bernardi (The Nephew); Francesca DeRose (The Niece)

*Tony, Paul and Sandra are out on a joyride, looking to raise a little hell. They get word that the secluded house of eccentric recluses Vittorio and Sara Corsini is loaded with valuables and decide to pay a visit, hoping to rob them blind. Sandra pretends to be stranded and asks for shelter and the Corsinis oblige her with hospitality. She then leaves the door open and allows her friends to come in after her. The robbery doesn't go as planned, and the old couple and their servant Peter are killed. When the three youths try to flee, they discover that they are prisoners—and that time itself seems to be running in reverse ...*

Right after completing *The Sweet House of Horrors*, Fulci dove straight into his next project. *The House of Clocks* is the stronger of the two television films he made back-to-back, and it remains one of his most engaging final works.

Fulci once again devised the story and it deals with the themes of time and fate, which are familiar concepts from his earlier films. Fulci entrusted the writing of the screenplay to an old collaborator and a new one, making the film into a symbolic changing of the guard: Gianfranco Clerici had already collaborated on the screenplays for *Don't Torture a Duckling*, *The New York Ripper* and *Murder-Rock: Dancing Death*, while Daniele Stroppa would go on to become one of the director's last trusted writing collaborators. This would mark the last time Fulci worked with Clerici, but Stroppa—whose earlier credits included

Lamberto Bava's *Delirium: Photos of Gioia* and Claudio Lattanzi's *Zombie 5: Killing Birds* (both 1987)—would go on to collaborate on the screenplays for *Voices from Beyond* and *The Wax Mask*.

Like *The Sweet House of Horrors*, the film experiments with a mixture of the brutal and the whimsical, but the effect feels less strained this time around. The opening scenes set the tone very well: A doddering old couple, Vittorio and Sara Corsini, goes about their daily routine, with the husband obsessing over his clock collection and the old lady pottering about in the garden, while their housekeeper walks on pins and needles trying to avoid displeasing them. Despite their outwardly placid and sweet demeanor, it's clear that there is something sinister about the couple. These suspicions are confirmed when the maid enters the family chapel and finds the decomposing bodies of a young man and a young woman, dressed in wedding attire, with spikes driven through their throats. Vittorio realizes that the housekeeper is wise to their little secret, and Sara responds by staking the woman through her crotch—shades of *City of the Living Dead*! They then go about concealing their crime and restoring their neatly ordered little world to its former condition. The contrast between the gruesome burst of violence and the sweetly doddering behavior of the old couple is nicely achieved and establishes a tone that will be followed through for the rest of the picture. The film is not a spoof, per se, but it is decidedly tongue-in-cheek; fortunately, this does not take the edge off of the suspense or the film's various shock sequences.

From here, the film introduces the ultimate '80s horror film cliché: horny teenagers. The trio of young protagonists is established as reckless and unsympathetic early on, but they will grow and become a little more endearing as the story develops. Fulci's anti-drug attitude is evident as the three spend a great deal of time smoking marijuana, but he stops short of implying that the narcotic is responsible for their behavior; instead, it is just indicative of their idle and aimless mentality. After ripping-off some food from a local supermarket, they make their way to the house—they've heard it's stuffed with rare antiques and want to make an easy score. Once they gain access to the house, all hell breaks loose: The robbery turns into a massacre and they end up killing the old couple and their faithful gardener Peter. The conflict between the stately older generation and the drug-addled younger one is a bit facile, perhaps, but it gets the point across: The trio of kids has no respect for their elders or what they represent, and are intent on feeding their own greedy interests at any costs. The theme is not quite as simple as that, however: As will soon become apparent, the older generation will not be so simply eradicated, nor are they free from criticism, either.

With the death of the time-obsessed Vittorio, the clocks begin running backwards. As the kids attempt to flee the house, they discover that they are not able to do so: They have become prisoners and are being set up for a little well-deserved retribution. As time continues to break down, logic and reality become similarly distorted. The dead come back to life, but not as conventional zombies: Time has simply allowed them to return to life and to heal their wounds, thus enabling them to take revenge on their attackers. Unfortunately for Vittorio and Sara, however, this also extends to their niece and nephew, laid out in the chapel; they, too, return to life and kill off their murderers. They then take their place as the new heads of the household, while the long-suffering housekeeper is returned to her post to serve under more benevolent masters.

The film ends with a twist that threatens to throw the film into the same category as *The Ghosts of Sodom*; it's revealed to have all been a bad dream—or rather a shared dream or premonition between the three teenagers. Just as the audience is ready to groan, however, Fulci and his cowriters toss in a welcome double-twist: The events of the night before may have been a nightmare, but it contains the seeds of a greater truth. The three teenagers try to alter the course of their destiny by avoiding the house and its horrors, but fate will not be double-crossed so easily; they are killed in a car crash, anyway. The notion of characters trying to alter their destiny is a familiar one

in Fulci's *oeuvre*, and can be seen in films like *A Lizard in a Woman's Skin*, *The Psychic* and *The Black Cat*, wherein dreams and visions serve as a baleful warning of what is to come, even as the characters try to avoid the inevitable. In Fulci's downbeat view of things, man's ultimate destiny is the grave—and no matter how hard one may fight to avoid this outcome, it will eventually come to us all.

Fulci's flair for creating atmosphere remains undiminished. He establishes the right ambience of doom and gloom in the eerie opening shots and does not allow the quirky humor to undercut this at any point. Nino Celeste's lighting is excellent and the camerawork by his operator Alessandro Grossi is of a similarly high caliber. Grossi had worked as an operator since the late 1970s and would soon be promoted to cinematographer, after assisting Luigi Ciccarese on *Demonia*; his first credits as a full-fledged director of photography would be Fulci's *Nightmare Concert (A Cat in the Brain)* and *Voices from Beyond*. The use of wide angle lenses and mobile camerawork recalls the glory days of Fulci's collaborations with Luigi Kuveiller and Sergio Salvati, but unfortunately such visual splendors would become more and more difficult to find in the director's subsequent, cash-strapped work. Special note should also be made of Elio Micheli and Paolo Faenzi's excellent art direction. The set dressings and overall attention to detail help to make the film look considerably more lavish than it really was. As such, it is one of the very few Italian horror films of its period to come close to recapturing the visual splendors of the "golden age" works by Mario Bava, Antonio Margheriti and Riccardo Freda.

*The House of Clocks* would meet the same fate as its predecessor, being effectively held hostage by Reteitalia for a period of time before eventually finding its way to home video; the films were deemed too violent to be shown on television as intended and the network did not reach out to Fulci for any further television movies. Even so, the director would later say that he enjoyed working on the two films and that he found them to be a refreshing challenge:

> In a way, it's much more demanding than making a film for the cinema. You have to respect certain rules like minimalizing the use of deep-focus shots, which play a vital role in thrillers and horror films and instead create tension in other ways, because a viewer tires of watching a television screen faster than he would in front of a cinema screen, which is coercive, whereas with the television, the viewer's attention is more liable to wander.[1]

For his next venture for the big screen, Fulci would revisit familiar terrain—but inadequate resources would nearly destroy the project before it ever reached cinema screens.

Notes:
1. Palmerini, Luca M. and Gaetano Mistretta, *Spaghetti Nightmares*, (Key West: Fantasma Books, 1996), p. 64.

# 1990

## *Demonia (Italy)*

Directed by Lucio Fulci; Produced by Ettore Spagnuolo, for Lanterna Editrice and A.M. Trading International S.r.l.; Screenplay by Lucio Fulci and Piero Regnoli [as Pietro Regnoli], from a story by Lucio Fulci, Piero Regnoli and Antonio Tentori [uncredited]; Director of Photography: Luigi Ciccarese; Editor: Otello Colangeli; Music by Giovanni Cristiani

Main Players: Brett Halsey (Professor Paul Evans); Meg Register (Liza); Lino Salemme (Turi DeSimone); Christina Englehardt (Susie); Pascal Druant (Kevin); Grady Clarkson (Sean); Carla Cassola (Lili, the medium); Ettore Comi (John); Pierluigi Conti [as Al Clever] (Porter)

Cameo appearance: Lucio Fulci (Inspector Carter)

*An expedition headed by Professor Paul Evans goes to Sicily to investigate the influence of Greek culture on the area. The locals warn Evans and his team not to mess around near the abandoned monastery in the area, but Evans' assistant, Liza, is drawn to the place. Eventually the spirits of the demonically possessed nuns in the monastery are freed and they set out on a mission to claim some new souls. More bloodshed will occur before the locals finally rebel and put a stop to the supernatural occurrences …*

*Demonia* marked Fulci's would-be return to the big screen; unfortunately for the director, however, the recent trend of his films sitting on the shelf would continue, as this film also failed to secure theatrical distribution anywhere in the world. In Italy, the film went straight to video; in America, it would not surface through "official" channels until 2001.

All the ingredients are in place, but something is seriously amiss with *Demonia*. In an interview with Brett Halsey included in this book, the actor notes that he does not believe that the film was ever properly completed; seeing the film, it's easy to see why he feels this way. The story by Fulci and veteran writer-director Piero Regnoli (more on him in a bit) offers a promising set-up, but it ultimately doesn't make a lick of sense. Fulci's best horror films of the 1980s showed a blatant and deliberate disregard for logic, but the director's flair for creating a dream-like atmosphere made sense of such an approach; *City of the Living Dead* and *The Beyond* are not plot-driven films, and their characters frequently do things which make no real sense, but it's all consistent with the mission of creating a nightmare on celluloid. *Demonia* is similarly senseless, but it doesn't feel as if this is deliberate or even consistent with a dream-like ambience. Instead, it feels as though there's a lot of connecting tissue that is missing. To put it metaphorically, the film is a skeleton without any flesh. Chances are that Fulci could have made this work to some degree if he had planned it out that way, but the fact that the film doesn't hold together seems to validate the argument that it was thrown together with reckless abandon once the production ran out of money. There are too many scenes that go nowhere, to say nothing of scenes that come out of left field and have absolutely no set-up. Fulci's propensity for shock effects is a running thread throughout his work, but he always displayed a degree of care with setting these effects up to maximize their effectiveness. In this film, however, there is a reckless attention to detail. Late in the film, for example, a child is put into danger when he is kidnapped by one of the possessed nuns; his father follows in hot pursuit. The child escapes from the evil nun and then suddenly, out of the blue, the father is seen strung up in the middle of the forest. The child runs to reunite with him and inadvertently trips a trap that tears the poor man in half down the middle; the child is splattered in blood as he stands by helplessly. There was a terrific shock effect to be had in this scene. As it stands, however, it's so arbitrarily and clumsily integrated into the film that it only succeeds in prompting nervous laughter. The remarkably slipshod special make-up effects credited to Giuseppe Ferranti (who is capable of much better), Franco Giannini, Mario Ciccarella and Elio Terribili do not help matters. Their combined efforts are generally amateurish and help to make *Demonia* one of the crudest and downright tackiest films in Fulci's filmography.

The script works in some allusions to Fulci's backlog of genre work—a séance scene is straight out of *City of the Living Dead*, the female protagonist is named after Catriona MacColl's character in *The Beyond*, the blonde-haired kid being splattered with his father's blood recalls a moment in *The House by the Cemetery*, etc.—but all the self-referencing in the world is not enough to overcome the overall air of lethargy which hangs over the proceedings. This is particularly dispiriting because, on the face of it at least, there is a good movie struggling to break free here. Fulci works hard to establish a moody atmosphere: The opening shots of the camera gliding through the abandoned monastery are very promising indeed, and there is some inventiveness in the staging of some of the kills. However, too much of it feels rushed—the flashback to the nuns being crucified by angry villagers is over before it even begins, for example, and this is precisely the kind of set piece Fulci would ordinarily dwell on in great detail. By contrast, dialogue scenes drag on and on, and the characters are so sketchy that they never generate much interest. The overall impression is of Fulci being compelled to fluff-off the big set pieces, while having to pad the movie out in other areas with boring dialogue scenes. Fulci's best films manage to create a sense of dramatic tension and suspense; *Demonia* just drags by and ultimately feels much longer than its relatively brief 85-minute running time.

The director would later hit on one of the film's major shortcomings when interviewed by Massimo Lavagnini. He described *Demonia* as:

> A wonderful movie, ruined from very bad photography. And that's that.[1]

**Modern fan-made art for *Demonia*; designed by Silver Ferox.**

Okay, so "wonderful" may be stretching it a bit, but there is little doubt that Luigi Ciccarese photographs the film with all the flair of an overeager amateur. He had already done a poor job on *Aenigma*, so why Fulci agreed to utilize him again is anybody's guess; both film were produced by Ettore Spagnuolo, however, and it's quite possible that he imposed Ciccarese on the production. In any event, his propensity for drowning night scenes in blue lighting is again in evidence, and his attempts at creating a dreamy ambience by placing a piece of gauze over the lens is bungled: This old-school technique requires great care, but it's so poorly thought out that the fabric is often in focus, creating a bizarre mosaic-like effect in the image. One can imagine Sergio Salvati, Luigi Kuveiller or Nino Celeste making a better job of the film, and it inevitably would have come off better as a result.

The most interesting addition to the technical crew is Otello Colangeli, who fills in for Fulci's favored editor Vincenzo Tomassi. Colangeli does the best he can with the material, but the often slap-dash results are not indicative of his strengths as an editor. Born in Rome in 1912, he

**Porter (Pierluigi Conti, aka Al Cliver) loses his head in *Demonia*.**

was a veteran of the movie industry since the late 1930s. He worked on an impressive number of films, including Luciano Emmer's *The Bigamist* (1956), Paolo Heusch and Mario Bava's *The Day the Sky Exploded* (1958), Riccardo Freda's *The Giants of Thessaly* (1960), Alberto De Martino's *The Blancheville Monster* (1963), Antonio Margheriti's *Castle of Blood* (1964) and its color remake *Web of the Spider* (1970) and Mario Bava's *Knives of the Avenger* (1966) and *Four Times That Night* (1969). *Demonia* was his penultimate editing job; he died in 1998.

Co-writer Piero Regnoli was born in Rome in 1921. He entered films in 1950 as an uncredited assistant director on *Sins of Pompeii*, which is where he likely first made the acquaintance of Fulci. He would become an incredibly prolific screenwriter, and also dabbled in directing; he assisted on the script for Riccardo Freda and Mario Bava's *I vampiri* (1957), then directed the first Italian knock-off of Bava's *Black Sunday* (1960), the irresistibly titled (and very profitable) *The Playgirls and the Vampire* (1960). He first collaborated directly with Fulci on the script for *White Fang*, and he also had a hand in a couple of the first—and most interesting—cash-ins on *Zombie*: Umberto Lenzi's *Nightmare City* (1980) and Andrea Bianchi's *Burial Ground: The Nights of Terror* (1981). Following *Demonia*, he would reunite with Fulci one last time on *Voices from Beyond*; he died in 2001. Antonio Tentori (born in Rome in 1960) also had a hand in developing the story, though he is not credited on the finished film. In addition to working on the script he served as one of Fulci's assistants, along with Camilla Fulci. *Demonia* marked Tentori's cinema debut, and he was rewarded for his hard work on this film with a more visible role on Fulci's next picture, *Nightmare Concert (A Cat in the Brain)*: Tentori had a significant role in developing the script for the *Maestro*'s most self-reflexive movie, and he was rewarded with his first screen credit. After that, he would go on to cowrite such films as Sergio Stivaletti's *The Three Faces of Terror* (2004), Bruno Mattei's *The Jail: The Women's Hell* (2006), *Zombies: The Beginning* and *Island of the Living Dead* (both 2007) and Dario Argento's *Dracula 3D* (2012).

The cast includes a number of Fulci veterans making their final bows for the director. American actor Brett Halsey came to work with Fulci rather late in the director's career on *The Devil's Honey*, but he was impressed by his fighting spirit and enjoyed a personal friendship with the filmmaker; that friendship would be compromised by a bit of shady business dealing involving Fulci's next film, but more on that in a bit. Al Cliver (his *nom de plume* misspelled as Clever in the end titles!) also pops up as a rival archaeologist who ends up getting shish kebabbed and beheaded by the ghosts. Neither actor is really given much of an opportunity to shine unfortunately, though the sight of the latter's head, covered in seaweed and perched atop a ship's anchor, is one of the few truly arresting images in the movie. Carla Cassola returns from *The House of Clocks* as one of Fulci's ill-fated mediums: Like so many "seers" in Fulci's movies, she sees too much and loses her eyes as a result; this instance of ocular violence is undone, however—like so much of the film—by a general air of carelessness. And lastly, brooding and imposing Lino Salemme returns from *The Sweet House of Horrors* to play the thuggish butcher who threatens the expedition. Salemme does his best, but he also gets stuck with one of the goofiest demises: He is attacked by slabs of meat (!) in the deep-freeze, then has his tongue (which looks impossibly large!) spiked to a tabletop. Fulci makes his first cameo appearance since *Aenigma*, and it's tempting to view him as playing the same character: a police inspector with a fondness for *Columbo*-like raincoats. It's nice seeing the director looking a little healthier and less gaunt, at least.

*Demonia* is one of Fulci's weakest films, an incoherent mishmash of the ghost story and nunsploitation genres (a staple of Italian exploitation, in which blasphemous fantasies about "naughty nuns" are given full rein; it came to prominence after the release of Ken Russell's scandalous *The Devils* in 1971), with only a few flashes of the director's distinctive style. Whatever misgivings he may have felt about the project, it did not slow him down, however, and his next picture would prove to be one of his most hotly debated.

Notes:

1. Retrieved from, http://www.shockingimages.com/fulci/interview.html

## *Nightmare Concert (A Cat in the Brain)* *(Italy)*

Aka *Un gatto nel cervello; Un gatto nel cervello (Nightmare Concert); A Cat in the Brain*

Directed by Lucio Fulci; Produced by Luigi Nannerini and Antonio Lucidi [as Anthony Clear], for Executive Cine TV; Screenplay by Lucio Fulci, Giovanni Simonelli [as John Fitzsimmons] and Antonio Tentori, from a story by Lucio Fulci and Giovanni Simonelli; Director of Photography: Alessandro Grossi; Editor: Vincenzo Tomassi; Music by Fabio Frizzi

Main Players: Lucio Fulci (Himself); Brett Halsey (The Monster); David L. Thompson (Professor Ego Swharz); Jeoffrey Kennedy (Inspector Gabriele Vanni); Malissa Longo (Katya Swharz); Paola Cozzo (Lilly); Shilett Angel (Filippo); Robert Egon (Second Monster/Himself)

*Film director Lucio Fulci is beset by horrible nightmares because of the horrific scenes of violence and mutilation included in his movies. He begins to fear that he is losing his grip on reality, so he seeks the service of a psychiatrist, Dr. Swharz. Swharz uses hypnosis on the hapless horror movie director and allows him to believe that he is responsible for a series of killings which is actually being carried out by the deranged psychiatrist ...*

Fulci was in a peculiar place in his life and career when he came to make *Nightmare Concert (A Cat in the Brain)*. He had long toiled in the film industry and had done some work he was fiercely proud of, but he viewed his legacy as "The Godfather of Gore" with an air of bemusement. When reflecting on his life in the cinema, he made the wry observation that:

> The films I wanted to make, like [*Don't Torture a*] *Duckling*, luckily, I got the chance to make. Two or three that I can say represent the kind of intelligence that purely represents me. Twenty-five years ago, when I made my more personal movies, critics didn't want to understand this intelligence. They called my art "shit." Now critics want to call my shit "art."[1]

Fulci's professional frustration is understandable—most of his films were coolly received by critics and the work of which he was the proudest had disappeared into obscurity, while the more popular gory horror movies became the topic of much discussion. Fulci did not view his genre work with distaste or disinterest, of course, but his being viewed as a purveyor of gory thrills did have its limitations; now into his 60s and finally rebounding after a period of devastating illness, he decided to strike back at the critics by making a personal little movie which would enable him to address some of the criticisms which had dogged him in recent years.

*Nightmare Concert (A Cat in the Brain)* appears to have originated as something of a peace offering by Fulci towards producers Luigi Nannerini and Antonio Lucidi. He had broken off a contract with them after the production of *Touch of Death*, though he continued to lend his name—if little else—to a series of low-budget horror films they bankrolled under the banner of "Lucio Fulci Presents." In order to satisfy his contractual obligations, Fulci devised a scenario with the aid of veteran screenwriter Giovanni Simonelli. Born in Rome in 1926, Simonelli started off as a screenwriter in the late 1950s. He dabbled in various popular genres, including *pepla* (*Goliath Against the Giants*, 1961), spy thrillers (*That Man in Istanbul*, 1965), Spaghetti Westerns (*Johnny Ringo*, 1966) and *gialli* (*Naked You Die*, 1969). He first worked with Fulci on the Nannerini/Lucidi production of *Hansel e Gretel*, which was part of the aforementioned "Lucio Fulci Presents" series. Fulci then brought in his youthful collaborator Antonio Tentori to help whip the script into good shape. It was decided to shoot the film in 16mm and then to blow it up to 35mm for anticipated theatrical play dates. The production would also utilize a wide array of stock clips from Fulci's various projects for Nannerini and Lucidi, meaning plenty of footage from *Touch of Death* and *The Ghosts of Sodom*, as well as scenes from the "Lucio Fulci Presents" titles. If

**Italian pressbook for *Nightmare Concert* (*A Cat in the Brain*); artwork by Enzo Sciotti.**

it all sounds like a bit of a mish mash, it really is in a way—and yet, there's something special about *Nightmare Concert (A Cat in the Brain)*.

The film starts off with an overhead view of the protagonist—Fulci, playing a variation on himself—sitting at his desk, jotting down ideas for some sadistic gore scenes for his latest horror movie. As the camera booms down and onto his baldhead, it seems to enter into the skull, exposing the inner-workings of the brain. Fulci's voice[2] continues with its grocery list of atrocities, only to be suddenly quieted by the arrival of a cat (in truth, a very tacky looking puppet) that tears the director's grey matter to shreds. It's an arresting opening on several levels: For one, it makes it clear that this is not going to be the usual Italian horror fare, and for another it makes it equally clear that this is going to be a bit ropey and rough around the edges, but that it won't skimp on the red stuff.

**Lucio Fulci takes center stage as the mentally unbalanced horror film director in *Nightmare Concert (A Cat in the Brain).***

The film then begins a back-and-forth between old film clips and new footage, as Fulci goes about trying to complete his latest opus even as his mental state deteriorates rapidly. The implementation of the old footage is inspired at times, insipid at others. Occasionally one gets the impression that Fulci is just trying to pad the film out to feature length, but at others he is able to use it to address past cinematic sins. One of the most enjoyable segments of the film shows him working on staging scenes from *The Ghosts of Sodom*. One might question the wisdom of utilizing footage from his weakest film, but on a purely practical level he was obliged to do so by the producers; on an artistic level, however, he manages to address the absurdities of that film by showing him shaking his head in disbelief after finishing a take and muttering, "Sadism ... Nazism ... Is there any point anymore?" Fulci makes it clear that he is aware of the tacky excesses of some of these films but, as a pragmatic professional, he is obliged to keep forging ahead. At one point he says, "I make horror films. If I made movies about love, nobody would buy a ticket!" (by way of explaining his *modus operandi*.) Still, make no mistake about it: *Nightmare Concert (A Cat in the Brain)* is not Fulci's open apology for making horror movies—instead he is using the material to send himself up a bit while also poking fun at the conservative mindset which criticizes these films.

Fulci's depiction of himself is interesting. He does not bring his family into the picture at all, so he appears to lead a very lonely, even sterile existence. He lives comfortably in a nice apartment and appears to be on good terms with his neighbors—he's even nice enough to assist his crippled neighbor to get down the stairs on a daily basis—yet he seems isolated and incapable of enjoying the good things in life. On the set, he depicts himself as indecisive and introverted—a far cry from the imposing, even aggressive figure he is known to have been in real life. In a way, it could be that Fulci simply bit off more than he could chew with this acting assignment; he wanders through the action looking vaguely disoriented much of the time. He had given some nice performances in the cameo roles of his earlier pictures, but perhaps the burden of carrying an entire picture on his sloped shoulders was too great to bear. And yet, the film simply wouldn't be the same without him at its core. He may seem a bit lost and aimless from time to time, but there is something irresistible about getting to spend so much time with Fulci on camera. He allows himself some nicely humorous moments—for example, slipping into one of his blackouts and assaulting a female producer—but for the most part the material requires him to keep a straight face. There's something vaguely pathetic about the way he comes across in the film, as if a long career in the cinema has brought him nothing but isolation and misery, as his mental state falls into disarray because of the constant flood of blood and gore surging through his recent movies.

In a move that serves to set the "film Fulci" apart from the "real Fulci," the director turns to a psychiatrist for assistance. Fulci's contempt for the psychiatric profession is evident in many of his films, and in a 1995 interview with Sergio Grmek Germani, he expounded on the matter even more:

> I've hated psychologists for years. What they don't know is that their entire discipline is based on one man's need for money, for cocaine. His name was Sigmund Freud, and he needed money. Therefore he invented, copying it from the Catholics, who were always first, the confession. Instead of conducting it collectively, he did it individually. He was successful, and now these charlatans won't stop jabbering.[3]

The "charlatan" on view in *Nightmare Concert (A Cat in the Brain)* is named Dr. Egon Swharz—and far from being just a harmless quack, he will prove to be a bloodthirsty killer. Swharz preys upon Fulci's vulnerability by promising to help him to come to grips with his neuroses. He puts the director under hypnosis and only then does he show his true colors: He conditions Fulci so that every time he hears a high-pitched whistle, he will slip into a trance; at that point, Swharz will commit a murder before the director's eyes and leave evidence at the scene which will incriminate Fulci—thus, Fulci will come to believe that he is committing the murders, while Swharz hides behind his façade of bland respectability. Swharz is well aware of Fulci's reputation for directing sadistic horror movies and uses this to his advantage; at one point he even cackles over the "stupid" assertion that watching violent acts on film will lead to violent behaviors in real life. Swharz is a cynical psychopath who betrays the trust which his clients place in him; his innate need for bloodshed is at odds with the basically gentle demeanor of Fulci, who earns a living putting his violent fantasies on celluloid. Fulci's message is clear: Nothing is off-limits in the arts, and a flair for visualizing violence and brutality on screen is not indicative of a violent or unbalanced nature in the artist.

*Nightmare Concert (A Cat in the Brain)* is often reviled for what it isn't, but it makes better sense to appreciate it for what it is. It is not a polished fever dream like Federico Fellini's masterpiece *8½* (1963). Fellini's film remains the high water mark in the subgenre of films about filmmaking; its existential drama of an artist who has lost his ability to create remains as vivid and engaging as ever. It is tempting to view Fulci's film as an extension, but one must be careful in this context. Fellini's film mixes comedy and pathos with reality and fantasy to create a truly extraordinary end result. Fulci's film is far less polished, and any attempt to approach it from a conventional point of view doesn't present it in a very favorable light. The reality is, the film was cobbled together rather crudely, and the resources do not permit Fulci to provide the kind of tremendous "final statement" on his career and his place in the industry that one would ideally wish for. It doesn't reach back to his days working with Steno, nor does it even show him working in the greater comfort and familiarity of his most beloved horror films of the 1980s. In essence, it shows him at the end of the road, cut off from most of his most treasured collaborators and unsure of where his career is going to take him next. As such, it paints a very interesting portrait of him at a vulnerable stage in his life; with this in mind, it makes sense that he depicts himself as a loner, sooner than trying to capture a more "realistic" portrait of him interacting with his friends and family away from the set. In *Nightmare Concert (A Cat in the Brain)*, Fulci has no real life away from the set; life has passed him by and now his career is hitting the skids, as well. For viewers familiar with the director and the full scope of his work, it presents an oddly touching portrait of the artist as a slightly disillusioned old man.

As a piece of filmmaking, *Nightmare Concert (A Cat in the Brain)* is crude and functional. The lighting by Alessandro Grossi—this was his first assignment as a director of photography, following working as a camera operator on *The House of Clocks*, *The Sweet House of Horror* and *Demonia*—is adequate in spots and amateurish in others. The mixture of old and new footage is well integrated at times and clumsy at others. The dialogue is stiff and the acting is not much better. As such, it's easy to understand why it is often derided as a low point among Fulci's admittedly problematic latter-day work. Viewers who thrive on polished cinema will not find much to admire here, but for the devoted Fulci cultist the film is still of great interest. Fulci's sardonic ruminations on psychiatry and the kneejerk manner in which horror films and their creators are attacked by the press have a real sting to them, and as a portrait of an artist at work—even if it is admittedly not a terribly truthful one—it remains unique in the director's body of work. If nothing else, it has an interesting central idea, and this is enough in itself to help it overcome some of its less-than-stellar technical attributes.

The film also benefits from the return of two of Fulci's most reliable collaborators. Vincenzo Tomassi is back on board as editor, following a brief period away from the director; he remained on the payroll with Nannerini and Lucidi following Fulci's departure and edited the "Lucio Fulci Presents" titles while the director busied himself with other projects. Tomassi does the best he can under the circumstances, mixing the assorted footage and managing to create some nice transitions where the use of clips isn't too forced and arbitrary. Fabio Frizzi also makes his

**An Italian lobby card and the cover for the soundtrack release utilized the same image of Professor Swharz (David L.Thompson) strangling his faithless wife (Malisa Longo).**

return to Fulci's crew for the first time since *Manhattan Baby* in 1982. His score is a similar patchwork of new and old elements: In addition to some familiar cues from *The Beyond*, he provides some new music, as well. His use of "Peter and the Wolf" for the murder scenes evokes memories of Fritz Lang's *M* (1931), which was one of Fulci's favorite films; it's an impish touch which lends a bit of levity to the proceedings. Sadly, this would be Frizzi's final collaboration with Fulci; the two men would part ways after this, though Frizzi continues to pay homage to his friend as he covers the most popular themes from the films they made together in various concert appearances. One final "collaboration" in the film proved to be more contentious: In utilizing many scenes from *Touch of Death*, Fulci elected to credit American actor Brett Halsey with appearing in the film as "The Monster." When Halsey later found out that his director friend had used his name and likeness in the film without his permission, he tried to reach out and clear the air, but Fulci would not return his phone calls. As Halsey told me when I met him at the Monster Bash in Butler, PA in 2011, Fulci undoubtedly thought that the actor was calling and insisting on being paid some exorbitant sum in exchange for turning a blind eye to the subterfuge; it proved to be a sad falling out, though Halsey retains a very positive view of his relationship with Fulci on the whole.

For Fulci, *Nightmare Concert (A Cat in the Brain)* would prove to be a pleasurable experience. He would often play the film up as one of his favorites in interviews and loved to claim that an American genre titan stole from the film. When asked why he made the film, Fulci quipped:

> So Wes Craven could copy me. [...] *New Nightmare* ... obviously *A Cat in the Brain*. Only my film was made in 16mm for $100,000. It's *Eraserhead* made by an old man. I haven't earned a single penny from that one, either. The owner of the company just went bankrupt. Craven made a lot of money on *New Nightmare*. I think he's seen *Cat* too many times. When I meet him, I'll tell him so.[4]

In a way, these claims seem a bit desperate—an attempt at validating a minor film by claiming that it had been ripped-off by a more popular (and profitable) movie. Fulci's likening of the film to *Eraserhead* has less to do with the concept than it has to do with the notion of creating a film under such duress, with so little resources. But the comparison is unfair: *Eraserhead* is an organic piece, beautifully crafted under less-than-ideal circumstances, while *Cat* is a hodgepodge largely comprised of clips from earlier movies. Even so, there is something oddly fitting about Fulci taking exception to the notion of a famed American genre filmmaker taking inspiration from one of his films, when one considers the regular claims of plagiarism which dogged Fulci's zombie movies in relation to those of George A. Romero, for example. Truth be told, the odds of Craven ever having seen the film are slim to nil: *Nightmare Concert (A Cat in the Brain)* barely received a theatrical release in Italy[5] and it would not make its official appearance in the U.S. until 1999, when it was released to laserdisc by Box Office Spectaculars. In 2009 Grindhouse Releasing released the film on DVD.

*Nightmare Concert (A Cat in the Brain)* remains Fulci's most hotly contested title: Some overeager fans have labeled it a masterpiece, while other more intolerant viewers deem it to be a train wreck of sorts. As is so often the case, the reality lies somewhere in between. For all its faults—and they are many—it's a peculiar and engaging work with some clever ideas struggling to break free of its sometimes haphazard construction. It isn't one of Fulci's truly great works, but it is one of his most important.

Notes:

1. Berger, Howard, "The Prince of Italian Terror," *Fangoria*, July 1997, p. 67.
2. Fulci's voice is dubbed on both the Italian and English soundtracks for the film.
3. Interview included on the Grindhouse DVD release of *A Cat in the Brain*.
4. Berger, Howard, "The Prince of Italian Terror," *Fangoria*, July 1997, p. 66.
5. Fulci was furious when the Italian distributor cut the ending of the film; in the Italian theatrical release, the audience is led to believe that Fulci is really crazy after all when he appears to kill a shapely young woman (played by the striking Paola Cozzo, from Lamberto Bava's *Demons*, 1985) who is with him on his sailboat; the original ending—preserved in the American release—reveals that this is one final sleight-of-hand, as the "murder" is just another scene being directed by Fulci for his latest movie.

# 1991

## *Voices from Beyond (Italy)*

Aka *Voci dal profondo*; *Voix profondes*

Directed by Lucio Fulci; Produced by Antonio Lucidi and Luigi Nannerini, for Scena Film and Executive Cine TV; Screenplay by Lucio Fulci and Piero Regnoli (as Pietro Regnoli), based on the short story by Lucio Fulci and Daniele Stroppa; Director of Photography: Alessandro Grossi [as Sandro Grossi]; Editor: Vincenzo Tomassi; Music by Stelvio Cipriani

Main Players: Duilio Del Prete (Giorgio Mainardi); Karina Huff (Rosy Mainardi); Pascal Persiano (Mario Mainardi); Frances Nacman [as Frances Nacmen] (Hilde Mainardi); Bettina Giovannini (Lucia Mainardi); Lorenzo Flaherty (Gianni); Paolo Paoloni (Grandfather Mainardi); Sacha Maria Darwin (Dorrie); Antonella Tinazzo (Rita)

Cameo appearance: Lucio Fulci (Pathologist)

*Giorgio Mainardi rules his family with an iron fist. When he dies mysteriously from an internal hemorrhage, the family is gathered for the reading of his will. His daughter Rosy begins seeing visions of him in her dreams and he assures her that he has been murdered, but he is not sure by whom. Rosy begins to investigate, while the other relatives sweat and bicker among themselves ...*

Lucio Fulci had been involved in writing in one form or another for all of his adult life: He worked as an art critic prior to entering films, then worked as a screenwriter on films directed by others before going on to collaborate on the screenplays for many of his own films. Late in his life, he began to write short stories and articles for various Italian publications, as well. These works allowed him to develop possible scenarios for proposed film projects, while also enabling him to share his strong opinions on an array of topics. "Voci dal profondo," written by Fulci with the collaboration of Daniele Stroppa (who had collaborated on the screenplay for *The House of Clocks*), was originally published in the *Gazzetta di Firenze*. It would later be included in the anthology of Fulci's short stories, titled *Le lune nere* and published in 1992; the other stories included in the collection were "I testimoni" (a tale of premonition which recalls elements of *The Psychic* and *The Black Cat*), "Buoni sentimenti" (co-written by Gabriele Marconi, it tells of a child staying home from school with a cold; her grandmother tells her various fairy tales hoping to make her better, but her condition only worsens as a result), "Porte del nulla" (co-written by Piero Regnoli, which Fulci would film as his next picture, *Door to Silence*), "Uomo di guerra" (in which a veteran becomes a celebrity on television for his insight into war when a conflict breaks out, only to commit suicide when the war concludes and people stop caring about him), "Trio" (in which a woman fantasizes about cheating on her dullard husband with a rugged movie star), "In assenza di Dio" (another piece of religious criticism, in which a man comes to Italy during Easter celebrations and agrees to play Jesus in a pageant, not realizing that he will be nailed to the cross for real), "Attesa" (in which a wife and her mother-in-law await the return of their husband/son) and "Gourmet (Sapore di coppia)," which was reportedly Fulci's personal favorite and tells the story of a henpecked husband who eventually kills his wife and eats her remains. The latter story would be reprinted in another volume dedicated to Fulci's writings, titled *Miei mostri adorati*, published in 1995; in addition to reprinting "In assenza di Dio" and "Gourmet (Sapore di coppia)," it also includes the stories "Infortunio sul lavaro," "Ecceso di Fede," "Vocazione" (a gruesome tale of a Nazi who slaughters children and feasts on their sexual organs; a girl falls in love with him and believes that he is protecting the children, so when the Liberation takes place and he is killed, she does her best to make him out to be a martyr and a hero), "Opera Italiana" (a *noir*-like tale of children being abducted in order to harvest their organs for transplants), "Vangelo apocrifo" (an ironic story of four people in search of sanctuary following the death of Jesus Christ; while on the road, they meet a man who may or may not be Christ resurrected—or he could be an alien) and several articles, including: "Effetti speciali" (which deals with his thoughts on the horror genre; for example, he reveals that some of his favorite films include Tod Browning's *Freaks*, 1932, Karl Freund's *The Mummy*, 1932, and James Whale's *The Invisible Man*, 1933) and "Totò e Orson Welles: l'impossibile coppia," which included his reflections on working on Steno's *L'uomo, la bestia e la virtù*, with particular emphasis on the problematic relationship between Totò and Welles.[1]

**Anglo export ad for *Voices from Beyond*; artwork by Enzo Sciotti.**

Like several of Fulci's other short stories, "Voci dal profondo" was written with an eye towards developing the story into a screenplay. When the time came to write the finished script, however, Fulci turned not to Daniele Stroppa (who would return to collaborate on the screenplay for Fulci's planned "comeback" picture, *The Wax Mask*) but to Piero Regnoli. Regnoli and Fulci had last worked together on the screenplay for *Demonia*, and apparently Fulci found working with him to be an agreeable experience; it would be one of the last films the veteran screenwriter and director ever worked on—he died in 2001. Producers Antonio

Lucidi and Luigi Nannerini elected to back the film, indicating that any hard feelings suffered over Fulci breaking his previous contract with them after the completion of *Touch of Death* had been forgiven and forgotten. They had collaborated smoothly on *Nightmare Concert (A Cat in the Brain)*, a film Fulci was rather proud of, and though they were unable to secure the film a theatrical distribution outside of Italy, they were comfortable rolling the dice on another picture together.

The film begins with a dash of eroticism that mutates into violence: Giorgio is making love to his younger, very attractive wife, Lucia, when their small son cries out for his mother. Giorgio does not take kindly to the interruption, so he arms himself with a knife and stabs the child to death. This is then revealed to be a dream, and this establishes the basic theme of the film right off the bat; the blurred line between dreams and reality, and the bits of truth which dreams can reveal to those who are open to interpreting them. The murder of the little boy may be a dream, but for Lucia (ironically, Lucia was the name of Fulci's own mother, with whom he "enjoyed" a very strained relationship) it indicates a propensity for violence on Giorgio's part, which is difficult to ignore. Giorgio is a petty tyrant who bosses people around and cheats on his wife. He is not concerned with what people think of him, nor is he bound by sentiment when it comes to his interactions with his family—including his wheelchair-bound father, who lives in a vegetative state following a serious stroke.

Giorgio is not a positive character, but then again the film is not exactly teeming with goodhearted people. Virtually everybody in the household has a strong motive for wanting to kill Giorgio. Fulci and Regnoli create a soap opera ambience in which everybody is fooling around or hiding some deep, dark secret. The red herrings are plentiful, but for one this actually works fairly well because everybody truly does seem capable of committing a murder. Rosy is the only exception to the rule—she has escaped from the viper's nest by going away to college and, when she is called back for the reading of the will, it is she whom her father reaches out to from beyond the grave to solve the mystery.

Fulci's fixation on death and the possibility of the afterlife is strongly felt in this film. Like *Aenigma*, it opens with the death of a main character—and it even repeats the camera movement of an overhead shot which cranes back, suggesting the release of the soul following Giorgio's demise. Like the tormented teen in *Aenigma*, Giorgio is not free to move on to the great beyond, as it were: He must discover who killed him if he is ever to rest in peace. Rosy acts as his go-between to make this possible, but the film makes it clear that his relationship with her was every bit as severe as anybody else who was unfortunate enough to be in his path. The audience is not encouraged to sympathize with him and his plight, but Rosy's devotion to unmasking her father's murderer provides the film with its only source of warmth and humanity. The final reveal that it was his "wicked stepmother," Hilde, who was responsible is satisfying, as is Rosy's decision to allow her to suffer with the knowledge of her own evil actions while providing Giorgio with the closure he needs in order to move on. As such, Rosy does not become corrupted by her family's evil influence. She is also able to end her relationship with her father on a positive note, as they attain a deeper understanding that goes beyond earthly concerns.

*Voices from Beyond* is one of Fulci's most disarming films. It tells a coherent and engaging story in a compelling fashion. Stylistically, it stands out as one of his best-realized later-period films: Alessandro Grossi's use of blown-out lighting is visually dynamic, and there are some beautifully composed dream and fantasy sequences. There isn't a tremendous amount of blood and gore, but the occasional violent outbursts are convincingly handled. Fulci's interest in the process of death is reflected in the way he keeps showing Giorgio's state of deterioration in his coffin; the images of bugs and maggots crawling over the body as the skin breaks down and the body begins to decay are certainly potent. The film also enables him to revisit his beloved zombies for one last time, when the character of Mario dreams that he is under attack by the creatures in the family crypt. The production values are very good, as well, making it one of Fulci's richer-looking films of the period; as actress Frances Nacman reveals in the accompanying interview, the crew were permitted access to the former villa of famed director Luchino Visconti. There is also a very good music score by Stelvio Cipriani, which would remain his only soundtrack for the director. Cipriani's distinctive style enlivened many key *gialli* (*Twitch of the Death Nerve*, 1971) and *poliziotteschi* (*La polizia ha le mani legate*, 1974), and he remains active to this day.

Fulci was pleased with the end results, albeit with reservations:

> I love it very much. It's a wonderful movie with the wrong cast. Karina Huff is unpleasant, Del Prete is completely out of the role, the mother-in-law is too wicked and you understand immediately that she is the killer.[2]

Truth be told, he is a little unfair with regards to some of the actors. While he is correct in his assertion that Karina Huff fails to make Rosy as engaging as she should be, Duilio Del Prete is very impressive as Giorgio and Frances Nacman is appropriately bitchy as Hilde. Huff had already appeared in *The House of Clocks* as one of the three delinquents, and she was much more effective in that role; here she seems a bit lost, and her one-note interpretation damages some of her scenes. Perhaps she was simply tiring of acting; she would only make one more minor film appearance before walking away from movies for good. Del Prete (1938-1998) had been in films since the late 1960s; he worked in a variety of different genres and racked up two appearances for American director Peter Bogdanovich, who cast him in *Daisy Miller* (1974) and *At Long Last Love* (1975). *Voices from Beyond* was also one of his last film roles. In addition to acting, Del Prete was also a popular recording artist. He gives a very good account as Giorgio—he is not a character the audience is supposed to warm to, anyway, and he is appropriately intimidating while also finding some pathos in the role where required. Frances Nacman[3] manages to be even viler as Hilde Mainardi; as Fulci notes, she is transparently evil, but given that so many characters of a similar nature surround her, it's not fair to suggest that she tips her hand too soon. Born in New York in 1935, Nacman established a solid reputation as a singer, then she decided to try her hand at acting fairly late in life; she moved to Rome in the 1980s and continued to live and work there until her death in 2008. Pascal Persiano (*The Sweet House of Horrors*), Paolo Paoloni (*The House of Clocks*) and Sacha Maria Darwin (*Touch of Death*) also put in final appearances for Fulci.

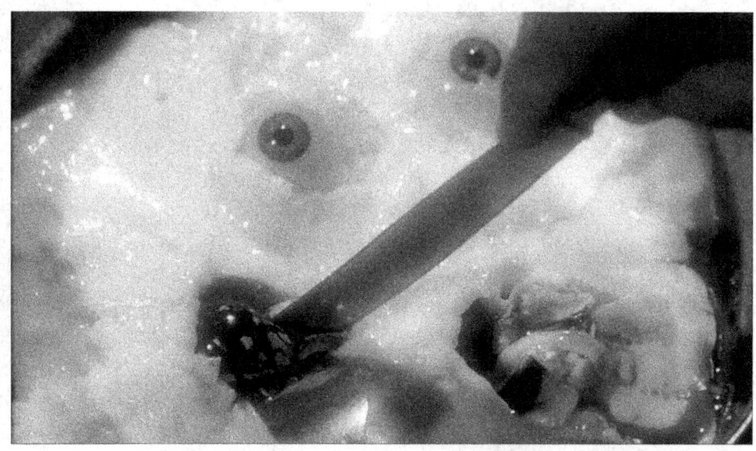

**Some disturbing nightmare imagery in *Voices from Beyond*, with a nod towards Fulci's propensity for ocular violence.**

**Mario's nightmare allows Fulci to revisit his beloved zombie imagery for one last time.**

*Voices from Beyond* also marks the end of Fulci's collaboration with editor Vincenzo Tomassi; this was the last film Tomassi edited in a lengthy career that extended back to the mid-1960s. He died in 1993. Fulci took his death hard, as he was—after Ornella Micheli—one of the few editors with whom he had a really good rapport. Films are often saved in the cutting room, and there's no doubt that the close relationship Fulci enjoyed with Tomassi helped to shape some of his best-loved movies. Fulci also makes his final cameo appearance in one of his own films, though this would not have been foreseen at the time: He appears as a pathologist carrying out the autopsy on Giorgio's body.[4] Fulci ultimately dedicated the film to British horror writer/director Clive Barker (*Hellraiser*, 1987) and film critic Claudio Carabba, whom he described as two of his "few real friends." Barker's nightmarish visions of hellish horror definitely owe a bit to Fulci's celebrated horror films of the 1980s, of course, while Carabba was one of the few critics in Italy who took Fulci and his work seriously. At this stage in the game, Fulci is clearly aware of his own cinematic mortality, and *Voices from Beyond* could almost have served as a final testament of sorts … but another project would still find its way to completion, while the promise of further work would help to sustain him as he entertained journalists and fans who were finally paying homage to him and his impact in the film industry.

Notes:

1. My thanks to Lionel Grenier for providing me with relevant information on Fulci's short stories.
2. Retrieved from, http://www.shockingimages.com/fulci/interview.html
3. The prolific voice artist Carolyn De Fonseca dubbed Nacman on the English track. De Fonseca also dubbed Florinda Bolkan in *Don't Torture a Duckling* and Dagmar Lassander in *The House by the Cemetery*, in addition to dubbing Daria Nicolodi in Dario Argento's *Deep Red* (1975) and *Phenomena* (1985), Bernice Stegers in Lamberto Bava's *Macabre* (1980), Conchita Airoldi in *The Strange Vice of Mrs. Wardh* (1970), Franca Bettoia in Sidney Salkow's *The Last Man on Earth* (1964) and Daliah Lavi in Mario Bava's *The Whip and the Body* (1963), among many others. She died in 2009.
4. He would, however, go on to make a cameo in the ill-fated horror comedy *Sick-O-Pathics* (1996), directed by Brigida Costa and Massimo Lavagnini. As Lavagnini explained in his piece "Beyond the Memory," included in Chas. Balun's *Beyond the Gates: A Tribute to the Maestro* (San Leandro: Blackest Heart Books, 1996, p. 77): "We were in the study of [Fulci's] house in Bracciano when I asked him to play a cameo in front of the video camera. He impulsively agreed […] He showed an uncommon sense of self-irony and he was incredibly nice when he told us that 'young people have to be helped.'" *Sick-O-Pathics* was released straight to video, and has become very difficult to see since the 1990s. In addition to Fulci, the cast also includes appearances by Antonella Fulci, Luigi Cozzi, Dardano Sacchetti, Aristide Massaccesi and David Warbeck.

# Frances Nacman
# Interview by Mike Baronas and Kit Gavin

Mike Baronas and Kit Gavin conducted the following interview with actress Frances Nacman on September 13, 2001. Ms. Nacman was born in America but immigrated to Italy in the 1980s, where she enjoyed some success as a singer and an actress on stage, TV and film. *Voices from Beyond* was her only collaboration with Lucio Fulci. Sadly, Ms. Nacman passed away in Rome in 2007, at the age of 73. We are very grateful to her for discussing her career and her experiences in working with Fulci.

**Mike Baronas**: When did you first come to Italy?
**Frances Nacman**: In 1980 I came here. I was 44, and said, "I would not be 45 in the United States."
**MB/KG**: You were 44 years old?!?
**FN**: Yes.
**MB/KG**: Are you serious?
**FN**: Yes (*smiles*). I'm 66 now. I feel like I'm almost strange because of it. I have no friends my age. I meet people that are even close to my age and I feel like I am talking to my mother and my father. They have no concept of the music of today, of what's happening today, of life today. I'm still trying to decide what to do when I grow up.

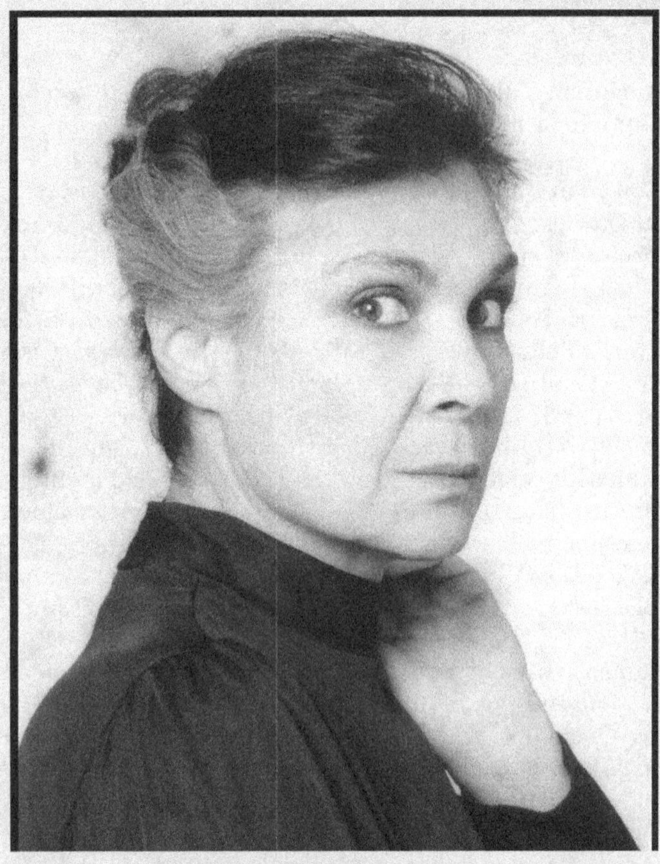

**A portrait of Frances Nacman.**

I like to think I live really well—I am a vegetarian, I exercise, I walk a lot, I don't have a car, if I have to go somewhere in the center I walk there—I live a very relaxed life. I married an Italian who died in 1986. My husband's name was Fernando Maria Imbert. He wrote movies, designed costumes and sets, was a Professor of Art History at the University of Rome, was an architect and spoke five languages. He was the most incredible man I have ever met, and that's what made me stay in Italy. I was just traveling. I didn't leave America and say, "I'm going to Italy," I said, "I'm going to see Europe."

I had been given a $10,000 inheritance in two increments; $5,000 each, and the first one I just pissed away—I bought a brand new car, I redecorated the house. With the second one I said to myself, "If I don't do something intelligent with this one, I'm going to regret it for the rest of my life." And then on May 18, 1980 I saw a television show about Picasso and saw the houses that he lived in and what he did with his life, and I said, "Why is there such a big difference between the way we are living, Mr. Picasso and me? Is it just because he can paint? That shouldn't make a big difference. I'm going to Europe, I'm going to go, and live an exciting life." And I gave away everything I had, including my Ford LTD, and I called and told everyone I knew—and you can tell by looking at my apartment that my apartment is interesting—and I said, "Come take anything in my apartment, I'm out of here."

I flew out of America on July 4. I bought a ticket on Independence Day and made a deal with my sister that if I called her and decided to leave, she would send me the money for a plane ticket home. I was going to stay here until the money ran out. She thought I was crazy. She said, "You don't speak any languages except English. You don't know anybody, etc. Why don't you just take a leave of absence from work and sublease your apartment. Why don't you just work for a company there like IBM? They have offices everywhere." I said, "No. That's what *you* want to do (*laughs*). I want to wash dishes in a Paris restaurant." I didn't want to work for IBM. I didn't want to sit in an office. I wanted to do something weird and interesting, and that's what I did.
**MB/KG**: So what did your sister think when you didn't call up and ask for the money?
**FN**: You know, I've been here 21 years, and she's never come to visit me. She has never set foot in Europe, because she always had a reason. "My husband doesn't like to fly" or "I could never leave him alone. He doesn't know how to boil an egg." You know, the usual crap excuses. And then he died and then it was, "I can't go now because I don't have the money and I can't afford it," so she's never

come. And I find that fascinating—maybe it would be admitting that I had done all right.

It's fine—my life here. I have lots of friends, Italians, all young people. And financially I'm fine—the apartment is mine. This was my husband's, I mean we lived here together and his mother had *usufrutto*. It means one person owns the walls and one person owns the inside of the apartment—so my mother-in-law owned the walls and I owned the inside. But what happens is when one of them dies, the other one automatically gets the apartment—it cannot be left to anyone else, in other words. So when my mother-in-law died, I automatically got the apartment. And so that really makes life nicer when you own an apartment in an area like this [Trastevere], right in the heart of Rome, a block from the river ... I mean, give me a break! I know people who are paying fortunes in rent because this is an area where everybody wants to live, and of course the taxes here are so low on apartments. If this apartment were in America, I would have to pay a fortune in taxes. But here it's like nothing. It's negligible.

And work is nice. My agent is really mellow, but when I made the movie with Lucio I had a different agent—an American woman—named Rita Haley, who was just starting out and didn't know a lot of things. And she had to learn a lot of things, mainly by error. She got me all the first movies I made, except the first one for a friend. And then she left Rome. She said she didn't want to be an agent anymore. She was a wealthy woman playing around and wanted to see if she could do it. And, of course, she knew Lucio. I think he had a yacht. I think she would go with him as friends on his yacht, but he was always talking about her negatively, saying things like, "Your agent is crazy," and stuff like that. But I had heard that he was such a screamer. When I told people I was going make a movie with Lucio Fulci, people said, "Oh God! He's gonna scream at you, and he curses people." But he didn't do that. I mean, he was a smartass—he would make remarks—but he didn't scream at people.

**MB/KG**: So you were an actress in the States before you came to Italy?

**FN**: I acted, but only in theater. I had never made a movie. I never was before a camera in America. I had an agent, Ernest Borgnine's daughter, who got me into a couple of studios, but everybody said, "If you don't have experience, we can't use you." I even auditioned, and when we had finished I was asked, "Who are you? And what have you done?" I had not done anything in film work. They said, "God! When you've done something, come back, because you're really good (*laughs*)." I just said, "Thank you." So I never did that, but I did other jobs. I graduated in California, Hull State University.

**MB/KG**: Is that where you grew up, California?

**FN**: Yeah, well, America. We lived everywhere—Arizona, Miami, Bethlehem, New Hampshire—but mostly California. Most of my schooling was in California. Although my first acting "thing" was in Tucson, Arizona, when I did my first theater piece in school. Anyway, I was a purchasing agent for a landscape company. I was working for the Music and the Arts Foundation of America. I just did everything.

I was born in Brooklyn, New York, but we left when I was 6 years old, so my memories of New York are minimal. I went back this June [2001], interestingly enough, for the first time in 12 years, and I was at the World Trade Center with a friend. We had lunch there and walked around. I never actually went in the buildings because it's not my cup of tea, but it was interesting to be there in hindsight. But I don't feel a New Yorker. I don't feel an anything ... I'm a "Where-I'm-At-er." So right now I'm feeling like a *Romana* (*smiles*). I would love to be considered Roman. I really love it here. I've been here 21 years.

**MB/KG**: Your birth name is Frances Nacman, correct?

**FN**: Exactly that, but on the cover of the film I made with Lucio it says "Frances Namen," because that was his thing, you know, to change the spelling of your name. I mean, he did it with almost everybody. And the film, it had a name in English, and it was *Voices from Beyomd* [*sic*] with an "M." And I loved it! Not only was my name misspelled, but the film was as well. I thought that was classic, so I bought the video. [Note: the title is accurately spelled onscreen.]

**MB/KG**: How did you get the role?

**FN**: I had an agent, and, by that time, when I made the film with Lucio, I had already made films. The very first thing I did in front of a camera was run down a beach and sing for a 12-minute short for a French film director friend of mine, and it was called *Desperately Seeking a Producer*. But I also sang the title song for that film. Because that's what I did—I was a jazz singer—I forgot to mention it. I was a jazz singer for years. Here in Italy as well.

The second thing I did was play the mother on a 13-episode TV series called *Chaira e gli altri*. I was the mother of Ottavia Piccolo, who is one of the biggest Italian actresses there is. I couldn't believe it ... I had no idea what I was doing. I mean, I was doing theater and I was over-the-top all of the time. And the very second film I did I was as Mrs. Rosenberg with Burt Lancaster in *The Hijacking of the Achille Lauro*. In America it was called (*deepens voice*) *Voyage of Terror*. It was a two-night television rucka-ducka thing, and I played part of one of the three couples that goes on the Achille Lauro ship. The main couple was Burt Lancaster and Eva Marie Saint. For the audition, I was 20 minutes late because I took a bus and there was a traffic jam. I ran in, making my apologies, and dropped my box of Tic Tacs—which went all over the floor and there was a scene—and I still got the part. I couldn't believe it. I was saying, "How could they be giving me this part, because I don't know anything," and then I was working continuously. I was never a walk-on. I started off as a person, a real person.

So I had made several films, and when I went out and met [Fulci] he immediately gave me the part. It was in an

**Frances Nacman in *Voices from Beyond*.**

office, and, again, I took a bus. I don't do that anymore. Now I go by taxi to auditions, because I believe if you go in feeling like you're an actress, you're somebody. You're not sweaty.

I was in awe of Lucio because I still didn't know what I was doing and he would say, "Errr, let's shoot again. Nacman is acting." He's the one who taught me how not to do it. The only thing I didn't like in the film was the last scene. I'm turning around, and she's [Karina Huff's] saying, walking around me, "You'll be living in this house alone, and the memory of my father ... babble, babble, babble." And I saw my character as not giving a shit, and looking at her as to say (*bemusedly*), "Oh really?!?" I mean, if I'm like a murderess, I would be laughing at her (*laughs demonically*). Instead, Lucio said, "Hunch over more. You're afraid. Keep looking at her in fear." And I thought it was horrendous. I thought it came out awful because it was out of character. For the whole movie I was hard and like a rock, and then suddenly a ghost threatens me and I'm scared to death? I didn't like it.

Since Lucio, I've done a lot of things. Now I'm currently involved in theater again, because theater is always your first true love. You get to do something through from the beginning to the end, and it's so different from film. Film is work, theater is just fun, and I'm with an English-speaking theater company that does repertoire. On top of that I do films, television shows and commercials.

**MB/KG**: Do you still sing now? And what sort of commercials have you made here in Italy?

**FN**: No. My husband died in 1986 and I stopped singing. I just stopped. I did a couple of concerts in France after that, but nothing really. I was singing with an 18-piece orchestra. They were all kids 18 to 20 years old, and I was double the age of anyone else in the orchestra. We did all the standards. It was really nice. [Note: Following this interview, Frances went on to make a number of successful concert appearances in and around Italy.]

In Italy I did a commercial for Real Azzurro Toilet Bowl Cleaner (*laughs*). And it was me speaking, which was so neat—speaking in Italian. Because they made me very British with a lorgnette in front of me, and a guy turns up with a new toilet bowl and I go (*in English accent*), "Finalemente [Finally]! Enough with the halfway cleaning, I have to have a cleaning agent all the way down to the bottom. You see?" And I point to the toilet bowl, and he says, "Oh—how disgusting." Then a maid comes in with a bottle of Real Azzurro. "Oh, but madam, don't you know you don't have to get a new toilet ... da, da, da" (*laughs*).

I also made a great one in Holland for Mazda cars that had no words. I'm just there with my husband, and he parks this beautiful car that you barely see—you don't really even see that it's a Mazda—and he puts his hand on my leg. I move it away, and he tries to put his arm around me, and I move it away. I look at him like to say, "Are you kidding?" And then goes to open my blouse and I stop him. Then he tries to kiss me and I slap him in the face twice, and his nose bleeds. He then looks over at me—and then I laugh, and he laughs. And then the voice over says, "Mazda. To get back those old feelings when you were young." They came over to Italy from Holland looking for an Italian Sophia Loren-type woman. I still had my hair dark then and I said, "Okay," let my hair down, put on big hoopy-doopy earrings, then I went in and got the part.

**MB/KG**: Quite a few of the films you've done have been American films shot in Italy.

**FN**: Um, yes. I did a six-episode thing shot for European television, *Pepe Carvalho*. At the end, believe it or not, I'm the killer. Isn't that funny? I'm such a nice person. It's interesting that I'm the killer.

**MB/KG**: A femme fatale.

**FN**: Yes, I'm a femme fatale always. I'm the one that they say, "Give her a whip and high boots! She looks like a dominatrix to me (*laughs*)." *Pepe Carvalho* did well in Europe, but I don't think it ever got to the States. Let's just not talk about the stars ...

**MB/KG**: Go on, what were the stars like to work with?

**FN**: Valeria Marini; I always felt so sorry for her, she was so concerned with what she looked like. I mean she was constantly asking for make-up and continually wondering, "How big is the frame?" and "What would you be seeing?" and she was so nervous and it was so difficult for her. I really felt for her. She was like out of her thing. It was not her style as an actress. Although she's as cute as a bug in a rug, when she acts she's a doll to watch, but she suffers so much to get that feeling out.

**MB/KG**: A highly acclaimed film you worked on was *A Month by the Lake*.

**FN**: With Vanessa Redgrave and Uma Thurman, I mean, come on! That was a hot movie. I lived on Lake Como for seven weeks making that movie. It was phenomenal, because I was only used for like 12 days and even when I was called for those days I wasn't used because it was May and the weather kept changing. They would say, "We are going to do the outdoor scene," and they would make you up, then the weather would change. Then they would say, "Okay, we're going to do the indoor scene," and I wasn't in the indoor scene, so I was being paid for not working. It was an incredible experience.

Vanessa Redgrave was phenomenal. She never walked off set at night without saying goodnight to the guys. She was an incredible woman to work with. Alida Valli was in that movie too—she was 73—on set, I think she had a birthday. Uma Thurman was so very beautiful but complaining because, you know, the Italians would get her in make-up and not use her for hours and hours, and she was complaining, "They're not paying me enough!" It was a fun movie. Alessandro Gassman was in that movie too, and I just adored him. When I met him on the plane—we flew to Como together—I had no idea who he was. I was on the plane and I heard people in the seats behind me talking and he introduced himself. When I first met him he was a really nice kid. I was shocked when I realized who he was.

And then—let me tell you this, because nobody's ever gonna know it—I was in a movie with Kim Basinger, *I Dreamed of Africa*. I'm in that movie, but you never see me. I shot three days in Venice. I was the nurse. He calls, "Nurse!" and I come in and take her pulse. The director said, "Do you think she would say a line?" I said yes. "Okay, hook her up with a microphone ... now, what would she say?"—"Uh, time for your pill?" "Yes, okay, time for your pill." And it was 100% cut. All you see are my hands taking her pulse. Those are my hands. In the credits of the movie it says "Nurse = Frances Nacman," but you don't see me at all. I contacted everyone in the States and said, "I'm in a Kim Basinger movie!" and then the whole thing was cut. It was a bit of a bummer.

**MB/KG**: Another cult director you worked with was Ruggero Deodato, for the ill-fated TV series *Oceano*.

**FN**: We made that on the Canary Islands with names you wouldn't believe; I mean Ernest Borgnine, Irene Papas. Martin Balsam kills me in that. It never came out. I heard it was impounded, but what for? Bad acting (*laughs*)?

[Deodato] was much more difficult to work for than Lucio Fulci was, but it was an absolute dream. He's nicer off the set. He's an artist and does art shows in galleries, really nice, with clocks, if I remember, clocks within things. My friend Cyrus Elias plays my husband in that movie. So I've had two movies that never came out. Are they trying to tell me something (*laughs*)?

**MB/KG**: *Voices From Beyond* is really a sort of "Cinderella versus the Wicked Stepmother" story. Did you approach it as such? Do you remember any of your co-stars from the film?

**FN**: Absolutely, because that's the way he gave it to me. My entrance was moving a curtain aside, so right away I was into it, and I saw this as a good introduction to the character. It's the evil stepmother. And the guy who plays my son [Pascal Persiano], I mean he was just so wonderful, with his hunched over shoulders and such a wishy-washy guy that it pushed me even more—not over-the-top—but it was just great.

I can't remember any of their names, but the girl who plays the wife [Bettina Giovannini]—the dark-haired girl who cries all the time throughout the whole film—we used to laugh about it because she used to say, "I've just got to stop crying." She said to Lucio, "Don't I do anything in this film but *cry*?" She is crying in almost every shot, and I found that hysterical, and so did she. And then the guy who plays my husband [Paolo Paoloni], the gray-haired guy, he's really good. I've seen him in a lot of things here. He was also really nice to work with, and very professional. And then the girl, the blonde lead girl [Karina Huff]—hectic—she was hectic all the time. She was like, "Oh my God!! Do you have any deodorant?!?" and so and such. She's an American, I think. They were a nice group. And where we were shooting was *phenomenal*! That's the house of the big director Visconti. The house is on Lake Albano. It's where the Pope's house is—Castel Gandolfo—it's about an hour's drive outside of Rome, near the Via Appia. The view was a great big lake, and it was just decorated to die for ... just beautiful. He had never lived there, maybe he had died there, but other people had bought the house. But it's as it was. I think the only thing that was added was the painting of the guy who dies that's hanging on the wall. And we had the dressing rooms down the hill. We were always dealing with little cars, bringing us up and down the hill. It was like another building, I think a barn or something like that.

**MB/KG**: Was this one of the more enjoyable shoots because of the location?

**FN**: One of the more enjoyable shoots was actually for those three weeks on the *Achille Lauro* ship, that's the most enjoyable shoot I ever had. Traveling up to Istanbul. We worked for a week in Genoa with the boat in the dock. We did the horrible scenes there, the shoot-up scenes. And then we went on a cruise with actual passengers and we shot the rest of the movie; some were thrilled to languish in swimming pools and be extras in a film with Burt Lancaster, and others were pissed off because they had booked a cruise with three swimming pools and half the time they couldn't go near them because we were shooting. So there was a lot of animosity, but for us, it was terrific. That was a terrific shoot. I mean, I was flown for three days to shoot in Israel, because Egypt would not give us permission to shoot some scenes there. All the scenes supposed to be in Cairo or in Alexandria were really shot in Israel.

**MB/KG**: What was your first impression of Lucio Fulci?

**FN**: Hmmm ... (*pauses*). He was homely (*laughs*). That was my first impression of him. I said, "Wow, what a homely guy!" I saw his daughter and I thought the same thing about her. She worked on the set with us. They had a problem with their teeth.

I was amazed at the way he shot. I was constantly saying, "Wow, what an idea, that's incredible." In a dream sequence, when the man who's dead is talking to me, he's reading the newspaper. Lucio sticks the camera so as the newspaper is up, someone else's hand would have to come into a frame and turn the page of the newspaper. When he set that up I said, "That's incredible!" I had never seen anything like that in my life. He was always doing these incredibly interesting shots—even that last one in the kitchen—even though I didn't like it, the idea of the camera going around me in a circle and having me follow the camera was really a great thing. I like to think I was constant on that one.

**MB/KG**: In the film, Fulci actually turns in a cameo role as a doctor.

**FN**: He said he was a real medical doctor, and so that's why he played the part. He said, "Nobody can play this part like I, because I know what really happens." The opening scene where the guy's in the hospital and he's spitting up blood, I mean, he said, "I know that's what would happen."

**Frances Nacman mugs for the camera while on a music tour.**

**MB/KG**: Did his daughter Camilla work from a wheelchair at the time?

**FN**: Oh no, she was running around like a crazy person. But they both had the same problem with their teeth. Their teeth were like black and everybody was thinking, "Why don't they take care of that?" And everybody thought it strange that somebody in this business would not think it worth it. But I know there was always something wrong with her. I mean, she walked strangely, and that some accident had to have happened. That was my first impression.

Also, his office was nothing special. Most of the offices I had been to had been really nice. And the billboards that were up were like, this cat thing, were so bizarre. Bizarre stuff up on the walls, and I thought, "This is strange."

**MB/KG**: It was his second-to-last film—the one you made with him.

**FN**: Oh, really? But even he said, "You know you're really lucky that you're making a movie with me now. I didn't used to be so nice." He said that. He was aware that he had changed, obviously.

He had a good crew. We did it on scratch track, not live. And then it was to be dubbed. The dubbing director's [Ted Rusoff's] wife [Carolyn De Fonseca] ended up doing my part. I was never called to dub my own voice. She called me after and said, "I just finished dubbing your role. I just want you to know that you're really great!" And I was like, "*Wow!* Thank you." Of course, I was aware that it would take them an age for me to do the dubbing, because I didn't know how.

**MB/KG**: So have you done any dubbing in Rome at all?

**FN**: I dubbed one main film for a big dubbing director here, Nick Alexander, and it just didn't work for me. It was interesting, but it just wasn't what I wanted to do. I did dub porno films, horrendous ones. I had no idea when I did the first one that's what it was. I was standing there and I was watching it and even before anything happened—just the initial people walking around and talking to each other fully-dressed in a park—I turned to the person next to me and said, "This a "fuck/suck movie," honey, that's what this is." There was no doubt in my mind that those people were going to be without clothes in about five minutes, because they were such bad actors. I mean, they were absolutely stilted. You know: "Well, you're looking lovely today," and the answers were, "Oh, really? I love when people tell me that." So you know already you're dealing with that kind of movie. I was 25-year-old blonde with big boobs for three hours, and got paid for it. I loved it. They said, "Thank you," and I said, "Thank *YOU*!"

And of course there were a couple of them—which is again true to my being the killer—where I was the prison warden, because I have a very deep voice. I had parts where my dialogue would be, "Put her in *there*!" and that kind of shit (*laughs*). "Take her clothes off! Internal examination!" So, yes, you do all that. That's part of the biz. How wonderful I think my life has been where I'm always doing something in front of people. I was on the stage at three. I was a ballet dancer. I won the Lester Horton Dance Scholarship when I was, like, 11. It was always okay for me.

**MB/KG**: So what's next for you?

**FN**: Oh gosh, I haven't the slightest idea. I don't even want to imagine. Sure, making films is good fun, but nothing is a drop-dead necessity for me. I'm having a lot of fun with theater at the moment, and see myself staying here and things continuing. I get involved in animal charities; you do what you can do. I often go to the church next to my house and say to the Madonna, "So far, so good!"

**MB/KG**: Finally, what's your fondest memory of Lucio Fulci?

**FN**: Wow, it's hard to pick one. I say, when he sets up the shoots—I think I said that before. It's when he sets up the shoots, watching him do it. When he gets the idea of what he's going to do with the camera, those are my fondest memories—those moments. What a fun man. [He] never screamed at me. *Ciao, Lucio!*

## *Door to Silence (Italy)*

Aka *Le porte nel silenzio; Door into Silence*

Directed by Lucio Fulci (as H. Simon Kittay); Produced by Aristide Massaccesi (as John Gelardi); Story and Screenplay by Lucio Fulci (as Jerry Madison); Director of Photography: Giancarlo Ferrando (John C. Fredericks); Editor: Rosanna Landi (as Kathleen Stratton); Music by Franco Piana

Main Players: John Savage (Melvin Devereux); Sandi Schultz (Death); Richard Castleman (Hearse Driver); Jennifer Loeb (Margie); Elizabeth Chugden (Sylvia Devereux); Joe 'Cool' Davis (Minister)

*Businessman Melvin Devereux is trying to make his way back home following a bad storm. The storm has many of the main roads flooded and inaccessible, so he is forced to use an alternate route. As he drives along, he comes upon a hearse—Melvin tries to pass the hearse, which tries to force him off the road. Now angered, Melvin pursues the hearse and is bugged by the feeling that the body it is transporting may be his own …*

Following the completion of *Voices from Beyond*, Fulci's old friend and colleague Aristide Massaccesi approached him. Massaccesi was born in Rome in 1936 and started off in the film industry as a camera operator before becoming known as a gifted cinematographer. He made the transition to directing in the early 1970s, and often signed his films under the pseudonym of Joe D'Amato. He directed quite a few horror and exploitation items before turning his talents primarily to hardcore pornography in later years. Among his better-known credits as a director are *Death Smiles on a Murderer* (1973), *Emanuelle in America* (1977), *Emanuelle and the Last of the Cannibals* (1977), *Beyond the Darkness* (1979), *Anthropophagus* (1980) and *Erotic Nights of the Living Dead* (1980). He died in 1999. With his undeniable flair for the exploitative, it's rather surprising that it was a story with very little commercial potential, which prompted him to back Fulci. As Fulci later explained:

> It was based on a short story I wrote; I have had two volumes of short stories published. Aristide Massaccesi read it and said, "Why don't we make this into a film?" I said, "Massaccesi … this film will be a flop! It's just the story of a man driving around in his car! The audience won't give a damn!" He insists we go into production in New Orleans with my daughter assisting the production to save money. None of the equipment works. First headache.[1]

Unfortunately, the problems were only just beginning.

Based on Fulci's story "Porte del nulla," the film is another meditation on fate and the futility of trying to escape one's destiny. Structurally, the film contains some similarities to *The Psychic*, but in many respects it remains a fairly unique entry in the director's eclectic body of work. The story focuses on a hotshot businessman, Melvin Devereux, who wants nothing more than to get back to the comfort of his own home. He is stuck on the road on a sweltering summer day and has to take a number of detours owing to some recent flooding. His run-in with a hearse driven by a mysterious driver threatens to push him over the edge. The driver nearly forces Melvin off of the road, and then it proceeds to play a long, drawn-out game of cat-and-mouse with the neurotic businessman. Melvin begins to experience flashes of subliminal imagery—but what is the significance of this? Could he be foreseeing something that has yet to happen, or is he remembering something that had already come to pass? Fulci films these little vignettes in much the same way as the visions which dog Virginia throughout *The Psychic*; unlike that character, however, Melvin is not psychically "in tune" to anything. He is a short-tempered, self-important prick who condescends to virtually everybody he encounters. He pretends to be a respectable businessman who is happily married, but at least twice he is tempted into nearly cheating on his spouse. Melvin has little enough insight into his life in general, so whatever "powers" of second-sight he could conceivably possess would be ill spent on him. The story follows a fairly predictable path, and the final revelation that Melvin is already dead and is remembering everything that led to his demise is hardly shocking. Fulci does not seem unduly concerned with building towards a big shock reveal, however; instead, he focuses on the futility of Melvin's quest, as it builds towards its inevitable conclusion.

Fulci's decision to undercut suspense in favor of evok-

**Door to Silence; original artwork by Scott Hoffman.**

**John Savage as the sweaty, twitchy Melvin.**

ing an almost drugged-out, nightmarish atmosphere almost certainly works against the film's chances of finding a wider audience. The film does not strive for the same macabre dreamscape one remembers from *City of the Living Dead* or *The Beyond*, however; this film's horrors are much more muted. Even so, he does a remarkably effective job of capturing the off-kilter feel of a man trapped in a dream which he does not understand until it is too late. Melvin's inability to comprehend what has happened to him condemns him to revisit the chain of events that ultimately lead him to his death. Many viewers therefore regard the film as an exercise in abject tedium; a big build-up to a punch line that is obvious pretty much from the get-go. However, it seems unlikely that Fulci really intended for the finale to be all that surprising. Certainly he has displayed a great flair for undercutting audience expectations in the past, and *Door to Silence* continues that trend: The film does not adhere to the path one would normally expect and succeeds instead in frustrating less-patient viewers. Seen through a more sympathetic lens, however, the film has much to offer as an exploration of one man's mission to outsmart fate. In a sense, the film is

**Opening titles frame grab from *Door to Silence*: for his final effort as a director, Fulci was obliged to use a pseudonym.**

closer in tone to an episode of *The Twilight Zone* than it is to one of Fulci's more popular films. The stately pacing helps to sustain the right air of ennui as Melvin stubbornly tries to escape from the inevitable.

Unfortunately, *Door to Silence* would become Fulci's last film. Many viewers therefore approach it with unfairly inflated expectations, as if imagining that Fulci approached it as his final work; in fact, he would spend the rest of his days planning future projects, but bad luck and his own failing health would undo these plans in the end. In a final bit of ignominy, Fulci was also obliged to sign the film with a pseudonym—a first in his career as a director.[2] Fulci would explain that:

> It was the fault of a woman with shitty breath, a despicable being called Lucaroni. She told Aristide that "In this moment Fulci isn't fashionable ... let's call him Simon Kittay." Even the Japanese asked me to explain about this matter. She isn't working for Massaccesi anymore, hah![3]

Thus, Fulci's final directorial work deprives him of any onscreen credit; he is credited as "Jerry Madison" as screenwriter and as "H. Simon Kittay" as director. The subterfuge extends to other members of the crew, as well, with editor Rosanna Landi billed as "Kathleen Stratton", cinematographer Giancarlo Ferrando as John C. Fredericks and producer Massaccesi as "John Gelardi."

The film allowed Fulci to revisit New Orleans, Louisiana for the first time since *The Beyond*. No doubt the pleasant experience he had working in New Orleans prompted him to set the story there in the first place. The film utilizes mostly American acting talent and appears to have been filmed almost entirely with live sound—another anomaly of sorts in Fulci's career. To play the lead role of Melvin, Massaccesi secured the services of intense method actor John Savage. Born in Long Island in 1949, Savage attended acting school before cutting his teeth on stage. He made his film debut in 1969 and went on to win acclaim for his work in such films as Curtis Harrington's *The Killing Kind* (1974), Michael Cimino's *The Deer Hunter* (1978), Harold Becker's *The Onion Field* (1979) and Oliver Stone's *Salvador* (1986). A politically committed actor, he also devoted much energy to supporting the anti-apartheid movement in South Africa. Later career highlights include the likes of Francis Ford Coppola's *The Godfather: Part III* (1990, also featuring another Fulci alum, Brett Halsey), Terrence Mallick's *The Thin Red Line* (1998) and Spike Lee's *Summer of Sam* (1999). Savage's intensity has yielded some remarkable performances, but it has to be admitted that he coasts through *Door to Silence* with an air of bemused disinterest; his performance creates a void at the center of the film, which definitely undermines Fulci's efforts. Fulci did not enjoy his experience directing Savage:

**VHS release for *Door to Silence*.**

> So this guy breaks my balls for the whole film. He is difficult with everyone. I plead with Massaccesi: "I will kill this John Savage!" In New Orleans, it is humid and raining all the time—Savage says we'll shoot regardless. I say "Savage—you are mad!" He makes us shoot so that nothing makes much sense. When we finish, Massaccesi says, "It's a good film." I say, "It's a flop! You'll still pay me, but it's a flop!"[4]

True to his expectations, *Door to Silence* failed to find an audience. It was dumped into Italian theaters for a very brief release in December of 1991, and foreign distributors didn't take an interest in it. The film didn't "officially" surface in America until it made its DVD debut in 2009.

And thus, Lucio Fulci's directorial career ends—not with a bang, but with a whimper. Perhaps if Massaccesi had had the faith to allow Fulci's name on the credits, it may have piqued a little more curiosity from foreign buyers—or not: After all, Fulci's last works were all commercial failures to one degree or another. Time helps to put things into better perspective, however, and the ever-decreasing quality of Italian genre fare makes some of these later works look more desirable than they have in the past. In reality, Fulci's best, most inspired work is pretty much confined to a 20-year period, covering 1966 to 1986, but what a period of creativity that proved to be. If *Door to Silence* does not seem the ideal swansong, it pays to remember that better things were seemingly within Fulci's grasp at the very end ... but fate, his old enemy, had other plans.

Notes:

1. Berger, Howard, "The Prince of Italian Terror," *Fangoria*, July 1997, p. 82.
2. The American release version of *The Beyond*—heavily altered and retitled as *The Seven Doors of Death*—credits Fulci as Louis Fuller; however, Fulci's name is credited on all other versions of the film.
3. Retrieved from, http://www.shockingimages.com/fulci/interview.html
4. Berger, Howard, "The Prince of Italian Terror," *Fangoria*, July 1997, p. 82.

# Films "Presented by" Lucio Fulci

## The Murder Secret (1988)

Aka *Non aver paura della zia Marta; El espejo roto; The Broken Mirror*

Directed by Mario Bianchi; Produced by Antonio Lucidi and Luigi Nannerini, for Alpha Cinematografica; Story and Screenplay by Mario Bianchi; Director of Photography: Silvano Tessicini; Editor: Vincenzo Tomassi; Music by Gianni Sposito

Main Players: Adriana Russo (Nora Hamilton); Gabriele Tinti (Richard Hamilton); Jessica Moore (Georgia Hamilton); Maurice Poli (Thomas); Sacha Maria Darwin [as Sacha M. Darwin] (Aunt Martha); Anna Maria Placido (Richard's Mother)

*A family goes to visit their Aunt Martha, who has just been released from an asylum for the criminally insane. When they arrive at Martha's house, they are told that the woman is not home. However, Thomas, the caretaker, assures them she will be there any time now – and so they spend the night. They may not live to see Aunt Martha, however ...*

## *Hansel e Gretel* (1989)

Aka *Die Saat des Teufels*

Directed by Giovanni Simonelli; Produced by Antonio Lucidi and Luigi Nannerini, for Cine Duck; Story and Screenplay by Giovanni Simonelli; Director of Photography: Silvano Tessicini; Editor: Luigi Gorini; Music by Lanfranco Perini

Main Players: Massimiliano Cipollone (Hansel); Silvia Cipollone (Gretel); Elisabete Pimenta Boaretto (Silvia); Maurice Poli (Commissioner Roy); Lucia Prato (Lina); Gaetano Russo [as Ronald Russo] (Fred); Giorgio Cerioni (Mario); Paul Muller (Procurer); Zora Kerova (Woman in bath) [uncredited]

*Hansel and Gretel are on their way home when they are kidnapped. It is revealed that the kidnappers are involved with a terrible scheme: They take body parts from unwilling "donors" and sell them off to wealthy people in need of a transplant. The children are murdered and their organs are harvested, but they return from the grave to exact vengeance ...*

## *The Red Monks* (1989)

Aka *I frati rossi; Sexorgien der roten Mönche*

Directed by Gianni Martucci; Produced by Pino Buricchi, for Natmas Productions; Screenplay by Pino Buricchi and Gianni Martucci, from a story by Luciana Anna Spacca; Director of Photography: Sergio Rubini; Editor: Vanio Amici; Music by Paolo Rustichelli

Main Players: Lara Wendel (Ramona Curtis); Gerardo Amato (Robert Garlini); Malisa Longo (Pricilla); Chuck Valenti [as Richard Brown] (Ben); Gaetano Russo [as Ronald Russo] (Richard Garlini)

*Ramona marries Robert and moves in with him to his creepy ancestral mansion. While there, the bloom comes off of their romance: He shows no amorous interest in her and disappears for long periods of time in the foreboding basement. In time, Ramona uncovers a terrible secret involving a family curse ...*

## *Escape from Death* (1989)

Aka *Luna di sangue*

Directed by Enzo Milioni; Produced by Antonio Lucidi and Luigi Nannerini, for Alpha Cinematografica; Story and Screenplay by Enzo Milioni and Giovanni Simonelli [as Gianni Simonelli]; Director of Photography: Silvano Tessicini; Editor: Vincenzo Tomassi; Music by Paolo Gatti and Alfonso Zenga

Main Players: Jacques Sernas (Dr. Marc Duvivier); Zora Kerova [as Ulla Z. Kesslerova] (Mary); Barbara Blasko [as Barbara Blasco] (Ann Moffett); Jessica Moore (Tania); Annie Belle (Brigitte Garré)

*Ann Moffett is in line to inherit a vast fortune. A group of greedy and immoral people set out to drive her insane, hoping that they will be able to get their hands on her money ...*

## *Massacre* (1989)

Aka *Massacro*

Directed by Andrea Bianchi; Produced by Antonio Lucidi and Luigi Nannerini, for Cine Duck; Story and Screenplay by Andrea Bianchi; Director of Photography: Silvano Tessicini; Editor: Vincenzo Tomassi; Music by Luigi Ceccarelli

Main Players: Gino Concari (Walter); Patrizia Falcone (Jennifer); Silvia Conti (Liza); Maurice Poli (Frank); Pier Maria Cecchini (Robert); Robert Egon (Jean); Paul Muller (Commissioner)

*The cast and crew of a low-budget horror film titled* "Dirty Blood" *take up residence in a secluded hotel while they are filming. The director, Frank, calls in a medium in the hopes of giving the film a little authenticity, and she inadvertently unleashes the spirit of a murderer ...*

## *Bloody Psycho* (1989)

Aka *Snake House*

Directed by Leandro Lucchetti; Produced by Antonio Lucidi and Luigi Nannerini, for Cine Duck; Story and Screenplay by Leandro Lucchetti and Giovanni Simonelli; Director of Photography: Silvano Tessicini; Editor: Luigi Gorini; Music by Lanfranco Perini

Main Players: Peter Hintz (Dr. Werner Vogler); Louise Kamsteeg [as Loes Kamma] (Micaela); Brigitte Christensen (Mrs. Rezzori); Sacha Maria Darwin (Sasha); Paul

Muller (Attorney Cohen)

*The wheelchair-bound Mrs. Rezzori, who resides in a creepy castle with some shifty relatives and domestic help, calls in Dr. Vogler. The castle is reported to be haunted, and in time a mysterious killer starts killing everybody off …*

Some directors work steadily and successfully without ever establishing much in the way of a public profile; others manage to establish a connection with the audience which gives their name an added weight. In his own way, Fulci falls into the latter category. True, he may have been pilloried by critics and ignored by the *intelligentsia*, but thanks in particular to the success of his latter-day horror films, Fulci became solidified as one of Italy's most significant genre film directors. Only Dario Argento would establish a higher profile for himself, and, for a period of time, he was able to parlay his reputation as Italy's premier *Maestro* of the macabre into a business empire which extended to various successful film productions (including Lamberto Bava's *Demons* films) as well as the merchandizing end of the business (he is co-owner of the *Profondo Rosso* shop in Rome, with his friend and colleague Luigi Cozzi). Fulci would not be quite as fortunate, but even so his name meant something. As such, producers could sometimes cash-in on the built-in audience amassed by popular directors by paying them for the use of their name. In America, this trend can also be seen in the various films "presented" by the likes of John Carpenter and Wes Craven; fans who regard their participation as a sort of artistic seal of approval will therefore be far more inclined to check out the likes of *Vampires: Los Muertos* (2002) and *Dracula 2000* (2000) for that reason than they would be for the films' individual merits. In reality, the participation of Carpenter and Craven in those films is pretty much a matter of signing a contract, cashing a check and allowing their names to be attached as producers. Lucio Fulci was by no means immune to the allure of such an arrangement himself.

In 1988, Fulci signed a contract with producers Antonio Lucidi and Luigi Nannerini; as part of the deal he struck with them, he was to direct several features and also lend his name to several other productions they had in the pipeline. Fulci was going through a difficult period in his career, and saw no harm in taking a little easy money in exchange for allowing the use of his name. However, after directing *Touch of Death* and *The Ghosts of Sodom* in rapid succession, he decided it was best to move on and find a classier venue in which to work. His name would still be attached to several of their productions, but his actual involvement in these films remains highly questionable.

The five films produced by Nannerini and Lucidi make use of the same basic technical crews that had worked on *Touch of Death* and *The Ghosts of Sodom*, including cinematographer Silvano Tessicini and make-up effects artist Giuseppe Ferranti. In common with those films, an air of indecent haste and inadequate production resources marked these productions. It would appear that Fulci was

**DVD sleeve for the Italian release of *Bloody Psycho*, from AVO Film; artist unknown.**

only directly involved with the first two: *The Murder Secret* and *Hansel e Gretel*. He is said to have "supervised" the filming of the gore effects in the former—though exactly what that entails is anybody's guess; there is certainly plenty of red stuff in the finished film, but the effects are not of an appreciably superior caliber to those in the later productions—while assistant director Michele de Angelis has verified that Fulci directed some additional material for the latter when the finished film proved to be too short. In almost every respect, however, the five films are interchangeable: They all feature an uncommonly disagreeable cast of characters (it's always nice to see familiar character actors like Maurice Poli and Paul Muller, even if they are generally squandered), they all suffer from glacial pacing and they all are marked by a general sense of malaise which indicates a lack of enthusiasm on the part of their filmmakers. *The Murder Secret* is the first and probably the best of the lot, and it benefits from a streak of gleefully mean-spirited sadism. The final twist is a bit tired, but Poli and Gabriele Tinti put in good performances and there's some gratuitous T&A courtesy of the shapely Jessica Moore. It's not high art, of course, but it works well enough as mindless entertainment. *Hansel e Gretel* is the most memorably nasty of the bunch in terms of concept, but in the hands of director Giovanni Simonelli—a screenwriting veteran who worked with Fulci on *Nightmare Concert (A Cat in the*

*Brain)*; this film is his only credit as a director—it emerges as a very flat soufflé indeed. It's a pity, really, as the idea of updating the Grimm fairy tale has merit, and the notion of killing off children as a means of keeping wealthy older people alive is an interesting one; interestingly, the story bears some similarities to one of Fulci's short stories, "Opera Italiana," which also uses the idea of children being sold for organ harvesting. Similarly, *Massacre* could have been a fun bit of meta-cinema as it deals with the filming of a low-budget horror movie, but exploitation veteran Andrea Bianchi—best remembered for irresistible sleaze like *Strip Nude for Your Killer* (1975) and *Burial Ground: The Nights of Terror* (1981)—directs with a noticeable lack of enthusiasm. By contrast, there isn't even the germ of a good idea to be found in *Escape from Death*, which plays like a very sluggish update of Clouzot's *Les Diaboliques* (1955). The usual story of an heiress being driven crazy by greedy relatives, it doesn't even have all that much gore or sleaze to help perk things up. This is particularly surprising since director Enzo Milioni had previously directed the incredibly sleazy and tacky *giallo The Sister of Ursula* (1978); both films are distinguished by a similar disregard for pacing and tension, however. *Escape from Death* would prove to be an undistinguished end to an undistinguished career for Milioni. The last—and probably least—of the bunch is *Bloody Psycho*, directed by Leandro Lucchetti from a script by Luchetti and Giovanni Simonelli. The story mixes in old dark house clichés with the paranormal and some of the silliest soft-core sex imaginable—the sequence in which Peter Hintz and Louise Kamsteeg work yogurt into their love-making must be seen to be truly (dis)believed!—to create an oddly inert and atmosphere-free viewing experience. The unappealing cast does not help matters, but ultimately the biggest villain is Lucchetti himself, who displays absolutely zero flair for this sort of thing.

The five Lucidi/Nannerini films are ultimately of more interest for providing Fulci with much of the stock footage he would put to use in *Nightmare Concert (A Cat in the Brain)*. In the interests of giving proper credit to which films provided which material, here follows a rundown of the scenes incorporated into Fulci's later film: *The Murder Secret* includes the footage of Jessica Moore's drawn-out shower, which climaxes with her being butchered with a knife; the scene of the boy riding through the house on a bicycle, which concludes with him losing his head to a chainsaw; the bit with the woman being (improbably) decapitated by a chest and the footage of the music box which leads into the sight of Poli kissing the rotting remains of Aunt Martha. *Hansel e Gretel* includes the scene Fulci is shown editing in his own film, with the middle-aged lady having her eye gouged out. *Massacre* includes the murder of the prostitute, who gets her hand and her head chopped off; the scene of the strange black mass with the tacky-looking demons in the park; the footage of the woman stripping in the window; the shots of the dead woman on the merry-go-round; the sequence of the older man making love to his mistress in a car, which ends with them both being butchered and the boat house murder of the young woman and her two male friends. *Escape from Death* includes the scene of a woman being decapitated by a scythe. *Bloody Psycho* includes the footage of the man being brutally stabbed in the stairwell; the scene of the rotting corpse in the wheelchair being pushed down the stairs; the bit with Paul Muller getting his throat slit, when he is run over by said wheelchair and the scene with the old woman having her tongue torn out in the bath house. Never let it be said that Fulci was not judicious in his use of clips from these films: He effectively boils down the best bits from these moth-eaten productions and utilizes them in a much more witty and self-reflexive context.

Around the same time, producer Pino Buricchi also approached Fulci and asked to use his name in relation to his production of *The Red Monks*. A tedious old dark house horror film with some added sleaze, it brings nothing new to the table and plays like a slightly sexed-up update of a 1960s Gothic-like Massimo Pupillo's *Bloody Pit of Horror* (1965), with a dash of Mario Bava's *Lisa and the Devil* (1973) tossed in for good measure. Amid doses of soft-core sex and amateurish doses of blood and gore, the film spends much of its running time on seemingly endless scenes of characters wandering around the castle setting, doing their best to look frightened. In addition to being credited with "presenting" the film, Fulci is also listed as having been responsible for the special effects. It's precisely the kind of film that would have sunk long ago were it not for the way Buricchi played-up Fulci's "involvement" in the advertising. Not surprisingly, Fulci later recanted his participation and claimed:

> The producers begged me to help promote the film. I don't even know the director.[1]

After this, Fulci was no longer asked to lend his name to other people's productions; perhaps in agreeing to put his name on the credits of these sub-par productions, he killed off any further interest in doing so. Those viewers who were roped into seeing these films because of his name surely felt duped, and, with the exceptions of *The Murder Secret* and *The Red Monks*, none of them would even be prepared for English-language distribution; instead, they sank without a trace, and if they continue to hold any cult appeal whatsoever, it's largely for the benefit of fans who want to see which clips originated from which picture in *Nightmare Concert (A Cat in the Brain)*.

Notes:

1. Thrower, Stephen, *Beyond Terror: The Films of Lucio Fulci* (Guildford: FAB Press, 1999), p. 283.

# Final Thoughts on Lucio Fulci

Following the release of *Door to Silence*, Lucio Fulci anxiously anticipated his next project. His health was failing, however, and he did not have the benefit of a recent success to guarantee further employment. The Italian film industry had long treated him as something of a marginal figure, anyway, and his own tempestuous behavior did not do him any favors in the long run. Former friends and colleagues went on with their careers but were either unable or unwilling to provide him with much support. He continued to busy himself writing articles and short stories, and was proud when two volumes dedicated to his writings were published: *Le lune nere* was brought out in 1992 by a small publishing house known as Granata Press (the same company would also publish the first serious, in-depth Italian-language study of Fulci's work, *L'occhio del testimone: Il cinema di Lucio Fulci*, written by Michele Romagnoli), while *Miei mostri adorati* would follow in 1995, from Pendragon. Around that same time, Fulci began working on his first novel, as well; in an interview with Massimo Lavagnini, he says that the book was to be titled *Caccia agli angeli cadut* (or, *Hunt of the Fallen Angels*).[1] It is unknown how much progress he made on the project, as it never saw the light of day. Fulci also continued developing ideas for possible film and TV projects; the book *I maestri del giallo*, published in 1996 by Nocturno Edizioni, gathers together several treatments he wrote in 1990 (including *Chiara e le voci* and *Gli occhi di Emma*, both co-written by Daniele Stroppa), hoping to attract the support of a producer—nothing ever happened with the idea, however. The failure of Fulci's final films to find an appreciative audience—and with some of them never securing a theatrical release altogether—surely annoyed the director, and he continued to hold onto the hope of making some kind of a triumphant comeback.

If there was a silver lining in the dark cloud, it came in the form of long overdue praise from fans and journalists from France, the U.K. and the U.S. Fulci basked in the attention, and regaled his fans with stories. In January of 1996, Fulci flew to the New York for his first-ever American convention appearance. He had no idea what to expect, but was gratified by a major turn-out—especially in light of a blizzard which was poised to dump snow on the East Coast—and hordes of adoring fans. Filmmaker Scooter McCrae was entrusted with looking after Fulci's needs that weekend and he has some very vivid recollections to share:

"I vividly remember the first time we met in the drab, ancient and huge lobby of the Hotel Pennsylvania on Seventh Avenue in Manhattan. I was standing about with my usual circle of like-minded film geek friends when Lucio Fulci got off the elevator. He recognized someone in our group and ambled towards us slowly with a pronounced limp (he had a cast on his foot from a recent accident), looked at us scalawags and asked the whole bunch of us loudly in his entrancingly thick accent: "Which one of you is ahh-scooooo-terrrrr?"

"Wide-eyed with ecstatic disbelief, I stepped forward to be received by this master of horror (as I was still years away from seeing more of his body of work and realizing what an all-around talented filmmaker he really was). And from that moment on, we were off and running like two old friends who were catching up on old times.

"One thing that I had heard about him is that he liked to give people little nicknames for whatever reason tickled him, something I got to witness first hand when he referred to fellow convention guest John Saxon as "Jurassic Saxon." There was a twinkle in his eye and an entertaining lilt in his voice when he said it, which made it playful and amusing to hear. I've since gathered that on-set some of his nicknames for actors who gave him a hard time were slightly less charitable. I have to admit to wondering if he ever concocted any kind of secret, derogatory nickname for me once we got to know each other a little bit.

"We rarely spoke about his (or anyone else's) movies,

**Lucio Fulci holds forth at his only American festival appearance, in January of 1996, with journalist Loris Curci along to help translate; Fulci would be dead a mere two months later. Photo courtesy of Jon Kitley.**

as I figured he must get enough questions about all of that from lots of other folks, so I let him lead the dialogue and I followed up in whatever direction he steered our discussions. He loved his daughters dearly, and they were often the point of our conversations as we kept coming back to them over the course of our dinners together. I feel the need to mention this detail as those who don't know or really understand his work still brand him and his movies as having a misogynist streak, which I don't think could be farther from the truth.

"In fact, at one point I leaned in and told him about my biggest issue with *The New York Ripper*. He focused the crosshairs of his gaze upon me as I warned him that I had a critical question about his work to ask him. "I have a big problem with that movie," I said. "There's not a single character I can identify with or feel sympathy for, and that makes it a difficult movie to enjoy." He nodded, listened and then told me I had been watching it incorrectly. "You're right, there's nobody for you to identify with and nothing to enjoy, and that's the point!" He turned his attention back to his food. And suddenly, the movie repositioned itself in my brain and made a lot more sense to me.

"For whatever reason, I kept fucking up saying his name incorrectly and would stumble on the last syllable, saying "Lu-chee" instead of "Lu-chee-oh," but he seemed to enjoy my ineptness on this count. I think he liked the fact that I called him "light" all the time (as this is what "luce" means in Italian). It made him smile and sometimes even laugh when I made this mistake, which was nice to see from someone who had such an infamous reputation for being a bit of a stern taskmaster on his film sets. I saw nothing like that at all from him, even as the circumstances of his time spent in NYC became a bit more irritating with each passing day.

"The blizzard that began on the last day of the convention (January 7, 1996) was brutal and dumped nearly two feet of snow onto the city, wreaking havoc with the transportation infrastructure and closing the airports. That, combined with Lucio's mobility issues meant there was not much for him to do but be trapped in that damned hotel all day. And as we sat in the hotel restaurant nibbling at our overpriced and undertasty food stuffs, he often expressed how much he wanted to go down to Chinatown and have a bowl of shark fin soup at a specific joint he remembered some years back while in town for one of his film shoots.

"Unfortunately, the furthest out we ever got from the hotel for a meal was across the street to some crappy Blarney Rock Pub for a warm beer, depressingly blah hamburgers and the kind of faux Irish atmosphere meant to tickle the tourists but becomes mostly nauseating to those of us who live in this town and know better. Lucio found the whole thing amusing on one level, but also frustrating. To have traveled all this distance and be stuck like this definitely tested his patience.

"One time when I came to pick him up for dinner, he was sitting on the edge of his bed totally transfixed by what was happening on the tiny television screen. The Channel Four news division had a helicopter with a camera attached to it that was flying especially low and quietly, providing extremely fluid and beautiful footage of the powdery white devastation that had blanketed New York City. Lucio could not get enough of it and quizzed me concerning what I might know about this camera set-up, as he thought it would be an incredible thing to work with on his next movie.

"Up until meeting Lucio and hanging out in his hotel room, I was not aware that he was diabetic. I discovered this the first time when I entered his bathroom and saw a bunch of empty needless all over the place. For a brief moment, a wave of panic shot through me as I wondered what the needles were for, but when I saw the size and type it was obvious these were not the objects of an illicit drug habit that I had stumbled across.

"But this was another point of exasperation that had to be dealt with, as Lucio had only brought along so many needles and enough insulin to get him along for a relatively short visit. Thankfully, he ended up having just enough to get him through this extended period, but not before I had ventured out to the pharmacy to find out exactly what could be done to get these extra supplies for someone who was visiting our country and didn't exactly have a written prescription from his doctor at the ready.

"Once enough snow had finally melted, getting Lucio on his homeward bound airplane was a whole adventure unto itself. Without belaboring all the excruciatingly annoying obstructions created by the hotel staff (really, they were assholes) and the still very slippery weather presented to us, we took our time for safety sake and eventually made it to the airport.

"I think the "geekiest" moment I experienced with Lucio happened when we arrived at the airport. After checking his bags I escorted him to his gate (oh, the days before 9/11) and, as we were passing through one particular space, something about it looked very familiar to me. I turned to Lucio and asked, "Luce, this looks just like the airport you shot a scene from for ...

"Before I could finish the sentence, Lucio had already given our location the once over and nodded his agreement to my assessment, answering the question before it had even been fully proffered. We were indeed now walking through the section of the airport where, some 17 years earlier, he had stolen a shot of Ian McCulloch and Tisa Farrow for *Zombie*. It was a bizarre moment, both electrifying and surreal.

"While waiting for his plane, our conversation got especially esoteric. He talked about being at some party where filmmaker Jess Franco was tickling the piano keys somewhere in Europe back-in-the-day. Also—and I believe this to probably be some kind of misunderstanding on my part, although I love this possibility too much to not share it—Lucio indicated that at some point he was either doing some minor crew work as a day laborer or just happened to be watching as Orson Welles was directing *The Lady from Shanghai* during its Acapulco shoot. Again, I probably just misunderstood what he was saying, as his English was sometimes very good and then sometimes not, but I do want to believe this story is true!

"Eventually, he got on the plane and left for home. And only a handful of months later, he was dead for reasons both sad and unnecessary.

"I was very lucky to have had these special moments with him and I'm honored to share them here with like-minded and curious readers. He was a complicated person, but also vibrantly alive and passionate about so many things besides cinema, and I was honored that in the midst of hard times he opened up and shared his thoughts with me. The fact that I was able to put together this remembrance nearly 30 years later from memory—without the aid of any notes—should give you some idea of the profound impression he left upon me."

The fan circuit brought Fulci back into contact with Dario Argento, with whom he finally mended fences and set about collaborating with on a film, *The Wax Mask*, which was already discussed in detail in the section of this book dedicated to the films written by Fulci. Rosario Prestopino, Fulci's old make-up wizard from films like *Zombie*, *City of the Living Dead*, *The Black Cat* and *The New York Ripper*, met with Fulci during this time frame:

> I went to Bracciano to visit him. He always had a problem with his foot because of his diabetes. He was submerged in his books and pens, writing, and I remember he was keeping busy with the preparation on *The Wax Mask*. [...] He was a little angry. Let's say angry with Dario because they had an agreement and there were delays with starting the movie, and he was impatient. He had energy, and that energy gave him courage, and that courage made him want to start over; to start over with the chance at an "A" type movie. [...] With Fulci's direction and Dario Argento's production [...], the two of them united could have been a great thing, but it wasn't meant to be.

Lucio Fulci passed away on the night of Wednesday March 13, 1996. He was 68 years old. The official cause of death was diabetic shock, sustained as he slept. Years of health problems had put a severe cramp on Fulci's financial resources, and his situation so moved Dario Argento that he insisted upon paying for the funeral services himself.

As his friend, the late writer Massimo Lavagnini, explained, Fulci's death was overshadowed by that of another filmmaker:

> Lucio was unlucky even in death, as the newspapers gave little coverage to the news because of the demise of another director, the Polish filmmaker [Krzysztof] Kieslowski, who died the same day.[2]

**Lucio Fulci's grave stone; photos courtesy of Andrea Rossi.**

One cannot help but be reminded of a similar story pertaining to Fulci's good friend, Mario Bava, whose death was overshadowed by that of Alfred Hitchcock, who died four days after the Italian *Maestro* in April 1980. Even in death, these significant artists of Italian cinema failed to reap the respectful notices that they deserved.

Journalist Jason Slater, whose love of Fulci stems from seeing *Zombie* at the age of 10 and who corresponded with the *Maestro* prior to finally meeting him in London just a short time before his death, was so moved by the loss that he went to Rome to attend the funeral. As he explained to me,

> I flew over to pay my respects with Antonella. Now I was to stay at Fulci's villa; I was very grateful, and was told I was going to sleep in her father's bed. I said I felt it wasn't right and would be happy to sleep on the couch, but she would not have it: I was to sleep in her father's room. I opened the door. It was a small bedroom with a *huge* poster for one of his comedies. Nothing else. Very basic. The bed? A single bed with a Disney cartoon for a quilt, I kid

you not.

According to Mark Thompson Ashworth, who attended the service at the Church of the Artists located in the Piazza del Popolo in Rome, there were many people in attendance. Not many of Fulci's professional colleagues attended, but Argento and his office staff were in attendance, as were old friends like actress Gabriella Giorgelli (who would go on to appear in *The Wax Mask*) and director Umberto Lenzi. As Mark recalled for the author, the services were held on an appropriately gloomy and rainy Saturday morning. Fulci's remains were interred in the Prima Porta Cemetery in Rome; Mario Bava (who preceded him in death by 16 years) is interred in the very same cemetery, albeit on the opposite side.

In the years since his death, Fulci's stock has not really risen among intellectual Italian film critics. Some journalists in France, the U.K. and the U.S., in particular, have done their best to pay homage to him and to cut through the snobbery surrounding his work to argue that he was a one-of-a-kind cinema artist, but the battle has been an uphill one. It's bad enough that he spent his career making "populist" entertainments, but even within that framework he is not recognized as an innovator. He is often dismissed as an imitative hack, but those who have taken the time to explore his work and appreciate what he did within a certain framework can appreciate the variety and the quality of much of his output. To this day, the debate wages as to whether he was an artist or a hack. Tomas Milian, the star of three of the films of which Fulci was proudest, would later remark that Fulci didn't fully utilize his gifts, that he was "making movies with his left hand" instead of truly pushing himself to the limit.[3] Similarly, his good friend and sometime actor Fabrizio Jovine also opined that Fulci cared too much about making the most money to support his lifestyle and that the films he made were therefore not always the most ideal projects as a result. No matter how one views his body of work, however, there is no denying that its impact is still being felt. Fan clubs exist all over the world, and his work continues to sell on DVD and Blu-ray, often in lavish special editions that celebrate the man's memory. And it is here, no doubt, that Fulci would have felt the most vindicated: Even if the critics continue to debate and deny his merits, his work is beloved by millions of fans the world over. As such, even though it has been nearly 20 years since his passing, a popular phrase among Fulci cultists irresistibly comes to mind: *Fulci Lives*!

Notes:
1. Retrieved from, http://www.shockingimages.com/fulci/interview.html
2. Balun, Chas., *Beyond the Gates: A Tribute to The Maestro*, (San Leandro: Blackest Heart Books, 1996), p. 77.
3. Quoted from "Fulci of the Apocalypse" (2001) featurette included on the Anchor Bay DVD release of *Four of the*

# Afterword by Fabio Frizzi

*Apocalypse*, directed by Gary Hertz.

When I met Lucio Fulci for the first time, in the screening room at Via Margutta in Rome, I could not imagine that it would be a defining moment for my career and my life in general.

Each new acquaintance is important in itself. The concept of "sliding doors" can often completely change one's life, either in a positive or negative way: Missing an airplane can either be a huge hassle or—as in the case of another film director friend, Aldo Lado—postpone one's appointment with the beyond.

However, back to that afternoon of so many years ago: The test screening of *Four of the Apocalypse* was an utterly important moment. I had already written the scores to a number of films, a couple of which had been good box-office results, and my music publisher Carlo Bixio had persuaded me to form a working trio with his brother Franco and Vince Tempera, an excellent arranger and composer from Milan who had been on the crest of the wave for a few years. Two experienced figures sat next to me, as I was a young film music composer in search of new and beautiful professional experiences.

There were all the three of us in the room, the Bixio-Frizzi-Tempera trio, excited and curious about this new meeting, this new opportunity.

Lucio was a complex, interesting, eclectic person. He was an author and filmmaker who always had very clear ideas on how to tell stories, on the use of film technique, on the feelings he wanted to communicate to his audience. To do so, he patiently put together a small army of collaborators, almost always the same, who had learned how to follow his instinctive creativity and overcome the technical difficulties and budget restraints that were typical of Italian cinema of that period. They were next to him even in moments of insecurity and anger.

Since that afternoon in the small screening room I became part of that army, first with my trio and then, a few years later, alone. Of course, I did not write the music for all of his subsequent projects, but there was a red thread that tied my career to Lucio Fulci's cinema for 15 years.

To Fulci, cinema was an important thing, central to his existence. Probably cinema was his true life, his way to overcome some difficult periods in his privacy. I often happened (almost always, actually) to know filmmakers who had rebuilt a family of sorts on the set. Vittorio Sindoni, Bruno Corbucci and Carlo Vanzina are the first who come to mind. When shooting starts it's party time: the production office, the exteriors, especially the studio sets and the editing room all become the many branches of that family—all parts of a big extended family whose members all know one another, with the pleasure of sharing moments of work, fun, trouble.

It was the same with Lucio: From the very first day of shooting to the final postproduction mix, he was followed and advised by his more loyal collaborators, and respected and pampered by everybody.

And even the tense moments that would happen during shooting (since Lucio did not have an easy temper) became anecdotes to share when the next film began.

And the friendship and esteem consolidated and grew, time after time.

I was one of the youngest in the crew. Lucio loved giving nicknames to his collaborators, and I became "the kid." It was also because of this age difference that, when I realized that our relationship had become something different, when he began to confide in me, telling me about his life, his beloved daughters and the good and evil that was behind the scenes, I felt flattered.

Our professional and personal ride went on for a long

**A portrait of Fabio Frizzi.**

**Cover sleeve for the Italian VHS release of Nightmare Concert (A Cat in the Brain) from Empire Video; artwork by Enzo Sciotti.**

time, through different genres, and eventually landed in horror films, giving my career a huge amount of experience, new certainties and a new, growing self-esteem. I believe that the professional growth I underwent, thanks to my collaboration with Lucio Fulci, is an essential part of my career as a film music composer.

We lost sight of each other after *A Cat in the Brain*. It should not happen, but it does. The Italian film industry was falling into a crisis from which it would never recover, and television was beginning to lay down the law.

When I heard he was gone, my heart stopped beating for a moment. We often think, "Well, it's been a long time, I haven't heard from that friend, sooner or later I'll make him a call ..." But since then, no more phone calls, no more lunches at the Celestina Restaurant gossiping about Rome's movie people. No more Lucio Fulci.

And yet, life is strange, and it may surprise you even when it seems there is nothing more to say on a certain topic.

I had the distinct feeling that Fulci had always been much more loved abroad than at home. Soon after *Zombie* I received letters from all over the world, where I received praise for my music and words of great appreciation for the film.

Even after he was gone, Lucio had not been forgotten. On the contrary, the Internet was his greatest ally. A network of fans that communicate with each other, exchanging feelings and opinions, and rediscovering forgotten pages of information ... This wave of love for Lucio Fulci, day after day, stood above me as well.

I was very fond of that period, for a way of writing scores that was so instinctive and fresh, for that moment of growth that I experienced. But I considered it a closed chapter of my past life. Driven by many new friends, as well as by having again met Antonella and exchanged messages with Camilla, I looked back, revisited that film and musical legacy, and in a sense I made it all mine once again.

And that beautiful friendship renewed. When I get on stage and begin to tell of those past days, it's as if Lucio is looking at me from the first row, ironic and irreverent as ever ... but happy.

# Index

Fellini, Federico, 22, 27, 28, 29, 30, 41, 42, 50, 52, 64, 75, 79, 86, 92, 93, 113, 137, 166, 191, 194, 200, 230, 329

**If you enjoyed this book,**
**write for a free catalog of**
**Midnight Marquee Press titles**
**or visit our website at**
**http://www.midmar.com**

**Midnight Marquee Press, Inc.**
**9721 Britinay Lane**
**Baltimore, MD 21234**
**410-665-1198**
**mmarquee@aol.com**

CPSIA information can be obtained
at www.ICGtesting.com
Printed in the USA
BVHW012038040819
555064BV00011B/1145/P

9 781936 168613